A
HISTORY
— *of* —
WARFARE

ALSO BY JOHN KEEGAN

The Face of Battle

The Nature of War (with Joseph Darracott)

World Armies

Who's Who in Military History (with Andrew Wheatcroft)

Six Armies in Normandy

Soldiers (with Richard Holmes)

The Mask of Command

The Price of Admiralty

The Second World War

A
HISTORY
— of —
WARFARE

John Keegan

Alfred A. Knopf   New York   1993

THIS IS A BORZOI BOOK
PUBLISHED BY ALFRED A. KNOPF, INC.

Copyright © 1993 by John Keegan

Library of Congress Cataloging-in-Publication Data
Keegan, John, [date]
A history of warfare / John Keegan.
p. cm.
Includes bibliographical references and index.
ISBN 0-394-58801-0
1. Military art and science—History. I. Title.
U27.K38   1993
355'.009—dc20   93-14884
CIP

Manufactured in the United States of America
FIRST AMERICAN EDITION

In memory of Winter Bridgman
Lieutenant in the Régiment de Clare
killed at the battle of Lauffeld
July 2, 1747

Contents

Illustrations   ix

Acknowledgments   xi

Introduction   xiii

1   War in Human History   1
Interlude: Limitations on Warmaking   61

2   Stone   77
Interlude: Fortification   137

3   Flesh   153
Interlude: Armies   219

4   Iron   235
Interlude: Logistics and Supply   299

5   Fire   317

Conclusion   386

References   393

Select Bibliography   411

Index   418

Illustrations

Pages 144 to 145
Easter Island (*Barnaby's Picture Library*)
Carl von Clausewitz (*Hulton Deutsch*)
Mameluke warrior (*British Library*)
Battle of the Pyramids (*Robert Harding Picture Library*)
Zulu warriors (*Mansell Collection*)
A Partisan's Mother (*Peter Newark's Military Pictures*)
Japanese swordsmen (*Victoria & Albert Museum*)
Mountain infantrymen in the Julian Alps (*Robert Harding Picture Library*)
Mark IV Panzer (*E. T. Archive*)
German infantrymen, 1942 (*E. T. Archive*)
Future Yanomamö warrior (*Sue Cunningham Photographic*)
New Stone Age hunters (*Mansell Collection*)
Aztec warriors (*British Museum*)
Egyptian archers (*Peter Clayton*)
Sethos I (*British Museum*)
Palette of Narmer (*Girauden*)
Rameses II (*British Museum*)
Assyrian victors (*C.M. Dixon*)
Assyrian hunters (*E.T. Archive*)
Walls of Jericho (*British School of Archaeology, Jerusalem*)
Great Wall of China (*G & A Loescher/Barnaby's Picture Library*)
Hadrian's Wall (*Barnaby's Picture Library*)
Porchester Castle (*Aerofilms*)
Krak des Chevaliers (*Aerofilms*)
Siege of Limerick (*Mansell Collection*)
Standard of Ur (*British Museum*)
Assyrian warriors (*C.M. Dixon*)
Assyrians in battle (*C.M. Dixon*)
Sarmatian warrior (*Peter Newark's Historical Pictures*)
Battle of Issus (*C.M. Dixon*)
Iranian horsemen (*Peter Newark's Historical Pictures*)
Coming of the stirrup (*E.T. Archive*)
Zouaves (*Mansell Collection*)

Janissaries (*Sonia Halliday*)
Swiss militia (*Popperfoto*)
John Hawkwood (*Mansell Collection*)
The Village Recruit (*Mansell Collection*)
Conscripts, 1939 (*Hulton Deutsch*)

Pages 272 to 273
Greek armour (*C.M. Dixon*)
Hoplite (*Mansell Collection*)
Hoplites in battle (*Peter Newark's Historical Pictures*)
Roman warship (*C.M. Dixon*)
Centurion (*E.T. Archive*)
Barbarian tribesman (*Robert Harding Picture Library*)
Frankish horseman (*Robert Harding Picture LIbrary*)
Crusaders (*Peter Newark's Historical Pictures*)
Escalade used in a medieval siege (*Hulton Deutsch*)
Roman centurion (*Mansell Collection*)
Cannon manufacture (*Peter Newark's Historical Pictures*)
Railroad construction (*M.A.R.S.*)
Krupp's trial range (*Mansell Collection*)
Atlantic convoy (*Peter Newark's Historical Pictures*)
Early cannon (*E.T. Archive*)
Gunpowder (*E.T. Archive*)
Knights of Malta (*Robert Harding Picture Library*)
The *Great Harry* (*Mansell Collection*)
Seventeenth-century Manual of Arms (*Mansell Collection*)
Siege cannon (*M.A.R.S.*)
Gunpowder mill (*Mansell Collection*)
Battle of Williamsburg (*Peter Newark's Historical Pictures*)
British soldier at the Somme (*E.T. Archive*)
German Junkers dive-bombers (*E.T. Archive*)
B–17s (*M.A.R.S.*)
Atomic bomb test at Bikini atoll (*Peter Newark's Historical Pictures*)

Acknowledgments

Great changes have occurred in the world since I began this book in 1989, and those changes should be acknowledged first. The Cold War has ended. A brief but dramatic air and ground war has been fought in the Gulf. A protracted and cruel civil war has broken out and still rages in former Yugoslavia. Several of the themes developed in this book have revealed themselves – at least to me – in the Gulf and Yugoslav wars.

In the Gulf a Clausewitzian defeat was inflicted by the forces of the coalition on those of Saddam Hussein. His refusal, however, to concede the reality of the catastrophe that had overtaken him, by recourse to a familiar Islamic rhetoric that denied he had been defeated in spirit, whatever material loss he had suffered, robbed the coalition's Clausewitzian victory of much of its political point. Saddam's continued survival in power, in which the victors appear to acquiesce, is a striking exemplification of the inutility of the 'Western way of warfare' when confronted by an opponent who refuses to share its cultural assumptions. The Gulf war may be seen in one light as a clash of two quite different military cultures, each with deep historical roots, neither of which can be understood in terms of abstractions about the 'nature of war' itself, since there is no such thing.

The horrors of the war in Yugoslavia, as incomprehensible as they are revolting to the civilised mind, defy explanation in conventional military terms. The pattern of local hatreds they reveal are unfamiliar to anyone but the professional anthropologists who take the warfare of tribal and marginal peoples as their subject of study. Many anthropologists deny that there is such a phenomenon as 'primitive warfare'. Most intelligent newspaper readers – on whom reports of 'ethnic cleansing', the systematic mistreatment of women, the satisfaction of revenge, the organisation of massacre and the voiding of territory then left unoccupied have made such an indelible impression – will be struck by the parallels to be drawn with the behaviour of pre-state peoples described in this book.

I am particularly grateful to Professor Neil Whitehead for the guidance he gave me in finding my way through the literature of the anthropology of warfare. The misunderstandings and misinterpretations that resulted are my own. The professional soldiers and military historians to whom I owe a debt of gratitude for my efforts to piece together a comprehensive picture of the forms warfare has taken across time and place are too numerous to mention. Not all may wish to be associated with such a personal view as the one I have come to hold. I should, however, like to remember my Balliol tutor, A.B. Rodger, who first taught me military history, Brigadier Peter Young, DSO, MC, head of the Department of Military History at the Royal Military Academy, Sandhurst, in which I first tried to teach the subject, and Dr Christopher Duffy, my Sandhurst colleague, whose deep knowledge of Habsburg and Ottoman military history first alerted me to the idea that warfare is a cultural activity.

I am deeply grateful to Elisabeth Sifton, my American editor, for the work she did on the manuscript, to my English editor, Anthony Whittome, for the meticulous care he has taken in turning it into a printed book, to Anne-Marie Ehrlich for once again assembling illustrations, to Alan Gilliland for devising and drawing the maps, to Frances Banks for typing from my increasingly difficult handwriting and, as always, to my literary agent, Anthony Sheil, a friend of thirty years. I particularly wish to thank Andrew Orgill and his staff at the Central Library, Royal Military Academy, Sandhurst, one of the great military libraries of the world to which I am lucky enough still to be allowed access, the staff of the Ministry of Defence Library and the staff of the London Library.

I owe personal thanks to many friends at *The Daily Telegraph*, including Conrad Black, Max Hastings, Tom Pride, Nigel Wade – who arranged for me to visit the Gulf in November 1990 and Yugoslavia between the Croatian and Bosnian wars – Peter Almond, Robert Fox, Bill Deedes, Jeremy Deedes, Christopher Hudson, Simon Scott-Plummer, John Coldstream, Miriam Gross, Nigel Horne, Nick Garland, Mark Law, Charles Moore, Trevor Grove, Hugh Montgomery-Massingberd, Andrew Hutchinson and Louisa Bull.

My brother Francis, by his interest in the history of our mother's family, the Bridgmans of Toomdeely, has established our relationship with several soldiers who went from Ireland to fight for France in the wars of Louis XV. As one of them, Winter Bridgman, exemplifies the type of international professional officer who features widely in what follows, it is to him that I have chosen to dedicate this book. I am deeply grateful to Francis for all the work he has done. My thanks finally to friends at Kilmington, particularly Honor Medlam, Michael and Nesta Gray, Don and Marjorie Davis, and my love as always to my children and children-in-law, Lucy and Brooks Newmark, Thomas, Rose, Matthew and Mary and to my darling wife, Susanne.

Kilmington Manor
June 9, 1993

Introduction

I was not fated to be a warrior. A childhood illness left me lame for life in 1948 and I have limped now for forty-five years. When, in 1952, I reported for my medical examination for compulsory military service, the doctor who examined legs – he was, inevitably, the last doctor to examine me that morning – shook his head, wrote something on my form and told me that I was free to go. Some weeks later an official letter arrived to inform me that I had been classified permanently unfit for duty in any of the armed forces.

Fate nevertheless cast my life among warriors. My father had been a soldier in the First World War. I grew up in the Second, in a part of England where the British and American armies gathering for the D-Day invasion of Europe were stationed. In some way I detected that my father's service on the Western Front in 1917–18 had been the most important experience of his life. The spectacle of the preparation for invasion in 1943–4 marked me also. It aroused an interest in military affairs that took root, so that when I went up to Oxford in 1953 I chose military history as my special subject.

A special subject was a requirement for a degree, no more than that, so that my involvement in military history might have ended at graduation. The interest, however, had bitten deeper during my undergraduate years, because most of the friends I made at Oxford had, unlike me, done their military service. They made me conscious of having missed something. Most had been officers and many had served on campaign, for Britain in the early 1950s was disengaging from empire in a series of small colonial wars. Some of my friends had soldiered in the jungles of Malaya or the forests of Kenya. A few, who had served in regiments sent to Korea, had even fought in a real battle.

Sober professional lives awaited them and they sought academic success and the good opinion of tutors as a passport to the future. Yet it was clear to me that the two years they had spent in uniform had cast over them the spell of an entirely different world from that they were set on entering. The spell was in part one of experience – of strange places, of unfamiliar responsibility, of excitement and even of danger. It was also the spell of acquaintance with the professional officers who had commanded them. Our tutors were admired for their scholarship and eccentricities. My contemporaries continued to admire the officers they had known for other qualities altogether – their dash, élan, vitality and impatience with the everyday. Their names were often mentioned, their characters and mannerisms recalled, their exploits – above all their self-confident brushes with authority – recreated. Somehow I came to feel that I knew these light-hearted warriors and I certainly wanted to know people like them very badly, if only to flesh out my vision of the warrior's world that, as I laboured over my military historical texts, was slowly taking shape in my mind.

When university life came to its end, and my friends departed to become lawyers, diplomats, civil servants or university tutors themselves, I found that the afterglow of their military years had cast its spell on me. I decided to become a military historian, a foolhardy decision since there were few academic posts in the subject. More quickly than I had any right to expect, however, such a post became vacant at the Royal Military Academy Sandhurst, Britain's cadet college, and in 1960 I joined the staff. I was twenty-five, I knew nothing about the army, I had never heard a shot fired in anger, I had scarcely met a regular officer and the picture I had of soldiers and soldiering belonged entirely to my imagination.

The first term I spent at Sandhurst pitched me headlong into a world for which not even my imagination had prepared me. In 1960 the military staff of the Academy – I belonged to its academic side – was composed, at the senior level, exclusively of men who had fought in the Second World War. The junior officers were almost all veterans of Korea, Malaya, Kenya, Palestine, Cyprus or any one of another dozen colonial campaigns. Their uniforms were covered with medal ribbons, often of high awards for gallantry. My head of department, a retired officer, wore on mess evenings the Distinguished Service Order and the Military Cross with two bars and his distinctions were not exceptional. There were majors and colonels with medals for bravery won at Alamein, Cassino, Arnhem and Kohima. The history of the Second World War was written in these little strips of silk that they wore so lightly and its high moments were recorded with crosses and medals which the bearers scarcely seemed conscious of having been awarded.

It was not only the kaleidoscope of medals that entranced me. It was also the kaleidoscope of uniforms and all that they signified. Many of my university contemporaries had brought with them scraps of military glory – regimental blazers or British Warm overcoats. Those who had been cavalry officers continued to wear with evening dress the morocco-topped patent-leather boots, slotted at the heel for spurs, that belonged to their Lancer or Hussar uniforms. That had alerted me to the paradox that uniform was not uniform, but that regiments dressed differently. How differently Sandhurst taught me on the first mess evening I spent there. There were Lancers and Hussars in blue and scarlet, but also Household Cavalrymen crushed by the weight of their gold lace, Riflemen in green so dark it was almost black, Gunners in tight trousers, Guardsmen in stiff shirts, Highlanders in six different patterns of tartan, Lowlanders in plaid trews and infantrymen of the county regiments with yellow, white, grey, purple or buff facings to their jackets.

I had thought the army was one army. After that evening I realised it was not. I still had to learn that the outward differences of dress spoke of inward differences of much greater importance. Regiments, I discovered, defined themselves above all by their individuality and it was their individuality which made them into the fighting organisations whose effectiveness in combat was proclaimed by the medals and crosses I saw all about me. My regimental friends – the ready friendship extended by warriors is one of their most endearing qualities – were brothers-in-arms; but they were brothers only up to a point. Regimental loyalty was the touchstone of their lives. A personal difference might be forgiven the next day. A slur on the regiment would never be forgotten, indeed would never be uttered, so deeply would such a thing touch the values of the tribe.

Tribalism – that was what I had encountered. The veterans I met at Sandhurst in the 1960s were by many external tests no different from professional men in other walks of life. They came from the same schools, sometimes the same universities, they were devoted to their families, they had the same hopes for their children as other men, they worried about money in the same way. Money, however, was not an ultimate or defining value, nor even was promotion within the military system. Officers, of course, hankered for advancement, but it was not the value by which they measured themselves. A general might be admired, or he might not. Admiration derived from something other than his badges of superior rank. It came from the reputation he held as a man among other men and that reputation had been built over many years under the eyes of his regimental tribe. That tribe was one not only of fellow officers but of sergeants and ordinary soldiers as well. 'Not good with soldiers' was an ultimate condemnation. An officer might be clever, competent, hard-working. If his fellow soldiers reserved doubt about him, none of those qualities countervailed. He was not one of the tribe.

The British army is tribal to an extreme degree; some of its regiments have histories which go back to the seventeenth century, when modern armies were only beginning to take shape from the feudal hosts of warriors whose forebears had entered western Europe during the invasions that overthrew the Roman empire. I have encountered the same warrior values of the tribe in many other armies, however, over the years since I first joined Sandhurst in my youth. I have sensed the tribal aura about French officers who fought the war in Algeria, leading Muslim soldiers whose traditions belong with those of the *ghazi*, Islam's frontier marauders. I have sensed it, too, in the recollections of German officers, re-enlisted to build Germany's post-war army, who had fought the Russians on the steppe and preserved a pride in the ordeal they had undergone that harked back to the wars of their medieval ancestors. I have sensed it strongly among Indian officers, above all in their quickness to insist that they are Rajputs or Dogras, descendants of the invaders who conquered India before its history had begun to be written. I have sensed it among American officers who served in Vietnam or the Lebanon or the Gulf, exponents of a code of courage and duty that belongs to the origins of their republic.

Soldiers are not as other men – that is the lesson that I have learned from a life cast among warriors. The lesson has taught me to view with extreme suspicion all theories and representations of war that equate it with any other activity in human affairs. War undoubtedly connects, as the theorists demonstrate, with economics and diplomacy and politics. Connection does not amount to identity or even to similarity. War is wholly unlike diplomacy or politics because it must be fought by men whose values and skills are not those of politicians or diplomats. They are those of a world apart, a very ancient world, which exists in parallel with the everyday world but does not belong to it. Both worlds change over time, and the warrior world adapts in step to the civilian. It follows it, however, at a distance. The distance can never be closed, for the culture of the warrior can never be that of civilisation itself. All civilisations owe their origins to the warrior; their cultures nurture the warriors who defend them, and the differences between them will make those of one very different in externals from those of another. It is, indeed, a theme of this book that in externals there are three distinct warrior traditions. Ultimately, however, there is only one warrior culture. Its evolution and transformation over time and place, from man's beginnings to his arrival in the contemporary world, is the history of warfare.

—1—
War in Human History

WHAT IS WAR?

WAR IS NOT THE continuation of policy by other means. The world would be a simpler place to understand if this dictum of Clausewitz's were true. Clausewitz, a Prussian veteran of the Napoleonic wars who used his years of retirement to compose what was destined to become the most famous book on war – called *On War* – ever written, actually wrote that war is the continuation 'of political intercourse' (*des politischen Verkehrs*) 'with the intermixing of other means' (*mit Einmischung anderer Mittel*).[1] The original German expresses a more subtle and complex idea than the English words in which it is so frequently quoted. In either form, however, Clausewitz's thought is incomplete. It implies the existence of states, of state interests and of rational calculation about how they may be achieved. Yet war antedates the state, diplomacy and strategy by many millennia. Warfare is almost as old as man himself, and reaches into the most secret places of the human heart, places where self dissolves rational purpose, where pride reigns, where emotion is paramount, where instinct is king. 'Man is a political animal,' said Aristotle. Clausewitz, a child of Aristotle, went no further than to say that a political animal is a warmaking animal. Neither dared confront the thought that man is a thinking animal in whom the intellect directs the urge to hunt and the ability to kill.

This is not an idea any easier for modern man to confront than it was for a Prussian officer, born the grandson of a clergyman and raised in the spirit of the eighteenth-century Enlightenment. For all the effect that Freud, Jung and Adler have had on our outlook, our moral values remain those of the great monotheistic religions, which condemn the killing of fellow souls in all but the most constrained circumstances. Anthropology tells us and archaeology implies that our uncivilised ancestors could be red in tooth and claw; psychoanalysis seeks to persuade us that the savage in all of us lurks not far below the skin. We prefer, none the less, to recognise human nature as we find it displayed in the everyday

3

behaviour of the civilised majority in modern life – imperfect, no doubt, but certainly cooperative and frequently benevolent. Culture to us seems the great determinant of how human beings conduct themselves; in the relentless academic debate between 'nature and nurture', it is the 'nurture' school which commands greater support from the bystanders. We are cultural animals and it is the richness of our culture which allows us to accept our undoubted potentiality for violence but to believe nevertheless that its expression is a cultural aberration. History lessons remind us that the states in which we live, their institutions, even their laws, have come to us through conflict, often of the most bloodthirsty sort. Our daily diet of news brings us reports of the shedding of blood, often in regions quite close to our homelands, in circumstances that deny our conception of cultural normality altogether. We succeed, all the same, in consigning the lessons both of history and of reportage to a special and separate category of 'otherness' which invalidates our expectations of how our own world will be tomorrow and the day after not at all. Our institutions and our laws, we tell ourselves, have set the human potentiality for violence about with such restraints that violence in everyday life will be punished as criminal by our laws, while its use by our institutions of state will take the particular form of 'civilised warfare'.

The bounds of civilised warfare are defined by two antithetical human types, the pacifist and the 'lawful bearer of arms'. The lawful bearer of arms has always been respected, if only because he has the means to make himself so; the pacifist has come to be valued in the two thousand years of the Christian era. Their mutuality is caught in the dialogue between the founder of Christianity and the professional Roman soldier who had asked for his healing word to cure a servant. 'I also am a man set under authority,' the centurion explained.[2] Christ exclaimed at the centurion's belief in the power of virtue, which the soldier saw as the complement to the force of law which he personified. May we guess that Christ was conceding the moral position of the lawful bearer of arms, who must surrender his life at the demand of authority, and therefore bears comparison with the pacifist who will surrender his life rather than violate the authority of his own creed? It is a complicated thought, but not one which Western culture finds difficult to accommodate. Within it the professional soldier and the committed pacifist find room to co-exist – sometimes cheek-by-jowl: in 3 Commando, one of Britain's toughest Second World War units, the stretcher-bearers were all pacifists but were held by the commanding officer in the highest regard for their bravery and readiness for self-sacrifice. Western culture would, indeed, not be what it is unless it could respect both the lawful bearer of

4

arms and the person who holds the bearing of arms intrinsically unlawful. Our culture looks for compromises and the compromise at which it has arrived over the issue of public violence is to deprecate its manifestation but to legitimise its use. Pacifism has been elevated as an ideal; the lawful bearing of arms – under a strict code of military justice and within a corpus of humanitarian law – has been accepted as a practical necessity.

'War as the continuation of policy' was the form Clausewitz chose to express the compromise for which the states he knew had settled. It accorded respect to their prevailing ethics – of absolute sovereignty, ordered diplomacy and legally binding treaties – while making allowance for the overriding principle of state interest. If it did not admit the ideal of pacifism, which the Prussian philosopher Kant was only just translating from the religious to the political sphere, it certainly distinguished sharply between the lawful bearer of arms and the rebel, the freebooter and the brigand. It presupposed a high level of military discipline and an awesome degree of obedience by subordinates to their lawful superiors. It expected that war would take certain narrowly definable forms – siege, pitched battle, skirmish, raid, reconnaissance, patrol and outpost duties – each of which had its own recognised conventions. It assumed that wars had a beginning and an end. What it made no allowance for at all was war without beginning or end, the endemic warfare of non-state, even pre-state peoples, in which there was no distinction between lawful and unlawful bearers of arms, since all males were warriors; a form of warfare which had prevailed during long periods of human history and which, at the margins, still encroached on the life of civilised states and was, indeed, turned to their use through the common practice of recruiting its practitioners as 'irregular' light cavalry and infantrymen. From the unlawful and uncivilised means by which these irregular warriors rewarded themselves on campaign and from their barbaric methods of fighting, the officers of the civilised states averted their gaze; yet without the services they offered, the over-drilled armies in which Clausewitz and his kin had been raised would scarcely have been able to keep the field. All regular armies, even the armies of the French Revolution, recruited irregulars to patrol, reconnoitre and skirmish for them; during the eighteenth century the expansion of such forces – Cossacks, 'hunters', Highlanders, 'border-ers', Hussars – had been one of the most noted contemporary military developments. Over their habits of loot, pillage, rape, murder, kidnap, extortion and systematic vandalism their civilised employers chose to draw a veil. That it was an older and more widespread form of warfare than that which they themselves practised they preferred not to admit; 'war . . .

the continuation of policy', once Clausewitz had formulated the thought, proved to offer the thinking officer a convenient philosophical bolt-hole from contemplation of the older, darker and fundamental aspects of his profession.

Yet Clausewitz himself saw with half an eye that war was not altogether what he claimed it to be. 'If the wars of civilised peoples are less cruel and destructive than those of savages', he conditionally began one of his most famous passages. It was a thought he did not pursue because, with all the considerable philosophical force at his disposal, he was struggling to advance a universal theory of what war *ought* to be, rather than what it actually was and had been. To a very great degree he succeeded. In the practice of warmaking it is to the principles of Clausewitz that the statesman and the supreme commander still turn; in the truthful description of war, however, the eye-witness and the historian must flee from Clausewitz's methods, despite the fact that Clausewitz himself was both an eye-witness and a historian of war, who must have seen and could have written of a great deal that found no place in his theories. 'Without a theory the facts are silent,' the economist F.A. Hayek has written. That may be true of the cold facts of economics, but the facts of war are not cold. They burn with the heat of the fires of hell. In old age General William Tecumseh Sherman, who had burned Atlanta and put a great swathe of the American South to the torch, bitterly delivered himself of exactly that thought, in words that have become almost as famous as those of Clausewitz: 'I am tired and sick of war. Its glory is all moonshine . . . War is hell.'[3]

Clausewitz had seen the hellish fires of war, had indeed seen Moscow burn. The burning of Moscow was the single greatest material catastrophe of the Napoleonic wars, an event of European significance akin in its psychological effect to that of the Lisbon earthquake of 1755. In an age of belief the destruction of Lisbon had seemed awful evidence of the power of the Almighty and had been the stimulus of a religious revival throughout Portugal and Spain; in the age of revolution the destruction of Moscow was seen to testify to the power of man, as indeed it did. It was taken to be a deliberate act – Rostopchin, the city governor, claimed credit for it, while Napoleon had the alleged incendiarists hunted down and executed – but Clausewitz, strangely, could not convince himself that the burning was a deliberate policy, a scorching designed to deny Napoleon the prize of victory. On the contrary: 'that the French were not the agents I was firmly convinced,' he wrote, 'that the Russian authorities had done the act appeared to me, at least, not proven.' He believed it instead to be an accident.

The confusion which I saw in the streets as the [Russian] rearguard moved out; the fact that the smoke was first seen to rise from the outer edge of the suburbs where the Cossacks were active, both convinced me that the Moscow fire was a result of the disorder, and the habit the Cossacks had of first thoroughly pillaging and then setting fire to all the houses before the enemy could make use of them . . . It was one of the strangest happenings of history that an event which so influenced the fate of Russia should be like a bastard born from an illicit love affair, without a father to acknowledge it.[4]

Yet Clausewitz must have known that there was nothing truly accidental about the fatherless act of Moscow's burning or any of the other numberless illegitimacies that attended Napoleon's campaign in Russia in 1812. The involvement of the Cossacks was in itself a guarantee that incendiarism, pillage, rape, murder and a hundred other outrages would abound, for to the Cossacks war was not politics, but a culture and a way of life.

The Cossacks were soldiers of the tsar and at the same time rebels against tsarist absolutism. The story of their origins has been called a myth and there is no doubt that they did mythologise their own beginnings as time drew on.[5] Yet the essence of the myth is both simple and true. Cossacks – the name derives from the Turkic word for freeman – were Christian fugitives from servitude under the rulers of Poland, Lithuania and Russia, who preferred to take their chance – to 'go Cossacking' – on the rich but lawless surface of the great Central Asian steppe.

By the time that Clausewitz came to know the Cossacks, the myth of their birth in freedom had grown in the telling but diminished in reality. At the outset they had founded genuinely egalitarian societies – lordless, womanless, propertyless, living embodiments of the free and free-ranging warrior band that is such a powerful and eternal ingredient of saga across the world. In 1570 Ivan the Terrible had had to barter gunpowder, lead and money – three things the steppe did not produce – in return for Cossack help in liberating Russian prisoners from Muslim enslavement, but before the end of his reign he had begun to use force to bring them within the tsarist system.[6] His successors sustained the pressure. During Russia's wars with Napoleon, regular Cossack regiments were raised, a contradiction in terms though all of a part with the contemporary European fashion for incorporating units of forest, mountain and horse peoples in the different states' orders of battle. In 1837 Tsar Nicholas I completed the process by proclaiming his son 'Ataman of All Cossacks', whose followers were represented in the Imperial Guard Corps by regiments of Cossacks of the Don, the Urals and the Black Sea, differentiated from other units of tamed frontiersmen, Lesquines, Musalmans and Caucasian Mountaineers, only by the details of their exotic uniforms.

Yet despite the lengths to which domestication went, the Cossacks were always spared the indignity of paying the 'soul tax', which branded a Russian subject a serf, and they were specifically exempt from conscription, which the serfs regarded as a sentence of death. Indeed, to the very end of tsardom the Russian government preserved the principle of treating with the various Cossack hosts as if they were free-standing warrior societies, in which responsibility to answer the call to arms fell on the group, not its individual members. Even at the outbreak of the First World War the Russian war ministry looked to the Cossacks to provide regiments, not heads, a perpetuation of a system, part feudal, part diplomatic, part mercenary, that in a variety of forms provided states with ready-trained military contingents almost from the beginning of organised warfare.

The Cossacks whom Clausewitz knew were much nearer to the free-booting marauders of original Cossackdom even than the dashing rovers whom Tolstoy was later to romanticise in his early novels, and their burning of the outskirts of Moscow in 1812, which led to the conflagration of the capital, was wholly in character. The Cossacks remained cruel people and the burning was not the cruellest of their acts, though cruel enough – it left several hundred thousand Muscovites homeless in the face of a sub-Arctic winter. In the great retreat that followed, the Cossacks showed a cruelty which stirred in their western European victims a reminder of the visitations of the steppe peoples, pitiless, pony-riding nomads whose horsetail standards cast the shadow of death wherever their hordes galloped, visitations that lay buried in the darkest recesses of their collective memory. The long columns of the Grand Army that straggled knee-deep through the snow toward the hope of safety were stalked just out of musket-shot by waiting squadrons of Cossacks who swooped whenever weakness overcame a sufferer; when a group succumbed it was ridden down and wiped out; and when the Cossacks caught the remnants of the French army that had failed to cross the Beresina River before Napoleon burned the bridges, slaughter became wholesale. Clausewitz told his wife that he had witnessed 'ghastly scenes . . . If my feelings had not been hardened it would have sent me mad. Even so it will take many years before I can recall what I have seen without a shuddering horror.'[7]

Yet Clausewitz was a professional soldier, the son of an officer, raised to war, a veteran of twenty years of campaign and a survivor of the battles of Jena, Borodino and Waterloo, the second the bloodiest battle Napoleon ever fought. He had seen blood shed in gallons, had trodden

8

battlefields where the dead and wounded lay strewn close as sheaves at harvest, had had men killed at his side, had a horse wounded under him and had escaped death himself only by hazard. His feelings ought indeed to have been hardened. Why then did he find the horrors of the Cossack pursuit of the French so particularly horrible? The answer is, of course, that we are hardened to what we know, and we rationalise and even justify cruelties practised by us and our like while retaining the capacity to be outraged, even disgusted by practices equally cruel which, under the hands of strangers, take a different form. Clausewitz and the Cossacks were strangers to each other. He was revolted by such Cossack habits as riding down stragglers at the point of a lance, selling prisoners to the peasants for cash and stripping the unsaleable ones to the bare skin for the sake of their rags. It probably inspired his contempt that, as a French officer observed, 'when we faced up to them boldly they never offered resistance – even [when we] were outnumbered two to one'.[8] Cossacks, in short, were cruel to the weak and cowardly in the face of the brave, exactly the opposite pattern of behaviour to that which a Prussian officer and gentleman had been schooled to observe. The pattern was to persist. At the battle of Balaclava during the Crimean War of 1854 two Cossack regiments were sent forward to oppose the charge of the Light Brigade; a watching Russian officer reported that, 'frightened by the disciplined order of the mass of [British] cavalry bearing down on them, [the Cossacks] did not hold, but, wheeling to their left, began to fire on their own troops in an effort to clear their way of escape.' When the Light Brigade had been driven out of the Valley of Death by the Russian artillery, 'the first to recover', reported another Russian officer, 'were the Cossacks, and, true to their nature, they set themselves to the task in hand – rounding up riderless English horses and offering them for sale'.[9] The spectacle would no doubt have reinforced Clausewitz's contempt, strengthening his conviction that the Cossacks did not deserve the dignity of the title 'soldiery'; despite their mercenary conduct, they could not even be called proper mercenaries, who are normally faithful to their contract; Clausewitz would have probably considered them mere scavengers, who made a living on the offal of war but shrank from the butchery.

For the real work of war in the age of Clausewitz was butchery. Men stood silent and inert in rows to be slaughtered, often for hours at a time; at Borodino the infantry of Ostermann-Tolstoi's corps are reported to have stood under point-blank artillery fire for two hours, 'during which the only movement was the stirring in the lines caused by falling bodies'. Surviving the slaughter did not mean an end to butchery; Larrey, Napoleon's senior surgeon, performed two hundred amputations in the night after Borodino, and his patients were the lucky ones. Eugène Labaume described 'the interior of the gullies' that crisscrossed the battlefield: 'almost all of the wounded by a natural instinct had dragged themselves thither to seek protection . . . heaped on top of each other and swimming helplessly in their own blood, some called on passers-by to put them out of their misery.'[10]

These slaughterhouse scenes were the inevitable outcome of a way of warmaking that provoked peoples whom Clausewitz found savage, like the Cossacks, to flight when it threatened to involve them but, if they had not witnessed it, to laughter when they had it described to them. European drill, when first demonstrated by Takashima, the Japanese military reformer, to some high-ranking samurai in 1841, evoked ridicule; the Master of the Ordnance said that the spectacle of 'men raising and manipulating their weapons all at the same time and with the same motion looked as if they were playing some children's game'.[11] This was the reaction of hand-to-hand warriors, for whom fighting was an act of self-expression by which a man displayed not only his courage but also his individuality. The Greek *klephts* – half-bandits, half-rebels against Turkish rule whom their sympathisers, the French, German and British Philhellenes, many of them ex-officers of the Napoleonic wars, tried to instruct in close-order drill at the outset of Greece's war of independence in 1821 – also reacted with ridicule, but in disbelief rather than contempt. Their style of fighting – a very ancient one, encountered by Alexander the Great in his invasion of Asia Minor – was to build little walls at a point of likely encounter with the enemy and then to provoke the enemy to action by taunts and insults; when the enemy closed, they would run away. They lived to fight another day, but not to win the war, a point that they simply could not grasp. The Turks also fought in ethnic style: theirs was to rush forward in a loose charge with a fanatical disregard for casualties. The Philhellenes argued that unless the Greeks stood up to the Turks they would never win a battle; the Greeks objected that if they stood in the European fashion, breasts bared to the Turkish muskets, they would all be killed and so lose the war in any case.

'For Greeks a blush – for Greece a tear' wrote Byron, the most celebrated of the Philhellenes. He had hoped with other lovers of liberty 'to make a new Thermopylae' at the side of the Greeks. His discovery that they were invincible only in their ignorance of rational tactics depressed and disillusioned him, as it did other European idealists. At the heart of Philhellenism lay the belief that the modern Greeks were, under their dirt and ignorance, the same people as the ancient Greeks. Shelley, in his preface to *Hellas* – 'The world's great age begins anew/The golden years return' – put this belief in its most succinct form: 'The Modern Greek is the descendant of those glorious beings whom the imagination almost refuses to figure to itself as belonging to our kind, and he inherits much of their sensibility, their rapidity of conception, their enthusiasm and their courage.' But Philhellenes who shared a battlefield with Greeks not only rapidly abandoned their belief in the common identity of ancients and moderns; among those who survived to return to Europe, 'almost without exception', writes William St Clair, the historian of Philhellenism, 'they hated the Greeks with a deep loathing, and cursed themselves for their stupidity in having been deceived'.[12] Shelley's naïvely poetic proclamation of the courage of the modern Greeks was particularly galling. The Philhellenes wanted to believe that they would display the same tenacity in close-order, in 'the battle to the death on foot', as the ancient hoplites had done in their wars against the Persians. It was that style of fighting which, by devious routes, had come to characterise their own brand of warfare in western Europe. They expected at the least that contemporary Greeks would show themselves willing to re-learn close-order tactics, if only because that was the key to winning their freedom from the Turks. When they found that they would not – that Greek 'war aims' were limited to winning the freedom to persist in their *klepht* ways of cocking a snook at authority in their mountain borderlands, subsisting by banditry, changing sides when it suited them, murdering their religious enemies when chance offered, parading in tawdry finery, brandishing ferocious weapons, stuffing their purses with unhonoured bribes and never, never, dying to the last man, or the first if they could help it – the Philhellenes were reduced to concluding that only a break in the bloodline between ancient and modern Greeks could explain the collapse of a heroic culture.

The Philhellenes tried but failed to make the Greeks accept their military culture. Clausewitz did not try but would have failed to make the Cossacks accept his military culture. What he and they failed to see was that their own Western way of fighting, typified by the great eighteenth-century French Marshal de Saxe in his acute critique of the military shortcomings of the Turks and their enemies as marked by *'l'ordre, et la discipline, et la manière de combattre'*, was quite as much an expression of their own culture as the 'live to fight another day' tactics of the Cossacks and the *klephts*.[13]

In short, it is at the cultural level that Clausewitz's answer to his question, What is war?, is defective. That is not altogether surprising.

We all find it difficult to stand far enough outside our own culture to perceive how it makes us, as individuals, what we are. Modern Westerners, with their commitment to the creed of individuality, find the difficulty as acute as others elsewhere have. Clausewitz was a man of his times, a child of the Enlightenment, a contemporary of the German Romantics, an intellectual, a practical reformer, a man of action, a critic of his society and a passionate believer in the necessity for it to change. He was a keen observer of the present and a devotee of the future. Where he failed was in seeing how deeply rooted he was in his own past, the past of the professional officer class of a centralised European state. Had his mind been furnished with just one extra intellectual dimension – and it was already a very sophisticated mind indeed – he might have been able to perceive that war embraces much more than politics: that it is always an expression of culture, often a determinant of cultural forms, in some societies the culture itself.

WHO WAS CLAUSEWITZ?

Clausewitz was a regimental officer. That requires some explanation. A regiment is a unit of military force, typically a body of soldiers about a thousand strong. In eighteenth-century Europe, the regiment was an established feature of the military landscape and it survives intact into our own time; indeed, some existing regiments, notably in the British and Swedish armies, have continuous histories of some three centuries. Yet at its birth in the seventeenth century the regiment was not merely a new but a revolutionary constituent of European life. Its influence became as significant as that of autonomous bureaucracies and equitable fiscal authorities, and interwoven with them.

The regiment – semantically the word connects with the concept of government – was a device for securing the control of armed force to the state. The complex reasons for its emergence derived from a crisis which had developed two hundred years earlier in the relationship between European rulers and their providers of military service. Traditionally kings had depended for the raising of armies, when needed, upon landholders in the countryside, to whom local rights of subsistence and authority were devolved in return for their promise to bring armed men, in numbers proportionate to the grants of land held, and for a stated period, on demand. The system was in the last resort determined by the subsistence question: in primitive economies, where harvesting and distributing are constrained by difficulties of transport, armed men must be planted on the land, with rights over the harvest, if they are not to relapse into labouring status.

This feudal system was never neat, however – its varieties in place and over time defy categorisation – and rarely efficient. By the fifteenth century it had become very inefficient indeed. A condition approaching permanent warfare afflicted much of Europe, the result of both external threat and internal fractiousness, which the feudal armies could not suppress. Attempts to make armed forces more effective, by conceding greater independence to landholders in the worst-troubled areas or paying knights to serve under arms, only heightened the problem; the landholders declined to muster when called, built stronger castles, raised private armies, waged war in their own right – sometimes against the sovereigns. Kings had long supplemented feudal with mercenary force – when they could raise the money. In mid-fifteenth-century Europe, kings and the great landholders alike found their territory ravaged by mercenaries who had been called into service by offers of cash which had then dried up. Unpaid mercenaries became a scourge, sometimes as greatly feared as the intruders – Magyars, Saracens, Vikings – who had inaugurated the militarisation and castellation of Europe in the first place.

The problem was circular: to raise more soldiers as a means of restoring order was to risk adding to the number of marauders (*écorcheurs* as the French called them, scorchers of the earth); to shrink from restoring order was to condemn the tillers of the soil to rape and pillage. Ultimately a king of France, the country worst afflicted, took the plunge. Recognising that the *écorcheurs* had 'become, despite themselves, military outcasts, yet hoping sooner or later to be recognised by the king or the great lords', Charles VII 'proceeded in 1445–6 not, as is sometimes said, to create a permanent army but to choose from the mass of available soldiers' the best on offer.[14] Mercenary companies with a uniform composition were formed and officially recognised as military servants of the monarchy, whose function would be to extirpate the rest.

The *compagnies d'ordonnance*, as Charles VII's creations were called, were made up of infantrymen, whose social inferiority to the feudal cavalry put them at a military disadvantage, enhanced in turn by prevailing doubts about their physical ability to stand against cavalry on the battlefield. Some infantry, notably the populist Swiss, had already shown a capacity to do down mounted men with edged weapons alone; when effective handguns came into general use at the beginning of the sixteenth century, the *moral* point, as the military historian Sir Michael Howard has characterised it, was settled by technology for good.[15] Thenceforward infantry consistently beat cavalry, which found itself marginalised on the battlefield, while continuing to insist on recognition of its ancient social standing. That social standing was, however, further and simultaneously undermined by the impact of gunpowder on the feudal cavalry chiefs' strongholds. Battery by mobile artillery, a new weapon first effectively deployed by Charles VII's successor, Charles VIII, spelt an end to the defiance of royal authority by lords with strong castles. The process began in the 1490s; by the early 1600s their descendants were pleased to accept colonelcies of infantry by royal favour.

Such colonelcies were attached to the 'regiment' – or command – of a collection of companies, the company itself having been proved by experience to be too small either to count on the battlefield or to attract, unless it were to a company of royal guards, a man of standing as commander. Thus regimental colonels in most European armies were also proprietors, as were the chiefs of the mercenary units that continued to exist side by side with the new royal regiments well into the eighteenth century. Proprietors were paid a lump sum from the royal treasury, spent it as they chose on pay and uniforms, and usually sold the subordinate offices, captaincies and lieutenancies, to supplement their incomes; 'purchase' of commissions persisted in the British army until 1871.

These new regiments rapidly acquired a character different from that of the mercenary bands of late feudalism and the Wars of Religion, which had usually disbanded when funds dried up (unless, as happened to numbers of Italian city states, the hirelings took control of government). They became permanent royal – eventually national – institutions, often acquiring a fixed headquarters in a provincial city, recruiting in the surrounding area and drawing their officers from a coterie of associated aristocratic families. The Prussian 34th Infantry Regiment, which Clausewitz joined in 1792, at the age of eleven, was just such a regiment. Founded in 1720 and garrisoned at the Brandenburg town of Neuruppin, forty miles from Berlin, it had a royal prince as colonel; its officers were drawn from Prussia's minor nobility, while the soldiers – conscripted for an indefinite term from the poorest in society – formed, with their wives, children and invalid comrades, more than half the town's population.

A hundred years later, the whole of Europe would be dotted with such garrison towns, some giving a home to several regiments. At their worst such regiments resembled that of Anna Karenina's lover, Vronsky, which Tolstoy depicts as a dandies' club, officered by idlers and swells who cared more for their horses than their men.[16] At their best, however, such regiments became 'schools of the nation', which encouraged temperance, physical fitness and proficiency in the three Rs. Clausewitz's regiment was a forerunner of the latter sort. Its

14

commander set up regimental schools to educate the young officers, to teach the soldiers to read and write and to train their wives in spinning and lace-making.

Such 'improving' regiments were a source of deep pride to their colonels, not least because they seemed models of social perfection, an idea deeply attractive to men of the Enlightenment. Though the soldiers were virtually enslaved, and effectively imprisoned in the garrison towns lest they desert, they made *en masse* a splendid spectacle, seemingly drawn from a species different from the brutish villagers who populated the countryside; and long service did eventually inure them to their lot. There are pathetic descriptions of Prussian veterans, too old and infirm to take the field, hobbling after their regiments as they departed on campaign, since they knew no other life but that of the ranks. Colonels who had formed such soldiers, even if by the drill book and the lash, may well have convinced themselves that they were instruments of social virtue. If they did so, however, they deluded themselves, for the paradoxical reason that the regiments succeeded all too well on their own terms. They had been founded to isolate society's disruptive elements for society's good, though that had been forgotten. They ended by isolating themselves from society altogether, differentiated by their own rules, rituals and disciplines.

The social failure of the Prussian army was unlikely to have troubled the young Clausewitz had it not also condemned the Prussian state to military catastrophe. Within a year of joining the army Clausewitz was pitched into battle against French soldiers animated by motives entirely different from those of the ex-serfs he was commanding. The armies of the French Revolution were bombarded by propaganda about the equality of Frenchmen as citizens of the Republic and about the duty of all citizens to bear arms. Their wars with Europe's surviving monarchical armies were characterised as struggles to overthrow the aristocratic order wherever it was found, not only so that the Revolution might be defended at home but so that its liberating principles might be implanted wherever men were still unfree. For whatever reason – the subject is extremely complex – the Revolutionary armies proved almost impossible to beat, and their military dynamism persisted even after the good republican General Bonaparte had made himself the Emperor Napoleon.

In 1806 Napoleon turned his attention to Prussia and overthrew its army in a few whirlwind weeks. Clausewitz found himself a prisoner on French soil and, when allowed to return home, an officer of a skeleton army that existed only by French tolerance. For a few years he conspired with his seniors, Generals Scharnhorst and Gneisenau, in a plot to flesh

15

out the army under Napoleon's nose, but in 1812 he rebelled against gradualism and took the path of the 'double patriot'. 'Double patriotism' impelled him to disobey his king's orders to serve under Napoleon in the invasion of Russia and instead to join the tsar's army in the cause of Prussian freedom. As a tsarist officer he fought at Borodino and, still in Russian uniform, returned to Prussia to fight in its War of Liberation in 1813. 'Double patriotism', incidentally, was to be the code of the ultra-nationalist Japanese officers who disobeyed the moderate policies of the Emperor's government before the Second World War in order, as they saw it, to obey the Emperor's true interests.

Only patriotic desperation could have driven Clausewitz to such a subversive course; having chosen that path he was thereby energised to embark on a career of intellectual subversion that had a worldwide effect. The disaster of 1806 had profoundly shaken his belief in the Prussian state; it had not, however, undermined his belief in the values of the regimental culture in which he had been raised. He had, indeed, no way of thinking of war except as a calling in which the soldier, by his conduct, and particularly the officer, defied nature. Nature argued for flight, for cowardice, for self-interest; nature made for Cossacking, whereby a man fought if he chose and not otherwise, and might turn to commerce on the battlefield if that suited his ends – this was 'real war' at its worst. The best-observed ideals of regimental culture, however – total obedience, single-minded courage, self-sacrifice, honour – most nearly approached that 'true war' which Clausewitz convinced himself a professional soldier should make his end.

As Michael Howard has pointed out, the distinction between 'real war' and 'true war' was not original to Clausewitz.[17] It was 'in the air' in the early nineteenth-century Prussian army, not least because it accorded with the idealist philosophy that pervaded Prussia's universities and cultural life. Clausewitz had no formal philosophical training; 'rather, he was a typical representative of his generation, who attended lectures on logic and ethics designed for the general public, read relevant nonprofessional books and articles, and drew scraps of ideas at second and third hand from the cultural environment.'[18] The cultural environment was conducive to a military theory founded on a dialectic between true and real war; it further afforded Clausewitz the language, the arguments and the mode of presentation best calculated to commend his theory to his contemporaries.

Clausewitz was in a dilemma after he returned to Prussia in Russian uniform in 1813. His career was blighted, yet he remained a fervent

Prussian nationalist. He wished to design for his country's army a theory of war that would ensure it victory in the future, yet his country showed no inclination to undergo the sort of internal change that had made France invincible during the Revolution. Clausewitz did not himself desire that it should; he despised the French, thought them inferior in national qualities to his own people – sly and glib where Prussians were truthful and noble – and remained too rooted in his monarchical and regimental upbringing to want revolutionary ideals transplanted to his kingdom. His rational powers told him, none the less, that it was the revolutionary fervour of the French armies that had brought them victory. In France during the Revolution, politics had been everything; in Prussia politics had been and very largely remained even after Napoleon's defeat nothing but the whim of the king. The dilemma was therefore: how might one have the forms of warfare practised by the armies of the French Republic and Napoleon without the politics of revolution? How might one have popular warfare without a popular state? Could he but find the language to persuade the Prussian army that warfare was indeed a form of political activity, that the more nearly it could approximate to 'true war' the better it served a state's political ends, and that any gap remaining between 'true war' and the imperfect form of 'real war' should be recognised simply as the deference that strategy paid to political necessity, then the Prussian soldier could be safely left in a state of political innocence, with the difference that he would thenceforward fight as if the fire of politics flowed in his veins.

Clausewitz's solution to his military dilemma approximates closely, in a sense, to the solution that Marx found to his political dilemma only a few years afterward. Both were raised in the same cultural environment of German idealism, though Marx had had the formal philosophical training that Clausewitz had not, and it is extremely significant that Clausewitz has always stood high in the favour of Marxist intellectuals, Lenin foremost among them. The reason is easy to see. Reductivism is the essence of Marxist methodology, and Clausewitz argued by reduction that in war the worse the better, because the worse is nearer to 'true' rather than 'real' war. Marx also was to argue that the worse the better, the worse in politics being the culmination of the class struggle, revolution, which overthrows the hollow world of 'real' politics and ushers in the 'true' society of proletarian victory.

The motives that impelled Marx to argue as he did were not the same as those that animated Clausewitz. He was the bolder spirit; while Clausewitz clung to the role of insider, hoped – vainly – to be appointed ambassador

17

to London or chief of the general staff, and gladly accepted promotions and decorations, Marx revelled in the role of outsider.[19] Exile, poverty, execration by the Prussian state were grist to his mill. Life on the outside strengthened his hand, while Clausewitz believed that only by remaining inside the system could he change it. Yet, intellectually, more united than divided the two men, for both had to overcome a similar philosophical difficulty, that of persuading a chosen audience to a point of view to which it was highly resistant. Marx was an apostle of revolution to a society whose progressive elements were profoundly disillusioned by revolution, who remembered that the French Revolution and the 1830 revolution had failed, who were to see the 1848 revolution fail, and who were oppressed on all sides by the power of the monarchical or bourgeois state. Clausewitz was the apostle of a revolutionary philosophy of warmaking, which sought to depict war as a political activity to a caste that held politics to be anathema. Both eventually found a means to overcome the intellectual resistance of the audience each sought to convert. Marx conceived a set of what he considered scientific historical laws which laid down for progressives not merely the hope but the certainty, the inevitability, of the proletariat's victory. Clausewitz conceived a theory which elevated the regimental officer's values – total dedication to duty, even to dying in the cannon's mouth – to the status of a political creed, thereby absolving him from deeper political reflection.

On War and *Kapital*, different as they are in subject matter, may therefore be seen ultimately as two books of a kind. Clausewitz no doubt hoped that *On War* would achieve the same status as Adam Smith's *Wealth of Nations*, that supreme work of the Enlightenment mind; he may indeed have thought that, like Smith, he had done no more than to observe, describe and categorise the phenomena before his eyes. Marx, too, did much describing, much of it accurate. Drawing on Adam Smith's brilliant identification of industry's division of labour, he went on to characterise the emotion such division engenders as 'alienation'; so that where Smith saw in the processes of pre-mechanical pinmaking – when one man drew the wire, another cut it to length, a third pointed the shaft, a fourth forged the head – only the miraculous working of the 'unseen hand' that directed a market economy, Marx had the inspiration to diagnose that the desperation such work implants in a thinking and feeling man's breast would lead to what he called 'class war'. Marx drew the conclusion that the processes of mass production in an economic system where the worker did not own the means of production made revolution inevitable; and he was right enough in his observation for industrialists in our own times to persist in the search for means to make the process worker's lot tolerable, even meaningful. Clausewitz, too, began with description. He took military uniforms, songs and drill for granted, and went on from that starting-point to argue that the soldier's alienation (though he did not use the term) from his lot – hardship, wounds, death – was destined to lead armies to defeat and collapse, the military equivalent of revolution, if they could not be convinced that the terrible experience of 'true war' better served their state than the easier obligation of 'real war', with which all men-at-arms were familiar.

Just as common sense tells us that protracted class war is intolerable to any society in which it persists, and that revolution causes ills beside which those of class war appear trivial, common sense also warns that 'true war' may prove worse than flesh and blood can bear. Of course, Clausewitz, as a thinker, never expected that the gap between 'real war' and 'true war' could be closed altogether. Indeed, the strength of his appeal to intellectuals, particularly Marxist intellectuals, has always lain in the delicacy of his emphasis on the intangible factors – chance, misunderstanding, incapacity, incompetence, political change of mind, failure of will or collapse of consensus – that make 'real war' rather than 'true war' the more likely form any actual war will take. 'True war' is indeed unbearable.

And yet, despite the room for escape from the harshness of 'true war' that Clausewitz allowed, the paradox was that *On War* succeeded beyond what may have been his wildest expectations. He died a disappointed man in 1831, a victim of the last great European cholera pandemic, unpromoted and largely unhonoured in his own country; the text of *On War* saw the light of day only through the editorship of his devoted widow. Marx also died a disappointed man, twelve years after the defeat of the Paris commune of 1871, which appeared to spell finis to his confident prediction that revolution was the inevitable outcome of the oppression of Europe's proletariat by Europe's bourgeoisie. Yet, only thirty-four years later, in a country so backward that Marx dismissed its suitability as a revolutionary seedbed, revolution not merely took root but flowered into the first dictatorship of the proletariat. That was at the height of a great war among the bourgeois states, a war without which the circumstances of the Russian Revolution would not have been created. The terrible nature of that war, not the terrible nature of industrial capitalism, exerted the push to revolution in Russia, and the war's terrible nature was, as much as anything else, the belated outcome of Clausewitz's literary insistence that armies must strive to make 'real war' and 'true war' the same thing.

On War had proved a book of long-delayed effect. Not until forty years after its publication in 1832–5 did it become widely known, and then in a roundabout way. Helmuth von Moltke, chief of the Prussian general staff, had apparently magical gifts of generalship which had toppled the power of the Austrian and then the French empires in campaigns of a few weeks in 1871. The world wanted to know his secret, of course, and when Moltke revealed that, beside the Bible and Homer, the book that had most influenced him was *On War*, Clausewitz's posthumous fame was assured.[20] That Moltke had been a student at Prussia's war college when Clausewitz was its director was overlooked and in any case irrelevant; the world seized on the book itself, read it, translated it, often misunderstood it, but thereafter believed that it contained the essence of successful warmaking.

On War's onward march derived much of its force from its apparent validation by much that had happened in warfare since its composition. The most important of these developments was the spread of that regimentalism in which Clausewitz had been raised. 'The business of war', he laid down, in one of those characteristic modifications of his central idea of war as a political act, 'will always be individual and distinct. Consequently, for as long as they practise this activity, soldiers will think of themselves as members of a kind of guild, in whose regulations, laws and customs the spirit of war is given pride of place.' That 'kind of guild' was, of course, the regiment, whose spirit and values he then proceeded to categorise:

> An army that maintains its cohesion under the most murderous fire; that cannot be shaken by imaginary fears and resists well-found ones with all its might; that, proud of its victories, will not lose the strength to obey orders and its respect and trust for its officers even in defeat; whose physical power, like the muscles of an athlete, has been steeled by training in privation and effort . . . that is mindful of all these duties and qualities by virtue of the single powerful idea of the honour of its arms – such an army is imbued with the true military spirit.[21]

For 'army' read 'regiments', its constituent parts. Prussia in the nineteenth century was positively swamped by regiments; in 1831 there had been only forty of them, but by 1871 there were more than a hundred, not counting rifle battalions or cavalry. Every fit Prussian was a member of a regiment, or had been in his hot youth, and all understood the 'single powerful idea of the honour of its arms'.

That 'single powerful idea' brought Prussian arms victory in wars against Austria and France, and immediately sent officers in other nations scurrying to raise regiments on the Prussian model, recruited from the best of a nation's young men and supported by droves of older reservists who looked back on their conscript days as the *rite de passage* which ushered them from boyhood to manhood. This *rite de passage* became an important cultural form in European life, an experience common to almost all young European males and, through its universality, its ready acceptance by electorates as a social norm and its inescapable militarisation of society, a further validation of Clausewitz's dictum that war was a continuation of political activity. If peoples voted for conscription or acquiesced in conscription laws, how could it be denied that war and politics indeed belonged together on the same continuum?

And yet, the God of War is not mocked. When in 1914 the conscript regiments of Europe marched off to war, dragging their tails of reservists behind them, the war that embroiled them was worse by far than anything for which the citizens had bargained. In the First World War 'real war' and 'true war' rapidly became indistinguishable; the moderating influences which Clausewitz, as a dispassionate observer of military phenomena, had declared always operated to bring a war's potential nature and actual purpose into adjustment dwindled into invisibility; Germans, French, British and Russians found themselves apparently fighting war for war's sake. The war's political objects – difficult enough to define in the first place – were forgotten, political restraints were overwhelmed, politicians who appealed to reason were execrated, politics even in the liberal democracies was rapidly reduced to a mere justification of bigger battles, longer casualty lists, costlier budgets, overflowing human misery.

Politics played no part in the conduct of the First World War worth mentioning. The First World War was, on the contrary, an extraordinary, a monstrous cultural aberration, the outcome of an unwitting decision by Europeans in the century of Clausewitz – which began with his return from Russia in 1813 and ended in 1913, the last year of the long European peace – to turn Europe into a warrior society. Clausewitz was not the architect of that cultural decision, any more than Marx was the architect of the revolutionary impulse which perverted liberalism during the same period, but each bears weighty responsibility. Their great books, purporting to be works of science, were in fact heady works of ideology, laying down a vision of the world not as it actually was but as it might be.

The purpose of war, Clausewitz said, was to serve a political end; the nature of war, he succeeded in arguing, was to serve only itself. By conclusion, his logic therefore ran, those who make war an end in itself are likely to be more successful than those who seek to moderate

21

its character for political purposes. The peace of the most peaceful century in European history was held ransom to this subversive idea, which bubbled and seethed like the flux of an active volcano beneath the surface of progress and prosperity. The wealth generated by the century paid, on a scale never before witnessed, for the works of real peace – schools, universities, hospitals, roads, bridges, new cities, new workplaces, the infrastructure of a vast and benevolent continental economy. It also generated, through taxes, improved public health, higher birth rates, and a new and ingenious military technology, the wherewithal to fight true war, through the creation of the strongest warrior society the world had ever known. When in 1818 Clausewitz began the manuscript of *On War*, Europe was a continent disarmed. The Grand Army of Napoleon had melted away after his exile to St Helena, and those of his enemies had dwindled proportionately. Large-scale conscription had effectively been abolished everywhere, the arms industry had collapsed, generals were pensioners, veterans begged in the streets. Ninety-six years later, on the eve of the First World War, almost every fit European male of military age had a soldier's identity card among his personal papers, telling him where to report for duty in the event of general mobilisation. The regimental depots bulged with spare weapons and uniforms to kit the reservists out; even the horses in the farmers' fields were docketed for requisition should war come.

At the beginning of July 1914 there were some four million Europeans actually in uniform; at the end of August there were twenty million, and many tens of thousands had already been killed. The submerged warrior society had sprung armed through the surface of the peaceful landscape and the warriors were to wage war until, four years later, they could wage it no more. And although this catastrophic outcome must not be laid at the door of Clausewitz's study, we are nevertheless right to see Clausewitz as the ideological father of the First World War, just as we are right to perceive Marx as the ideological father of the Russian Revolution. The ideology of 'true war' was the ideology of the First World War's armies; and the appalling fate that those armies brought upon themselves by their dedication to it may be Clausewitz's enduring legacy.

Yet Clausewitz was not merely an ideologist but also a historian, to whose hand there lay available much else besides his own experience as a regimental officer in a monarchical army and its peremptory treatment by the soldier-citizens of revolutionary France. Reflecting at the end of the 1820s on the whirlwind events of his youth, he ascribed them to the people's new share in the great affairs of state; their participation, in turn, resulted partly from the impact that the Revolution had on the internal conditions of every state and partly on the danger that France posed to everyone. Will this always be the case in the future? From now on will every war in Europe be waged with the full resources of the state, and therefore have to be fought only over major issues that affect the people? Or shall we again see a gradual separation taking place between government and people? Such questions are difficult to answer . . .[22]

Good historian though he was, Clausewitz allowed the two institutions – state and regiment – that circumscribed his own perception of the world to dominate his thinking so narrowly that he denied himself the room to observe how different war might be in societies where both state and regiment were alien concepts. That was not a mistake Moltke would make. He espoused the ideology of Clausewitz for purely utilitarian ends, knowing that war in the further corners of the earth – in Egypt and Turkey, for example, where he had soldiered in the service of the Sultan – could take forms utterly strange to his ideological master, and yet appropriate enough to, indeed indivisible from, the nature of the societies that practised them.

   In the first form, theocratic inhibitions on the waging of war were eventually overwhelmed by material necessity. This becomes apparent in the mysterious history of Easter Island. In the second, where warriordom assumed an extreme form in the Zulu kingdom, it was ambient social chaos that transformed the comparative benevolence of a primitive pastoral society. In the third, that of Mameluke Egypt, religious prohibitions on members of the same creed waging war on each other gave rise to the strange institution of military slavery. In the fourth, samurai Japan, an available improvement in the technical means of waging war was outlawed in the interests of preserving the existing social structure. Much of this history was, of course, closed to Clausewitz. Even if it was theoretically possible for him to have read something of the institutions of the Polynesian Easter Islanders and of samurai Japan from the literature of voyagers to the Pacific which aroused widespread interest in eighteenth-century Europe, he could have known nothing of the Zulus, whose rise to dominance in southern Africa was only beginning at the time of his death. Of the Mamelukes, nevertheless, he should have known a good deal, if only because they were among the most celebrated subjects of the Ottoman Turks whose empire, even in Clausewitz's lifetime, remained a major military factor in the international politics of Europe. He would certainly have known of the Ottomans' personal military slaves, the

23

Janissaries, whose existence testified to the paramountcy of religion, rather than politics, in Turkish public life. His decision to ignore Ottoman military institutions flawed the integrity of his theory at its roots. To look beyond military slavery into the even stranger military cultures of the Polynesians, the Zulus and the samurai, whose forms of warfare defied altogether the rationality of politics as it is understood by Westerners, is to perceive how incomplete, parochial and ultimately misleading is the idea that war is the continuation of politics.

WAR AS CULTURE

Easter Island

Easter Island is one of the loneliest places on earth, a dot in the southern Pacific more than 2000 miles from South America and 3000 from New Zealand, the nearest large land masses. It is also one of the world's smallest inhabited places, a triangle of extinct volcanoes about seventy square miles in extent. Despite its isolation, it belongs firmly within the culture of Polynesia, a highly developed New Stone Age civilisation of the central Pacific which in the eighteenth century embraced the thousands of islands which lie between Easter Island, New Zealand and Hawaii, the three apices of the Polynesian triangle, distant from each other by thousands of miles in space and hundreds of years in date of original settlement.

Polynesian civilisation was extraordinarily adventurous. Its European discoverers and early ethnographers could not at first believe that a people without a written language could have colonised such an enormous area – thirty-eight major archipelagos and islands spread over twenty million square miles of ocean; elaborate explanations, all false, were devised to deny that the Polynesian canoe sailors had achieved feats of navigation akin to those of Cook and La Pérouse. Polynesian culture remained, nevertheless, remarkably congruent: not only were the languages of widely separated islands evidently cognate, but the social institutions flourishing on Hawaii, New Zealand and Easter Island remained constant and startlingly similar.

Polynesian society is theocratic in structure. Chiefs, who are believed to be descended from the gods, in turn deified or supernatural forefathers, also hold the office of high priest. As high priest the chief mediates between god and man to bestow on his people the fruits of the soil and the sea; his power of mediation – *mana* – entitles him to sacred rights (*tapu* or taboo) over land, fishing-grounds, their produce and much else

24

that is good or desirable. *Mana* and taboo assured remarkably stable and peaceful societies in normal circumstances and in the happiest Polynesian islands theocracy safely regulated relations between chiefs and people, as well as among the clans that had descended from the original chief.[23]

Yet there was never a Polynesian Golden Age. Even in the benevolent Pacific, circumstances were not always normal, if normality means that resources were always sufficient to accommodate populations. Populations grew, though islanders regulated their numbers by birth control, infanticide and the encouragement of emigration, which they called 'voyaging'. Times came when fertile land and productive fishing-grounds were fully exploited and no nearby or known island beckoned. Then serious trouble began. The word for a warrior, *toa*, is identical with that for the ironwood tree, from which clubs and other weapons were made – and used to settle the quarrels, over insults, property, women and succession to position, to which man is naturally prone. The *mana* of a chief had always been enhanced if he were a notable warrior. But in times of trouble warriors who were not chiefs broke taboo to seize what they needed or wanted, with disastrous effect on the Polynesian social structure. Sub-clans might become dominant and in extreme circumstances a clan might be driven from its territory altogether.

The worst case was played out on Easter Island, and with particular deadliness. How the Polynesians, perhaps in the third century AD, had found the island, 1100 miles distant over open ocean from the next nearest settled place, remains a mystery. Find it they did, however, bringing with them the staples of island life, sweet potatoes, bananas and sugar cane. They cleared land under the three peaks, harvested fish and seabirds and founded settlements. About AD 1000 they also embarked on the most elaborate veneration of the theocratic principle found in the Polynesian world. Though the population of Easter Island seems never to have exceeded 7000 souls, it succeeded over the course of the next 700 years in carving and raising more than 300 giant statues, typically five times life-size, on extensive temple platforms. In the final stage of statue-raising on Easter Island, during the sixteenth century AD, the islanders also invented a script, which appears to have been used by priests to help memorise oral traditions and genealogies. This was the culmination of a civilised time in which the perceived power of the gods, mediated through living chiefs, imposed peace and order.

Then something went wrong. Imperceptibly a growing population de-nuded the island's environment. Forest clearance reduced rainfall, and the fields yielded less; it also reduced the yield of timber from which canoes were built, thus diminishing the harvest of the sea. Life on Easter Island started to become brutish. A new artefact appeared, the *mata'a*, a flaked obsidian spearhead of deadly effect.[24] Warriors, called *tangata rima toto*, 'the men with bloodied hands', became dominant. The pyramid of clans descended from the founding chief coalesced into two groups, which from separate ends of the island warred incessantly. The paramount chief, descendant of the founder, became a symbolic figure, whose *mana* no longer impressed. In the course of social disintegration through warfare, the statues were systematically toppled, either as an insult to the *mana* of an enemy clan or as a token of rebellion by commoners against the chiefs whose *mana* had failed them. Eventually a bizarre new religion, utterly at odds with the stately theocracy of Polynesia, emerged: 'the men with bloodied hands' competed to be the first to find an egg of the sooty tern, thus winning chieftainship – for a year only.

When the Dutch voyager Roggeveen landed on Easter Island in 1722, anarchy was already far advanced; by the end of the nineteenth century, degeneration – compounded by European slave-raiding and the diseases the Europeans had introduced – had reduced the population to 111 persons, who retained but the sketchiest oral traditions of their remarkable past. From what they told, and from the dramatic archaeological evidence, anthropologists reconstructed a doleful picture of Easter Island society in what they called its Decadent Phase. Not only did it show endemic warfare and betray signs of cannibalism; it also revealed the physical extent of the efforts some islanders made to escape from the effects of warfare altogether. Many of the natural caves and tubes in the lava had been closed with dressed stones taken from desecrated statue platforms, to make personal or family refuges, and at one end of the island a ditch had been dug to separate a peninsula from the mainland, surely a strategic defensive undertaking.

Refuges and strategic defences constitute two of the three forms of fortification that military analysts recognise; only the third, the regional stronghold, is missing from Easter Island. Its absence does not denote a missing dimension of warfare that the Easter Islanders failed to practise. It is merely an index of how small the theatre of war was. Within the island's tiny compass, the islanders appear to have taught themselves the full logic of Clausewitzian warfare by bloody experience. They certainly learnt the importance of leadership, which Clausewitz so emphasised; the existence of the entrenchment at the Poike peninsula suggests that some of them agreed with his dictum that the strategic defensive is the strongest form of warfare; they may even, given the extraordinarily sharp decline in their numbers during the seventeenth century, and the mass-production of the newly invented obsidian spearhead, have attempted Clausewitzian warfare's crowning act, the decisive battle.

Yet to what self-defeating purpose! Clausewitz may have believed that war is the continuation of politics. Politics, however, is practised to serve culture, and the Polynesians, in their wider world, had devised a culture as beneficent as any within which men have lived. Bougainville, when he arrived at Tahiti in 1761, proclaimed that he had found the Garden of Eden and his account of beautiful people living happily in a state of nature became so influential that it contributed to the cult of the 'noble savage' which nourished intelligent European society's impatience with their own ordered but artificial eighteenth-century world. Out of that impatience grew the political dissent and Romantic ideology that together overthrew the kingly states in which the devotees of noble savagery had been raised.

Clausewitz, in his exaltation of the dramatic act – decisive battle – and of the egotistic individual – the leader, Napoleon in particular – was as Romantic as any enemy of the *ancien régime*. In his dedication to king and regiment, however, he remained bound by *mana* and taboo to an extent of which he was quite unaware. In monarchical Europe, before the French Revolution, the regiment was a device for restraining the violence of warriors and harnessing it to the purposes of kings. Because Prussia, of which Clausewitz was a servant, was peculiarly disfavoured with the good things of this world, its greatest king, Frederick the Great, had encouraged his officers to practise warfare with a ruthlessness which exceeded the bounds other kings thought proper. The propagation of his *mana*, as it were, required a violation of taboo which fellow kings thought improper.

Frederick, however, never put himself beyond the pale. He merely pushed warfare in the prevailing code to the limits of acceptable ruthlessness. Clausewitz, raised in a world in which royal *mana* and military taboos had been extinguished apparently for good, found the words to legitimise the new order. That it was no order at all, and that his philosophy of warfare was a recipe for the destruction of European culture, he failed to perceive altogether. How can he be blamed? The Easter Islanders, isolated in space and time from the larger, more benevolent Polynesian world, no doubt felt, had they been able to articulate the idea, that changed circumstances required a cultural revolution. They may even have invented a word equivalent to 'politics' to describe the ferment of loyalties which followed the succession to power of the annual finder of the first egg of the sooty tern. We cannot now say. The degenerate state

27

to which the survivors of endemic warfare found by the first anthropologists had been reduced was not conducive to a measured analysis of the
evolution through which their culture had passed. Nevertheless, there is
this observation to be made. Clausewitzian warfare did not serve the ends
of Polynesian culture. That culture, though it was not free, democratic,
dynamic or creative in any of the Western senses of those words, nevertheless adjusted local means to chosen ends in a fashion almost perfectly
adapted to the conditions of Pacific island life. *Mana* and taboo fixed a
balance between the roles of chief, warrior and clansman, to the benefit
of all three; and if their interrelationships can be called the 'politics' of
Polynesian life, then war was not its continuation. War, when it came in
a 'true' form to that corner of Polynesia called Easter Island, proved to
be a termination first of politics, then of culture, ultimately almost of life
itself.

The Zulus

The Easter Islanders played out their deadly, self-invented experiment
in total warfare unseen by the outside world. The Zulus, by contrast,
were drawn through the military revolution their society underwent at the
beginning of the nineteenth century into a highly coloured confrontation
with Western civilisation, in a tale which has grown with the telling. Its
beginnings were a little too late for Clausewitz to have been aware of the
drama unfolding in southern Africa – as he ought to have been of the
story of the Mamelukes which comes next. Its culmination has become
one of the great popular history stories of modern times, and a potent
element in the myth of the Afrikaner people, in whose great marble shrine
at Pretoria the figures of the Zulu warriors the Voortrekers fought are quite
as idealised as those of the Boer heroes themselves. That is not surprising;
the myth of the Afrikaners requires that their enemies should have been
both noble and terrible and, in the course of their rise as a nation at the
beginning of the nineteenth century until their catastrophic overthrow in
the war of 1879, the Zulus became very terrible warriors indeed.

In their origins the Zulus led a gentle, pastoral way of life. The
Nguni people from whom they rose, cattle-herders who had migrated
to the south-east African coast from the distant north in the fourteenth
century, were described by shipwrecked Europeans three centuries later
as 'in their intercourse with each other . . . very civil, polite and talkative,
saluting each other, whether male or female, young or old, whenever they
meet'.[25] They were kind to strangers, who might travel in perfect safety

among them, as long as they took the precaution not to carry iron or copper, which were so rare that they gave 'inducement to murder', and they were notably law-abiding, particularly in personal relations. Slavery was unknown, revenge had 'little or no sway', and disputes were referred to the chief, whose word was accepted 'without a murmur'. Chiefs themselves were subject to law, and might be fined by their counsellors or have their decisions overturned by a higher chief.

Though their early European visitors noted that *ubuntu* – humanity – was their most important value, the Nguni did fight and they did wage war. The *casus belli* was usually a quarrel over grazing, the essential resource in a society where cattle may well outnumber people, and the loser ended up on new and poorer land. As is typical with primitive people living in underpopulated country, the result was not slaughter but displacement.

Battles tended to be ritualised, conducted under the gaze of old and young, begun with an exchange of insults and finished when casualties were inflicted. There were natural as well as customary limitations on the level of violence: because metals were scarce, weapons were made of fire-hardened wood, thrown rather than used hand-to-hand; and should a warrior happen to kill an opponent, he was obliged at once to leave the field and undergo purification, since the spirit of his victim would certainly otherwise bring fatal illness to him and his family.[26]

Suddenly in a few decades at the beginning of the nineteenth century, this typically 'primitive' style of warmaking was overturned. Shaka, chief of the Zulu, a small Nguni tribe, became the commander of an army of savagely disciplined regiments that waged battles of annihilation, and his Zulu kingdom became a power in southern Africa; the chiefdoms it displaced were reduced to fugitive tribes, wandering hundreds of miles in a chaos of social disorganisation to find some place of refuge.

Europeans who witnessed the rise of Shaka, like the navigators baffled by the Polynesians' mastery of maritime skills, sought some explanation for it which denied a spontaneous cause. Shaka, it was said, had met Europeans and learnt of European military organisation and tactics. That was certainly untrue.[27] But what was true was that the benevolent conditions enjoyed by the northern Nguni in their idyllic pastoral phase changed for the worse at the end of the eighteenth century. Cattle, by which the Nguni measured their wealth, had grown in numbers to exceed the supply of 'sweet' grazing. To the west rose the dramatic barrier of the Drakensberg, approached by 'sour' grazing inhospitable to a pastoral economy. The tsetse fly belt, on the Limpopo River to the north, denied expansion in that direction. The introduction of maize, brought to Africa from America in the sixteenth century, led to an increase in population among the southern Nguni, and further south the Boers of the Cape were blocking, with firearms and grim determination to find *Lebensraum*, any opportunity to move in that direction. To the east lay the sea.[28]

Some adjustment of their free-and-easy way of life had already occurred before Shaka rose to fame. A previous chief had abolished the system by which warriors, when called to serve their chief in war, went with others from their locality to muster at his kraal. Instead he formed 'age regiments', of men born in the same years. Their separation, during military service, from their potential brides reduced the birth rate; it also increased the power of the chief and the amount of the tribute – in cattle, produce and hunted game – due to him, since the warriors' labour was his while they were under arms.

Shaka institutionalised these changes to an extreme degree. 'Age regiments' became permanent bodies, living apart from civil society in military barracks. Warriors were denied marriage not for the duration of a campaigning season or two but until their fortieth year, when they were allotted wives from the equivalent of women's regiments that Shaka also formed.

The old restraints on battle were also cast aside. Shaka designed a new weapon, a stabbing spear, with which he trained his men to close with and kill their opponents. (It may be that, with the advance of the Boers out of the Cape, iron had become more plentifully available than thitherto; this is an aspect of the intensification of Nguni warfare which does not seem to been explored by historians. The stabbing assegai would certainly have required more iron in its manufacture than the throwing spear previously used.)

Hand-to-hand fighting with edged weapons requires close-order tactics. These Shaka invented also. He had already obliged his men to discard sandals and learn to run long distances on hardened feet. In battle he formed his regiments into two wings with a strong centre and a reserve in the rear; when the moment for engagement came, the centre charged in dense ranks to fix the enemy, while each wing raced to encircle him from a flank. The purification ritual was abandoned until after the battle was over.[29] When the killing started, a warrior disembowelled his victim, to ensure death, and then went on to the next. Disembowelling was the traditional means of releasing the spirit of the dead, which it was believed would otherwise drive the killer insane.

Shaka did not shrink from killing women and children, a practice repugnant to his Nguni forebears, but in general he was content to

30

kill the men of a neighbouring tribe's ruling family, together with the warriors who gave battle; survivors were incorporated into his growing kingdom. His purpose was to build a nation out of the Nguni kin who would accept his authority, and to extend the lands they occupied.

Beyond the spreading borders of Zululand this system caused catastrophe. Shaka's methods cured overpopulation in Zululand, but among his neighbours his methods set in train a series of displacements which robbed one people after another of their traditional homelands and their settled ways of life. 'The rise of the Zulu kingdom had repercussions from the Cape Colonial frontier to Lake Tanganyika. Every community throughout approximately a fifth of the African continent was profoundly affected, and many were utterly disrupted.'[30]

These awful effects of Zulu imperialism became known as the *Difaqane*, 'forced migration'. 'By 1824 most of the country between the Tukela and the Mzimkhulu [rivers], the Drakensberg and the sea, was devastated. Thousands of people had been killed; others had fled further south; and others had been absorbed into the Zulu nation. In Natal organised community life virtually ceased.'[31] This is not a small area; it measures about 15,000 square miles. Its dimensions are as nothing, however, to the distances over which fugitives from the Zulus fled. One group terminated their flight on the shores of Lake Tanganyika, 2000 miles from their starting-place. In the course of their wanderings, some groups had lost their cattle altogether and been forced to subsist on weeds and roots; some had been driven to cannibalism; many had found themselves caught up in 'hordes', which stripped the land like locusts, marking the course of their passage by a trail of dead and dying.

Young Zulus remained true to Shaka's military system and ethos for some time after his fall in 1828. It is a besetting fault of triumphant warrior systems that fail to fund economic and social diversification from the fruits of victory, that they become fossilised in their moment of glory. Why that should be is a theme of this book; in the case of the Zulus it was undoubtedly the result of their having to live, as was said of the Prussians, *toujours en vedette* – so threatened by equally potent military powers (which happened in nineteenth-century southern Africa also to be at a more advanced stage of economic development) that they continued to concentrate all their energies in an exclusively military form. As so often elsewhere, the form was that which had determined their rise. The Zulus did eventually acquire firearms but they failed to adapt their tactics to the new weapon, persisting in the mass attack with the stabbing assegai as their means to battlefield supremacy.

Shaka was a perfect Clausewitzian. He designed a military system to serve and protect a particular way of life, which it did with dramatic efficiency. Zulu culture, by making warrior values paramount, by linking those values to the preservation of a cattle-herding economy, and by locking up the energies and imagination of the most dynamic members of the community in sterile military bondage until well past maturity, denied itself the chance to evolve and adapt to the world around it. In short, the rise and fall of the Zulu nation offers an awful warning of the shortcomings of the Clausewitzian analysis.

The Mamelukes

Bondage, in a stronger or weaker form, is a common condition of military service. Among the Zulus it reached an extreme. Shaka's warriors were not slaves, since it was custom, reinforced by terror, rather than law that bound them in servitude. Nevertheless they were, in a functional sense, slaves to Shaka's will. Soldiers might, however, be slaves under the law in past times, however contradictory their status seems to us today. Slavery in the modern world implies the absolute deprivation of the individual's liberty, while possession of weapons and mastery of their use are means to the individual's liberation. We do not perceive how a man may be armed and at the same time bereft of his freedom. In the medieval Muslim world, however, no conflict was perceived between the status of slave and soldier. Slave soldiers – Mamelukes – were a feature of many Muslim states. In the nature of things, they often became the rulers of such states, their leaders remaining in power for generations, yet far from using the power they enjoyed to make themselves legally free, they were adamant in perpetuating the Mameluke 'institution' and resisted all pressure to change its nature. There were understandable reasons for their resistance. They owed their dominance to their monopoly of elaborate skills of horsemanship and archery, which to abandon for the commoner practices of musketry or fighting on foot might have toppled them from their position. It was the narrowness of their military culture, like that of the Zulus, which nevertheless brought them down in the end. Though their political power derived from their military exclusivity, they preferred to persist in their outmoded warrior style rather than adapt to new ways in warfare. The Clausewitzian analysis, in their case as in that of the Zulus, was stood on its head. The holders of power made politics a continuation of warfare. Practically that was a nonsense. Culturally the Mamelukes had no alternative.

32

In the Islamic as in the Greek and Roman worlds, slavery took many forms, some quite benign; a slave might be a respected craftsman, a teacher, a businessman trading in part for himself, a confidential secretary. Islam, however, took the diversity of slavery further than the Greeks or Romans had done. Under the government of the caliphs – the 'successors' of Muhammad who exercised worldly as well as religious authority – a slave might become a high government official. It was an extension of this practice that made slaves soldiers and it was only within the Islamic world that such soldiers were to form a military élite.

That they came to do so derives from the conflict that quickly emerged within Islam between the morality of warmaking and its practice. Muhammad, unlike Christ, was a man of violence; he bore arms, was wounded in battle and preached holy war, *jihad*, against those who defied the will of God, as revealed to him. His successors perceived the world as divided into *Dar al-Islam* – the House of Submission, submission to the teachings of Muhammad, collected in the Koran – and *Dar al-Harb*, the House of War, which were those parts yet to be conquered.[32] The early Arab conquests of the seventh century extended the frontiers of *Dar al-Islam* in whirlwind leaps, so that by AD 700 the whole of what is now Arabia, Syria, Iraq, Egypt and North Africa had been brought within it. Thereafter the progress of *jihad* became more difficult and more problematical. The original Arab conquerors were few in number, too few to sustain the pace of conquest at its initial intensity. They also proved in victory to be prone to the weaknesses of ordinary humanity, keen to enjoy victory's fruits in peace yet ready to quarrel over the succession to their leadership.

Leadership was invested in a caliph, or 'successor' to Muhammad. The early caliphs found a means to satisfy the claims of their veterans, who wanted ease without war, in the *diwan*, a pension list for Arab warriors financed from the fruits of conquest. They were less successful in averting conflict among those who disagreed about who should be caliph. They quickly fell into a passionate dispute on the matter, in a fundamental disagreement on the nature of authority – should it be hereditary, from Muhammad, or should it derive from the consent of the community, the *umma*? – which persists to this day in the division between Shi'i and Sunni Muslims. What made the dispute irresolvable was a third and indisputable factor in Muslim belief, the prohibition on Muslim fighting Muslim. War, to the Muslim, could only be *jihad*, a holy struggle with those who would not submit to revealed truth. War between those who had submitted was a blasphemy.

Yet some Muslims persisted in carrying their disagreements over the

33

caliphate to the point of war, while divided Islam later came to wage outright struggle for territory. In the face of both developments many pious Muslims withdrew from secular life altogether. Arabs of the heroic tradition would not serve as soldiers because the *diwan* made it not worth their while, while most Muslim converts would not serve either, out of piety; and yet claims to the succession by dissidents, as well as the continuing imperative of *jihad*, made war unavoidable. The caliphate was driven to expedients. Quite early in the conquests Islam had made use of warriors who were not Arabs, converts who had attached themselves to an Arab master (later these converts inevitably formed the majority of Muslims).

Islam had also, by the same principle, made use of slaves, since they too were attached to Arab masters, and now it became a natural alternative to enlist slaves directly. How early is a matter of dispute, but certainly by the middle of the ninth century Islam instituted what was to be a unique policy in military recruitment: the acquisition as slaves of non-Muslim youths to be raised in the faith and trained as soldiers.[33]

These Mamelukes were recruited, almost exclusively, on Islam's border with the great steppe of Central Asia, between the Caspian Sea and the mountains of Afghanistan (later also from the northern shore of the Black Sea), an area populated, when the Caliph al-Mu'tasim began systematic enlistment in the ninth century, by Turks. 'No people in the world', he is supposed to have said, 'are braver, more numerous or more steadfast.' The Turks were a tough lot, as modern Turks remain, and were themselves already on the march westward, in what was to become a tide of conquest even wider than that of the Arabs. They had other qualities to commend them to the caliphs. If they were not yet Muslims, they knew of Islam, because the steppe frontier was not a fixed barrier, but a diaphragm through which Turk and non-Turk raided and traded and, in the case of Turks, frequently emigrated to better themselves. The Islam they knew, moreover, retained its heroic character. The *ghazis*, frontier warriors, prosecuted the holy war in easy conscience, without any of that tendency to what Daniel Pipes has called 'inwardness', the alienation from the secular power of Islam, which Muslims in the heartlands displayed.[34] But what was most admired in the Turks was less their personalities than their practical skills: mastery of the horse and of the techniques of fighting from horseback. The riding horse originated on the steppe; the Turks rode it as if part of themselves – legend had it that Turkish women conceived and gave birth on horseback – and they used with unmatched deadliness the mounted warrior's weapons, the lance, the composite bow and the curved sabre (on which, in a forgotten tribute to the steppe warriors' invincibility, the British general officer's Mameluke sword is patterned). The Turks had their drawbacks. They were insatiable plunderers, by reaction from the extreme frugality of their life on the steppe, which yielded little but milk and meat, and the chance to plunder was a strong inducement to a Turk to accept enslavement; indeed, once the 'Mameluke institution' was a going concern, much of the supply of military slaves was undertaken by Turkish rulers and heads of families, whose willingness to curry favour and profit with the power of Islam by the trade was matched by the readiness of those they sold to take up a secure and respected career.

Most of the great Muslim states employed military slaves. By far the most important of them was the Abbasid caliphate of Egypt, restored there after the overthrow of the Baghdad caliphate by the Mongols in 1258, whose Mamelukes ruled the country under their own sultans from the middle of the thirteenth until the beginning of the sixteenth century. The Mamelukes had chosen the right side in a dynastic struggle. They held on to it because they won a truly decisive battle at Ain Jalut in 1260, which established them as the saviours of the Muslim and, indeed, much of the rest of the civilised world, their opponents being the same Mongols, kinsmen of the recently deceased Genghis Khan, who had dethroned and murdered the Baghdad caliph two years before, and whom no other military power, not even the professional Christian warriors who had the Crusader kingdom in the Holy Land, had been able to withstand. What made the Mamelukes' victory particularly remarkable was that many of the horsemen in the Mongol army were themselves Turks, the Mongols' steppe neighbours, who were enthusiastically exploiting the chance to plunder that Genghis Khan's break-out from Central Asia had brought; thus at Ain Jalut they were, as the Arab historian, Abu Shama, observed, 'defeated and destroyed by men of their own kind'.[35] It would be truer to say they were defeated by men of their own race, for upbringing and training made the Mamelukes soldiers of a very special kind indeed.

Most of the Mamelukes at Ain Jalut were Kipchak Turks from the north shore of the Black Sea (Baybars, the greatest of them, was a Kipchak), who had been sold as slaves in childhood or adolescence and brought to Cairo for their training. Secluded like novices in a monastic barracks, they were first taught the Koran, the code of Islamic law and the Arabic script; at manhood, they began instruction in the *furusiyya*, the system of riding, horsemastership and mounted skill-at-arms which underlay Mameluke prowess on the battlefield.[36] The *furusiyya*, in its emphasis on uniting horse and rider, inculcating dexterity and precision in the handling of weapons from the saddle and fostering tactical cohesion among mounted comrades, bore close comparison with the schooling of men-at-arms in Christian Europe; indeed, to what extent chivalry as a code both of arms and honour was common to the knight of the Cross and the *faris* of the Crescent is a fascinating question of medieval military history.

Yet, this devotion to cavalry warfare was to spell their doom. As a group they were shielded from military developments in the wider world, which might have warned them that the days of the horsemen were numbered; unlike the armoured knights of western Europe, they made no encounter either with primitive gunpowder weapons or with upstart, common infantrymen demanding their rights. Until the end of the fifteenth century their status, both political and military, remained unchallenged, to such an extent that, though a Mameluke would go nowhere but on horseback, the exercises of the *furusiyya* fell into decay.

There was one excellent feature of the Mameluke system. It was entirely unhereditary. Though Mamelukes could marry and father free children, indeed themselves became legally free on graduation (though not free to leave the institution or choose another master than the sultan), no son of a Mameluke could become one. That ought to have ensured an infusion of new ideas as well as of new blood. In practice it did nothing of the sort. New Mamelukes continued to arrive in Egypt from the steppe frontier throughout the fourteenth and fifteenth centuries, but after their training in the novitiate and the *furusiyya*, they became indistinguishable from their predecessors. There were good reasons for that. The status of the Mameluke was highly privileged. The institution had seized power and privilege, as it was in the logic of military slavery that it should. No doubt its members thought that these were best retained by an unwavering dedication to the practices that had made them great in the past.

Then, at the beginning of the sixteenth century, the Mamelukes were simultaneously confronted by the gunpowder revolution in its developed form from two different directions. Their control of the Red Sea was contested by the Portuguese, who had sailed around Africa in ships mounting heavy cannon. And the security of the frontiers of Egypt was threatened by the Ottoman Turks, whose cavalry armies had been heavily supplemented by well-trained musketeers. In haste, the Mameluke sultan tried to repair a century of military neglect. Large numbers of cannon were cast. Units of gunners and musketeers were formed. The *furusiyya* exercises were revived and the Mamelukes set to re-learning the skills of lance, sword and bow with intensity. But, fatally, the re-militarisation of the Mamelukes and the espousal of gunpowder were kept quite separate.

36

No Mameluke was trained or would train in any use of firearms whatso-ever; gunners and musketeers were recruited from outside the Mameluke caste, from black Africans and people of the Maghreb, the Arab west.[37]

The outcome was predictable. The gunners and musketeers who went to the Red Sea achieved considerable success against the Portuguese, who were fighting in confined waters, which did not favour their ocean-going ships, and at the extreme limit of their lines of communications. The Mamelukes who rode out to confront the Ottoman gunpowder armies at the battles of Marj Dabiq in August 1515 and Raydaniya in January 1516 were utterly defeated. The 'institution' was overthrown and Egypt became a province of the Ottoman empire.

The two defeats at Marj Dabiq and Raydaniya took a similar form. In the first the Ottomans, commanded by Sultan Selim I, placed their artil-lery on the flanks and their musketeers in the centre, and waited for the Mamelukes to attack them. They did so in the traditional Turkish crescent deployment and were thrown back in rout by Ottoman firepower. In the second, the Mamelukes, who had assembled some artillery, hoped that the Ottomans would attack them but found themselves outflanked and were tempted to make a cavalry charge again. Its impetus broke one Ottoman wing, but firepower saved the day; 7000 Mamelukes were killed and the survivors fell back on Cairo, which they were shortly forced to surrender.

The tactics of the two battles are much less interesting than subsequent Mameluke lamentation over the means by which they were defeated. Ibn Zabul, the Mameluke historian who deplored his caste's downfall, speaks for generations of *preux chevaliers* in the speech by the Mameluke chief-tain, Kurtbay, which he contrives:

> Hear my words and listen to them, so that you and others will know that amongst us are the horsemen of destiny and red death. A single one of us can defeat your whole army. If you do not believe it, you may try, only please order your army to stop shooting with firearms. You have here with you 200,000 soldiers of all races. Remain in your place and array your army in battle order. Only three of us will come out against you . . . you will see with your own eyes the feats performed by these three . . . You have patched up an army from all parts of the world: Christians, Greeks and others, and you have brought with you this contrivance artfully devised by the Christians of Europe when they were incapable of meeting the Muslim armies on the battlefield. The contrivance is that musket which, even if a woman were to fire it, would hold up such and such a number of men. . . . And woe to thee! How darest thou shoot with firearms at Muslims![38]

Kurtbay's lament echoes the disdain for mechanical weapons of the

French knight Bayard, *chevalier sans peur et sans reproche*, who habitually had crossbowmen prisoners killed, and anticipates the spirit of the 'death charge' of von Bredow's cavalrymen into the muzzles of the French rifles at Mars-la-Tour in 1870. It is the defiant cry of the warrior horseman, in the twilight of the warhorse, from around the world. Yet there was more to Kurtbay's outburst than caste pride, resistance to change, religious orthodoxy or contempt for underlings. There was recent and solid experience that edged weapons could overcome gunpowder by their mediation through the martial qualities which the Mamelukes believed made them fit to lord it over the rest of the world. In 1497 a boy sultan, Sa'adat Muhammad, had formed in Cairo a regiment of black slave musketeers, accorded them privileges and used them in faction fights. It may be that he foresaw the gunpowder revolution; it may be simply that he thought firearms made him strong. Whatever the case, the Mamelukes were outraged and when Sa'adat married a favourite black, Farajallah, to a Circassian slave girl – most Mamelukes were by then Circassians – their temper broke.

> The Royal Mamluks [recorded the historian al-Ansari] expressed their disapproval to the Sultan, and then they put on their steel and armed themselves with their full equipment. A battle broke out between them and the black slaves who numbered about five hundred. The black slaves ran away and gathered again in the towers of the citadel and fired at the Royal Mamluks. The Royal Mamluks marched on them, killing Farajallah and about fifty of the black slaves; the rest fled; two Royal Mamluks were killed.[39]

Yet as the Mamelukes were to discover, when men of equal worth fight on unequal terms, the side with the better weapons wins. That was the lesson of Marj Dabiq and Raydaniya. That was to be the lesson, 400 years later, of the Japanese war against the Americans in the Pacific when, at their last gasp against the power of American industry, Japanese suicide pilots wore their samurai swords in the cockpits of the *kamikaze* aircraft they flew against the enemy's aircraft-carriers. It was to be the lesson of both Germany's world wars in the twentieth century, when their military caste's contempt for their enemies' superiority in the *Materialschlacht* – battle of attrition – ultimately availed their soldiers' courage not at all.

The Mamelukes would not take this lesson to heart. The Ottoman victories of 1515–16 did not mean the end of the Mameluke institution, since its form was too useful for the Ottomans to dispense with it. Indeed, it could be argued that Islam, until infected by the essentially antipathetic concept of nationalism in the twentieth century, could accommodate no system of professional military organisation not based on slavery. In any event subordinate Mameluke dynasties not only crept back to power in Ottoman Egypt but achieved it also in other distant conquered provinces like Iraq, Tunis and Algiers. Though they might regain position, however, they proved irreformable as soldiers. When Napoleon invaded Egypt in 1798, the Mamelukes again rode out to oppose cannon and musket with the exercises of the *furusiyya* and were, of course, routed in the Battle of the Pyramids; Napoleon, enchanted by their noble savagery, took one of them, Rustum, to be his personal attendant to the end of his reign. The surviving Mamelukes, still ready to defy the modern age from horseback, were eventually massacred by the ruthless Muhammad Ali, an Ottoman satrap who had no qualms about practising 'Christian' methods of warmaking, in Cairo in 1811.[40]

The Battle of the Pyramids certainly, the Cairo massacre of the Mamelukes probably, were events of which Clausewitz was aware. Each ought to have been an indication that culture is as powerful a force as politics in the choice of military means, and often more likely to prevail than political or military logic. But Clausewitz, if he knew the facts, did not draw the inference. By an odd twist of circumstance, his pupil, Helmuth von Moltke, was to witness the culmination of Muhammad Ali's role as an agent of Ottoman power in the old Mameluke lands, in a series of events which demonstrates how much more persistent culture is than political decision as a military determinant.

Moltke was sent in 1835 by the Prussian army on a mission to help modernise Turkish military organisation and practice. He found the experience dispiriting. 'In Turkey,' he wrote, 'even the least gift becomes suspect, as soon as it comes from the hand of a Christian. . . . A Turk will concede without hesitation that the Europeans are superior to his nation in science, skill, wealth, daring and strength, without it ever occurring to him that a Frank might therefore put himself on a par with a Muslim.' In military affairs this attitude translated into mulish disrespect. 'The colonels gave us precedence, the officers were still tolerably polite, but the ordinary man would not present arms to us, and the women and children from time to time followed us with curses. The soldier obeyed but would not salute.'

Moltke was to accompany the Turkish army in the expedition which the Ottoman sultan sent to Syria to bring Muhammad Ali, the rebellious ruler of Egypt, to heel in 1839. It was a bizarre encounter. The Ottoman army was superficially modernised, or 'Christianised', but the Egyptian one very much more so. Muhammad Ali was, indeed, himself a European, a Muslim Albanian, who had first learned the superiority of 'Christian' methods in the Greek War of Independence; some of his confederates in the war against the Mamelukes, like the French Colonel Sève, were renegade Philhellenes. Muhammad Ali's army disposed of the Ottomans in a battle, at Nezib, in Syria, at which Moltke found himself a bystander; the spectacle of the Turks – mainly conscript Kurds – fleeing in disorder before the Egyptians sent him back to Prussia profoundly disillusioned by the resistance of the Ottoman sultan's peoples to necessary reform.

Ottoman Turkey did nevertheless eventually succeed in creating a modern army, though only at the expense of restricting membership of it to ethnic Turks proper. That arbitrary limitation of the relationship between his peoples and the sultan greatly undermined the authority of the Ottoman government over its Muslim but non-Turkish subjects. That narrowing of his basis of power was certainly a major contribution to the strains that the Ottoman empire underwent when, as commander of a 'Christianised' army, the Sultan-Caliph was drawn into war on the side of Germany in 1914. The outcome of the war left Turkey without an empire, and soon without a sultan or caliphate. All that was left of it was the army it had sacrificed everything to create.

There was an ultimate irony in any impatience that the successors of Clausewitz and Moltke felt with their Turkish pupils. For the collapse of the Turkish empire in 1918 coincided, of course, with the collapse of their own, and through exactly the same medium: the deliberate choice of war for misconceived political ends. The 'Young Turks' – all deeply involved in the 'Christianisation' of the Sultan's army – went to war on Germany's side because they believed that would help to make Turkey strong. Germany had gone to war because it believed that going to war was a means in itself of making Germany strong. Clausewitz, too, would doubtless have felt the same. This cultural distortion of outlook spelled death equally to traditional German culture and to that of the servants of the Caliph.

The Samurai

At much the same time that the Mamelukes were going under to gunpowder, another military society at the opposite end of the world assured its survival by outrightly defying the circumstances that threatened it. In the sixteenth century the Japanese sword-bearing class was confronted by the challenge of firearms; it contrived means to rid Japan of firearms and thereby to perpetuate its social dominance for another 250 years. While the Western world, which touched it briefly in the sixteenth century, commercialised itself, voyaged, industrialised and underwent political revolution, the Japanese samurai closed their country to the outside world, extirpated such bridgeheads of foreign religious and technical influence as had intruded, and entrenched the traditions by which they had lived and ruled for a thousand years. The impulse is not without parallels – it was strongly felt in China in the nineteenth century – though the achievement is unique. For all its uniqueness, however, the achievement is evidence that political logic need not dominate warmaking, that, on the contrary, cultural forms, when they find strong champions, may prevail against the most powerfully besetting temptations to choose technical expedients as a means to victory, particularly when the price of victory is that of overturning ancient and cherished values.

The samurai were, in crude terms, Japan's feudal and knightly class. They owed their origins to Japan's insular isolation and to the internal subdivision of the Japanese islands by their mountain chains. The leaders of Japan's valley clans (akin to the 'valley lords' of Ottoman Anatolia) gave allegiance to an emperor whose ancient lineage was deeply revered but whose power was purely nominal. From the seventh century AD, when a clan chief, Fujiwara Kamatari, instituted a central government modelled on that of the T'ang dynasty in China, it was effectively administered by a clan family, at first his own, later by more successful rivals. Rivals could compete for and eventually usurp the Fujiwaras' power because of their tax-raising powers: in a misguided concession to Buddhism, a state-sponsored import from China, the Buddhist monasteries had been exempted from tax, and their secular neighbours soon extracted similar rights for themselves, at the same time enforcing the practice of making the peasants pay tax directly to the local clan lord. With the wealth that tax-raising brought, first one, then another lordly family came to dominate the imperial court, until in the twelfth century the current power-holder prevailed on the then ruler, a boy emperor, to grant him the title of *Sei-i tai-Shogun*, or generalissimo. Yoritomo, the first shogun, had already established a new seat of government, the *Bakufu*, literally the 'camp office', and thereafter it exercised central authority until the nineteenth century, when, at the Meiji restoration, real power was returned to the court, if not the emperor, by its overthrow and then that of the last valley magnates.

The shoguns, the leaders of the other military clans who repetitively competed with them for dominance, and their samurai followers (the large warrior class whose members, distinguished by their right to wear two swords, insisted on their gentlemanly status) were not mere thugs, as their equivalents in medieval Europe so often were. They were certainly fierce and talented warriors. Proof of that was originally given by their decisive defeat of the Mongols who, at the opposite extremity of their push into the Arab world in 1260, succeeded in setting foot on the Japanese archipelago in 1274. When they returned in 1281 a typhoon destroyed much of their fleet and they departed never to return.

'Style' was central to the samurai way of life – style in clothes, armour, weapons, skill-at-arms and behaviour on the battlefield; in that they did not much differ from their chivalric contemporaries in France and England. In their cultural outlook, however, they differed very greatly. The Japanese were a literate people and the literary culture of the samurai was highly developed. The greatest nobles of Japan, those who resided at the court of the powerless god-emperor, did not seek military reputation at all, but strove for literary glory. Their example set the tone for the samurai, who commonly wished to be known both as swordsmen and poets. Buddhism in its Zen form, that adopted by the samurai, encouraged a meditative and poetic outlook on the universe. The greatest warriors of feudal Japan were therefore also men of the mind, the spirit and the cultivated senses.

Feudal Japan was politically chaotic, because of the endemic competition for the shogunate, but chaotic within accepted limits. By the beginning of the sixteenth century, however, feuding had got out of hand and the social order was threatened; established leaders were being overthrown by upstarts, some mere bandits; the shogun's power became as fictional as the emperor's. Order was restored in the years 1560–1616 by a succession of three outstanding strongmen, Oda Nobunaga, Toyotomi Hideyoshi and Tokugawa Ieyasu, acting in the name of the shogun. They systematically put down the power of the Buddhist monasteries, the errant clan leaders, and the lawless bands of lordless men. Ieyasu's pacification concluded with the siege of the fortress of Osaka in 1614, last stronghold of his opponents, after which he decreed the destruction of all non-residential castles in Japan. Such was his authority that decastellation, which took kings decades in Europe, was completed in a few days.

Superior generalship was not the only explanation of the restoration of central power. The three strongmen were also exponents of a new weapon. Portuguese voyagers had brought cannon and firearms to Japan in 1542. Oda Nobunaga was greatly impressed by the power of gunpowder, rapidly equipped his armies with muskets and peremptorily deritualised the mode of battle-fighting in Japan. Thitherto Japanese battles had traditionally begun, in the ancient and almost worldwide fashion of warmaking between champions, by the leading men on each side shouting challenges to each other, identifying themselves and displaying their weapons and armour. The ritual continued even after the introduction of firearms, but Oda Nobunaga would have none of it. He taught his musketeers to unleash volleys in ranks of up to a thousand and, at the decisive battle of Nagashino in 1575, swept away the enemy in a torrent of fire.[41] This was a revolutionary change from the battle of Uedahara, in 1548, when the side possessing firearms missed the chance to use them because the other charged with swords the instant the rituals had been concluded.

The dominance established by the strongmen might have ensured that of firearms, but exactly the contrary was the outcome. By the end of the seventeenth century the use of firearms had become almost extinct in Japan, the weapons themselves great rarities. Only a handful of Japanese knew how to make firearms or to cast cannon, and most surviving cannon dated from before 1620. That state of affairs continued until the middle of the nineteenth century, when the arrival of Commodore Perry's 'black ships' in Tokyo Bay in 1854 peremptorily reintroduced the Japanese to the imperatives of gunpowder. In the intervening 250 years, however, the Japanese had done without gunpowder altogether. The impetus to self-denial had come from the last of the strongmen, Tokugawa Ieyasu, whose campaign of pacification had culminated in his accesssion to the shogunate. How and why had he outlawed the gun?

The 'how' is simple to explain. First came a general disarming of the populace instituted in 1587 by Ieyasu's predecessor, Hideyoshi, who decreed that all non-samurai were to hand in all weapons – swords and guns alike – to the government, which it was announced intended to use the metal in the construction of an enormous statue of the Buddha. The purpose of the programme was, of course, to further the pacification of Japan by restoring a monopoly of arms to the military class, which was under government control. European governments enacted similar measures in the gunpowder age, though they took decades to achieve their object. In Japan, where justice was savage and peremptory, it was achieved at once.[42]

Then, from 1607 onward, Ieyasu instituted a system that centralised the manufacture of firearms and cannon and denominated the government as the only authorised purchaser. All gunfounders and gunsmiths were ordered to take their workshops to the city of Nagahama, the four chief gunsmiths were promoted to samurai rank, thus securing their loyalty to the sword-bearing class, and a decree was promulgated that no order for a weapon could be filled unless approved by the Commissioner for Guns. He, in turn, proved willing to approve only those orders placed by the government, which in its turn progressively decreased its purchasing, until by 1706 Nagahama production in even years was 35 large matchlocks, in odd years 250 small ones. Distributed among a warrior class of some half a million – by which they were used chiefly in ceremonial processions – such numbers proved insignificant. Gun control had worked. Japan retreated from the gunpowder age.

But why? This is a much more complex question. Guns were unquestionably a symbol of foreign intrusion. They were associated, illogically but inescapably, with the spread of Christianity by Portuguese Jesuit missionaries, who were judged to be harbingers of invasion – invasion on the scale which had recently made the Philippines a Spanish possession – and Ieyasu's successor, Hidetada, rigidly enforced the suppression and expulsion orders that his predecessors had belatedly introduced. The shogunate's suspicion of Christianity and all its appurtenances was reinforced by the Shimbara Rebellion, raised by native Christians in 1637 and fought with gunpowder. When it was over, the Tokugawa shogunate's authority was not challenged again for more than 200 years, and the closing of the country against foreigners and foreign influences it had imposed the previous year became complete.

An additional inclination towards chauvinism may have been exerted by Japan's only foreign-policy adventure, an invasion of Korea in 1592, apparently intended as the preliminary to an over-ambitious aggression against China, which ended unsuccessfully in 1598. Yet more important than the rejection of things foreign, and profoundly underlying it, was the recognition that the gun made for social instability. A gun in the hands of a commoner or freebooter could topple the lordliest noble, as every European knight of the gunpowder age knew. Cervantes has Don Quixote condemn 'an invention which allows a base and cowardly hand to take the life of a brave knight'.[43]

The third reason for gun control in Japan was that it could actually be imposed. European warriors might deplore the effects of gunpowder on their chosen way of life, but with an open frontier to the south-east, against which the Ottoman Turks battered enthusiastically with great cannon, they had no option but to batter back if Christendom were to survive. Once Christendom was divided by the Reformation at the precise moment when technology made cannon mobile and personal firearms reliable, inhibitions against Christian shooting at Christian were dissolved. No such factors impinged on Japan. Distance and the military reputation of its people protected it from the European voyagers; China had neither the navy nor the inclination to invade it; there were no other potential invaders. Domestically, the Japanese, though divided by class and faction, formed a single cultural unit. Gunpowder was therefore not essential to national security, nor was it sought as a means to victory by factions opposed to each other ideologically.

Gunpowder was also irreconcilable with the ethos of the Japanese warrior when that ethos had strong protectors. The Tokugawa shogunate was more than a political institution. It was a cultural instrument. The cultural historian G.B. Sansom wrote:

> Not confining [itself] to the functions of raising revenue and keeping order, [it] undertook to regulate the morals of the people and to prescribe their behaviour in the minutest detail. It is doubtful whether previous history records a more ambitious attempt on the part of a state to interfere with the private life of every individual and so to control the thoughts as well as actions of a whole nation.[44]

Particular attention was given to regulating the thoughts and actions of the sword-bearing class, and the only manual of arms compatible with polite learning in Japan was that of the samurai sword. The Tokugawas and their predecessors may have used gunpowder for reasons of *Realpolitik*; once it served their purpose of winning them power, it and all firearms became detestable.

The cult of the sword had many sources. It was fostered by Zen Buddhism, which stressed 'two supreme ideals – fidelity and an indifference to physical hardship'. It was reinforced by the culture of the warrior class, 'a culture that paid meticulous attention to the formal, the ceremonious, and the elegantly expressed in life and art'; Japanese swordplay, like that of the European fencing-master, was as much an art as a skill, governed by rules of deportment and gesture which epitomised the Japanese concern for 'style' in every aspect of existence.[45] It seems to have partaken of the Japanese belief in the importance of unity with nature and natural forces, since muscular effort is 'natural' while the chemical energy of gunpowder is not. It undoubtedly coincided with the Japanese respect for tradition, since not only was swordplay traditional, but the best swords themselves were often ancient heirlooms with their own personal names, handed on from father to son just as the family name – in itself a distinction restricted to sword-owners – was as well.

Such swords have become collector's items today. Yet they remain more than beautiful antiques. First-quality samurai swords were the best edged weapons that have ever been made. Observes a historian of the anti-gunpowder campaign:

> There exists in Japan a film showing a machine-gun barrel being sliced in half by a sword from the forge of the great fifteenth-century maker,

Kanemoto II. If this seems improbable, one must remember that smiths like Kanemoto hammered and folded and rehammered, day after day, until a sword blade contained something like four million layers of finely forged steel.[46]

It is, of course, impossible to disarm a population completely when scythes and flails lie to hand. But the tools of everyday life make poor implements of combat against such specialist weapons. In ensuring that warriors had a monopoly of swords, the Tokugawa were guaranteeing the samurai's place at the pinnacle of Japanese society.

The Tokugawa's logic was not Clausewitz's logic. Though he apparently believed that his analysis of the nature of warfare was value-free, he had nevertheless been infected by the contemporary European belief that mankind is naturally drawn to 'politics' or 'political activity' and that politics is intrinsically dynamic, indeed 'progressive'. This was a view that the Duke of Wellington, a natural conservative and principled opponent of the French Revolution, endorsed with the full weight of his disapproval. Clausewitz did indeed seem to perceive politics as an autonomous activity, the meeting-place of rational forms and emotional forces, in which reason and feeling are the determinants but in which culture – that great cargo of shared beliefs, values, associations, myths, taboos, imperatives, customs, traditions, manners and ways of thought, speech and artistic expression which ballast every society – plays no determining role. The Tokugawa reaction proves how wrong he was, demonstrating as it does so well the truth that war may be, among many other things, the perpetuation of a culture by its own means.

A CULTURE WITHOUT WAR

Clausewitz's belief in the primacy of politics rather than culture was not, however, personal to him. It was the position of Western philosophers from Aristotle onward and it received in Clausewitz's own lifetime powerful reinforcements from the spectacle of pure political ideas – themselves the product of living philosophers like Voltaire and Rousseau – in free action against passion and prejudice in the streets of Paris. The wars Clausewitz knew, the wars in which he fought, were the wars of the French Revolution, and the 'political motive' for which he always looked as the precipitating and controlling factor in warmaking was, at the outset at least, always present. Europe's dynastic states correctly feared that the French Revolution was a threat to monarchy; war clearly appeared to be 'a continuation of politics'.

46

It must also be recognised that Clausewitz as a historian had nothing to guide him toward the importance of cultural factors in human affairs. Comparative history, of which cultural history is the child, was not an approach adopted by any of the leading historians whom he might have taken as model. Sir Isaiah Berlin in one of his salutes to the father of comparative history, Giambattista Vico, perfectly sums up the spirit of the Enlightenment as a belief that 'a universally valid method had been found for the solution of the fundamental questions that had exercised men at all times – how to establish what was true and what was false in every province of knowledge'.[47]

The greatest publicist of the Enlightenment, Voltaire, even while he advocated the widening of historical inquiry to embrace social and economic activities and their effects, strongly believed that the only objects worthy of historical study were the peaks, not the valleys, of the achievements of mankind . . . 'If you have no more to tell us', Voltaire declared, 'than that one barbarian succeeded another on the banks of the Oxus or Ixartes, what use are you to the public?'[48]

Where Voltaire led, who was Clausewitz not to follow? In the decades of the nineteenth century after his death, German historians became pioneers of the comparative method in history and politics, but in his lifetime, the Enlightenment ruled. 'We see, therefore, that under all circumstances war is to be regarded not as an independent thing, but as a political instrument; and it is only by taking this view that we can avoid finding ourselves in opposition to all military history,' he wrote.[49] What more perfectly Enlightenment, more purely Voltairean view could possibly be expressed?

Yet Voltaire, in his contemptuous dismissal of the importance of events on the banks of the Oxus, strikes Clausewitzian theory a blow. Military historians now recognise that the banks of the Oxus are to warfare what Westminster is to parliamentary democracy or the Bastille to revolutions. On or near the banks of the Oxus – the river that separates Central Asia from Persia and the Middle East – man learned to tame the horse, to harness it for driving, and eventually to ride it under a saddle. It was from the Oxus that conquerors rode forth to found 'chariot empires' in China, India and Europe. It was on the Oxus that the cavalry revolution, one of the two indisputable revolutions in warmaking, took place. It was across the Oxus that successive waves of Central Asian conquerors and despoilers – Huns, Avars, Magyars, Turks, Mongols – broke into the Western world. It was at Samarkand, just north of the Oxus, that Tamerlane, the most pointlessly destructive of the horse chieftains, began his reign of terror.

The early caliphs recruited their slave soldiers on the Oxus; so too did the Ottoman sultans. The Ottoman siege of Vienna in 1683, threatening the heartland of Christendom, remained the most disruptive military episode in the memories of Clausewitz's contemporaries. A theory of war that did not take into account the Oxus and all it stood for was a defective theory. Clausewitz constructed such a theory, none the less, and with calamitous effects.

In the years after the First World War, radical military writers held Clausewitz circumstantially if not directly responsible for the recent carnage. The British historian B.H. Liddell Hart, for example, inculpated him of urging the largest possible offensive with the largest possible numbers as the key to victory. But in the years after the Second World War, he was raised to new heights, in a virtual apotheosis, as the greatest military thinker, past, present and – here was the indication of the infatuation he had rekindled – future also. Academic strategists of the Cold War years proclaimed that, in the gloom that a nuclear winter threatened, Clausewitz offered a guiding light of universal truth. His detractors were given short shrift: Liddell Hart's notorious attack on him was dismissed, for example, as a 'caricature'.[50]

The academic strategists were conflating an observation with a hypothesis. The observation is that war is a universal phenomenon, practised at all times and all places since the retreat of the last Ice Age; the hypothesis is that there is a universally true theory of the objects of war, and of how those objects may best be achieved. It is easy to see why they were seduced by Clausewitz: under threat of nuclear attack, a state has no option but to align its foreign policy as closely as possible with strategic doctrine, and to extrude from the interstices all modifying qualifications. A nuclear state must appear to mean what it says, since deterrence depends upon convincing an adversary of one's fixity of purpose, and mental reservation is the enemy of conviction.

Nuclear deterrence was and is abhorrent to humane sentiment, however, since it implies that a state, if required to defend its own existence, will act with pitiless disregard for the consequences to its own and its adversary's peoples. Little wonder that, in the Western world at least, where politics in the last 2000 years has institutionalised the Judaeo–Christian belief in the unique value of the individual, deterrence theory evokes the deepest repugnance, often from patriots devoted to the national defence, even from professional warriors who have shed their own blood for their countries.

To invent a philosophy that would integrate nuclear-deterrence theory and the common morality and political ethics of the democratic states was a task that might well have defeated the ingenuity even of the cleverest theorists. But they did not need to do this. In Clausewitz they found ready to hand a philosophy and vocabulary of military extremism to which history had given currency. With nuclear weapons, 'real war' and 'true war' were believed to be the same thing; and the contemplation of the horror of such an identification was believed in itself to guarantee that war would not occur.

There was a double weakness in this logic, however. First, it was entirely mechanistic; it depended upon the procedures of deterrence working faultlessly in all circumstances. Yet if there is one observable truth of politics, it is that mechanistic means have a poor record of controlling the behaviour of governments. Second, it required the citizens of states with nuclear weapons to cultivate a schizophrenic outlook on the world: while sustaining their beliefs in the sanctity of human life, respect for the rights of the individual, tolerance of minority opinion, acceptance of the free vote, accountability of the executive to representative institutions and everything else that is meant by the rule of law, democracy and the Judaeo-Christian ethic – nuclear weapons were deployed to protect these values – they were at the same time expected to acquiesce in the code of the warrior, of which physical courage, subordination to the heroic leader and 'might is right' are the ultimate values. This schizophrenia, moreover, was to be permanent since, in the catchphrase of the nuclear theorists, 'nuclear weapons cannot be disinvented'.

Robert McNamara, Secretary of Defense in President John F. Kennedy's administration, epitomised Clausewitzian deterrent logic in a speech he gave in 1962 at the University of Michigan, in the heartland of American humanist values. 'The very strength and nature of the alliance [NATO, but essentially American] forces makes it possible for us to retain, even in the face of a massive surprise attack, sufficient reserve striking power to destroy an enemy society if driven to it,' he said.[51] This threat to visit 'true war' on an enemy that initiated 'real war' had a philosophical purity that Clausewitz might well have cheered. But the cheer would have been a cry from the past. For Clausewitz, as I have said, was even in his time an isolated spokesman for a warrior culture that the ancestors of the modern state were at pains to extirpate within their own borders. Naturally they recognised its value for state purposes, but they allowed it to survive only by localising it within a collection of artificially preserved warrior bands; the regiments were wholly different in ethos from that of the civil society in which they were garrisoned.

In earlier times European society had been heavily suffused by warrior values and practices; then, from the seventeenth century, through a sustained policy of depriving the population of firearms, destroying the castles of the provincial grandees, appropriating their sons as regular officers, creating specialist corps of artillerists officered from the non-warrior classes and monopolising the production of battlefield weapons in state arsenals, the sort of governments of which Clausewitz was a servant effectively demilitarised European society everywhere west of the Oder and Drava rivers, that is to say from Berlin and Vienna to the Atlantic.

When in response to forces released by the French Revolution, European states were progressively impelled to remilitarise their own populations, they did so from above, and it was accepted with varying degrees of enthusiasm. Universal service eventually came to be associated, entirely understandably, with suffering and death: there were 20,000,000 deaths in the First World War, 50,000,000 in the Second. Britain and America abandoned it altogether after 1945; when it was reintroduced by the United States in the 1960s, to fight what became an unpopular war, the eventual refusal of the conscripts and their families to ingest warrior values caused the Vietnam War to be abandoned. Here was evidence of how self-defeating is the effort to run in harness in the same society two mutually contradictory public codes: that of 'inalienable rights', including life, liberty and the pursuit of happiness, and that of total self-abnegation when strategic necessity demands it.

Indeed, all attempts to bring about profound social change from above have proved difficult in the modern world; many have failed altogether, notably those seeking to alter rights of private property or the relationship of the cultivator with the land. Social change engineered from below – the forte of reformist religious movements – has had a better record of success. It is instructive to follow, therefore, the course of twentieth-century efforts to remilitarise societies from below, of which two deserve particular attention. They are those of Mao Tse-tung in China and his followers in Vietnam, and of Tito in Yugoslavia. Both were rooted in Marx's directive to 'create popular armies' as a means to bring forward the inevitable revolution; both followed remarkably similar patterns; both brought about the political results to which they were directed; neither had anything but calamitous cultural effects.

In the years after the dethronement of the last emperor in 1912, China descended into an anarchy in which a nominally sovereign republican government disputed authority with local warlords in all the provinces. A third party to the conflict was the nascent Communist party, one of whose leaders, Mao Tse-tung, early put himself at cross-purposes with the Central Committee and its Russian mentors. His opponents were set upon capturing cities. He, by close study of the real grievances of the rural populations among whom his soldiers moved, decided that the best means of capturing cities was by permeating the countryside that surrounded them with revolutionary guerrillas. Out of such guerrilla forces, he came to believe, victorious armies could be created. In a memorandum he wrote in 1929, he described his methods:

> The tactics we have derived from the struggle of the past three years are indeed different from any other tactics, ancient or modern, Chinese or foreign. With our tactics, the masses can be aroused for struggle on an ever-broadening scale, and no enemy, however powerful, can cope with us. Ours are guerrilla tactics. They consist mainly of the following points: Divide our forces to arouse the masses, concentrate our forces to deal with the enemy . . . Arouse the largest number of the masses in the shortest possible time.[52]

Mao was wrong about the unique nature of his tactics. In their emphasis on isolating towns by dominating the surrounding countryside, they derived directly from the methods of the horse peoples who had been such peristent enemies of China for nearly two thousand years. But there were novel features in Mao's methods: first, his belief that the 'classless' – 'soldiers, bandits, robbers, beggars and prostitutes' – were grist to the revolution's mill, 'people capable of fighting very bravely and, if properly led, a revolutionary force'; second, his perception that in the face of a more powerful enemy a war could nevertheless be won if one had the patience to avoid seeking a decision until the enemy's frustration and exhaustion robbed him of the chance of victory.[53] This theory of 'protracted war' will be remembered as Mao's principal contribution to military theory. After his triumph over Chiang Kai-shek in China, it was adopted by the Vietnamese in their wars, first against the French, then against the Americans.

Between 1942 and 1944 Josip Broz Tito, General Secretary of the Yugoslav Communist Party, also used this process in the mountains of Montenegro and Bosnia-Herzegovina. The Axis occupiers of Yugoslavia were already engaged against a guerrilla army loyal to the royal government in exile, Mihailovic's Chetniks. Chetnik policy was to lie low until the Axis had been sufficiently weakened in the war outside Yugoslavia for a general national rising to succeed. Tito would have none of that; for a variety of reasons, including the hope of relieving pressure on the Soviet Union but also his policy of implanting a Communist party apparatus throughout Yugoslav territory, his Partisans campaigned as widely and actively as they could. 'Wherever the Partisans . . . occupied a region, they . . . organised committees of peasants to run local affairs and to maintain law and order. Even when the Partisans lost control of an area, these political auxiliaries remained active.'[54] Sir William Deakin, then a British liaison officer with Tito, thus described his observation of the process in action soon after a successful German sweep against Tito's headquarter brigade in 1943: 'In the immediate moment of our tired escape from destruction, [Milovan] Djilas [a leading Communist intellectual but also a warrior who had killed Germans] departed with a handful of companions southwards to the desolation of the battlefield. It was an unwritten rule of Partisan war that in a lost free territory the bare elements of Party work must continue, and cells be re-formed in anticipation of a future return.'[55]

This 'heroic' aspect of the Partisan struggle, deeply inspiring to scholars-turned-soldiers like Deakin, reads well on the page. But in practice the policy of waging a politico-military campaign over the length and breadth of Yugoslavia brought untold suffering to its peoples. Their history was already one of bitter and violent rivalry, which the war had reawoken. In the north leaders of the Catholic Croats had taken advantage of Italian sponsorship to unleash a campaign of expulsion, forced conversion and extermination against the Orthodox Serbs. Muslims in Bosnia-Herzegovina took a hand in the civil war also, while in the south the Serbs of Kossovo were attacked by their Albanian neighbours. The Chetniks, for their part, contested authority in the Serb lands with the Partisans, with whom they had failed to agree a joint strategy, but did not open war with the German occupiers lest that provoke reprisals. Tito hardened his heart against reprisals; indeed, he saw Axis atrocities as a spur to recruitment. He deliberately drew the Germans after him in seven so-called 'offensives' that left the countryside through which his Partisans marched a wasteland. The villagers had either to follow the Partisans 'into the woods' (a traditional description of the whereabouts of resisters to the Turks) or stay and await reprisals. Kardelj, Tito's deputy, was emphatic about the desirability of confronting the uncommitted with such a dilemma: 'Some commanders are afraid of reprisals and that fear prevents the mobilisation of Croat villages. I consider the reprisals will have the useful result of throwing Croatian villages on the side of Serb villages. In war we must not be frightened of the destruction of whole villages. Terror will bring about armed action.'[56]

Kardelj's analysis was correct. Tito's policy of superimposing a pan-

Yugoslav, pro-Communist, anti-Axis campaign on the web of local ethnic and religious, collaborationist and anti-collaboration conflicts already raging, but also of disrupting all truces where he found them, did indeed have the effect of turning many small wars into a single large war, in which he became the principal commander on the anti-Axis side. At his behest most Yugoslav males, and many Yugoslav women, were forced to choose sides. The population was indeed remilitarised from below. At the war's end, at least 100,000 of those who had chosen the wrong side were as a direct consequence killed by the Partisans, joining in death the 350,000 Serbs killed by the pro-Italian Croats. Yet, since the Royal Yugoslav Army had collapsed in only eight days in 1941, most of the 1,200,000 other Yugoslavs who died between 1941 and 1944, in a total of 1,600,000, must be reckoned active or passive victims of the policy of Partisan warfare. It was a terrible price to pay so that Tito should make his political point.

The externals of such warfare – whether Yugoslav, Russian, Chinese or Vietnamese – have made arresting raw material for the art of Socialist Realism. The life-size bronze of the young defiant, trembling with the urge to die for his country, that dominates the central hall of the Yugoslav military museum in Belgrade, brilliantly dramatises the idea of popular resistance; in a different mood so too do Sergei Gerasimov's canvas of the *Partisan Mother*, pregnant with a new combatant, impassively confronting the German soldier who has burnt her house, Tatyana Nazarenko's *The Partisans Have Arrived*, an ironic pietà of help brought too late to a scene of German atrocity, and Ismet Mujesinovic's *Liberation of Jacje*, which, through an episode of Tito's war, evokes Géricault's magnificent denunciations of Ottoman oppression painted during the Greek War of Independence. There is much in the same, if very imitative, vein from Mao's and Ho Chi Minh's wars in the east: People's Army men, in neat, worn campaign dress, comforting the victims of Chiang Kai-shek, working shoulder to shoulder with peasants to gather the harvest from their threatened fields, or massed for the advance to final victory under the Red Dawn.[57]

Partisan art is, nevertheless, the art of the freeze-frame, literally the cliché, a moment of apparent realism plucked from an entirely contradictory reality. Indeed, the experience of popular struggle, of forcing peaceable and law-abiding citizens to bear arms and draw blood against their will and in defiance of their interests, is unspeakably awful. The people of the West were mostly spared it in the Second World War, the Americans and British absolutely. The few who witnessed what it meant in practice have left gruesome records of what they saw. William Deakin, a young historian from Oxford who parachuted into Yugoslavia to join Tito in 1943, described an encounter with some captured Chetniks:

> During the action that night, Partisan troops captured the commander of the Chetnik Zenica *odred*, Golub Mitrović, and two of his staff. I was faced with this group of prisoners in a woodland clearing. It was proposed that I should interrogate them personally. This was the first, and only, occasion that such a situation arose. I refused. The British could not be a party to civil war. The evidence was clear. It was beyond my responsibility to to be implicated in questioning Chetnik prisoners about to be executed. I turned away and walked through the trees. A short burst of rifle fire closed the incident. We advanced past the three bodies a few minutes later. This episode was ill-received by the Partisan command. I had long anticipated such a confrontation, and knew that I should have to assume such an attitude, from which I never deviated – at the price of lack of comprehension and a certain ill-will on the part of our Partisan allies. They felt that we were fighting another war.[58]

So, indeed, he should have been. There are no circumstances, in any code of justice which the British army recognises, that justify the shooting of unarmed men, not convicted of capital crimes by a court of law, who have fallen into one's power.

Milovan Djilas had the honesty in his magnificent memoir of the realities of the Partisan experience, *Wartime*, to disclose how much more deeply he had been corrupted by the code of guerrilla combat. This is how he, for his part, treated unarmed prisoners who fell into his hands:

> I unslung my rifle. Since I didn't dare fire, because the Germans were some forty yards above – we could hear them shouting – I hit the German over the head. The rifle butt broke and the German fell on his back. I pulled out my knife and with one motion slit his throat. I then handed the knife to Raja Nedeljković, a political worker whom I had known since before the war, and whose village the Germans had massacred in 1941. Nedeljković stabbed the second German, who writhed but was soon still. This later gave rise to the story that I had slaughtered a German in hand-to-hand combat. Actually, like most prisoners, the Germans were as if paralysed, and didn't defend themselves or try to flee.[59]

The brutality that Djilas learned in the mountains of Yugoslavia was taught to tens of millions wherever 'people's war' was practised. Its cost in lives scarcely bears contemplating. Tens of millions died, either as participants or more often as unhappy bystanders, in China, Indo-China and Algeria. On Mao's Long March from south to north China in 1934–5, only some

8,000 of the 80,000 people who set out survived; those who did were to become, like Djilas, pitiless executives of a social revolution which measured its thoroughness in the number of 'class enemies' it did to death.[60] About one million 'landlords' were killed in the year after the Communists came to power in China in 1948, usually by their fellow villagers at the instigation of party 'cadres', often survivors of the Long March. This holocaust was inherent in the doctrine of people's war from the outset.

Perhaps most tragic of all remilitarisations from below was that played out between 1954 and 1962 in Algeria, where veterans of the first Indo-China war – French officers on one side, ex-soldiers from the French Algerian regiments on the other – inflicted the doctrine of people's war on whichever sections of the population they managed to bring under control. The Army of National Liberation, in conscious imitation of Mao, deliberately implicated villagers in acts of rebellion wherever they could. Selected French officers (many of whom had been forced to study Marx in Vietnamese prison camps) responded by training 'their' villagers as counter-insurgents and swearing with their lives that the loyalists would never be abandoned by France. When the moment of abandonment came, at least 30,000 and perhaps as many as 150,000 loyalists were murdered by the victorious ALN. It had lost 141,000 killed in combat and, during the eight years of war, had itself killed 12,000 of its own members in internal purges, 16,000 other Muslim Algerians and presumably another 50,000 enumerated only as 'disappeared'. The Algerian government itself today sets the cost of the people's war at 1,000,000, out of a pre-war Muslim population of 9,000,000.[61]

The warrior generations to which the remilitarisations gave birth in Algeria, China, Vietnam and what was once Yugoslavia, are growing old today. The revolutions for which they and millions of unwilling participants paid such a terrible price in blood and anguish have withered at the roots. South Vietnam, the prize of Ho Chi Minh's long war, has refused to abandon its capitalist habits. The Chinese greybeards of the Long March have preserved the authority of the party only by conceding economic freedoms wholly at variance with Marxist doctrine. In Algeria a spawning population looks for a solution to economic hardship either in Islamic fundamentalism or in emigration to the richer world on the other side of the Mediterranean. The peoples of former Yugoslavia whom Tito sought to unite by bloodying their hands in a common struggle against the Axis now bloody their hands against each other in a struggle reminiscent of nothing so much as the 'territorial displacement' anthropologists identify as the underlying logic of much 'primitive' warfare in tribal society. In the borderlands of the dissolved Soviet Union, from which modern revolutionaries took their inspiration, a similar pattern discloses itself, as newly independent 'minorities' use their freedom from Russian control to revive ancient tribal hatreds and to re-fight wars, sometimes within rather than between tribes, which to outsiders appear to have no political point whatsoever.

As we contemplate this end-of-the-century world, in which the rich states that imposed remilitarisation from above have made peace their watchword and the poor states that suffered remilitarisation from below spurn or traduce the gift, may war at last be recognised as having lost its usefulness and deep attractiveness? War in our time has been not merely a means of resolving inter-state disputes but also a vehicle through which the embittered, the dispossessed, the naked of the earth, the hungry masses yearning to breathe free, express their anger, jealousies and pent-up urge to violence. There are grounds for believing that at last, after five thousand years of recorded warmaking, cultural and material changes may be working to inhibit man's proclivity to take up arms.

The material change stares us all in the face. It is the emergence of the thermonuclear weapon and its intercontinental ballistic missile-delivery system. Yet nuclear weapons have, since 9 August 1945, killed no one. The 50,000,000 who have died in war since that date have, for the most part, been killed by cheap, mass-produced weapons and small-calibre ammunition, costing little more than the transistor radios and dry-cell batteries which have flooded the world in the same period. Because cheap weapons have disrupted life very little in the advanced world, outside the restricted localities where drug-dealing and political terrorism flourish, the populations of the rich states have been slow to recognise the horror that this pollution has brought in its train. Little by little, though, recognition of the horror is gaining ground.

There was little television coverage of the war in Algeria, which ended in 1962, but a great deal of the war in Vietnam, where the effect of the medium worked largely to reinforce the resistance of men of draft age and their families, rather than to mobilise repugnance for war itself. But the televised spectacle of starving Ethiopians fleeing from soldiers scarcely better-fed than themselves, of the savageries of the Khmer Rouge in Cambodia, of the wholesale slaughter of Iranian child soldiers in the marshes of Iraq, of the destruction of Lebanon as a society and of a dozen other squalid, cruel and pointless conflicts has had a different result. It is scarcely possible anywhere in the world today to raise a body of reasoned

56

support for the opinion that war is a justifiable activity. Western enthusiasm for the Gulf War dissipated in a few days when visual evidence of the carnage it had caused was presented.

Russell Weigley, in an important recent study, has identified the onset of what he calls an impatience with the 'chronic indecisiveness of war'. Taking as his subject of study the period from the early seventeenth to early nineteenth centuries, when states had at their command reliable instruments of military power in a condition of technical equipoise, he argues that war showed itself not as 'an effective extension of policy by other means . . . but the bankruptcy of policy'. The frustration engendered by the failure to achieve a decisive result led on, he implies, to 'the calculated and spontaneous resort to deeper and baser cruelties' in succeeding centuries, 'to the sack of cities and the ravishing of countrysides both in search of revenge and in the usually vain hope that larger cruelties [would] break the enemy's spirit'.[62] The trend of his argument and that advanced in this chapter lie in the same direction. It may be summarised in the following terms.

In the century that began with the French Revolution, military logic and cultural ethos took divergent and contradictory courses. In the developing industrial world, conditions of growing wealth and the rise of liberal values encouraged the expectation that the historic hardship under which mankind had laboured was on the wane. That optimism proved insufficient, however, to alter the means by which states settled disputes between themselves. Much of the riches that industrialism generated went, indeed, to militarise the populations that it benefited, so that when war came in the twentieth century its 'recalcitrant indecisiveness', as Weigley observes, reasserted itself with even greater force. The reaction of the rich states was to embark on an ever more intense militarisation of their populations from above, in an attempt to break the deadlock. As the tide of war spilled over into the poor world, militarisation began from below, as the leaders of movements dedicated to winning freedom from European empires and an equivalent to Western economic well-being compelled peasants to become warriors. Both developments were fated to end in frustration. The appalling human cost of mass militarisation suffered by the industrialised states in the second of the two world wars led to the development of nuclear weapons, designed to end wars without the commitment of manpower to the battlefield, but proving once deployed to threaten the end of everything. Mass militarisation in the poor world resulted not in liberation but in the entrenchment of oppressive regimes raised to power at the cost of widespread suffering and death.

It is in this state the world finds itself now. Despite confusion and uncertainty, it seems just possible to glimpse the emerging outline of a world without war. It would be a bold man who argued that war was going out of fashion. The resurgent nationalisms of the peoples of the Balkans and of former Soviet Transcaucasia, which have found expression in warmaking of a particularly abhorrent kind, give the lie to that. Such wars, however, lack the menace raised by similar conflicts in the pre-nuclear world. They provoke not the threat of sponsorship by opposed great-power patrons, with all the danger of ramification that such sponsorship implies, but a humanitarian urge to intervene in the cause of peace-making. Prospects of peace-making may be illusory. The Balkan and Transcaucasian conflicts are ancient in origin and seem to have as their object that 'territorial displacement' familiar to anthropologists from their study of 'primitive' war. Such conflicts by their nature defy efforts at mediation from outside, since they are fed by passions and rancours that do not yield to rational measures of persuasion or control; they are apolitical, to a degree for which Clausewitz made little allowance.

Yet the fact that the effort is being made betokens a profound change in civilisation's attitude to war. The effort at peace-making is motivated not by calculation of political interest but by repulsion from the spectacle of what war does. The impulse is humanitarian, and though humanitarians are old opponents of warmaking, humanitarianism has not before been declared a chief principle of a great power's foreign policy, as it has now by the United States, nor has it found an effective supranational body to give it force, as it has recently in the United Nations, nor has it found tangible support from a wide body of disinterested states, willing to show their commitment to the principle by the despatch of peace-keeping, and potentially peace-making forces to the seat of conflict. President Bush may have overreached himself in proclaiming the appearance of a New World Order. The elements of a new world resolution to suppress the cruelties of disorder are, nevertheless, clearly visible. Such resolution, if it persists, is the most hopeful outcome of the events of our terrible century.

The concept of cultural transformation has pitfalls for the unwary. Expectations that benevolent change – rising living standards, literacy, scientific medicine, the spread of social welfare – would alter human behaviour for the better, have so often been dashed that it may seem unrealistic to foresee the arrival of effective anti-warmaking attitudes in the world. Yet profound cultural changes do occur and their occurrence can be documented. As the American political scientist John Mueller has observed, the institution of human slavery was created at the dawn of the human race, and many once felt it to be an elementary fact of existence. Yet between 1788 and 1888 the institution was substantially abolished . . . and this demise seems, so far, to be permanent. Similarly the venerable institutions of human sacrifice, infanticide and duelling seem also to have died out or been eliminated. It could be argued that war, at least war in the developed world, is following a similar trajectory.[63]

Mueller, it must be said, is a disbeliever in the proposition that man is biologically disposed towards violence, one of the most fiercely contested issues in behavioural science, from which most military historians prudently distance themselves. It is not necessary, however, to take the disbelieving view in order to be impressed by the evidence that mankind, wherever it has the option, is distancing itself from the institution of warfare.

I am impressed by the evidence. War, it seems to me, after a lifetime of reading about the subject, mingling with men of war, visiting the sites of war and observing its effects, may well be ceasing to commend itself to human beings as a desirable or productive, let alone rational, means of reconciling their discontents. This is not mere idealism. Mankind does have the capacity, over time, to correlate the costs and benefits of large and universal undertakings. Throughout much of the time for which we have a record of human behaviour, mankind can clearly be seen to have judged that war's benefits outweighed its costs, or appeared to do so when a putative balance was struck. Now the computation works in the opposite direction. Costs clearly exceed benefits. Some of these costs are material. The superinflationary expense of weapon procurement distorts the budgets even of the richest states, while poor states deny themselves the chance of economic emancipation when they seek to make themselves militarily formidable. The human costs of actually going to war are even higher. Rich states, as between themselves, recognise that they are not to be borne. Poor states which fall into war with rich states are overwhelmed and humiliated. Poor states which fight each other, or are drawn into civil war, destroy their own well-being, and even the structures which make recovery from the experience of war possible. War truly has become a scourge, as was disease throughout most of human history. The scourge of disease has, almost within living memory, been very largely defeated and, though it is true that disease had no friends as war has had friends, war now demands a friendship which can only be paid in false coin. A world political economy which makes no room for war demands, it must be recognised, a new culture of human relations. As most cultures of which we have knowledge were transfused by the warrior spirit, such a cultural transformation demands a break with the past for which there are no precedents. There is no precedent, however, for the menace with which future war now confronts the world. Charting the course of human culture through its undoubtedly warlike past towards its potentially peaceful future is the theme of this book.

Interlude 1
Limitations on Warmaking

To look forward to a future in which recourse to war has been brought under rational limitation should not lead us into the false view that there have been no limitations on warmaking in the past. The higher political and ethical systems attempted to impose legal or moral restrictions both on the use of war and its usages from early times. The most important limitations on warmaking, however, have always lain beyond the will or power of man to command. They belong within the realm of what the Soviet General Staff used to call 'permanently operating factors', and such factors – weather, climate, seasons, terrain, vegetation – always affect, often inhibit and sometimes altogether prohibit the operations of war. Other factors, loosely categorised as 'contingent' and including difficulties of supply, provisioning, quartering and equipment, have strictly limited the scope, intensity and duration of warmaking in many periods of human history. As wealth increased and technology developed, some were reduced or largely overcome – the soldier's rations, for example, may now be preserved in convenient form for almost indefinite periods – but none can be said to have been eliminated altogether. How to feed, how to shelter, how to move an army in the field remain today the first, chief and most persistent problems that a commander has to solve.

Perhaps the effect of both 'permanent' and 'contingent' factors in limiting the scope and intensity of offensive or defensive operations is best illustrated from naval warfare. Man may fight with his fists on land, but to do even that on the surface of the water he requires a buoyant platform. Purpose-built platforms we must guess, since of their nature they decompose, appeared comparatively late in human history. The earliest to be found has been dated only to 6315 BC and given the effort, probably cooperative effort, needed to construct the simplest raft or dugout, we may presume that the bone and stone tools which provide evidence of man's earliest industry predate boatbuilding by a very long period indeed.[1]

Specialised warships, even ships suitable for war, are relatively recent in origin. They have always been expensive to build and they require handling by specialist crews. Their construction and operation therefore demands considerable disposable wealth, probably the surplus of a ruler's revenue; and if the earliest form of fighting at sea was piratical rather than political in motive, we must remember that even the pirate needs capital to start in business. The first navies may or may not have been anti-piratical in purpose – the advantages conferred by the ability to move forces or supplies along rivers or coasts may have first prompted rulers to maintain warships – but navies are, by definition, more costly than individual ships. Whichever way it is looked at, fighting on water has cost more than fighting on land from the start.

Wealth, or the lack of it, is not the only factor to limit the ability to wage war at will on water; others are weather and deficiencies of propulsive power. Wind comes free and the earliest representation we have of naval warfare – of a fight between warriors of the Pharaoh Rameses III and the Sea Peoples in the Nile delta in 1186 BC – shows the Egyptians in a ship with sails.[2] Sailing-ships, however, were not to make suitable fighting platforms before the invention of the gun, since the management of sails precluded engagement at the short ranges where pre-gunpowder weapons could take effect. Oared ships were much more manoeuvrable in encounters where crews sought to close hand-to-hand with swords and spears. The advantages of the oared ship went further: by mounting a ram, and working up to full rowing speed, it could actually sink another if it caught it broadside on, which a wooden sailing-ship stout enough to bear the shock of impact could not do. Light winds would not impart the necessary speed; strong winds raise seas in which no captain with a thought for the survival of his ship would risk such an encounter.

The oared ship had serious deficiencies as a ship of war, however; in confined waters, like those of the Mediterranean, dominated from the second millennium BC onward by a succession of rich states that could afford the manpower costs, it was to set the terms of naval warfare until the coming of the gun. Yet it could not keep the seas in bad weather and so was essentially a summertime weapon. Worse, it could not work away from a port of re-supply for more than a few days at a time, since the hull form which made it fast in smooth waters – long but shallow and narrow – deprived it of the carrying space required to feed and water the large crew needed to row it at ramming speed. True, it was later to be used outside the inland seas as a vehicle of marauding in oceanic waters by nihilists like the Vikings – once they had mastered the technology of deep-keel construction and the technique of star-sight navigation – where it spread terror, devastation and death over coasts and riverine lands hundreds of miles from base. The Vikings, however, flourished in an era when states were weak, particularly at sea, and in any case they depended on the wind to carry their longships to undefended shores, using oars only for auxiliary purposes.

In consequence, as John Guilmartin has demonstrated in his brilliant analysis of Mediterranean naval warfare, galley navies were never autonomous instruments of strategy but extensions, or more accurately partners, of armies on land.[3] The inshore wing of a galley fleet normally hinged on the coastward flank of an accompanying army, in operations that were amphibious in the strict sense of the term. The fleet manoeuvred so as to isolate an enemy coastal base from support by its own naval forces, while the army advanced with supplies to positions from which the galleys could be re-provisioned. This symbiosis explains why the great Mediterranean sea battles, from Salamis in 480 BC to Lepanto in AD 1571, were all fought within sight of land. Why, though, once the big-gun sailing-ship came to exercise mastery of the seas – that is, from the sixteenth century onward – were most naval battles still fought within sight of land, or very close to it? Two of the victories won by the greatest of sailing-ship admirals, Nelson, were gained against fleets lying inshore at anchor – the Nile and Copenhagen – while the third, Trafalgar, was the result of an encounter only twenty-five miles off the Spanish coast. The tendency for sailing-fleets to fight inshore had nothing to do with endurance. The wooden man-of-war, unlike the galley, carried stores and water sufficient to keep it at sea for many months, so that as early as 1502 Portuguese ships, which had sailed round the Cape of Good Hope, were able to fight and defeat the fleet of a local ruler off the west coast of India. In the 1650s Cromwell's admiral, Blake, could campaign in the Mediterranean, where England then had no base, while by the middle of the next century Britain and France were conducting intensive naval campaigns against each other off the east coast of India, six months' sailing-time from home. Despite their distance from base, all these fleets continued to do battle in coastal waters.

Several reasons combine to explain this circumstance. One is that battle under sail could not be conducted in rough weather (an exception was Quiberon Bay, fought in Atlantic squalls in November 1759) and inshore waters are more often calm than the high seas. Another is that the objects for which naval battles are fought – free access to the high seas from port, protection of coastwise shipping, defence against invasion – have their locus in coastal waters. A third is that sailing-fleets, operating exclusively by visual communication, have extreme difficulty finding each other in great waters. Even with a chain of frigates, the visual link between each was at most twenty miles; many fleets missed each other with the greatest ease, as Nelson found at the Nile in 1798. It is significant that in two real but rare deep-sea encounters – the second battle of Finisterre, 1747, fought 200 miles off Ushant, and the Glorious First of June, 1794, fought again off Ushant but 400 miles into the Atlantic, both between the British and French – the French fleets were in both cases encumbered by convoys, the latter 130 ships strong, covering so large an area of sea that they made a much more prominent target for a pursuer than their escort of warships would have done if sailing alone.

The supersession of sail by steam as a means of propulsion might be thought to have loosened the link between the warship and the land, since a steam warship could manoeuvre to engage even in flat calm, and remained a stable gun-platform at wind speeds that forced sailing-warships to reef and close their gunports. Paradoxically, however, the steam ship actually restored the logistic dependency under which the galley had lain and greatly diminished the operating range of steam fleets relative to that of sailing-fleets. The reason was that until the comparatively late adoption of oil fuel, steam warships burnt coal at an enormous rate – HMS *Dreadnought* of 1906 emptied its bunkers in five days' steaming at twenty knots – and so were tied to their coaling-stations.[4] A naval power like Great Britain, which acquired its worldwide network of bases in sailing-ship days, could keep fleets in all the oceans because they could coal at hundreds of ports; even so, they were local, not oceanic, in range. A state without such a chain of bases could either not project naval power at all, or was dependent on the goodwill of allies to do so. When Russia sent its Baltic fleet to the Far East in 1904–5, at a time when it was on bad terms with Britain, the ships managed the voyage only by piling their decks so high with coal that, between stops at French colonial ports, they could not have used their guns.

It is an extra paradox that coal-fired fleets, though in theory capable of oceanic encounter (two days' steaming would carry them 500 miles from land), continued in practice to clash near coasts. In part the same strategic factors affected them, but they also continued, like their sailing predecessors, to be virtually blind until the coming of wireless; indeed, the real extension of their line of sight had to wait upon the arrival of the wireless-equipped, shipborne aircraft. As a result, all the sea battles of the First World War were fought within a hundred miles of land; the pattern repeated itself in the Second World War, despite the advent of radar, the aircraft-carrier and the long-range patrol submarine, and the mastery of the technique of replenishment at sea. The ultimate explanation derives from the vastness of the oceans; fleets could rarely count upon defeating distance in the vasty deep. The American aircraft that sank the Japanese carriers at Midway – one of the few true oceanic encounters in the history of the world – were guided to them by shrewd guesswork; the *Bismarck*, eventually sunk a thousand miles off Brest in May 1941, had twice shaken off the whole of Britain's Home Fleet; while the mid-Atlantic battles between Allied escorts and surfaced German U-boats were brought about because large, slow convoys made abnormally conspicuous targets. Given the resistance offered to surveillance systems by the movements of oceanic storms, such as the large weather fronts which the Japanese used to cover their approach to Pearl Harbor in December 1941, and the persisting difficulty of coordinating long- with short-range target-acquisition equipment, the seas may well keep their secrecy for a long time to come.

The facts of the past are more surely and very simply stated. Seventy per cent of the globe's surface is covered by water, most of it open sea, and most large sea battles have taken place in but a fraction of that area. If we draw up a list of Fifteen Decisive Sea Battles, to match Creasy's famous *Fifteen Decisive Battles of the World*, taking 'decisive' to mean 'of durable and more than local importance', it might read as follows:

Salamis, 480 BC: defeat of Persia's invasion of Greece
Lepanto, 1571: Muslim advance into western Mediterranean checked
Armada, 1588: Spain's offensive against Protestant England and Holland frustrated
Quiberon Bay, 1759: Anglo-Saxon success in struggle with France for dominance in North America and India ensured
Virginia Capes, 1781: victory for the American colonists guaranteed
Camperdown, 1797: Dutch naval competition with the British extinguished for good
The Nile, 1798: Napoleon's ambition to dominate both shores of the Mediterranean and reopen struggle for India thwarted
Copenhagen, 1801: mastery of North European waters conveyed to Britain
Trafalgar, 1805: Napoleon's naval power finally destroyed
Navarino, 1827: inaugurated dissolution of Ottoman empire in Europe
Tsushima, 1905: established Japan as dominant power over China and in North Pacific
Jutland, 1916: collapsed Germany's ambition to operate an oceanic navy

Midway, 1942: denied Japan control of the Western Pacific

March convoy battles, 1943: forced withdrawal of Germany's U-boats from the Battle of the Atlantic

Leyte Gulf, 1944: established incontestable power of the United States over Imperial Japanese Navy

These are shorthand notes of the significance of the battles chosen; what is remarkable about this list – though experts may quarrel with it – is how close and often the sea battles cluster in the same corner of the map. Camperdown, Copenhagen and Jutland, for example, were all fought within 300 miles of each other; Salamis, Lepanto and Navarino, the first and last separated by 2300 years in time, took place near the Peloponnese at points scarcely more than a hundred miles apart. The Armada battle, Quiberon Bay and Trafalgar were fought within a hundred miles of Longitude Five West, between Latitudes Fifty and Thirty North, a comparatively tiny patch of the globe – much of it occupied by dry land. The Virginia Capes were to be the scene of much naval fighting after 1781, as Tsushima had been before 1905, notably during the Mongol offensive against Japan in 1274–81, while the coast where the Nile was fought had been a magnet for naval operations since the Pharaohs. Of the fifteen 'decisive' sea battles cited, therefore, it emerges that only two, Midway and the March convoy battles, took place in previously unviolated water far from land.

Equally, most of the globe's dry land has no military history. Tundra, desert, rain forest and the great mountain ranges are as inhospitable to the soldier as to the traveller; indeed, even more so, for the soldier's necessities are more cumbersome. Military manuals may contain entries on 'desert' or 'mountain' or 'jungle' warfare, but the truth is that to attempt to fight in terrain that is waterless or roadless defies nature and that such fighting as does take place is usually mere skirmishing between expensively over-equipped specialists. Rommel's and Montgomery's desert armies of the Second World War clung to the coast of North Africa; Japan's conquest of the dense forest land of Malaya in December 1941–January 1942 was achieved along the colony's excellent roads and by amphibious 'hooks' down its coastline; China's seizure of parts of India's mountain frontier in 1962, when attacks were mounted at heights above 16,000 feet, was staged by troops who had acclimatised for a year on the Tibetan plateau – many of the Indian defenders who had recently come up from the plains were incapacitated by altitude sickness.

In all, about seventy per cent of the world's 60,000,000 square miles of dry land is either too high, too cold or too waterless for the conduct of

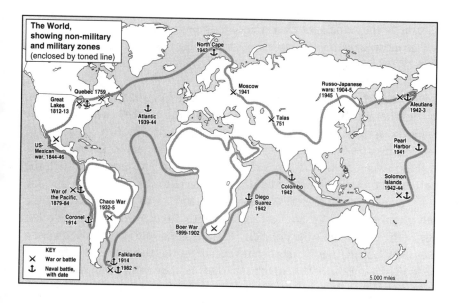

The World, showing non-military and military zones (enclosed by toned line)

North Cape 1943
Quebec 1759
Great Lakes 1812-13
Moscow 1941
Russo-Japanese wars: 1904-5, 1945
Aleutians 1942-3
Atlantic 1939-44
Talas 751
Pearl Harbor 1941
US-Mexican war, 1844-46
War of the Pacific, 1879-84
Chaco War 1932-5
Colombo 1942
Solomon Islands 1942-44
Coronel 1914
Diego Suarez 1942
Boer War 1899-1902
Falklands 1914 1982

KEY
× War or battle
⚓ Naval battle, with date

5,000 miles

military operations. The poles, North and South, demonstrate the effect of such conditions with starkness. The Antarctic continent's inaccessibility and the extreme climatic conditions that prevail there secluded it from warmaking for millennia, though several states laid claim to territory; the icecap, moreover, is known to cover valuable mineral deposits. Since the signing of the Antarctic Treaty of 1959, all territorial claims have been put into abeyance and the continent has been declared demilitarised. The North Pole, by contrast, is not demilitarised and, indeed, the icecap is regularly undersailed by nuclear-propelled submarines. But the length of the polar night – three months in winter – the extreme winter cold and the absence of any resource of value makes it improbable that fighting will ever be conducted on its surface. The most northerly military incidents to have taken place on land in polar regions were the skirmishes fought in 1940–3 to capture or defend weather stations, set up by German or Allied parties, on the east coast of Greenland and on Spitzbergen, near Latitude Eighty North; casualties were inflicted by both sides but, under the attack of the elements, they were at times compelled to assist each other to survive.[5] Beyond that, intense military activity has been concentrated into a fraction even of that space where conditions do favour the movement and maintenance of armed forces. Battles not only tend to recur on sites

69

close to each other – the 'cockpit of Europe' in northern Belgium is one such area, the 'Quadrilateral' between Mantua, Verona, Peschiera and Legnano in northern Italy another – but have also frequently been fought on exactly the same spot over a very long period of history.

The most arresting example is Adrianople, now Edirne, in European Turkey, where fifteen battles or sieges have been recorded, the first in AD 323 and the last in July 1913.[6]*

Edirne is not now and never has been a large city; its population remains under 100,000. Its curious distinction as the most frequently contested spot on the globe has been conferred on it not by its wealth or size but by its peculiar geographical position. It stands at the confluence of three rivers, whose valleys provide avenues of movement through the mountains of Macedonia to the west, Bulgaria to the north-west and the Black Sea coast to the north, and which then flow to the sea through the only extensive plain in the most southeasterly tip of Europe. At the other side of the plain stands the great city of Constantinople (Istanbul), on a site chosen by Constantine for his capital because it was the most easily fortified position on the Bosphorus, which separates Europe from Asia. Adrianople and Constantinople are therefore strategically twin cities, together guarding movement from the Black Sea to the Mediterranean and from southern Europe to Asia Minor, or vice versa. Because Constantinople defied attack from the sea, particularly after the building of the walls of Theodosius in

* Adrianople I was fought between the Roman Emperor Constantine and the pretender Licinius, who approached from west and east respectively; at Adrianople II, 378, one of the catastrophes of history, the Emperor Valens and the last great Roman army were overwhelmed by the Goths, who had invaded the empire across the Danube (in flight from the Huns, a horse people, who had broken out of the steppe); at Adrianople III, 718, the recently arrived Bulgars defeated a Muslim army attempting to take Constantinople from the rear – an outcome of crucial importance for Christian Europe; Adrianople IV, V and VI were fought by the Bulgars in their attempts to attack Constantinople, in 813, 914 and 1003; Adrianople VII, 1094, was a battle between a Byzantine emperor and a pretender; at Adrianople VIII, 1205, the Bulgars defeated the Crusader Baldwin, who had made himself Byzantine emperor, and the Doge Dandolo (whose family house in Venice is now that city's most expensive hotel); Adrianople IX, 1224, ended in a victory by the restored Byzantine imperial house over the Bulgars; Adrianople X, 1255, was an internal Byzantine struggle; Adrianople XI, 1355, ended in victory by the Byzantines over the Serbs, who had recently become a Balkan military power; Adrianople XII, 1365, marked a successful stage in the Ottomans' advance from Asia Minor into Europe; following the consolidation of Ottoman power, there was no further battle until 1829, when at Adrianople XIII a Russian army took the city from them; in the last two battles, in 1913, Ottoman Turkey first lost and then regained Adrianople from the Serbs and Bulgars.

the early fifth century, all invaders of southern Europe from Asia Minor found themselves compelled to land in the plain to its rear; invaders starting north of the Black Sea were driven to hug its western shore by the barrier of the Carpathians on their inland flank, and so also ended up in the plain of Adrianople; while invaders from Europe, drawn by the prize of Constantinople, the richest place in the Western world between the fall of Rome and its sack by the Crusaders in 1204, had no choice but to cross the same plain in their approach march. Adrianople, in short, is the European end of what geographers call a land bridge, by which Asia gives on to Europe along two major routes, and it was fated to be fought over whenever there was a major outflow of military force, east–west or west–east, by way of either; in the circumstances, it is not surprising that the city never grew to any size.

Few other places exemplify the effect of permanent or contingent factors on the course of warfare as well as Adrianople does; nevertheless, in a weaker form their influence can be traced throughout the course of history on most landscapes where military activity has been high. Large rivers, highland barriers, dense forests form 'natural frontiers' with which, over time, political boundaries tend to coincide; the gaps between them are avenues along which armies on the march are drawn. Once through such gaps, however, armies rarely find themselves free to manoeuvre at will, even if no apparent obstacles stand in their way. A more subtle geography comes into play, reinforced by climate and the season, and adapted by the roadmaker and bridge-builder, even if not by the fortification engineer. Thus the German *Blitzkrieg* into France in 1940, apparently an unconfined romp across open country once the tanks that led it had broken the barrier of the Ardennes forests and the River Meuse, turns out to have followed very closely the line of *Route nationale* 43, which for much of its length is the Roman road laid out soon after Caesar's conquest of Gaul in the first century BC.[7] Neither the Romans nor those who built on their work made a point of quarrelling with geography; we may infer, therefore, that the German tank commanders, whatever their illusion of pursuing a free trajectory, were in fact obeying topographical dictates as old as the last reshaping of the earth's surface in northern France, laid down at the retreat of the glaciers 10,000 years earlier.

A similar pattern of obedience to the laws of nature presents itself in the study of the German army's campaign into Russia in the year follow- ing the *Blitzkrieg* in France. Western Russia appears to offer the invader, particularly a mechanised invader, free movement at will. Between its 1941 frontier and the three cities of Leningrad (St Petersburg), Moscow and Kiev, 600 miles distant, the surface of the land nowhere rises above 500 feet, while the rivers that cross that enormous and almost treeless plain tend to flow with the line of advance rather than across it. Nothing solid should impede the onset of the invader. Nothing solid does. In the centre, however, rise two of Russia's greatest rivers, the Dnieper and the Niemen, flowing respectively into the Black and Baltic seas; their headwaters, with many tributaries, combine to form the Pripet marshes, a swamp 40,000 square miles in extent and so resistant to the conduct of military operations that its position on the situation map became known to German staff officers as the 'Wehrmacht hole'(*Wehrmachtloch*), containing no German military units of worth whatsoever. As a result it became a main base area for Soviet partisan operations against the Wehrmacht's rear areas and, doubtfully effective though such operations were, a source of persistent unease to the German army as long as its front line in Russia was drawn further to the east.

The *Wehrmachtloch*, though a permanent feature of the Russian theatre of war, was a minor influence on German operations. A major and repetitive factor was the appearance of the seasonal swamp, created by the spring snowmelt and the autumn rains, across its whole front of engagement. The *rasputitsa*, as Russians call the twice-yearly liquefaction of the face of the steppe, brings military movement to a halt for a month at a time. As Golikov, the Soviet commander of the Voronezh Front, signalled to a subordinate who had enquired about the prospect of a counter-offensive reaching the line of the Dnieper in March 1943, 'There are 200–230 miles to the Dnieper and to the spring *rasputitsa* there are 30–35 days. Draw your own conclusions.'[8] The inescapable conclusion was that the onset of the snowmelt would outpace the Soviet advance, leaving the line of the Dnieper in German hands. So, indeed, it turned out. But the *rasputitsa* more often worked to the Germans' disadvantage. It was prolonged in the spring of 1941, thus delaying the start of the invasion by several critical weeks, and again in the autumn, forcing a postponement of the advance on Moscow. The late arrival that year of the winter frosts, which restore a weight-bearing crust to the surface of the steppe, left the Wehrmacht's tanks literally bogged down just too far from Moscow to ensure the capture of the capital by the timetabled date. Tsar Nicholas I called January and February 'two generals in whom [Russia] can confide';[9] the March and October *rasputitsa* proved better generals to Russia in 1941 and may, indeed, have rescued it from catastrophe that year.

How may the discussion be summarised so far? What is clear is that the congruence of 'permanently operating' and contingent factors –

climate, vegetation, topography and the alterations that man has made to the natural landscape – imposes on Mercator's projection of the world map a sharp division between military and non-military zones, the latter vastly exceeding the former in extent. Organised and intensive warfare has been carried on over extended periods of time along an irregular but continuous band of the world's surface lying between the tenth and fifty-fifth degrees of latitude in the northern hemisphere, and stretching from the Mississippi valley in North America to the Philippines and their outliers in the western Pacific, or from 90 degrees West of Greenwich to 135 degrees East. *The Times Atlas of the World* classifies vegetation into sixteen categories, including (before land-clearing for agriculture) Mixed Forest, Broadleaf Forest, Mediterranean Scrub and Dry Tropical Forest.[10] If a line is drawn to enclose those four vegetation zones in the northern hemisphere and the land and sea routes between them, one may quickly see that almost all of history's battles have been fought within the space the line encloses and very few outside. If the battle locations are dated by month, a seasonal concentration will superimpose itself, varying from place to place with highs and lows of temperature and rainfall, and dates of harvesting. By way of illustration, the first three battles of Adrianople were fought in July, August and July respectively and the last three in August, March and July; March is unusually early for campaigning even in the southern Balkans, when the rivers run high with snowmelt, but the other dates, immediately following the Mediterranean harvest, are exactly as to be expected.

Is it true, then, that the zone of organised warfare coincides, inside seasonal variables, with that which geographers call 'the lands of first choice', those easiest to clear of forest and yielding the richest crops when brought under cultivation? Does warfare, in short, appear cartographically as nothing more than a quarrel between farmers? In the sense that serious warmaking requires wealth, and intensive agriculture has always yielded the largest and most consistent return on any of man's activities until very recent times, there is something to that view. On the other hand, while farmers are implacable in disputes about boundaries and water rights, and sturdy fighters when called to arms by superiors, they are also, by common observation, implacable individualists who abandon servitude to their animals and their fields only with the greatest reluctance. Marx regarded the peasants as 'irredeemable', by which he meant that he saw no prospect of enlisting them in the revolutionary armies with which he hoped to overthrow the capitalist order.[11] Mao thought differently; and Victor Davis Hanson, in his breathtakingly original study of warmaking in classical Greece, is persuasive that it was the small landholders of the Greek city states who invented the idea of the 'decisive battle' as Westerners have practised it ever since. Nevertheless, Marx had a point. The farmer is indeed rooted in his plot, his village and his grumbles, and naturally resists the summons to march to some distant border between the lands of first choice and the unploughed region that lies beyond, however good the reason that he should.

We should note that plough people of the same language and religion rarely fight each other on a major scale. On the other hand borders between ploughed and unploughed land, throughout the temperate zone, are very frequently defined by long and expensive works of fortification: the Roman Antonine Wall just short of the Highland Line in Scotland; the *limes* marking the line between plough and forest in Roman Germany; the *fossatum Africae* which defended the fertile Maghreb from Saharan raiders; the Roman 'Syrian' frontier of forts and military roads separating plough from desert along the line of the Jordan and the Tigris-Euphrates headwaters; the Russian *cherta* lines running for 2000 miles from the Caspian Sea to the Altai mountains as a defence against steppe raiders; the Habsburg Military Frontier in Croatia separating the plains of the Sava and Drava from the Turkish-controlled mountain zone to the south; above all, the Great Wall of China, built to exclude the steppe nomads from the irrigated lands of the Yangtse and Yellow rivers on so extensive a scale and over so long a period that archaeologists have as yet failed to map all its complexities.[12]

These fortified boundaries suggest a fundamental tension between the haves of ploughed land and the have-nots of soils too thin, cold or dry to be broken for cultivation. To recognise that tension is not to fall into the false perception that the motive underlying major warmaking is mere expropriation. Man the warrior is a more complex being than that. Cultivators who are ethnic kin do fight each other, sometimes with the deadliest ferocity; have-nots from the wastes beyond the fertile zone may fight apparently for an idea alone – for example, the Arab followers of Muhammad expropriated with a will, but it was the urge to extend the frontiers of the House of Submission, rather than a base material motive, that drove them to their extraordinary exploits. The greatest of conquerors, Alexander of Macedon, was already comfortably established as ruler of the cities of Greece before he set off to the ends of the earth, and seems to have pillaged the Persian empire largely for the pleasure of it. The Mongols, even wider-ranging than Alexander in their assaults on settled states, showed virtually no capacity to consolidate the fruits of their victories:

some of the descendants of the Diadochi, Alexander's generals, were still in power in Bactria 300 years after his death, while none of the regimes founded by Genghis or his immediate successors lasted for more than a century. Tamerlane, a Tartar claiming Mongol ancestry – from Genghis, no less – appears to have valued the rich lands he overran absolutely not at all but, like a slash-and-burn harvester, to have moved on as soon as he had exhausted the soil where he ravaged.

Yet to note that the have-nots often misuse what they expropriate is not to invalidate the general point that the tide of war tends to flow one way – from poor lands to rich, and very rarely in the opposite direction. That is not simply because poor lands offer little worth fighting over; it is also because fighting in poor lands is difficult, sometimes impossible. Poor people from what William McNeill calls 'food-deficit areas' – desert, steppe, forest, mountains – will fight among themselves, and their fierce military skills have been valued and purchased by the rich for as long as we have records of organised warmaking. Hence the exotic names – hussar, uhlan, jäger – that some European regiments proudly bear to this day, and the even more exotic scraps of barbaric clothing – bearskin caps, frogged jackets, kilts and lionskin aprons – that continue to be worn for ceremony. The warfare of poor peoples, nevertheless, was limited in scope and intensity by their very poverty. It was only when they broke into the rich lands that they were able to accumulate the stocks of provender which made deeper penetration, and eventual conquest, a possibility. Hence the wealth and labour expended by cultivators in fortifying their borders, to exclude the predators before they could make serious trouble.

The causes underlying the operation of 'permanent' and 'contingent' factors on warfare may therefore be seen to be exceedingly complex. Man the warmaker is not an agent of unbounded free will, even though in warmaking he may burst the limits that convention and material prudence normally impose on his behaviour. War is always limited, not because man chooses to make it so, but because nature determines that it shall be. King Lear, railing at his enemies, may have threatened to 'do such things – what they are yet I know not – but they shall be the terrors of the earth'; as other potentates in straitened circumstances have found, however, the terrors of the earth are hard to conjure up. Wealth lacks, the weather worsens, the seasons turn, the will of friends and allies fails, human nature itself may revolt against the hardships that strife demands.

Half of human nature – the female half – is in any case highly ambivalent about warmaking. Women may be both the cause or pretext of warmaking – wife-stealing is a principal source of conflict in primitive societies – and can be the instigators of violence in an extreme form: Lady Macbeth is a type who strikes a universal chord of recognition; they can also be remarkably hard-hearted mothers of warriors, some apparently preferring the pain of bereavement to the shame of accepting the homeward return of a coward.[13] Women can, moreover, make positively messianic war leaders, evoking through the interaction of the complex chemistry of femininity with masculine responses a degree of loyalty and self-sacrifice from their male followers which a man might well fail to call forth.[14] Warfare is, nevertheless, the one human activity from which women, with the most insignificant exceptions, have always and everywhere stood apart. Women look to men to protect them from danger, and bitterly reproach them when they fail as defenders. Women have followed the drum, nursed the wounded, tended the fields and herded the flocks when the man of the family has followed his leader, have even dug the trenches for men to defend and laboured in the workshops to send them their weapons. Women, however, do not fight. They rarely fight among themselves and they never, in any military sense, fight men. If warfare is as old as history and as universal as mankind, we must now enter the supremely important limitation that it is an entirely masculine activity.

—2—
Stone

WHY DO MEN FIGHT?

WHY DO MEN FIGHT? Did men wage war in the Stone Age, or was early man unaggressive? Men – but also women – fight, with ink and paper, very fiercely over these questions. They are not the military historians, who rarely concern themselves with the well-springs of the activities they chronicle, but the social and behavioural scientists. Perhaps military historians would be better historians if they did take time to reflect on what it is that disposes men to kill each other. The social and behavioural scientists have no choice but to do so. Man and society are their subjects, yet most human beings for most of the time cooperate for the common good. Cooperativeness must be taken as the norm, and why that should be so requires some explanation, though of no very profound sort, since common observation will establish that cooperation is in the common interest. If there were no departure from the cooperative principle, therefore, social and behavioural scientists would have little to do. They would be explaining the predictable, an unrewarding and unrewarded task. It is the unpredictability of human behaviour, in individuals and in human groups, which challenges them to supply explanations, and the unpredictability of violent behaviour most of all. The violent individual is the principal threat to the norm of cooperativeness within groups, the violent group the principal cause of disruption in wider society.

Studies of individual and group behaviour take different directions. They share, however, a common ground, to which debate eventually returns: is man violent by nature or is his potentiality for violence – about such potentiality there can be no dispute, if only because man can kick and bite – translated into use by the operation of material factors? Those who hold to the latter view, loosely categorised as 'materialists', believe that their perceptions demolish the naturalist position. The naturalists unite to oppose the materialists but divide sharply between themselves. There is a minority whose members insist that man is naturally violent; though most would not concede the analogy, theirs is the argument of

79

Christian theologians who hold to the story of the Fall and the doctrine of original sin. The majority reject such a characterisation. They regard violent behaviour either as an aberrant activity in flawed individuals or as a response to particular sorts of provocation or stimulation, the inference being that if such triggers to violence can be identified and palliated or eliminated, violence can be banished from human intercourse. The debate between the two schools of naturalists has aroused strong passions. At a meeting at Seville University in May 1986, a majority of those present issued a statement, modelled on the United Nations Educational, Scientific and Cultural Organisation's Statement on Race, condemning belief in man's violent nature in absolute terms. The Seville Statement contains five articles, each beginning 'It is scientifically incorrect', to which affirmation is expected. The articles together amount to a condemnation of all characterisations of man as naturally violent. In succession they deny that 'we have inherited a tendency to make war from our animal ancestors' or that 'war or any other violent behaviour is genetically programmed into our human nature' or that 'in the course of human evolution there has been a selection for aggressive behaviour more than for other kinds of behaviour' or that 'humans have a "violent" brain' or, finally, that 'war is caused by "instinct" or any single motivation'.[1]

The Seville Statement has found weighty support. It has, for example, been adopted by the American Anthropological Association. It does not, however, much help the layman who is aware that war has ancient origins, knows that surviving 'Stone Age' peoples like the highlanders of New Guinea are undeniably warlike, is conscious of violent impulses in himself but lacks the expert knowledge of genetics or neurology necessary to take sides. Yet the debate between the two naturalist parties is important, indeed fundamental, as is that between the naturalists and the materialists. At a hopeful time in human history, a time of effective disarmament and of the adoption of humanitarianism as a principle in world affairs, the layman naturally seeks reassurance that the drafters of the Seville Statement have right on their side. Mankind's success over the the last two centuries in altering for the better the material circumstances of life would then encourage support for the materialists' explanation of organised human violence, in the anticipation that a continuation of the efforts that have largely defeated disease, want, ignorance and the hardship of manual labour might eliminate warfare also. Its history, from the Stone Age onward, would then become an antiquarian interest, of no more relevance to everyday life than that of world exploration or of pre-Newtonian science. If, on the other hand, the drafters of the Seville

Statement are wrong, if their condemnations of the naturalist explanation of human violence are mere expressions of optimism, then the materialist explanation is wrong as well, and our end-of-the-century expectations of an end to war entirely misplaced. It is important to know what both the pessimists and the optimists in the naturalist school have to say.

WAR AND HUMAN NATURE

The scientific study of violence and human nature centres on investigation of what scientists, perhaps by prejudgement, denote as 'the seat of aggression', found in the area of the brain known as the limbic system. This area, located low in the central brain, contains three groups of cells, known as the hypothalamus, the septum and the amygdala. Each, when damaged or electrically stimulated, produces changes in the behaviour of the subject. Damage to part of the hypothalamus of male rats, for example, reduces their aggressive behaviour and abolishes sexual performance, while electrical stimulation increases aggression – though 'stimulated animals attack only [less] dominant animals, which shows that the direction of aggression is controlled by another part of the brain'.[2] The reference to less dominant animals is important, because it is an observation of great antiquity that groups of gregarious animals arrange themselves into a pecking order, so called from hierarchy among domestic fowl, asserting or conceding rank in accordance with it. Damage to the amygdala of monkeys may decrease fear of and therefore aggressive behaviour towards 'novel or unusual objects' but increase fear of fellow monkeys, thus causing the damaged animal to lose rank in its group.

Neurologists cautiously conclude that the reactions to fear, aversion or threat that resolve themselves as aggression – but also as defence – have their origin in the limbic system. They also emphasise, however, the complex relationship of that system with the 'higher' parts of the brain, such as the frontal lobes where incoming sensory information is first and most elaborately processed. The frontal lobes, according to A.J. Herbert, appear to be responsible for the 'regulation and use of aggressive behaviour', since it is known that damage to the frontal lobes in man may cause 'uncontrollable outbursts of explosive aggression . . . not followed by remorse'.[3] What neurologists have established, crudely speaking, is that aggression is a function of the lower brain, amenable to control by the higher brain. But how do the different parts of the brain communicate? Two means are through chemical transmitters and hormones. Scientists have discovered that reducing a chemical called serotonin heightens aggression, and they suspect that there may be a peptide which induces its flow. The peptide, however, has not been found, and variations in the level of serotonin are rare. Hormones, the secretions of the ductless glands, are by contrast easily identifiable and one of them, testosterone, produced in the male testes and closely identified with aggressive behaviour, varies widely in concentration. Its administration to humans – whether male or female – heightens aggression. On the other hand, its administration to female rats that are nursing young reduces their aggressiveness towards males, while their maternal protectiveness is stimulated by another hormone altogether. Generally speaking, high levels of testosterone in males make for heightened masculinity, of which aggressiveness is one feature; low levels, however, do not correlate with an absence of courage or combativeness. Evidence for that, for example, is found in the reputation of eunuch bodyguards and the successes of the famous Byzantine eunuch general, Narses. Finally, scientists emphasise, hormonal effects tend to be moderated by context; calculations of risk, that is to say, will offset, both in animals and man, the operation of what may be called instinct.

Neurology has not, in short, yet succeeded in clarifying how aggression is generated or how controlled within the brain. In genetics, on the other hand, there has been some success in showing how context and 'selection for aggression' correlate. Since Darwin first proposed the idea of natural selection in 1858, scholars in many disciplines have sought to establish it on an incontestable scientific basis. Darwin's original work was based merely on the external observation of species, which led him to suggest that individuals best adapted to their surroundings were the more likely to survive to and in maturity, that the offspring of such survivors, by inheriting their parents' characteristics, would survive in larger numbers than those of the less well adapted, and that their inherited characteristics would eventually dominate within the species as a whole. What made his theory revolutionary was the argument that the process was mechanistic. Parents, he stated, could pass on only those characteristics they inherited, not – as his contemporary Lamarck contested – those that they acquired. How such characteristics underwent change for yet better adaptation – by the process we call 'mutation' – he could not yet explain. Indeed, there is still no explanation of how mutation occurred in the primary organisms from which the myriad varieties of species descend.

Mutation is nevertheless an observable phenomenon; mutation for aggression is one of its forms and aggressiveness is clearly a genetic inheritance that may enhance the chance of survival. If life is a struggle, then those who best resist hostile circumstances are likely to live the longest and produce the largest number of resistant offspring; a recent and enormously popular book, *The Selfish Gene,* by Richard Dawkins, ascribes this process not merely to the product of genetic inheritance but to the gene itself.[4] Genetic experimentation, moreover, demonstrates that some strains of laboratory animals are verifiably more aggressive than others and that aggressiveness breeds true into subsequent generations. Geneticists have also identified rare forms of genetic constitution which correlate with exaggerated aggressiveness, the best known of which is the XYY chromosome pattern in human males: about one male in a thousand inherits two Y chromosomes rather than the normal one, and the XYY group yields a slightly disproportionate number of violent criminals.[5]

Evidence culled from genetic exceptions and even more so from animals bred in laboratory conditions does not, however, supply answers to questions about the aggressive disposition of any existing creature, including man, in its environment. Successful adaptation through mutation, however mutation occurs, is a response to environment, or context, and while it might prove possible, through the new science of genetic engineering, to make 'point mutations' in a genetic inheritance and so breed creatures which lack aggressive responses altogether, it would be necessary for their survival to hold them in conditions from which all threat was entirely absent. No such conditions exist in the natural world, nor could they be created. Even were a wholly unaggressive breed of humans to evolve to live in wholly benevolent circumstances, they would still be obliged to kill the lower organisms that cause disease, the insects and small animals that harbour them and the larger animals which compete for food supplies in the stock of vegetation. It is difficult to see how the necessary system of environmental control could be carried on by creatures which lacked aggressive responses altogether.

What is apparent is that the opponents and the proponents of the thesis that 'man is naturally aggressive' both pitch their case too strong. Opponents fly in the face of common sense. Observation demonstrates that animals kill members of other species and also fight among themselves; the males of some species fight to the death. It is necessary to deny all genetic connection between man and the rest of the animal world – a position now held only by strict Creationists – in order to discount the possibility that aggression may be part of man's genetic inheritance. Proponents also go too far, though for different reasons. One is that they tend to draw the boundaries of aggressiveness too wide. Thus a major group of classifiers, who uncontroversially differentiate between 'instrumental or specific aggression', defined as 'concerned with obtaining or retaining particular objects or positions or access to desirable activities' and 'hostile or teasing aggression', which is 'directed primarily towards annoying or injuring another individual', also include 'defensive or reactive aggression' which is 'provoked by the actions of others'.[6] There is a logical distinction, of course, between aggression and self-defence, which is not invalidated even if the classifiers can show that all three sorts of behaviour they classify together have their origin in the same area of the brain. Such indifferentism also suggests that the proponents of the view that man is naturally aggressive give too little importance to the moderating influence of parts of the brain beyond the limbic system. As has been observed, 'all animals which show aggressive behaviour carry a number of genes which modify its level of expression' – so that aggressive impulses are offset by calculation of risk or by matching threat to chance of escape, in the well known 'fight/flight' patterns of behaviour – the ability to modify the expression of aggression being particularly marked in humans.[7] It seems, therefore, that scientists have so far done little more than identify and categorise emotions and responses which have been eternally familiar. True, we now know that fear and rage have a neural seat in the lower part of the brain, that it is stimulated by the identification of threat in the higher part of the brain, that the two neural areas communicate through chemical and hormonal links and that certain genetic inheritances predispose towards greater or lesser violent response. What science cannot predict is when any individual will display violence. What, finally, science does not explain is why groups of individuals combine to fight others. For some explanation of that phenomenon, in which lie the roots of war, we have to turn elsewhere, to psychology, ethology and anthropology.

WAR AND THE ANTHROPOLOGISTS

A psychological basis for a theory of aggression was advanced by Freud, who originally regarded it as the frustration of the sexual drive by the ego. After the First World War, in which two of his sons served with distinction but which marked him by its tragedy, he adopted a darker view.[8] In a famous correspondence with Einstein, published as *Why War?*, he states bluntly that 'man has within himself a lust for hatred and destruction' and offered as the only hope of offsetting it the development of 'a well-founded dread of the form future wars will take'. These observations, adopted by Freudians as the theory of the 'death drive', principally concerned the

84

individual. In *Totem and Taboo* (1913), Freud had proposed a theory of group aggression which drew heavily on literary anthropology. He suggested that the patriarchal family was the primal social unit and that it had ramified by the working of sexual tensions within it. The patriarchal father was supposed to have had exclusive sexual rights over the family women, thus driving his sexually deprived sons to murder and then eat him. Ridden by guilt, they then outlawed or tabooed the practice of incest and instituted that of exogamy – marrying beyond the family circle – with all its potentiality for wife-stealing, rape and consequent inter-family and then inter-tribal feud of which the study of primitive societies yields so many examples.

Totem and Taboo was a work of the imagination. More recently the new discipline of ethology, in which psychological theory is combined with the study of animal behaviour, has produced more rigorous explanations of group aggression. The founding 'territorial' idea derives from the work of Konrad Lorenz, a Nobel prizewinner, who argued from his observation of animals in the wild and in controlled environments that aggression was a natural 'drive', deriving its energy from the organism itself, which achieves 'discharge' when stimulated by an appropriate 'releaser'. Most animals of the same species, however, possessed in his view the ability to palliate the aggressive discharge in others of their own kind, usually by displaying signs of submission or retreat. Man, he argued, originally behaved in the same way; but by learning to make hunting weapons he succeeded in overpopulating his territory. Individuals then had to kill others in order to defend a patch, and the use of weapons, which emotionally 'distanced' killer from victim, atrophied the submissive response. Such was the process, he believed, by which man had been transformed from a subsistence hunter of other species into an aggressive killer of his own.[9]

Robert Ardrey elaborated Lorenz's territorial idea to suggest how individual aggression might have become group aggression. Being more effective as hunters than individuals, groups of humans, he argued, learnt to hunt cooperatively over common territories as hunting animals had adapted to do, so that cooperative hunting became the basis of social organisation and supplied the impulse to fight human interlopers.[10] From Ardrey's hunting thesis, Robin Fox and Lionel Tiger have gone on to propose an explanation of why males provide social leadership. Hunting-bands, they say, had to be exclusively male in composition, not just because males are stronger but because the presence of women would be a biological distraction; because hunting-bands had to accept leadership for reasons of efficiency and were for millennia the principal providers of sustenance, aggressive male leadership thereafter determined the ethos of all forms of social organisation.[11]

The theories of Lorenz, Ardrey, Tiger and Fox, which drew heavily on the work of human and animal behavioural scientists, were not welcomed by the practitioners of the oldest discipline in social science, anthropology. Anthropology is an extension of ethnography, the study of surviving 'primitive' peoples in their habitats; from ethnography it attempts to supply explanations of the origins and nature of civilised societies. Early ethnographers, like Latifau and Demeunier, had recognised in the eighteenth century that warfare was an intrinsic feature of the societies they studied and in their work on, for example, the American Indians they provided now invaluable descriptions of 'primitive' warfare.[12] Descriptive ethnography became anthropology because, in the nineteenth century, it was invaded by proponents and opponents of Darwinian theory; thus was born the great 'nature versus nurture' debate which continues to divide social scientists to this day. In the course of the nature/nurture debate – it was opened by Francis Dalton, Darwin's cousin, in 1874 – war was quite soon extruded as a subject of study. That was an achievement of the nurture school which, determined in a typically nineteenth-century way to prove that man's higher powers were dominant over his lower nature and that reason would lead him to foster ever more cooperative social forms, managed to fix the focus of anthropological enquiry on to the origin of political institutions. Those, they said, were to be found within the family, clan and tribe, rather than in their external relations (of which warmaking was a type). Some in the nature school, who became known as Social Darwinians for their dedication to the concept of struggle as a means of change, disagreed, but they were marginalised.[13] The nurture school contrived to draw discussion into what they had identified as the key issue, that of kinship in primitive society, from which they believed it could be shown how all higher, more complex, non-blood relationships derived.

Kinship concerned the relationship between parents and their children and their children's relationships with each other and more distant relatives. It was not at issue that such relationships pre-dated the formation of the state. It was equally not at issue that family and state were different organisations. The problem was to show how the state had developed from the family and whether family relationships determined those that states adopted. The essentially liberal philosophy of the nurture school demanded evidence that relationships within a state could be established by rational choice and fixed by legal form. Anthropology came under pressure, therefore, to produce examples of primitive societies in which patterns of kinship anticipated those in the politics of modern liberal states. There was a great deal of malleable evidence available, particularly of the sort in which myth and ritual were used to reinforce bonds of kinship and obviate recourse to violence, and the nurture school made full use of it. By the end of the nineteenth century, indeed, the energies of anthropologists were largely devoted not to debating whether kinship was the root of human relations, but whether the creative cultures they took as a model of human organisation had developed spontaneously at a number of separate places or had been diffused – that argument was called 'diffusionism' – from an original centre to others.

This search for origins was essentially self-defeating, since not even the most primitive societies available for study, it had to be admitted, existed in a primeval state. All must have evolved in some way or been altered by contact, however tenuous, with others. The wasteful diffusion of energy among anthropologists in what was essentially a sterile debate was ended peremptorily at the beginning of the twentieth century by a German emigrant to the United States, Franz Boas, who simply denied that a search for origins was productive. Anthropologists, he said, would discover if they searched widely enough that cultures merely perpetuated themselves. Since perpetuation was not rational, it was futile to sift between cultures in the search for historical endorsement of a preferred modern political form. Man should be free to choose among the widest variety of cultural forms and adopt that which best suited him.[14]

This academic doctrine, which became known as Cultural Determinism, quickly achieved enormous public popularity through the work of his assistant, Ruth Benedict, whose *Patterns of Culture*, published in 1934, became the most influential work of anthropology ever written, even allowing for the widespread attention drawn to the universality of human myths by Sir James Frazer through *The Golden Bough* (eleven volumes, 1890–1915).[15] Benedict proposed the existence of two main cultural forms, Apollonian and Dionysian, the former authoritarian, the latter permissive. The idea of the Dionysian mode, however, had already aroused widespread attention as a result of a visit made by a young pupil of Boas, Margaret Mead, to the South Seas in 1925. In *Coming of Age in Samoa* Mead reported that she had found a society which existed apparently in perfect harmony with itself, where the bonds of kinship attenuated almost into invisibility, where parental authority was dissolved within the affections of the extended family, where children did not compete for primacy and where violence was virtually unknown.

For feminists, progressive educationists and moral relativists *Coming of Age in Samoa* remains today a gospel text, whether they are aware of it or not. Cultural Determinism also had a profound effect on Boas' fellow anthropologists in the Anglo-Saxon world, but for a different reason. The British in particular, leaders in ethnography because of the opportunities for fieldwork that the enormous extent of their empire offered, accepted the importance of its thrust but recoiled from its intellectual imprecision; they were dissatisfied above all by the refusal of the Cultural Determinists to admit that human nature and man's material needs might be as important as freedom of choice in determining within which culture he lived. Under the influence, therefore, of another German-speaking émigré, Bronislaw Malinowski, who had also done his first fieldwork in the South Seas, but ten years before Margaret Mead, they offered an alternative which has come to be known as Structural Functionalism.[16] The clumsy title reflected a conflation of two philosophies. The first was evolutionary and Darwinian: it laid down that any society's form was a *function* of its 'adaptation' – the term is a pure Darwinism – to its surroundings. Thus, to suggest a crude example, 'swidden' (slash-and-burn) agriculturalists pursued their apparently feckless way of making a living because they found themselves in forested areas where soil fertility was low but other people thin on the ground. It therefore made sense to hack out a clearing for a season or two, grow yams, fatten pigs and then move on. The ability of such societies, however, to remain 'adapted' to their surroundings is sustained by their cultural *structure*, which may appear simple at first glance but, to the ethnographer prepared to devote sufficient time to living among them, may reveal itself as surprisingly elaborate.

The Structural Functionalists got down to a far more detailed analysis of society than the Cultural Determinists thought necessary. The raw material they collected to show how structure supported function turned out, however, to fall into those two now familiar categories, myth and kinship. Over the interrelationship of the one with the other they were to debate in increasingly complex and private language up to the Second World War and beyond. The debate became all the more agitated after the war with the intervention of a brilliant Frenchman, Claude Lévi-Strauss, who succeeded in making structure seem much more important than function. Starting with Freud's favoured concept of taboo, he set out to give it the anthropological foundation that psychoanalysis had always failed to supply. There was indeed, he said, a taboo, supported by myth, against incest in primitive societies; they accommodated it by arranging mechanisms of exchange, between families, tribes and so on, in which women were the most valuable commodity. Exchange systems evened out rancours and resentments; the exchange of women, in the avoidance of incest, was the ultimate emollient.[17]

Anthropology had got itself into a situation where explanations of how societies remained stable and self-sustaining dominated all other ways of looking at them. Anthropologists knew that disputes over women were the chief cause of trouble among primitives; they refused, however, to apply themselves to the study of its consequence, which was war. This was perverse. Lévi-Strauss was writing in the aftermath of the worst war in the world's history, and numbers of leading anthropologists, notably Edward Evans-Pritchard, the outstanding British anthropologist of his generation, had fought in it; Evans-Pritchard had actually led a band of ferocious tribesmen against the Italians in Ethiopia in 1941 and the horrors of the revenge they took on their former rulers caused him anguish for the rest of his life.[18] In any case, the nature of the two world wars, particularly the morbidly ritual character of the trench offensives of the First World War, cried out for anthropological investigation. It was a cry that anthropologists chose not to heed.

Part of the reason for that may have been because the first anthropologist to lose patience with his colleagues' collective refusal to recognise the importance of warfare had done so in a book deliberately intended to cause intellectual offence. *Primitive Warfare*, published in 1949, was the work of Harry Turney-High, an American anthropologist who, like many of his generation, did his fieldwork among native Americans – some of whom were among the most warlike people known to ethnographers. In 1942, however, Turney-High left his university to enter military service and had the good luck to be posted to the horsed cavalry at the moment that it was about to disappear for good. The warhorse and the horsed warrior's weapons must draw the thoughts of an educated man with an informed imagination back to the very beginnings of man's relationship with the animal world; 'you have to have ridden with a squadron to understand the fascination of horses *en masse*, for the horse is a herd animal by instinct,' wrote Alexander Stahlberg, a contemporary of Turney-High's in one of the last German cavalry regiments.[19] Turney-High's exercises with the sword opened his eyes to the inadequacy of almost everything professional ethnographers had written about early warfare.

The persistence with which social scientists have confused war with the tools of war [he wrote on his opening page] would be no less astounding did their writing not reveal . . . complete ignorance of the simpler aspects of military history. . . . It would be hard to find a noncommissioned officer in the professional armies of the second rate powers who has been as confused as most analysts of human society.[20]

Turney-High was right; I constantly recall the look of disgust that passed over the face of a highly distinguished curator of one of the greatest collections of arms and armour in the world when I casually remarked to him that a common type of debris removed from the flesh of wounded men by surgeons in the gunpowder age was broken bone and teeth from neighbours in the ranks. He had simply never considered what was the effect of the weapons about which he knew so much, as artefacts, on the bodies of the soldiers who used them. 'This civilian attitude', Turney-High remarked, 'has resulted in hundreds of museum cases holding weapons from all over the world, catalogued, marked with accession number, and uncomprehended.'[21] He was determined to make his brother and sister anthropologists comprehend the dark and violent side of the life of the peoples they studied, the bone-crushing, flesh-piercing purpose of the weapons they carried in ceremony, and the lethal consequences of breakdown in the exchange mechanisms with which they were alleged to sustain their kinship systems in perpetual equilibrium.

Turney-High did not deny that some primitive peoples were 'premilitary'. He was even prepared to admit that some peoples, if left to themselves, were happy to choose as peaceful and productive a way of life as Margaret Mead said she had found among the Samoans.[22] He was insistent, however, that war was a timelessly universal activity, give or take the odd exceptions, and he was pitiless in rubbing his fellow anthropologists' noses in that fact.

The ethnographer has not hesitated to describe, classify, and co-ordinate all culture, material and non-material, to the best of his ability. Neither has he hesitated to discuss war at length, for it is one of man's most important non-material complexes. The core alone, 'How does this group fight?', is excluded. The field researcher has been meticulous regarding the icing and has overlooked the cake.[23]

The anthropologist-turned-cavalryman served up in man-sized helpings the ethnographic record of how groups fought. Moving in great swoops from Polynesia to the Amazonian basin, from Zululand to the America of the Plains Indians, from the sub-Arctic tundra to the West African forests, Turney-High described in bloody detail the practises of captive torture, cannibalism, scalp-taking, head-hunting and ritual evisceration wherever they were to be found. He analysed the exact nature of combat in dozens of different societies, explaining how the New Hebrideans appointed champions to stage ritual duels before the assembled warring sides, the North American Papago chiefs nominated some men to be 'killers' and others to protect the killers in the fight, the Assinboin accepted the war leadership of men who had had a dream of victory over a customary enemy and the Iroquois maintained a battle police to hold the shirkers in a war party to their duty. He was relentless in tabulating the exact effect of spear, arrow, club and sword on human flesh; lest any faint-hearted colleague flinch from contemplating what the function of a flint warhead might have been, he pointed out that its lineal descendant was the bayonet, the development, he alleged, of a weapon system which had been responsible for the destruction of more human life than any other artefact in history.[24]

Turney-High's purpose was, however, a larger one than that of confronting anthropology with evidence that primitive man had blood on his hands. He postulated from the evidence he presented an agonising crux: most of the societies which ethnographers preferred to study, he said, existed 'below the military horizon' and it was only when the sun of their future rose above it that they emerged into modernity. At a stroke he challenged all the theorisings of the Cultural Determinists, the Structural Functionalists and the disciples of Lévi-Strauss (whose seminal *Structures élémentaires de la parenté* also appeared in 1949). What Turney-High boldly asserted was that it was pointless to look for the origins of the liberal state in any freedom of choice among available cultural systems, structural adaptation to habitat or mythic management of exchange systems. All societies trapped at that level, he insisted, were bound to remain primitive till kingdom come. It was only when a society moved from the practice of primitive war to what he called true war (sometimes he called it civilised war) that a state could emerge, and it was only, by inference, when a state had come into existence that choices could be made about the nature that it should take – theocratic, monarchic, aristocratic or democratic. The key test of transition from primitivity to modernity, he concluded, was 'the rise of the army with officers'.[25]

Since Turney-High had on his opening page demoted most of his fellow anthropologists to an intellectual level below that of non-commissioned officers, it is scarcely surprising that they repaid him by ignoring his book altogether. David Rapaport, the political scientist who wrote the foreword to the second edition (1971), explained their response as a '"disciplined incapacity" to recognise original work'.[26] But the explanation was much simpler. They knew when they were being insulted and collectively turned their backs on the name-caller. That might be a reasoned response were his book to appear today. Turney-High is an unreformed Clausewitzian, whose test of a society's military standing is whether it practises a form of war that leads to victory: territorial conquest and disarming of the enemy. Clausewitzian victory in the nuclear age (Turney-High wrote before the Soviet Union had exploded its first atomic bomb) has come to seem, even to the least sentimental of strategic analysts, a very dubious aim, and it is doubtful whether many of them would embrace the concept of 'civilised war' in the spirit that Turney-High offered it forty years ago. Nevertheless, in his own time he put his profession on the spot. He had demanded that it think how warmaking transformed the stateless societies it loved so well into the states that paid the expenses of its field trips, and he would brook no refusal to answer.

An answer did come – in time. The pressure of external events forced anthropologists to look at their primitives as warriors and not exclusively as gift-givers or myth-makers. The pressure was felt most strongly in the United States not simply because it was a principal nuclear power and a leading combatant in Vietnam but because it had become in the years after 1945 the heartland of anthropology. Ethnographic fieldwork, in its increasingly scientific guise, is enormously expensive and it was to the rich American universities that most scholars had to look for funds. To such scholars, moreover, whose mission was to probe the deepest and oldest secrets of human behaviour, the students at the American universities, where opposition to the nuclear arms race and the Vietnam War was strongest, began to pose the eternal questions: What makes man fight? Is man naturally aggressive? Have there been societies without war? Do any still exist? Can a modern society embrace perpetual peace and, if not, why?

Only five articles on the anthropology of war had appeared in learned journals in the 1950s.[27] From the 1960s onward they appeared thick and fast. In 1964 the veteran Margaret Mead issued a rallying-cry for Cultural Determinism in an article entitled 'Warfare is only an invention'.[28] A new generation of anthropologists did not think that it could be that simple. New theories had impinged on their subject. Mathematical games theory was one, which allotted numerical values to possible choices in any given conflict of interests and proposed that the 'strategy' accumulating the highest total would prove the most successful. Games theory operated at an unconscious level, its proponents insisted, so that it was not necessary for humans to know that they were playing a game for it to be carried on; the survival of those who made the larger number of correct choices was the 'pay-off'.[29] This was merely an attempt to put Darwinian natural selection on to a quantitative footing; because of its intellectual ingenuity, nevertheless, it attracted supporters. Others became involved in the developing discipline of ecology, the study of the relationship between a population and its habitat; young anthropologists quickly saw that certain ecological concepts, such as carrying capacity, which limits population in a given region to that which its consumables will support, could be of great value to them. Consumption implies population growth, population growth leads to competition, competition provokes conflict and so on. Was competition itself the cause of war? Or was war, through its 'function' of reducing population or displacing the defeated from the conflict zone, a cause in and of itself?

This dance along the well worn paths of 'origins' and 'functions' might have continued for a long time. What changed its pace and direction were two things. First, the American Anthropological Association devoted a symposium at its 1967 meeting to warfare at which, eighteen years after he had proposed it, Turney-High's distinction between 'primitive' war and 'true' or 'civilised' or, as it was now to be known, 'modern' war was at last accepted.[30] The second was that from the 1960s onward a group of anthropologists who had tacitly accepted the validity of Turney-High's insight and had gone to look at primitive warriors through his eyes returned from their field expeditions and began to write up their findings. They did not, of course, agree about how to explain what they had seen. Nevertheless, they had undoubtedly studied warriors who used primitive weapons and it was with primitive weapons – spear, club, arrow – that war had certainly first been fought. It was open to argument whether such weapons had been simple wooden artefacts, or had been tipped with bone or stone, or whether fighting between humans in any style recognisable as warfare had had to await the development of metallurgy. Not even the most dedicated opponent of the idea that technology determines the nature of humanity's social forms could deny, however, that spear and club, and even bow and arrow, limit the harm that humans can do to each other in combat, particularly by limiting the range at which harm can be done. The warfare of contemporary people who still used spears, clubs and arrows to fight provided, therefore, at the very least some insight into the nature of early combat. Combat is the heart of warfare, the act by which men are maimed or killed in numbers, the activity that divides war from mere hostility, the source of the moral crux – is man good or bad? Does he choose war or is it chosen for him? The young anthropologists who had set off to answer Turney-High's key question, 'How does this group fight?' had also produced the first solid observations of the nature of combat with primitive weapons and, in that respect at least, some insight into how war might have begun. This is the point to look at what they reported. The case-studies chosen have been arranged in developmental progression, the most primitive forms of warfare first.

SOME PRIMITIVE PEOPLES AND THEIR WARFARE

The Yanomamö

The Yanomamö, a people of some 10,000 souls, live in an area of dense tropical forest some 40,000 square miles in extent, on the headwaters of the Orinoco River, straddling the borders of Brazil and Venezuela. When Napoleon Chagnon spent sixteen months there in 1964, he was one of the first outsiders to have made contact with them, while they had as yet received almost no artefacts from the modern world. The Yanomamö are swidden (slash-and-burn) agriculturalists, who hack out temporary gardens from the forest, grow plantains and make new clearings when soil fertility falls. Their villages, holding groups of 40–250 closely related people, are set up about a day's march from each other, though at a greater distance when enemies are neighbours, and hostilities, which are frequent, often cause moves. A typical move is by a small village away from a larger, hostile one toward a strong, allied village.

The Yanomamö have been called 'the fierce people', and their behaviour is, indeed, extremely ferocious; they have a code of ferocity (*waiteri*) by which individual men demonstrate their aggressiveness, while whole villages also seek to convince others of the dangers of attacking them. Boys are encouraged to be violent from an early age, by taking part in fierce games, and grow up to be very violent to women. Though women are the principal prizes in exchange and fights, the men who possess them treat them badly. They are beaten, burnt or even shot with arrows when a man gets into a rage, the rage itself often being staged to demonstrate *waiteri*; wives can hope for protection only if they have brothers in the village whose reputation for fierceness is greater than that of their tormentors.

Despite *waiteri*, the event in the Yanomamö year to which villages

94

look forward is the season of inter-village feasting. During the wet season the villagers tend their gardens; when the dry season comes they prepare to feast with a neighbouring village or to be feasted. Trade provides the basis of trust, such as it is, in which agreement to feast originates; though the Yanomamö's material culture is crude in the extreme – they make little more than hammocks, clay pots, arrows and baskets – not all villages make the same things and they depend on others to make up the deficiencies. Successful feasting may then lead on to the most important form of exchange, that of women.

Exchange of women, though it palliates the ferocity that both individual Yanomamö and their villages display to each other, does not obviate outbreaks of violence. Men constantly seek to seduce the wives of others, which makes for violence within a village, perhaps causing a village group to leave and set up on its own as a separate and now hostile village. A large village in a woman-exchange relationship with a smaller one may demand an unfair ratio. Or a given woman who has been too brutally treated by her husband may be reclaimed by a relative from her original village.

It is in circumstances like these that the 'fierce people' become violent and Yanomamö violence commonly takes a stylised form. It is a widely held belief that combat among primitive peoples is largely ritual but, while there is much to that view, it needs careful qualification. Nevertheless, the practice of violence among the Yanomamö does tend to escalate through carefully graded stages, the levels being the chest-pounding duel, the club fight, the spear fight and the inter-village raid.

Chest-pounding duels, which usually take place at the inter-village feasts, 'are always conducted between members of different villages and arise over accusations of cowardice or in response to excessive demands for trade goods, food or women'.[31] The procedure is unvarying: after the feasters have taken hallucinogenic drugs, to foster a fighting mood, a man steps forward and thrusts out his chest. A representative of the other village who accepts his challenge steps forward, seizes him and hits him a violent blow in the chest. The recipient of the blow usually does not respond, since he wants to demonstrate his toughness, and may receive as many as four blows before demanding his turn. The exchange goes on blow for blow, until one party is disabled or both are too sore to continue, in which case they may continue with a side-slapping duel, which normally ends quickly when the loser is winded. In the aftermath, if the duel was prearranged, the contestants cradle and chant to each other, swearing eternal friendship.

Club fights, which are usually spontaneous, are nastier but still ritualised.

'These usually result from adultery or suspicion of adultery.'[32] The plaintiff, bearing a ten-foot pole, goes to the centre of the village – which may be his own – and shouts insults at the offender. If his challenge is accepted, he plants his pole in the ground, leans on it and awaits a blow on the head. Once delivered, it is his turn to respond. The sight of blood, quickly drawn, turns the fight into a free-for-all, with men picking sides and wielding clubs. There is then the real danger of wounding or death, since the challenger's club has a sharpened end – the sign that he meant business – and someone may be run through. At this stage it is the village headman's role to intervene with his bow, threatening to shoot an arrow into anyone who will not stop. Fatal wounds are sometimes inflicted, however, which means that the culpable party must fly the village to another, or, if the fight was between villages, that the attackers will retreat. The consequence, however, is a war of raiding in either case.

Chagnon considers that raiding constitutes Yanomamö 'war' but describes a stage intermediate between that and the chest-pounding duel, the spear fight, of which there was only one incident while he was in the field. A small village, defeated in a club fight over a woman – her headman brother took her back from a husband who treated her too badly – allied itself with some others and made a concerted sortie. They succeeded in driving the inhabitants of the larger village out of their homes under 'a hail of spears' and chased them as they fled. The large village re-formed, the attackers turned tail and a second spear fight took place some miles farther away. Both sides then retired 'after nearly losing their tempers'. Several men had been wounded and one subsequently died.

Both villages later raided each other, but Chagnon regards the raid rather than the spear fight as the more warlike activity, on the grounds that Yanomamö who set out on a raid do so with the intention of killing, and do not much mind how, even in some circumstances whom, they kill. Typically they lie in wait outside the target village until they find a defenceless victim – someone 'bathing, fetching drinking water or relieving himself' – kill him and then fly. Flight is well organised, through a chain of rearguards, and necessarily so, for one raid provokes another. The raiding pattern may lead to what Chagnon considers the ultimately hostile act, a treacherous feast, when a warring village prevails on a third village to invite its enemies to a feast and then surprises them. As many as possible are killed and the widows distributed among the victors.

Chagnon interprets the Yanomamö style of fighting as a cultural response to their surroundings. It is, he says, absolutely not designed to secure territory, since villages never appropriate the habitat of a defeated neighbour; the point, rather, is to emphasise what he calls 'sovereignty', measured by a village's ability to prevent another taking its women or to establish its right to acquire women on favourable terms. Hence the displays of 'fierceness', which are intended to deter seducers, wife-stealers or raiders at the start.

The Yanomamö behave differently against their non-Yanomamö neighbours, however, and have in recent years expanded successfully into new territory and almost exterminated one tribe. Such genuine fierceness toward others derives from the Yanomamö's belief that 'they were the first, finest and most refined form of man to inhabit the earth' and that all other peoples are a degeneration from their pure stock.[33] The 'enemy' are in general those not related by marriage, for the Yanomamö, though collectors of women if 'fierce' enough, observe kinship rules designed to avoid incest. Kinship is not, however, so strong a force as to prevent warfare between related groups, who fight frequently. What makes them do so, Chagnon suggests, is the practice of female infanticide, common among primitives but followed by the Yanomamö to maximise the number of 'fierce' males in the endless rondo of women-taking.

Since his first visits to the Yanomamö, Chagnon has altered his view of the function of their warfare, and now inclines to see it, in neo-Darwinian terms, as 'selected for reproductive success': more killing brings more women and so more offspring.[34] Objectively, however, there seems something for all theorists in his account. Warfare undoubtedly adjusts the population to available territory – losses accounted for twenty-four per cent of all recent male deaths in three related groups he studied – as the ecologists would expect. The relative weakness of the kinship system would seem significant to Structuralists, who might argue that warfare was a result of a failure in reciprocity. The Structural Functionalists would see both the practice of warfare and the use of myth to sustain it as evidence that Yanomamö culture was a total adaptation to their environment. Ethologists would take 'fierceness' as proof of their point, that man has a violent drive that seeks discharge.

Military historians would be interested above all by the externalities of Yanomamö combat. Taking as their starting-point the observable fact that people are fearful, and that fearfulness is enhanced by the deadliness of weapons, they would emphasise the carefully ritualised nature of Yanomamö armed encounter, and perhaps reverse Chagnon's hierarchy. The 'raids' and 'treacherous feasts' that he sees as the acme of their warfare look in perspective more like murder, as known to societies regulated by codes of public law. Chest-pounding duels, club fights and spear fights, on the other hand, approximate to ritual conflict, regulated by an appreciation of how dangerous it is, first, to expose any but selected fighting men to injury; second, of how rapidly a fight may escalate into general violence if there is not a limitation on what weapons may be chosen – hence no use of sharpened clubs except by the challenger – or if deadly weapons, such as spears, are used at close range.

The Yanomamö, in short, seem to have got intuitively to Clausewitz's point and to have passed beyond it. Kinship groups might have embarked on a warfare of decisive battles designed to establish a hierarchy of 'sovereignties' once and for all, had they so chosen. To have done so, however, would have been to risk annihilation, once their 'real', which is to say ritual, battles escalated into 'true' war. Preferring mutual prudence, they have settled for a routine of endemic fighting, much of it symbolic in character, which brings death to some but spares the majority to live, even if to fight another day.

The Maring

Of all discoveries about primitive societies made by ethnographers, that of ritual battle is of the greatest interest to military historians, if only because traces of it are so evidently present in what we know about 'civilised' war. Too often, however, the picture of ritual battle is over-generalised, implying a strength of ritual that reduces battle to a harmless game. Here is a description of primitive war, written by a bibliographer with a wide variety of sources in mind, but primarily based on the warfare of the mountain peoples of New Guinea:

> the pitched battle . . . involved anywhere from two hundred to two thousand warriors and was held in a pre-defined area of no man's land along the borders of the warring groups. Each army was composed of warriors, usually related by marriage, from several allied villages. Even though large numbers of warriors were involved, there was little or no military effort; instead, dozens of individual duels were engaged in. Each warrior shouted insults at his opponent and hurled spears or fired arrows. Agility in dodging arrows was highly praised and young warriors pranced about. The women often came to watch these wars and would sing or goad their men on. Women also retrieved spent enemy arrows so that their husbands could shoot back at their foes. Regularly occurring pitched battles were generally found among advanced tribal people in fairly dense populations. For instance, this type of warfare was not found in Amazonia, but it was common in highland New Guinea where population density is ten times that of the former area . . . In spite of the huge array of warriors involved

in these pitched battles, little killing took place. Because of the great distance between warriors and the relative inefficiency of primitive weapons, combined with a young warrior's agility to dodge arrows, direct hits rarely occurred. In the event that someone was badly wounded or slain, the battle would usually cease for that day.[35]

Some of the elements in this description are uncontentious: for example, the statement that all fighting, until the coming of close-order tactics with standardised weapons, was an affair of individual duels. It is indeed a feature of ritualised battle that casualties tend to be low, and even 'civilised' warfare yields examples of something like resort to recognised fields of encounter, if only because geography is sparing with sites where armies can be assembled. Nevertheless it is an idealisation, as the nastier elements in the warfare of the very primitive Yanomamö reveal. It provides an excellent starting-point for a comparison of popular impressions of ritual warmaking with its more complex reality.

The Maring, among whom Andrew Vayda worked in 1962–3 and 1966, then numbered some 7000, living in an area of 190 square miles astride the forested crest of the Bismarck range in central New Guinea. They subsisted by growing tubers in forest 'gardens', moved regularly for fallowing, by raising pigs and by a little hunting and gathering, a typical 'slash and burn' pattern. Population density was quite high, over a hundred to the square mile – much higher than the Yanomamö's, and the social unit was a cluster of clans, nominally descended from the same paternity, who took wives from outside. The size of a cluster varied between 200 and 850, occupying a defined area of cultivation along one of the streams rising from the watershed. Borderlands were thinly occupied and some clan clusters benefited from primary forest in their territory, which provided a reserve of untilled land. Below the mountain zone the terrain was unhealthy and population – of quite different language groups – became dense again only at the coast. Before the 1940s, they had no access to metal and the best of their tools and weapons were stone artefacts.[36]

In material culture, however, the Maring were superior to the Yanomamö, as the nature of their warfare reflected. Besides plain wood bows, arrows and spears, they also possessed polished stone axe-heads and large wooden shields. With these they conducted fights which passed through what the Maring themselves recognised to be carefully regulated phases. The first was what they called 'nothing' fights, the second 'true' fights, and the third and fourth, not a necessary escalation from fighting, 'raids' and 'routs'.

'Nothing' fights, as Vayda described them, most resembled the harmless ritual battles casually supposed to typify primitive warfare.

> In these the warriors repaired each morning from their homes to pre-arranged fight grounds at the borders of the lands of the two main belligerent groups. The opposing forces took up positions close enough to each other to be within the range of arrows. Thick wooden shields, as tall as the men and about 2½ feet wide, afforded protection in combat. Sometimes the bottoms of the shields were made to rest on the ground and warriors darted out from behind their shields to shoot their arrows and then darted back. Some men also emerged temporarily from cover in order to taunt their foes and to display their bravery by drawing enemy fire. At the end of each day's fighting, the men returned to their homes. Although these small bow-and-arrow fights sometimes continued for days or even weeks, deaths or serious injuries in them were rare.[37]

'True' fights differed from 'nothing' fights in both tactics and the weapons used. Men brought axes and thrusting spears to the fight ground, and narrowed the range to that of hand-strokes. While bowmen in the rear kept up a hail of arrows, fighters in the front rank duelled from behind their shields, occasionally changing places with the bowmen for a rest; individual warriors were also at liberty to take a breather altogether when their efforts exhausted them. Arrows or throwing-spears might sometimes bring down a man in the front line; then, if the enemy timed a short charge right, he could be finished off with axes or thrusting-spears. However, casualties were still rare, and the battles dragged on for days.

> Each morning when there was to be fighting, the able-bodied men . . . assembled near their hamlets and went *en masse* to the fight ground for their day's combat, while the women remained behind to attend to routine gardening and domestic tasks. The men themselves did not fight daily during the period of warfare. When it rained, both sides stayed in their houses, and, by mutual agreement, all combatants sometimes took a day off to repaint their shields, to attend to rituals in connection with casualties, or simply to rest. There could even be intervals as long as three weeks during which active hostilities were suspended and the men worked at making new gardens.[38]

These rituals, almost incomprehensible as they are to modern man for all the echoes of the fighting under the walls of Troy that they bring, occasionally petered out with the final exchange of arrows. They might, however, lead on to more bloody 'routing' when a war party set out from one clan region to deal death and destruction in another; 'raiding', a murderous but more limited sort of expedition, seems to have been an alternative to the 'true' fight in the ladder of escalation. Routs, on the other hand, were a consequence of 'true' fights and resulted in many deaths, of women and children as well as of men, and in the headlong flight of the victims from their settlement.

Maring warfare requires considerable explanation, which Vayda attempts to supply. 'Nothing' fights occurred, he says, when slights and offences accumulating during a peaceful cycle eventually merited revenge: they might be as mild as an insult or as serious as murder, with rape, abduction or suspicion of spell-casting somewhere in between. The point of the 'nothing' fights was twofold: to test the military strength of the opposition but also to negotiate. Much of the shouting was from mediators, who urged peace. These mediators were often allies, for whom clansmen always looked when war was in the air. They provided an impartial voice, but also evidence of the extra strength available to a party if the other insisted on proceeding to 'true' fighting.

'True' fighting could bring its own result, which was an acceptance of stalemate; 'raiding' might have the same effect. 'Routing', however, normally resulted in the displacement of the victims from their settlement, and in the destruction of their houses and gardens. It was the ultimate test, therefore, of which was the stronger party and who might encroach on the territory of a neighbour, an important assessment in a society short of land. Maring fighting, it would seem, was thus 'ecological' in motivation: it redistributed land from the weak to the strong. But Vayda also points out that important features of Maring warfare contradicted this. One is that victorious Maring rarely occupied all or even some of a defeated clan's territory, out of fear that lingering bad magic made it unsafe to do so. Another is that the timing of warmaking always coincided with the readiness of a clan cluster to offer the necessary sacrificial thank-offering to their ancestor spirits for assistance in the fight.

Such thank-offerings took the form of killing and eating mature pigs, in the ratio of one for each member of the clan cluster. Since it takes about ten years to raise and fatten such a number of surplus pigs, fights only occurred about every ten years; and, strangely, it was only toward the end of a ten-year period that neighbouring clan clusters began to offer each other the slights and injuries which were the occasion of war. To undertake war without the means of thanking ancestor spirits was to court defeat; on the other hand, to have a surplus of pigs without an excuse to eat them was to lose the point of fattening them. Vayda noted that Maring population densities had actually been in decline during their last extended period of fighting, thus calling into question his own explanation that it was shortage of land that caused the Maring to fight. It might indeed be thought that the

Maring fought out of habit, perhaps even for the fun of it, rather than for any reason that anthropological theory can advance.

The depiction of war as fun can, of course, too easily slide into trivialisations. Nevertheless, the 'play' element in warfare has been taken very seriously by historians of chivalry, for example, while, casting backward in time, any search for the 'origins' of fighting inevitably carries us back to man's early life as a hunter. The weapons of hunting for sport and the toys of play and games originated in the tools of subsistence hunting. Once agriculture, however crude, began to alleviate the relentless necessity to track and kill animals for daily nourishment, hunting, sport, games and even war were destined to achieve a psychological co-existence in early cultures, as indeed the first three do in our own today. It is, in that perspective, not surprising that the Maring should, with the weapons they had to hand, have devised a system of warfare in which the game or play element was so strong; the means to transform the effect of wooden spears and stone axes, wielded by men in a mutually supporting group, from that of mere wounding to true killing agents derived not from those weapons' intrinsic lethality but from the intentions of the combatants. What should impress us about Maring warfare is not its 'primitivity' but its sophistication. At the individual level it must have done much, in a society without aesthetic achievements, to satisfy the human need for self-expression, display and competition, and even, if one accepts that theory, the 'drive-discharge' of aggression. At the group level, it provided a medium for impressing on an opposing group the degree of gravity with which transgressions of good-neighbourliness were regarded, and the unpleasant consequences that would flow from a failure to recognise superior might, displayed initially in a symbolic style and in a mood that invited not escalation but diplomacy.

Military historians must fix on the characteristics of the Maring's weapons above all. Stone axes and bone arrowheads, 'catalogued [but] uncomprehended' in Turney-High's penetrating phrase, imply a human past red in tooth and claw. Confronted by lumps of cunningly flaked flint, the modern mind leaps instantly to the thought of cloven skulls and shattered spines. It may well be that these were the injuries our prehistoric ancestors inflicted on their enemies at whatever risk to their own skins. What we know about the Maring suggests, by contrast, that peoples with Stone Age weapons do not necessarily have a disregard for their own survival. Weapons that are deadly only at close quarters do not thereby impose on those who wield them a necessity to fight at close quarters; to leap to that conclusion would be to adopt a 'technological determinism' in human behaviour to which the cautious, tentative and procrastinating character of the Maring's tactics gives the lie. If the Maring showed reluctance for the decisive battle, showed indeed that they did not consider the point of battle necessarily to be outright victory on the battlefield, then it is permissible to suppose that other peoples at a similar level of material culture did likewise. It is with that thought in mind that we should continue to consider how wooden, stone and bone weapons might have been used in the prehistoric past.

The Maoris

It is a large step to move from consideration of the warfare of peoples as simple in social organisation as those of mountain New Guinea to that of the hierarchical and theocratic chiefdoms of New Zealand, centre of the largest settlements of the Polynesian diaspora across the southern Pacific. It is a leap not merely in time and across cultures but also over a yawning abyss of disagreement among anthropologists about the stages by which primitivity becomes modernity.

The classic anthropological view is that prehistoric human society evolved through the stages of Band, Tribe, Chiefdom to early State. In this typology, the Band is defined as a small group whose members know, or at least believe, that they are related to each other by blood, typically the social organisation of timid and reclusive hunters or gatherers, living under paternal authority, like the Bushmen of South Africa. The Tribe normally shares a belief in common ancestry but is principally united by language and culture and does not necessarily accept headship, though there may be some recognition of authority, usually reinforced by myth, through a father (patrilineal) or mother (matrilineal) descent; tribes tend toward egalitarianism, by anthropological theory.[39] But Chiefdoms are hierarchical and usually theocratic, individual members ranking themselves by the distance at which their descent originates from a founding father of divine ancestry. The State, under which most inhabitants of the world live today, is held to have developed from the Chiefdom. Anthropologists, using Max Weber's famous differentiation, distinguish between chiefdoms and states by their founding of legitimacy in, respectively, 'traditional' (or occasionally 'charismatic') and 'legal' codes.[40]

Fortunately for the lay person, anthropologists have recently come to prefer a simpler system of classification, which recognises only 'egalitarian' and 'hierarchical' societies in the stage before statehood.[41] The reason for this change of view – not universally accepted – is that many of the simpler societies found by ethnographers in the less accessible regions of the world – mountains, forests, arid and desert zones – have now been identified as refugees from oppression by stronger neighbours; their social structures have been degraded by flight, dispersion, economic hardship and the devaluation of their myths and authority systems by the ordeal that displacement brought. This interpretation is galling to those who have committed themselves to belief in the existence of stateless societies formed by cultural choice or by adaptation to their surroundings, but the star of that sort of anthropology is in decline.[42] It is made galling to others, however, by the greater importance the new interpretation accords to warfare, particularly when the motivation to war is harshly defined as a competition for scarce resources.[43]

While the society of the Maring is not like a state at all (that of the Yanomamö is thought by some to be that elusive thing, pristine aboriginality), that of the Maoris of New Zealand approached very closely to statehood, if only by the tests of capacity to construct major public works and conduct large-scale warfare over extended distances. The Maoris were certainly not short of food, even though they succeeded in their first 600 or 800 years of settlement in New Zealand in exterminating some eighteen species of bird, including the giant, flightless moa.[44] On the other hand, inter-island migration probably had as its principal cause a progressive rise in population densities which, when intensification of production, infanticide, 'voyaging' and warfare failed to stem the pressure, led to the extrusion of whole groups. The Polynesians who arrived in New Zealand, possibly about AD 800, may have been 'voyagers' of the Viking sort, adventurous young men, landless like Leif Ericksson and seeking a Vinland to the south, or they may have been refugees from a victorious chief in their home island; perhaps they were lucky castaways.[45] By whatever means they made their landfall, they brought with them the staples of Polynesian life, and also its institutions, chiefdoms descended by myth from the gods, social rank and military specialisation. They brought, too, the artefacts of island life, including wooden weapons – the spear and the club – to which worked shell, coral, bone or stone lent deadly edges. It was with these weapons that the Maori, in the wide spaces of the North and South Islands, were eventually to practise a form of warfare from which rulers of states in the ages of iron or even gunpowder would have had little to learn.

The source of a Polynesian chief's power was twofold: it derived from *mana*, his priestly duty to mediate between man and god, and from taboo, his right to dedicate a portion of the fruits of the earth and the waters given by the gods to a religious purpose. That might be ritual feasting, sacrifice or temple-building, but it effectively entailed taxation and often the direction of labour. Chiefs could therefore demand, and even compel, an important extension of the powers of mere headship in simpler and more egalitarian societies, whose members looked to the headman only for mediation, advice and leadership. The need to intensify production on islands experiencing population pressure empowered a Polynesian chief to demand communal effort in farming, fishing, building, even irrigation works; if rising population pressure fomented war, it further empowered the chief, particularly if he acquired a reputation as a *toa*, warrior, to compel men to accept his military commands.[46]

It has been convincingly argued that the Maori chiefdoms in New Zealand found it easier to relieve population pressure by making war on neighbours with productive land than to hack into virgin forest, of which much remained even at the coming of the European settlers in the 1840s. Chiefs could wage such wars because they could demand their followers' presence, could provide campaign supplies, could mobilise long-distance transport, such as fleets of canoes, and, if they had political skills, could articulate communal grievances against an enemy.

Maori warfare followed a familiar pattern. The occasion of war was always a desire for revenge, which might or might not be satisfied by a raiding party finding and killing a single member of the enemy. Maori war parties could do battle in a very brutal way. After a public meeting at which 'offences would be recounted vehemently', warlike songs chanted and weapons displayed, the war party would set out. If it met the enemy in the open and succeeded in breaking his ranks, the rout that followed had gruesome consequences:

> the great aim of these fast-running warriors . . . was to chase straight on and never stop, only striking one blow at one man, so as to cripple him, so that those behind should be sure to overtake and finish him. It was not uncommon for one man, strong and swift of foot, when the enemy was fairly routed, to stab with a light spear ten or a dozen men in such a way as to ensure their being overtaken and killed.[47]

The Maoris might, by such methods, have gone far toward exterminating each other, had it not been that their warfare was limited in two ways. Materially, Maori fighting turned on the attack and defence of fortifications. The strength and number of Maori forts – at least 4000 have been found – reflects the power of their chiefs to organise communal labour among a population of forty tribes, numbering altogether between 100,000 and 300,000, and shows how politically developed their culture was. Militarily, however, the existence of the forts worked to spare the Maoris the worst of the warfare they practised among themselves. Built typically on hilltop sites, the forts incorporated extensive food-storage chambers, which allowed the occupants to survive depradation of their fields, and also strong palisades, deep ditches and high banks. Since the Maoris had apparently no instruments of siege warfare, a resolute defence could hold attackers at bay until their campaigning stores ran out.[48]

Culturally, Maori warfare limited itself because of its very simple objects. Anthropologists have satisfied themselves that the Maoris went to war in order to redistribute land from the weaker to the stronger. The Maori war plan, however, was to eat the fallen enemy (except for their heads, which were kept as trophies). This disparity between what the subjects of ethnography were doing and what anthropologists concluded was the deeper purpose of their actions provides the basis for some of the angriest academic debates. For military historians, it seems clear that the Maori military culture was one of revenge. Male children from the earliest age were taught that insult, to say nothing of robbery or murder, was unforgivable, and the Maori were implacable in storing up a memory of grievance, sometimes from generation to generation, that was satisfied when the enemy was killed, his body eaten and his head mounted on the palisade of the fortified village, where it would be symbolically insulted. This revenge warfare was not conducted on a one-for-one basis; simply to have eaten the enemy and taken a head or heads would be enough to expunge a long-held grievance over even more deaths than were inflicted in reprisal.[49]

Here is another example of how a cultural ethic, even of the most savage sort, may have the paradoxical effect of limiting the harm warriors will do to each other. When reinforced by material constraints, such as those provided by fortification, its eventual result with the Maoris was to ensure that the potentiality of the chiefdom to transcend the technology of club and spear in a drive towards island-wide conquest did not take place. With the arrival of the musket, several Maori chiefdoms evolved towards statehood with terrifying rapidity, but that is a different story. Meanwhile, in a society of pre-Columbian America far more sophisticated than that of the Maoris, a cultural ethic limited its greater potentiality for Clausewitz's decisive battle to an even more arresting degree.

The Aztecs

There is a cruelty in the warfare of some pre-Columbian peoples of

North and Central America that has no parallel elsewhere in the world. Turney-High considers the Melanesians of the South Pacific to be foremost in 'simple cruelty' – the evidence lacks to prove that one way or the other – and perhaps some South Americans to be the worst cannibals (he was an early exponent of the belief that cannibalism was explained by protein deficiency, a view that later gained many but is now losing supporters).[50] Neither group, however, went in for the ritual torture of captives, to be followed by cannibalism or not, as was practised by, among others, some Plains Indians and the Aztecs. Turney-High relates:

> The Skidi Pawnee strove to capture a beautiful enemy maiden on each of their raids. This girl was then adopted into some very honourable Pawnee family where, to her surprise, she was treated with more consideration than the real daughters of the lodge. She became the pampered darling. Yet late one night she was rudely seized, stripped of her clothing, and her body half painted down its length from head, through groin, to foot with charcoal. She thus symbolised the junction of day and night. She was then strung up between two upright poles . . . Her adopted father was then compelled to shoot an arrow through her heart just as the sacred Morning Star was rising. The arrows of the priests soon followed, and her body was horribly mangled before it had served its purpose. This rite of appeasement to the Morning Star was considered essential to Pawnee welfare, to success in all things and agriculture in particular.[51]

A Jesuit missionary to the Huron described an even more ghastly ritual murder of one of their Seneca captives in 1637. He, too, had been adopted into a chief's family but had then been rejected because he bore wounds. He was consigned to die by fire and was brought into the council house, after his captors had feasted, for a night of agony. The Huron chief announced how his body would be divided, while he sang his warrior songs, and then 'he began to run a circuit around the fires, again and again, while everyone tried to burn him [with firebrands] as he passed; he shrieked like a lost soul; the whole cabin resounded with shrieks and yells. Some burned him, some seized his hands and snapped bones, others thrust sticks through his ears'. Yet, when he fainted he was 'gently revived', he was given food, he was addressed in kinship terms, in which he himself answered those who seared his flesh, and all the while he 'gasped out his warrior songs as best he could'. At dawn, still just conscious, he was taken outside, tied to a post and burned to death by the application of heated axe-heads to his flesh. Then his body was divided and the pieces distributed as the chief had promised.[52]

107

There are descriptions from the Algerian war of young French para-troopers patting and consoling a Muslim captive whom they had tortured for information, but such behaviour bears no relation to the Huron rituals. The paras tortured for a practical purpose, but the Huron and their victim were complicit partners in a ghastliness inexplicable to anyone outside their myth system. The horror of the night of the Seneca's death has been resurrected by the cultural historian Inga Clendinnen to introduce her brilliant reconstruction of the ethos of the Aztecs of central Mexico, for whom human sacrifice was a religious necessity, warfare the principal means to acquire sacrificial victims, and the captives of warfare, like the heroic Seneca, themselves complicit devotees of the cult which required their protracted death-agonies. The Aztecs were formidable warriors who, between the thirteenth and sixteenth centuries AD, succeeded in making themselves masters of the valley of central Mexico and in building the most brilliant material civilisation of all pre-literate, pre-metallic cultures; its splendours, as the awe-struck conquistadors reported, exceeded those of their native Spain. To military historians, however, the fascination of the Aztecs' civilisation resides in the extraordinary limitations on their capacity for warmaking that they imposed on themselves, through their

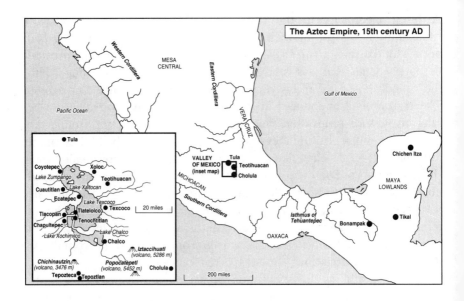

religious beliefs, and the restraints those beliefs imposed on their warriors in battle.

The Aztecs originally entered the Mexican central valley as humble seekers after subsistence. By making themselves useful as soldiers to the Tepanec, one of the three recognised powers in the valley, and by finding a place of settlement on a thitherto unadopted island in Lake Texcoco, they succeeded in establishing themselves as a power in their own right. Those who then accepted their primacy were incorporated into their empire; those who resisted were forced to fight. Aztec armies were extremely well organised and supplied, as befitted a highly bureaucratic culture; typically they were divided into commands of 8000 men, several of which could march on parallel routes along the empire's excellent roads at a speed of twelve miles a day, carrying rations for an eight-day campaign.[53]

It is possible to speak of Aztec 'strategy', as Clausewitz would have understood the word. Their wars began, writes R. Hassing,

> with what were essentially demonstrations of military prowess in which equal numbers of soldiers from both sides fought in hand-to-hand combat to display their skills. If this failed to intimidate one side into surrendering, the wars escalated in ferocity, in the number of combatants, and in the use of weapons . . . such as bows and arrows . . . Even while ongoing, these wars pinned down dangerous enemies while their forces were decimated in these wars of attrition that the numerically superior Aztecs were bound to win, and they allowed Aztec expansion to continue elsewhere . . . opponents were gradually encircled until, cut off from outside support, they were defeated.[54]

Clendinnen represents Aztec warfare in an altogether more complex light. Aztec society was intensely hierarchical – 'ranked', as anthropologists say, not by the simpler division of age but by status. At the bottom were slaves, unfortunates who had fallen to the bottom of the economic system; then commoners, the ordinary agriculturalists, craftsmen and merchants of countryside and town; then nobles; then priests; finally the monarch. All males, nevertheless, were born as potential warriors and had the chance to rise to high warrior status through the training-schools of their city districts – *calpulli*, which were part club, part monastery, part guild. A few novices became priests, but the majority took up everyday life while retaining the obligation to serve as warriors if necessary, and a minority – from noble houses founded on martial exploits – were destined to continue familial tradition. The monarch was chosen from those who achieved the rank of war leader.

The monarch was not simply a soldier, however; nor was he a priest, though priests surrounded him and regulated his grisly daily routines. Nor again was he a god, though he was believed in some sense to be inhabited by godly power. On his accession he was recognised, in a chilling formulary, as 'Our lord, our executioner, our enemy', an exact representation of his power over his subjects, some of whom, purchased infants or slaves, were destined to ritual and bloody sacrifice in his presence.[55] He is best regarded as an earthly being considered in the possession of the gods, to whom he had to offer blood sacrifice for their benevolent performance of the rhythms – particularly the daily rising of the sun – by which the Aztec people were permitted to carry on their lives. Aztec society itself, however, could not yield a sufficient number of acceptable victims to satisfy the needs of sacrifice. They had to be won in war.

Pitched battle was the central act of Aztec warfare, and it was fought at close range. But it was a form of battle strange to us because of its highly ritualised nature and the mutual acceptance of its codes by Aztecs and their enemies alike. The Aztecs were magnificent goldsmiths but had not discovered iron or bronze. They used the bow and arrow, the spear and the *atlatl*, the lever that adds range to the thrown spear. Their favoured weapon was a wooden sword, studded along its cutting edge with slivers of obsidian or flakes of flint, designed to wound but not to kill. Warriors wore quilted cotton 'armour' which could keep out arrows – the Spaniards later adopted it when fighting the Aztecs, when they found that their steel breastplates were not only too hot but also superfluous in Mexico – and carried small round shields; the object of the warrior was to close with an opponent and strike a disabling blow beneath the shield at his legs.[56]

Aztec armies were as ranked as Aztec society. The majority of the warriors jostling for place in the battle line would be novices, fresh from the training-schools and organised in groups to learn how to take a captive. Superiors made sure that they yielded station to the experienced warriors, graded according to the number of captives each had taken in previous battles. The most senior, who had taken seven captives, fought in pairs and were distinguished by the most magnificent of the warrior costumes; should one die and the other turn tail, he would be killed by his companions. These warriors have been called the 'berserkers' of Aztec warfare, those who set an example of courage on the field and were permitted a roughness of manner in the ordered city life of the Aztecs to be tolerated in no one else.

Yet 'the great warriors were solitary hunters', who 'searched through the dust and confusion of the battle for an enemy of equal, or ideally just

110

higher, rank'. (Classicists and mediaevalists will recognise this ethic from the annals of Homeric and chivalric combat.)

> The matched duel was the preferred mode . . . what [the warriors] strove to do was to bring their opponent down, most often by a blow to the legs – cutting a hamstring, crippling a knee – so that he could be grappled to the ground and subdued. It is possible the seizing of the warrior lock . . . was enough to effect submission, although there were usually men with ropes on hand to bind the captives and lead them to the rear.

So central to Aztec warfare was the act of individual captive-taking that for a man to give a captive to a comrade who had not made a capture, as a favour to promote him in rank, carried the death penalty for both.[57]

A battle that began with an exchange of arrows, to sow the confusion in which these individual duels might be fought, ended with those taken prisoner being led to the great city of Tenochtitlan. The victors went their way – the champions to rest until the next ordeal, warriors of middle rank perhaps to retire honourably to bureaucratic posts, those who had failed at the second or third attempt at captive-taking to be expelled from the warrior school and to sink to the status of load-carrier, plying for hire, the lowest place in Aztec society. The ordeal of the captives had only just begun.

Aztec battles might yield many thousands of captives, if conquest followed victory; after the suppression of one revolt by a subject people, the Huaxtecs, perhaps 20,000 were brought to the capital, to be sacrificed in dedication of the new pyramid temple, having their hearts torn out when they climbed to its summit. Some captives, together with bought or tribute slaves, were kept for sacrifice at the four great festivals of the year. At the first, the Feast of the Flaying of Men, Tlacaxipeualiztli, however, were slain a select group of victims whose manner of capture and style of execution epitomised both the form and philosophy of Aztec warmaking. This particular military transaction was stylised to an extreme degree: the 'flower' or 'flowery' battle, fought between the Aztecs and their neighbours, all speakers of the Nahuatl language, specifically for the taking of captives of the highest warrior class who were fit to undergo sacrificial death. The battles were prearranged and the fate of the victims was known.[58]

One out of 400 captives taken by each warrior-school might be selected for 'striping'. In the period of preparation before he was brought to the execution place, he was treated as an honoured guest, 'constantly visited, adorned and admired by his captor and the captor's

111

devoted entourage of local youth' – though also 'taunted' with reminders of the terrible fate that lay before him. When the day of the festival came, he was taken, surrounded by priests, to a killing-stone, mounted on a platform high enough for the public to view, tethered with a rope, and there equipped for his death agony.[59] The stone gave him a height advantage over the four warriors who were to attack him, and he was provided with four throwing-clubs which he might launch at them. His principal weapon, however, was a warrior sword, edged not with flint but feathers.

> The victim, elevated above his opponent and released from the inhibition against killing which prevailed on the battlefield, could whirl his heavy club and strike at the head of his antagonists with unfamiliar freedom. The [Aztec] champions were also presented with a temptingly easy target. The victim could be disabled and brought down with one good blow to knee or ankle, as on the battlefield. But such a blow would simultaneously abort the spectacle and end their glory, so the temptation had to be resisted. Their concern under these most taxing and public circumstances was rather to give a display of the high art of weapon handling: in an exquisitely prolonged performance to cut the victim delicately, tenderly with those narrow blades, to lace the living skin with blood [this whole process was called 'the striping']. Finally the victim . . . exhausted by exertion and lack of blood, would falter and fall.

He was finished off by the ritual opening of his chest and the tearing of his still-beating heart from its seat.[60]

His captor took no part in this lethal mutilation but watched from below the execution stone. As soon as the body was decapitated, however, so that the skull could be displayed at the temple, he drank the dead man's blood and carried the body back to his home. There he dismembered the limbs, to be distributed as sacrifice required, flayed the body of its skin, and watched while his family

> ate a small ritual meal of maize stew topped by a fragment of the dead warrior's flesh, as they wept and lamented the likely fate of their own young warrior. For that melancholy 'feast' the captor put off his glorious captor's garb, and was whitened, as his dead captive had been, with the chalk and feathers of the predestined victim.

Later, however, the captor – who had addressed the victim as 'beloved son' during the waiting-time and been addressed in return as 'beloved father', and who had provided an 'uncle' to attend him during the 'striping' – changed his garb again. He took to wearing the flayed skin of the dead man and to lending it out 'to those who begged the privilege', until it and its scraps of attached flesh rotted into deliquescence. This was the last tribute paid to 'our Lord the Flayed One' who, in the four days preceding his death, had been rehearsed in the ritual of the killing-stone, had four times had his heart symbolically dragged from his chest and, on his last night, had kept vigil with his 'beloved father' until the time came to go to the stone and watch those before him on the sacrificial list fight their doomed struggle.

What bore the victim up during his unspeakable ordeal, Clendinnen suggests, was the knowledge that 'if he died well, his name would be remembered and his praises sung in the warrior houses of his home city'. This has just enough resonance with European epic and saga to carry psychological conviction, at least as far as the behaviour of the warrior is concerned; one is reminded of Colonel Bigeard's *'plutôt crever'* when told to parade before the Vietminh cameras at the surrender of Dien Bien Phu, or of the veteran Australian, winner of a Victoria Cross in the First World War, setting off alone towards Japanese lines at the fall of Singapore with grenades in his hands and 'no capitulation for me' on his lips, never to be seen again. It does not suffice as an explanation of what the warriors were about *en masse* on the battlefield, not at any rate for moderns who expect wars to have a material point, and loss of human life to bear a proportionate relation to it. But Inga Clendinnen suggests that ultimately there was nothing material about Aztec warmaking. They believed that they were the heirs of the legendary founders of the civilisation of the central Mexican valley, the Toltecs, and that it was their calling to revive the splendours of the Toltec empire. They achieved that object, but they had been led to it, and could only be sustained in it, by their gods, who demanded sacrifices, of everything and anything of value, even of the most trivial value, but above all of human life itself. Thus while they sought 'to exact from towns in their immediate vicinity . . . maximum tribute [as evidence] of acquiescence . . . in [their] claim to Toltec legitimacy', far more important was the outward demonstration of an inward acceptance through the test of cooperation in the bloody rituals their gods demanded. What the Aztecs wanted from their neighbours was recognition of their own 'account of themselves and their destiny'.[61]

Because such a destiny – to be bound to the wheel of endless propitiation of an unloving and blood-hungry divinity – coincides with no vision of the world to which any modern holds, the temptation is to dismiss Aztec warfare as an aberration, having no connection with any system of strategy or tactics that we would consider rational. That, however, is because we have come to separate the need for security from trust in a divine yet immediate intervention in worldly affairs. The Aztecs saw things in an exactly contrary light: only by repetitive satisfaction of divine needs could divine harshness be held at bay. Their warfare, as a result, was limited by a belief about the object it should achieve – the taking of prisoners, some of whom should be voluntary participants in their own ritual murder – and, as a further and even more arresting consequence, Aztec weapons of the first quality were designed within the limitation that they should wound but not kill.

There is an important qualification to be set against this account of Aztec warfare: it tells us only about the warfare of the Aztecs at the height of their power and not of how they fought when they were struggling to achieve it. The probability is that then they slaughtered those who opposed them, as all conquerors have always done. The 'flower battle' is an institution not only of a very sophisticated but also of a self-confident society, which could afford to ritualise warmaking because it was not challenged at its borders by potential usurpers. It was also an enormously rich society, which could afford the wastefulness of sacrificing captives in thousands, rather than putting them to productive work or selling them into slavery elsewhere. The Maya of Central America, whose monuments exceed those of the Aztecs in scale and quality, seem to have done the opposite, sacrificing only noble captives and putting the rest to labour or into the market. Mayan practice was far more of a pattern with that of other martial peoples, for whom slave-taking was normally an important reward of warmaking and sometimes a principal motivation for it.[62]

The Aztecs who fought were warriors, not soldiers; that is to say, they expected and were expected to fight because of the place they held in the social order, not because of obligation or for pay; they also fought with stone weapons. These two conditions further define the sort of warfare we are examining. Aztec warfare no doubt represents pre-metallurgic warfare in the most refined and one of the most eccentric forms it could take. It still belongs, all the same, with that of the Maoris and even of the Maring and the Yanomamö, rather than with that which the discovery of metal and, later, the raising of armies ushered in. All four were warfares of encounters fought at close range, with weapons of little penetrating power and therefore without the dense bodily protection needed to stop puncture wounds to the head or trunk. They accorded a high degree of ceremony and ritual to combat, the spur to and ends of which bore scant relation to the causes and results which modern man perceives in the wars he fights. Revenge and the expiation of insult were commonly the spur, satisfaction of mythic necessity or divine demands equally commonly the end. Such causes and results can subsist only below what Turney-High called the 'military horizon'. But when and how and – if we dare ask it – why did war begin?

THE BEGINNINGS OF WARFARE

We date 'history' from the moment when man began to write or, more precisely, from when he left traces of what we can recognise as writing. Such traces, left by the people of Sumer, in what is now Iraq, have been dated to about 3100 BC, though the precursors of the symbols used may be 5000 years older still, and originate at the time, around 8000 BC, when man was ceasing in certain favoured areas to live by hunting and gathering and had begun to farm.

Modern man, *homo sapiens sapiens*, is much older than the Sumerians, of course, and his hominid ancestors – those to whom he is recognisably related in size, carriage and capabilities – so much older again that the time distance which separates them from us cannot easily be invested with meaning. One historian, J.M. Roberts, who has tried to chart prehistory – the aeons before writing – in a way that has graphic sense, suggests that we think of the birth of Christ as an event that happened twenty minutes ago, of the appearance of the Sumerians as forty minutes earlier, the establishment in western Europe of 'recognisable human beings of a modern physiological type' five or six hours before that and the appearance of 'creatures with some manlike characteristics' two to three weeks from the present.[63]

The history of warfare begins with writing, but its prehistory cannot be ignored. Prehistorians are as sharply divided as anthropologists by the issue of whether man – and 'pre-man' – was violent toward his own species or not. It is a dangerous debate to enter, but we must at least see what they are arguing about. The debate may be said to begin with the differentiation of social roles between male and female. *Australopithecus*, an ancestor of man of whom traces have been found from perhaps as long ago as 5,000,000 years and who has left verifiable traces of his existence 1,500,000 years old, appears to have taken food from the place where it was found to the place where it was eaten, perhaps to have made a shelter at the eating-place and certainly to have fashioned and used the first tool, a roughly flaked and therefore edged pebble. Excavations in the Olduvai gorge in Tanzania have revealed the bones of animals smashed for the extraction of marrow and brain.

It has been suggested that the offspring of *Australopithecus* lost the capacity to cling to its mother for long periods, while she roamed abroad with her mate as nursing primates usually do, and that the eating-place was therefore a home to which the males brought food. In *homo erectus*, who descended from *Australopithecus* about 400,000 years ago, this trend was heightened. The size of its brain and therefore head greatly increased, without proportionate increase in body size before birth. The infant *homo erectus* remained immature for much longer than *Australopithecus* had done, in consequence, thus tying its mother more tightly to the feeding-place; the skeletal change the female underwent to accommodate the larger head in pregnancy further unfitted her to range with food-gatherers. It has been suggested that it was at this stage of evolution that females underwent loss of oestrus – fertility only at restricted periods, as in all other mammals – and became attractive to males at all times; they were therefore more likely to be singled out as – and themselves to single out – long-term mates and to avoid, or to be forbidden, sexual relations with close blood relations. It seems certain that loss of oestrus, by liberating the female from the frenzy of the rut, allowed her to persist in the careful maternity which her slow-maturing, large-brained offspring needed to grow to adulthood.

This, at any rate, is one explanation of the growth of the family unit, of its needs for shelter and transported food, and of its solidarity. *Homo erectus* has left us traces of his family and perhaps his social life, according to Roberts, in relics of 'constructed dwellings (huts, sometimes fifty feet long, built of branches with stone-slab or skin floors), the earliest worked wood, the first wooden spear and the earliest container, a wooden bowl'.[64] This, of course, from a time when he not only gathered edible roots, leaves, fruits, grubs, but also hunted small and large mammals, in an environment of climate fluctuations that drew game animals across an enormously wide range of territory as vegetation flourished or withered with the advance and retreat of the ice-sheets.

These fluctuations were spaced at vast intervals in time – four intermissions have been identified in an ice age that lasted 1,000,000 years and ended only some 10,000 years ago – and many small human groups must have failed to survive changes in their environment and died out. Some, nevertheless, adapted, learnt the use of fire, and acquired the skills – probably cooperative skills – to trap and kill very large mammals that would provide food for many. It is supposed that hunting-parties combined to drive elephants, rhinoceroses or mammoths over cliffs or into swamps, where they would die from their injuries or from cumulative wounding by early man's primitive weapons.[65]

The earliest stone tools to be found could not have been used as weapons of the chase, and therefore certainly not of war. *Australopithecus's* was a hand-held pebble, roughly chipped to give it a cutting-edge. Chipping, however, produces flakes – particularly from flint, identified early as the most rewarding stone with which to work – and once man had identified that both nucleus and flakes were valuable he began to produce the two deliberately. As his skill increased, and he learnt to use first a stone anvil and then a bone point as a pressure tool, he was able to fashion large tool-heads and fine, long blades, sharpened where needed on both edges. These indeed provided hunting-weapons, the spear point for throwing or thrusting and the axe-head for dismembering fallen carcasses. Tools of this refinement are found in sites dated to the end of the Old Stone Age, 10,000 to 15,000 years ago.

Those were violent times, as were the hundreds of thousands of years in which man pitted himself against large animals. At Arene Candide, in Italy, has been found the skeleton of a young man who died at the end of the Old Stone Age, at least 10,000 years ago. Part of his lower jaw, his collar-bone and the shoulder-blade, together with the top of the thigh bone, had been carried away by the bites of a large, savage animal, perhaps a bear which had been cornered in a pit or cave that the hunters dug or adapted as a trap. The wounds had been inflicted in life, for the body had been carefully buried, with a cosmetic application of clay or yellow ochre over the damaged parts.[66] The victim may have been unlucky in a bear drive, for the discovery of a flint point in the skull of a bear found at Trieste, and dated to the last interglacial period 100,000 years ago, indicated that Neanderthal man, *homo sapiens sapiens's* ancestor, had already learnt how to fix a blade into a handle at right-angles and to deliver a skull-smashing blow from close quarters.[67] From the same period dates a spear of yew wood found lodged in the ribs of an elephant killed in Schleswig-Holstein, while the pelvis of a Neanderthal skeleton excavated in Palestine bears the unmistakable trace of a deep penetration by a spear point.

All this suggests that man the hunter was brave and skilful. There was, suggest the prehistorians Breuil and Lautier, no

great abyss separating [him] from the animal. The bonds between them were not yet broken, and man still felt near the beasts that lived around him, that killed and fed like him . . . From them he still retained all the faculties that civilisation has blunted – rapid action and highly trained senses of sight, hearing and smell, physical toughness in an extreme degree, a detailed, precise knowledge of the qualities and habits of game, and great skill in using with the greatest effect the rudimentary weapons available.[68]

These, of course, are the qualities of the warrior across the ages, which modern military training-schools of Special Forces seek to re-implant in their pupils at the cost of much time and money. The modern soldiers learn to hunt to live; but did the prehistoric hunters fight men? The evidence is scant and often contradictory.

The Neanderthal pelvis with the spear wound is no evidence at all, since it might have been inflicted by accident among a hunting-party in the tumult of the kill; everyone who handles weapons knows that the most dangerous ones are those held by immediate neighbours. Does the wonderful cave art which began to appear during the last ice age, some 35,000 years ago, offer any proof of man's inhumanity to man in what was still a hunting culture? All the human inhabitants of the earth were by then *homo sapiens sapiens*, who had appeared only some 5000 years earlier but rapidly supplanted the Neanderthals in a way which no prehistorian has succeeded in explaining. Several thousand cave paintings have been found at sites all over the world – dating from a time when the human population was under a million – and in 130 of the earliest, which may be 35,000 years old, there are representations of man or man-like beings. Some interpreters of the paintings believe that they show dead or dying men; some also think that the reverently depicted animals bear spear, dart or arrow symbols. Others disagree; the majority of the human figures shown are in peaceful scenes, while the arrow symbols may be of 'sexual significance – or meaningless doodles'.[69]

The men of the Old Stone Age, in any case, had not yet invented the bow.[70] At the beginning of the New Stone Age, however, some 10,000 years ago, there occurred 'a revolution in weapons technology . . . four staggeringly powerful new weapons make their appearance . . . the bow, the sling, the dagger . . . and the mace'. The last three were refinements of weapons already in existence: the mace derived from the club, the dagger from the spear point and the sling from the *bolas*, the last a pair of stones covered with leather and joined by a thong, thrown to entangle the legs of deer or bison which had been herded into a killing-place.[71] The *atlatl*, or spear-throwing lever, was probably also an indirect precursor of

118

the sling, since it worked by the same principle. The bow, however, was a real departure. It may be seen as the first machine, since it employed moving parts and translated muscular into mechanical energy. How the men of the New Stone Age hit upon it we cannot guess, though it spread very rapidly once invented; why they did so has most probably to do with the progressive retreat of the last ice-sheets. The warming of the temperate zones completely changed the movement and migration patterns of the hunters' prey, abolishing the old pelagic areas where game was predictably found, and, by liberating animals to roam and feed further and more widely, forced the hunter and the hunting-party to find a means of bringing down a more fleeting target over longer ranges.

The simple bow, as the original is called, is a piece of homogeneous wood, typically a length of sapling, and it lacks the opposed properties of elasticity and compression that gave the later composite and long bows, made of both sapwood and heartwood, their greater carrying and penetrative power. Even in its simple form, however, the bow transformed the relationship of man with the animal world. He no longer had to close to arm's length to dispatch his prey, pitting at the last moment flesh against flesh, life against life. Henceforth he could kill at a distance. In that departure ethologists like Lorenz and Ardrey perceive the opening of a new moral dimension in man's relations with the rest of creation but also with his own kind. Was man the archer also man the first warrior?

Cave art of the New Stone Age undoubtedly shows us scenes of bowmen apparently opposed in conflict. Arthur Ferrill claims to perceive in the painting from caves in the Spanish Levant roots of battlefield tactics, with warriors forming columns behind a chief, shooting arrows in a ranked formation and even practising an outflanking movement in an encounter between what he calls the 'army of four' and the 'army of three'. It should be clear from what we know about both the Yanomamö (who knew the bow even though they did not fashion stone) and the Maring that all three scenes are explicable in terms of the formal displays of force they practise. The Yanomamö chief, for example, produces his bow and threatens club fighters with it when violence takes a dangerous turn. The Maring shoot arrows from the rear in both 'nothing' and 'true' fights, but at distances which threaten little harm to anyone; the apparent proximity of the archers of the 'armies' of both 'four' and 'three' has less to do with reality than with the cave artists' treatment of perspective.

If we are to think of the bowmen of the New Stone Age as prototypical of the hunters who still survive in the modern world, it is certainly not safe to invest them with strong warrior qualities; it is equally unsafe to argue that they were peaceful people. Ethnographers who have devoted themselves to the study of some still-existent groups are champions of the view that hunting-gathering is compatible with an admirably pacific social code, and that the former may indeed foster the latter. The San (Bushmen) of the South African Kalahari Desert are commonly held up as models of unassertive gentleness, and a similar claim has been made for the Semai who seclude themselves in the Malaysian jungle.[72] The trouble, however, with attempting to argue backward from the characteristics of surviving hunters to the behaviour of our common ancestors is that the survivors are probably very unlike Stone Age men. The Semai, for example, supplement hunting with crop-raising, a means of subsistence unknown in the times of cave art, while the Bushmen are unquestionably 'marginalised': they have been thrust into the arid zones they now inhabit by the advance of the cattle-herding Bantu and they may owe their evasive and uncontentious habits to a decision not to attract the attention of their aggressive neighbours.

The ethos of societies centred on the hunting-party may, indeed, quite ambivalently vary between the cooperative and the contentious. Frederick Selous (1851–1917), the archetype of the Great White Hunter, found his party swelled almost uncontrollably when he was shooting game in what is now Zimbabwe in the 1880s, as native people hungry for meat tailed on to the retinue of someone who was known to be a dead shot. Ethnographers note, by contrast, that a hunter whose luck leaves him may quickly lose his authority in a hunting-band and even become the victim of those who had come to depend on him for food. Equally, neighbours may learn to share hunting, according to migration patterns or in acceptance of the succession of lean with fat years; or they may do no such thing, but rather guard their hunting-grounds as if they were private property and kill those who cross the boundaries. Hugo Obermaier, an early interpreter of cave art, believed one scene showed Stone Age man defending his territory.[73] Egyptologists interpret the contents of the notorious Site 117 at Jebel Sahaba in Upper Egypt in a similar way: in the graves there fifty-nine skeletons have been excavated, many of which, notes F. Wendorf, show signs of wounding. The skeletons are in direct association [with] 110 artifacts, almost all in positions which indicate that they had penetrated the body either as points or barbs on projectiles or spears. They were not grave offerings. Many of the artifacts were found along the vertebral column, but other favored target areas were the chest cavity, lower abdomen, arms and the skull. Several pieces were found inside the skull, and two of these were still embedded in the sphenoid bones [at the base of the skull] in positions which indicate that the pieces entered from under the lower jaw.[74]

Since the skeletons were those of males and females in almost equal number, and the absence of callusing around the bone injuries indicated that wounding had been fatal, one conclusion drawn was that the dead were victims of a fight between hunters over territory, perhaps brought on by a sudden desiccation – return of arid conditions – in the Nubian region during the climatic instability at the end of the Ice Age.

'We may have in this site', thinks Ferrill, 'the first extensive skeletal evidence for warfare in prehistoric times.'[75] Equally, however, we may not. The bodies may have been interred over a period of time, as another interpreter suggests. They may, again, belong to people of an altogether different culture from those who killed them, since the upper reaches of the Nile valley were a melting-pot in the New Stone Age, and so bear not at all upon the bellicosity of Stone Age hunters. An uncanvassed fourth possibility is that the graves do indeed reveal evidence of a fight between hunters, but one that falls into the category of 'raiding' or 'routing' as practised by the Yanomamö and Maring. The fact that the victims were both male and female is consistent with this interpretation, and so is what Ferrill calls the 'overkill', the infliction of multiple wounds, as on the body of a young woman inside whose skeleton twenty-one arrow or spear points were found. The Maring, in particular, set out on a 'rout' with the intention of slaying all they can trap in the target village, without distinction of age or sex; and if the wounding evidence suggests a massacre, that, alas, is consistent with human behaviour from many places over many centuries. One of the most gruesome discoveries made at the disinterment of the mass grave on Gotland, containing 2000 bodies from the battle of Visby of 1361, was that many of the dead had been extensively mutilated – typically by repeated sword-cuts down their shins – and such cuts could only have been inflicted after they were disabled. But as I have argued before, moreover, neither 'raiding' nor 'routing' is a true act of warfare. Each subsists 'below the military horizon' and is better thought of as multiple murder than as an episode in a campaign. If the dead of Site 117 and those who attacked them were both from hunting-cultures, as the original excavators supposed, and if the dead were all killed at one time, then the ghastly outcome of their encounter reinforces the view that the hunting men of the New Stone Age were no more than primitive warriors, members of groups without a distinguishable military class and without a 'modern' concept of warfare. Fight they no doubt did, ambush, raid and perhaps 'rout' as well; but organise themselves for conquest and occupation they almost certainly did not.

Yet those people of prehistoric Nubia, inhabitants of a region which then as now straddles the meeting-place of fertile and infertile land, may be a key to our understanding of how 'primitive' eventually became 'true' or 'modern' or 'civilised' war. For another interpretation of the evidence at Site 117 is that it memorialises not a fight between hunting-peoples over game-bearing territory, but a conflict of entirely different economies. The upper Nile valley is one of the areas in which the benevolent change of climate that followed the end of the last ice age best favoured the adoption of a new and more settled way of life for Stone Age man. There are indications from the stone implements found that the inhabitants had begun to harvest wild grasses and to grind the extracted grains into meal; there are subtler indications that they had begun if not yet actually to domesticate, then to tend the animals on which they depended for a living.[76] They were trembling on the brink of pastoralism and agriculture, the two activities which transform man's relationship with his habitat. Hunters and gatherers may have 'territory'; pastoralists have grazing and watering-places; agriculturalists have land. Once man invests expectations of a regular return on his seasonal efforts in a particular place – lambing, herding, planting, reaping – he rapidly develops the sense of rights and ownership. Toward those who trespass on the places where he invests his time and effort he must equally rapidly develop the hostility of the user and occupier for the usurper and interloper. Fixed expectations make for fixed responses. Pastoralism, and agriculture even more so, make for war. That, at any rate, is one meaning that has been placed on the relics of Site 117 where, it is suggested, a sudden fluctuation of climate, characteristic of the earth's warming at the time, cast a group of hunters or gatherers, driven back towards the Nile, into conflict with proto-pastoralists or farmers over the same piece of territory. From which group came the bodies of those who are buried there, we must be left to guess.

Superior skill at arms should have rested with the hunters. 'We may speculate', thinks J.M. Roberts, 'that the dim roots of the notion of aristocracy are to be sought in the successes (which must have been frequent) of hunter-gatherers, representatives of an older social order, in exploiting the vulnerability of the settlers, tied to their areas of cultivation.'[77] Certainly it is a universal phenomenon that rights of hunting are always arrogated by those who have authority over the tillers of the soil, that aristocrats who monopolise such rights also enact brutal penalties against those who violate them, and that the overthrow of aristocratic hunting-rights has often been a chief demand of revolutionaries. Hunter-gatherers had many centuries of decline ahead of them, however, before their putative descendants could lord it – as Grand Falconers or Chief Foresters or Masters of the Horse – over the cottagers and ploughboys of the feudal establishment. In the meantime, the trend of events in the ecologically favoured zones of human habitation lay with those who would work to alter the surface of the land rather than with those who were content to skim its offerings. Agriculture was the way of the future.

In the 7000 years between the retreat of the ice and the appearance of writing at Sumer, man – though still working with stone tools – painstakingly, erratically and with many false starts taught himself the techniques of land clearance, tilling and reaping in half a dozen regions which were to become the centres of great civilisations, in the valleys of the Tigris and Euphrates, the Nile, the Indus and the Yellow River. Of course, he did not make a leap directly from his ice-age way of life to intensive cropping. Historians generally agree that he began by bringing gregarious animals under a measure of control – there is evidence of shepherding in northern Iraq as early as 9000 BC – and there was clearly a cumulative progression from systematic collection of wild grains to planting and eventually to the selection of better-cropping strains. Historians do not agree, however, as to where and how man first established agricultural settlements – understandably, since the evidence is so patchy. An early assessment was that he chose the uplands of the Near Eastern river valleys, healthier and drier than the ground below, where slash-and-burn clearance could make successive fertile openings in the tree cover.[78] This theory is supported by evidence of the contemporaneous appearance of a new sort of stone tool, fashioned from heavy basalt or granite, and ground by abrasion – the magnificent 'polished' axes and adzes of the New Stone Age. Some historians advanced the idea of a Neolithic Revolution, in which the demands of agriculture called forth novel tool-working skills or, alternatively, new tools made advances into the forest possible. Certainly it is the case that chipped tools of flint do little damage to large trees, while a heavy polished axe can fell a tree of almost any size. The neat technological determinism of this theory, however, did not last long, even though it suggested that an even neater pattern of agricultural advance occurred with our New Stone

Age ancestors: from the hilly flanks of the Fertile Crescent down into the alluvial plains of the great rivers themselves, and from slash-and-burn to the seasonal cultivation of flood-fertilised lowlands.

Undoubtedly such a movement occurred, but from a very early period, perhaps as early as 9000 BC, man hit upon an altogether different pattern of agricultural life. At Jericho, 600 feet below sea level in the arid valley of the Jordan, archaeologists have found the remains of what by 7000 BC was an eight-acre town, housing 2000 or 3000 people, who made their living by cultivating the fertile zone in the surrounding oasis; their strains of wheat and barley were imported from elsewhere, as was the obsidian for some of their tools. Only a little later, at Çatal Hüyük, in modern Turkey, a much larger town grew up, eventually covering thirty acres and accommodating between 5000 and 7000 people, living a life of considerable sophistication. Digging has disclosed the presence of a wide variety of imported goods, presumably traded, an equally wide variety of locally produced craft goods, suggesting a division of labour, and most arresting of all, traces of an irrigation system, indicating that the inhabitants were already practising a form of farming previously thought characteristic only of the much larger and later settlements in the great river valleys.

Of key significance to military historians is the structure of these two towns. Çatal Hüyük is built with the outer walls of its outermost houses presenting a continuous blank face, so that even were an intruder to have broken a hole through it, or through a roof, he 'would find himself not inside the town but inside a single room'.[79] Jericho, even more impressively, is surrounded by a continuous wall ten feet thick at the base, thirteen feet high and some 700 yards in circumference. At the foot of the wall lies a rock-cut moat thirty feet wide and ten feet deep, while inside the wall at one point stands a tower that overtops it by fifteen feet, providing a look-out place and, though it does not project beyond to form a flank as later bastions would, a dominant fighting-platform. Moreover, Jericho is built of stone, not the mud of Çatal Hüyük, indicating that an intense and coordinated programme of work, consuming tens of thousands of man-hours, had been undertaken. While Çatal Hüyük's conformation might have been chosen simply to keep out the occasional robber or raider, Jericho's is quite different in purpose: incorporating as it does two elements that were to characterise military architecture until the coming of gunpowder, the curtain wall and the keep, as well as the even longer-lived moat, it constitutes a true fortified stronghold, proof against anything but prolonged attack with siege engines.[80]

The discovery of Jericho in 1952–8 compelled a complete reappraisal of

124

prevailing scholarly assumptions about when intensive agriculture, urban life, long-distance trade, hierarchical society and warfare first began. Hitherto it had been thought that none of these developments emerged until the foundation of the irrigation economies in Mesopotamia, and those believed to have derived from them in Egypt and India, sometime before 3000 BC. After the excavation of Jericho it was clear that warfare at least – for what could be the point of walls, towers and moats without a purposeful, well-organised and strongly armed enemy? – had begun to trouble man long before the first great empires arose.[81]

And yet between Jericho and Sumer we have but the scantiest evidence of how military developments progressed. That was perhaps because, in a still largely empty world, *homo sapiens* was devoting his energies to colonisation rather than conflict. In Europe there were already farming villages as early as 8000 BC and agriculture was advancing westward at the rate of about a mile a year in the more fertile zones, reaching Britain about 4000 BC. There were urban settlements on Crete and the Aegean coast of Greece in 6000 BC and a developed pottery industry in Bulgaria about 5500 BC, while by 4500 BC the cultivators of Brittany were beginning to raise the megalithic tombs that still commemorate their ancestors. By the same date five of the six distinguishable ethnic groups that inhabit India were established throughout the subcontinent, pursuing a New Stone Age way of life in scattered settlements. There was a thriving New Stone Age culture in the fertile highlands of north and north-west China in 4000 BC, based on the wind-driven (loess) soils of the Yellow River. Only Africa, Australia and the Americas then remained solely in the hands of hunter-gatherers, nowhere numerous, though the Amerindians who had crossed the Bering Strait from Siberia about 10,000 BC, bringing with them advanced hunting techniques from the Old World, had nevertheless succeeded in extinguishing the continent's spectacular big game, including the giant bison and three species of mammoth, in about a thousand years.

Almost everywhere population densities remained very low. Though the number of people in the world rose from about 5–10 million in 10,000 BC to perhaps 100 million in 3000 BC, they were almost nowhere densely concentrated. Hunter-gatherers typically needed between one and four square miles of territory to support each individual. Farmers could support themselves and their families on much smaller spreads: at the Egyptian city of El-Amarna, for example, founded by the pharaoh Akhenaten about 1540 BC, it has been estimated that people were living at a density of about 500 per square mile of productive soil.[82] That, however, was on the hand-watered gardens of the rich Nile valley and, in any case, at a date that lay in the future. Between 6000 and 3000 BC the scattered agricultural settlements in eastern Europe did not exceed a size of fifty or sixty households each; in the Rhineland of the fifth millennium BC, farmers were subsisting by slash-and-burn in the great forests, periodically abandoning and then reoccupying settlements which never housed more than 300–400 people.[83]

In such stringent and yet paradoxically such ample circumstances, the urge to fight cannot have been strong. Land was effectively free, to anyone willing to shift a few miles and burn some forest – as poor peasants were still doing in nineteenth-century Finland. Yields, on the other hand, must have been so low as to produce little worth robbing, except immediately after the harvest, and then difficulties of transporting the loot – lack of pack or draught animals, lack of roads, lack perhaps even of containers – would have robbed the exercise of its point.[84] Robbery, particularly robbery with violence, justifies the risks involved only if the reward comes in a compact form of high intrinsic value. Ship cargoes meet those criteria; but there were no cargo ships to pirate in the fourth millennium BC. Large agricultural surpluses do so as well, particularly if they are stored at points easy of access and for escape, and all the more so if held in a transportable form – in bales, pots, sacks or baskets or as flocks on the hoof. Then, of course, the land which is the source of such bounty itself becomes a target, even if the interlopers lack the skills to manage it, as was so often to prove the case. In the millennia when man was teaching himself to farm and colonising the empty lands of the Near East and Europe, there was only one region that produced large surpluses exposed to predation across approach routes that favoured easy movement. That was the lower alluvial plain of the Tigris and Euphrates rivers, known to ancient historians as Sumer. It is from the Sumerians that we derive the first hard evidence of the nature of warfare at the dawn of written history and can begin to perceive the outlines of 'civilised' war.

WAR AND CIVILISATION

The Sumerians, like the Aztecs, achieved civilisation within the constraints of a technology of stone. It is, however, not their tools – and in any case they early became metallurgists – but their powers of organisation that laid the basis for their warmaking, as both defenders and aggressors. Historians believe that settlers first began to establish themselves on the alluvial plain of Iraq once they dared to leave the rainfall line at the foot of the surrounding hills – in what are now Syria, Turkey and Iran – and begin to experiment with grain-growing and herding on unwooded land. Mesopotamia – the land between the rivers – offered rich advantages to settlers. It was fertile, and its fertility was renewed by the annual flood of snowmelt from the rivers' mountainous source. It was level – it falls only 112 feet in 210 miles – and it needed no clearing, since no trees grew there. There was no frost during the growing season, and, if the sun shone too hot for comfort in summer, there was unlimited water to swell cultivated plants. The limitlessness of the water supply, however, was what forced the early settlers to coordinate their efforts to bring the soil under cultivation, in a pattern of activity entirely different from that of the independent slashers-and-burners who had already begun to penetrate the great European forests. The floods formed swamps in some places but elsewhere left the rainless alluvium parched. To drain the marsh and water the dry land required ditches to be dug, and not only dug but dug to a plan, and not only planned but kept in constant repair, as each year the flood brought silt to clog the channels. Thus was born the first 'irrigation society'.

An elaborate political science of irrigation (called by some 'hydraulic') societies has been constructed by ancient historians, almost all of it from archaeological discovery. The Sumerians left an enormous buried treasure of dwellings, temples and city walls – built roughly in that order – and of manufactured and trade goods, together with many carved objects and a vast archive of inscribed clay tablets, the latter all relating to the receipt, storage and disbursal of produce and all found within temple limits. From this record, it has been proposed that Sumerian civilisation developed along the following trajectory.

The first settlers formed small, self-sufficient communities. Because of the tendency for the rivers to change their beds, irrigators were obliged to cooperate, linking one system with another as the waters moved and thus progressively enlarging the size of their settlements. The organisation of linkages and the regulation of disputes fell to those with traditional priestly functions and, because the timing and volume of the flood's annual arrival was ascribed to the favour or disfavour of the gods (who may have been new gods), mythic intercession with the divine by the priests progressively invested them with political power. Such priest-kings naturally used their power to have temples raised, both as dwellings for themselves and as centres of the cults they served, and their power to direct labour for temple-building further translated into the power to elaborate irrigation systems and other public works. The temples, meanwhile, became centres of administration, since large bodies of farmers giving their labour to public works needed feeding from a central source, and at such a source the collection of agricultural surplus and its distribution to the labourers had to be methodically recorded. Different forms of produce, as well as different quantities, had to be noted by distinguishable marks, and from such notations on impressible clay derived the symbols which provided the first form of writing.

Hence the argument that by about 3000 BC the Sumerian irrigation societies had built the first cities, that such cities may properly be called city states, and that such states were theocracies. The power of the priest-kings derived from their 'ownership' of the unprecedented wealth that irrigation farming yielded – 200 grains harvested in the ear for each one sown – and then from the use to which they put their share of the surplus. It paid for the temple staffs, for the slaves which indebtedness may have brought, and for the funding of trade which the temples presumably dominated: the Mesopotamian plain being deficient in stone, metal and almost every sort of wood, all those materials had to be brought from a distance to satisfy the Sumerians' need for essentials and also their desire, soon generated in a society where some were liberated from daily labour, for luxuries as well. The archaeology of Sumer yields evidence of luxuries brought from far away: gold from the Indus valley, lapis lazuli from Afghanistan, silver from south-eastern Turkey, eventually copper from the coasts of the Arabian Sea.[85] The one thing it does not reveal, at least from the earliest stages of the Sumerian cities' rise to statehood, is any evidence of warmaking. None of the thirteen cities known to have existed at the beginning of the third millennium, including Ur, Uruk and Kish, then had walls. Sumeria at that stage seems to have had a civilisation spared domestic strife by the awesome authority of its priest-kings, inter-city war perhaps by the absence of any clash of interests, and external aggression by the harshness of the landscape that surrounded the fruitful valley and by the lack of any means of mobility – neither the camel nor the horse had yet been domesticated – available to potential interlopers from the western desert or the eastern steppe.[86]

In the same millennium that Sumer was achieving statehood, similar irrigation societies were growing up, or were about to do so, in the valleys of the Nile and the Indus; Chinese and Indo-Chinese civilisation, later so dependent on irrigation technique, had not yet moved to that economic level. The key to the rise of theocracy in the Indus valley, it has been suggested, lay in the invention there of baked brick, which permitted the construction of flood-control works on a scale large enough for half a million square miles of land to be brought under cultivation around the

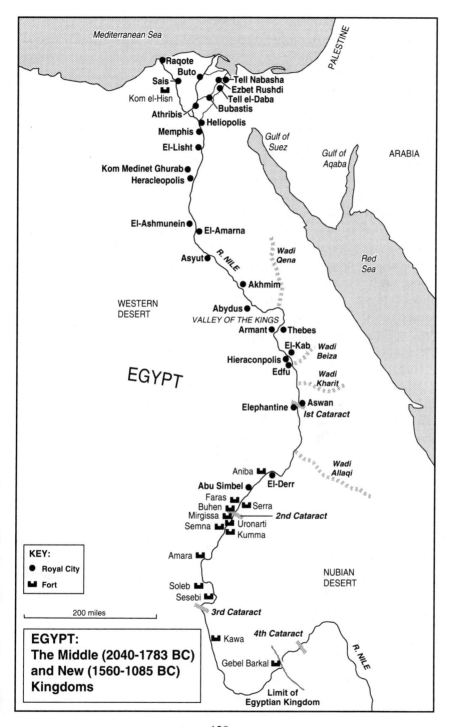

Mediterranean Sea

PALESTINE

Raqote
Buto
Sais
Kom el-Hisn
Tell Nabasha
Ezbet Rushdi
Tell el-Daba
Bubastis
Athribis
Heliopolis
Memphis
El-Lisht

Gulf of
Suez

Gulf of
Aqaba

ARABIA

Kom Medinet Ghurab
Heracleopolis

El-Ashmunein
El-Amarna

R. NILE

Wadi
Qena

Asyut

Red
Sea

Akhmim

WESTERN
DESERT

Abydus
VALLEY OF THE KINGS
Armant Thebes
El-Kab
Hieraconpolis
Edfu

Wadi
Beiza

Wadi
Kharit

EGYPT

Elephantine Aswan
1st Cataract

Wadi
Allaqi

Aniba
Abu Simbel El-Derr
Faras
Buhen Serra
Mirgissa
Semna Uronarti
Kumma

2nd Cataract

Amara

NUBIAN
DESERT

Soleb
Sesebi

3rd Cataract

KEY:
● Royal City
⊔ Fort

200 miles

Kawa 4th Cataract

R. NILE

Gebel Barkal

EGYPT:
The Middle (2040-1783 BC)
and New (1560-1085 BC)
Kingdoms

Limit of
Egyptian Kingdom

now vanished cities of Harappa and Mohenjo-Daro toward the end of the third millennium.[87] But excavation has only begun to lay bare the secrets of the ancient Indus. In Egypt, by contrast, where systematic archaeology started, over a century of digging has allowed us to reconstruct the anatomy of its civilisation with some certainty and from an early date.

Site 117 has alerted us to Egypt's violent prehistory. The evidence lacks to prove one way or another how the Egyptians' way of life developed between 10,000 BC and the unification of their settlements along the Nile under a single king about 3200 BC – whether peacefully or not. Scholars agree, however, that it was the particular environment of the river valley rather than political events within it that did most to make Egypt the civilisation it became. Egypt lives by the silt-bearing flood that descends from Lake Tana in the Ethiopian highlands immediately after the spring monsoon; the fact that it varies in volume and date of arrival was crucial in bringing the Egyptians to venerate their kings as gods. Until about the fourth millennium, the desert that borders the Nile along its 600 miles between the delta and the Second Cataract approached the river less closely than it does today and the valley people dwelt higher up on the banks, combining cultivation with herding. Then there was an unexplained desiccation, driving the population down into the flood plain, on which in future it came entirely to depend for a living. Scholars suppose a period of warfare between the chiefs of population centres along the valley, as they struggled for control of the migrants from the extending desert's fringe; then, about 3100 BC, the local big men lost their authority to a single ruler, conventionally called Menes, who united Lower and Upper Egypt – the delta and the southern Nile – and founded the kingdom that was to survive, under the rule of the pharaohs, for nearly 3000 years.[88]

Military Egypt had a style as distinctive to itself, and almost as long-lasting, as its own civilisation; quite different from that of Sumer or the regimes that succeeded to dominance in Mesopotamia, it was long marked by technological backwardness and a studied indifference to external threat. Both features had their root in Egypt's unique location. Even to this day, the country is virtually unapproachable by an invader except through narrow corridors to the north and south. To the east the arid highlands that divide the Nile valley from the Red Sea form a natural barrier a hundred miles wide, while to the west the sands of the Sahara remain a no man's land for any army. The first pharaohs began to deal with the threat from the south by a campaign of conquest into Nubia, and by the Twelfth Dynasty (1991–1785 BC) they had secured the frontier between the First and Second Cataracts with an extensive complex of forts;

the threat from the north originally did not exist, since few people dwelt on the eastern Mediterranean coast and those who did lacked means of mobility.[89] When the threat became manifest during the second millennium, the pharaohs attempted to deal with it, eventually successfully, by withdrawing the capital from Memphis to Thebes, by raising a standing army and by exploiting the difficulties of the terrain in the delta as a natural barrier.[90]

Until the founding of the regular army under the New Kingdom (1540–1070 BC), Egyptian warfare remained strangely old-fashioned. Its weapons were 'clubs and flint spears even in the Middle Kingdom', during the internal wars over succession to kingship. In that period (1991–1785 BC) bronze weapons were widely in use elsewhere, and the Egyptians had themselves been making first copper and then bronze weapons for several hundred years.[91] The reason for the Egyptians' tendency to cling to a superseded technology is hard to find; that they undoubtedly did so is proved by the many depictions of their warfare left to us in their sculpture and wall-painting. Their soldiers do not wear armour of any sort, but march to battle bare-chested and bare-headed, with only short shields for protection; it is only quite late in the New Kingdom that we find any representation of even the pharaoh wearing armour.[92] Now, it is a simple fact of biology that the naked human flinches from a blow with an edged weapon (Shaka's extraordinary and probably unique achievement, millennia later, was to make his Zulus behave otherwise); we may therefore presume that Egyptian combat, until the appearance of invaders of a different culture at the end of the Middle Kingdom, was stylised and perhaps even ritualised. Scarcity of metal may be an alternative explanation, of course, but it is more likely to be ancillary to the reason why the warriors of a highly sophisticated civilisation chose to equip themselves scarcely better than their Old Stone Age ancestors. The probability is that in a rigidly stratified society, whose kings had progressed from the status of priests to that of gods and where almost every aspect of public and indeed private life was regulated by ceremony, battle too partook of the ceremonial.

It is extremely significant, for example, that representations of the proto-pharaoh Narmer, dating from about 3000 BC, and of the New Kingdom pharaoh Rameses II, who ruled nearly 2000 years later, show both with an upheld mace about to dispatch a cringing captive; the posture of the captives is closely similar, the stance of the pharaohs identical.[93] Even when allowance is made for the very long-lasting conventions of Egyptian art, the similarities may not easily be dismissed. What both may represent is an actual, not merely symbolic, killing of a captive at the end of battle. The practice of human sacrifice disappeared early in Egyptian civilisation, but it may well be that it persisted on the battlefield, that warriors fought unprotected because they rarely came to hand strokes (a characteristic, as we have seen, of 'primitive' warfare), but that it was the fate of those disabled or captured to be ceremonially slaughtered by a great warrior – perhaps the pharaoh himself – once victory had been conceded.[94] The possibility of a parallel with the Aztecs' 'flower battle' is there to see, and is supported by the Egyptians' persistence in a choice of weapons – mace, short spear, simple bow – which eventually, after nearly 1500 years of continuous pharaonic rule, achieved an almost antiquarian oddity.

Battle was certainly not ceremonial when fought against foreigners; the mummified body of Seqenenre the Brave, a pharaoh who defended the kingdom against invaders just before the founding of the New Kingdom in 1540 BC, reveals a terrible head wound, presumably suffered in defeat.[95] But the preceding 1400 years, a span of time which takes modern Britons back to a century when their islands were ruled from Rome and today's Americans to an age when the territory of the United States was not ruled at all, the Egyptians maintained a stable and almost unvarying way of life, based on the three seasons of inundation, growing and drought, regulated by the rule of a king who took a major place among their 2000 gods, and dedicated, in the time and with the labour that could be spared from irrigation and cultivation, to raising and furnishing the palace, temple and tomb architecture, still unsurpassed in monumentality, that the necessities of passage to the afterlife, as they conceived it, required. Within that ordered world, deeply beautiful in its artistic achievement for all the harshnesses that the act of creation laid on those at the bottom of the artistic process, the hewers of stone and drawers of sledges, warfare must have been relegated to a lowly and unimportant role. 'Ultimately kingship was the outcome of force,' suggests one analyst but it may have been a form of force quite unClausewitzian in character, a stylised clash of arms brought on by the manifest incapacity of a regnant king to perform his functions and thus no more than a spectacular physical event by which authority was transferred to one better qualified to exercise it.[96] The people of Egypt, over the space of 1400 years, fourteen centuries of what must have seemed a fixed normality to the generations which lived and died within their span, may very well have been spared the reality of war, as other people later experienced it elsewhere, altogether.[97]

The people of Sumer were not so fortunate. The river plain of the

Tigris and Euphrates, unlike that of the Nile, is not protected by geography from invasion – the Sumerians themselves were probably migrants in the first place – nor does it lend itself to central control. In Egypt a ruler who can plug the top and bottom of the valley has the whole river for his kingdom. In Mesopotamia, not only do the rivers wander seasonally across the face of the land; it is flanked to its east and north by highlands that act not as barriers but as points of dominance to those settled there, who find in the tributary valleys of the great rivers easy lines of approach to the rich flood plain at their feet. The political effects of this geography are easy to depict: Sumerian cities early began to dispute among themselves over boundaries, water and grazing rights, all subject to the vagaries of flood; the Sumerian kings also early found their authority challenged by the arrival of immigrants from the hills who set up cities of their own. Between 3100 BC and 2300 BC, as a result, warfare increasingly dominated Sumerian life, leading to the supplanting of priest-kings by war leaders, military specialisation, the accelerated development of a weapons metallurgy and, probably, the intensification of combat to the point where we can begin to speak of it as 'battle'.

These are, of course, suppositions, to be pieced together from fragments of evidence – the appearance of walls at city sites, the discovery of metal weapons and helmets, the frequency of the inscription for 'battle' on clay tablets, records of the sale of slaves, who were perhaps captives, the gradual replacement of the prefix *en* (priest) by *lugal* (big man) in the titles of rulers, and so on.[98] Particularly important is the evidence for the infiltration of Semitic peoples from the north, the Akkadians, who first founded cities of their own on the plain and eventually, after some centuries of conflict between their cities and those of the Sumerians, supplied the world's first emperor, Sargon of Agade.

It has been suggested that Sumer also supplies the first evidence of long-distance campaigning, in the saga of Gilgamesh, king of the city of Uruk about 2700 BC. He appears to have gone on a military expedition to bring cedar wood from the mountains – 'I will cut down the cedar. An everlasting name I will establish for myself! Orders . . . to the armourers will I give' – and to have killed the ruler where the cedar trees grew.[99] It is difficult to see, however, how he might have transported a quantity of cedar wood any distance, so that the saga provides little support for the practice of either war or trade over long distances at that time. Nevertheless Uruk appears to have acquired walls in the time of Gilgamesh, and walls more than five miles round, which speaks for his powers to direct labour, while within the next 200 years hard evidence of serious warmaking begins to accumulate.[100] We have the so-called Vulture stele, which shows Eanatum II, king of Lagash, defeating the people of Elam, early inhabitants of what was to become the mighty Persian kingdom; his soldiers wear metal helmets and are arrayed in column on a six-man front.[101] The Standard of Ur, from the same period, shows soldiers similarly equipped – they wear cloaks and fringed kilts which appear to be strengthened with pieces of metal, claimed by some scholars to be prototypical armour, though very ineffective it must have been – and are led by others driving four-horse, four-wheel carts. Excavations at the 'death pits' of Ur have produced relics of metal helmets which appear to have been worn over leather caps.[102]

The helmets are copper, the first non-precious metal that man learnt to work, because it can be found in large and relatively pure ingots in a natural state. It is not of much military use, being easily penetrated if used as bodily protection in sheet form and quickly losing its edge if beaten into a weapon.[103] Some natural copper, however, occurs in an ore that contains tin and, as man learnt during the fourth millennium that metals could be melted, the technique of combining common copper with scarce tin to produce hard bronze evolved; it was widely in practice by the end of the third millennium, and in Mesopotamia smiths were busy inventing most of the metal-working methods on which we still depend today, including smelting from ore, casting, alloying and soldering.[104] One of the earliest products of alloying and casting was the socket axe, a bronze head into which a wooden handle could be securely riveted, thus producing a durable edged weapon of formidable penetrative power when wielded by a muscular and determined warrior. The 'chalcolithic' period, in which copper (Greek *khalkos*) and stone (Greek *lithos*) co-existed, was rapidly superseded by the coming of the age of bronze, as man bent to the almost universal rule that a superior technology obliterates an inferior one as fast as the necessary techniques and materials can be acquired. One of the necessary materials in this case – tin – was scarce and localised; it occurs in Mesopotamia only as an impure ore called cassiterite, a river-washed mineral, but adequate supplies of the pure ore seem to have arrived quickly from the shores of the Caspian Sea and perhaps even from central Europe. By the time Sargon of Agade (or Akkad, a city so-called from his Semitic ancestors and yet to be discovered by archaeologists) had made himself ruler of Mesopotamia, about 2340 BC, bronze had become the weapon of conquerors; Sargon was a man of bronze.

The Sumerian King List, our principal source of knowledge about Sumerian history, has been interpreted to show that he ruled from 2340 to 2284 BC; alternatively he is said to have ruled for fifty-six years. What seems certain is that he fought a series of wars against neighbouring cities and then against neighbouring peoples – thirty-four wars are mentioned – and that he eventually succeeded in establishing the boundaries of his empire roughly where those of modern Iraq lie today. In the eleventh year of his reign he campaigned as far as Syria, the Lebanon and southern Turkey and may have reached the Mediterranean. One inscription suggests that he had an army of 5400 soldiers and his army was undoubtedly kept busy putting down revolts among the Sumerians who rebelled against rule by a Semitic incomer; Sargon called himself 'He Who Keeps Travelling the Four Lands', that is the universe, and he certainly appears to have lived *toujours en vedette.*

Sargon's grandson, Naram-Sin (2260–23 BC), called himself 'King of the Four Quarters', a truly imperial title, and he is known to have campaigned into the Zagros range, the mountains that separate Mesopotamia from northern Persia. By the time of his reign, and despite his need to defend the frontiers of his empire, the empire had then become an established fact, and was indeed the most important fact in the developing life of the Middle East. Its wealth was a magnet to jealous predators living beyond the magic circle, among whom, nevertheless, some elements of its civilisation took root, as a result partly of war, partly of trade. The outcome was that 'by about 2000 BC . . . Mesopotamia had come to be ringed around by a series of satellite civilisations, or proto-civilisations' which, as they acquired the military means, supplied the waves of conquerors – Gutians, Hurrians, Kassites – who conquered part or all of the great plain during the next thousand years. Such peoples were making their own transition to a different economic life even before they came down from the high ground, refining their mastery of pastoralism, which began to supply the animals – asses, oxen and horses – through which they acquired military mobility, and developing techniques of agriculture on rain-watered land that provided them with a surplus on which to support the beginnings of civilised life.[105]

Certain military equipments, attributes and techniques were common to those who lived both within the empire and on its fringes. They had abandoned stone weapons for bronze and had begun to acquire metallic armour; they made increasing use of the bow and, if a rock sculpture depicting Naram-Sin has been accurately interpreted, may have developed the powerful composite bow by the middle of the second millennium BC; they were familiar with the architecture of fortification and had also learnt some of the methods – breaching and scaling – of siegecraft; they had accepted the need, within Mesopotamia at least, for the ruler to maintain out of his revenue bodies of armed men ready to go to war; the same revenue may have supplied the funds for the manufacture of standardised weapons; they must, given the distances over which they campaigned, have learned the rudiments of logistics, at least to the extent of being able to supply themselves with food for man and beast for some days' campaigning within enemy territory; above all, they had learned to improve the physique of domesticated horses – domestication had begun on the steppe during the fourth millennium – by care and selective breeding.[106] Such horses, when used to pull a greatly improved war cart, which had shed two of its four original wheels to become the chariot, were truly to revolutionise warmaking, above all by putting the rich and stable but sedentary valley civilisations at risk from the predators who hovered in the horse-breeding lands beyond. After the end of the second millennium BC, such predatory charioteers disrupted the course of civilisation in Mesopotamia, Egypt, the Indus Valley, and wherever else it had put down roots.

Interlude 2
Fortification

Charioteers were the first great aggressors in human history. Aggression, by an opposite if not always equal reaction, stimulates defence, and so, before we consider how the charioteers and the horse-riding peoples who succeeded them altered the world in which civilised arts of peace had begun to flourish, we ought to examine the means by which the settled inhabitants of the rich lands sought to preserve what they had won from nature against theft and devastation.

The evidence from Jericho indicates that the very first agriculturalists were able to find the means to protect their dwellings against enemies, though who such enemies might have been remains obscure. Were they raiders who wished to plunder stored produce, perhaps on a regular, parasitic basis, or would-be agriculturalists who wanted Jericho's fields and perpetual water-source for themselves, or mere vandals who threatened to plunder and destroy? The first seems the likeliest; people from the wilderness rarely want, let alone know how, to turn farmer and, while history is full of pointless vandalism, it more usually shows that raiders had the sense to see that parasitism profited better than rape and pillage. If that were the case at Jericho, we should probably see its walls and tower not simply as a *refuge* – the first of the three forms that fortification may take – but also as the second, a *stronghold*.

A stronghold is a place not merely of safety from attack but also of active defence, a centre where the defenders are secure from surprise or superior numbers, and also a base from which they may sally forth to hold predators at bay and to impose military control over the area in which their interests lie. There is a symbiosis between a stronghold and its surroundings. A refuge is a place of short-term safety, of value only against an enemy who lacks the means to linger in the vicinity or who operates a crude strategy of raiding against soft targets: the medieval *villes perchées* of south-eastern France, built on the summits of the precipitous coastal hills of Provence as sanctuaries against the visits of Muslim sea raiders, are perfect examples of the type.[1] A stronghold, by contrast, must command an area productive enough to support a garrison in normal times but itself be sufficiently large and secure to house, supply and protect the garrison when under close attack. The builders of strongholds, therefore, have always had to make a nice judgement between the false economy of building too small and the extravagance of conceiving defences too expensive to be completed or, if completed, too extensive to be defended with the manpower available. The Crusader kingdoms, particularly in their years of decline, perpetually teetered on the brink of over-fortifying the shrinking garrisons that they could deploy.

Strongholds differ from refuges also in the features they must incorporate. It suffices if a refuge is strong enough to deter an attacker from the trouble of mounting assault; 'primitive warriors', like the Maring inside their palisaded villages or the Maoris inside their hilltop *pa*, were safe from 'routing' or 'raiding' because their enemies lacked siege engines and had no means to support themselves for any length of time away from their own homes.[2] Strongholds, typically the constructions of more advanced and therefore richer societies, must be able to withstand siege from attackers who bring their own rations or command a line of communications along which they can be supplied and who also deploy machinery. The circumference of a stronghold should therefore enclose a water-supply – especially if it is to be a protection for flocks – as well as storehouses and living-space.[3] Above all, it must provide means for the garrison to wage an active defence – fighting-platforms that command a field of fire over prepared killing-grounds and strong gates through which counter-attacks can be mounted at moments of opportunity.

Until the coming of gunpowder, all attacks on strongholds had to be mounted at close range. That was true by definition of the simplest sort of attack – escalade – by which the besiegers sought to scramble over the walls with scaling-ladders, but also true of what siege engineers later called 'deliberate siege' – mining, battery with rams or projectile-throwers and counter-fortification with siege towers. Projectile-throwing, let it be said at once, rarely repaid the effort: a stout wall can easily absorb the energy directed against it by engines that depend on counter-weights or torsion springs to launch their missiles. Of their nature, moreover, such engines throw their projectiles at an inefficient angle of attack; the superiority of the gunpowder missile over all its predecessors was that, since it travelled in a flat trajectory, it could be directed at the one point where a high wall is vulnerable to collapse, at its foundations.

The designers of strongholds always sought, therefore, to deny an attacker easy access to a wall's foundations and to provide the defenders with superior fire positions. One of the fascinations of Jericho is that its builders, in the dawn of fortification practice, appear to have perceived all the dangers by which it might be threatened and to have furnished it with protection against each. Thus the dry moat deprived the attackers of a platform from which to approach the walls' foundations, while it also formed a prepared killing-ground (in an environment with impermeable soil, less evaporation and more water, it might have been made a wet moat). The walls, over three times the height of a man, required any attacker to bring scaling-ladders, a very insecure footing from which to launch an assault; it is likely that the walls were also furnished with fighting-platforms. Finally the tower, which overtopped the walls, gave the defenders a further advantage of height.

To these three defensive features – walls, moat, tower – fortification engineers were to add little in the 8000 years between the building of Jericho and the introduction of gunpowder. The principles were established; all subsequent improvements were no more than refinements of what Jericho's builders conceived. Outer walls were to be set around inner ones – 'multivallation'; obstacles were to be set at the lip of the moat (as they may indeed have been at Jericho, the evidence perhaps

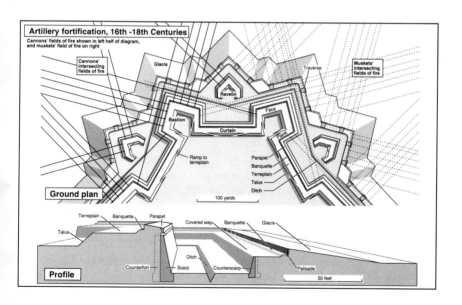

having perished); inner strongholds – 'keeps' or 'citadels' – were to be added and towers set on the outer rather than inner faces of the walls, to allow flanking fire; at very important sites, detached outworks – themselves strongholds in miniature – were to be built as a protection for gates or to deny points of advantage to an attacker. In general, however, it may be said that later fortification engineers made no greater improvement over Jericho than subsequent printers have over Gutenberg's Bible.

Strongholds are a product of small or divided sovereignties; they proliferate when central authority has not been established or is struggling to secure itself or has broken down. Thus the Greek fortifications on the coasts of modern Turkey and Sicily were built to protect individual commercial settlements in the early years of colonisation; the castellation of England by the Normans – 900 castles may have been built between 1066 and 1154, varying in size between those that needed as few as a thousand and as many as 24,000 man-days for their construction – was undertaken as a deliberate means of enforcing Norman rule on the Anglo-Saxons;[4] the Roman forts of the 'Saxon Shore', such as Reculver and Pevensey, were built to deny the estuaries of south-east England to Teutonic sea raiders emboldened by the decline of Roman power during the fourth century AD.[5] More properly, however, we should regard the forts of the Saxon shore not as individual strongholds but as elements in the third form that fortifications may take: strategic defences. Strategic defences may be continuous, as Hadrian's Wall was when kept in repair, or more commonly may comprise individual strongpoints so positioned as to be mutually supporting and to deny avenues of attack to an enemy across a wide front. Of their nature, strategic defences are the most expensive form of fortification to construct, to maintain and to garrison, and their existence is always a mark of the wealth and advanced political development of the people who build them.

The fortified cities of Sumer, once Sargon brought them under central control, may be seen as forming a strategic system, though they did so by the process of accretion, not design. The first deliberately conceived strategic system would appear to be that of the Nubian forts built by the pharaohs of the Twelfth Dynasty from 1991 BC onward. They eventually stretched for 250 miles along the Nile, between the First and Fourth Cataracts, constructed so as to command both the river and the desert and at distances from each other which allowed intercommunication, perhaps by smoke signals. Again, the archaeological evidence reveals a concept of fortification to which subsequent builders of strategic defences found little to add. The early forts, located in a region around the First Cataract where the valley is wide enough to support an agricultural population, were designed to protect it as well as dominate the river. The later forts, which followed the line of the Egyptian advance into barbarous Nubia and the much narrower upper Nile, were more strictly military in function. Surviving written records reveal that the upstream forts were conceived as a truly military frontier. Senusret III erected a statue of himself and raised an inscription: 'I have made my boundary, having sailed further south than my fathers. I have increased what was bequeathed to me. As for any son of mine who shall maintain this boundary . . . he is a son of mine who was born to My Majesty . . . But as for whoever shall abandon it, and who shall not fight for it, he is no son of mine.' The inscription was found at the fort of Semna and dates from 1820 BC. The statue has been lost but in the same fort has been found a cult statue of Senusret III which dates from 1479–26, clear evidence that his admonition to hold what he had won had been taken to heart.[6]

Egyptian frontier policy in Nubia was a model for later imperialists everywhere. At Semna three forts are situated so as to control the river from both banks, and there are tunnels so that water can be drawn from it; a mud-brick wall protected the road to the south on the landward side for several miles. All the forts contain large granaries, two sufficient to supply several hundred men for a year; they were probably restocked from the rear supply centre at Askut, an island fortress apparently purpose-built as a grain store. Another inscription reveals what the garrison's duties were: 'to prevent any Nubian from passing . . . when faring northward, whether on foot or by boat, as well as any cattle of the Nubians. An exception is a Nubian who shall come to barter at Iken, or one with an official message.' Forward of the forts, the Egyptians maintained a desert patrol recruited from Nubian desert men, named Medjay. (Among the 'Semna Despatches' found on papyrus at Thebes is a typical desert patrol report: 'The patrol which set out to patrol the desert edge . . . has returned and reported to me as follows: "We have found a track of 32 men and 3 donkeys."') British officers with experience on India's North-West Frontier would recognise Egyptian practice instantly. Like the Egyptians, the British maintained an administered zone where large garrisons protected the settled population, a forward zone where the garrisons held purely military forts, and forward of that again a 'tribal' zone where only the roads were defended and the surrounding areas were policed by tribal militias – Khyber Rifles, Tochi Scouts – recruited from the peoples against whom the whole elaborate defensive structure had been erected in the first place.

It is not surprising that the plans of both Jericho and the Second

Cataract forts perpetuated and reproduced themselves over time and distance; it is not even very surprising that they emerged so early. Given that man turns his mind to integrating the various but limited elements of architecture and town-planning into a system of self-protection, it almost inevitably follows that something like Jericho or the Semna complex will emerge; similarly, though this has psychological rather than material roots, the practice of turning poachers into gamekeepers – Medjay, Khyber Rifles – follows almost immediately from the recognition that primary control of a frontier between civilisation and barbary is best exercised by bribing those who live on the wrong side of it.

It would be wrong to surmise, however, that the principles that underlay the construction of Jericho and Semna were rapidly or widely disseminated. The people of Jericho were rich in their time, the pharaohs of the Twelfth Dynasty richer still. Elsewhere mankind remained poor and thinly settled until well into the second millennium BC and it is only in the first millennium that defended settlements came to be built over a wide area. Archaeologists have noted the appearance of a fortified Greek settlement at Old Smyrna, within a defensive wall furnished with cut-stone bastions, in the ninth century BC, and of walled settlements at such widely distant spots as Saragossa, Spain, and Biskupin, Poland, in the sixth century.[7] Hilltop enclosures – the 'Iron Age forts' so familiar in Britain, where 2000 have been identified – may have been dug in south-eastern Europe as early as the third millennium, but it was only in the first that they became widespread.[8] Historians continue to disagree about their function – proto-towns or places of temporary refuge? – and about the political conditions that prompted their building. The probability is that, like the Maori *pa*, they were the products of a society that had become tribalised and in which neighbouring groups sought to secure their movable goods against raiding; but we cannot be sure. All we know is that fortification spread from south-east into north-west Europe during the first millennium, matched by the establishment of defended ports along the coasts of the Mediterranean and the Black Sea as Greeks and Phoenicians voyaged to establish trading colonies beyond their homelands. Fortification undoubtedly followed trade; indeed Stuart Piggott, the leading expert on urban prehistory, suggests the existence of a major two-way trade route leading from the fortified Mediterranean coastal ports to the inland hill-forts of France and Germany, along which passed wine, silk, ivory (and even apes and peacocks – a Barbary ape reached a king of Ulster in prehistoric times) on the northward leg, and amber, furs, hides, salt meat and slaves in return.[9]

By the end of the first millennium fortifications pimpled the face of

144

...ve: Carl von Clausewitz
...30–1831), Prussian
...eral and military thinker.
...book *On War* has largely
...rmined how the Western
...d has thought about
...are since his death.

...t: A Mameluke warrior
...e Fourteenth Century AD
...ising the exercises of the
...siyya, the most refined
...of the steppe horse-
...'s skill-at-arms.

...w: An *image d'Epinal* of
...Mamelukes of Egypt in
...at with Napoleon's
...s at the battle of the
...mids, 1798. *Furusiyya*
...idualism was defeated
...illed musketry.

Left: Zulu warriors charging with the stabbing assegai in war of 1879. After their victory at Isandhwlana they were destroyed by British firepower.

Below: A Partisan's Mother, S. Gerasimov, 1943. This heroine of Socialist Realism defies the Nazi invader with future partisan in her arms.

Left: Mountain infantry of the Austro-Hungarian army scaling a peak in the Julian Alps. There was prolonged fighting in these ranges and in the Carpathians and Vosges in 1914–18.

Below: A Mark IV Panzer of the Afrika Korps in the battle of El Agheila, April 1941. Free movement in the open desert was limited by logistics.

: German infantrymen manhandling a staff car across the roadless steppe in spring, 1942. The seasonal *rasputitsa* halts military ıent in western Russia twice each year.

ıpanese swordsmen and the art of the duel. The cult of the sword in Japan held the gunpowder revolution at bay until the ·enth Century.

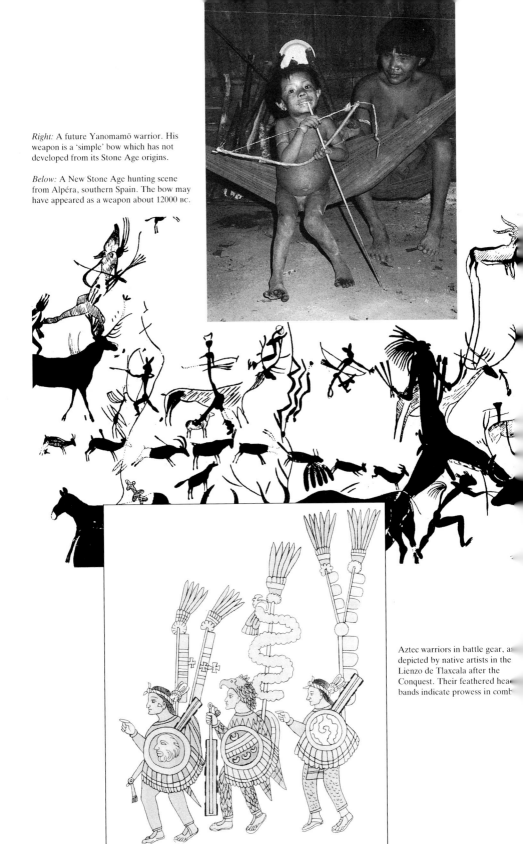

Right: A future Yanomamö warrior. His weapon is a 'simple' bow which has not developed from its Stone Age origins.

Below: A New Stone Age hunting scene from Alpéra, southern Spain. The bow may have appeared as a weapon about 12000 BC.

Aztec warriors in battle gear, as depicted by native artists in the Lienzo de Tlaxcala after the Conquest. Their feathered headbands indicate prowess in comb...

Egyptian archers from
[tom]b of Mesehti at Assiut,
[Middl]e Kingdom (1938–
[175]0 BC). Their lack of
[body] protection indicates
[tenta]tive nature of early
[Egypti]an warfare.

[S]ethos (Seti) I in battle with the Libyans at Karnak, Four-
[teenth c]entury BC. The coming of the chariot brought a novel
[element] to Egyptian warfare.

[T]he Palette of Narmer (Menes) shows the unifier of Lower
[a]nd Upper Egypt, reckoned the first pharaoh (c. 3100 BC),
despatching a captive.

Above: Rameses II, in a similar pose seventeen centuries later, despatches a Nubian. Ritual slaughter may have been a feature of Egyptian, as of Aztec, warfare.

Below: The Assyrian victors of the Chaldean campaign (late Seventh Century BC) counting heads. was not a ritual but evidence of a new ruthlessnes warmaking.

Below: Assyrians hunting the large-horned ox from a chariot, Seventh Century BC. The chariot may originally have been developed for hunting.

Left: The walls of Jericho, excavated in 1956, which have been dated to 7000 BC. The fortifications also include a rock-cut dry moat and tower.

Below: The Great Wall of China near Peking, in its reconstructed state. A strategic defence, it was constantly extended to protect the empire from the steppe nomads.

n's Wall at its centre near Cuddy's Crags. Begun in 122 AD, it is the best-preserved of the frontier fortifications of the Roman e.

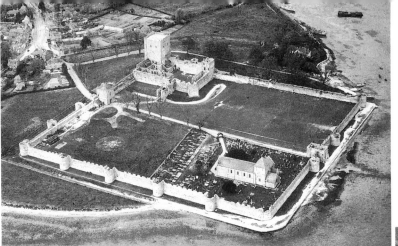

Porchester Castle, a Norman stone-built ke[...] inside a Roman fort of the Saxon Shore, one o[...] the Empire's major defensive systems.

Right: Krak des Chevaliers, greatest of Crusader castles. The problem of the Christian knights was to find the garrisons for the strongholds they built.

Below: The siege of Limerick, 1691; the plan shows 'artillery' bastions added to a mediaeval wall with towers, and the besiegers' approaches. parallels and star earthworks. My Bridgman ancestors were given land nearby for service in this siege.

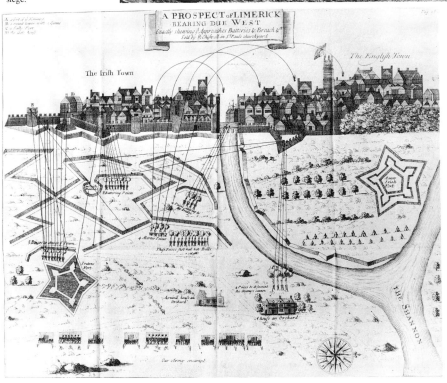

A PROSPECT OF LIMERICK BEARING DUE WEST

The Standard of Ur,
the Sumerian king-
about 2500 BC. The
rt is drawn by
s, not horses, and
rriors are wearing
armour.

Mounted
an warriors of the
f Shalmaneser III
4 BC). They ride
t saddles and have
learnt the forward

Assyrians in battle
abs, c. 650 BC.
abs are riding the
y domesticated
while the Assyrian
now ride from the
'control'

Left: A Sarmatian mounted warrior, kin to the [A]ans who were enemies of Rome and Persia. H[is] armour points the way to the development of [?] plate.

Below: Alexander the Great confronts Darius [at the] battle of Issus, 333 BC. The Persian emperor i[n his] chariot flies from Alexander on Bucephalus i[n a] graphic symbolisation of the cavalry revoluti[on.]

Above: Iranian horsemen of the steppe, first millenium BC. Their elaborate horse-furniture indicates their mastery of their mounts, whose slender Caspian build anticipates that of the Arab horse.

Right: The coming of the stirrup: mounted warriors of the Carolingian empire, from the St Gall Psalter, couch lances for the charge.

Left: Warriors: the Zouave in the foreground is a Frenchman wearing the dress of a North African tribe, tribute to the reputation of 'primitive warriors' among Nineteenth-Century European armies.

Slave soldiers: Janissaries ('new soldiers') of the Ottoman ...re parading at Lake Van in the Sixteenth Century; Janissaries ...enslaved by the Sultan from Christian children of the Balkans.

...: Militia: Swiss citizen soldiers on parade. Switzerland ...ues to make the performance of military service a condition – ...les – of the enjoyment of electoral rights.

Left: Mercenary: John Hawkwood, painted by Uccello in 1436, English commander of the White Company, who sold his service to Florence, Milan and the papacy in the Fourteenth Century.

Below: Regular: *The Village Recruit,* after Wilkie; drink, flattery and the King's shilling tempt a landless labourer into long service in George III's army.

Below: Conscript: Londoners line up to register for compulsory military service at King's Cross, May, 1939, on the eve of the Second World War.

NOTICE.
HAVE YOUR BIRTH CERTIFICATE
READY.
IF YOU HAVE NO CERTIFICATE
BE PREPARED TO GIVE:
I. DATE and PLACE OF BIRTH
II. NAMES OF YOUR PARENTS
III. MOTHER'S MAIDEN SURNAME

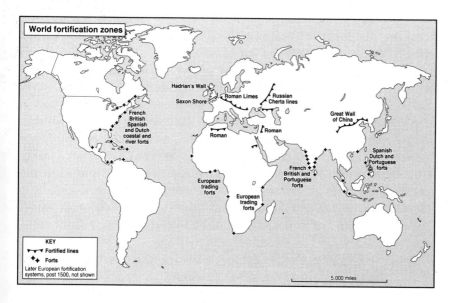

the temperate zone. In China, where the first towns had been unwalled and where, in the treeless loess plains even the basic materials are lacking, towns walled with beaten earth (*pisé*) nevertheless appeared during the Shang dynasty (*c.* 1500–1000 BC), which exercised the earliest centralised authority; interestingly, the Shang ideograph for a city, *yi*, incorporates the symbols for an enclosure and a man kneeling in submission, suggesting that, as was often the case elsewhere, the fort in China was an institution of social control as well as of defence.[10] In historic Greece, following the Dark Ages brought on by the collapse of Minoan civilisation, the emergent city states walled themselves as a matter of course; so too did those in contemporary Italy, including, of course, Rome. By the time Alexander the Great set off on his march of conquest through Persia to India in the fourth century BC, strategists expected to find their path blocked by strongholds whenever they campaigned in settled terrain.

The general principle held, however, that a multiplicity of strongholds indicated a weakness or absence of central authority. Alexander conducted at least twenty sieges between 335 and 325 but none within the confines of the Persian empire; as befitted a great state, its interior was defended at its periphery. Alexander's three battles with the Persian army, at the

145

Granicus, Issus and Gaugamela, were fought in open country. It was only when he had subdued Persia and pushed on into the fractious lands between it and India that he had to revert to the siegecraft he had practised when breaking into the empire during 334–2. The Romans conducted one siege after another when building their empire, from Agrigentum – one of the early fortified ports of Sicily – during the First Punic War in 262 BC to Alesia, a gigantic Celtic hill-fort, where Caesar overthrew Vercingetorix in 52 BC. They also, in the course of their advance from the Alps to Scotland and the Rhine, dotted the landscape with the rectangular legionary forts that their soldiers were trained to throw up at the end of each day's march in hostile territory. These standardised designs – with their four gates and central ceremonial square they strangely resemble the classical Chinese city – also formed the model for the principal Roman cities of conquest: under the modern centres of London, Cologne and Vienna lie the remains of the square legionary forts on which they all grew up.

Within the pacified Roman empire, however, the conquerors did not fortify: 'the majority of Gallic cities developed as open settlements and were left undefended'.[11] That was what was meant by *pax Romana* – open cities, safe roads, the absence of internal boundaries over the great extent of western Europe. It was assured by fortification elsewhere, of course, though exactly how remains one of the most contentious issues in the writing of Roman history. The physical evidence of fortification at the frontiers is there for all to see, most visibly in the central stretches of Hadrian's Wall. Traces of the Antonine Wall, by which the Romans marked an even deeper advance into north Britain, are still detectable, as are parts of the *limes* along the Rhine and the Danube, the *fossatum Africae* on the desert edge in Morocco, Algeria, Tunisia and Libya and the *limes Syriae*, which stretched from the Gulf of Aqaba and the north of the Red Sea to the headwaters of the Euphrates and Tigris. Were these 'scientific frontiers', as some modern historians think, or merely marks of the limits of effective control established by Roman armies campaigning to pre-empt the forces of disorder, some merely local, some strategically threatening, which they met at the effective economic boundaries of the Mediterranean world? Edward Luttwak, in his *The Grand Strategy of the Roman Empire*, has successfully propagated the belief that the Romans, like the British in India, firmly conceived a scheme of what could and could not be defended, though varying the method by which it was defended in practice – strong central army first, then strong local defence, finally an unsatisfactory mixture of the two – as their fortunes dictated.[12] Luttwak's opponents deny any such consistency, particularly where the eastern frontiers were concerned. Benjamin Isaac believes that Rome sustained an aggressive policy against Persia and Parthia over a very long period, and that the fortifications in the east should therefore be seen as defended lines of communication for expeditionary armies; C.R. Whittaker thinks that there were permanent local troubles on many frontiers and that Roman defences, like those of the Egyptians in Nubia or the French in Algeria during the war of 1954–62 (the Morice Line), were principally intended to keep malefactors at arm's length from peaceful cultivators.[13]

What is certain is that the growth of central authority was almost everywhere and at all times marked by the construction of strategic defences, from those as simple as Offa's Dyke between Anglo-Saxon England and Celtic Wales – though a mighty undertaking it must have been in its time, consuming tens of thousands of man-digging days – to the still-unravelled complexities of the Great Wall of China. The exact function of such defences is more difficult to define, varying so much as to defy generalisation. Thus the Habsburg Military Frontier with the Ottoman lands – the *krajina* – was certainly meant to keep the Turks out; but building it was a tribute more to Turkish strength than to that of Austria, though the Habsburgs were the older dynasty. By contrast, the chain of fortresses erected at great expense to protect the British ports on the south and east coasts in the 1860s (seventy-six were completed or under construction by 1867) was a response to a phantom threat from France, perhaps evidence of a neurotic distrust of the power of ironclad warships to supply the defence which the English had always confidently expected from wooden walls.[14] Louis XIV's chain of fortresses along the eastern border of France was an aggressive device, designed to extend French power step-by-step into the Habsburg lands; even more so was the *cherta*, a line of improvised fortifications pushed eastward by the tsars from the sixteenth century on into the wild lands of the steppe, intended to press the nomads south of the Ural mountains and to open a path of settlement into Siberia. The *cherta* could only be extended, however, with the half-willing assistance of the Cossacks, and one of its functions, which they were slow to perceive, was that of bringing their free settlements under Muscovite control.[15]

That prescription – half defensive, half oppressive – describes, in the view of Owen Lattimore, who with Frederick Jackson Turner was the greatest of frontier historians, the role of China's Great Wall. Turner, in a famous paper of 1893 to the American Historical Association, argued that the idea of the moving frontier, which offered free land to anyone prepared to venture westward, had been decisive in shaping the American national character – exuberant, energetic and inquisitive – and in assuring that the United States would remain a great democracy. Lattimore, by contrast, represented the Great Wall as a different sort of frontier in every way. Admittedly it moved: beginning by the interconnection of a number of local walls, raised by regional rulers to protect their embryo states, its line was eventually fixed along the boundary between the soils of irrigated agriculture and those of pastoralism – roughly river valley and steppe – by the Chin dynasty in the third century BC. Neither they, however, nor any subsequent dynasty, in Lattimore's view, could get the line of the Great Wall right: sometimes it pushed northward to enclose the Ordos plateau in the great bend of the Yellow River, sometimes that was abandoned, while there were numerous extensions to and realignments of its western end where it reached out toward the Tibetan plateau; eventually all its arms and branches ran to a total length of nearly 4000 miles.[16] Lattimore argues that all these twists and turns are evidence less of the waning or waxing power of dynasties than of the pursuit of a chimera. Successive emperors did indeed seek a 'scientific' frontier, on the line where land suitable for peasant farming met that which ought to be abandoned to the herding nomads. No such line, however, was to be found, since the two zones were not only separated by one of mixed ecology, but that third zone itself shifted with changes of climate – desiccation, humidification – in the interior of the great Eurasian land mass. Attempts to dictate ecology by colonising the border zone with peasant Chinese produced a *Schlimmbesserung* – worsening by improvement. The settlers, particularly those implanted in the great bend of the Yellow River, tended to nomadise themselves when desiccation set in and thus to swell the numbers of the horse peoples who beat in successive waves against the Wall; offensives by the horse peoples also undid the efforts of the frontier commanders to sinicise the semi-nomads whose natural home the inter-zone was.[17]

It was not surprising, in the circumstances, that the Chinese never unwalled the cities around which their irrigated settlements had first grown up. In times of dynastic strength they served as centres of imperial administration; during periods of turmoil, brought on by nomadic assaults on the throne, they remained sanctuaries of the imperial tradition which always reasserted itself to tame and sinicise the conquerors. City walls were rightly regarded as symbols of civilisation – under the Ming (AD 1368–1644) 500 were completely reconstructed – as was the Great Wall itself.[18] Both, however, were no more than props to the imperial system, whose ultimate strength reposed in the philosophical beliefs of the Chinese about how society should properly be ordered. Such beliefs could retain their force not so much because they permeated society from top to bottom – they tended to remain the cultural property of the land-owning and official class – as because the numbers of outsiders who succeeded to power were comparatively small, and came from steppe societies which, to an extent that they themselves did not often recognise, had themselves been subtly sinicised by sustained contact with the target civilisation at its fortified edge. In that sense, the Great Wall was itself a civilising instrument, a diaphragm through which potent ideas flowed outward to moderate the barbarism of those who beat perpetually at the gates.

The classical civilisation of the West was not so lucky. Unlike the Chinese, the Romans were assaulted by a sustained surge of barbarians in very large numbers, too few of whom had been romanised by continuous and mediating contact with civilisation to ensure its preservation. From the middle of the third century AD, as barbarian raiders struck more frequently and deeply into Gaul, provincial officials began to wall inland towns; even by the fifth century, however, only forty-eight cities had been fortified, mostly in frontier or coastal areas; in Spain only twelve had been walled, while in Italy south of the Po valley Rome alone retained its defences.[19] Chains of forts were thrown up along the North Sea, Channel and Atlantic coasts, and the *limes* down the Rhine and Danube were strengthened. Once these frontier defences were overrun, the western empire lay ripe for the taking. The barbarian kingdoms that succeeded to Rome did not at first need, even had they known how, to fortify. Successive irruptions by wholly unromanised intruders – Scandinavian sea raiders, Arabs, Central Asian steppe peoples – met no strategic defences to bar the way and few internal fortifications. Little wonder that Charlemagne's brave effort to recreate a pan-European state was whittled away piecemeal by their assaults.

Eventually western Europe was re-fortified, but in a pattern that would have rightly caused a Chinese dynasty nothing but alarm. The mysterious revival of trade between 1100 and 1300, itself perhaps due to an equally mysterious rise in the European population from about 40,000,000 to about 60,000,000, in turn revived the life of towns, which through the growth of a money economy won the funds to protect themselves from dangers beyond the walls; Pisa, for example, surrounded itself by a ditch dug in two months in 1155 and completed a continuous wall with towers the following year. The newly walled towns, however, used their immunity not to underpin royal authority but to demand rights and freedoms; Pisa was walled as an act of defiance against the emperor Frederick Barbarossa.[20] Meanwhile, in a process the Chinese emperors would have found even more alarming, local strongmen were busily covering the face of western Europe with castles, at first simple entrenchments, then from the tenth century onward more dominating mottes, finally true stone strongholds. Some of these places were owned by a king or his trusted vassals, but progressively the majority must be classified as the illegal ('adulterine') creations of the disobedient or upstart. Their justification was always that threats from the ungodly – Vikings or Avars or Magyars – required them to have a secure place in which to stable their warhorses and house their men-at-arms. The reality was that, in a Europe which lacked both strategic defences and strong central authorities, they were profiting from circumstances to make themselves local overlords.

Castellation on such a scale – there were three castles in the Poitou region of France before the Vikings began to raid, thirty-nine by the eleventh century; none in Maine before the tenth century, sixty-two by 1100; and the pattern repeats itself elsewhere – eventually cancelled out the advantage it gave in local struggles for power.[21] When every strong man kept his court armed, the result was not overlordship, and mutual support of central authority against intruders even less, but endemic local warfare. Kings issued licences for castles and, with their great vassals, overthrew the adulterine whenever they could. Castles, however, could be built very quickly – a hundred men might throw up a small motte in ten days – but a castle once built was much more difficult to reduce if its castellan dug in his heels.[22] The strength of castles greatly exceeded the force of siegecraft, a truth not to be overturned until the coming of gunpowder and that had held good since the building of Jericho.

Ancient historians are fascinated by the representations of siege practices and siege engines that excavations in Mesopotamia and Egypt have revealed – battering-rams, scaling-ladders, siege towers, mineshafts. Written accounts of Greek siege warfare disclose the appearance of the catapult, earliest of projectile-throwers, in 398–7 BC.[23] The earliest representation of a ram – of very flimsy type, though apparently protected by a roof – is from Egypt and dated to 1900 BC; the scaling-ladder was depicted about 500 years earlier. A much more formidable battering-ram, mounted in a wheeled carapace, is shown in a palace relief sculpture from Mesopotamia of about 883–59 BC, together with a scene of engineers undermining a wall. A mobile siege tower, also Mesopotamian, is shown in another relief dated to 745–27 BC, by which time the construction of ramps to fill a moat and reach the crest of the wall had also been brought into use; large siege-shields, to protect archers shooting at the defenders on the parapet, were apparently also by that time an item of siegecraft.

There are also allusions to the use of fire to attack gates, and possibly also the interior of a fortification, while interruptions of the water supply, where practicable, and, of course, starvation had become standard siege techniques.[24]

All the works of siegecraft available to commanders before the invention of gunpowder were, therefore, devised between 2400 and 397 BC. None, except starvation, offered a certain, or even very effective, means of bringing a fortification to surrender. A besieger's best hope of a quick result, according to the classical strategist Polybius, lay in exploiting the defenders' complacency or achieving surprise. Treachery was another device – it brought the fall of Antioch to the Crusaders in 1098, for example, and that of many other strongholds as well.[25] Those methods apart, an attacker might sit for months outside the walls, unless he could find a weak spot or create one himself. Chateau-Gaillard was taken in 1204 through an unguarded latrine tunnel; Rochester, on the other hand, besieged by King John in 1215, lost the southern corner of its keep to undermining and the firing of the tunnel timbers – which consumed the fat of forty bacon pigs – but was eventually taken only because the garrison had run out of food after fifty days of continuous investment, the greatest siege in England up to that time and for long after.[26]

The taking of Jerusalem by the Crusaders in 1099 with a siege tower was an exceptional event, ascribed in part to the weakness of the garrison, in part to the religious inspiration of the attackers. In general, the advantage in siege warfare before gunpowder always lay with the defender, as long as he took the precaution of laying in supplies, and to such an extent that it was a convention of siege warfare in the medieval West for the parties to agree on a time limit, at the expiry of which, if the siege had not been raised by a relieving force, those inside the walls were allowed to march out without penalty.[27] Since the attackers might themselves run out of food, or even more probably succumb to disease in their unhealthy encampments, such an agreement was a sensible option for any garrison.

We ought, therefore, to treat with extreme reserve all representations of siegecraft and siege engines, if offered as evidence of their importance in 'the art of war' at any time before the gunpowder age. Warfare in art always calls forth from the artist the representation of the potential and the sensational, rather than that of documentary realities; in that light, Egyptian and Assyrian wall-paintings and sculpture reliefs of royal triumphs under the walls of cities are no more to be relied upon as testimony of contemporary actualities than the heroic portraits of Napoleon by David and Le Gros are to be taken as depictions of his behaviour as a general in the field; between war art and the war comic interposes a very narrow gap, and probably has done so since the first court painter was commissioned to paint the first king-conqueror. Fortifications, and all actions to bring them low, are a ready subject for the war artist, whose misrepresentation of what passed between defender and attacker may well have imposed a grave distortion on our understanding of defensive warfare in the pre-gunpowder age.

The subject of fortification may be left with these thoughts in mind: stoutly defended and well provisioned strongholds were difficult to take at all times before the gunpowder age; such strongholds were often as much instruments of defiance of central authority – or, a subject to be explored later, a means to overawe free citizens or cultivators – as components of a strategic defence; strategic defences, never easy to align with natural frontiers and always costly to build, maintain, provision and garrison, ultimately depend for their strength on the will and the capabilities of the power they were conceived to defend. 'They labour in vain who build' defences that are expected to stand by themselves.

—3—
Flesh

FEW FORTIFICATIONS YET STOOD when charioteers first drove forth to topple thrones and found dynasties of their own. Such as did exist offered little obstacle to their conquests. About 1700 BC a Semitic people, known to us as the Hyskos, began to infiltrate Egypt through the Nile delta and soon set up a capital of their own at Memphis. A little later, Mesopotamia, then united under the Amorite dynasty founded by Hammurabi about 1700 BC, was overrun by people from the northern mountains between modern Iraq and Iran; they appear to have made themselves overlords of the ancient inter-riverine kingdom by 1525 BC. Shortly afterward Aryan charioteers from the steppe lands of eastern Iran, speaking an Indo-European language, entered the Indus valley and utterly destroyed its civilisation. Finally, about 1400 BC, the founders of the Shang dynasty, perhaps also originating from the Iranian steppe, arrived with their chariots in northern China and set up the first centralised state, based on a superior military technology and the institution of the walled camp.

The adoption of the war chariot and the imposition of the power of war charioteers throughout the centres of Eurasian civilisation in the space of some 300 years is one of the most extraordinary episodes in world history. How did it come about? It depended on many developments – in metallurgy, woodworking, tanning and leatherworking, and the use of glues, bone and sinew – but above all on the domestication and improvement in physique of the wild horse. Even today, when mankind everywhere expects to travel by internal combustion engine, horseflesh engages passions and mobilises money on a vast and universal scale. The richest men in the world compete to display their wealth through the ownership of thoroughbred horses. Horseracing is 'the sport of kings', on which republican multimillionaires rejoice to expend fortunes; but few kings or millionaires ever risk as much of what they have as the common man who believes he knows a winner. In the world of the horse the poorest feel themselves the potential equals of the wealthiest in the land because, as the saying goes, 'animals can make fools of us all'. The

155

horse, however pampered, whatever its bloodlines, may choose to repay an owner's expectations in hypochondria or ill-will; contrarily, an unknown horse may stay the course against all odds, make its rider, trainer, breeder and owner men of stature overnight, bring joy to the hearts of a thousand humble punters and send bookmakers home with lighter pockets than they set out with. The modern thoroughbred is a force to be reckoned with, and the great thoroughbred may end his days more famous than most statesmen of his lifetime. The greatest of thoroughbreds acquire regal and dynastic status: pilgrimages are made simply to see them run, while the descent of their genes into subsequent generations is catalogued with all the care taken to establish the legitimacy of a Bourbon or Habsburg. A great horse, in a sense, becomes a king. It is not surprising that kings were made by the first great horses.

THE CHARIOTEERS

The horse that *homo sapiens* first knew was a poor thing; so poor, indeed, that man hunted it for food. *Equus*, the ancestor of *equus caballus*, our modern horse, was actually hunted out of existence in the Americas by the Amerindians who crossed into the New World at the end of the last ice age. In the Old World the return of the forests after the end of the ice age drove *equus caballus* out of Europe on to the treeless steppe, where it was first hunted and then domesticated for its flesh. In the settlements of the so-called Srednij Stog culture on the River Dnieper, above the Black Sea, the bones of apparently domesticated horses form a majority among those excavated from village sites dated to the fourth millennium BC.[1] Stone Age man chose to eat the horse rather than drive or ride it, because the animal they knew was almost certainly not strong enough in the back to bear an adult male human, while men themselves had not yet designed a vehicle to which a draught animal might be harnessed. The relationship between man and the equine species is, in any case, extremely complex. Unlike the dog, which, though a pack animal, appears to associate itself as an individual quite easily with a human individual, and may have begun to do so about 12,000 years ago, the horse has to be cut out of a herd and tamed if a useful 'mutualism' is to arise between it and its human master.

There was no reason, moreover, why Stone Age man should have identified the horse as potentially more useful to him than its equine cousins – the widespread donkey or ass, the hemione of Mongolia and Turkestan, the kiang of the Tibetan plateau, the khur of western India or the onager of Mesopotamia and Turkey – which we now know lack, for genetic reasons, the potentiality for selective breeding to larger, stronger or faster varieties. The early *equus caballus* outwardly resembled the still-existent *equus przewalskii* (Przewalski's horse) and the *equus gmelini*, the tarpan which survived on the steppe until the last century; all in turn resembled the asses, hemiones and onagers, in colour, size and shape. Genetic analysis now tells us that *equus caballus*, with 64 chromosomes, is a different beast from Przewalski's, with 66, from the donkey, with 62, and from the hemiones, with 56; to Stone Age man, however, there can have been little to choose between them.[2] *Caballus*, in particular, with its short legs, thick neck, pot-belly, convex face and stiff mane must have defied distinction from the tarpan, which apparently resisted before its extinction all efforts to refine its appearance or performance.

Man seems to have approached neither driving nor riding through the horse or its allied equids at all, but via the cow and perhaps the reindeer. Cultivators in the fourth millennium BC discovered that castrating the male domesticated cow, to produce the ox, gave them a tractable animal that could be harnessed to a simple plough such as men themselves pulled; the attachment of such draught animals to a sledge, in treeless environments like the steppe and the alluvial plains, was a natural development. Mounting the sledge on captive rollers then followed, and from the captive roller the wheel, rotating on a fixed axle as the potter's already did, must have evolved quite simply.[3] A set of pictographs from the Sumerian city of Uruk, dated to the fourth millennium BC, shows the progression from the sledge to the sledge-on-wheels in a fairly direct line. A famous representation known as the Standard of Ur, of the third millennium BC, shows a four-wheeled cart drawn by four onagers as a vehicle for a king and a platform for his weapons – axe, sword and spear – on the battlefield. This cart, with its two-piece wooden wheels, descends from the solid-wheeled prototype, and we may suppose that the Sumerians had recognised the onagers as superior draught-animals – faster and more spirited than oxen.

As anyone who has kept a donkey as a childhood pet knows, however – and the onager is only a slightly larger and leggier donkey – this lovable animal has severe drawbacks. Its stubbornness can outlast that of its master; it has a very high pain threshold and therefore easily resists whip, spur and bit; it can carry weight only over its hindquarters and cannot therefore be ridden from the forward, 'control' position; it has only two gaits – the walk and the run – the first being slower than an even human pace, the latter tending to breakneck speed. These characteristics, which no amount of selective breeding succeeds in altering, relegate the ass, with the hemione half-asses, to a menial role. As a beast of burden both its range and load-carrying capacity are limited; as a mount it is an animal of last choice.

It is therefore not surprising that, about the beginning of the second millennium BC, the domesticated horse should have begun to have its role transformed from that of meat-giver to load-puller. Even the small horses of the wild vary in size, and while small mares of the Stone Age stood less than twelve hands at the shoulders (a hand is four inches), the larger stallions could exceed fifteen hands.[4] Herdsmen had already learnt the rudiments of selective breeding through their management of sheep, goats and cows; to apply it to the horse was a natural step. It may not, however, have had the immediate effects expected from it. The first strains of selectively bred animals tend to diminish in size, which in the case of the horse would reduce its suitability for riding and even more so its tractive power.[5] There was, moreover, a new difficulty in using the tractive power of the horse. The donkey, though its tractive power is low, is fairly easily controlled by reins to a nose band and sensibly will not pull any more heavily against neck harness than it finds comfortable; the placid ox needs only the touch of a whip to set it in forward motion, which is easily transferred to a cart through a yoke shaped to fit its prominent shoulders. But the much more spirited horse can be controlled only by fitting its mouth with a bit – and over the proper design of the bit horsemen continue to debate to this day; its narrow shoulders slip through a yoke while a neck band constricts its windpipe. Man would very slowly discover that the correct method of harnessing a horse for traction is either with a breast band – attributed to the Chinese – or by a padded collar encircling its whole neck. Until he did so, his methods of controlling and harnessing the horse actually worked against each other: constricting its mouth, to guide it but also to vary its pace, threw it against its neck band which, by tending to choke it, slowed it down.

The harnessed horse was therefore unsuitable as a draught-animal both for the heavy waggons and the deep-furrowing plough that began to appear in Europe in the second millennium BC.[6] That meant that the vehicle to which it was harnessed should be made as light as possible. The result was the chariot. The historian Stuart Piggott, in an arresting and highly convincing reference to what appears to be a timeless and universal psychology of transport – that the fast and dashing vehicle confers on its possessor social prestige and undoubtedly also sexual allure, as well as material advantages and physical thrills – has suggested that a light chariot with two spoked wheels appeared suddenly and almost

simultaneously throughout a 'technological *koine*' which embraced all the
lands of civilisation from Egypt to Mesopotamia.

> The new factor involved was speed provided by a new motive force, which
> in the instance of the small horses of antiquity could only be exploited by a
> combination of lightness and resilience of a new kind. To adopt a concept
> from structural engineering, the disc-wheeled ox-wagon might be seen as a
> slow, heavy, timber-built compression structure, and the chariot as a fast, light
> wood structure, largely in tension with its bent-wood felloes [tyre segments] and
> frame.

As Piggott points out, the appearance of such a chariot cannot have
failed to be revolutionary, if only psychologically: 'speed for human
transport on land was suddenly multiplied by something like 10 – from
the [2 miles] an hour for ox-transport to the [20 miles] an hour reached
with ease with a modern representation of an ancient Egyptian chariot
with a pair of ponies, the chariot itself with its harness weighing only [75
lbs].' (It is worth remembering in this context that only two centuries ago
Dr Johnson, who thought driving in a carriage with a pretty woman the
best of pleasures, gave it as his opinion that the human frame could not
sustain a speed of motion of more than twenty-five miles an hour.)

The effect of the chariot was not, however, merely psychological.
It led to the emergence of a chariot-warrior group, skilled fighters who
monopolised the use of their specialised and extremely expensive vehicles,
together with complementary weapons, such as the composite bow, and
who dominated an entourage of secondary specialists – grooms, saddlers,
wheelwrights, joiners, fletchers – essential to keeping war chariots and
horses on the road.

Whence came these charioteers? Clearly not from the still-forested
lands of western Europe, even though pockets of wild horses may have
survived there; its forests formed an obstacle that delayed the arrival of
chariot aristocrats for at least 500 years. Nor again from the alluvial plains
of the great rivers, since there the horse did not roam. The steppe – dry,
treeless and offering good going in all directions – was unquestionably the
main home of the wild horse but, though highly suitable for the passage of
wheeled vehicles at all periods outside the spring and autumn *rasputitsa*, it
is so deficient in the metals and woods necessary for chariot construction
that it too may be discounted as the place of origin. By a process of
elimination, therefore, the proposition that chariots and charioteers first
appeared in the borderlands between the steppe and the civilised river
lands seems convincing.

The historian William McNeill, following the generally accepted view that a warlike 'battleaxe' folk, speaking Indo-European languages, migrated from the western steppe to dominate the 'peaceful megalith builders of the Atlantic coast' in the second millennium BC, goes on to argue that the metalworkers who sold them the high-priced and mystic skills that gave them dominance over Europe's Stone Age peoples also migrated, but in the opposite direction, from Mesopotamia to the edge of the steppe in northern Iran.

> From the fourth millennium BC, agricultural communities had clustered on the better-watered patches of this plateau; and agriculture probably increased in importance there during the second millennium. On the grasslands around and between these agricultural settlements lived barbarian pastoralists, linguistically akin to the warriors of the western steppe. Through the mediation of agricultural communities in their midst, these pastoralists became increasingly exposed to influences radiating from the distant Mesopotamian culture centre. In this setting, not long before 1700 BC, a critically important fusion of civilised technique with barbarian prowess seems to have occurred.[7]

This was the invention, or perfection, of the chariot.

Why should charioteers, or the pastoralists from whom they directly or indirectly descended, have been more warlike than their hunting ancestors or agricultural neighbours? The answer requires a consideration of factors not for the squeamish, all having to do with how man has killed – or not killed – fellow mammals. It may be taken for granted that the adoption of agriculture reduced the proportion of meat in the human diet; not only is it known that a switch to cereal production always reduces protein intake, as cultivators devote land to crops rather than grazing; it is also a widely observable fact that cultivators seek to prolong the lives of their domesticated animals – so as to maximise their milk yields, carcass weights or muscular power – rather than cull them for food as soon as they reach maturity. As a result, the farmer lacks skills both as a butcher of slaughtered meat and as a killer of young, nimble animals likely to evade his lethal intentions. Primitive hunters, though no doubt excellent butchers, were probably no more skilled in the techniques of the kill; their preoccupations were rather with tracking and cornering their prey than with the precise method by which they struck the fatal blow.

Pastoralists, on the other hand, learn to kill, and to select for killing, as a matter of course. They must be quite unsentimental about their sheep and goats, which are to them no more than food on the hoof: milk, and its derivatives, including butter, curds, whey, yoghurt, fermented drinks and cheese, but chiefly meat and perhaps blood. It is not certain whether the steppe nomads of antiquity siphoned blood from their animals, as East African cattle-herders do, but it seems possible; they certainly killed the annual crop of young animals and the older breeding-stock, together with injured, deformed or ailing individuals, on a rotational basis. Such a programme of killing demanded an ability to dispatch a living creature with the minimum of damage to the carcass and its valuable contents, and with the minimum of disturbance to others in the flock. Dealing the lethal blow, once, quickly and neatly, was a principal pastoral skill, heightened no doubt by anatomical knowledge gained in regular butchery; the need to castrate most of the males in the flock taught another lesson in cutting flesh, as also did lambing and the rough veterinary surgery of flock management.

It was flock management, as much as slaughter and butchery, which made the pastoralists so cold-bloodedly adept at confronting the sedentary agriculturalists of the civilised lands in battle. Battle between the two, therefore, may have been not much different from the tentative and procrastinating encounters of the Yanomamö and the Maring, perhaps formalised with ceremonial elements. Even if there were a specialist warrior class, this supposition is not invalidated; lack of armour and truly lethal weaponry speaks for the persistence of 'primitive' habits of combat in the Nile kingdom, too, and the Sumerians' equipment was not much advanced over theirs. In such technological circumstances, battle formations were likely to have been loose, discipline weak and battlefield behaviour crowd- or herdlike. Working a herd, however, was the pastoralists' stock in trade. They knew how to break a flock up into manageable sections, how to cut off a line of retreat by circling to a flank, how to compress scattered beasts into a compact mass, how to isolate flock-leaders, how to dominate superior numbers by threat and menace, how to kill the chosen few while leaving the mass inert and subject to control.

All pastoralists' methods of battle as described at later dates in history disclose just such a pattern. We must make an allowance for the fact that the Huns, Turks and Mongols known to European and Chinese writers had graduated from the chariot to the riding-horse, which made their tactics even more effective; the essentials, nevertheless, must have remained constant. These people, the writers say, did not form lines of battle or commit themselves irrevocably to attack. Instead they approached their enemy in a loose crescent formation, which threatened less mobile opponents with encirclement around the flanks. If strongly resisted at any point, they would stage a withdrawal, the object of which was to draw the enemy into an ill-judged pursuit that would break his ranks. They closed to hand strokes only when the battle was clearly going in their favour, and when they did so they inflicted wounds with superlative edged weapons which often decapitated or dismembered; they thought so little of the quality of enemy steel that they disdained to wear any but the most exiguous armour themselves. To turn the battle in their favour, they harried and intimidated the enemy with volleys of arrows shot at long range with their terrifyingly superior arm of choice, the composite bow. Ammianus Marcellinus wrote of the Huns in the fourth century AD, 'In battle they swoop upon the enemy, uttering frightful yells. When opposed they disperse, only to return with the same speed, smashing and overturning everything in their path . . . there is nothing to equal the skill with which – from prodigious distances – they discharge their arrows, which are tipped with sharpened bones as hard and murderous as iron.'[8]

Scholars dispute how to date the appearance of the composite bow; it may have been in use as early as the third millennium BC, if a Sumerian stele has been correctly interpreted; it was certainly in existence by the second, since its distinctive ogival or 'recurved' shaped – familiar to us as the 'Cupid's bow' whose arrows transfix Watteau's and Boucher's lovelorn courtiers – is clearly depicted in a golden bowl of 1400 BC, now in the Louvre.[9] It cannot have appeared overnight, for the complexity of its construction, like that of the chariot, speaks of a variety of prototypes, and decades, if not centuries, of experimentation. In its finished form, which did not vary between its perfection in the second millennium BC and its supersession as a weapon of war in the nineteenth century AD (it was last used by Manchu bannermen), it consisted of a slender strip of wood – or a laminate of more than one – to which were glued on the outer side ('back') lengths of elastic animal tendon and on the inner side ('belly') strips of compressible animal horn, usually that of the bison. The glues, compounded of boiled-down cattle tendons and skin mixed with smaller amounts reduced from the bones and skin of fish, might take 'more than a year to dry and had to be applied under precisely controlled conditions of temperature and humidity . . . a great deal of art was involved in their preparation and application, much of it characterised by a mystical, semi-religious approach'.[10]

The composite bow began as five pieces of plain or laminated wood – a central grip, two arms and two tips. Once glued together, this timber 'skeleton' was then steamed into a curve, opposite to that it would

162

assume when strung, and steamed strips of horn were glued to the 'belly'. It was then bent into a complete circle, again against its strung shape, and tendons were glued to its 'back'. It was then left to 'cure' and only when all its elements had indissolubly married was it untied and strung for the first time. Stringing a composite bow, against its natural relaxed shape, required both great strength and dexterity; its 'weight', conventionally measured in 'pounds', might amount to 150, against only a few for a simple or 'self' bow made from a length of sapling.

Similar 'weights' characterised the long bow, when toward the end of the Middle Ages west European bowyers learnt to use a billet containing both heart and sap wood to fashion their weapons; it worked by the same principle of opposing the forces of elasticity and compressibility, stored by the archer's arm when he bent the bow, and released by his fingers, to drive an arrow forward. The disadvantage of the long bow, however, was precisely its length; it could only be used by an archer on foot. The composite bow was short, reaching only from the top of a man's head to his waist when strung, and therefore suiting itself perfectly to use from a chariot or horse. It shot a lighter arrow – the best weight was about an ounce – than the long bow would, but could still carry to 300 yards with great accuracy (far longer ranges in free flight have been recorded) and penetrate armour at a hundred yards. The lightness of the arrow was actually an advantage, since it allowed the pastoral warrior to carry a large number – up to fifty in his quiver – into battle, which he counted on winning by subjecting the enemy to a disabling hail of missiles.

The simple accoutrements belonging to a chariot or mounted archer did not vary for more than 3000 years. The essentials were the bow itself, the arrow and the thumb ring, which protected his skin from flaying at the moment of the arrow's release; important accessories were the quiver and the bow case, which shielded weapons not in use from variations in temperature and humidity (both degraded the weapon's range and accuracy). This equipment can be seen in some of the earliest depictions of composite-bow archers; exactly the same objects are displayed as principal parts of the regalia of the Ottoman sultans of the eighteenth century AD in the Topkapi Palace in Istanbul today.[11] Many other items also did not vary in the horse world – including tents, floor coverings, cooking-vessels, clothing and the nomads' simple pieces of furniture. The pastoralists stored their possessions in chests, which could be slung in pairs athwart a pack animal, and used round-bottomed pans and kettles, which could be bundled into nets; the kettle drum, on which the

Turks would beat the note of battle, was no more than a nomad's camp cauldron with skin stretched across its mouth.

Quite as much as the charioteers' equipment and their familiarity with animals, their ability to move and readiness to do so fitted them for aggressive warmaking. All war requires movement, but for settled peoples even short-range moves impose difficulties. Their gear is clumsy and heavy; they lack readily mobilisable means of transport, particularly draught-animals – which are needed in the fields; and food both for man and beast comes in an awkward and bulky form. Settled people expect to sleep with a roof over their heads, but do not possess tents; they take shelter when the weather turns inclement, lack weather-proof clothes, and relish regular, cooked meals. The farmer is hardier than the artisan – the Greeks thought it was *ponos*, agricultural toil, that fitted the tiller of the soil alone to be a warrior – but even he is soft by comparison with the nomad.[12] The nomad is constantly on the move, eats and drinks when he can, braves all weathers, is grateful for small mercies. Everything he possesses can be bundled up at a moment's notice and his food moves with him, as grass and water call his flocks, whenever he shifts camp. Even the nomads most favoured by circumstances, those whom regular availability of summer and winter grazing at fixed locations allows to practise transhumance, are tougher by far than the settled farmer. The ancient nomads of the arid steppe, where tribe had to compete against tribe for what scraps of grazing there were, must have been among the toughest people in creation.

The American sinologist Owen Lattimore crossed the 1700 miles of arid zone between India and China in 1926–7 – following part of the route which those who brought their chariots to China in the second millennium BC may have taken, oasis by oasis, over several generations. The caravan men among whom he travelled, he recalled,

> become nomads. Many of their propitiatory rites and self-defensive tabus are not only taken over from the Mongols, but from the most primitive instincts of nomadic people. They strive to propitiate the powers and spirits that follow at the heels and lurk about the tents of savage, wandering people at grips day and night with the harsh menace and niggardly resources of a raw, unmastered country. From the moment that the tent is pitched at the first camp . . . fire and water assume a different importance. Each time that the tent has been set up in a new place, a little of the first water boiled and the first food cooked must be thrown out of the door.

This was always done even though the food and water available to the caravan men was grossly unpalatable.

164

We began the day at dawn by making tea . . . of the coarsest grade of twigs, leaves and tea-sweepings . . . In this tea we used to mix either roasted oaten flour or roasted millet – looking like canary seed, which in fact it was – stirring it into a thin slush and drinking it down. About noon we had the one real feed of the day. This would be made of half-cooked dough. We carried the white flour along with us, and would make the same sort of dough every day. We would moisten the flour, roll it and thump it, and then tear it up into little blobs or cut it into a rough kind of spaghetti . . . The reason we drank so much tea was because of the bad water. Water alone, unboiled, is never drunk . . . Our water everywhere was from wells, all of them more or less heavily tainted with salt, soda and, I suppose, a number of mineral salts. At times it was almost too salt to drink, at other times very bitter. The worst water . . . is thick, almost sticky and incredibly bitter and nasty.[13]

Lattimore's nomads probably differed in their habits from those of the second millennium in using tea and flour; in other respects there can have been little to choose between their ways of life, characterised in both cases by its subjection to natural forces, unpredictability and extreme harshness. Anything that alleviated that harshness must have been welcome, and it is in that light that we should consider why – perhaps rather than how – the two extraordinary artefacts, the chariot and the composite bow, appear to have originated in the borderlands where civilisation touched the nomadic world.

The elements of the chariot – wheels, chassis, draughtpole and their metal fittings – were 'civilised' in origin, in that they derived from clumsier prototypes developed for work in farming and building. Archaeologists continue to disagree about who then refined the elements into the light, cross-country chariot itself, but they do not address the question of what the chariot was for.[14] That may be clarified if we ask how the chariot was used: for war, of course, but also for hunting. It could be driven across rough ground, and it was used as a platform for huntsmen to shoot game with the composite bow, as much pictorial evidence from many Egyptian and Mesopotamian sources attests; Chinese poetry of the Chou dynasty also makes it clear that the chariot was a hunting-vehicle.[15]

That being so, we may perhaps suggest that the chariot and the composite bow appeared together because they served a crucial need of the nomad pastoralist: to give him a means of herding his flocks at a pace faster than his feet could carry him, and also to put him on near, if not equal, terms of mobility with the predators, wolf and perhaps bear and the large cats also, that harried their flanks. It would certainly have made an excellent platform for the composite bowman out after wolf, who would have found accurate shooting at moving targets no more difficult, perhaps easier, than the horseman was later to do from the saddle. Settled people were later to marvel at the horseman's ability to drop his reins and pick off a victim with an arrow without checking pace. John Guilmartin ascribes it to '[the infinity] of time the steppe nomad . . . spent herding and guarding livestock, which kept him in the saddle but not otherwise occupied . . . unless by constant archery practice . . . In view of the number of targets – human and animal, edible and otherwise – which the steppe presented, constant practice made economic sense.'[16] If we substitute 'chariot' for 'saddle' in that passage, the sense remains the same and the argument quite as convincing.

Toward the middle of the second millennium BC, the peoples who had learnt the skills of making and using chariots and composite bows discovered – by what means we cannot surmise – that the defenders of the settled lands could not stand against the aggressive methods they had initially devised to oppose the predators that attacked their flocks. Charioteers who descended from the highlands to the open and level plains were able to inflict crippling casualties on the Mesopotamians and Egyptians with impunity. Circling at a distance of 100 or 200 yards from the herds of unarmoured foot soldiers, a chariot crew – one to drive, one to shoot – might have transfixed six men a minute. Ten minutes' work by ten chariots would cause 500 casualties or more, a Battle of the Somme-like toll among the small armies of the period. In the face of such an attack by an enemy against which it could not manoeuvre out of trouble, the stricken host had only two choices: to break and run or to surrender. In either case, the outcome for the charioteers would have been a large booty in prisoners, probably rapidly destined to become chattel slaves.

It is widely suggested that the first interpenetrations of steppe and civilised societies were brought about by long-range traders, who carried cloth, trinkets and worked metal to exchange for the objects of value that the barbarian world yielded, including furs, tin – and slaves. No one knows how slave-trading began. It would have come naturally to pastoralists used to herding four-footed animals, particularly if foreigners adopted the habit of taking their goods to sites at which the herdsmen gathered for seasonal festivals, which, as Lattimore noted, 'tend to become the scenes of fairs', and such fairs may have been the first slave markets.[17] If the pastoralists had learned to accumulate and convoy slaves for sale on the steppe, one may suppose that when they eventually descended from the highlands on campaigns of conquest, they were attuned to slave-taking and slave management and well prepared to impose their authority over the people they conquered through an intermediate stratum of slaves attached to themselves.

That would be one explanation of how quite small groups of aggressive intruders not only overthrew but for a time sustained power among peoples who greatly outnumbered them. That the chariot rulers were also slave-masters appears indisputable. Of course, slavery was known in pre-chariot Mesopotamia and Egypt, but its practice, particularly on a trade basis, may have been intensified there by the arrival of the chariot conquerors, while its transmission into Europe may have derived from the migration of the Mycenaeans from Asia Minor, who did not bring the chariot with them but acquired it about the middle of the second millennium BC, at the time when it suddenly came to dominate warmaking in the Middle East.[18] Slavery in China is dated to the arrival of the Shang dynasty, while, according to the Rig-Veda, the chariot conquerors of the Indus valley made slavery the basis of what would later become caste.

The rapid dispersion of the chariot ought not to surprise us. Indeed, there may have been a chariot industry and chariot market – akin to the high-technology arms industry and market that has equipped new Third World states with what are called 'state of the art' arms in our own time, light, easily transportable and judged by the purchaser worth every unit of hard currency expended to buy them. Once perfected, the technology of the chariot would have been easy to replicate and even easier to transport and sell; an Egyptian bas-relief of *c.* 1170 BC shows a chariot being carried on the shoulders of one man – no feat if it weighed, as a reconstruction did, less than a hundred pounds – and such a highly marketable product would have stimulated production wherever craftsmen with the necessary skills resided. The check on overproduction of such a saleable and high-priced item would have been, in practice, not shortages of skills or raw material but a dearth of suitable horses. The chariot horse had to be a selected and highly schooled animal. The earliest known schooling of horses, apparently to dressage standard if an elaborate contemporary vocabulary of horsemastership is a reliable indication, can be dated from a group of Mesopotamian texts to the thirteenth and twelfth centuries BC; then as now, the young horse was intransigent in any language spoken to it.[19]

Language supplies one clue as to who the first conquering charioteers may have been. The Hyskos who invaded Egypt originated on the semi-fertile northern fringe of the Arabian desert and spoke a Semitic language.[20] The Hurrians and Kassites who divided and overthrew Hammurabi's Mesopotamian empire came from the mountainous headwaters of the Tigris and Euphrates, still ethnically one of the most complex regions in the world; the Kassites spoke an unidentified tongue, classified as 'Asianic', while the Hurrians – and the Hittites who established an empire in what today is Turkey – spoke Indo-European languages. So, too, did the Aryan invaders of India, and it is possible that the charioteers who founded the Shang dynasty in China may have made their way thither from northern Iran also – though perhaps from some proto-Iranian heartland in the Altai.[21]

The obscure identity of the chariot rulers is an indication of their chief characteristic: they were destroyers rather than creators and, in so far as they civilised themselves, it was through the adoption of the manners, institutions and cults of their subjects rather than by developing any culture of their own. Within Mesopotamia the empire of Hammurabi, which had emerged from a time of troubles brought by border peoples known as the Gutians and the Elamites, succeeded in re-establishing the authority once exerted by Sargon, in rebuilding a bureaucracy and a professional army akin to his and in ruling from Babylon. The army of this Amorite empire, however, remained an infantry force which was no match for the charioteering Kassites and Hurrians when they broke through the frontiers in the seventeenth century BC. The Hyskos invaders of Egypt, though they became effective rulers of northern Egypt, did so only by Egyptianising themselves, taking an Egyptian deity as their state god and adopting pharaonic administrative practice. The Shang, too, seem to have taken over a pre-existing culture in northern China, rather than to have brought one of their own. Inscriptions reveal that they were hunters from the chariot, killing game as big as the tiger and the horned ox with the composite bow, and that they practised human sacrifice, probably of slaves though perhaps also of prisoners of war. Grave goods found in excavation indicate that they monopolised the use of bronze, while the cultivators who were their subjects continued to use stone tools. Eventually the Shang were overthrown in 1050–25 BC by a native southern dynasty, the Chou, which had learnt the use of the horse and the chariot from another source.

The tyranny of the charioteers was everywhere short-lived. The Aryan rulers of the Indus civilisation seem to have been the only charioteer invaders not overthrown from within; some scholars, however, regard the appearance of Buddhism and Jainism as a native reaction against the tyranny of caste that the Aryans had introduced. The Hyskos were cast out of Egypt by a revival of pharaonic power under Amosis, founder of the New Kingdom, about 1567 BC. Other charioteers, the Hittites of Anatolia – modern Turkey – and the Mycenaeans of modern Greece, who were perhaps responsible for the destruction of Minoan civilisation in Crete and may have inspired Homer's story of the Trojan War, were both toppled by peoples from northern Greece, Phrygians and Dorians, about 1200 BC. Most significant of all, however, the native Mesopotamians, under the kingship of Ashuruballit, concluded about 1365 BC a protracted campaign against their Hurrian overlords and re-established their ancient kingdom, known to us from its capital city of Assur as Assyria.

Our image of the Assyrians, derived from their magnificent royal art excavated at Nineveh and Nimrud, is of a charioteering race. So, indeed, their kings and nobles were and the pharaohs of the New Kingdom became. Their ancestors, however, had not been. It is this transformation of the role of kings in the civilised world that we must regard as the most significant, lasting and baleful effect of warrior domination of the ancient theocratic states. The Egyptians of the Old and Middle Kingdoms had scarcely been warriors at all; even Sargon's standing army was a bumbling and ineffective organisation by comparison with its Assyrian successor. To the Assyrians and Egyptians the chariot peoples taught both the techniques and ethos of imperial warmaking, and each within its own orbit became an imperial power. The impulse that drove the pharaohs of the New Kingdom to expel the Hyskos carried their armies in the years that followed to plant Egypt's frontiers far from the Nile, in the uplands of northern Syria. After the expulsion of the Hurrians, the Assyrians solved the besetting problem of Mesopotamian civilisation – the encirclement of its rich but naturally defenceless land by predators – by going over to the offensive, and progressively extending the boundaries of what became the first ethnically eclectic empire to include parts of what today are Arabia, Iran and Turkey, together with the whole of modern Syria and Israel. Thus the legacy of the chariot was the warmaking state. The chariot itself was to be the nucleus of the campaigning army.

THE CHARIOT AND ASSYRIA

At the height of its powers, say in the eighth century BC, the Assyrian army revealed features on which many of those of successor armies in other empires were to be modelled; some of them have come down to our own day. Foremost among them were its logistic arrangements: supply depots, transport columns, bridging-trains. The Assyrian was the first true long-range army, able to campaign as far as 300 miles from base and to move at speeds of advance that would not be exceeded until the coming of the internal combustion engine.

Assyrian resources did not extend to the paving of roads – of little point, in any case, in a climate which is excessively dry but, when wet, washes away untarred road metal – but the kingdom had an extensive network of royal highways, often mentioned as boundaries to fields in the land registration documents that cuneiform scribes wrote in vast numbers on the clay tablets which provide archaeologists with their information.[22] Along these roads the horsed elements of an army might move as fast as thirty miles a day – a good march even for a modern force. Of course, the roads deteriorated in quality beyond the central plain and inside enemy territory, where military engineers would have to improve the going up hillsides and through mountain passes. The army also made use of water transport where appropriate, though both the Tigris and Euphrates are difficult to navigate, because of shoals and uneven seasonal water-flows. In the early seventh century, Sennacherib brought Syrian shipbuilders to construct ships at Nineveh for a campaign against the Elamites, in what is now southern Iran. He apparently wanted sea-going craft, as used in the Mediterranean, which were beyond the skills of the riverside boat-builders of Mesopotamia. Once launched, they were sailed by Phoenician seamen as far down the Tigris as it was navigable, manhandled to a canal leading

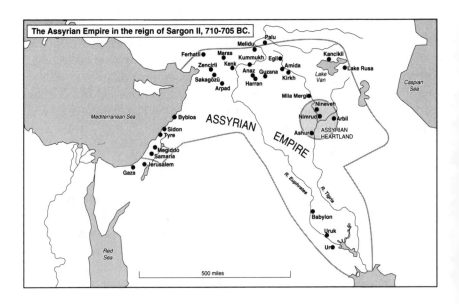

to the Euphrates and then sailed into the Persian Gulf, where they loaded troops and horses for a landing in Elamite territory.[23]

Stores, war material of all sorts, chariots and horses were held at central depots, called the *ekal masharti*, 'palace of the place for marshalling forces'. That at Nineveh was described by Esarhaddon in the seventh century BC as made by 'the kings who preceded me . . . to provide proper arrangements for the camp, to look after the steeds, the mules, the chariots, the battle equipment and enemy booty'; it had 'become too small for horse training and chariot exercises'. It is not known how much prepared food the army took with it on the warpath; the Assyrians seem to have expected largely to live off the country in enemy territory.[24] In his campaign against the powerful northern state of Urartu in 714 BC, Sargon II records that he sent to one captured fortress 'corn, oil and wine' but his son Sennacherib, when fighting the Chaldaeans in southern Mesopotamia in 703 'let [the] troops eat up the grain and dates in their palm groves, and their harvest in the plain'. Laying waste the enemy's land, after the army had eaten its fill and taken what it could carry, was then as later a standard practice. In his final campaign against Urartu, Sargon destroyed irrigation systems, broke open granaries and cut down fruit trees.

Sargon's ire may have been aroused by the difficulty of the campaign: his troops 'had crossed and re-crossed mountains innumerable' and had 'turned mutinous. I could give no ease to their weariness, no water to quench their thirst.' He was campaigning north of the Zagros range, in the broken lands between Lakes Van and Urmia, a region still regarded today as almost impenetrable by formed units. It was in such difficult country that the Assyrian engineering arm came into its own. Sargon recorded that during the Urartu campaign 'I equipped my sappers with strong copper [probably bronze] picks, and they shivered the crags of steep mountains to fragments as though limestone, and made a good way'. The army was even better at negotiating waterways: Ashur-nasir-pal, campaigning against the always troublesome southern power of Babylon centuries before, 'crossed the Euphrates at the town of Haridi . . . by means of the boats I had made – boats of skins that had moved along the roads with me'. These skin boats, used in Iraq into modern times, may have been one-man inflated sheepskins or, more probably, *kelek* rafts, a wooden platform supported by a number of such skins. The army also made use of reed boats, still in use by the Marsh Arabs who live in the confluence of the Tigris and Euphrates. Assyrian bas-relief representations show disassembled chariots being conveyed in them across waterways.

Assyrian military organisation also foreshadowed that of later imperial armies. For one, Assyria appears to have been the first power to recruit troops without ethnic discrimination. Ruthless in its population policy – it resettled dissidents far from their homelands in order to assure internal security, as the Ottomans and Stalin were later to do – it was at the same time quite prepared to integrate into the army both subject peoples and prisoners of war, as long as it was sure it could count on their loyalty. Language and a common religion were the adhesives: Assyria propagated a primitive monotheism, through the cult of Assur, and opened its official language to loan words from others, which it allowed to be used in tandem in the interests of intercomprehensibility. For another, subject peoples often entered the army, as Rome's were later to do, with their own distinctive weapons – slings or bows – and formed corps ancillary to the army's main fighting-force. They may also have provided the siege engineers, whom Assyrian artists portray attacking the foundations of walls, digging mineshafts, building siege-ramps or working siege-engines. The Syrians were great besiegers. Sennacherib described his siege of Hezekiah in Jerusalem – and it is recorded in the Old Testament, 2 Kings 18 – as follows: '[he did] not submit to my yoke. I besieged and captured forty-six of his strong walled towns with innumerable surrounding villages, by consolidating ramps to bring up battering rams, by infantry attacks, mines, breaches and siege engines . . . He himself I shut up inside Jerusalem, his royal city, like a caged bird.' Hezekiah, rather than face the consequences, capitulated and paid tribute.[25]

For all its imperial accretions, the Assyrian army remained at heart a charioteering force. Sennacherib, fighting the Elamites in 691 BC, had his court historiographer describe how he 'transfixed the troops of the enemy with javelins and arrows'.

> The commander-in-chief of the king of Elam, together with his nobles . . . I cut their throats like sheep . . . My prancing steeds, trained to harness, plunged into their welling blood as into a river; the wheels of my battle chariots were bespattered with blood and filth. I filled the plain with the corpses of their warriors like herbage . . . [There were] chariots with their horses, whose riders had been slain as they came into the fierce battle, so that they were loose by themselves; those horses kept going back and forth all over [the battlefield] . . . As to the sheikhs of the Chaldaeans [Elamite allies], panic from my onslaught overwhelmed them like a demon. They abandoned their tents and fled for their lives, crushing the corpses of their troops as they went . . . [In their terror] they passed scalding urine and voided their excrement in their chariots.[26]

This was a battle to the death, as the highly realistic details convey, brought only perhaps because the Elamites had positioned themselves so as to deny Sennacherib's army access to the Tigris and thus, as his scribe points out, to drinking-water also; as was to prove so often the case in the future, battle in these circumstances was a matter of necessity, not choice. Sargon's final battle against Urartu, however, had revealed a trace of chivalry: Rusa, the king, had sent a message to challenge the Assyrians to meet him.

Chariot grandees, like later cavaliers, thus may have already begun to reckon that quarrels between them were best settled by chivalric encounter, leaving the footmen and other hangers-on to form a rough line of battle in their rear, heap up the spoils if victory came, or suffer the consequences if it did not. Chinese charioteers of the Chou period were clearly infected by chivalry, as is recorded also in the succeeding Spring and Autumn period. In a battle between the rival states of Ch'u and Sung in 638 BC, the Duke of Sung's minister of war twice asked permission to attack the enemy before they had formed ranks, making the perfectly reasonable point that 'they are many but we are few'; he was refused. After the Sung had been defeated and the Duke wounded, he justified himself as follows: 'The gentleman does not inflict a second wound, or take the grey-haired prisoner . . . Though I am but the unworthy remnant of a fallen dynasty, I would not sound my drums to attack an enemy who had not completed the formation of his ranks.' Other practices deemed unchivalrous among Chinese chariot aristocrats were taking advantage of a fleeing enemy who was having trouble with his chariot (he might even be assisted), injuring a ruler, or attacking an enemy state when it was mourning a ruler or was divided by internal troubles.[27]

Exemplary behaviour between charioteers is typified by an incident from a later Sung war, when the then duke's son found himself opposite a warrior with an arrow already notched to his bow. He shot, missed and notched another arrow before the duke's son was ready to shoot. The duke's son then called out, 'If you don't give me my turn, you are a base fellow' (literally, not a gentleman). His opponent gave him his chance and was shot dead.[28]

These are the manners of the duel, or of the ceremonial encounter of champions, encounters that require arrangement. And arrangement seems to have been accepted in chariot warfare. Not only did Urartu challenge Assyria to fight; the Chinese of the Spring and Autumn period disdained those who launched surprise attacks while they themselves normally sent messengers to arrange a time and place for battle; they also asked for fields to be ploughed in such a way as to allow chariots easy movement, and there are repeated inscriptions about the need to fill in wells and cooking-pits before a battle so that the chariots should have free passage. Even in modern warfare battlefields need preparation if there is to be a test of arms, and there are legal prohibitions against, for example, laying unmarked minefields. In the ancient world, where logistic difficulties – the labour of getting an army into proximity with another, the near impossibility of keeping it fed in one place for more than a day or two – were paramount, it made sense to remove obstacles to the manoeuvre of the leading warriors' principal weapons. At Gaugamela, the battlefield near the Tigris where Alexander the Great defeated the Persians in 331 BC, his opponent Darius not only levelled the area thoroughly before the encounter but also built three 'runways' for his chariots. Alexander, it might be added, had earlier dismissed entreaties by his subordinates to make a night attack, on the grounds that if he lost it would mean obloquy but that, even if he won, victory would carry the taint of unfairness.

Chariot fighting was an activity nearly 1500 years old when Alexander – riding his legendary horse Bucephalus – defeated Darius. It was by then fading into obsolescence: only peoples at the margin of the civilised world – like the Britons who opposed the Roman invasion – continued to think it a useful way of making war. Despite all the years it had been practised, however, we lack any clear idea of its nature; historians of the ancient world differ sharply over how the chariot was used. Professor Creel, for example, thinks that it provided a 'mobile point of vantage' in Chinese battle and he quotes Professors Oppenheim, Wilson and Gertrude Smith to the effect that it was used in Egypt as a command post and in Mesopotamia and Greece as battlefield transport; Professor M.I. Finley, on the other hand, thinks that Homer's descriptions of the chariot as a 'taxi' to battle represented practice in Homer's time only, and that the heroes of the *Iliad* had fought otherwise.[29]

It would be odd if Finley were wrong. Court art may triumphalise; it may also perpetuate as symbolic the purely antique; it must not, of its nature, ridicule. Thus it was just possible, at a time when the idea and trappings of chivalry had come back into fashion, to depict the Prince Consort in armour without provoking Victorians to laughter; the representation of Hitler, mounted and armoured, was an absurdity.[30] Pharaohs, Assyrian kings and Persian emperors clearly did not think it absurd that they should be shown shooting the composite bow from a chariot. Their court artists may have exaggerated their masters' prominence in the battle line; but if it was as chariot archers that these great men wished to have themselves depicted, we must therefore infer that chariot archery was a dominant means of winning battle over a considerable period of time, from the first appearance of the chariot about 1700 BC to its supersession by horsed cavalry about a thousand years later.

It has already been suggested that the initial advantage of the chari-oteer lay in the suddenly and very greatly increased speed of movement he enjoyed on the battlefield, on the long-range lethality of his composite bow and on a cultural readiness to kill. All these advantages would have eroded with time. Familiarity with a novel weapons system ought not to breed contempt, but it does stimulate counter-measures. Those attacked by charioteers acquired chariots; non-charioteers learnt to target the horses of the enemy's chariots, to form chariot-proof ranks, to carry arrow-proof shields, to make use of broken ground on which charioteers could not manoeuvre. Nevertheless, while the great men of opposed armies reckoned charioteering glamorous, there must have been a complicity between friend and foe to see that battles were so fought that chariots got their chance. Ritualism or ceremonialism are, as we have seen, deep-rooted in man's conception of how combat should be conducted and are suppressed only by the necessities of battle to the death – not something that war is always about.

The first chariot battle of which we have an account, the battle of Megiddo in northern Palestine, fought in 1469 BC between the pharaoh Tuthmosis III and a confederation of Egypt's enemies under Hyskos leadership, was concluded with almost no bloodshed on either side. Megiddo is also generally counted as the first battle of history, in that we can date it, locate its site, identify the contestants and follow its course. Tuthmosis, who had just come to the throne, was pursuing the new Egyptian strategy of vigorous offensive against the outsiders who had violated the immunity of the river kingdom. Collecting an army, he marched in stages of ten or fifteen miles a day – an impressive speed of advance – along the Mediterranean coast, through Gaza and then up to the mountains on the Syrian border. The enemy seems to have counted on the difficult terrain forming a barrier against his attack. There were three routes through the mountains to the town of Megiddo; the pharaoh chose the most difficult, against advice, on the ground that he might thereby surprise them. The approach march took three days, the last spent negotiating a pass of less than two chariots' width. Late in the evening he camped on the plain in front of Megiddo and next morning deployed his army for battle. The enemy had also come forward, but, when they saw the extent of the Egyptian line, with one wing on each flank of the valley and the pharaoh commanding from his chariot in the centre, their morale collapsed and they fled in panic to the protection of the walls of Megiddo in their rear. Tuthmosis ordered a pursuit, but his soldiers stopped to plunder the enemy's abandoned camp on the way and two of the principals in the opposing army managed to get inside Megiddo. Since the city had an ample water supply within its massive walls, it managed to hold out against the Egyptians – who constructed a line of circumvallation around it against any relief operation – for seven months. Only eighty-three of the enemy had been killed in the battle and 340 taken prisoner; the fugitives, however, did not rally and the besieged kings eventually surrendered, sending their children out as hostages and begging the pharaoh that 'the Breath of Life be given to their nostrils'.[31]

The most valuable booty of the victory came in the form of horses, of which the Egyptians captured 2041; as they were perhaps still importers of bloodstock, such numbers would have been an important addition to their chariot arm. We have no indication of how many chariots were committed by either side at Megiddo. When, however, 200 years later in 1294 BC Rameses II defeated a Hittite army at Qadesh on the River Orontes in southern Syria – sustaining the New Kingdom's policy of aggressive warmaking at the far limit of strategic outreach from the Nile delta – the Egyptian army appears to have had fifty chariots and 5000 soldiers. It is said that the much larger Hittite army had 2500 chariots, which must be an exaggeration – its front of attack would have been 8000 yards wide – but an Egyptian bas-relief of the battle depicting fifty-two chariots indicates that the numbers committed were very considerable.[32]

There is some doubt whether the Hittites used the composite bow. Their chariot crews are usually represented as spearmen, which may explain why the Egyptians were able at Qadesh to extricate themselves from potential defeat. In any case, both at Megiddo and Qadesh chariot fighting had not yet reached the developed form it did at the height of Assyria's imperial power in the eighth century BC. Weapons systems take long periods to be assimilated, the more complex the longer, and the chariot system, which comprised not only the chariot itself, but also the composite bow, the horse, and all its trappings – all foreign to the lands where the chariot kings ruled – was a very complex system indeed. It is not surprising if both the Egyptians and the Hittites were as yet clumsy charioteers and that the system had to wait until comparatively late in the development of Assyrian battlecraft before it achieved its full potential. By then it may well have become, as the scribes of Sargon and Sennacherib describe, a weapon of shock and terror, manipulated by the driver to charge at breakneck speed behind a team of perfectly schooled horses and used by the archer as a platform from which to launch a hail of arrows; squadrons of chariots, their drivers trained to act in mutual support, might have clashed much as armoured vehicles have done in our time, success going to the side that could disable the larger opposing number, while the footmen unlucky or foolhardy enough to stand in their way would have been scattered like chaff.

THE WARHORSE

At the apogee of its effectiveness, the chariot was overtaken in importance by a single element in the chariot system, the horse itself. It has been suggested that the Assyrians themselves were responsible for this ironic revolution, which brought the downfall of their empire.

Horses had been ridden in the civilised world since the second millennium. Riding is represented in Egyptian art as early as 1350 BC and reliefs from the twelfth century show mounted soldiers, one of whom is taking part in the battle of Qadesh.[33] None, however, is a cavalryman. All ride bareback, without stirrups, and straddle the horse toward its rump, not a control position. That indicates, indeed, that the horses were not yet strong enough in the back to be ridden in the modern style. By the eighth century BC, however, selective breeding had produced a horse that Assyrians could ride from the forward seat, with their weight over the shoulders, and a sufficient mutuality had developed between steed and rider for the man to use a bow while in motion. Mutuality, or perhaps horsemanship, was not so far advanced, all the same, that riders were ready to release the reins: an Assyrian bas-relief shows cavalrymen working in pairs, one shooting his composite bow, the other holding the reins of both horses. This, as William McNeill observes, is really charioteering without the chariot.[34]

Out on the steppe, however, man may have been riding even earlier than in the civilised lands, and it is possible that the use of the bow from horseback bled back from the Assyrians across the steppe frontier and was taken up by peoples who were better advanced in horsemanship. We know that as late as the reign of Sargon II the supply of horses still ran from the steppe, where unbroken foals were caught yearly for training and then sale, to Assyria; it is not improbable that the skills of mounted archery went in the opposite direction.[35]

At any rate, the fall of the Assyrian empire was due to the irruption, at the end of the seventh century BC, of a horse people known to us as the Scythians, an Iranian race whose place of origin may have been as far away as the Altai mountains in eastern Central Asia. They appear to have ridden on the heels of another Iranian horse people called the Cimmerians, who raided into Asia Minor about 690 BC, leaving a shaken world behind them; the Assyrians themselves, at the moment of the Scythians' appearance, were hard pressed at the borders of their empire – to the north in Palestine, to the south by the allegedly vassal state of Babylon and to the east by the Medes of Iran. All these pressures might have been resisted, for Assyria had recovered from troubles before. In 612 BC, however, the Scythians joined the Medes and Babylonians in a siege of the great city of Nineveh, which they succeeded in taking. Two years later, despite help from Egypt, the last Assyrian king was again defeated by an alliance of Scythians and Babylonians at Harran and in 605 the power of Assyria passed to Babylon.

Babylonia's power shortly passed to Persia, the last of the great empires to arise in the heartland of civilisation, but Persian power was not rooted in any advanced military technique. It ultimately rested on the chariot: despite the recruitment of mercenary infantrymen and the training of Persian noblemen to fight as cavalry, it was as charioteers that the Persian emperors chose to go to battle and when the Persian emperor Darius met an enemy with revolutionary military means at his disposal, he was overcome. His empire passed to Alexander's successors, and a fragile form of the Alexandrian military system defended it for a century and more after his death. Along the 1500 miles of borderland that separates the steppe from settled land between the Himalayas and the Caucasus, however, neither charioteering nor Alexander's European tactics were appropriate once the horse peoples had learned that civilisation was vulnerable to their attack. Thus the first Scythians who made their raid into Mesopotamia at the end of the seventh century BC were harbingers of what was to be a repetitive cycle of raiding, despoliation, slave-taking, killing and, sometimes, conquest that was to afflict the outer edge of civilisation – in the Middle East, in India, in China and in Europe – for 2000 years. These persistent attacks on the outer edge of civilisation of course had profoundly transforming effects on its inner nature, to such an extent that we may regard the steppe nomads as one of the most significant – and baleful – forces in military history. The innocent agents of the harm they were to do were the descendants of the little, rough-coated ponies which man had been breeding and eating on the Volga only a few dozen generations before the Scythians made their first ominous appearance.

Flesh

THE HORSE PEOPLES OF THE STEPPE

What is the steppe? To those who live in settled and temperate lands, the steppe means the enormous expanse of empty space that fills the map between the Arctic Ocean to the north and the Himalayas to the south, between the irrigated river valleys of China to the east and the barriers of the Pripet marshes and Carpathian mountains in the west. On the civilised man's mental map, it appears as not only featureless but climatically undifferentiated, a zone of sparse and uniform vegetation, without mountains, rivers, lakes or forests, a sort of waterless ocean without known voyagers.

This impression is quite incorrect. In modern times its western reaches have been settled by Russian and Ukrainian city-dwellers in the millions; yet even before they began to populate the banks of the western steppe's great rivers – Volga, Don, Donetz, Dnieper – travellers who ventured into the wilderness recognised that climate and topography marked it out into several distinct regions. Geographers generally denote three: the *taiga* or sub-Arctic forest, which runs from the northern Pacific to the Atlantic's North Cape; a wide band of desert, touching the Great Wall in the east and the salt marshes of Iran in the west; in between the two, the steppe proper.

The *taiga* is forbidding territory; the climate is extreme – near Yakutsk the ground has been found to be permanently frozen to a depth of 446 feet – and the fishermen and hunters who survive on the banks of the rivers that drain the plateau to the Arctic Ocean – Ob, Yenisei, Lena and Amur – are shy forest-dwellers; among them only the Tungu, who live in eastern Siberia and the basin of the Amur River, are known to history, principally as the Manchu who captured the Chinese throne in the seventeenth century AD.

In the desert belt,

none of the rivers reaches the sea; they lose themselves in the sand or flow into salt marshes. The Gobi Desert is a cheerless solitude of sand, rock or gravel that extends 1,200 miles, inhabited, in popular belief, only by demons, whose thundering wailings are more plausibly attributed to the noise of shifting dunes, dislodged by strong winds.

Vegetation is confined to scrub and grassy reeds; the climate is extreme; icy sandstorms blow furiously in winter and spring; rain falls but seldom, though after a brief shower the desert floor suddenly blooms with small green plants. The Takla-makan is a smaller Gobi, so swept in summer by choking dust storms that travel across it is tolerable only in winter. The Dasht i-Kavir, or

Persian desert, 800 miles wide, consists less of sand than of salt swamps, but [is] dotted with oases.

These oases were the nodal points, in William McNeill's theory, by which the Indo-European charioteers made their way to China.

The true steppe is an elongated belt of grassland, 3000 miles long and averaging 500 miles in depth, bounded to the north by the sub-Arctic and to the south by desert and mountains; it gives at its eastern end on to the river valleys of China and at its western on to the approach routes to the fertile lands of the Middle East and Europe. It forms

a treeless pasture, a grassy plain between the mountains, unsuited to agriculture unless expensively irrigated, but admirably suited to the breeding of cattle, sheep and goats, the sub-alpine valleys of the Altai providing exceptionally fine grazing-grounds. The vegetation consists principally of rich grass; the surface of the soil varies from gravel to salt and loam; the climate, though severe, and in the high steppe appallingly cold in winter [below freezing in the Altai mountains for 200 days in the year], is dry and therefore bearable, and the shepherds of these regions often live to extreme old age.[36]

Geographers distinguish between a high and low steppe, respectively east and west of the Pamirs, which outcrop from the Himalayas. The 'gradient' therefore runs westward, and the grazing improves in that direction, thus encouraging migration towards Europe and the Middle East. Historically, however, there has been much movement in the opposite direction; the Dzungarian gap to the south of the Altai mountains, the steppe heartland, offers a natural gateway toward the Chinese plains. This is easier of passage than the western gateways – at each end of the Caucasus mountains, in the gap between the Caspian and Aral seas, and around the top of the Black Sea into the Adrianople corridor – which are narrower and easier to defend.

The Scythians, the first steppe people of whom we know, probably originated in the Altai and followed the steppe gradient westward to attack Assyria. Of those who came later, the Turks seem certainly to have come from the Altai, and their tongue (to which those of the Kazaks, Uzbeks, Uighurs and Kirghiz among others are allied) was, and remains, the principal speech of Central Asia; the Huns who appeared outside Rome in the fifth century AD spoke a language that belonged to the Turkic group. Mongolian, by contrast, spoken by comparatively few steppe peoples, apparently originated in the forest lands north of Lake Baikal and east of the Altai; Manchu, also Tungusic, derives from eastern Siberia. Some of the first horse peoples were, however, like the original charioteers, Indo-Europeans, and spoke what has become Persian; allied languages, now forgotten but spoken by warriors in their time, were Sogdian and Tocharian, and another was that of the people known to the Romans as Sarmatians.[37]

What drew the horse nomads out of the steppe? We cannot easily fit their warmaking behaviour into any of the patterns discerned in other societies by social anthropologists. They were certainly not 'primitive warriors': from the start they fought to win, so that explanations couched in terms of kinship quarrels or ceremonialism do not fit them. Territoriality also seems an inappropriate concept; though nomadic tribes undoubtedly were attached to certain grazing-lands and conceded the claims of others to theirs, it was also a salient characteristic of nomadism that tribal composition was fluid; chiefship was precarious and followings split or coalesced unpredictably. Perhaps the most useful idea is the ecological one of 'carrying capacity'. William McNeill has persuasively argued that life on the steppe was subject to sudden and highly disruptive climatic change: warm, moist seasons, making for good grazing and a higher survival rate of animal – and human – offspring, were commonly followed by harsh times, which left larger flocks and families stranded for sustenance. Migration within the steppe did not help, since neighbours suffered similarly and resisted incursions. The obvious means of escape was therefore outward, into gentler climes where cultivated land offered emergency rations.[38]

The perceptible flaw in this explanation – perceived and allowed for by McNeill himself – is that nomads would in time have learnt to anticipate the intermission of bad with good times and made their homes elsewhere than on the steppe, which ought in consequence, after their acquisition of the riding-horse, to have reverted to emptiness. In some sense it did so: the widest-ranging aggressors among the steppe peoples – the Mongols and Turks – did establish tribute-yielding empires over settled peoples that liberated them from the cycle of famine on the sea of grass. Nevertheless, the nomads had a weakness: they liked the nomadic way of life and despised the weary cultivator, bound to his furrows and his plough-ox. What the nomads wanted was the best of both worlds: the comfort and luxury that settled ways yielded but also the freedom of the horseman's life, of the tented camp, of the hunt and of the seasonal shift of quarters.

The persistence of the nomadic ethos is nowhere better caught than in the Topkapi at Istanbul, palace of the Ottoman Turkish sultans, where, until the beginning of the nineteenth century, the rulers of an empire that stretched from the Danube River to the Indian Ocean spent their days as they might have done on the steppe, seated on cushions on carpeted floors of makeshift pavilions set up in the palace gardens, dressed in the horseman's kaftan and loose trousers, and having as their principal regalia the mounted warrior's quivers, bow cases and archer's thumb rings. Planted though it was in the capital city of the eastern Roman empire, the Topkapi remained a nomadic camp, where the horsetail standards of battle were processed before great men, and stables stood at the door.

Another explanation has been offered for the nomads' warmaking: that it was a means of forcing the civilised lands to trade. The steppe peoples certainly learnt to trade at an early time and in their horses, and probably also slaves, had commodities that professional merchants were eager to buy or exchange against manufactured goods; one of the conditions for peace that the Huns requested from the Romans in the middle of the fifth century AD was that a market on the Danube be reopened 'as in former times'.[39] The success of commercial interests at both ends of the Silk Road that linked China to the Middle East, first opened in the second century BC, in maintaining traffic along it for over a thousand years also suggests that the nomads generally perceived the advantage in encouraging rather than plundering a flow of goods through their lands. Nevertheless, it was frequently interrupted, when local greed got the better of commercial sense; and, moreover, forced trade does not work when there is a structural imbalance between what is sought and what can be offered in return. The steppe simply did not produce enough of what civilisation wanted for transactions initiated by military means to become self-sustaining by normal commercial incentives. As the British found when they sought to foist unwanted opium on China in the nineteenth century, a demand to sell, backed up by force of arms, inevitably leads the seller into imposing his political will on the unwilling buyer, and so becoming an imperialist in substance if not name. Such a sophisticated two-step was, in any case, probably beyond the early horse peoples.

THE HUNS

The first steppe people of whom we have any detailed knowledge were the Huns, who invaded the Roman empire in the fifth century AD. If they can be identified with the Hsiung-nu, they had seriously destabilised the unified China of the Han dynasty in the second century BC. The Huns, who probably spoke a Turkic language, were without writing; their religion was 'a simple nature worship'. They may have used shamans – spirit callers who were believed to mediate between god and man whom we also

182

know among the northern forest peoples who migrated to North America – and are certainly known to have practised scapulimancy, the telling of omens from patterns on sheeps' shoulder-blades. Foretelling the future was important to the Huns; it was apparently for Hunnish mercenaries in his service that Litorius took the omens before the battle of Toulouse in 439, the last Roman general known to have performed the ancient pagan rites.[40] The Huns' social system was simple: they recognised the aristocratic principle – Attila prided himself on being well born – and they kept a limited number of slaves but accepted no other divisions.

They sold slaves, of course, and in very large numbers after they had made a conquest: their inhumanity in breaking up families for the market appalled Christian writers in the fifth century.[41] Slave-selling certainly exceeded in profitability the trade in both horses and furs as soon as the Huns established themselves in the outer provinces of the Roman empire, but they also derived an enormous income in gold by way of ransom for military and civilian captives, as well as in straight bribes from the later emperors: during the period AD 440–50 the eastern provinces paid them 13,000 pounds of gold, about six tons, to buy peace.[42] It is these sort of transactions that cast doubt on the interpretation of horse peoples' excursions from the steppe in terms of 'escaping climatic change' or 'enforcing trade'. The truth seems much simpler: nomads – physically tough, logistically mobile, culturally accustomed to shedding blood, ethically untroubled by religious prohibitions against taking the lives or limiting the freedom of those outside the tribe – learnt that war paid.

Whether the conquests that successful warmaking brought could be sustained was another matter. Nature seems to impose limits on the depth of penetration that nomads can make into settled land. Nomadic demand on irrigated land for grazing rapidly disrupts the system and returns it to a state where it will support neither beast nor man; if cleared from forest, the land reverts to woodland when the ploughing population is dispersed. (The trend became disastrous in Mesopotamia after the arrival of the Turks in the thirteenth century.[43]) Nomadic expansion could be consolidated, therefore, only in the borderlands between steppe and agriculture, but such lands support only small populations. In the Far East, where the conquering nomads were halfway to being Chinese already, they were easily assimilated, even if as a ruling class. In the west, where religion and civilised custom imposed a much sharper differentiation between them and the agriculturalists, the borderlands became a permanent battleground, where use of the soil had to be sustained by force of arms.

To Attila's Huns, the ploughed fields of Gaul and the gardened floodplain of the Po must have presented bewildering environments. Food they would have found in abundance, but not of the accustomed sort, and not in varieties that regenerated after foraging. Grass does not replace wheat or beans in a single season. Attila is said to have brought his following of families in waggons, but he cannot have brought his sheep or any large number of his horses; his traditional economic base must have been left behind, perhaps as far away as the lower Danube valley. It may have been the pull of his flocks and herds that explains his mysterious departure from Italy in 452, when the peninsula lay undefended before him. A return to the grasslands in such circumstances would have made logistical sense. It was not his retreat which shook the Roman empire, however, but his advance, and before that the thrust of the Huns into eastern Europe, which provoked a massed assault by the Germanic tribes on the Danubian frontier. The sequence of the Hunnish offensive from the steppe gives us a clear example of how disruptive a campaign by horse people could be once they took to the warpath.

If the Huns were the Hsiung-nu who menaced China in the second century AD (the identification rests on a single piece of Scythian evidence), nothing was heard of them between the first century BC and AD 371, when they defeated the Alans, an Iranian people, at the battle of the Tanais River, between the Volga and the Don; many Alans joined the Huns, others reached the Roman borders and became mercenary cavalrymen.[44] In 376 the Huns advanced from the Volga to invade the Gothic lands between the Dnieper and the Roman frontier on the Danube. The Goths were the most aggressive of the German tribes who had been pressing against the border of the Roman empire for at least a century. Their western (Visigoth) branch was established on territory which had been Roman between 106 and 275 – the province of Dacia (modern Hungary) – and, in this time of troubles for the empire, its leaders had been treating on equal terms with the emperors. The advancing Huns, driving the eastern (Ostrogoth) Goths in front of them, turned the Visigoths into supplicants overnight. Reluctantly – there were too many barbarians inside the empire already – the Romans gave them permission to cross the Danube, and their cousins followed in their wake. Local officials badly mistreated them, however, and though they had given up their arms as a condition of entry, they conjured up other weapons and stood to fight at the Willows, near the Danube delta. The Romans might easily have overcome them but, panicked by a rumour, true or false, that the Goths had made an alliance with the Huns, who were camped across the Danube, they retreated into the Balkan mountains.

184

Trouble, perhaps fomented by the Goths, now flared up along the whole of the Roman frontier with Germany and while the youthful emperor Gratian tried to contain the Alemanni on the Rhine, Valens, emperor in the east, collected the best army he could and moved to restrain the Goths who were pillaging eastern Greece. On 9 August 378, he came up against their fortified camp outside Adrianople, was wounded in the course of a chaotic battle and died in the massacre that followed it. The death of an emperor in battle, all too soon after that of Julian in a Persian war (363), was a grave blow to Rome. The irretrievable consequence of Adrianople, however, was neither the moral nor material damage it caused but the enforced barbarisation of the Roman army, imposed upon the new eastern emperor, Theodosius, by the Visigoths as condition of their good behaviour. In return for being allowed to settle south of the Danube (382), inside the empire and with their weapons, the Visigoths agreed not only to keep the peace but to fight for the emperor as 'federate' allies.

'The settlement was . . . a grave breach with precedent.'[45] The Romans, as the Assyrians had done before them, had traditionally incorporated barbarian contingents into the army, but as specialists and in small numbers. As the pressures on the empire had increased, so had the numbers – there may have been 20,000 'Roman' Goths at Adrianople, and some mercenary Huns were serving in the cavalry, along with representatives of other horse peoples – but thitherto the Romans had always retained control of the leadership, either by appointing imperial officials as generals or by elevating barbarians to the still greatly coveted – and well paid – higher ranks of the Roman army. Theodosius's settlement changed that: thereafter barbarian armies operated autonomously within the empire and, in circumstances where a continuous press of barbarian numbers from outside provoked successive crises of leadership within, the barbarian chiefs threw their weight this way and that between competitors for the imperial title, with catastrophic economic and military results.

Thus, though Theodosius succeeded in reuniting the empire under a single throne, he allowed more Goths to enter the empire in the course of his pacification campaigns, and this Visigothic contingent under Alaric, after the death of Theodosius in 395, caused irreparable damage to what remained of the imperial structure in the west. In 401, from a base in Greece, Alaric invaded Italy across the Alps, opening a campaign of despoliation which Stilicho, the last but one great Roman general, took three years to bring under control. At its end Stilicho's army was so depleted in numbers that he lacked the strength to move against the next major threat. During 405 the largest barbarian host yet seen, a collection of Germanic peoples including Vandals, Burgundians, Swabians and Goths under the leadership of Radagaisus, crossed the Danube and then the Alps to winter in the Po valley. They had apparently been displaced from northern Germany by Huns who were pushing upward from the homeland they had established in Dacia – which forms the last extension of the steppe grassland on the edge of forest Europe. Stilicho was eventually able to confine Radagaisus's horde into an area near Florence, starve it into surrender and drive the remnants back across the Alps into southern Germany. Thence, in the next few years, the separate tribes made their way across the Rhine to initiate the culminating barbarisation of Gaul.

Roman loss of control over the remaining western provinces proceeded apace, with Alaric playing a malign role. In 410 he captured and sacked Rome and then marched south to cross to Roman Africa but died before he could find ships. Meanwhile the eastern empire also came under threat from the Huns who had briefly invaded Greece in 409. Fortunately some Huns proved willing to change sides for the right inducement and these mercenaries provided Aëtius, 'the last of the Romans', with much of the force with which he sustained imperial authority in the second quarter of the fifth century.[46] From 424 onward, campaigning largely in Gaul, he succeeded in holding the Teutonic invaders at bay, even while Spain and Roman Africa were crumbling under the attack of the Vandals. Between 433 and 450 Aëtius's war in Gaul was almost continuous.

In 450 he was confronted by a new challenge. The Huns of Hungary had been acting as an independent power on the flank of the eastern Roman empire for twenty years, taking tribute from the emperor but also raiding his territory and cooperating with the Teutonic rulers to their mutual advantage. In 441 they had raided into Greece again, under the leadership of their king's nephew, Attila, who in 447 appeared under the walls of Constantinople. In 450 he transferred his effort to Gaul and in 451 was laying siege to Orléans. Siegecraft was not an art that the Huns had yet mastered, or that any horse people before the Mongols were to do, and while Attila was engaged under the city's walls, Aëtius, by frantic diplomacy, assembled an army of Franks, Visigoths, Burgundians and Alans and drew him into battle on the open plains of the Champagne between Troyes and Châlons.

Châlons, fought in June 451, has been called one of 'the decisive battles of history'. There were Teutons and horse people on both sides and it was Aëtius's Alans who succeeded in holding Attila's Huns in a pitched struggle. When Attila detected that Aëtius had profited from this check to make an encircling move toward his rear, he took refuge in his waggon laager and, under cover of Hun archery, succeeded in disengaging and beating a retreat to the Rhine. In the following year he moved from the Rhine to Italy, his appearance driving people from the plain of the Po to take refuge on the islands which would become Venice and, also in popular supposition, causing Pope Leo I to visit his camp and dissuade him from attacking Rome. In the event Attila did not march further south but, after agreeing to ransom his more important captives, turned about and retreated. Within two years 'the scourge of God' was dead and the Hunnish empire collapsed.

There were circumstantial reasons for Attila's decision to leave Italy. It had just suffered famine, while pestilence had broken out in his army and an eastern Roman force had crossed the Danube to campaign in Hungary. Such circumstances do not, however, explain why the Hunnish empire failed to survive Attila's death or why, on the death of his sons, the Huns disappeared from history. One suggestion is that, during their sojourn on the borders of the Roman empire, they had abandoned their steppe habits, adopted Teutonic methods of fighting and so become absorbed.[47] This is dismissed by Maenchen-Helfen, the most meticulous collater of Hunnish data: 'Attila's horsemen were still the same mounted archers who in the 380s had ridden down the Vardar valley into Greece.' Another explanation is that the Hungarian plain is not large enough to support horse herds of the size the Huns needed to sustain their cavalry organisation. Horse peoples certainly need very large strings. Marco Polo, who crossed Central Asia in the thirteenth century, noted that a single rider might keep as many as eighteen changes of mount. It has been calculated, moreover, that the Hungarian plain can graze only 150,000 horses, too few, even allowing ten horses per rider, to have mounted Attila's horde. That calculation, however, leaves out of account the much milder climate that prevails there by comparison with the steppe, making for a richer and longer growth of pasture. In 1914 Hungary mounted 29,000 cavalrymen at one horse per man and, though the horses would have been larger than Attila's and partly grain-fed, such differences are not sufficient to explain a tenfold diminution of requirements.[48] Hun horses must have thrived in the seventy years they were there and it is most unlikely that Attila was short of them when he set out for the west in 450.

On the other hand, it is highly probable that a large proportion of the horses he took were ridden to death and that they could not be replaced down his line of communications. Cavalry campaigns kill horses in huge numbers if they cannot be regularly rested and grazed. During the Boer War of 1899–1902, for example, the British army lost 347,000 out of the

518,000 that took part, though the country abounded in good grazing and has a benign climate. Only a tiny fraction, no more than two per cent, were lost in battle. The rest died of overwork, disease or malnutrition, at a rate of 336 for each day of the campaign.[49] Attila, moreover, had no means of moving his horses by waggon or ship, as the British transported theirs to and within South Africa. The likelihood is, therefore, that any remounts he received along the overland route from Hungary arrived in little better shape than those his men were already riding, and that the retreat to the grasslands finished off many of the survivors. The Scourge of God may have been an even worse enemy of his own army. He seems to have left little substantial force to his sons, and their deaths in battle, one at the hands of the Goths, the other against a general of the eastern Roman empire in 469, is the last news we have of the Huns.[50]

THE HORSE PEOPLES' HORIZON, 453–1258

Yet despite the abrupt disappearance of the Huns from history, the horse peoples had arrived. They were to remain an ever-present menace to the civilisations of Europe, the Middle East and Asia for the next millennium. Theirs had been an extraordinary rise to power in little more than 1500 years. They were, moreover, truly a new sort of people, previously unknown to the world. Military force was, of course, already established as a principle before their coming but as a resource available only to governments and the settled populations they ruled, and one strictly limited by the yields of the economies they controlled.

Armies that were fed from an agricultural surplus and limited in range of manoeuvre by their pace and endurance on foot simply could not undertake free-ranging campaigns of conquest. Nor did they need to: enemies similarly constrained could threaten them with defeat in battle but not with *Blitzkrieg*.

The horse people were different. Attila had shown an ability to shift his strategic centre of effort – *Schwerpunkt*, as Prussian general staff doctrine later denoted it – from eastern France to northern Italy in successive campaigning seasons, 500 miles apart as the crow flies and considerably further in practice, since he was operating along exterior lines. No such strategic manoeuvre had been attempted or had been possible before. Freedom of action on this scale lay at the heart of the 'cavalry revolution'.

The horse people fought unconstrained in another sense. They did not seek, as the Goths did, to inherit or adapt to the half-understood civilisations they invaded. Nor – despite a suggestion that Attila contemplated marriage with the daughter of the western Roman emperor – did they seek to supplant others' political authority with their own. They wanted the spoils of war without strings. They were warriors for war's sake, for the loot it brought, the risks, the thrills, the animal satisfactions of triumph. Eight hundred years after the death of Attila, Genghis Khan, questioning his Mongol comrades-in-arms about life's sweetest pleasure and being told it lay in falconry, replied, 'You are mistaken. Man's greatest good fortune is to chase and defeat his enemy, seize his total possessions, leave his married women weeping and wailing, ride his gelding [and] use the bodies of his women as a nightshirt and support.'[51] Attila might have spoken thus; he certainly behaved in that spirit.

The horse and human ruthlessness together thus transformed war, making it for the first time 'a thing in itself'. We can thenceforth speak of 'militarism', an aspect of societies in which the mere ability to make war, readily and profitably, becomes a reason in itself for doing so. Yet militarism is a concept that cannot be applied to any horse people, since it presumes the existence of an army as an institution dominant over but separate from other social institutions. There was no such separation among Attila's Huns, nor would there be among any horse people until the Turks espoused Islam. The fit and adult males of a horse people *were* the army, but not the sort of army by which Turney-High measured a society's position above or below the 'military horizon'. All the horse peoples who beat a path of conquest off the steppe into the lands of civilisation fought 'true war' by all the tests – lack of limitation in the use of force, singularity of purpose and unwillingness to settle for anything less than outright victory. Yet their warfare had no political object in the Clausewitzian sense, and no culturally transforming effect. It was not a means to material or social advance; indeed, precisely the contrary, it was the process by which they won the wealth to sustain an unchanging way of life, to remain exactly as they had been since their ancestors first loosed an arrow from the saddle.

None of the horse peoples that kept a base on the steppe ever willingly altered its habits; at best, their most successful leaderships became absorbed as a ruling class in the settled societies they conquered, without abandoning their nomadic ethos, and that was true even of the islamicised Turks, despite the degree to which they sustained Byzantine forms of government within their empire after their capture of Constantinople in 1453. The Mameluke system, despite the degree of autonomy the Mamelukes enjoyed, was, as we have seen, merely a means of perpetuating the horseman's way of life, with all the wealth and honour that military power brought in its train. Most horse peoples, moreover, for most of the time that the frontiers of China, the Middle East and Europe lay open to their assault, succeeded neither in finding individual employment nor in imposing themselves as conquering rulers on more advanced societies. The steppe life remained rooted in war, but the warpath was a hard one, blocked in almost every direction by the defences of states which fought all the more fiercely to keep the horse peoples confined within the limits of the steppe. They had learned the ghastly consequences of dropping their guard.

In the wake of the Huns' disappearance, there remained no strong horse people in contact with civilised powers in Europe or the Middle East. The most significant were the Ephthalites, the so-called White Huns, who seem to have been displaced on to Persia's northern border by the Hsiung-nu when both lived far away on the fringe of China.[52] The Ephthalites had at least one spectacular success, in part because Persia's energies were devoted to waging its endemic war with Byzantium, but in 567 the Persians eventually succeeded in beating them off; deflected eastward, they appear to have made their way into Hindu India and planted the roots of future Rajput power.

Meanwhile Byzantium was holding at bay various horse peoples extruded westward by the perpetual tribal discords in the steppe heartland. These included the Bulgars and the Avars, the former pushed by the latter, who in turn were displaced by the growing power of the Turks. The Bulgars eventually settled in the Balkans, where they were to be a cause of trouble until the Ottomans finally brought them under control. The Avars migrated to Hungary, caused widespread disruption, and, though occasionally allied to Byzantium, laid siege to Constantinople in 626; with Persian help, they very nearly succeeded in entering it. They were repulsed but remained a powerful source for harm until they were eventually overcome by Charlemagne in the eighth century; their place was then taken by the Magyars, the last horse people to migrate from the steppe into central Europe.

Until they were turned westward, the Avars may, however, have already learnt the habit of warring against imperial power, if they can be identified with the Juan-Juan who at the beginning of the fifth century had fallen out with the dynasty known as the Northern Wei in northern China. The Northern Wei were one of a group of sinicised steppe people who, on the fall of the unified Han empire in the third century, had ruled north of the Yangtse; the circumstances of their rise to power are so complex

190

that the period is known as the 'Sixteen Kingdoms of the Five Barbarians' (304–439). By 386, however, the Northern Wei had emerged as dominant and begun to reunify northern China. In the process, they came into conflict with the Juan-Juan people living above the Gobi Desert, and expelled them from their territory. They were helped in this by a subject class of the Juan-Juan who worked for them as ironsmiths; these were the Turks. The Turks bore a recent grudge: after helping their masters to put down a revolt by another subject tribe, their chief sought as his reward the hand of the Juan-Juan chief's daughter. He was refused. The Northern Wei offered him a noble daughter of theirs and then together they fell on the Juan-Juans, who were broken. The Turks took their territory, and their chief the title of *khagan* or *khan*, which later became that of most steppe rulers.

The Turkish khan and his successors founded a great empire. They were 'the first barbarians to create a kingdom so extensive as to touch at different points the four great civilised societies of the day: China, India, Persia and Byzantium'.[53] By 563 they had advanced as far as the Oxus River, on Persia's eastern border, and with the Persians they made common cause against the Ephthalites. By 567 the Turkish khan, Istemi, had got a share of the Ephthalite lands as the spoils of victory. In the following year he was an important enough figure for the Byzantine emperor, Justin II, not only to receive an embassy from him but to send one of his own in return on the enormous journey to the centre of the steppe. Fatally, the Turks then fell to quarrelling over authority within their empire, the besetting fault of horse peoples and the main cause of dissolution of their structureless polities. In this period of disunion they lost much of their eastern territory to the rising power of the T'ang dynasty in China, which extended its control as far as the Oxus River by 659. By then, however, the Turks had encountered a new enemy in the west which was also reaching out into the steppe, making great conquests and striking to contest control of Central Asia with the Chinese. In the course of the next century and of this struggle for power for the steppe heartland, which culminated in the battle of the Talas River in modern Kirghizstan in 751, the Turkish empire was to be overthrown.[54] The new enemy were the Arabs.

Arabs and Mamelukes

The Arabs were not a horse people, though they were to become their principal employers in the civilised world. If only for that reason they would deserve the attention of military historians, but they deserve it for very much more. First, at the time the Turks encountered them, they were just completing one of the greatest campaigns of conquest in history, a campaign which had transformed an almost unknown tribal group from the deserts of inner Arabia into rulers of most of the Middle East, and the whole of North Africa and Spain. They had shaken the Byzantine empire, destroyed the Persian, and founded one of their own. Only Alexander the Great – and he had been the first long-range conqueror in history – had captured territory of a similar extent and with an equivalent rapidity. Their pattern of conquest, moreover, was creative and unifying. Though the Arabs would later fall out among themselves, the original empire was a single whole and one which rapidly dedicated itself to the arts of peace. The Arab rulers were to become great builders, beautifiers and patrons of literature and science. Unlike the rough horse peoples whom they were later to enlist as soldiers, they showed an astonishing ability to emancipate themselves from the campaigning way of life, to embrace civilisation and to cultivate sophisticated manners of thought and behaviour.

More than that, however, they stood out among military peoples because they demonstrated an ability to transform not merely themselves but warfare itself. There had been military revolutions before, notably those brought by the chariot and the cavalry horse. The Assyrians had established the principles of military bureaucracy, on which the Romans had built. The Greeks, as we shall see later, had evolved the technique of the pitched battle, fought to the death on foot. The Arabs transfused warfare with a new force altogether, the force of an idea. Ideology, it is true, had played its part in warfare before. The Athenian Isocrates had urged a Greek 'crusade' against Persia during the fourth century BC, in which the idea of liberty was implicit.[55] During the Emperor Theodosius's struggle with the Goths in 383, the Roman Themistius had argued that the strength of Rome lay 'not in breastplates and shields, not in countless masses of men, but in Reason'.[56] The Jewish kings had fought in covenant with their single and almighty God, while Constantine had invoked the image of the cross to bring him victory against a pretender at the battle of the Milvian Bridge. These had all been muted or limited ideas none the less. Though the Greeks took pride in their freedom and despised the subjects of Xerxes and Darius for their lack of it, their hatred of Persia was at root nationalistic. The appeal to reason lacked force at a time when Rome's armies were already heavily barbarised, their ranks filled with savage soldiers who had never heard reason's name. Constantine, moreover, was not yet a Christian when he uttered the appeal to conquer in the sign of the cross; and while the warrior kings of Israel may have drawn strength from the old Covenant in their small and local wars, the Christians of the new Covenant were to agonise for centuries over the issue of whether warmaking was morally permissible or not. Christians, indeed, have never found unanimity in the belief that the man of war may also be a man of religion; the ideal of martyrdom has always been as strong as that of the justified struggle and remains strong to this day. The Arabs of the conquest years were not caught on that crux. Their new religion, Islam, was a creed of conflict, that taught the necessity of submission to its revealed teachings and the right of its believers to take arms against those who opposed them. It was Islam that inspired the Arab conquests, the ideas of Islam that made the Arabs a military people and the example of its founder, Muhammad, that taught them to become warriors.

Muhammad was not only a warrior himself, who had been wounded in a battle at Medina against the men of Mecca in 625. He preached as well as practised war. In his last visit to Mecca in 632 he laid down that, though all Muslims were brethren and should not fight each other, they should fight all other men until they said 'There is no god but God'.[57] The Koran, which Muslims believe to have been taken down from his words by disciples, elaborates this command extensively. Even more specifically than Christ had done, Muhammad insisted that those who accepted the word of God thereby formed a community (*umma*) whose members owed each other responsibilities; thus it was not enough simply to avoid fratricide: Muslims were under an obligation to do positive good to less fortunate Muslims by assigning a certain portion of their income to charity; they also had a duty to care for each other's consciences. Beyond the *umma*, however, the obligation was reversed: 'O you who believe, fight the unbelievers who are near to you.'[58] This was not a call to forcible conversion. Non-believers who were prepared to live under Koranic authority were positively entitled to protection and, in strict theory, those outside the *umma* who kept the peace ought not to be attacked. In practice, however, the bounds of the *umma* came to coincide with the House of Submission (*Dar el-Islam*), while outside inevitably lay the House of War (*Dar el-Harb*). Against the House of War, Islam fell into conflict from the moment of the Prophet Muhammad's death in 632.

Conflict with the *Dar el-Harb* shortly became *jihad*, 'holy war'. It was not simply the command of the Prophet that made Muslims wage it so successfully, though wildly successful they were as warriors. There are at least two other reasons to explain the ease of their early victories. First, there is no conflict in Islam between devotion and material well-being.

193

Christ, to the great moral perturbation of his followers ever afterward, held up poverty as a holy ideal. Muhammad, by contrast, had been a merchant, had a keen understanding of the value of wealth, properly used, expected the *umma* to accumulate it and saw it as a means of doing good, both collectively and individually. He himself raided the caravans of the rich, unbelieving merchants of Mecca, and spent the loot to further his cause. That was an example that his holy warriors followed in their assault on the rich kingdoms of Byzantium and Persia.

Secondly, Islam dissolved the two principles on which war had so often been fought before: territoriality and kinship. There could be no territoriality in Islam, because its destiny was to bring the whole world to submission to the will of God. Islam means submission and 'Muslim', formed from the same word, someone who is under it. Only when the whole of the House of War had been brought within the House of Submission would Islam's destiny be complete. Then all men would be Muslims and therefore also brothers. In practice, the first Arab Muslims, still enmeshed by the powerful clan kinships of the desert world, resisted the principle of brotherhood, so that converts from beyond their tribes had to accept the status of clients (*mawali*) for a time.[59] Eventually, however, it was to prove one of the glories of Islam that it dissolved barriers of race and language to an extent that no religion or empire – and Islam comprehended both concepts – had succeeded in doing before.

Another factor greatly assisted the Arabs who, in the last years of Muhammad's life, set out to extend the boundaries of Islam: the kingdoms on which their force fell were in decline. Byzantium had expended much of its strength in resisting the Avars on its northern boundaries; more wearingly, it had been engaged since the beginning of the seventh century in the last of its great wars with Persia (603–28), a war that exhausted both empires. As for Persia, historically a great power, it had also suffered historically from the weakness of its geographical position, poised between the steppe on the one hand and the rich lands of the Middle East on the other. Before the rise of the horse peoples, it had frequently been able to profit from decline or collapse on its western borders to extend its imperial frontiers. A millennium before, in Alexander the Great, it had met an opponent of such towering skill and determination that its native dynasty had been supplanted and its imperial possessions divided among his generals. Seleucus, the Alexandrian general to whom the Persian heartland fell, succeeded in sustaining Hellenistic power but not in Hellenising Persian society. His empire eventually passed to the Parthians, another Iranian people who had begun in Central Asia. Though a horse people – it was their cavalry

194

prowess that overthrew the Seleucid infantry – they readily assimilated to civilisation, founded a great empire, and, between the first century BC and the beginning of the third AD, were Rome's chief enemies in the east. The wars between Persia and Rome were often marked by Persian victories: the campaign of 363, in which the emperor Julian the Apostate was killed in Mesopotamia, was almost as great a disaster for Rome as the Gothic victory at Adrianople fifteen years later. But the strain of constant warfare depleted Persia's wealth, manpower and resilience, and the empire was thereafter increasingly harried by nomads on their steppe frontier.

When, therefore, in 633 an Arab army invaded northern Mesopotamia, the Persian army was not what it had been; neither was the Byzantine. Audaciously, the Arabs chose to operate against both simultaneously and, though compelled to transfer forces between the two fronts, they succeeded in holding their own; in 637 at Qadisiyah, near modern Baghdad, they won a victory that ensured the triumph of Islam in Persia; the significance of that victory remains so great in the Arab world that in the 1980s it was constantly evoked by Saddam Hussein during his war of attrition with Iran. Meanwhile other Arab armies were conquering Syria (636), Egypt (642) and pressing westward along the Mediterranean coast toward the Byzantine provinces in North Africa. In 674 Mu'awiya, the fifth caliph or 'successor' to Muhammad, decided to lay siege directly to Constantinople, and though the Arabs gave up the effort in 677, they returned in 717. By that year, they had taken the whole of North Africa (705), crossed to Spain (711) and reached the Pyrenees, over which they shortly invaded France. In the east they conquered Afghanistan, raided into north-west India, annexed part of Anatolia (modern Turkey), pushed their northernmost boundary to the line of the Caucasus mountains and crossed the Oxus into Transoxiana where, at the Talas River in 751, they fought a decisive battle with the Chinese for dominance over the great caravan cities of Bokhara and Samarkand, on the Silk Road which led to the Great Wall.

What made the Arab victories all the more astonishing was the relatively poor quality of their armies. The Arabs, despite centuries of desert feuding, had no real experience of intensive warfare; they were indeed 'primitive warriors' whose preferred form of operations was the raid (*ghazwa*).[60] Nor does their generalship seem to have been particularly cunning. They certainly enjoyed no advantage in equipment or military technique. The Arab horse was already a fast, spirited and elegant beast, pampered and often hand-fed, in appearance almost a different animal from the shaggy steppe pony, but there were few of them. The camel, domesticated during the first millennium both in its single-humped (Arabian) and double-humped (Bactrian) species, was available in larger numbers but, though its powers of endurance were high, it was relatively slow and decidedly unwieldy.[61] Strategically, the camel enabled Arab armies to cross terrain civilised armies thought impenetrable, and to appear on the field of battle quite unexpectedly; tactically, it was of limited use at close quarters. Arab tactics, therefore, were to make the approach march on camelback and to transfer to the led horses – there may have been as few as 600 at Qadisiyah – only at the moment of contact.[62] These were the methods by which Khalid, one of the leading generals of the conquests, brought his army from Mesopotamia to deliver a crushing blow at the side of his comrade-in-arms, Amr, at the major victory of Ajnadain over the Byzantines in Palestine in July 634. On the battlefield itself, Arab armies chose positions defended by natural obstacles where their dismounted soldiers, armed with the composite bow, could fight behind some protection; they also preferred ground from which they had an easy escape route into the desert.[63]

These two characteristics of their warmaking style – dependence on obstacles and readiness for flight – are typically 'primitive'; as we have seen, they were those that so infuriated the Philhellenes in their encounter with the Greeks during the war of independence from Turkey. Here is a problem. If the Arabs were 'primitive warriors', why then were they so successful in their wars against the disciplined, organised armies of Byzantium and Persia, 'regular' armies as we would denote them in any system of military classification? We know that Persia and Byzantium had exhausted each other in the course of a long war. Nevertheless, it is a general rule that primitives lose to regulars over the long run; harassment is an effective means of waging a defensive war, but wars are ultimately won by offensives and the Arabs were certainly on the offensive during the era of the conquests. The conclusion must be that it was Islam itself, which lays so heavy an emphasis on the fight for the faith, that made them so formidable in the field. 'Primitive' tactics become effective if the warrior is inspired by a belief in the certainty of victory and is always willing to return to the struggle, however often he disengages when a particular fight goes against him. Casting forward in time, this was Mao's perception also. His tactics were 'primitive' to begin with, and he saw no indignity in retreat as long as his soldiers retained their belief in eventual victory. Another pillar of his strategy was to win the support of the populations among which he operated. The Arab armies benefited greatly from the presence in the settled lands they invaded of the *musta'riba*, Arabs who had given up the desert life but who felt strong cultural bonds with them and proved willing to fight at their side as soon as they heard a doctrine of brotherhood preached in the name of Islam.[64]

Yet, as we have seen from the story of the rise of the Mamelukes, Islam itself was eventually to be the undoing of Arab power. The prohibition against Muslim fighting Muslim was broken very early and this breach was eventually, though perhaps inevitably, to result in the loss of military authority by the later caliphs to subject soldiers who came to rule in their place, in fact if not in name; the great majority of these soldiers were recruited from the horse peoples of the steppe. The title Caliph, we already know, meant 'successor' to the prophet Muhammad and brought supreme authority both in the world and in religion. The early caliphs found no conflict in practice between their roles, as doctrinally there should be none. That was because the first Muslims were settled by tribe in new military 'camp' cities – one would become Cairo – where religious life was ordered by the word of the caliph and worldly needs supplied by the booty of conquest or a tax on unbelievers.

Tribal camp life could not be perpetuated once Islam's success swelled the number of Muslims. Muhammad had left no son, an obvious cause of quarrels over succession among tribes, and the quarrel over the succession to the fourth caliphate caused a division in the Muslim community – which split into a Sunni majority and a Shi'i minority – of great bitterness. Further division was caused by the resentment of newer converts that the original tribal families continued to be supported by payments from a military register (*diwan*) which had originated as a means of distributing the spoils of conquest to further holy war.[65] The dispute over the succession was smoothed out, allowing the Ummayid caliphs of Damascus to prosecute the campaigns into Spain and Central Asia, but the tensions persisted. Stability was only restored under the Abbasid caliphs who transferred the capital to Baghdad after victory in a civil war in 749. The Abbasids had triumphed in part because they promised to dissolve the distinction between the original Muslims and later converts, a distinction which turned on membership of the military register. Once, however, the military register was abolished, as it effectively was by the Abbasids, soldiering in the name of the successors to Muhammad brought reduced worldly profit but aroused strong religious scruple whenever the caliphs were defied by dissident Muslim subjects. They were defied often during the eighth and ninth centuries, when Spain and Morocco broke away to found rival caliphates claiming closer descent from Muhammad's family. Deprived of traditional tribal support and unable to raise armies among convert Muslims who took seriously the prohibition against fighting fellow believers, the Abbasids were compelled to find soldiers elsewhere. The solution was to make a virtue of the expedient of arming slaves for warfare and to use state revenue to buy recruits to slave armies.

The caliph al-Mu'tasim (833–42) is regarded as the founder of the Muslim military slave system. In fact, slave soldiers had fought beside free Muslims even in the days of the Prophet but they had come from many sources; some had been the personal attendants of their masters.[66] The Abbasids recognised that they could no longer sustain their power through such a haphazard system of recruitment. Al-Mu'tasim went out into the market on a large scale, buying the best material available, which was Turkish manpower from the edge of the steppe; he is said eventually to have had 70,000 Turkish military slaves under command.[67] The development of such a large slave army resolved for the time being the besetting military dilemma of Islam, which was how to follow its call to *haram*, the exercise of unlimited authority, without setting Muslim against Muslim brother. It did not resolve the problem of how to make the caliphs obeyed by Muslims who had set up rival caliphates on the fringes of empire in Central Asia and North Africa. That needed effective and dynamic leaders for the new slave army. They were provided first by the Buyid family, stalwart defenders of the Central Asian frontier who set up a caliph of their own choosing in Baghdad in 945. Even more effective leaders were to be provided, however, by a tribe of the very Turkish peoples against whom the Buyids had won their reputation, the Seljuks. In 1055 the Seljuks, in the name of Sunni orthodoxy, entered Baghdad, overthrew the Shi'i Buyids and declared themselves the caliph's new protectors. They were soon to be called sultans – 'holders of power'.

The conversion of the Seljuks to the Sunni form of Islam has been called 'a change as momentous as the conversion of the Franks under Clovis to Christianity nearly five centuries earlier'.[68] It was to result in the destruction of most of the Byzantine empire that remained in Asia, and the consequent crisis for Christianity was to call forth the Crusades. The Seljuks had been converted as a body, through the efforts of Islamic missionaries working on the steppe frontier, only in 960, when they were but one of several Turkic horse peoples – including the Karluks, Kipchaks and Kirghiz – struggling for dominance in Central Asia. The Karluks were to find fortune as the Ghaznavid rulers of Afghanistan and later as founders of the Slave Kingdom of Delhi, one of the most important of the Mameluke states.[69] Even their exploits, however, did not compare with those of the Seljuks who, in Toghril Beg, Malik Shah and Alp Arslan, produced commanders of ferocious competence. Malik Shah, with his famous vizier Nizam al-Mulk, was responsible for a major extension of Abbasid power into Central Asia between 1080 and 1090. Alp Arslan, campaigning in the opposite direction, struck into the mountains of the Caucasus and in 1064 captured the capital of Christian Armenia. Pushing on through the formidable Caucasus mountains, he secured positions from which to threaten the eastern border of Byzantium. In August 1071, at Manzikert, he found the Byzantine army and fought and won a battle of incontestable importance for the future political geography of the Near East and of Europe, a battle that would make the Byzantine domain in Asia 'a land of Turkish speech and Islamic faith – in short "Turkey"'.[70]

The Abbasid experiment in dependence on slave armies had had, therefore, paradoxical results. By drawing the Turkic horse peoples into the service of the caliphate it had restored its power; by its choice of warrior nomads as its principal servants it had unwittingly surrendered its competence, even if not its nominal authority, and so separated for ever the leadership of Islam from its Arab roots. The Abbasids would continue to rule in name and even, in al-Nasir (1180–1225), find a caliph whose energy seemed to promise a revival of the dynasty's early years. The mistake had been made, however, of recruiting as slave soldiers a strain of proud, hardy, highly intelligent but alien warriors who eventually saw no reason to persist in subservience, who consequently took the means at hand to make themselves masters of the empire, and who, moreover, had the wit to devise a formula which preserved the dignity of the caliphate but delivered its substance to themselves.

Other alien Muslims would follow where the Seljuks had shown the way, once their power waned, as it did towards the end of the twelfth century. In the east the lands the Seljuks had secured fell to the Ghaznavids and to new Turkic intruders from the steppe, known as the Turkomans. In the west the caliphate was to find an outstanding military protector in Salah el-Din (Saladin), a Kurd from the Iranian northern mountains, who rose to prominence through the crisis of the Crusades. Manzikert, as we have seen, had driven the Byzantine armies from Asia and so terrified the Emperor Michael VII that, despite centuries of division and distrust between the eastern Orthodox and western Latin branches of Christianity, he had launched a cry for help to the Pope. The appeal had been slow to mature but had borne fruit in the end. In 1099 an army of Christian knights from France, Germany and Italy, and from many other western lands, had arrived outside Jerusalem, taken the city and established a bridgehead in the Holy Land from which the Crusaders intended to launch a campaign for the reconquest of the formerly Christian East from Islam. In the ensuing wars between the Crusading kingdoms and their Muslim enemies the tide of advantage flowed one way and another for nearly a century. Under the leadership of Saladin, appointed to command in Egypt in 1171, the balance seemed to swing decisively to the Muslim side. For the next eighty years, despite constant renewals of the Crusading effort, the Crusaders fought constantly on the defensive, their foothold shrinking to the point of extinction. The counter-offensive launched by Saladin appeared ready to culminate in a conclusive Muslim victory. Islam, however, had been looking in the wrong direction. Intent on solving a border problem in the west, the caliphs had neglected their security in the east. There, unperceived at first, a new menace began to grow out of the steppe at the beginning of the thirteenth century. In 1220–1 much of Central Asia and Persia fell to a strange horse people; in 1243 what is now Turkey fell also. The conquerors were not Muslims and campaigned with a terrifying ruthlessness against all who opposed them. In 1258 they entered Baghdad and put al-Muzt'asim, last of the Abbasid caliphs, to death. These conquerors were the Mongols.

The Mongols

Why the Mongols, any more than similar horse peoples of the steppe world who preceded them on the paths of invasion into the civilised lands, should have exceeded them all in the extent and rapidity of their conquests defies easy explanation. Exceed them nevertheless the Mongols did; indeed, no sequence of campaigns by a single people before or since has ever subjected so large an area to military domination. Between 1190, when Temujin, later to take the name Genghis Khan, began the unification of the tribes of Mongolia, and 1258, when his grandson stormed Baghdad, the Mongols successively overran the whole of northern China, Korea, Tibet, Central Asia, the Khwarezemian state in Persia, the Caucasus, Turkish Anatolia and the Russian principalities, and raided into northern India; in 1237–41 they campaigned extensively in Poland, Hungary, East Prussia and Bohemia and sent reconnaissances toward Vienna and Venice. They withdrew from Europe only when news reached their armies there of the death of Genghis Khan's son and successor. Under his heirs, the Mongols further extended their domains to include all of China, where Genghis Khan's grandson Kubla Khan founded the Yuan dynasty that reigned until the end of the fourteenth century; they also exerted control over parts of Burma and Vietnam, attempted – though failed – to invade Japan and Java, and continued to intervene in India, where in 1526 Babur, a descendant of Genghis, founded the Moghul (Mongol) empire. The title of Empress of India, assumed by Queen Victoria in 1876, derived directly from this Moghul conquest 350 years earlier and so ultimately from the ambitions of Genghis Khan, who in 1211, on the eve of his departure from the steppe on his first campaign, emerged from the tent where he had communed with heaven, to proclaim to his people, 'Heaven has promised me victory.'[71]

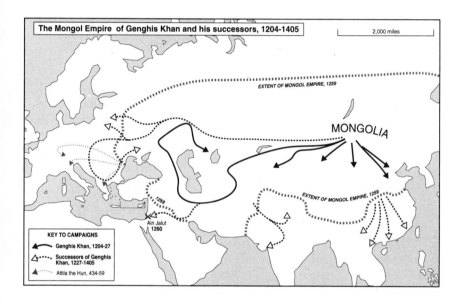

It is, however, towards China, not India, that the Mongols first set their course, since they were borderers of that empire. From the time of the earliest unification under the Ch'in in the first millennium BC, Chinese dynasties had always been menaced, and often usurped, by peoples from north of the Yellow River. In time the dynasties devised a dual system of coping with these irruptions: using the Great Wall, first consolidated by the Ch'in, and frequently rebuilt, realigned and extended, as a primary line of demarcation between civilisation and nomadism, the Chinese rulers encouraged the border peoples – inevitably partly sinicised by contact with Chinese traders, officials and soldiers, and directly rewarded for their services by grants of protection, subsidies and territory (sometimes within the Great Wall) – to act as primary defenders of the settled lands; then, if that primary line of defence was penetrated, they counted on the superior attractions of their own civilised Chinese life to disarm the invaders in the course of time. The policy was based 'on a set of assumptions, all of which reinforced the notion of the supremacy of Chinese institutions and culture and of their acceptability to the barbarians; the idea that the latter might not have had any need for Chinese culture was never entertained.'[72]

For more than a thousand years the policy worked. Though often invaded, at times divided and in some periods seriously disrupted, China was never wholly subjected to non-Chinese rule; foreigners who succeeded in carving out an area of authority were indeed, through acculturation and intermarriage, always absorbed into the civilisation. Periods of disruption often resulted in a positive and creative reaction when central power was re-established. Thus the Sui dynasty (581–617) and the succeeding T'ang (618–907), dominated though they were by aristocracies whose roots lay in the barbarian and largely Turkic invasions from the steppe that had caused the divisions of the third to fifth centuries, not only extended and strengthened the Great Wall but constructed huge public works, including the Grand Canal which linked the Yellow and Yangtse rivers above their navigable points. All this was achieved, moreover, without a militarisation of the regime, which stands in remarkable contrast to the experience of the Romans, who suffered first the barbarisation of their army and then the supplanting of their polity by warrior kingdoms that lived by the sword.

Though the Chinese ruling dynasties and aristocracies esteemed skill-at-arms and horsemanship, they did not confuse military leadership with administrative skills. And under the Sui and T'ang dynasties the gradualist military strategy first propounded by the fourth-century writer Sun Tzu took root. Sun Tzu drew on an existing corpus of ideas and practices in formalising his theory; it would not otherwise have recommended itself to the Chinese mind. In its emphasis on avoiding battle except with the assurance of victory, of disfavouring risk, of seeking to overawe an enemy by psychological means, and of using time rather than force to wear an invader down (all concepts recognised to be profoundly anti-Clausewitzian by twentieth-century strategists, when the campaigns of Mao Tse-tung and Ho Chi Minh drew Sun Tzu to their attention) his *Art of War* encouraged the integration of Chinese military with political theory in an intellectual whole.[73] And gradualism in any case best suited the Chinese armies of the Sui and early T'ang periods, which were recruited on a militia basis, and reinforced at the frontiers by contingents of non-Chinese but sinicised auxiliaries.

At the height of its power in the early eighth century, the T'ang achieved greater success than any Chinese dynasty had done before or was to do afterward. Through its material and intellectual ascendancy, in particular as a result of the proselytising energies of Chinese teachers of Buddhism, who had overtaken the Indians and Ceylonese as exponents of its beliefs in East and South Asia, the T'ang empire extended its borders to include wide areas beyond the Great Wall, parts of Indochina and the eastern borderlands of Tibet, then a troublesome neighbour. The T'ang dynasty's very success, however, was to prove its undoing. Military success, perhaps inevitably, elevated military men, often non-Chinese, to prominence, and a struggle for power between the mandarinate and the *generalität* ensued, leading in 755–63 to a military rebellion of such severity that the emperor was forced to flee his capital, and his successor succeeded in restoring authority only by enlisting Tibetan and nomad help. These events immediately followed the Arabs' defeat of the T'ang army at Talas in 751, which was the decisive moment in the struggle between the Middle and Far East for control of Central Asia. The Chinese commander at Talas had been a Korean, while the leader of the rebellion of 755, An Lu-shan, was of mixed Sogdian and Turkish birth. In Chinese terms, both came from the barbarian world.

This reappearance of non-Chinese men at the centre of Chinese imperial affairs presaged ill for the future. Though from the eighth century on there was an enormous expansion of rice production through intensive irrigation, and from it a doubling of the Chinese population, these developments were largely confined to the Yangtse valley and the south. In the north the military rebellion led to famine, the diffusion of imperial power into the hands of local commissioners of the military regions, and the recruitment of mercenary armies composed of 'the rootless, of those on the loose, and of convicts granted a conditional amnesty'.[74] From this period dates the Chinese distaste and contempt for the trade of soldiering that persisted until the victory of the People's Liberation Army in 1949. At the beginning of the tenth century, imperial authority broke down; though unity was restored by the Sung, that dynasty (established in 960) did not succeed in recovering the territories in the north-west and north that had come under the control of the Mongolian Khitay and the Siberian Jürchen (the latter, in the seventeenth century, would conquer China as the Manchus). Meanwhile, the Sung's western provinces fell to the Western Hsia or Tanguts, a people of mixed Turkish, Tibetan and Siberian origin.

Thus 'Han' China, so called from the dynasty which had forcibly populated so much of its empire with ethnic Chinese, was in an unstable condition when Genghis Khan was given heaven's assurance of victory in 1211. The Great Wall was in the hands of a non-Han people, the western flank was occupied by another barbarian group, while the Sung's army was 'overmanned and inefficient, although military expenditure absorbed most of the budget' to pay mercenary wages, was short of horses and was deprived of the support of auxiliary barbarian contingents, since the dynasty no longer exerted influence on the steppe border.[75] Yet these circumstances still do not explain how the Mongols overran so much of China so quickly, let alone their equally whirlwind victories in the west.

Much was undoubtedly due to the character of Genghis Khan himself and to the single-mindedness with which he enforced Mongol tribal customs and tribal prejudices against outsiders. Mongol sexual morality was strict: adultery was punished by the death of both parties, and the taking of captive women was also disfavoured. This code eliminated quarrels over wife-stealing so characteristic, and disruptive, of primitive societies.[76] The Mongols, and Genghis Khan in particular, were nevertheless quick to take offence and brutal in taking revenge on outsiders; indeed, Genghis's life is largely a history of revenge-taking, and Mongol warfare may be viewed as an extension of the primitive urge to vengeance on an enormous scale. Yet the Mongols were perfectly ready to enlist the expert help of outsiders and, indeed, to add foreign contingents to their army; necessarily so, since the size of the Mongol nucleus of the force with which they began the second phase of their conquest of northern China in 1216 has been estimated at only 23,000.[77] The majority in the 'Mongol' armies that terrorised the West were Turks, while the Tartars (with whom the Mongols are so often confused, a confusion that ethnolinguists have difficulty in disentangling) were neighbours whom Genghis subjected.[78]

Much is made by students of Genghis of the sophistication of his military organisation: his offer to his followers of a 'career open to talents' and his logical division of the army into tens, hundreds and thousands – there were eventually to be ninety-five 'thousands' – which anticipated the modern Western system of subordinating sections to squadrons and squadrons to regiments.[79] All this was no doubt significant; by disengaging appointment to command from considerations of heredity – except where his immediate family was concerned – and by making it dependent on performance, he was breaking with tribalism. These innovations, nevertheless, were internal to a tiny people, quite lacking in the numbers necessary to overwhelm populations hundreds of times larger. None of the horse peoples from the steppe ever exceeded a few hundred thousand, but the extent of their conquests do not bear comparison with those of the Mongols and it seems unlikely that, had they been better organised, they would have equalled them in warmaking. Other factors were at work.

These did not include a superior technology. The Mongols – like the Huns, the Turks and the Chinese aristocracies who preserved the love of the horse they had inherited from their steppe ancestors – knew no way of fighting but that which depended on the composite bow and a string of ponies; it has been suggested that their army included contingents of armoured cavalry, but this is most unlikely. Admittedly, the Mongols enlisted the help of foreigners who understood the techniques of siege warfare; nevertheless, siege engineering in the pre-gunpowder age was a laborious and time-consuming method of breaking into strongholds whose defenders were determined to resist. Since, despite speculation to the contrary, it is almost certain that the Mongols had not yet learned the use of gunpowder – if, indeed, anyone had at that period – and none the less overwhelmed a whole succession of fortified places in the East and West – Utrar in Transoxiana (1220), Balkh, Merv, Herat and Nishapur in Persia (1221), and Ning-hsia, the capital of the Western Hsia (1226) – we must conclude that the garrisons generally gave up without a struggle.[80] It is significant that at the one place where the Mongols met resolute resistance, the Persian city of Gurganj, the siege lasted from October 1220 to April 1221, exactly the sort of delay that feudal warriors in the West would have anticipated in a similar action at that time.

What seems likely in the circumstances is that the word got about that the Mongols could not be beaten. We know that Bokhara and Samarkand capitulated at their very appearance; in Bokhara, Genghis, perhaps evoking the spectre of Attila, preached a sermon in the chief mosque describing himself as the 'flail of God'. What made for this reputation of invincibility? The Mongols knew the use of the stirrup, which Attila's Huns did not, but the stirrup had been in general use for 500 years. The Mongol horse had over time probably been bred to a higher standard than the Hun, and by improved horsemastership they could possibly maintain larger stocks, but these advantages would have been enjoyed also by the Turks. Genghis and his sons imposed a ferocious discipline on their tribesmen; the *yasa*, their code of law, laid down that booty was to be held collectively, and made it a capital offence for a warrior to abandon a comrade in battle, and these sanctions against personal enrichment and the habit of flight in the face of danger so characteristic of 'primitive' warfare may allow us to regard the Mongol cavalry swarm as an army, operating above the 'military horizon', and not just a war band.[81] Nevertheless, the reasons for the fear in which they were quickly held still seem elusive.

Focus is supplied if we discard the notion that the Mongol invasions were a sort of military pandemic, erupting almost simultaneously throughout the whole area of affliction, and recognise that they developed sequentially from small beginnings and were conducted with ruthless skill. Vengeance has been suggested as the Mongols' motive, and it is certainly true that their first successful campaign was against the Chin, who had insultingly demanded that Genghis should do them homage as a notional vassal, and their second against the Khwarazamians, who had treacherously killed envoys requesting rights to trade. Genghis did not attack without calculation, however; like Alexander the Great, he was a voracious consumer of intelligence about his intended victims and maintained a wide network of spies. He was also, like Alexander, a rational strategist. Before he set off to attack the Chin, he dismissed the option of a march across the Gobi Desert, the direct but difficult route, in favour of a roundabout approach through the Kansu corridor, the continuation of the Silk Road east of the Dzungarian gap which gives on to the end of the Great Wall. The need to fight and win an initial campaign against the Western Hsia he accepted as a necessary preliminary.

It may also have appeared desirable. It has been suggested that the Western Hsia, or Tanguts, were but one of a group of horse peoples all engaged in an undeclared, and to outside eyes unrecognised, struggle to recreate that unified steppe empire which the Turks had first brought into being in the sixth century. 'When and how these attempts to recreate a unified steppe empire began are clouded in myth and legend, as well as by the subsequent embellishments by the Mongols themselves of [Genghis Khan's] career.'[82] The Mongols, by this interpretation, were drawn into this struggle and ended as the undisputed leaders of their language group: from that victory their subsequent history flowed. If we accept this version, and it is tempting to do so, it clears away the last and chief difficulty in understanding how the Mongols rose to world empire. They cease to appear as a people 'remote from the centres of civilised life [and] almost untouched by cultural or religious influences from the cities of eastern and southern Asia', and emerge instead as participants in a struggle that ran along the whole steppe horizon; the struggle was the medium through which, however indirectly, notions of military discipline and organisation from beyond the horizon transformed their methods of warmaking.[83]

Most of these must have been Turkish in origin, fed back in altered form from the Islamic Middle East and China. Over the centuries Sinicised

206

or Islamicised Turks must have made their way back on to the steppe as successful veterans returning home, as failures or outcasts, as fugitives fleeing punishment, as escorts to merchants, or even as official emissaries. Old soldiers' tales always find a ready audience and knowledge of foreign military expertise is a currency of universal value. The idea that the Mongols knew nothing of their enemies' strengths before they set out, or that they learned nothing from them, cannot be entertained.

The most important of the strengths they may have learned was an abstract one: that infusion of warmaking by Islam with the force of an idea. It is significant that the Turks whom the Mongols are most likely to have known or heard of were Islam's frontier warriors, the *ghazis* who taught the Koran with the sword. Genghis himself is said to have believed that his mission was divine, sanctioned and demanded by Heaven, to have taught his followers so, to have required the shamans to support his position and even to have preached a sort of primitive nationalism which held the Mongols to be a chosen race.[84] Yet, more important still, he accepted none of Islam's palliating morality. The tools of warmaking already at his disposal – the horse warrior's mobility, the long-range lethality of the composite bow, the do-or-die ethos of the *ghazi*, the social élan of exclusive tribalism – were formidable enough. When to those ingredients was added a pitiless paganism, untroubled by any of the monotheistic or Buddhist concerns with mercy to strangers or with personal perfection, it is not surprising that Genghis and the Mongols acquired a reputation for invincibility. Their minds as well as their weapons were agents of terror, and the terror they spread remains a memory to this day.

THE DECLINE OF THE HORSE PEOPLES

Yet ultimately the besetting inability of horse peoples to translate initial conquest into permanent power overtook the Mongols as it had overtaken the Huns and the Buminid Turks. Genghis is credited with great administrative ability but it was extractive, not stabilising, designed to support the nomad way of life, not to change it. His system included no means for legitimising the rule of a single successor, even in the eyes of the Mongols themselves, let alone that of their subjects. Nomadic custom was for the ruler's appanage – territory, followers, flocks – to be divided equally between his sons and, when Genghis died in 1227, that is what happened. His empire was shared out between the four sons of his chief wife, Börte. The youngest, according to custom, received the ancestral lands, while the conquered territories were shared between the others.

Over the next generations the Mongol rulers of Russia went their own way but those of Central Asia and China were drawn into disputes over the succession that resulted in civil war among Genghis's grandsons. It was resolved when Hülegü, ruler of Central Asia, agreed to support the claim of his brother Kubilai (Kubla Khan) to the title Genghis had held. That did not, however, restore unity in the Mongol heartland. Kubla Khan was already engaged in the war that would establish his branch as the Yuan dynasty of China, a struggle that eventually consumed all his energies and progressively detached the Mongols who followed him from their old steppe life. Hülegü, meanwhile, in pursuing the challenge for primacy in Central Asia, increasingly involved himself in the endemic warfare on the eastern border of the Islamic lands and so committed himself to an eventual campaign against the caliphate itself.

Though the Mongol empire's disintegration can be seen with hindsight to have begun from the moment when Kubla Khan turned to China, its disintegration was not apparent at the time either to Islam or to the Christian West; both correctly identified the Mongols as a power still greatly to be reckoned with, yet from entirely opposed perspectives. Locked in their own struggle, a century and a half old, for possession of the Holy Land, news of the approach of Hülegü's Mongol horde from Central Asia brought, respectively, fear and hope.

Hope was what the Crusaders of the Latin kingdoms of the East felt. The Crusades have been described as constituting no more than 'a border problem' for Islam, one among many, and it is true that the Crusaders had never succeeded in enlarging the foothold they had won at Jerusalem in 1099 to any extent. They had even lost Jerusalem to Saladin in the twelfth century, clinging on by their fingernails to a few enclaves along the Syrian coast in the aftermath of his counter-offensive. Yet the appeal of the Crusade had never died in the West. Constantly renewed, it had called forth five 'official' Crusades by the thirteenth century; numerous others had been aborted or else directed against enemies of the Church in other lands. It had led to the founding of powerful military orders of knights under religious vows, to the building of a system of strong castles for them to garrison on the Crusading kingdoms' borders and to the dissemination and refinement of a code of 'chivalry' among the horse-riding knightly class throughout Christian Europe. Between the eleventh and the thirteenth centuries chivalry had become unquestionably the most important element in the military culture of the West, at a time when the energies of the Western aristocracies were almost wholly directed to warmaking. The regular renewals of the call to go Crusading, to which kings lent as ready an ear as landless knights hoping to win fame and wealth in the East, therefore paid off. By the middle of the thirteenth century, when Hülegü's Mongols stood poised to break out of Central Asia, Jerusalem had been recaptured and the integrity of the Latin kingdoms restored. Their fortunes seemed to have been revived and the original Crusading vision to stand in the ascendant again. Crusading hopes had been dashed so often, however, that no Crusader would confuse a temporary alleviation of difficulty with a permanent reversal of the balance of power. Power still rested with Islam, which had an apparently inexhaustible capacity to mobilise new offensive efforts from within its own spiritual and physical resources. In a one-front war, it enjoyed the advantages. Rumours of the approach of Hülegü's Mongol horde from Central Asia, promising the opening of a second front against the Crusaders' enemy, inevitably kindled expectations of a change of circumstances. To such effect, indeed, that the Crusaders leapt at a confusion of names of the mysterious horse peoples to invent a Christian king, Prester John, who was riding to their rescue from the interior of the steppe.[85] Hülegü was not Prester John. The Crusaders were right, nevertheless, to perceive him as a threat to their enemies. Islam, which had felt a tremor of fear at news of his approach, was equally right to regard the Mongol advance as a menace. How greatly they were to be feared it had yet to learn.

Saladin's success against the Crusaders in the twelfth century had shifted the effective centre of Islamic life to Egypt and Syria, where his descendants ruled as the Ayyubid dynasty. The legitimate Abbasid caliphate still had its seat at Baghdad, however, and it was that city that lay in the Mongols' immediate path. At the outset, Hülegü's approach in 1256 did not arouse alarm, since it seemed to be directed against the murderous sect of the Assassins; his destruction of their strongholds was widely welcomed and prompted the Christian Armenians to send a contingent to join his horde. In 1257, however, he entered Persia, which he quickly conquered, and by the end of the year stood poised to enter Mesopotamia. The Abbasid caliph, al-Muzt'asim, quaked before his coming but could not quite bring himself to submit to the unvarying Mongol demand: capitulation or extinction. In January 1258, Hülegü crossed the Tigris from Persia, brushed aside the Caliph's army and captured Baghdad. Al-Muzt'asim was put to death by strangulation, a steppe practice that the Ottoman Turks would later institute as a succession procedure in their court life at Istanbul.[86] Hülegü also had many of the Baghdad citizens massacred, though they had been guaranteed their lives, a breach with Mongol custom perhaps intended to transmit a shock wave ahead of him. The inhabitants of Aleppo in Syria, to which he next moved, were massacred also, but they had defended their city. The citizens of Damascus and many other Muslim places were more prudent and were spared. The spectacle of the collapse of Islamic power all about them encouraged the Crusaders to persist in their view that the Mongols aided their cause and even persuaded Bohemond, mightiest of Crusaders, to join their army for a while. When it pressed on into the Holy Land, however, they thought better and withdrew into their coastal forts. In the absence of Hülegü, who had been recalled to the steppe to take part in the selection of a Great Khan, they came to a hasty understanding with the equally anxious Ayyubids of Egypt and agreed, despite their bitter memories of defeat by Saladin, to allow an Egyptian army to enter their territory, make camp near Acre and prepare to oppose the Mongols, now led by Hülegü's subordinate, Kitbuga. While they waited, Baybars, the Egyptian commander, was actually received at the Crusading court.

Baybars was a Mameluke and a ferociously ambitious character, who had already asserted the power of the Mameluke institution in Egypt by murdering one sultan and replacing him with another. He may have had a hand in the decision taken to murder the Mongol envoys who had been sent by Kitbuga with the usual demand for submission. This act of defiance, particularly provocative in view of the Mongols' known commitment to vengeance as a *casus belli*, ensured that battle would ensue. So it did; the Mongols advanced from their encampments in Syria into northern Palestine and on 3 September 1260, at Ain Jalut (the Spring of Goliath) north of Jerusalem, they and the Egyptian army, commanded by the sultan Qutuz and Baybars, clashed. In a single morning of fighting the Mongols were defeated, Kitbuga captured and killed and the survivors scattered, never to return.

Ain Jalut, the first pitched battle that the Mongols lost, caused a sensation at the time throughout the Christian, Muslim and Mongol world and it continues to be closely studied by historians. Its result is disputed: did it save the Near East from Mongol domination, or was the Mongol horde already at the limit of its strategic and logistic outreach? The tactics of the battle, too, divide historians: was it a brilliant feat of arms by Baybars or did the Egyptian army win by weight of numbers? There is certainly substance to the argument that the Mongol horses had eaten out Syria, as cavalry armies always tended to eat out cultivated land when they left the steppe, and it does appear that Hülegü had taken much of his force with him when he left for Central Asia.[87] On the other hand, recent estimates are that as many as 10–20,000 remained under Kitbuga.

At the same time, it is now thought that the size of the Egyptian army may have been exaggerated, and that its core of Mamelukes may have numbered no more than 10,000 in a force of 20,000.[88] In short, Ain Jalut may have been fought on equal terms and thus have been a truly significant encounter, if not because of its immediate strategic outcome, then because it marked the power of one horse people, organised as a professional force and supported by the revenues of a sedentary state, to overcome that of another still living by pillage and animated by the primitive values of tribalism and vengeance.

We have already noted the judgement of Abu Shama that 'it was a remarkable thing that the [Mongols] were defeated and destroyed by men of their own kind', a reference to the presence of large numbers of Turks on both sides. Certainly the battle appears to have been fought in traditional steppe fashion, with the Egyptians advancing to contact with the Mongols, feigning retreat at the moment of action and drawing their pursuers to follow them to a site where the ground favoured a sudden counter-attack. Nevertheless, the turning-point seems to have been the moment when Sultan Qutuz launched himself into the mêlée with the cry 'O Islam' – a reminder to us that the Mamelukes were the military servants of a war-making religion while their opponents shared no common creed.[89] It was also supremely important that Baybars' men had a great deal of military experience, won against the still-formidable Crusaders, and reinforced by the endless drill and discipline of the Mameluke school of war. If it is not correct to speak of Baybars' Mamelukes as an army in the modern sense, their tactics had not yet fossilised into the anachronism they were later to become when confronted by Ottoman gunpowder, were quite appropriate to the challenge the Mongols presented and demonstrate in retrospect the 'value-added' effect of training lent to one force when engaged with an equivalent relying instead on élan and reputation.

After Ain Jalut, the Mongols had no further surprises to unleash on the civilised world, nor did any other horse people. That judgement may seem to do less than justice to Tamerlane who, in his time as conqueror (1381–45), spread even more terror than Genghis had done, and over almost as wide an area. Tamerlane, however, lacked even such administrative ability as Genghis had shown and, in his practice of exemplary terror, destroyed the foundations of anything he might have built upon.[90]

Tamerlane possessed the warrior spirit; born Timur, he became known as Timur-leng or Tamer the Lame after an early wounding that left him with a limp. He encouraged a pitiless quality of atrocity in his soldiers; it is from his campaigns, rather than those of Genghis, that derive the memories of towers and pyramids of skulls.[91] He seems, however, to have been possessed by nothing more than the warlike urge, refusing his followers all opportunity to enjoy the fruits of victory, but seeking forever new worlds to conquer. It was a thankful relief to the civilisations on the steppe border when he died just before setting out to contest possession of Kublai Khan's conquests with the restored native Ming dynasty in China. By the end of the fourteenth century, Mongol power had effectively been extinguished wherever it had spilled over the edge of the steppe; only in India, and then in a form so heavily Islamicised as to make its Genghisid and Timurid origins unrecognisable, was it to have a future.

What, then, was the Mongol legacy? To have caused the dispersion of Turkic peoples to three corners of the earth – China, India and the Middle East – is thought by one historian to have been the principal outcome, with all that that implied for the military histories of those three regions. Certainly, Genghis Khan, by displacing westward the then insignificant tribe of Ottomans, initiated a sequence of events that devastated the established order in the Near East, replaced it with another that survived into this century, and held Europe under threat of an Islamic offensive that persisted from the fall of Constantinople in 1453 until the raising of the siege of Vienna 230 years later.

Through their intimate involvement with the European world, however, the Ottomans were forced into a military compromise between the steppe *Blitzkrieg* and the sedentary warfare of fortifications and heavy infantry whose opposed tendencies they never managed to reconcile. They succeeded in founding their own disciplined, regular heavy infantry force, but only on the basis of a slave system (the Janissaries), which eventually fossilised it as it fossilised the Mamelukes; at the same time they persisted in encumbering themselves in their Asiatic domains with a horse-riding aristocracy whose nomadic lawlessness proved ineradicable; these Anatolian chieftains became effectively independent of the Turkish sultan in the eighteenth century.[92]

Nevertheless, it is in the Ottomans' attempts at compromise between their steppe heritage and the challenge of their confrontation with the urban and agricultural West that one perceives the true significance of what the horse peoples brought to warfare. No doubt the ecological explanation of their failure to carry their conquests off the grasslands, or, if they did so, of their subsequent abandonment of steppe culture, is correct. Permanent pasture can be maintained only by intensive effort in irrigated or naturally forested lands; such effort requires a settled population that needs agriculture to support it; agriculture and pasturage are incompatible; therefore invaders intent on grazing large strings of horses had either to retreat to their proper habitat or change their ways. The horse peoples, as we have seen, did one or the other. Whatever the outcome, however, the military habits of the worlds into which they made their irruptions were changed by the experience for ever.

The horse-riding peoples, like the charioteers before them, brought to warmaking the electric concept of campaigning over long distances and, when campaigning resolved itself into battle, of manoeuvering on the battlefield at speed – at least five times the speed of men on foot. As protectors of their flocks and herds against predators, they also preserved the spirit of the hunter, lost to agriculturalists except of the lordly class; in their management of animals they showed a matter-of-factness – in mustering, droving, culling, slaughter for food – that taught direct lessons about how masses of people on foot, even inferior cavalrymen, could be harried, outflanked, cornered and eventually killed without risk. These were practices that primitive hunters, with their empathetic relationship with their quarry and mystic respect for the stricken prey, would have found intrinsically alien. To the horse peoples, equipped with their principal weapon, the composite bow, itself a product of the animal tissues which supported their way of life, killing at a distance – of emotional detachment as well as physical space – was second nature.

It was the emotional detachment of the horse warriors, ultimately manifest in their deliberate practice of atrocity, which the settled peoples found so terrifying. It nevertheless rubbed off on them. Of the two characteristics of 'primitive' warfare that persisted well into the development of civilisation – tentativeness of encounter and association of ritual and ceremony with combat and its aftermath – the horse peoples had truck with neither. They may have made a practice of retreating before an enemy who showed fight; but this was a feigned manoeuvre, designed to draw an opponent out of a chosen position, disorder his ranks and expose him to a disabling counter-attack; in no way did they equate with the primitive warrior's unwillingness to come to hand strokes. When a horse horde closed in for the kill, it slaughtered without compunction. There was absolutely no hint, moreover, of ritual or ceremony in the actions of a horse horde. The horse peoples fought to win – quickly, completely and quite unheroically. Eschewal of heroic display was, indeed, almost a nomad rule. Genghis himself, though wounded by an arrow early in his rise to power, was physically timid and later took no exposed part in the battles where he was nominally in command.[93] Western warriors found it a most bewildering characteristic of nomad tactics that the leader's position in the typical crescent formation was unidentifiable, since he usually rode inconspicuously far from the centre, where an Alexander or a Lionheart would have put himself on view.

The habit of heroic display clung to Western concepts of military leadership for a very long time.[94] If the horse peoples failed to dissuade would-be heroes among their enemies from taking the attendant risks, they were undeniably successful in transmitting their unceremonious concern to win. In Eastern Europe, as the military historian Christopher Duffy has noted, warfare on the European continent first assumed the racialist and totalitarian character that insidiously came to pervade it everywhere; he ascribes this to Mongol influence on 'the Russian character and Russian institutions, [leading to] the brutalisation of the peasantry, a denial of human dignity and a distorted sense of values which reserved a special admiration for ferocity, tyrannical ways and slyness'.[95] Steppe ferocity also made its way into Europe by a southerly route, first through the Seljuk advance into Anatolia, then by the Ottoman conquest of the Balkans; war on the Ottoman frontier was for centuries the fiercest in Europe. It may also have filtered back through the Crusaders' encounter with Islam.

If Crusading may be seen as the mirror image of *jihad*, it was not until Saladin confronted the Latin kingdoms that they found themselves with a real fight on their hands; but Saladin was a product of Islam's energetic response to the challenge from the steppe, while the core of his army of Turkish slave soldiers were expert in the ferocious tactics of mounted archery. Crusading in the East brought back into Europe habits learned there; they may have been translated into the northern Crusades against the pagan Slavs – themselves under attack by the steppe peoples from the opposite direction; eventually they penetrated Spain, where the knights of the Reconquista fought Islam with a ruthlessness Genghis would have applauded. War *à outrance* certainly took root in Spain; it is not fanciful to suggest that the awful fate of the Incas and the Aztecs – the latter still trapped in the pathetically inappropriate ceremonialism of the flower battles – at the hand of the Spanish conquistadors ultimately harked back to Genghis himself.

In China, the empire with which the horse people of the steppe were most intimately connected, Mongol habits of warmaking perhaps had their most durable effect. 'The Chinese Way of Warfare', as John King Fairbank has reminded us, preserved from primitivism practices of ritual and ceremony – including divination and displays of prowess by champions before battle – that persisted much longer than in any other great civilisation;[96] but it also included a unique ethical component, derived from the

Confucian code central to Chinese public life, that was best expressed by the idea that 'the superior man should be able to attain his ends without violence'.[97] The Turkic invaders whom the Chinese absorbed during the first millennium AD were brought to accept that ethic, even though they retained their pride in the steppe warrior's skills of riding and archery. By the violence of the reaction necessary to overthrow the Mongols, after the conquest by Kublai, however, the Ming emperors were obliged to impose on their fellow Chinese a regime more absolutist than any known before. The Ming, in effect, militarised China and created a hereditary military class; it was under the Ming that China embarked on its only sustained effort at overseas expansion, and its largest effort to control the steppe by direct offensive action; five great expeditions were mounted by the dynasty north of the Great Wall, which was also then rebuilt in the form we see today. The military effort to restore traditional China had an unattended and largely contrary result: 'the Ming regime which cast out the Mongol Yüan dynasty became more despotic in its image, imitated some features of the Yüan military system, and remained transfixed by the menace of a revival of Mongol military power.'[98]

The Ming were right to persist in their fear of the barbarians from the steppe, but when a new menace appeared to overthrow them in the seventeenth century, it was mounted, ironically, not by the Mongols but by one of their hereditary enemy peoples, the Manchus.

The Manchus were not strictly a horse people, since they had become largely settled, sinicised and mercantile before they left Manchuria. But the core of their army was cavalry, and they brought to perfection the Mongol technique of using military power to make the Chinese administrative system work for them.

> This was an achievement not only on the military level but even more on the level of political organisation. The secret of this in turn was the nomads' capacity to work with Chinese of the border region and through this collaboration combine under one regime the skills of violent warfare by non-Chinese and of administration through trustworthy Chinese underlings – how to seize power and how to keep and use it.[99]

Unfortunately the power of the Ming dynasty that the Manchus seized in China was a heavily Mongolised version of the Chinese ideal of government, and they kept and used it by the principle of altering it not at all. The best of the Ch'ing emperors became, in the eighteenth century, paternal despots, who patronised the intelligentsia, encouraged the arts, sponsored the rise of trade and banking, and instituted the mildest fiscal regime the peasantry of China had ever known. The penalty for this benevolence, however, was 'hypertrophy of the centralised bureaucracy'. Nothing could be decided except by reference to Peking, while the civil servants trapped within the regime were the products of a system of competitive examination and education which 'strengthened inhibitions'.[100] Hypertrophy arrested the Chinese genius for adaptation. China had once been a civilisation of scientific enquiry and technical development, but under the Manchus all attempts at change, material as well as intellectual, fell under suspicion. In Japan, in the same period, technological change was outlawed in the interests of preserving a certain social order and the dominance of a native ruling class; in China, to preserve an alien ruling class, technological change was stifled rather than outlawed. Whereas in Japan the samurai eventually came to see that their future lay in embracing Western science and industry, the Manchus and their mandarins could not make the leap into modernity. We can assemble evidence of many influences to suggest why not. Ultimately, however, the failure was due to the Manchus' very foreignness, their origins as conquerors from the steppe, and the consequent ossification of their military system which, as the basis of their power, they shrank from updating. There is no more pathetic episode in military history than that of the Manchu bannermen of the nineteenth century pitting their outmatched composite bows against the rifles and cannon of the European invaders.

A long telescope allows us to see that the fighting powers of the Europeans who waged the nineteenth-century opium wars against China had been sharpened long ago and far away by their ancestors' encounter with the Manchus' horse-people ancestors. The European armies of the age of imperialism owed one pillar of their efficiency to a principle established off the steppe: that of bureaucratic organisation, founded in Sumer and Assyria, translated through Persia to Macedon, Rome and Byzantium, and artificially revived from classical sources at the Renaissance. They owed another, that of commitment to the pitched battle, to the Greeks. All the others – long-range campaigning, high-speed manoeuvre on the battlefield, effective missile technology, the application of the wheel to warfare and, above all, mutuality between horse and warrior – had their origins on the steppe and its borderlands. We may even ascribe to the later Turks and Mongols credit for taking from Islam that creed's revolutionary contribution to warmaking – its detachment from considerations of family, race, territory or particular political forms – and investing it with the force of an idea: that war could be an autonomous activity and the warrior's life a culture in itself. It was that culture, in a diluted but still recognisable form, which Clausewitz encountered among the Cossacks whose 'unmilitary' ways so affronted him during the Moscow campaign of 1812. 'Unmilitary' it may have been; it had troubled the world nevertheless, for much longer than Clausewitzian strategy was to do, while, in the transmission of its ruthlessness, ferocity and obsession with unconditional victory to the warfare of settled peoples, Clausewitz himself owed much more to it than his ordered mind would ever allow him to recognise.

Interlude 3
Armies

Clausewitz was unable to recognise an alternative military tradition in the Cossacks' style of warmaking because he could recognise as rational and worthwhile only one form of military organisation: the paid and disciplined forces of the bureaucratic state. He could not see that other forms might equally well serve their societies, and well defend them – or extend their power, if that was their ethos. The gunpowder armies that he knew were, of course, irresistible by the undrilled, and even by weaker versions of themselves. He could not foresee the stalemate they would impose on each other as they multiplied their firepower during the next century in pursuit of those battlefield victories he laid down it was their purpose to achieve; nor could he foresee that, for example, 'the Chinese Way of Warfare' would, in the twentieth century, inflict on Western armies and their commanders, schooled in his teachings, a painful and long-drawn-out humiliation.

Yet Clausewitz had under his eyes examples of military organisation, each rational in its own terms, which differed markedly from the regimental order in which he had trained and served. That of the Cossacks was one; another was that of the *opolchenie*, the militia of serfs raised by the Russian landowners to harry Napoleon's retreat. Inadvertently, he admitted the part the *opolchenie* played in driving the Grand Army's soldiers to their fate when he noted the 'armed people around them'.[1] He himself was an ardent exponent of the militia principle when it came to freeing Prussia; his *Essential Points on the Formation of a Defence Force* (January 1813) formed the basis for the raising of the national *Landwehr*, a conscript force. Equally important were the volunteer *Jäger* and *Freischützen* units, formed by romantic young patriots eager to wage irregular warfare against the French. Elsewhere in the great mobilisation of peoples that the Napoleonic wars had brought about, Clausewitz would have known a whole variety of allies and auxiliaries, enlisted directly as emigrés, who might have joined for national reasons but more often because they were lost and hungry, or loaned, willingly or unwillingly, as formed units by their home states to the Emperor.[2] The best of them were the Swiss regiments, which were transferred under the *capitulation* arrangements by which the Swiss made a living as mercenaries in many armies of the *ancien régime*; excellent also were the Polish lancers, whose origins lay in the feudal cavalry of their ancient kingdom. Many excellent regiments were the playthings or personal bodyguards of minor German princes whose independence Napoleon had extinguished. (An officer of one of them, Captain Franz Roeder of the Lifeguard of the Grand Duke of Hesse – in his dabblings with Ossian and Goethe and his Philhellene daydreams by no means untypical of the sort of young German of his time who thought soldiering an occupation for gentlemen – has left us one of the very best memoirs of the retreat from Moscow.)[3] The French garrison of Prussia also included regiments of Croat military colonists from the Habsburg Military Frontier with the Turks, who were in fact refugee Serbs from the Ottoman lands, while the Imperial Guard contained a squadron of Lithuanian Tartars, recruited from Turkic remnants of the Golden Horde. The unit most illustrative of the transformations a military organisation might undergo in a single existence was the *Bataillon de Neufchâtel*. Raised in the Swiss canton of which Napoleon had made his chief of staff, Marshal Berthier, prince and sovereign duke, it survived Napoleon's fall to be taken into Prussian service, eventually to become the *Gardeschützenbataillon* of the Kaiser's Imperial Guard and so in 1919 to yield some of the recruits for the *Freikorps*, the levies of ex-soldiers with which right-wing generals and Social Democrat politicians put down the 'Red Revolution' in Berlin. As it was among the *Freikorps* veterans that Hitler found the nucleus of the Nazi party's strongarm units, it is not fanciful to trace a descent from the paintbox little army of Berthier's principality to the praetorians of the Waffen SS panzer divisions.[4]

Bodyguards, regulars, feudatories, mercenaries, military colonists, conscripts, serf militias, remnants of warrior tribes from the steppe – to say nothing of the Frenchmen of the Grand Army itself, some of whom had entered service as the citizen-soldiers of the Revolution whose irresistible élan had first fired Clausewitz with his vision of 'war as the continuation of politics' – can we impose any order on this medley? To a drillmaster they may have looked merely like soldiers, some good for the hardest tasks, some useful in the special duties of skirmishing or reconnaissance, some scarcely worth their pay, some a danger to their friends and a menace to all peaceful citizens. In the variety one can find much material to illustrate the interrelationship between military and social forms. What theories explain the variety?

Military sociologists take as their premise the proposition that any system of military organisation expresses the social order from which it springs – and that this holds true even when the bulk of a population is held in thrall by an alien military hierarchy, of the sort that dominated Norman England or Manchu China, for example. The most elaborate of these theories is the work of the Anglo-Polish sociologist Stanislav Andreski – significantly the son of a military emigré – who is best known for having suggested the universal existence of a Military Participation Ratio (MPR) by which, when other factors are taken into account, the degree to which a society is militarised may be measured.[5] Unfortunately Professor Andreski's work is not 'accessible' – now, alas, an adjective of contempt in the academic world, where 'accessibility' is confused with shallowness – to the general reader, since he has invented an elaborate vocabulary of new-coined words to define his terms. To offset that, he otherwise writes with clarity and panache, while he takes no moral position about his findings: though he clearly prefers to live in a society with a low MPR, where the armed forces are subject to the rule of law, he is refreshingly free of the delusion that military dictatorships can be abolished by writing articles in journals of political science. Indeed, if anything, he takes a pessimistic, Hobbesian view of human nature, holding that struggle is a natural condition of existence and, like Dr Johnson, that 'no two people can be half an hour together, but one shall acquire an evident superiority over the other'.

Andreski begins with Malthus, the father of population theory, who argued that, since populations increase geometrically, but food and living space do not, life can only be made tolerable if births are limited or if deaths are hastened by disease or violence. He thinks this is the origin of warmaking (had he written after the publication of McNeill's *Plagues and Peoples*, which argues that imported diseases are more lethal than fighting, he might not have been so sure).[6] In primitive societies, he suggests, strong men limit birth rates by appropriating the women of the weak; but as the upper stratum's birth rate increases, it must either extrude the surplus into the lower, which it continues to limit in size by violence, or else carry violence into the territory of neighbours. By either means a military class, dominant in its own society or conquering over another, is created. Its relative size – the Military Participation Ratio (MPR) – will then be determined by its success, after having satisfied its own – potentially extortionate – needs of consumption and ownership, in accommodating those of the lower strata.[7] In victorious tribes, which subdue their surrounding neighbours, all fit males may be warriors; in economically benevolent conditions, where the ruling stratum can provide for an expanding population from trade, industry or intensive agriculture, the armed forces will shrink to the size merely necessary to defend the people's good fortune, and something we call democracy may even emerge to disguise the realities of power. It is, however, between these two extremes of MPR, he says, that most social systems lie. Their exact nature will then depend on two other factors: the degree to which the rulers find it necessary or are able to exert control over the ruled – what Andreski calls *subordination*; and the degree to which those who possess military skills and equipment are united among themselves – *cohesion*.[8]

To give some of his examples: the Trek Boers, who left the region of British rule in South Africa at the beginning of the nineteenth century to find free land and hold it against attack by the local Africans, formed a society characterised by high MPR – every man was a mounted shot – low subordination, because the republics they founded were almost without government, and low cohesion, since the patriarchal family remained the unit of loyalty. The Cossacks, on the other hand, had an equally high MPR, low subordination – since leaders had few means to enforce their will – but high cohesion, because the dangers of steppe life held the bands together. More common forms have been low MPR, low cohesion, low subordination – such as the knightly societies of medieval Europe in the long periods of weak monarchical rule – or high MPR, high subordination and high cohesion, which describe the militarised industrial societies of the two world wars.

Andreski's brief book takes the breath away by its boldness and sweep. In a series of intricate but apparently logical steps, he leads the reader to accept that there can be only six forms of military organisation and then, by a whirlwind gallop through world history, musters every known society, from the most primitive tribes to the most affluent democracies, within one or another. It is only when the reader has come up for air that doubt supervenes. In a general way, Andreski's scheme looks too mechanistic: though contemptuous of Marx – 'purely economic factors produce, no doubt, fluctuations in the height of stratification, but . . . the long-term trends are determined by the shifts of the locus of military power' – his analysis is brutally dialectic.[9] More particularly, if the reader has any precise knowledge of the societies Andreski so peremptorily dragoons, the fit between them and his categories looks less exact. For example: the Boers may appear to have lacked cohesion, and they were and remain a stiff-necked and quarrelsome lot, but no one who has fought them doubts that, what their laws lack, the power of the Dutch Reformed Church supplies; they have a biblical, not political, cohesion. Again, Cossack insubordination had its limits: expulsion from the band, at the dictate of elders or comrades, exposed the misfit to a dangerous isolation.[10] Andreski, moreover, accords little importance to what fellow sociologists call 'value systems'. Though he concedes that 'magico-religious beliefs [provided] the earliest foundations of social inequalities', he then drops the subject.[11] He takes no account of the deprecation of violence we have noted among some primitive tribes – which attempt to control it through ritual combat – or among monotheistic creeds, such as Islam, which was forced to create a social order of slaves in order to square the demands of power with those of religion, or in Chinese civilisation, which heroically persisted in the belief, however often deflected from it, that 'the superior man', by which was meant the ideal ruler, 'should be able to attain his ends without violence'.

It seems more profitable to proceed by a different method: to accept that there are a limited number of forms which military organisation has taken, and that there is indeed an intimate relationship between a particular form and the social and political order to which it belongs, but that what determines the relationship may be exceedingly complex. Tradition, for example, plays a preponderant role. Andreski admits that 'an egalitarian society where all men bear arms may resist the introduction of more efficient methods which make universal military service useless'.[12] It is more usual, if we take only the samurai and the Mamelukes as examples, for exclusive military minorities to cling to antique skills-at-arms, which they may do quite irrationally for hundreds of years. Such minorities – termed by sociologists 'élites', but incorrectly, since they are chosen only by themselves – may on the other hand pursue a relentless and extravagant policy of innovation; thus the officers of the Victorian Royal Navy, once they had accepted the steam ironclad, declared new models obsolete at ever narrower intervals, until warship-building became one of the most contested issues in British budgetary politics.[13]

Their 'navalism' reflected Britain's geographical circumstances: as a rich island it needed to defend itself against invasion, and as the seat of a maritime empire it needed to protect its trade and overseas possessions. Geography, however, is a universal influence on military forms, which only intermittently is Andreski prepared to recognise: thus he has spotted that it was Egypt's peculiar isolation that retarded its transition from stone to metal weapon technology and spared it the burden of maintaining a standing army until late in its civilised life. He seems to have missed, however, that it was Europe's exposure to irruption from the steppe – or later from Viking sea raids – that gave the knightly class so much of its power, that the unchanging steppe habitat made the nomads, once they had bred a man-carrying horse, what they were, that land hunger called the Scandinavians from their narrow coastal fields to go 'Aviking' or that it was the absence of any other secure natural harbour in the Adriatic that allowed Venice – a military power that interests him – to dominate that sea and then extend its commercial tentacles as far away as Crete and the Crimea.[14]

Above all, he discounts the allure that the warrior life exerts over the male imagination. This is a failing common among academics who interest themselves in military affairs but never leave their university surroundings. As those who know soldiers as members of a military society recognise, such a society has a culture of its own akin to but different from the larger culture to which it belongs, operating by a different system of punishments and rewards – the punishments more peremptory, the rewards less monetary, often, indeed, purely symbolic or emotional – but deeply satisfying to its adherents. I am tempted, after a lifetime's acquaintance with the British army, to argue that some men can be nothing but soldiers. The feminine parallel is with the stage: some women are fulfilled only theatrically – as *prima donna*, *diva*, icon of the photographer or couturier – yet, through that fulfilment, embody a universal ideal of femininity that earns the adulation of women and men alike. Such adulation is not enjoyed by male actors, however much admired; a stage hero merely simulates the running of risks. The warrior hero is admired by both sexes for running real risks; but the man of soldierly temperament – how blinkered social scientists are to the importance of temperament – will run risks whether admired by the outside world or not. It is the admiration of other soldiers that satisfies him – if he can win it; most soldiers are satisfied merely by the company of others, by a shared contempt for a softer world, by the liberation from narrow materiality brought by the camp and the line of march, by the rough comforts of the bivouac, by competition in endurance, by the prospect of *le répos du guerrier* among their waiting womenfolk.

The intoxication of the warpath helps to explain to us the ethos of the primitive warrior. Success on the warpath explains also why some primitives became warrior peoples. The rewards of success – if not outright conquest, the appropriation of territory and the subjection of outsiders, then booty or at least the right to trade on dictated terms – are enough in themselves to validate a rejection of settled ways. Yet it is important not to exaggerate the drives to the warrior life. As we have seen, many primitives strove to contain the impulse to violence, while even the most ferocious peoples ascended their pyramids of skulls in the more tentative footsteps of others; Tamerlane could not have become what he did had not earlier horse peoples tested the limits of civilisation's powers of resistance. Warrior peoples, moreover, have always been a minority among all peoples, whatever the allure – so much overlooked by the bellicose Anglo-Saxons, who prefer to regard themselves as donors to others of parliamentary institutions – of possessing a name that inspires awe; while warriors always form an absolute minority within populations which have passed beyond the primitive stage. There is what sociologists call a countervailing tendency in human nature, which opposes resort to violence. Aldous Huxley said that an intellectual was a person who had discovered something more interesting than sex. A civilised man, it might be said, is someone who has discovered something more satisfying than combat. Once man moved beyond the primitive, the proportion of those who preferred, to fighting, something else – tilling the soil, making or selling things, building, teaching, thinking or communing with the other world – increased as fast as the resources of the economy would stand. One must not idealise; the least fortunate found themselves bound to service or even servitude, while the privileged, as Andreski robustly points out, always rested their position on the power of arms, borne by themselves or loyal subordinates. Post-primitive man, however, did accord a particular value to the unviolent life, exemplified by that of the artist, scholar and, above all, holy man and woman. It was for that reason that the atrocities of the Vikings in particular, despoilers of monasteries and convents, aroused such disgust in the Christian world; even Tamerlane, who had respectfully received the great Arab scholar, Ibn Khaldun, did not descend to their bloody level.[15]

To modulate Andreski's analysis, therefore: let us concede the prevalence of warmaking in the primitive world – while making allowance for the existence of peoples who scarcely knew warfare, and for the attempts to moderate it by ritual and ceremony among those who did – and proceed forthwith to the post-primitive world. Our survey of military history so far reveals six main forms that military organisation may take: warrior, mercenary, slave, regular, conscript and militia. It is purely coincidental that Andreski also believes in the existence of six forms, which he calls homoic, masaic, mortasic, neferic, ritterian and tellenic (all neologisms), since few of the categories match. The warrior category is self-explanatory, but I use it to include such groups as the samurai and the Western knightly class, the nucleus of which may almost always be identified as the remnant of a warrior tribe, alien or native; warrior cults, like the original Muslims and the Sikhs, and self-made warrior polities, like the Zulu or Ashanti, include themselves. Mercenaries are those who sell military service for money – though also for such inducements as grants of land, admission to citizenship (offered by both the Roman army and the French Foreign Legion) or preferential treatment. Regulars are mercenaries who already enjoy citizenship or its equivalent but choose military service as a means of subsistence; in affluent states, regular service may take on some of the attributes of a profession. We have already examined the slave system. The militia principle lays the duty of performing military service upon all fit male citizens; failure or refusal to do duty usually entails loss of citizenship. Conscription is a tax levied upon a male resident's time at a certain age of life, though to citizens payment of such a tax is also usually represented as a civic duty; selective conscription, especially if for long periods of service to an unrepresentative government – twenty years was the term in Russia before the emancipation of the serfs – is difficult to differentiate from the slave system.

How warrior societies came into being does not require elaboration, nor do we need to examine how warrior groups acquired or perpetuated their power over non-warriors. Typically they monopolised the use of an expensive weapons system – as the chariot conquerors did – or perfected a difficult skill-at-arms, which was the reason for the horse peoples' long reign of terror. It is the transitions to the alternative forms which have a more complex rationale. That such transitions are necessary if a society is to evolve is self-evident, since warrior governments tend to be intensely conservative. They, like the samurai, Manchu and Mamelukes, fear to tamper with anything in the system they control, lest in so doing they bring the whole edifice down. As we have seen, however, obsolete military systems cannot resist change in perpetuity; when change comes, however, the new rulers – who may be the enlightened survivors of the old warrior order – confront two central problems. One is how to pay for the new military system. The other is how to assure the loyalty of those who belong to it. The two are intimately connected. Warriordom supports itself by direct exaction, either on the rest of society or on outsiders; hence the horse peoples' obsessions with taking booty or tribute or demanding the right to trade on dictated terms. Once the military specialism is devolved away from the direct centre of power – which is the beginning of warriordom's dilution – an intermediate method of rewarding soldiers has to be found. Genghis was scrupulous in seeing that all booty was centrally collected and equally distributed.[16] Even in his own lifetime, however, as the empire expanded, he was obliged to grant local powers to trusted subordinates and soon after his death such men acquired the right to tax as well as to rule. Genghis's tax-collectors had brought the revenues to a central treasury; that was an important reason why the Mongol army remained so formidable in his lifetime. In the time of his grandsons, a sort of feudalism had begun to emerge and with it the decline of Mongol power.

Feudalism is a common stage in the transition of warrior societies to other forms. It appeared in two principal varieties. One, which characterised its rise in the West, was the grant of land to military subordinates, on condition that they supported on it the appropriate military force to be brought into the sovereign's service when required, but carrying with it the right to bequeath the land, under the same conditions, to the feudatory's descendants. The other, more common outside Europe, was that of the non-hereditary fief, which could be taken back into the sovereign's hands at his dictate; it was prevalent in the Islamic world as the *iqta* system, and was much used by the Seljuks, Ayyubids and Ottomans. Both had their disadvantages. The *iqta*, because it was non-hereditary, encouraged the holder to enrich himself while the going was good; his taxpayers were exploited and his military obligation skimped.[17] Feudal vassals in the West, on the other hand, though they had an interest in the good management of their fiefs, since one might be passed on to a son, had an equally strong interest in improving a fief's military value. A vassal thereby strengthened his position in any dispute over rights or duties with his sovereign; by taking on vassals of his own and building castles, he might hope eventually to raise his house, in fact if not law, to sovereign status itself. Such was to be the history of much of western Europe between the division of the Carolingian empire in the ninth century and the coming of the gunpowder kings in the sixteenth.

Feudalism in whatever form was therefore a blind alley in the move away from warriordom. A much more effective system was the regular. It first appeared, surprisingly early, in Sumer and was brought to a scarcely improvable form by the Assyrians. The Assyrian army, as we have seen, included contingents of all the varieties of soldier then available, including, besides infantry, charioteers, mounted archers, engineers and waggoners. Its core, however, was the royal bodyguard, in which the origins of regular service may lie. The army of Sumer was probably first a royal bodyguard, around which other units congregated as need arose, and such 'nearest guards' were to persist thereafter in every state where power was personalised, however symbolically and however representative the basis of government, even down to our own times.

229

Bodyguards nevertheless were to follow a line of separate and sometimes divergent development from those of other regular forces. Those of rulers who set up fixed places of residence tended to become sedentary themselves, often to lose their warlike functions and sometimes to become kingmakers; rulers in consequence frequently recruited their bodyguards abroad, from warrior peoples who did not know a language in which to conspire with native malcontents. An example that readily suggests itself is that of the Varangian guard of the Byzantine emperors, originally formed of Swedes and Norwegians who had followed the trade routes of the 'Rus' down the great Russian rivers to Constantinople, but after 1066 largely of emigré Anglo-Saxons. They developed a patois of their own and have left their most celebrated memorial in the runes carved on the Lion of St Mark, exported as booty from the Piraeus after its capture from the Turks by Francesco Morosini in 1668, which now stands outside the Arsenal at Venice.[18] Other famous foreign guards were the Scottish Archers of the French kings, the Arab Guard of Frederick II Hohenstaufen (General Franco raised a Moorish Guard from the Moroccan *regulares* who did so much to win the Spanish Civil War of 1936–9), and the Swiss guards of several European sovereigns, including, of course, the popes. It is a little advertised function of the modern Special Air Service (SAS) Regiment to provide bodyguards to foreign rulers the British government has an interest in keeping in power.[19]

Such bodyguards, but also those recruited from a ruler's subjects which became sedentary in a capital, regularly tended to fossilise, often in a grotesque form: the British Yeomen of the Guard and the Papal Swiss Guard exhibit the trait, as did the vanished Bavarian Trabanters, who carried battleaxes into the nineteenth century. Some monarchs actually raised archaic guard units to exaggerate the length of their lineage, as the Hohenzollerns did with the *Schlossgardekompagnie*, which attended the last Kaiser dressed as if for the court of Frederick the Great. Not unnaturally, well-born young men of spirit turned their noses up at such service. They preferred to show their loyalty to a ruler in a 'nearest guard' that closed with the enemy. Some bodyguards thereby survived as fighting-units and many others were raised on the same model: the Prussian and Russian – Preobajensky, Semenovsky – regiments of footguards belonged to that tradition, as the British still do.

The loyalty of such units – that of the *Gardes françaises* in 1789 after it had been rotted by overlong residence in Paris was an exception – rarely fell into doubt. The difficulty remained, however, of how to pay for such forces, and was even more acute in the case of the regulars of the ordinary field army. It is a central element of the contract between ruler and regulars that they are fed, housed and paid in peace as well as war. Rich states with an efficient taxing power may succeed in doing so for long periods; if militarily over-ambitious they may nevertheless overtax their inhabitants, while it is frequently the case that the attempt to reduce the size of an expanded regular force at the end of a long war drives it to mutiny, as the Irish Free State found in 1923. It is therefore a temptation, particularly felt by rich states of small population, to sidestep the burden of supporting a regular army and, instead, to buy in military services as needed. That is the basis of the mercenary system. It is not the only basis; historically, many states have supplemented their forces by hiring mercenaries, often on long-term contracts, with results perfectly satisfactory to both parties, as the former relationship between the French and the Swiss, and that current between the British and the Gurkhas of Nepal, demonstrates. It is also possible to buy into a well regulated mercenary market, to which hirelings return after the expiry of their term of service; such a market existed at Cape Taenarum in the Peloponnese during the fourth century BC, supplied by landless soldiers thrown out of work after the city-state wars of the previous century, and it worked perfectly well as long as the demand for military professionals held up in Persia and then the Hellenised East.[20] Alexander the Great employed some 50,000 Greek mercenaries in 329, many recruited by the market system.

The danger inherent in the resort to mercenaries is that the funds necessary to support them may dry up before the contract reaches its agreed term, or that a war goes on longer than expected, with the same result, or that, if a state has been so miserly, complacent or supine as to depend exclusively on hired soldiers, the mercenaries come to see that they constitute the effective power within it. That, of course, was the issue in several Italian city states of the fifteenth century, where citizens had become too mercantile to do duty themselves but were too mean to pay for a standing force. In such circumstances it is their employers rather than the enemy that mercenaries confront with threat: they take sides in internal quarrels, they strike or blackmail for outstanding or extra pay, they may even go over to the enemy; at the very worst they seize power for themselves, as the *condottieri* Pandolfo Malatesta, Ottobuono Terzo and Gabrino Fondulo did, respectively, in Brescia, Cremona and Parma.[21]

Some earlier city states, as if they had foreseen the dangers of reliance on mercenary hire, though that was not the reason, chose an alternative method of providing for their defence: they made it a condition of citizenship that all free men of property should purchase arms, train for war and do duty in time of danger. This was the militia system. It may take other forms. The term is loosely applied to the levies of peasants raised by sedentary states of many kinds, including the Chinese and Russian empires, over long periods of history; it also includes the *fyrd* of Anglo-Saxon England and its equivalents in continental Europe, which were based on the principle, later known as the *jus sequellae* or *Heerfolge*, that free men must bear arms. It had been brought from Germany by the barbarian invaders, was carried on by the kingdoms which succeeded to Roman rule and remained in force until, in the military crises of the ninth and tenth centuries, it was overtaken in importance by the summons (*ban*) to the horse-keeping vassals. In remote regions with weak aristocracies, such as Switzerland and the Tyrol, it survived much longer; indeed, in Switzerland it survives to this day.

Yet it is not with the barbarian but the classical world that we associate the militia idea; with the phalanxes of Greek farmer-citizens who fought each other in their small states' quarrels, but who might combine against a common danger, such as that offered by the Persian empire in the sixth and fifth centuries BC. It is tempting to imagine that the Germans and the Greeks derived their idea of the freeman's military duty from a common source, even more tempting to propose that the Greeks' principal contribution to warmaking – that of the pitched battle, fought on foot at a fixed site until one side or the other conceded defeat – made its way back to the Germans, via Rome, in barbarian times. The evidence, however, may not stand such a weight of supposition. What does seem certain is that Rome, in pre-republican years, imported its tactics from the Greeks and that the Roman army of the Servian Constitution, from which that of the Caesars descended, therefore had its origins in phalanx warfare.[22] Politically and culturally thereafter Greece and Rome were to diverge. Rome's farmer-soldiers would progressively yield place to paid professionals, as it set its course for empire. The Greek 'genius for discord' would preserve the individual city militias, thus ensuring that a stronger power, that of the semi-barbarian Macedonians, would eventually do them all down. Nevertheless, as with so much else that was Greek, the militia idea would survive. With the rediscovery of classical learning in Renaissance Europe, it came to seem as good as that of the rule of law or civic pride, with both of which it was of course intimately connected. Machiavelli, whose political thought was rooted in the perception that sovereignty derives from arms, did not merely write books on the subject; he actually drafted the Florentine militia law (the *Ordinanza* of 1505) which was intended to liberate his city from the mercenary scourge.[23]

There was, however, a military defect in the militia system. Because it laid duty on the property-owning alone, it thereby limited the number of men a state could put into the field to a number lower than that of all its able-bodied male residents. The Greeks accepted that limitation for two reasons; the first was that it solved the besetting problem of how to pay for the army, since the soldiers in effect paid for themselves; the second was that it ensured the army's reliability: the property test united those who passed it, whatever their political differences, against all who did not, the landless and the enslaved, who as non-citizens were not allowed to bear arms. When emergency struck, however, such élitism could prove a crippling disadvantage, as the Spartans – who took to extremes the principle of exclusivity – found in the war with Thebes in the fourth century BC.

Conscription is not exclusive; by definition, it includes all who can march and fight, irrespective of wealth or political rights. For that reason it has never recommended itself to regimes which feared armed subjects might take power, nor to those which found difficulty in raising funds. Conscription is for rich states which offer rights – or at least the appearance of rights – to all. The first state to meet those conditions in full was the First French Republic. Some others – Frederick the Great's Prussia, for example – had imposed something like conscription before, but it had worked only by using the regular part of the army to recruit the rest. In August 1793, the French Republic declared that until the moment 'when enemies have been driven from the Republic's territory, all Frenchmen are permanently requisitioned for the service of the armies'; a former property test, which limited duty only to 'active citizens', had already been abolished.[24] Henceforth all Frenchmen might be soldiers and by September 1794 the Republic had 1,169,000 under arms, a size of force never before seen in Europe.

The whirlwind successes of the Revolutionary armies designated conscription as the military system of the future; they were, after all, what prompted Clausewitz to argue that 'war was the continuation of politics'; the grave drawbacks of the system – that it militarised society and entailed enormous costs – went unforeseen or were disguised. The Revolutionary armies paid for themselves for long periods by loot (Bonaparte's Army of Italy, at the time when the Republic's paper notes had driven coin out of circulation, became its principal source of hard currency); the other European governments that adopted conscription from the mid-nineteenth century onward concealed from themselves the financial burden by paying conscripts less than pocket money.

It is in that sense that conscription may be seen as a form of tax. Like all taxes, however, it had ultimately to make a beneficial return to those who paid. In France the benefit was citizenship for all who served. The monarchical governments that adopted it during the nineteenth century could not concede that weakening of their power. They offered the exhilarations of nationalism as a substitute, in the German states with great success. Nevertheless, the French idea that only the armed man enjoyed full citizenship had taken root, and rapidly became transmuted into the belief that civic freedoms were both the right and the mark of those who bore arms. Thus in some states where civic freedoms were already enjoyed but conscription was not imposed, such as Britain and the United States, there arose in mid-century the odd phenomenon of citizens foisting themselves on governments as volunteer soldiers; and in those struggling to resist the growth of representative institutions while imposing conscription, particularly Prussia, the middle-class militias brought into being by the wars against Napoleon sought to survive as outposts of rights against the powers of the king and his regular army.

In the long run, the establishment of universal conscription in the advanced states of continental Europe was matched by the extension of the vote, though for parliaments generally less responsible than those of the Anglo-Saxon countries, and by processes that had no direct and visible connection. The result, however, was that, at the outbreak of the First World War, Europe was composed of states in most of which some form of representative institutions existed and all of which maintained large conscripted armies. The loyalty of such armies, headily reinforced by national feeling, was to hold up throughout the first three years of the war's terrible ordeal. By 1917, the costs, psychological as well as material, of making every man a soldier began to have their inevitable effects. There was a large-scale mutiny in the French army in the spring of that year; in the autumn the Russian army collapsed altogether. In the following year the German army went the same way; at the November armistice, on its return home, the army demobilised itself and the German empire was thrown into revolution. It was the almost cyclical outcome of a process begun 125 years earlier, when the French had rescued a revolution by appealing to all citizens to support it with arms. Politics had become the extension of war and the age-old dilemma of states – of how to maintain efficient armies that were both affordable and reliable – had revealed itself to be as far from solution as when Sumer had first laid out its revenues to pay for soldiers.

—4—
Iron

STONE, BRONZE AND THE horse – the principal means through which war was waged in the era when states were being established and when they were being assaulted by warrior peoples living beyond the settled zone – were by nature limited resources, though in different ways. Stone is laborious to fashion. Bronze is a product of scarce metals. The horse can be kept, in the numbers necessary to mount a fighting army, on grazing lands that are found only in restricted areas of the world. Had stone, bronze and the horse remained the means by which war was fought, its scope and intensity might never have exceeded the levels experienced during the first millennium BC, and human societies, except in the confined and benevolent conditions that prevailed in the great river valleys, might never have evolved far beyond pastoralism and primitive husbandry. Man needed some other resource with which to attack the face of earth in the temperate, forested zones but also to contest possession of the lands already settled with the rich and strong minorities which had monopolised the expensive technology of warmaking in the Bronze Age.

Iron supplied the need. It is now a scholarly fashion to doubt the onset of an 'Iron Age revolution', in part because it was proposed by Marxist scholars whose vision of history was determinist and mechanistic. But one does not have to be a determinist to perceive that a sudden and very large increase in the supply of a material that could take and keep an edge, when previously such materials had been the perquisite of the few because of their cost and rarity, was bound to change social relationships. Not only sharp weapons but tools also became available to men who had laboured before with stone and wood to clear forests and break the surface of the soil. Iron tools not merely allowed but encouraged man to tackle soils that previously resisted him and in so doing to colonise regions distant from existing areas of settlement, to exploit more intensively those already brought into use or simply to colonise where the charioteers had conquered before them.

That iron is such a material does not need much demonstration. Bronze is an alloy of common copper and scarce tin; tin's scarcity and very localised sources made it a substance on which it was easy to levy high market prices and heavy transport tolls and taxes at the point of delivery. In consequence, warriors readily monopolised bronze and thus usually made themselves rulers as well. Iron is not scarce; its ores form some 4.2 per cent of the earth's mass, and it is widely distributed.[1] But in pure form, which primitive man could recognise and use, it is even scarcer than tin, appearing only as meteoric iron or as certain very isolated so-called telluric deposits. Nevertheless, primitive man knew and worked with meteoric iron, and when – by what chapter of accidents we cannot guess – he discovered how iron might by heat be extracted from its earthy bed, civilised man knew what could be done with it. It has been suggested that iron was first smelted by Mesopotamian smiths of about 2300 BC who were seeking to extract pigments, such as ochre, from the associated ore.[2] Smiths were a secretive lot, practising a mysterious craft and usually working under the direct protection of warriors whom they supplied with their precious products. The first smelted iron was almost surely monopolised, and it did not come into general use until about 1400 BC. At that time production seems to have been centred in Anatolia, where rich ores occur in profusion at surface sites, and it was through their consequent access to worked iron that the local Hittites were able to launch their aggressive campaigns against the valley kingdoms.

About 1200 BC, it has been suggested, the Hittites had ceased to be sole proprietors of the emergent iron industry when their kingdom was destroyed. The Anatolian iron-workers, scattered in the process, took their skills elsewhere to seek new purchasers and protectors. It may also be that iron-working itself had by this time reached a point of technical take-off. It had had to go through several stages. The first was to perfect a furnace in which ores could be smelted to produce ingots of economic size for an economic expenditure of fuel (the preferred fuel remained charcoal until early modern times, when first the Chinese and then the Europeans discovered how to transform coal into coke). Iron ores melt at a much higher temperature than copper or tin, requiring a forced draught; the first furnaces were sited on windy hilltops, until bellows were brought into use. They yielded about eight per cent iron for a given weight of ore, in a spongy mass known as a 'bloom', which could be made into tool- or weapons-grade ingots only by constant reheating and hammering; even then, unless the ore contained exceptionally large traces of nickel, its products were soft and quickly lost their edge. Cold-hammering to restore the edge, the bronzesmith's technique, did not work with iron.

It was only when it was discovered around 1200 BC that hot-hammering and quenching in water gave iron a durable and lasting edge that it at last emerged not merely as a competitor to bronze, but as its clear superior. That stage may have been reached at the moment when the Anatolian smiths were dispersed about the Near Eastern world.

The appearance of the skills of smelting and smithing had varied military effects. It better equipped warrior peoples to mount assaults on the rich and settled states and may therefore have contributed to the turmoil that engulfed the Middle and Near East at the beginning of the first millennium BC. Equally it eventually equipped the empires to strike back, since plentiful iron meant that larger numbers of men could be kept under arms, in states where revenues sufficed to support them. The Assyrian army was an iron army; even technologically backward Egypt embraced iron under the later pharaohs.

The most impressive weapons found in early Iron Age sites come not from the East but from Europe. They are the swords of the so-called Hallstatt culture, which date from as early as 950 BC.[3] Modelled originally on bronze patterns, these swords rapidly assumed exaggerated lengths, evidence of how much more extravagantly the new, cheap and plentiful iron could be used than the old bronze. Though iron spearheads have been found in Hallstatt culture graves, as well as traces of shields bound and riveted with iron, it is swords that predominate. The Hallstatt people seem to have been aggressive swordsmen, who counted on a sharp edge and long point to overcome an opponent.

The Hallstatt culture – so called from the first excavated site in Czechoslovakia – belonged to the Celts, that mysterious people who came to occupy most of western Europe by 1000 BC; in the third century BC they also migrated eastward into Anatolia. In their heyday, the Celts were conquerors, or at least colonisers, and their iron weapons were eagerly adopted by neighbours living across the mountains from the great European plain, notably the Greeks.

THE GREEKS AND IRON

The Greeks, like the Celts, are of mysterious origin, but they probably began to voyage from the southern shores of Asia Minor for Cyprus, Crete and the Aegean islands toward the end of the fourth millennium BC; at much the same time, mainland Greece began to be settled by other Stone Age people from the same regions. Then, in the middle of the third millennium, a northern people appeared in Macedonia, perhaps from the banks of the Danube, whose culture remained Neolithic when the first settlers had already entered the Bronze Age; it was they who brought the language that eventually all Greeks would speak.

It took time for the northerners and the settlers from Asia Minor to become one. Until the end of the second millennium BC, the islanders remained not merely a people apart; the Cretans in particular ascended to cultural heights the mainlanders could not match. At Knossos, in Crete, sheltered from invasion by the seas which also brought rich trade goods to the island, a sumptuous civilisation grew up. Then about 1450 BC catastrophe overwhelmed this Minoan world; archaeologists have long sought to explain why – without agreement, though the recent discovery of Minoan fortifications along Crete's shores suggests that they had not been as isolated from attack as was previously thought. They may have been subjected to raids before; in a single great descent, perhaps by the piratical 'Sea People' of Asia Minor, perhaps by Greek mainlanders jealous of the Cretans' dominance of Mediterranean trade, the great palaces, warehouses or workshops were destroyed.[4]

Meanwhile an advanced Bronze Age culture had taken root on the mainland, where a scattering of small kingdoms grew up along the eastern shore and particularly in the Peloponnese. One of the most important, Mycenae, has given its name to this civilisation, and by the end of the first millennium Mycenaean cities were also established on the shores of Asia Minor and as far away as Troy, on the straits that lead to the Black Sea. These cities were rich enough to support well-equipped chariot armies, if the Linear-B tablets, which are incised with the first traces of written Greek, may be taken as evidence; the accounts of the palace at Pylos record the presence of 200 pairs of chariot wheels in the royal arsenal.[5] Whence the chariots came we cannot guess. They may have been brought by charioteers who made themselves masters of the coastal kingdoms; those kingdoms' trading wealth may have allowed them to buy into the international market in advanced military technology. At any rate during the thirteenth century BC, chariots were important enough in the Greek world to play a significant part in an extended war between mainland Greece and Troy. So at least Homer describes in the *Iliad* when his heroes drive to battle behind their warhorses.

As is a commonplace now among ancient historians, however, Homer – composing his great poem in the eighth century about events 500 years earlier – seems to have misunderstood the role that chariots played in the heroic age. A modern scholar writes:

240

The real advantage of the war-chariot lay in massed attacks at speed. This is how it was used by the Mycenaeans and by the kingdoms of the Near and Middle East which maintained large forces of chariotry both in the Bronze Age and after the Mycenaean collapse. The Homeric picture could not be more different. There the warriors use the chariots merely as transport vehicles from which they dismount to fight on foot, and they are equipped either with the bow or the lance, the two weapons which made chariotry so formidable an arm after the invention of a light and fast spoke-wheeled chariot in the first half of the second millennium.[6]

Homer's misunderstanding is currently explained by the distance in time at which he stood from the Trojan War, which, it is now accepted, indeed took place and was not simply the stuff of myth, and was probably fought to resolve disputes over trading-rights in the Aegean and surrounding waters. But distance in time may not be the only explanation for the difficulty Homer had in recreating the heroic past. He was separated from it, too, by a time of troubles in Greek life, a Dark Age that severed connections between the thirteenth and eighth centuries even more absolutely than the European Dark Ages obscured Rome from the Carolingians; it even appears that the knowledge of writing was lost on the Greek mainland during the 300 years after 1150 BC.[7] The agents of this disastrous upheaval were a fresh wave of invaders from the north, known to later Greeks as the Dorians, who spoke Greek but were in every other way barbarian. The first wave may have come by sea; later arrivals seem to have brought the horse and iron weapons and so presumably arrived by land routes, perhaps pushed ahead of other horse-riding peoples who originated on the edge of the steppe.

Before these invaders a few Mycenaean Greeks, notably those living in Attica, around Athens, succeeded in holding their fortified places; their recolonisation of the islands (the Ionian migrations) later re-established Greek culture in the Aegean all the way to the shores of Asia Minor, where, during the tenth century BC, they built twelve strong fortified cities which looked to Athens as their place of origin and communicated with it and each other by sea. On the mainland, none of the Mycenaean kingdoms survived in independence. The Dorian invaders seized the best land, enslaved the inhabitants and worked them as serfs; however, they seem to have found little unity among themselves. 'Village fought against village, and men went about their business wearing arms.'[8]

This typical pattern of warrior conquest and settlement laid the basis for the rise of that most distinctive and influential Greek institution, the city state. Its origins have been best traced to the Dorian settlements on Crete, where constitutions that granted political rights to those who bore arms, descendants of the conquerors, and denied them to the rest, came into force in the period 850–750 BC; 'the remarkable feature of these Cretan constitutions was the orientation of the citizens not towards their family group but towards the state alone.'[9] At the age of seventeen the sons of leading families were recruited into troops, and were disciplined and trained to athletics, hunting or mock warfare. The unfortunates who failed to be accepted were excluded from the franchise and enjoyed lesser rights at law. At nineteen the successful graduates were granted membership of a men's mess, and thereafter fed and campaigned together. The messes were maintained at public expense and became effectively their members' homes; though they were allowed to marry, the wives were kept segregated and family life was reduced to a minimum.

Those outside this warrior class were held in various degrees of subjection. The descendants of the original conquered population were serfs, tied to their owners' estates or to public land; estate-owners also owned personal slaves whom they bought at market. People who had been conquered subsequent to the first invasions were allowed rights of property but paid tribute and were excluded from the franchise. As a Cretan drinking-song of the ninth century expressed it, 'My wealth is spear and sword, and the stout shield which protects my flesh; with this I plough, with this I reap, with this I tread the sweet wine from the grape, with this I am entitled master of the serfs.'[10]

> The origin of the *polis* (city-state) endowed it with pronounced characteristics. It inherited a strong sense of kinship from its constituent elements, the *komai* (village), so that citizenship was generally defined by hereditary descent on both sides. It perpetuated the distinction between master and serf and maintained the privilege of the citizen class in the community. It fostered the agricultural economy which was the source of self-sufficiency, and it ensured for its citizen class an adequate degree of leisure to practise the arts of peace and war.[11]

In the form nearest to its Cretan origins this *polis* and its constitution migrated to the Greek mainland and there took root most notably as Sparta, the greatest warring state in Greece. In Sparta the division between free warriors and disarmed and largely rightless serfs reached its most extreme, as did the disproportion between the two groups. The boys' initiation into training troops began at the age of seven; girls, too, were segregated and followed a regime of training in athletics, dancing and music. Until marriage, however, the girls lived at home, while the

242

boys were kept apart under the leadership of head boys and under the supervision of a state superintendent. Their life was designed to inure their bodies to hardship and they competed with other groups of their own age at sport and tests of endurance. At the age of eighteen they began their formal training for combat, and for a period were employed in secret service against the serfs. At twenty they took up residence in barracks – though they might marry at that age, they could not reside with their wives – and at thirty they proceeded to election to full citizenship. Only those candidates unanimously chosen became full citizens and embarked on the main duties of a Spartan 'equal': to hold the serf (helot) class in restraint and to stand in readiness for war. Each year the 'equals' actually waged an internal war against the helots, disposing of those the secret service had identified as unreliable.

Little wonder that Sparta rose to dominate its less warlike neighbours; perhaps no society known to historians has ever better perfected the warrior system. During the eighth century BC the Spartans first made themselves masters of the hundred villages that surrounded their own original five and then went on to conquer the neighbouring region of Messenia in a war that lasted twenty years (940–20 BC). Thereafter her rise to power in the Peloponnese ran less smoothly. The Spartans were challenged by the neighbouring state of Argos, and suffered defeat at Hysiae in 669, after a period in which subject cities had revolted against her rule. For nineteen years Sparta struggled for survival, but by the sixth century, after a battle with Argos which developed from a conflict between 'Three Hundred Champions' on each side, she had survived the ordeal to become the greatest military power in the Peloponnese.

Meanwhile the other leading cities of Greece were developing in a different way and in quite different directions, which carried their spheres of influence away from the mainland, into the islands and back to the shores of Asia Minor; eventually these Greek sea lanes stretched out to link the founding centres with colonies as far away as Sicily, the southern coast of France, the inland waters of the Black Sea and the shores of Libya. While Sparta was perfecting the weapons, tactics and military organisation that would dominate warmaking among Greeks on land, other states, notably Athens, were making themselves naval powers and building the ships with which they would contest for control of the Aegean and eastern Mediterranean with the Persians and their subject sea peoples.

The Persian wars (499–448 BC) took time in the making, for not until the rise of Cyrus the Great did Persia succeed in establishing a unified kingdom. During the sixth century BC, war for the Greeks was largely war between Greeks, as the city states perpetuated their quarrels over land, power and control of trade. It became in the process a new form of warfare, fought with iron weapons, affordable by many more men than had composed the armies of the Mycenaean world, wielded by small farmers who were equal citizens, and used to wage battles of an intensity and ferocity perhaps never before seen. The battles of earlier and other peoples – even those of the Assyrians, though we lack exact details of their conduct on the battlefield – had continued to be marked by elements that had characterised warfare since its primitive beginnings – tentativeness, preference for fights at a distance, reliance on missiles and reluctance to close to arm's length until victory looked assured. The Greeks discarded these hesitations and created for themselves a new warfare that turned on the function of battle as a decisive act, fought within the dramatic unities of time, place and action and dedicated to securing victory, even at the risk of suffering bloody defeat, in a single test of skill and courage. So revolutionary was the effect of this new spirit in warmaking that the foremost historian of the tactics of the Greek city states has proposed the arresting, if much contested, thought that the Greeks were the inventors of 'the Western way of war', by which the Europeans were eventually to subdue every area of the world into which they carried their arms.[12]

PHALANX WARFARE

Greece is a mountainous land, which lends itself to agriculture only in the valleys and in the few expanses of level ground to be found in the northern Peloponnese, Thessaly and along its western coast. Olive trees and vines can be cultivated on the slopes, where terracing, too, will yield fields. Grain, the other staple of Greek life, besides oil and wine, can be grown in quantity only in the wider spaces of the valleys or plains. The intense attachment of the Greek citizen-soldier to his smallholding, usually of fifteen acres or less, is thus easily understood. From it he drew both his livelihood and the surplus that allowed him to equip himself as an armoured spear-carrier and so, in turn, to take his place among those who voted for the city's magistrates and passed its laws. Any threat to invade his fields, destroy his trees or vines, or trample or burn his crops therefore menaced not only his survival during a following winter of hardship but his status as a free man. Devastation, 'laying waste', was a recurrent feature of Greek city-state warfare, and the provocation it offered has long been thought to explain the novel ferocity of its battles. More recently the American classicist Victor Hanson has proposed an alternative interpretation. Raised in a California family of vine-growers, he came to doubt whether 'laying waste' had economic effects so dire as had been imagined. From his own experience, he knew that a vine, however mistreated, has an almost miraculous power of regeneration; even if cut to the roots, in the following spring it will throw out green shoots and by summer be rampant in growth. To uproot the vine, the only effective means of destroying it, takes time: he calculated that to put a one-acre vineyard, containing as many as 2000 vines, out of production would require thirty-three man-hours of work.[13] The olive tree is even more resistant to attack; in maturity it is a hard and gnarled plant, which cannot be made to burst into flames simply by setting a fire at its base, while its thick trunk, which can reach a diameter of twenty feet, stoutly resists an axe. Like the vine it recuperates well, if not as rapidly, from lopping, and dies for good only if uprooted; uprooting is even more laborious in an olive grove than a vineyard.[14] For an invading enemy to disrupt the agricultural cycle of a collection of Greek farms, therefore, it had to strike at a more vulnerable source of produce; that meant the grain fields, from which the loss of a year's crop would entail want, the loss of two in successive years, after stores had been exhausted, starvation.[15] Yet there were difficulties also about ravaging fields. In the spring the corn was too green to burn, while trampling, sometimes attempted by invaders who had horses with them, was both time-consuming and ineffective. After harvest, the ears would be stored in secure barns ready for threshing. Therefore only a brief interval presented itself when dry standing crops, readily inflammable, could be found waiting for the torch. It was as short as a few weeks in May.

The Greek field pattern, however, resisted rapid overrunning by a raiding-party bent on harm; Greek farmers generally embanked or walled their holdings, often the constituent plots as well, and did so even if they lived apart from their neighbours; as a result, 'ravagers could not gallop wildly through the Greek countryside, spreading fire and ruin at will . . . Fences, hills, small orchards and vineyards all made progress slow.'[16] In short, the territory of the Greek city states was defensible, so defensible as to make common effort for the defence of the whole a rational military choice. If the enemy, who in the nature of things came from close at hand and could not therefore keep preparations for war secret, could be checked at the border, during the brief span of time when he might wreak his worst, the farms of the landholders, whose product supported them as citizens and warriors as well as heads of families, might collectively be spared damage.

This analysis was widely accepted before Hanson began his studies, if not in the detail he supplied. To it, however, he added a transforming idea. Given the extreme brevity of time in which attack could be made effective in the Greek farming world – and, as he points out, at least eighty per cent of those we call 'citizens' of the city states were countrymen and not town-dwellers – and given also that the attackers left their own fields vulnerable to spoliation when they marched off on campaign, the highest premium was placed, or placed itself, in settling matters as quickly and decisively as possible.[17] The 'idea' of military decision thus planted itself in the Greek mind beside those other ideas of decision – by majority in politics, of outcome by the inevitability of plot in drama, of conclusion by logic in intellectual work – which we associate with our Greek heritage. It is important not to advance effect over cause. The intellectual glories of Greece belong to an age at least two centuries beyond that when the Greeks began to fight in the massed ranks of the phalanx, in a narrow field of battle, shield against shield, spear against spear. Also, civilised though they were, they remained closely enough in touch with their past to have preserved the primitive passion for revenge, a response to insult which the great gods of their pantheon practised without remorse in the myths all Greeks knew by heart. As a result, suggests Hanson,

> the Greek manner of fighting [may] be explained as an evolving idea, a perception in the minds of small farmers that their ancestral lands should remain at all costs inviolate – *aporthetos* – not to be trodden over by any other than themselves, land whose integrity all citizens were willing to fight over on a moment's notice . . . most Greeks felt that revenge in the old form of pitched combat was the most honourable and expedient way of resolving an insult to their sovereignty. Their tradition, their duty, indeed their desire, was for a ritualistic collision, head-on with the spears of the enemy, to end the whole business quickly and efficiently.[18]

It may be also that another form of competition, whose origins the modern world finds in the Greeks, further helped to supply them with the idea of fighting for an unequivocal result on the battlefield. That was competitive athletics, and the associated contests of chariot- or horse-racing, boxing or wrestling which in 776 BC began to be organised among the established Greek states, at four-yearly intervals, at Olympia in the western Peloponnese, in the territory of the city of Elis; they were carried on uninterruptedly for more than a thousand years until AD 261. Competition at sport and games already had a long history in Greece; Homer depicts the heroes of the Trojan War engaging in two-horse chariot races, boxing, wrestling, weight-throwing and running at ceremonies held by Achilles 'to accompany the burial rites of his comrade Patroclus, killed by Hector in individual combat before the gates of Troy'.[19]

Many other peoples had or were to develop similar customs: the Hopi of Arizona held races in which the runners symbolised clouds and rain in the hope that the event would bring one from the other during the growing season; numerous hunting peoples, like the North American Huron and Cherokee, devised games or tests of skill which prepared the players for the chase by either ritual or practical means; even the individualistic steppe nomads rode against each other in contests to carry an object over a winning-line.[20] Yet, in general, competitive sport was alien to the horse peoples, especially if it involved rough physical contact, which the Greeks believed they associated with personal insult, if a contrived dialogue between Solon and a Scythian visitor to the Olympic games is reliable evidence. Carvings from tombs of the Egyptian New Kingdom show soldiers wrestling, but the competition is between Egyptians and Syrians or Numidians, who are represented as conceding defeat. It is not a depiction of struggle between equals, which the Greeks thought supplied games with their point.[21] When Herodotus visited Egypt from Greece in the fifth century BC 'he was astonished to find no organised games; [but] open competition in games is incompatible with such rigidly stratified societies as those of the ancient Near East, with their Pharaohs and other absolute monarchs at the apex, divinely sanctioned and sometimes gods themselves.'[22]

Games, particularly the violent games of boxing and wrestling, had their critics in the Greek world, whose objections were similar to those we hear today: that successful athletes were over-rewarded, set an example of asocial individualism, and suffered disabling injuries which unfitted them for active life. Plato flatly stated that the tactics of boxers or wrestlers 'are worthless in wartime and do not deserve discussion'. His judgement was too idealistic. Harsh sports, fought for a clear-cut result, reinforced the Greek military ethic; and in any case, Greek warfare was itself so brutal that no simulation was rough enough to unfit men to bear its horrors.[23]

Greek warriors took their place in the battlefield ranked shoulder to shoulder in a compact mass, usually eight rows deep. After the eighth century they were equipped in uniform style, though with weapons and armour the individual supplied for himself; the cost of the equipment, particularly of his bronze helmet, breastplate or the greaves that protected his shins, was a costly charge on his income and could be borne only by a man of property.[24] (The survival of bronze armour into the Iron Age is explained by the inability of contemporary ironsmiths to produce metal of sufficient malleability to form large sheets of an equivalent resilience; though iron was elsewhere already being used to armour soldiers with scales or hoops fixed to a leather tunic, and iron helmets appear to have been in common use in the Near East, neither provided the protection afforded by bronze.) Such protection was essential to the man who took his place in the phalanx – the word (literally 'a roller') is cognate with that for the finger, perhaps because fingers project like parallel spears from the hand – since the shock he had to withstand was not that of a sword or arrowpoint which might be deflected by a glancing surface but of a sharpened iron point, mounted at the end of a solid shaft of ash which, when thrust with all the muscular strength an opponent could muster, would penetrate anything but the best metal.

The man in the phalanx also protected himself with a round, convex shield, the *hoplon*, from which derives the word hoplite used to identify the Greek soldiers of phalanx warfare. It was made of wood reinforced with iron, measured three feet in diameter, and was suspended from his shoulder by a leather strap and manipulated by a grip for the left hand. The right hand was thus left free to couch the spear between elbow and ribs and drive the point at the man opposite in the enemy ranks. It is a famous observation, first remarked by Thucydides, that the phalanx in motion tended to slip to its right, as each man moved closer to the protection of his neighbour's shield. In contact with each other, two opposed phalanxes might be seen to wheel gradually about an invisible axis under the collective force of this individual urge to self-protection.

Phalanx did not meet phalanx without the preliminaries that all Greeks felt necessary. Sacrifice was one of them. 'For the Greeks no undertaking was without its appropriate ritual, giving assurance or approval or, at least, the withholding of hostility on the part of the supernatural powers . . . every stage of the process that led up to a clash of hoplite phalanxes on the field of battle was marked by attention to the gods.' An army marching out to war drove sheep with it to be sacrificed at the crossing-places of rivers or borders, at camp-sites and eventually on the battlefield itself. This *sphagia*, 'the rites of bloodletting', may have been performed 'in the hope of securing assurance by signs that the outcome would be favourable; it may have been a ceremony of placation; it may have been something much cruder, an anticipation of the bloodshed of the battle [which] marked its ritual beginning, offered in a spirit of appeal to the gods: "We kill. May we kill."'[25] By the time the moment came to perform the *sphagia*, however, the hoplites had usually reinforced their courage by more than ritual. It was common practice for both sides to eat a ceremonial mid-morning breakfast before the clash of arms; this last meal certainly included a wine ration, perhaps a larger one than on normal days. Drinking alcohol before battle is an almost universal practice where wine or spirits are available. The hoplites would also have heard the exhortations of their commanders and then, immediately after the ritual slaughter of the *sphagia*, moved forward themselves, uttering the *paean*, the battle-cry reproduced by Aristophanes as a ululating 'eleleleu'.

Whether the commanders took their place in the front rank is much debated; in the Spartan phalanx it appears that they did, as Homer has his heroes do in his descriptions of what is now called the 'proto-phalanx' in the *Iliad*. Thucydides, a veteran as well as a historian of battle, implies as much, for he says that the tactical subdivisions within the Spartan shield wall could be identified by the distinctive dress of the commanders standing in first line. That they chose the post of maximum danger chiefly reflects the strength of the warrior ethic in their society. Elsewhere, particularly at Athens, customs were different. 'An officer class simply did not exist in classical Greek cities' – military posts were as elective as civilian – and there was no tactical point in the leading men putting themselves at the front. Phalanx warfare was won not by encouragement by example, but by the united courage of equals in a terrifying, short-lived clash of bodies and weapons at the closest range.[26]

Hanson has brilliantly and imaginatively reconstructed this ghastly and wholly revolutionary style of warmaking. He discounts the significance of preliminary skirmishing by the light-armed infantry, propertyless men who could not meet the cost of armour, and equally that by the few, rich mounted warriors who may have accompanied the army. The Greek countryside, which could not carry a horse population, does not lend itself to cavalry action. Once the opposed phalanxes arrived at one of those few level sites which it was recognised provided the conditions for a test of strength – 'once the Greeks go to war', Herodotus wrote, 'they choose the best and smoothest place and go down and have their battle on that' – they wasted no time.[27]

Crossing a no man's land perhaps 150 yards wide at a clumsy run, under a weight of armour and weapons of seventy pounds, the ranks drove straight into each other. Each individual would have chosen another as his target at the moment of contact, thrusting his spear point at some gap between shield and shield, and seeking to hit a patch of flesh not covered by armour – throat, armpit or groin. The chance was fleeting. As the second and subsequent ranks were brought up short by the stop in front, the phalanx concertinaed, throwing the weight of seven men on to the back of the warriors engaged with the enemy. Under this impact, some men inevitably went down at once, dead, wounded or overborne from the rear. That might create a breach in the shield wall. Those in the second or third ranks strove to open it wider with their spears, thrusting and jabbing from their relatively protected position at whoever they could reach. If it widened, there followed the *othismos*, 'push with shield', to widen it further and to win room in which swords, the hoplite's secondary weapon, might be drawn and used to slash at an enemy's legs. The *othismos* was the more certain method, however: it could lead to the *pararrexis* or 'breaking', when those most heavily beset by the enemy's pressure began to feel the impulse to flight, and either broke away from the rear ranks or, more shamefully, struggled backward from the point of killing to infect their comrades with panic also.

Once the phalanx broke, defeat inevitably ensued. The opposing hoplites who found free space in front of them would aim to spear or cut down those who had turned their backs; 'there was even greater danger from the entrance of both cavalry and light-armed skirmishers . . . now for the first and only time since the minor pre-battle skirmishing, it was possible for them to enter the battlefield and demonstrate that they were, after all, effective fighters as they rode or ran down the helpless prize troops of the enemy.'[28] Escape from the light-armed was difficult. The hoplite might throw away his shield or spear as he ran, but could scarcely divest himself of his armour in flight. Men would if they could; Thucydides remarked that after an Athenian defeat during the Sicilian expedition in 413 BC 'more arms were left behind than corpses'; at the moment of choice between life and death the citizen-soldier would certainly discard even the costly body-armour which marked him out as a man of standing at home, if that offered survival.[29] Yet to do so might not greatly hasten his flight. After the mere half-hour or hour that the clash of arms had lasted, the hoplite was physically exhausted, perhaps as much by draining terror as muscular effort, and could not outpace the fresh light-armed men who harried his footsteps. The bold and well disciplined might make a fighting retreat in small groups; the philosopher Socrates, who survived the Athenian defeat at Delion in 424 BC, did so by taking a party under command and 'making it clear even from a distance that if anyone were to attack such a man as he, he would put up considerable resistance'.[30] Most men who left ranks that had been broken, however, simply ran for their lives, often to be cut down as they lumbered to safety.

It has been estimated that a phalanx might lose fifteen per cent of its strength by defeat, either through outright killing, death from wounds – typically brought on by peritonitis, following a penetration of the gut – or in the massacre which followed flight. The losses might, nevertheless, have been far greater had the winners pressed home their victory. Generally they did not. 'Pursuit of fleeing hoplites was [not thought] crucial: most victorious Greek armies saw no reason why they could not repeat their simple formula for success and gain further victory should the enemy regroup in a few days and mistakenly press their luck again.' As a result, 'both sides were usually content to exchange their dead under truce' – it was held a sacred duty by all Greeks that those who fell fighting should receive honourable burial – and then 'the victors, after erecting a battlefield trophy or simple monument to their success, marched home triumphantly, eager for the praise of their families and friends on return'.[31] Why, since Greek battle partook of such unprecedented ferocity, did Greek war lack what moderns would see as a justifying culmination in destruction of the defeated army? That it did not is a point on which Hanson is adamant: 'Ultimate victory in the modern sense and enslavement of the conquered was not considered an option by either side. Greek hoplite battles were struggles between small landholders who by mutual consent sought to limit warfare [and hence killing] to a single, brief, nightmarish occasion.'[32]

We can propose two explanations for this strange incompleteness of Greek warfare in the classical age, one with very old roots, the other to which the novel character of the Greek *polis* had itself given birth. For all its deadliness, so alien to the primitives, with whose tentative evasive or indirect tactics we are now familiar, there nevertheless remained strong traces of primitivism in Greek warmaking. One was the impulse to revenge: Greeks may not have made war over wife-stealing – though even modern scholars accept that such an episode might have been the occasion, if not the deeper cause, of the Trojan War in the heroic age – but they may have considered invasion of a city state's fields an affront as outrageous, in a different way, as the violation of tabu. If that were the essence of the provocation, it partly explains the immediacy of the hoplite response. The taking of satisfaction, also a very primitive emotion, may then explain why the response stopped short of Clausewitzian decision. It was already an extraordinary leap into the future for the Greeks to overcome the natural human dread of pushing personal exposure to its tolerable limits, and that is how their adoption of hoplite tactics ought to be seen: fighting face-to-face with death-dealing weapons defies nature, and they bore it only because all shared the risk equally, and sustained each other's courage, as well as place in the battle line, by pushing shoulder against shoulder. After that risk had been undergone it ought not to surprise us that the survivors felt they had done enough. To press on from the battlefield, to run to ground those who had opposed them, had the exhausted hoplites' powers allowed such an extra effort, would add an additional dimension to warmaking for which even the ever-open Greek mind might not have been ready.

Moreover, it is by no means certain that the idea of conquest in the modern sense was acceptable to the Greeks, at least as between Greek and Greek. The conflicts among the city states – Argos, Corinth, Thebes and especially Athens and Sparta – were real enough in the so-called 'age of tyrants' in the seventh and sixth centuries BC; even so, the object of warmaking was usually that of enlarging a league of allies rather than of subjecting a principal opponent to domination. From the earliest times, 'the Greeks were always conscious that they were different from other peoples . . . Greek prisoners of war, for example, were not in theory to be enslaved, unlike "barbarians" . . . The great religious festivals of the Greek year, when people of many cities came together' – the Olympic games pre-eminently – 'were occasions to which only the Greek-speaker was admitted.' For the Greeks, particularly for the Athenians and their Ionian cousins in Asia Minor who looked to the *metropolis* (mother-city) for inspiration, conquest was something imposed on others across the seas. They conquered widely, at least as much as was necessary to plant colonies on foreign shores; but at home, though they fought often and bloodily, they did not – with perhaps the exception of Sparta – seek to deprive each other of their acknowledged rights. By the sixth century, the city states were set in the direction of collective government; 'oligarchies, constitutional governments or democracies spread everywhere.'[33] While all states retained the institution of slavery, recent researches suggest that the proportion of slaves to freemen in the *polis* has been exaggerated. By the fifth century, for example, slaves in Athens were greatly outnumbered by free citizen-farmers; this explodes the supposition that Greek hoplites – except the Spartan – were set at liberty to wage war by the labours of the unfree in their smallholdings.[34]

During the seventh century Sparta had, through its remorselessly efficient military system, made itself an unchallengeable power in southern Greece; only through a pattern of shifting alliances could its chief rivals, Argos, Athens, Corinth and Thebes, hold it in check. But then, in 510 BC, the contest was heightened when Sparta directly intervened to attempt to set back Athens's decisive espousal of democracy; this ensured the onset of a contest of principle, between its warrior élitism and the representative example offered by its principal rival, that lasted for more than a hundred years. Yet for much of this period Sparta and Athens were thrown into alliance by patriotic impulse. The rising power of the Persians, who by 511 BC had consolidated an empire that included the whole of Mesopotamia and Egypt as well as lands reaching up to the Oxus and Jaxartes rivers, led them on to attack the Ionian settlements in Asia Minor. These cities had earlier been subjected by Croesus of Lydia, then passed to Persian control, and in 499 BC, with Athenian support, they rebelled to assert their independence. Darius, the reigning Persian emperor, crushed the rebellion in 494 BC but was determined to deal with the root of the trouble, which he identified as emanating from mainland Greece. In 490 BC, at the head of a well-equipped army of 50,000, he took ship aboard the formidable Persian navy and landed in the plain of Marathon, thirty-six miles north of Athens. The Athenians at once marched out to oppose the Persian advance inland, joined by their allies from Plataea, but sent an urgent appeal for help to Sparta. The Spartans replied that they would arrive as soon as an impending religious ceremony had been completed. By the time their leading troops reached the scene of action, the battle of Marathon was over. The Athenians had destroyed one-seventh of the Persian host, for little loss to themselves, and the enemy withdrew into his ships.

This was the first direct conflict between the Greek phalanx and the more uncertain ranks of a dynastic Middle Eastern army, composed of subject soldiers of very uneven worth. Hanson has suggested how unnerving the enemy must have found the Greeks' advance. He notes that Herodotus has Mardonios, the nephew of the emperor Darius and commander of the fleet that beached at Marathon, remark on the unnatural bloodthirstiness of the Athenians and their Plataean allies.

All the various contingents of the Great Army of Persia, with their threatening looks and noise, had a very different and predictable outlook on battle . . . But the Persians suffered from that most dangerous tendency in war: a wish to kill but not to die in the process . . . At Marathon they thought a 'destructive madness' had infected the Greek ranks as they saw them approach on the run in their heavy armour. Surely, as the outnumbered Greek hoplites crashed into their lines, the Persians must have at last understood that these men worshipped not only the god Apollo, but the wild, irrational Dionysus as well.[35]

The Spartans bitterly reproached themselves for their absence at Marathon, all the more because of the glory that victory brought to Athens. Nevertheless, they accepted that Persian aggression, with the threat it carried of extinction of Greek rights, obliged them to persist in their offer of assistance, and they proceeded with the Athenians to coordinate plans for resistance should the common enemy reappear. The Persians had not abandoned their determination to do so. Between 484 and 481 BC Xerxes, who had succeeded as emperor on Darius' death, drew Carthage into an alliance that ensured the Greek colonists in Sicily would not come to their mainland cousins' assistance, while completing elaborate logistic arrangements, including the building of a bridge of boats across the straits between Asia and Europe, to secure communications for the advance of his troops. At this news, many of the smaller Greek states sought to make their peace with Xerxes. Only Athens and the Peloponnesian states persisted in patriotic defiance. Sparta attempted to persuade Athens to send its forces south of the easily defensible Isthmus of Corinth into the Peloponnese to join those of the other cities in the Peloponnesian League. The Athenians, led by Themistocles, declined to do so, since that would mean abandoning their city; instead, they argued, their very strong navy should protect the seaward flank of a League expeditionary force, which would oppose the Persian advance much further north.

Reluctantly, for few of the allies wanted to send their troops out of the Peloponnese, Sparta fell in with Athenian strategy and agreed to hold a line where the coastal route from the plain of Thessaly passes through the defile of Thermopylae. Offshore the fleet, of which two-thirds was Athenian and under the direct command of Themistocles, inflicted a check (August 480 BC) on the Persian, which had suffered heavy losses in a gale; in the pass of Thermopylae itself Leonidas, the Spartan king, successfully blocked the Persian army's advance, until by treachery he was taken in the rear. In an act of self-sacrifice that was to become a byword for hopeless courage, Leonidas and his bodyguard – 'the three hundred at the pass' – held on nevertheless, while the fleet disengaged, evacuated the population of Athens to the island of Salamis and awaited action. The rest of the League forces had by now retreated south of the Isthmus of Corinth, leaving Themistocles to demonstrate that the Persians might indeed be defeated by sea power. He, by a devious if forgivable exercise in misinformation, persuaded Xerxes that the Athenians would come over if the Persian fleet moved to action, thus tempting it into confined waters where its superior numbers, of some 700 against 500 fighting-ships, gave it no advantage. In a single day of fighting (probably 23 September 480 BC), the Athenians destroyed half of it, with the loss of only forty ships of their own, and forced the remainder to withdraw northward.

254

THE GREEKS AND AMPHIBIOUS STRATEGY

Xerxes' invasion had not been completely defeated. That outcome was not achieved until the following year when, in the land battle of Plataea in July and the sea battle of Mycale in August, Athens and Sparta jointly disposed of the rest of the Persians' expeditionary force with its Greek (chiefly Theban) allies and not only chased it off the Greek mainland but recaptured and held the Black Sea Straits.

The campaign of 480–79 BC reinforced what had first been demonstrated to outsiders at Marathon ten years earlier, that to defeat a Greek phalanx required either Greek courage, or the enlistment of Greeks themselves, or a new and more complex tactical method. Greek courage resisted transplantation, but Greek mercenaries found a market even readier for their services than they had already established – the Persians had employed Greeks in their conquest of Egypt in 550 BC – and tactical experimentations, particularly with armoured cavalry, henceforth proceeded apace. The larger legacy of the campaign of 480–79 BC, however, was not military but naval. It elevated the power of fleets to a level equal to that held by armies in states that bordered an inland sea, and so set the style for a new method of warmaking, truly strategic in character, that dominated the struggle for position in the eastern Mediterranean for the rest of the century; its principles eventually passed into the lore of all maritime peoples.

The instrument of Greek, chiefly Athenian, naval strategy was the oared fighting-ship, probably developed by the Phoenicians of the Syrian coast from earlier local or even Cypriot models during the beginning of the first millennium BC. The Phoenicians were Persian subjects by the time of Xerxes, but their technology had already migrated to Greece, where at Athens the trireme, a heavy vessel with a strong armoured beak, 120 feet in length, fifteen in beam, was rowed by oarsmen sitting in three superimposed ranks, who could drive it at speeds sufficient to sink an opponent in a ramming attack.[36] Athens recruited its sailors from a lower census class than that of the hoplites, who supplied the galley with fighting marines. In close action, the oarsmen might join in the fight which, as ship locked with ship, took the form of a body-to-body rather than hull-against-hull struggle for advantage.[37]

The strength of the Athenian navy, and the military importance the city came to attach to it, derived from the direction in which its economy and foreign relations had developed during the previous two centuries. While Sparta had maximised the military advantages supplied by its exclusive social order to make itself pre-eminent in the Peloponnese, Athens, impelled in part by the difficulty it found in feeding its population off its poor soils, had turned itself into a trading, and increasingly a political, empire with allied or dependent cities as far away as Asia Minor. It was through this system of alliances that Athens took the leadership in the continuing war with Persia that followed Salamis and Plataea, and which in 460–54 BC involved its naval and expeditionary forces in a struggle for control of Egypt. Sparta, secure and self-sufficient, dropped out of the war, while Athens, at the head of the Delian League of smaller cities, prosecuted it with vigour, largely by levying ever heavier demands for subsidy on its supporters; eventually 150 cities were paying tribute.

By 448 BC Athens had exhausted Persia's will to sustain the war and peace was made. Peace abroad, however, did not bring peace at home. Athenian exactions had widely disaffected the tax-paying classes in the cities of the Delian League. Where Athenian intervention sometimes provoked revolution to install Athenian-style democracy, the combined effects of Athenian extortion, political subversion and widening strategic and commercial dominance eventually turned first Corinth, and eventually one city after another, against Athens and provoked an outbreak of hostilities, in which Sparta aligned herself with Corinth and Thebes. This First Peloponnesian War was concluded in 445 BC without heavy cost to either side. But Athens had set itself on a course which made a resumption inevitable. By barricading itself behind fortifications – the 'Long Walls' enclosing both Athens and its port of the Piraeus – that made it impregnable from the land, while, at the instigation of its dynamic leader, Pericles, concentrating its financial and military resources on expansion overseas, it set itself up as a city apart, ruthless in imposing its dominance over its former allies in the Delian League and in challenging both the interests of the other large commercial cities and the status of Sparta as chief military power on the mainland. In 433 BC war broke out between Athens and Corinth. In 432 BC Sparta joined in, bringing with her the cities of the Boeotian and Peloponnesian Leagues.[38]

This conflict, the Peloponnesian War proper, lasted until 404 BC, when it culminated in Athenian defeat and Spartan victory, but it exhausted the Greek city-state system for good; the residual hostilities that persisted in its aftermath laid Greece open to conquest and enforced unification at the hands of the Macedonians, brothers to the Greeks but semi-barbarians in their eyes, after which the splendour of Greek independence as a civilisation of free peoples on the periphery of an expansionist, Asiatic empire, and the glories of the intellectual and artistic life it had inspired, were finally overlaid. The war itself was a conflict of opposites, land power against sea power, in which advantage eluded either side. In the opening stages Sparta attempted to bring Athens down by starvation, invading its hinterland almost annually; Athens rode out this strategy of blockade by effectively abandoning its rural population and surviving on maritime imports, particularly those brought down the route from the grain centres around the Black Sea. When Sparta in 424 BC sent an army to capture the Thracian ports by which this route was maintained, Athens was driven to seek a truce, but Sparta failed in the diplomacy which might have brought lasting peace. Some of its allies deserted, reviving Athenian hopes of eventual victory and prompting the city in 415 to enlarge the war with the object of bringing on a decisive crisis. Athens launched an expedition against Syracuse in Sicily, in the hopes of capturing the whole island and so ensuring itself of a centre of supply that would conclusively secure its economic position.

The Sicilian expedition brought on a crisis, but one far larger than that for which Athens had bargained. Perceiving that the issue was now which city should hold primacy in the Greek world, Sparta abandoned the patriotic position it had sustained since Thermopylae and invoked the aid of Persia. Between 412 and 404 BC, in a series of land and sea campaigns that ranged as far as the entrance to the Black Sea, the Spartan army and the Persian navy inflicted a series of defeats on the Athenians which eventually drove their forces to take refuge within the Long Walls. The Persian fleet, after destroying the Athenian at the battle of Aegospotami in 405, appeared off the Piraeus; in April 404, under blockade by both sea and land, Athens was forced to surrender.

MACEDON AND THE CULMINATION OF PHALANX WARFARE

The end of the Peloponnesian War did not mean the end of war between Greeks. The fourth century was, indeed, to be a doleful time, both on the mainland and in the overseas colonies, as the protagonists persisted in their struggles for advantage, shifting alliances in increasingly arbitrary fashion and involving Persian help in a self-interested spirit wholly at variance with that of the patriotic movement which had united the Greeks in the face of Darius and Xerxes. Between 395 and 387 Athens and its confederates allied themselves with Persia against Sparta, which had taken up the cause of the Greek cities in Asia Minor: a combined Athenian–Persian fleet destroyed Sparta's navy at the battle of Cnidus, in 384. The consequent resurgence of Athenian power then alarmed Persia into sending surreptitious help to Sparta, and through the resulting stalemate, the Greeks were actually brought to recognise nominal Persian suzerainty at home and abroad. Sparta nevertheless persisted in attempts to sustain the decision of the Peloponnesian War, particularly by efforts to subdue Thebes, now its chief rival on land. Thebes won two remarkable victories, at Leuctra in 371 and Mantinea in 362, where its outstanding general, Epaminondas, demonstrated that the phalanx system could be adapted to achieve decisive tactical manoeuvre in the face of the enemy. At Leuctra, outnumbered 11,000 to 6000, he quadrupled the strength of his left wing and, masking his weakness on the right, led his massed column in a charge. Expecting the battle to develop in normal phalanx style, when both sides met in equal strength along the whole front of engagement, the Spartans failed to reinforce the threatened section in time and were broken, for considerable loss to themselves and almost none to the Thebans. Despite this warning, they allowed themselves to be surprised in exactly the same fashion at Mantinea nine years later and were again defeated. Epaminondas was killed in the moment of victory, an effect in part of the greater degree of exposure risked by a commander who experimented with the phalanx form, leaving Thebes bereft of leadership while the crisis persisted.

Power in Greece was now shifting from the established cities of the south and centre to the north, where Macedon, under an energetic new king, Philip, was transforming itself into a local hegemony. Philip, who had known and admired Epaminondas, reorganised the Macedonian army along lines that enhanced its powers of tactical manoeuvre, subdued enemies on his western and northern borders, and then turned to involve himself in Greek affairs. In the Third Sacred War (355–46) he achieved leadership of the Amphictyonic (north-eastern) Council, after defeating Athens and seizing many of its allied cities. Once he had consolidated his position and extended his conquests outside Greece, he was placed to extend his authority further. Demosthenes had warned his fellow Athenians and the rest of Greece that the Macedonian danger challenged them to unite, as they had once united against Persia, but he had gone unheard. In 339, in a renewed effort, Athens and Thebes declared war against the Amphictyonic Council, were met by Philip at Chaeronea (338) and utterly crushed. In the following year he summoned a council of all the Greek city states, at which all but Sparta accepted his leadership and his challenge to join Macedon in a campaign to throw off Persia's influence over the Greek lands by an expedition to Asia Minor.

Philip's eighteen-year-old son, Alexander, had been present at Chaeronea, where he led the cavalry of the left wing in what proved the day's decisive stroke. Two years later he was king himself; whether or not he was party to the conspiracy through which Philip met his death tantalises his biographers to this day. No breach in Macedonian policy followed from the succession. Indeed, Alexander took up the challenge of a Persian 'crusade' even more energetically than his father had promised to do. Having conclusively subdued Philip's old enemies on Macedon's northern border, and put down a resurgence of Theban defiance, he marshalled the Macedonian army, strongly reinforced with mercenary contingents recruited from the surplus of soldiers left unemployed by the Greek wars, crossed to Asia in the spring of 334 and set out to topple Darius III, the ruling Persian emperor. It was an undertaking of breathtaking audacity. Persia had made itself master of the lands of all previous Middle Eastern empires and its boundaries extended to enclose not only Persia proper but Mesopotamia, Egypt, Syria and Asia Minor with its Greek colonies. The Persian army, though still centred on a chariot nucleus, included heavy cavalry forces and large numbers of Greek mercenary infantry.

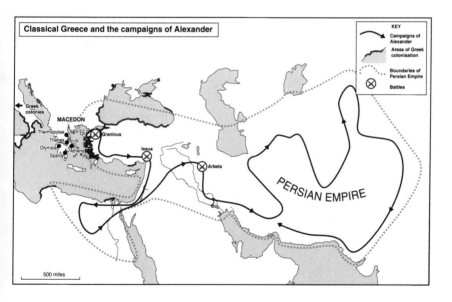

Alexander's own army mirrored in organisation that of the Persians. Though it had no chariots, which had long fallen out of fashion in Greece, it included regiments of heavy cavalry, mounted on horses bred

259

on the grasslands beyond the Macedonian mountains; his own shock force of Companions, horsemen (still without stirrups and riding rudimentary saddles) who wore armour and wielded spear and sword; and a powerful phalanx core, whose soldiers wore the traditional Greek body-armour but carried an even longer spear, the *sarissa*, so allowing the phalanx to be ranked at twice the depth of the old. Its component units were formed on a tribal basis but, more important, the Macedonian element was informed by a strong national spirit, while Alexander achieved remarkable success in implanting a sense of common patriotism among the Greeks he took to Persia with him. Altogether his soldiers numbered some 50,000 – this was enormous compared to the numbers who had opposed each other in the largest campaigns of the Peloponnesian War, when Sparta rarely found more than 10,000 troops – of which most were infantry.[39]

Alexander campaigned in Asia for twelve years, and his restless spirit eventually carried him as far away as the plains of northern India in search of new conquests. The decisive strokes against Persia were laid early on, however, in the three battles of the River Granicus (334), Issus (333), and Gaugamela (331), which progressively destroyed the Persian imperial army's capacity to resist and eventually overwhelmed it. The Granicus was a preliminary engagement, chiefly remarkable for the dynamic leadership displayed by Alexander at the head of his cavalry. 'It was a cavalry struggle,' wrote his biographer, Arrian, 'though on infantry lines; horse pressed against horse . . . trying to push the Persians from the brink and force them onto level ground, the Persians trying to bar their landing and hurl them back onto the river.'[40] Alexander chose his point of attack by observing how the Persians had sought protection behind the river banks, clear evidence of faint-heartedness and an interestingly 'primitive' survival of evasive tactics, which we know continued to permeate the ethos of Middle Eastern armies for another millennium. Alexander's Greek impatience with anything but face-to-face fighting impelled him to charge where the Persians looked strongest, a risk proved exactly justifiable when they broke before him. The Greek mercenary phalanx in second line, 'rooted to the spot by the unexpected catastrophe', was surrounded and hacked down.[41] Alexander himself was wounded, but in the totality of his victory that was forgotten. He had demonstrated that a Greek phalanx, combined with armoured cavalry, could carry war into Persian territory and press home its advantage. At Issus in the following year he reinforced the point. Outnumbered three to one (if the best estimate that Darius, who was present in person, had 160,000 men under command is correct), Alexander once again chose to attack on the strongest sector, picked out for him because 'in some parts [the Persians] had built up palisades [so that] Alexander's staff perceived Darius to be a man of no spirit'.[42] Crossing the enemy's missile zone at speed, and so braving what ought to have been a disabling barrage from the arrows of the Persian composite bowmen, he led the cavalry directly against the flank where Darius stood. In the centre his phalanx collided and was stopped by its Greek mercenary equivalent, but, after putting Darius to flight, he turned his horsemen to roll up the enemy infantry's flank and complete the victory.

The third confrontation was delayed while Alexander invaded and occupied those sections of the Persian empire – Syria, Egypt and northern Mesopotamia – that Darius had by now abandoned. It was not until twenty-three months after Issus that Alexander ran the Persian army to ground again, at Gaugamela, on 1 October 331 BC. The Macedonians were now at what seemed to be the extreme limit of their logistic outreach, having left their supporting fleet far behind by crossing the Euphrates to enter Mesopotamia proper. Darius calculated that, could he hold Alexander on a strong position, the Macedonians would either be defeated there or might disintegrate as an army if forced into retreat. He made his position at Gaugamela very strong, clearing an area on a tributary of the Tigris eight miles square, to give his chariots – which may have had scythed wheels – unimpeded room for manoeuvre, and making three parallel avenues down which they were to charge (the Chinese, as we have seen, also believed in thus preparing a battlefield). His army included not only charioteers (he himself paraded in a chariot, in continuation of the Middle Eastern imperial tradition) but contingents from twenty-four different subject or mercenary nationalities, among which were a few remaining Greeks, Scythian horsemen from the steppe, some Indian cavalry and even a group of elephants. As at the Granicus and Issus it outnumbered the Macedonian army considerably – there were at least 40,000 Persian cavalrymen present – and stood on well protected ground of its own choosing.[43] Success looked assured, and might have followed, had Alexander not first played Darius at his waiting-game and then effected an altogether novel tactical stroke. He delayed advancing to action for four days, leaving the Persians idle in their positions; when he eventually did so, he matched his deployment to that of Darius, cavalry on the wings and infantry in the centre, but then, in a creative adaptation of Epaminondas's manoeuvre at Leuctra, led it across the face of the Persian line to menace the enemy's left flank. Surprised, the Persians delayed counter-charging until the Macedonians had made contact; when at last they charged, Alexander was close enough up with his Companion cavalry to lead it into the gap thus created and panic Darius, who stood immediately in Alexander's path, into headlong flight.

It was not until ten months later that Alexander caught up with the emperor, then to find him dead from wounds just inflicted by his cowardly courtiers. Alexander, who had already proclaimed himself both Pharaoh of Egypt and King of Babylon, and had already taken the title of Persian emperor, now began to call himself King of Asia. At home, where outbursts by the ever-dissident Spartans and Athenians had been crushed, the Greek League had reaffirmed his appointment as overlord for life; he now set forth to make good his claim. He had already assessed the courses of action open to him:

> [to] withdraw to the Euphrates lines, leaving the military and economic strength of Persia broken; [to] stop, as Trajan was to do later, content with control of the rich plains of Mesopotamia; or [to] go on to conquer the rest of the Persian empire. Alexander took the third course. For the Persian empire resembled Macedonia herself, in that its rich plains were exposed to the attacks of the vigorous mountain peoples of the north and its further provinces formed a barrier against pugnacious nomadic peoples.

In short, Alexander had unwittingly inherited the strategic problems of those earlier valley emperors of whom he was now the successor, problems indeed that were replicated in China's relationship with the peoples north of the great bend of the Yellow River, in Rome's and Byzantium's wars on their Asiatic borders and ultimately in Christian Europe's efforts to define and hold its eastern steppe frontier. Alexander appeared to solve his inherited difficulties by a brilliantly positive policy of driving his line of control ever eastward, thus allowing none of the potential invaders into the Persian heartland to hold a footing from which attacks could be launched. In truth, however, his long military wanderings through Central Asia and northern India were the pursuit of a chimera. A new enemy presented itself after each conclusive victory until his army, at last tiring of exile, obliged him to turn for home. Behind he left a string of superficially Hellenised satellites that his generals ruled for themselves after his death at Babylon in 323 BC. But their foundations were insecure, their rulers fell to quarrelling among themselves, and during the following century most lapsed from Hellenism and reverted to their native state.

Alexander had struck at a propitious moment. His principal target, Achaemenid Persia, had overextended its power and was vulnerable to attack at its periphery, particularly when, to oppose the ferocious face-to-face fighters of the Macedonian phalanx and Alexander's armoured cavalrymen who, as Arrian perceptively remarked, fought like hoplites on horseback, it had to depend in bulk upon soldiers who belonged culturally to the Middle Eastern tradition of avoiding close combat, fighting behind a missile screen and trusting to obstacles to impede the enemy's advance. It was fortunate for Alexander, too, that when he struck out into Central Asia after his conquest of the Persian heartland, he campaigned among societies that had not yet acquired the strengths they were to find in the next millennium from Islam and their accumulated experiences of successful horse warfare. Alexander's life was indeed an epic; if his Byzantine successors, however, failed to repeat his successes in their struggle to sustain the frontiers of their empire to the Caucasus and the Nile, it was not because they lacked his will, capacity or resources, but because they were confronted by a far more formidable military problem.

ROME: MOTHER HOUSE OF MODERN ARMIES

The collapse of Alexandrian Hellenism in the East was matched at home also, though not through the quarrels of his successors. The power of the house of Macedon in its heartland, and over Greece also, was eventually overthrown by a people insignificant in Alexander's time, the Romans. Rome owed much to Greece for its rise. In the sixth century BC it was little more than a village on the banks of a river, where three tribes bearing Etruscan names, evidence of the dominance of Etruria to the north, lived under the rule of a king. During the reign of Servius Tullius, 580–30 BC, the population was supposedly organised into five military classes drawn from the propertied, and a militia was founded which certainly practised hoplite tactics.[44] The Romans later claimed that they took their tactics from the Etruscans, but it seems more probable that they were imported from the Greeks, probably those living in sizeable numbers in southern Italy. At about the same time a republican form of government replaced the monarchy, and it was under the republic that Rome first began to extend its area of control, initially by conflict with the Etruscans, themselves under pressure from the Gauls of northern Italy, then with the Gauls directly, finally with the Samnites to the south. When Rome's southern expansion brought her into contact with the Greek colonies in Calabria and Apulia, in the third century BC, they sent for help to Pyrrhus, ruler of one of the Alexandrian successor kingdoms in Greece; though victorious, he was so shaken by the costs of fighting a Roman army, particularly in the battles of Ausculum (299) and Beneventum (295), that he abandoned the campaign.

The Roman army had by now moved far in organisation from the hoplite model on which it was based. During their wars with the Gauls, who fought in a loose but dynamic open order, the Roman commanders had found that the tight ranks of the phalanx put their troops at a disadvantage. They had therefore introduced a system which allowed subsections, 'maniples' or handfuls, to manoeuvre on the battlefield and had progressively abandoned the thrusting spear in favour of a javelin, the *pilum*, which, when thrown, the soldier followed sword in hand. Increasingly, too, the soldiers of the legion, as the groups of maniples which constituted a division came to be called during the fourth century BC, dispensed with the heavy hoplite equipment; they adopted a light, oblong shield and, eventually, standard and much lighter body-armour of hooped iron, which would not have been proof against the pike-thrusts of phalanx fighting but served adequately to deflect sword-blows and missile-points. As important for the long-term efficiency of the Roman army as this change in equipment and tactics was the introduction of a new basis of service. Though by their frequent hiring of mercenaries the Greek city states had eventually compromised the principle that the citizen supported himself in the field, and while some were even driven to equip and pay their servicemen at public expense – by 440 Athens was paying its galley crews and overseas garrisons – the duty of the hoplite to campaign at his own expense remained an ideal.[45] By the fourth century Rome had abandoned it, and was paying the legionaries a daily stipend. This development marked the most important divergence of the Roman from the Greek military system. Rome's smallholders, at the dictate of an increasingly dominant political class, ceased to be attached to and supported by their land and became a recruiting pool for a professional army which campaigned, year after year, farther and farther from home, as the Roman republic extended to form an empire.[46]

Rome's imperial motives are much disputed by scholars. It was the traditional view, certainly one supported by Roman sources, that an economic motive lacked. Rome certainly did not need to find food for a growing population, as Athens did, since rich lands were easily annexed within a short campaigning distance of the city. On the other hand, Rome grew rich by conquest, and its empire's expansion fed on itself. Certainly, at the outset of the period of expansion, there was great enthusiasm for the acquisition of new land in Italy, both to provide estates for the political class and plots for the cultivators, and the state found no shortage of takers to buy or rent what it acquired by conquest; the agricultural colonies it founded were quickly settled and generally flourished. Yet arguments that

Rome's wars were deliberately undertaken to amass slave populations as a labour force on the expanding estates of the political class appear far-fetched, as do those that Roman governments thought in such primitive terms as loot; the Italy which succumbed to Roman conquest was a largely moneyless region, and had little to yield in precious metals or minerals or rich artefacts. Nevertheless, 'it was scarcely possible for a Roman to disassociate the expectation of gain from the expectation of successful war and conquest'. The two went together in the Roman outlook, as is best expressed by the classical historian William Harris: 'Economic gain was to the Romans . . . an integral part of successful warfare and of the expansion of power.'[47]

What most distinguished the warfare of the Romans from that of their contemporaries and neighbours was not its motivation – in that respect it was the headstrong and individualistic Greeks who stood apart – but its ferocity.[48] So ferocious were the Romans of the later first millennium BC that, in broad historical perspective, their behaviour bears comparison only with that of the Mongols or Timurids 1500 years later. Like the Mongols, they took resistance, particularly that of besieged cities, as a pretext justifying wholesale slaughter of the defeated. Polybius, the foremost Roman historian of the city's early military history, describes how Scipio Africanus, after storming New Carthage (Spanish Cartagena) in 209 during the Second Punic War,

> directed [his soldiers], according to the Roman custom, against the people in the city, telling them to kill everyone they met and to spare no one, and not to start looting until they received their order. The purpose of this custom is to strike terror. Accordingly one can see in cities captured by the Romans not only human beings who have been slaughtered, but even dogs sliced in two and the limbs of other animals cut off. On this occasion the amount of such slaughter was very great.[49]

The experience of New Carthage was widely repeated, sometimes in cities that had capitulated in the hope of averting a massacre, and even on the field of battle; Macedonians who fell in the campaign of 199 BC were later found by their companions as dismembered corpses, a sacrilege to all Greeks, who thought it a duty to bury the dead of battle, whether friend or enemy. The practice persisted into the first century AD, if the archaeological evidence for a massacre at Maiden Castle in Dorset, during the second Roman invasion of Britain, bears the interpretation usually put on it.

Harris concludes:

> In many respects, [the Romans'] behaviour resembles that of many other

non-primitive ancient peoples, yet few others are known to have displayed such an extreme degree of ferocity in war while reaching a high level of political culture. Roman imperialism was in large part the result of quite rational behaviour on the part of the Romans, but it also had dark and irrational roots. One of the most striking features of Roman warfare is its regularity – almost every year the Romans went out and did massive violence to someone – and this regularity gives the phenomenon a pathological character.[50]

In the context of comparative military history, this should not surprise us. The impulse to violence takes many forms, we have seen, and if most people shrank from expressing it directly when to do so entailed risk to their own bodies, a minority did not. Phalanx warfare, though it limited its effects by its essentially ponderous nature, inflicted appalling violence at the moment of contact, and to engage in it demanded a violation of both the instinct of self-preservation and the widespread cultural inhibition against face-to-face killing. What the Greeks learned to overcome in one fashion, the Romans learned in another. For all their social and political sophistication, they seem to have preserved from somewhere in their primitive past sufficient of the psychology of the hunter to fall on fellow humans as if on animal prey, and do their victims to death with as little regard for life as is sometimes shown by one wild species for another.

Yet Roman warfare, for all its episodic extremism, never achieved the levels of inhumanity and destructiveness reached later by that of the Mongols and Timurids. The Romans worked by piecemeal annexation and consolidation of territory – Caesar's conquest of Gaul was an isolated exception – and after the Punic wars they did not set out to rampage, terrorise and destroy as Tamerlane was to do. They built no pyramids of skulls; and if they set up military colonies on the boundaries of their possessions, as in Liguria in the third century BC, Roman citizens willingly settled this land, not displaced subject populations shifted from their homelands as a punishment for untrustworthiness – the practice instituted by the Assyrians and carried on by Mongols, Turks and eventually Russians.

The comparative restraint of their imperial method has several explanations. The first was that the Roman army lacked mobility of the order displayed by the horse peoples. A Roman legion of the fourth century BC included a sizeable cavalry contingent, but thereafter it declined to an auxiliary fragment, for both social and material reasons: Italy, like Greece, will not bear a large horse population, while the original knightly class progressively abandoned campaigning in the field to pursue politics in the city.[51] On the march, the legions displayed from the start of the era of expansion a remarkable ability to cover ground at a regular pace, day after day, and the state to provide it with pay and *matériel*. By its nature, however, an infantry army proceeds deliberately, not by dynamic surges, as conquering nomads do, so that Rome's expansion was cumulative rather than cascading in character.

Moreover, the cumulative pattern of expansion was determined by the nature of the Roman army itself, which became 'regular' and bureaucratic at an early stage and, by the time of the Punic wars against Carthage, had achieved a form from which it was not to diverge until the onset of the empire's troubles with the Teutonic barbarians in the third century AD. Historians credit Assyria with having inaugurated the regular system, and it indeed seems probable that the practices it instituted, including those of regular payment of full-time servicemen, establishment of arsenals and depots, building of barracks and centralised manufacture of equipment, did set a pattern for that of other, later empires; it percolated from the Middle East to zones of intense military activity farther west during the sixth and fifth centuries BC, partly through the Persians' contact with the Greeks, partly through the rise of the market in mercenaries who had to be supported from state treasuries. No army before that of the Roman republic, however, achieved its level of legally and bureaucratically regulated recruitment, organisation, command and supply. From the Punic wars onward, it stood apart from all other institutions in the civilised world – perhaps its only, though invisible, equivalent was the Chinese mandarinate – as a phenomenon of confident self-sufficiency.

Its ability to persist successfully in unrelenting warmaking, whether in wars thrust upon Rome or deliberately undertaken, derived in large measure from the state's solution of all centralised governments' besetting military difficulty: that of assuring a steady source of reliable and effective recruits. By the time of the Punic wars, the militia obligation, though theoretically still in force, had lapsed and the legions were manned by a selection process, the *dilectus*, by which the best of willing citizens who presented themselves were enrolled for a six-year term of service (which might be extended to as many as eighteen years). The adoption of the *dilectus* reflected a worsening of the small farmers' circumstances, and indeed the expanding estates of the rich were extinguishing the basis of smallholding; nevertheless, paid voluntary service seems to have been a popular enough alternative to farming for there to have been no need for laws reducing the term of service until the late second century BC.[52] There was no need to apply the *dilectus* to those assigned high rank in the legions since the Roman political system, at least until then, made it a condition of candidature for elective political office, leading to that of the ruling consulate, that young men of good birth must have first completed a statutory period of duty as a tribune, of which there were six to each legion; ten years of service, or ten campaigns, seem to have been the qualifying norm. In the later empire, and particularly during the military crises of the third century AD, the imposition of the qualification would lapse, but neither republic nor empire ever shed the view that right to rule was ultimately legitimised by ability to command in the field.[53]

Yet the ultimate strength of the Roman army, and the characteristic that made it the model, a millennium later, for those raised in the dynastic states of Europe, following the revival of classical learning at the Renaissance, from which the great modern armies descend, was supplied neither by its system of recruitment nor by its high command but by its legionary encadrement, the centurionate. The Roman centurions, long-service unit-leaders drawn from the best of the enlisted ranks, formed the first body of professional fighting officers known to history. It was they who imbued the legions with backbone and transmitted from generation to generation the code of discipline and accumulated store of tactical expertise by which Roman arms were carried successfully against a hundred enemies over five centuries of almost continuous warmaking.

The Roman historian Livy has preserved for us the record of service of a republican centurion which exactly conveys the ethos of this remarkable body of men, and it emphasises how revolutionary was the institution of the centurionate in a world where hitherto military service had been largely an intermittent, emergency or mercenary business; indeed, it might, with appropriate substitutions, stand as that of a regular warrant officer in any great modern army. Spurius Ligustinus told the consulate of 171 BC:

> I became a soldier in the consulship [of 200 BC]. In the army which was taken over to Macedonia, I served two years in the ranks against King Philip; in the third year because of my bravery [I was given] a post as centurion in the tenth maniple of the *hastati* [a term, with those of *triarii* and *principes*, surviving from the original ranking of legionary maniples by property qualification]. After Philip's defeat, when we had been brought back to Italy and released, I immediately set out for Spain as a volunteer with the consul M. Porcius [195 BC]. This commander judged me worthy to be assigned as centurion of the first century of the *hastati*. For the third time I enlisted again as a volunteer in that army which was set against the Aetolians and King Antiochus [191 BC]. By Manicus Acilius I was made centurion of the first century of the *principes*. When Antiochus had been driven out and the Aetolians subdued, we were brought back to Italy. And

twice after that I served in campaigns where the legions were in commission for a year. Then I campaigned twice in Spain [181 and 180 BC] . . . I was brought home by Flaccus along with the others whom he brought with him from the province to take part in the Triumph because of their bravery. Four times within a few years I held the rank of *primus pilus* [centurion of the first century of the *triarii*]. Four and thirty times I was rewarded for bravery by my commanders. I have received six civic crowns. I have served out twenty-two years in the army and am more than fifty years old.[54]

Ligustinus, who had six sons and two married daughters, was petitioning for further office or promotion, and, on the strength of his record, was made *primus pilus*, senior centurion, in the First Legion.

With an officer corps of the quality represented by Ligustinus, formed of men whose life was soldiering, who entertained no expectation of rising into the governing class, and whose ambitions were entirely limited to those of success within what could be perceived, for the first time in history, as an esteemed and self-sufficient profession, it is not surprising that Rome's boundaries came to be extended from the Atlantic to the Caucasus; it succeeded, by whatever means, in transforming the warrior ethos of a small city state into a true military culture, an entirely novel *Weltanschauung*, one shared by the highest and the lowest levels of Roman society, but rooted in and expressed through the values of a separate and subordinate corporation of specialists. Theirs was not a privileged life by any material test. For all the mechanistic efficiency of the legion in battle, Roman warfare remained a bloody and intensely dangerous business. The centurion, quite as much as the legionary, fought at close range to the enemy, often hand to hand, and accepted the danger of wounding as an inescapable hazard of the life he had chosen. Julius Caesar, for example, writing of his battle against the Nervii on the River Sambre in modern Belgium, in 57 BC, describes the critical moment:

The soldiers were crowded too closely together to be able to fight easily, because the standards of the Twelfth Legion had been massed in one place. All the centurions of the first cohort had been killed, together with its standard bearer, and its standard had been lost. In the other cohort almost all the centurions were dead or wounded and the chief centurion, Sextius Baculus, a very brave man, was so exhausted by the wounds, many and severe, that he had suffered, that he could hardly stand up.[55]

This graphic depiction of the reality of legionary warfare, in which the unvarying daily order of the camp, with its set duties of guards and fatigues and the regular comforts of the kitchen and the bath-house – no different at all from the routines maintained by European garrison armies a hundred years ago – could be suddenly interrupted by confrontation with a yelling crowd of unshaven and unkempt strangers, perhaps daubed with paint, brandishing deadly weapons, reeking of dirt and fear and sweating with the intense exertion of muscle-power warfare, conveys without the need for further demonstration that the Roman professional soldier did not serve for the monetary rewards enlistment brought him.[56] His values were those by which his fellows in the modern age continue to live: pride in a distinctive (and distinctively masculine) way of life, concern to enjoy the good opinion of comrades, satisfaction in the largely symbolic tokens of professional success, hope of promotion, expectation of a comfortable and honourable retirement.

As the empire grew and as the army revised its terms of enlistment to admit recruits who were not of Italian origin, whether as legionaries or as cavalry or as light infantry auxiliaries, the military profession became multinational in character, its members united largely by the duty they owed to Rome. In a remarkable survey that was made of the careers of ten Roman soldiers who died in the service of the empire during the first two centuries AD, as revealed by their gravestones, we find a cavalryman from Mauritania (modern Morocco) who died on Hadrian's Wall; the standard-bearer of the II Legio Augusta, born at Lyon, who died in Wales; a centurion of the X Legio Gemina, born at Bologna, who was killed in Germany at the disaster of the Teutoburg forest; a veteran of the same legion born near the headwaters of the Rhine, who died on the Danube at modern Budapest; and a legionary of the II Legio Adiutrix, born in modern Austria, who died at Alexandria.[57] Perhaps the most touching of funerary records that show how widely the legions were recruited comes from the gravestones of a wife and her soldier husband found at opposite ends of Hadrian's Wall: she was a local girl; he had been born in Roman Syria.

It was a regular army, nevertheless, made for regular, not dynamic, empire-building. The process by which the legions came to serve at such distance from the Roman army's birthplace and to embrace so wide a range of recruits as members – many from localities which lay in 'barbary' at the start of Rome's rise to empire – began in earnest during the Punic wars with Carthage. That city, a colony of the Phoenicians, first fell into conflict with the Romans when the latters' success in subduing their Italian neighbours drew them south to Sicily, which Carthage regarded as within its sphere of influence; Rome's confrontation with Pyrrhus, also an enemy of Carthage, weakened its position in the island. In 265 BC the two powers found themselves at war over it, and the war rapidly extended, by both land and sea, until the Carthaginians were obliged to concede defeat and the establishment of Roman control over western Sicily. While Rome added Corsica and Sardinia to these beginnings of its overseas empire, and made its first inroads into the lands of the Gauls, Carthage responded by campaigning along the Mediterranean coast of Spain, against cities that were Rome's allies. The siege of Saguntum in 219 BC brought on war afresh; it lasted for seventeen years, ended in Carthaginian defeat only after Rome had stared catastrophe in the face, and established the Romans as the dominant power in the Mediterranean world.

Carthage, with a large fleet, depended principally on mercenaries to provide her army, recruited from the North African coast and paid from the revenues of her trading empire, whose connections extended as far as the tin-producing regions of Britain. Fortuitously, she was during the Second Punic War to produce two commanders of outstanding ability, the brothers Hannibal and Hasdrubal, whose powers of leadership and tactical innovation transcended the limitation which the mercenary character of their soldiers imposed on their capacity to operate at long range from base. Hannibal opened operations with what was to become one of the most famous campaigns in history – his lightning march from Spain through southern Gaul, across the Alps and into central Italy, bringing with him a train of elephants. Defeating one Roman army at Lake Trasimene in 217 BC, he bypassed Rome, found allies in the south, rode out a delaying campaign by Fabius Maximus and took up a position in which he hoped to be joined by the Macedonian King Philip V, one of Alexander's successors. The Romans had now lost patience with Fabian tactics, and in 216 BC their field army advanced to contact with the Carthaginians near the Apulian town of Cannae. There on 2 August, sixteen legions, comprising some 75,000 troops, advanced to the attack. Varro, the Roman commander, had put his infantry mass in the centre, with cavalry at each wing, the standard classical deployment. Hannibal reversed arrangements, leaving his centre weak but massing his best infantry on either flank. When the Romans came forward, they were swiftly enveloped, their line of retreat cut off by a cavalry charge across their rear and the fugitives, to the number of 50,000, massacred as they fled. It was from the example of Cannae that the nineteenth-century French tactical analyst Ardant du Picq first proposed the important perception that it is in retreating that an army exposes itself to disabling losses.

By a stroke of diversionary strategy the Romans were able to ride out the disaster at Cannae. At home new legions were formed from the propertyless, normally exempt from service, and even from slaves, which provided enough force to confine Hannibal to southern Italy, where the Carthaginians had allies. In Spain, where the consul Cornelius Scipio had presciently stationed two legions to prevent Hannibal's drawing reinforcements from that region, the Romans went over to the offensive. In 209 Scipio's son, later to be famous as Scipio Africanus, launched a lightning attack against Cartagena, where the atrocities his troops committed had the effect of drawing the city's uncommitted neighbours to his side. When Hasdrubal beat a fighting retreat to the Adriatic, along the route his brother Hannibal had followed eleven years earlier, he was run to ground and defeated at the River Metaurus. His successor in Spain, another Hasdrubal, suffered the indignity of being beaten in a battle where Scipio applied against him the tactics that had won Cannae. This setback, from which Scipio profited to cross to Africa, impelled Carthage to call Hannibal home, and at Zama, in modern Tunisia, their two armies met in 202 BC. A Carthaginian elephant charge was nullified by the chequerboard formation in which Scipio disposed his troops; when he launched them in a counter-attack, the Carthaginian army was overwhelmed and Hannibal fled the field.

The final destruction of Carthage was to wait fifty years, during which Rome's military energies were consumed by interventions in Greece and the rest of the Hellenistic world. By 196 BC the Greek cities accepted a Roman protectorate, and when the Hellenistic kingdom of Syria intervened to reverse events, Rome transferred the legions first there and then to Asia Minor, most of which shortly fell under its control; Ptolemaic Egypt, most important among the surviving kingdoms once controlled by Alexander's generals, also fell by 30 BC.

By that date the most famous of Romans, Julius Caesar, had added Gaul to the empire, in a series of campaigns that lasted from 58 to 51 BC. Following its earlier expulsion of the Gallic tribes from northern Italy as early as 121 BC, Rome had gained a foothold in Gaul by expanding its province in Spain. In 58, to forestall the first recorded large-scale migration the Romans had encountered, that of the Helvetii from modern Switzerland, Caesar set up blocking positions in the Rhône valley and accepted help from the Gauls to resist the invasion. Having defeated the Helvetii, he now found his new area of control threatened by another invasion, that of a Teutonic tribe under Ariovistus, and he marched north to the Rhine to turn it back. His success, though welcome to the Gauls of the south, alarmed those of the north, whose tribal systems extended across the Rhine into Germany. Against these extremely warlike

272

Greek helmet and cuirass
[ei]ghth Century BC, the
[dis]covered suit of hoplite
[...] Bronze was preferred for
[pr]otection long after its
[...]tion by iron in the
[...]ure of weapons.

[Rig]ht: A hoplite of the Sixth
[...]C; his shield has not yet
[...] the distinctive bowl
[...] which the wounded – or
[...]rrior was brought back
[...]attlefield.

[...]plites preparing for
[fro]m a vase painting of
[...]e shield protected the
[...]nd thighs from spear
[wh]en the massed ranks

Above: A Roman oared warship,
descendant of the Greek trireme,
advancing to battle; its prow is armed
with a ram and its upper deck manned
by marines.

Right: A centurion of the XX Legion,
one of the four which conquered
Britain, who died at Colchester about
45 AD. He carries his vinestick of
authority.

Terracotta of a barbarian enemy of Rome
...e Puy-de-Dôme, Third Century AD; a fore-
...of the tribesmen who overwhelmed the
...in the Fifth Century.

...A Frankish horseman on his warhorse, in
...ail and with shield and lance as depicted
...andinavian enemy – who was unaware of the
...– in the Eighth Century.

Crusaders in chain mail charging Muslim horsemen, Fourteenth Century; in practice, Middle Eastern light horsemen avoided the clash of arms.

A late Fifteenth-Century depiction of escalade at the siege of a fortified city; the soldiers wear plate armour but there are cannon entrenchments.

Legionaries ...a bridge of ...om Trajan's ... Second Cen- ...the Legions, ...Assyrian army, ...with a bridg- ...on campaign.

...annon manu- ...the Ameri- ...l War; the ...ns were the ...strial nation ...mass-produc- ...ods in

...orthern rail- ...ers at work ...ange and ...a line during ...ican Civil ...road construc- ...d destruction ...y the North's

Alfred Krupp's trial range at Meppen, 1879; his steel cannon revolutionised artillery equipment in the years before the First World W

An Atlantic convoy bringing war supplies from America to Britain, 1943; the escorting aircraft was the instrument of the U-boats' defeat.

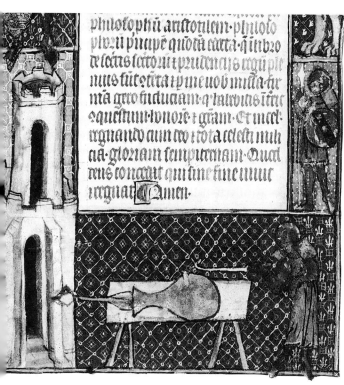

The earliest known representation of a cannon, 1326; the
gingerly application of lin-
stock to touchhole indicates
how unfamiliar the weapon
was.

ings of mutuality between man and the gunpowder weapon, about 1400; a century later the soldier would be putting it to his

Tunnage....1000.

MEN
Soldiers ......
Mariners ....
Gunners ....

alleys of the Knights of Malta
spitallers of the Crusades) in
ith the Ottoman fleet, early
enth Century; land warfare at

eft: The *Great Harry*, one of
ships built – for Henry VIII
and in 1514 – to fire cannon
de; they would dominate naval
until the 1850s.

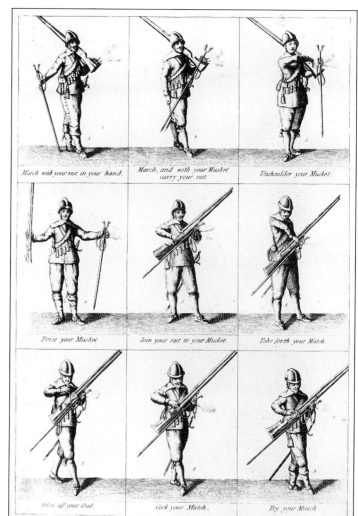

March with your rest in your hand.   March, and with your Musket carry your rest.   Unshoulder your Musket.

Poize your Musket   Join your rest to your Musket.   Take forth your Match.

Blow off your Coal.   Cock your Match.   Try your Match.

MANUAL EXERCISE OF THE MUSKETEERS. Pl.1.

Seventeenth-Century manual
step-by-step procedure in the
of the musket by ranked men
tial to avoid fatal accidents.

iege cannon, hitched to
rawn by trains of horses, on
a position, 1702; cannon
ese inaugurated the artillery
a two hundred years earlier.

A gunpowder mill, from *The Universal Magazine*, December, 1773; the monopolisation of gunpowder production by governments was a key to the rise of the modern state.

A British trench sentry on the Somme, 1916,
eeping comrades; even routine trench warfare
ngerous and exhausting.

A German Junkers 87 dive-bomber launches
b at a French tank during the blitzkrieg of
portent of the air domination of the battle-

battle of Williamsburg, May 5, 1862,
n Civil War; despite the North's material
y, Southern musketry and digging saved
d in this Peninsula Campaign.

Flying Fortresses (B-17s) in the strategic air campaign against Germany, 1944; the condensation trails are from their escorting fi

Test explosion of an atomic bomb at Bikini atoll, July 25, 1946; no military thinker has explained how nuclear warfare might
continuation of politics.

people he fought for four years, interrupted by expeditions against the Veneti of Brittany and their Celtic cousins in Britain (56–4 BC), but eventually he succeeded in imposing nominal peace throughout Gaul. Then, in 53 BC, the pacified Gauls rebelled *en masse* in a desperate effort to avoid incorporation into the empire and, under the leadership of Vercingetorix, obliged Caesar to repeat his efforts. This final stage of the Gallic wars, fought against an enemy who had learned much from Roman methods, lasted a year, when Vercingetorix retired into a vast fortified camp at Alesia, near the source of the Seine. This decision was a mistake; the Romans had formidable experience of and skills in siege warfare – it may be that some of the techniques they knew had been transmitted to them at several removes from their Assyrian inventors, via the international market in military science that had permeated the Middle East for centuries – and they quickly insulated the Alesian camp from any prospect of relief by constructing an even larger encirclement of fortifications (lines of 'circumvallation' and 'contravallation'), each about fourteen miles in circumference, to enclose it. Legionaries were masters of the spade; on the march in hostile territory, a legion automatically threw up for itself an entrenched camp of uniform pattern each night. When a relieving Celtic army appeared, estimated to have been a quarter of a million strong, Caesar supplied his 55,000 out of the stores he had accumulated within his own fortifications, held the attackers at bay, and persisted with his investment of Vercingetorix's position. Eventually, after three attempts to break out, the Gallic chieftain offered his surrender, was taken to Rome for Caesar's triumph, and then executed. With his death, native resistance to the inclusion of Gaul within the Roman empire collapsed.

The Roman empire was now almost as large as it would ever be in the west and had achieved nearly its fullest extent in Africa and the Near East; only on the frontier with the Middle East, where the kingdoms of Parthia and Persia were still powerful enough to contest control with Rome, would there be conquests still to be made. The very success of imperial expansion had thrown the social and political order at home into crisis, however. The relentless search for recruits, particularly among the Italians to whom incorporation in Roman territory had not brought the privileges of citizenship, and the growing power of consuls returning victorious from their annual campaigns to confront the magistrates in Rome with demands for money and authority, rendered the old systems of legionary enlistment and elective government increasingly obsolete. There had been a foretaste of trouble at the end of the second century BC when the brothers Gracchus had attempted to reduce both the burden of the military levy and the independence of the military authorities. Trouble became serious in 90 BC, when the Italian non-citizens revolted against the levy and were pacified only by grant of full citizenship. The difficulties in supplying the legions with manpower nevertheless persisted, even though there had been an effective dispensation with the ancient property qualification at the end of the first century, when the consul Marius opened the ranks to volunteers from the lowest census class. This measure paradoxically heightened the developing conflict between campaigning consuls and the city's political class, since it attached landless legionaries more closely to a commander, identified their interest with his (particularly if, as Marius did, he promised land as a reward for successful service) and thus strengthened the hand of generals against senate and magistrates.[58]

The crisis came to a head on Caesar's completion of his Gallic conquests. When he sought to prolong his period in command, the senate refused him; when he left his province, outside which his powers of command legally lapsed, at the head of the XIII Legion to return to Rome, he effectively threw down a challenge to civil war. The war lasted seven years (50–44 BC) and was fought as far afield as Spain, Egypt and Africa, as the senate found legions and generals, notably Pompey, to resist Caesar's rebellion. It culminated in his triumph and then, at the hands of principled opponents of dictatorship as well as disgruntled enemies, in his assassination. In the struggle for power that followed, Caesar's nephew, Octavian, overcame all opponents in a renewal of the civil war and in 27 BC, having already been granted the title of Emperor (though nominally 'Princeps', first citizen) by a compliant senate, added to it that of Augustus. Republican forms, though preserved in name, were effectively extinguished from that moment and henceforth Rome was an empire in substance as well as extent.

The imperial system resolved the anomalies inherent in the attempt to govern a military state through the competitive politics of an exclusive and no longer representative electoral class. The first effects were felt in the army itself. Augustus found it grossly swollen by civil war, to a size of half a million men, many of them little better than mercenary followers of rival commanders; he sharply reduced its numbers and stabilised it at a strength of twenty-eight legions. To assure the security of the central government against a repetition of Caesarism, he formed a new force, the Praetorian Guard, to garrison Rome. The field army was distributed largely to the frontiers, with the heaviest concentrations on the lower Rhine, opposite Germany, from which population pressure was already felt; on the upper

Danube, another region disturbed by the barbarians; and in Syria; smaller garrisons were maintained in Spain, Africa and Egypt. Equally important were the alterations he introduced into the basis of service. The fiction of the militia obligation was abolished and the legions became professional by enlistment. Preference was given to citizens, but suitable non-citizens were granted citizenship on recruitment; the term of service was fifteen years (often twenty in practice), during which legionaries were forbidden to marry – though families naturally, if illegally, attached themselves to the camps; pay was fixed and regular and, on discharge, the veteran received a retirement gratuity sufficient to provide him with a living. New taxes, actuarially calculated, found the large sums necessary to settle the veterans and so to provide the serving soldiers with a consequent incentive to loyalty and good conduct.

The numbers in the Augustan army settled at about 125,000 men. A similar number served in the legions' auxiliary units of cavalry and light infantry. Rome had employed such units since the start of the Italian conquests, but the auxiliaries had not been citizens and their terms of service had been irregular. Henceforth, certainly from the reign of Claudius, the successor of Augustus, they were properly paid, but the great inducement was that, at the end of twenty-five years' service, the discharged soldier received a grant of citizenship; so, too, since he was allowed to marry, did the sons of one wife, whenever born. These provisions greatly improved the quality of auxiliary troops, some of which were to perform so well that their members would be granted citizenship *en bloc*. As time went on, moreover, the cavalry wings and infantry cohorts ceased to be recruited at the point of service (a tendency that assimilated their quality much nearer to that of the legions), passed from the command of local chiefs to imperial officers, and were posted for duty anywhere in the empire.[59]

Augustus did most to secure the future reliability of the army by the arrangements he made for its command. Under the republic the proconsul of a province had commanded the legions within it. Augustus appointed himself proconsul of most of the provinces, so that he directly commanded their legionary garrisons, while decreeing that for the rest, to which the senate still appointed its nominees to govern, the legions came under his command also, through legates who were his personal representatives. To administer and finance this complex and highly centralised system, Augustus created an imperial civil service, staffed at its head by members of the political class, for whom it provided welcome responsibilities as well as state salaries. To these imperial officers fell the duty of raising taxes to support the provincial administrations and garrisons, to make the transfers to the imperial treasury and, in Egypt and Africa, to buy and collect the grain which supplied the city's families with free rations; 400,000 tons were imported each year.

This Julio-Claudian system, as historians call it, served well under his immediate successors, but contained unperceived perils. With a disputed imperial succession, or defeat in war, authority tended to revert to the army, on which the whole structure rested. The Roman empire's success committed it inevitably to go to war, since it could not tolerate disorder on its borders, while the growing prosperity it fostered encouraged envious outsiders to seek entry by force. Disorder was the principal danger in the east, where ancient kingdoms and the surviving rival empires of Parthia and Persia resented Rome's efforts to establish a stable line of control; intrusion was the danger in the west, along the Rhine and Danube, where the great movements of population, impelled by pressures from the steppe, were already being felt during the first century AD.

In AD 69 the predictable crisis supervened. There had been military successes under the Julio-Claudians. Britain (invaded in AD 43) had been added to the empire and Armenia had in 63 accepted Roman suzerainty. Equally there had been revolts, notably in Germany, where Arminius had destroyed a Roman army in the Teutoburg forest (AD 9), and in Judaea, where the Jews rose against Roman rule in 66. In 68 the eccentric, perhaps mad, reigning emperor, Nero, lost his soldiers' confidence and was overthrown by military insurrection; this led to civil war, competing claims to the succession and the eventual emergence of a soldier-emperor, Vespasian, not of Julio-Claudian birth. Able and cautious, he restored imperial stability but, as a military usurper, lacked legitimacy. That was revived by his eventual successor Nerva, who established the principle of appointing strong rulers by the process of formal adoption of a promising heir. Thus four adoptive successors, Trajan, Hadrian, Antoninus Pius and Marcus Aurelius, were all gifted administrators and successful commanders. Under these Antonine emperors (AD 98–180) the Roman armies won a string of victories and added Mesopotamia, Assyria and the trans-Danubian province of Dacia (modern Hungary) to the empire.

The success of the Antonines derived from their adoption of a policy of military stabilisation wherever it could be achieved, which meant everywhere except on the open border with Parthia and Persia. This has been called 'a grand strategy based on preclusive security – the establishment of a linear barrier of perimeter defence around the Empire'.[60] Historians differ bitterly over the complexities of the strategy. Some deny that it had any basis in Roman consciousness, and that the apparent drive to

276

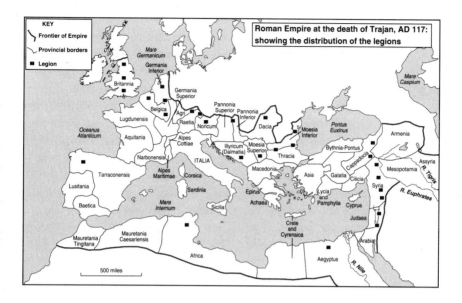

reach and hold 'scientific' frontiers, on the Rhine, Danube, north British highlands and edge of the Sahara, signified by the building of the fortifications whose sometimes massive relics still mark their outline, reveals nothing more than the desire of local commanders or visiting emperors to establish police posts and customs control at the edge of a zone of formal administration.[61] Those who hold such views deserve attention, since their knowledge of the details of Roman military policy is extensive and exact; the strength of their views is also reinforced by the terms in which they characterise the Roman military outlook: always informed by 'a desire for glory' rather than by strategic theory. That perception rings true. Clausewitz and his contemporary ideologues may have been inspired by Roman military practice, but the notion that Roman warmaking, any more than Alexander's, was Clausewitzian in essence bears very little weight. However logical his analysis of particular military situations, Alexander was drawn eastward by vainglorious impulse; Rome, perhaps also vainglorious, certainly entertained no conception of 'war as the continuation of politics' since it granted to none of its enemies, not even the Parthians or Persians, the dignity of civic status. Like the Chinese, the Romans divided the world into civilisation and the lands beyond its sway, and while they sometimes of necessity resorted to diplomacy (in their dealings with the Armenians and other old-established kingdoms, for example), they did so for reasons of expediency alone, not as one state treating with its equivalent. There was, indeed, no reason for them to do so. Not only by the tests of military and bureaucratic organisation did the Romans surpass every other people against whom their borders abutted. The 'idea' of Rome, which in AD 212 extended citizenship to all free men within its imperial boundaries, had no parallel elsewhere; nor did the extraordinary infrastructure of roads, bridges, aqueducts, dams, arsenals, barracks and public buildings by which Roman military power, civil administration and economic life were sustained.

Nevertheless, the existence of Rome's fortified frontiers, like much of China's Great Wall, is a fact. The Chinese learned that the building of a fixed line of defence does not of itself guarantee security, which can be maintained only by the simultaneous execution of a 'forward' policy, as by the T'ang into Dzungaria and the Manchu on to the steppe; the failure of the intervening dynasties of non-steppe origin to pursue or succeed in such a policy did not invalidate the building of the Wall in the first place, since it marked the outline of the cultural zone that all Chinese governments sought to preserve. Equally, the retrospective denials by some modern scholars that the Roman effort at fortification was a subordinate and secondary characteristic of the empire's real strategic purposes stumbles on the stones of the fortifications themselves. It may well be that in the first two centuries after Augustus the empire depended on the strength of the legions, variously deployed, to sustain security by indirect means. That is the view of Edward Luttwak, who suggests that the policy of the Julio-Claudians, who were still fighting wars of expansion, was to use the legions as a source of ultimate guarantee for a defence organised in first line by newly subdued clients, such as those in northern Greece, Asia Minor and Africa; while under the Antonines the legions were distributed at the frontiers to garrison barriers which then became the primary obstacle zone on which external threats were intended to break. Particular crises, he argues, were met by the concentration at the point of danger of legions withdrawn from borders where peace prevailed. His view is disputed by others who variously claim that the Romans remained expansionist on the frontiers where enemies challenged their power, notably those with Parthia and Persia, or that the army's main preoccupation was with local disorders which had their roots in habits of endemic brigandage, piracy or the indisciplines of transhumant herding tribes.

Nevertheless, no one denies that from the third century AD onward, when population pressure in the west and the strains of war with Persia in the east intensified, the identification of the legions with the fortified frontiers became absolute. There was a rationalisation of borders, particularly on the Danube, where the province of Dacia was abandoned in 270, on the River Rhine, on the lower Nile, where the Romans found the Numidians as implacable as the pharaohs had done, and in Africa, where parts of Mauritania were evacuated in 298. On the shorter lines, however, the legions were to fight for another century, and Roman strategy centred on the protection of the internal territories whose integrity the fortified frontiers defined. That being so, it is not factitious to argue that, even if in diluted strength, the outline of the frontiers, which shifted little between the accession of Augustus in the first century BC and the abandonment of Britain at the beginning of the fifth AD, exerted throughout a determining influence on the Roman military outlook. Historians with a particular knowledge of a period or a province, even of the Roman empire as a whole, may be able to show explicit inconsistencies in the view, perhaps bequeathed to us by Gibbon, that Rome saw itself as the still centre of a world of barbaric disorder. But to do so is to overlook the influence that the psychology of a professional army exerted on the imperial policies of the governments it served. Once frontiers are defined by fortifications which then become the permanent places of garrison of formal and named units, or at least familiar stopping-places through which such units rotate, they take on a symbolic significance for the soldiers who defend them; the emergence of such a symbolism is easily discernible in the history of the Roman army when, for example, we find that the VI Legio Victrix, which arrived in Britain about AD 122 from the Rhine, was still there sixty years later, that III Legio Cyrenaica, raised by Julius Caesar on the Nile, was still based in Egypt in the third century, and that two cavalry regiments, Ala Augusta Gallorum Petriana and Ala I Pannoniorum Sabiniana, raised respectively in Gaul and Pannonia (modern Hungary), served from the second to the third centuries on Hadrian's Wall, the latter throughout at what is today Stanwix.[62] The examples elaborate: between AD 69 and 215, III Legio Gallica was in Syria, from AD 85 to 215, II Legio Adiutrix was in Hungary, and from AD 71 to 215 VII Legio Gemina was on the Rhine.[63]

Within an army whose backbone was supplied by a body of professional soldiers on whose tongues circulated from generation to generation the litany of the legions' cantonments and the lore of the life lived there, it is impossible that the soldiers' consciousness did not eventually come to be circumscribed by the geography of the frontiers. There was, of

279

course, much to distract their attention from imperial defence, notably the recurrent disputes over the imperial succession which, during the third century, called legion into conflict with legion in the service of usurpers and provincial pretenders who laid claim to it. The reorganisation of the garrisons under Constantine (AD 312–37), who succeeded to the imperial title by victory in one of these civil wars, withdrew the legions into several central reserves, reduced them in size and added sizeable formations of cavalry to the army.[64] These changes drastically altered the composition of the army, diluting for good the strength of the infantry foundation on which it had rested since republican times. It remained, nevertheless, an imperial army, supported, if with greater difficulty in their collection, by imperial taxes, and still dedicated, though at a greater distance from base, to the defence of the frontiers. The quality of the auxiliaries, left by the Constantian reforms in uncomfortable isolation on the ever more contested borders, declined as a result of their detachment from contact with the legions; increasingly these units of *limitanei* were formed from locally enlisted peasant militias, who were farmers before they were soldiers. The military worth of the regulars remained, nevertheless, formidable.

After Diocletian (284–305), the empire was divided for administrative purposes into western and eastern halves, with a consequent and progressively separative effect on their military forces. But the next and eventually disabling crisis of the imperial armies was not felt until the fifth century. Despite the disasters of the Persian campaign of 363, in which the emperor Julian the Apostate was killed, and the catastrophe of Adrianople (396), in which Valens died at the hands of the Goths, order within the empire and the defence of its borders was restored by the titanic efforts of Theodosius, who reunited the eastern and western halves and waged a succession of campaigns to repel the outsiders from its territory. Nevertheless, as we have seen, it was Theodosius who took the fatal step of compromising the Romanity of the army by accepting under his command large units of barbarian 'federates' who served, not as the auxiliaries of old had done in units raised and officered by imperial officials, but as allies under their own leaders. This step, once taken, could not be withdrawn. Throughout the first half of the fifth century Teutonic soldiers poured into the western empire, and, though the imperial structures there remained nominally in place, and local generals such as Constantius or Aëtius retained sufficient force under command to confine some tribes to limited areas of conquest, and at times even to set barbarian against barbarian, control of the frontiers had to be abandoned altogether, while control within was feeble and erratic. The 'Roman' armies of Constantius and Aëtius were Teutonic in composition, carried Teutonic weapons, lost all semblance of legionary drill, and even adopted the German warcry, the *baritus*.[65]

In the face of Attila and the Huns, some of these barbarian invaders, who had suffered at Hunnish hands outside the empire, came to Aëtius's aid; they formed a large proportion of his army at Châlons in 451. While that victory spared Gaul, and perhaps Rome, from devastation by a horse people, Italy and the capital now came under threat from another direction. Gaiseric, leader of the tribe of Vandals who had crossed Gaul and Spain to found a kingdom in North Africa, took to the sea, seized Corsica and Sardinia and from that base captured and sacked Rome in 455; a counter-offensive mounted against him by Leo, the eastern emperor, ended in failure; and the Vandals established a piratical regime that controlled Mediterranean waters from their bases in Sicily and Africa; it was carried on by Saracen and Barbary successors for a thousand years. In Gaul and Italy power passed to three German chieftains, Ricimer, Orestes and Odoacer, who set up a succession of puppet emperors. One of them, Marjorian (457–61), actually reasserted a brief imperial authority in southern Gaul but was then forced off the throne. In 476 Odoacer, who disposed of the largest force in Italy, nominally a Roman army owing obedience to the puppet emperor Romulus, defeated Ricimer in a struggle for power, deposed Romulus and proclaimed himself not emperor but king. The senate, which still survived in shadow form, returned the imperial regalia to the eastern emperor at Constantinople; the Roman army in the west had already long ceased to exist.[66]

EUROPE AFTER ROME: A CONTINENT WITHOUT ARMIES

The Roman army did not cease to exist in the east; it defended Byzantium, at greatly varying distances from Constantinople – sometimes as far away as the Caucasus or the Nile, sometimes under the foot of its Cyclopean walls – until its remnants were overcome in the great siege of Constantinople by the Ottoman Mehmet the Conqueror in 1453. But from the start of the eastern empire's autonomy, it was a different army from that of the legions. Under Belisarius and Narses, the generals through whom the great emperor Justinian (527–65) recovered control in Italy and North Africa (destroying Vandal power in the process), it very closely resembles that of Aëtius and Marjorian. At Tricameron (453), where Belisarius overthrew the Vandal Gelimer, and at Taginae (455), where Narses won the victory that returned Ravenna and Rome to imperial rule, the bulk of both generals' armies was formed of non-Romans, including Huns in Africa and a body of Persian archers in Italy.[67] Once the borders of Byzantium had been stabilised, however, roughly on the line of the Danube and Caucasus and a sea frontier that enclosed Cyprus, Crete and the toe of Italy (Egypt, Syria and North Africa were lost to the Arabs between 641 and 685), the empire's military organisation could be put on a different basis. It resembled in structure that of Augustus: the empire was divided into provinces, called themes, under commanders who, with their troops, answered to the emperor direct. The troops were organised into units that derived from those of the Constantian reforms of the fourth century rather than from the heavy marching legions; they were small and independent infantry and cavalry regiments that could be combined as needed to reinforce the frontier militias. In the second century there were thirteen themes, seven in Asia Minor, three in the Balkans and three in the Mediterranean and Aegean; by the tenth century the number had grown to thirty, but the size of the army remained constant at about 150,000 men, half foot, half horse, about as large as that of the legionary army under Augustus. Supported by an efficient bureaucracy and taxing system, and fed and supplied by a prosperous peasantry, the Byzantine army effectively sustained a surviving, if greatly changed and, of course, Christianised Roman empire until the onset of the Turkish assaults in 1071.[68]

In the west no such army was revived to preserve the remnants of that Roman civilisation for which its destroyers professed such a strong admiration. Indeed revival was impossible, for the basis on which the army had been supported, regular and equitable taxation – very inequitable though it had become in the late empire – had been destroyed. The barbarian kings taxed as best they could, but the returns were insufficient to support disciplined soldiers; in any case the conquerors were deeply antipathetic to discipline, preserving in their hearts a rough Teutonic belief in the freedom of the arms-bearing warrior, and of his equality with his fellows. The Goths, Lombards, and Burgundians had been farmers before pressure from the steppe had pushed them across the Rhine, and they expected to live by farming when they came into their inheritance. In Italy each was allotted a third of the occupant's plot on which he was settled, an extortionate adaptation of the old imperial system of assigning a third of an occupant's premises to a billeted soldier; in Burgundy and southern France the allotment was set at two-thirds. Thus the soldiers settled down to plough unwelcome on scattered farms, frittering away

282

the military virtues which had made them so formidable in attack, without yielding to the government the regular surplus by which a civilised, peace-keeping army might have been rebuilt. 'The barbarian kingdoms combined the characteristic vices of the Roman empire' – principally the corrupt expropriation of smallholdings to swell the estates of the rich – 'and of barbarism . . . To their old abuses were now added the lawless violence of the barbarian tribesman and of [the surviving] Romans who aped their manners.'[69]

In retrospect, how easy it is to see that Rome's principal contribution to mankind's understanding of how life may be made civilised was its institution of a disciplined and professional army. Of course, it had had no such end in view when it embarked on its campaigns of expansion within Italy and then undertook the wars against Carthage; the army was transformed from a citizen militia into a long-range expeditionary force under the demands of the battlefield, not by conscious decision. Its adoption of a system of regular enlistment, offering 'a career open to talents' throughout the empire and to citizens and non-citizens alike, had its origins in necessity; the reforms of Augustus merely rationalised a situation that already existed. As if by the workings of an unseen hand, however, the evolution of the Roman army exactly served that of Roman civilisation itself. Rome, unlike classical Greece, was a civilisation of law and of physical achievement, not of speculative ideas and artistic creativity. The imposition of its laws and the relentless extension of its extraordinary physical infrastructure demanded not so much intellectual effort as unstinted energy and moral discipline. It was of these qualities that the army was the ultimate source and often, particularly in the engineering of public works, the direct instrument. Inevitably, therefore, the decline of the army's powers – even if brought about as much by internal economic and administrative failures as by military crises at the borders – entailed that of the empire's also, and the army's collapse that of the western empire itself.

The successor kingdoms in the west did not learn how priceless was the institution they had destroyed and how difficult to replace. Yet moral authority in post-Roman Europe did not altogether lose a home; it migrated to the institutions of the Christian church, firmly established in its Roman rather than Nestorian form thanks to the conversion of the Franks in 496, and in the Church the idea, if not the substance, of the empire found a continuum. Without swords, however, the Christian bishops could not give the Christian covenant force; and though their royal patrons had swords, they used them to make war on each other rather than to establish and keep a Christian peace. The history of western Europe in the late sixth and seventh centuries is a doleful one of constant quarrels among the royal houses of the successor kingdoms, moderated only when, at the beginning of the eighth century, the first of the Carolingians established their primacy in the Frankish lands on both sides of the Rhine. The emergence of the Carolingians was the outcome of an internal struggle, but it may be seen also as a response to the new threats – notably the advance of the Muslims from Spain into southern France and the assaults of pagan Frisians, Saxons and Bavarians on the eastern borders. Charles Martel's victory over the Muslims at Poitiers in 732 repelled them beyond the Pyrenees for good; the campaigns of his grandson Charles the Great, Charlemagne, consolidated a border as far away as the Elbe and upper Danube in Germany and brought the Italian kingdom of the Lombards, which included the city of Rome, within the new empire established by his coronation by Pope Leo III on Christmas Day, 800.

Charlemagne's legitimacy derived from his recognition by the Pope as successor to the Roman emperor through fictive descent; his power depended on his armed forces, which resembled the Roman army, even in its final state of decay, not at all. Earlier Frankish kings, like the other barbarian rulers, had maintained as the military core of their retinues groups of chosen warriors who could be depended upon to fight bravely and on demand – the equivalent of Alexander's Companion cavalry. In the era of the conquests the problem of how they were to be maintained did not arise, and in unsettled times they lived by extempore means. But once a kingdom acquired borders, however ill defined, and sought to maintain stability within them, the ruler's warriors required a steadier source of support than loot or temporary expropriation. The solution was to accommodate members of the Germanic war band (termed, in the Latin that supplied the new kingdoms with so many of their legal terms, the *comitatus*) within the old Roman practice of the *precarium*, effectively the lease by which cultivators tilled plots on a landowner's estate. In the days of the Roman empire's prosperity, a *precarium* had been held for money rent; as the disorders of the fifth and sixth centuries drove money out of circulation, the payment of rent gave way to the performance of services of various sorts. It was not a complex process, though in practice it proved gradual, for a ruler's followers, who already owed him a personal obligation and in return benefited by his patronage (*patrocinium*), to translate the relationship into one where military service was returned for patronal favour, but the *patrocinium* was expressed by the grant of a *precarium*.

The relationship suited both parties: the vassal (from the Celtic word for dependant) received a means of livelihood; 'the ruler was assured of his military services; and the bond between the two was sealed by the performance of an act of homage which, when Christianised by the intervention of the Church, became known as the oath of faithfulness or "fealty".'[70]

The arrangement known to us as feudalism (from the beneficiary *feudum*, or fief, that the patron granted to the vassal) became the general basis on which kings raised armies and the military class held land in Carolingian Europe from the middle of the ninth century onward; by then it was also established custom that fiefs were heritable within families as long as service continued to be done. The formalisation of these elements is conventionally dated to the year 877, when Charles the Bald, king of the West Franks and grandson of Charlemagne, decreed in the Capitulation of Kiersey that fiefs might pass from father to son; he had already decreed that every free man, which in effect meant those who had land or bore arms, must have a patron or lord, and that every man who had a horse, or ought to have one, should come mounted to the assembly at which, at least annually, the army was mustered. 'When every man had to have a lord, when every holder of a benefice had to serve as a mounted soldier, and when offices, benefices and military obligations became hereditary, feudalism was complete.'[71]

Carolingian feudalism, despite the emphasis it laid on horse-owning, should not be equated with the military system of the nomads. The cultivated lands of western Europe could support a horse population of no large size, and the feudal armies that answered the summons to arms resembled a horse people's horde in no way at all. The difference derived in great measure from the distinctive military culture of the Teutonic tribes, which encouraged face-to-face fighting with edged weapons, a tradition reinforced by their encounters with the Roman armies before they had lost their legionary training. This culture had been preserved when the Western warriors took to horseback, and it was reinforced by the potentialities of the equipment they wore and the weapons they used from the saddle. The saddle itself had developed into a solid seat, in part because from the early eighth century it became the point of attachment for the newly introduced stirrup.

The origins of the stirrup may have been Indian, but in the fifth century it was adopted by the Chinese and then by the peoples of the steppe, whence its use rapidly migrated to Europe. Its significance is fiercely debated, between those who argue that in giving the horseman a firm seat it transformed him into a mounted lancer, and the sceptics who deny that the stirrupless nomad had united himself with the horse any less well; since contemporary evidence is lacking to validate either view, it is not an argument into which the uncommitted should enter.[72] But we do know that in the West, from the eighth century onward, the mounted warrior bestrode his horse from a high saddle, lodged his feet in stirrups, and in consequence could manage weapons and wear equipment hitherto associated exclusively with the foot soldier. True, the Persians and then the Byzantines had fielded squadrons of armoured horsemen and even armoured horses at an earlier date, but we do not know how they were outfitted or how they fought, and to ascribe the origin of heavy cavalry warfare to them is risky.[73] By contrast, there is no doubt that by the ninth century the feudal horseman of western Europe wore a coat of iron chain-mail, carried a shield and had sufficiently free use of his hands to manage it and a lance or sword while in motion.

These innovations were timely, for during the ninth century a new wave of assaults on the West began that could not have been withstood by the cumbersome, infrequently summoned and largely horseless warrior hosts of the post-Roman successor kingdoms. These assaults had three points of origin: the Islamic lands, the steppe and the still pagan and barbarian coasts of Scandinavia. From the Islamic lands was mounted a regime of Mediterranean piracy and despoliation which recalled that of the Vandals in the sixth century and depended on the use of the same North African ports. The Saracens, as the Islamic intruders became known to the West, operated as freely as they did because, since the dissolution of the Roman fleet in the fifth century, there had been no state navy in the western Mediterranean to protect the coasts and ensure safe use of the sea. In 827 Sicily, so often before the *point d'appui* for powers on the rampage – Athens, Carthage, the Vandals – was occupied; shortly afterward pirates set up bases in the toe of Italy and in southern France; in the tenth century Corsica, Sardinia and even Rome were attacked. Eventually the Saracens were driven out of southern Italy by the efforts of the Byzantines, the only power still to maintain a galley fleet, but only after they had pillaged and destroyed, often deep inland, from the Rhône to the Adriatic.

The threat from the steppe was mounted by the Magyars who, displaced westward by the rising power of the Turks, appeared in the Danubian plain, Attila's former grazing-land, in 862. From it they launched a series of typical, but even by Hunnish standards extraordinarily far-ranging nomad raids, which in 898 carried them into Italy and drew Berenger, King of Italy, and his army of 15,000 armoured horsemen into a disastrous battle on the River Brenta in September 899. In 910, they confronted the general levy of the East Franks, called by the last Carolingian emperor, Louis the Child, near Augsburg and won a great victory that allowed them for the next ten years to roam in Germany largely at will. Henry the Fowler, king of Germany in 919–36, gradually constricted their depradations by extensive fortress-building on the eastern frontier, but they nevertheless managed to penetrate as far as France and Burgundy in 924 and 926 and, despite a defeat at his hands in 933, again into Italy in 954. The following year Otto I, Holy Roman emperor, at last found sufficient force at a moment of opportunity to fix and fight them against an obstacle, one of the few means by which heavy cavalry could crush the much more mobile light cavalry in combat. With an 8000-man army of mostly Bavarians and Swabians, sizeable for the time, he bypassed their camp outside Augsburg, which they were besieging, crossed the River Lech to bar their line of retreat and awaited attack. The Magyars, who like the Huns had retained the composite bow as their principal weapon and the loose steppe swarm as their tactical formation, despite their long acquaintance with the western style of warmaking, did as Henry hoped. Crossing the Lech to fight for an escape route, they were drawn into a confused battle with their backs to the river and ridden down to destruction by their armoured enemies. The scattered remnants were harried home by the armed people of the countryside and were never again able to mount a major raid out of the Hungarian plain into the cultivated lands of the west.[74]

The Scandinavians could not be so summarily despatched, for their assaults were launched by a means to which none of the west European kingdoms had an antidote, the sea-going warship. The peoples of the north European coasts had been adventurous seafarers for centuries; the Romans had maintained a fleet on the 'Saxon Shore' in Britain and Gaul to keep their piracy in check; it was the collapse of that fleet in the fifth century that had allowed the Angles, Saxons and Jutes to settle Britain from Denmark and north Germany.[75] The emptying of the lands beyond the Rhine in the barbarian migrations then brought on a lull in maritime emigration, but at the end of the eighth century land hunger in Norway and Sweden impelled the pagan northerners to renew their search for places of settlement, for loot and for opportunities to trade on dictated terms, and this was at precisely the moment when they had perfected a ship that would carry warriors long distances over stormy seas. The keys to the longship's superiority over contemporary coast-hugging craft were its narrow profile and deep keel, allowing it to be sailed to windward, together with its broad cross-section amidships, which made it suitable to row when winds failed and to beach on the open coast away from defended ports.[76]

In short, it was the perfect ship for sea raiders, always provided that they were hardy enough to bear the discomforts of long passages in an uncovered hull on cold rations between stopping-places. The Vikings – so called from the Norse *Viking*, piracy – were among the hardiest and most warlike peoples ever to assault civilisation, their terrifying readiness to close to hand-to-hand combat heightened in a century of land quarrels that preceded their era of voyaging.[77] Moreover, from about 840 onward they began to ship horses, thereby giving them the means to mount deep inland raids from unexpected directions that outwitted local defenders. Beginning with their first descent upon the monastery of Lindisfarne in northern England in 793 the Vikings ventured ever farther afield, raiding Seville in Muslim Spain in 844 and pushing deep into the Mediterranean in 859. In 834 they devastated the great trading-place of Dorstadt, at the mouth of the Rhine, and by 877 began an invasion of Anglo-Saxon England that eventually made the whole of the midlands and north into a Danish overseas kingdom by the mid-tenth century. Wider voyaging – which by astonishing leaps of navigation, akin in their daring to those of the Pacific Polynesians, carried them to Iceland in 870, and to Greenland in the next century – somewhat relieved the relentlessness of their assaults on western Europe, but it did not limit their intrusions in the ungoverned lands of central and eastern Europe. The Vikings, there known as 'Rus', took to a life of armed trading, from Sweden across the Baltic and thence down the great Russian rivers that led them into contact with Islam and Byzantium. In the west the Norsemen, at the same time as they were conquering central England, seized a foothold in northern France, which in 911 the king was obliged to cede to them as a fief. From this acquisition, Normandy, the Normans in the eleventh century conquered England in 1066 and from 1027 onward established near Naples the outposts of their future kingdom in Italy and Sicily.

Military means alone could not have sufficed to contain the devastations wrought by the various raiders of the ninth and tenth centuries. Western Europe stood in need, as China did in the face of the steppe nomads, of some cultural force with which to neutralise their nihilism and assimilate them within the governed world. The Saracens could not be assimilated; they raided and pillaged with the moral assurance of the *ghazi*, Islam's frontier warriors. The pagan Vikings and Magyars, however, still resided in the primitive world of vengeful or unlistening gods to which the Teutons and steppe peoples belonged before they heard the word of Christ or

Muhammad. The Christian church had already achieved an extraordinary work of pacification in western Europe, beginning with the conversion of the Franks in 496, and it had progressively brought all the invaders of the Roman lands within a single faith; it brought them also to respect the Christian institutions – papacy, episcopate, monastic foundations – that survived from Rome and, by a heroic mission, as much civilising as religious, carried Roman Christianity north and eastward to the farther Germans and Slavs. Conversion had often been imposed at the point of the sword, but Christian men and women, like the English St Boniface, Apostle of the Germans, had also died as martyrs in the effort to plant the word among savage peoples. It was by such means that the Magyars were converted by the end of the tenth century, after which Hungary became a bastion of resistance to steppe invasions, and the Scandinavians by the eleventh and twelfth.

A post-Roman Europe without the Roman church would have been a barbarous place indeed; the remnants of Roman civil institutions were too weak to provide a framework for a reconstitution of order, and in the absence of disciplined armies, the whole continent might have fallen back below the 'military horizon' into endemic conflict over territory and tribal rights. There were limits, however, to what the Church could achieve in its work of pacification, which derived in almost equal measure from its aspirations to power for itself and its doctrinal inhibitions about how power in practice is exercised in the world. In the east the Christian bishops persisted in the Constantian practice of deferring to the Byzantine emperor; in the formerly Christian lands that fell to Islam, religious and secular authority united in the person of the caliph. But in the west the papacy resisted either such accommodation. Successor to Rome and seated in Rome, the papacy sought from the moment of Rome's fall to establish the distinction between worldly and religious authority and to justify the subordination of the former to the latter. Charlemagne restored the Roman empire in name by the sword, but his title as emperor owed its legitimacy in the eyes of the popes to his coronation by Leo III at the see of St Peter.

While emperors were strong and popes weak, at least in worldly terms, no conflict between the power of the one and the claims to authority of the other arose. By the eleventh century, however, the Church had everywhere grown more wealthy and more confident. Its lands, often acquired by charitable bequest, supplied rulers with many of their military fiefs; its monastic institutions, equally founded on charitable legacies, became centres of a strong theology that found the arguments to reinforce papal claims to primacy. Such arguments deprecated the development of the practice by which emperor and kings, who appointed or 'invested' bishops and abbots to their offices, used pliant men as instruments of civil government, notably in the raising and maintenance of military forces. Theologians reluctantly conceded the morality of combat when conducted to impose or restore a sovereign's lawful rights; Christ's admonition to 'render unto Caesar the things that are Caesar's' provided, by enlargement, the necessary justification. Nevertheless, it held both killing and wounding to be a sin for which penance must be done – after Hastings in 1066 the Norman bishops imposed on their own knights a year's prayer and fasting for killing a man, forty days for wounding one – even though William the Conqueror had fought Harold and the Anglo-Saxons with the pope's approval of his claim that he was seeking restitution of his sovereign rights.[78] In the great 'investiture conflict' between Pope Gregory VII and the Holy Roman emperor Henry IV, in the eleventh century, whose manifest issue was that of precedence in appointing bishops, Gregory showed no reluctance at all in concerting an alliance of Normans and Germans to fight against the emperor. Forever in the background, however, lurked the Christian doubt of how Christ's blessing of the peacemakers might be reconciled with the impulse of the man on horseback, even if he rode under a papal banner, to yield to blood lust when he confronted a fellow soul, sword in hand.

It was a matter of conscience that could not be avoided in Europe where half of the upper society that did not labour wore godly cloth while the other half wore armour and kept warhorses. The knightly class of the eleventh century was still rough-hewn and the manners of chivalry lay in the future.[79] Only 200 years earlier the Carolingian decree that 'every man who had a horse should come mounted to the host' had 'brought with the ranks of the landed nobility a horde of upstart adventurers, whose chief title to nobility . . . was they rode a noble beast'. Europe remained a warrior society at heart. The law of God fell on deaf ears when men's blood was up and when the civil law had no wider jurisdiction than a lord's power to impose the rights that in title it gave him.

It was therefore a relief to Church and kings alike when at the end of the eleventh century the quarrel over investiture was overlaid by a new call to arms against a common, un-Christian enemy. A new pope, Urban II, a monk of Cluny, one of the monasteries where the theology of papal power had its seat, was elected in 1088 and at once set out by diplomacy to restore good relations with the Holy Roman emperor; at the same time he began to preach the sinfulness of Christian fighting Christian. At the Council of Clermont in 1095 he recalled the idea of the Truce of God, the armistice of Lent and holy days, and went on to urge that Christians should 'leave off slaying each other and fight instead a righteous war'. He reminded his listeners that, in the wake of the disaster of Manzikert twenty-four years earlier, the Byzantines had appealed to the West to come to the defence of Christendom in the East, that the Muslim Turks were continuing their advance into the Christian lands and that the holy city, Jerusalem, was in Muslim hands. He appealed for a campaign to be mounted without delay to restore it to the Church.[80]

The idea of 'Crusade', for that was what Urban launched, was already in the air. During the tenth century the Muslims of Spain, under the dynamic al-Mansur, had won territory from the tiny Christian kingdoms that survived in the northern part of the Iberian peninsula, and devout young knights from elsewhere in Europe, including Normans, Italians and Frenchmen, went there to fight; they were encouraged by the abbots of Cluny, who took a special interest in the welfare of pilgrims to the threatened shrine of the apostle James at Compostela; patron of the expedition of 1073 was Gregory VII, papal protagonist in the investiture conflict, who while reminding the world that 'the kingdom of Spain belonged to the see of St Peter, declared that Christian knights might enjoy the lands they conquered from the infidel'. Thus

> by the close of the eleventh century the idea of the holy war had been carried into practice. Christian knights and soldiers were encouraged by the authorities of the Church to leave their petty quarrels and to journey to the frontiers of Christendom to fight against the infidel. To reward them for their service they might take possession of the lands they reconquered and they received spiritual benefits . . . [Moreover] the Papacy was taking the direction of the holy wars. It often launched them and named the commander. The land that was conquered had to be held under ultimate papal suzerainty. Though the great princes were apt to remain aloof, western knights responded readily to the appeal of the holy war. Their motives were in part genuinely religious. They were ashamed to continue fighting among themselves; they wanted to fight for the Cross. But there was also a land-hunger to incite them, particularly in northern France, where the practice of primogeniture was being established. As a lord grew unwilling to divide his property and its offices, now beginning to be concentrated around a stone-built castle, his younger sons had to seek their fortunes elsewhere. There was a general restlessness and taste for adventure in the knightly class in France, most marked among the Normans, who were only a few generations removed from nomadic freebooters. The opportunity for combining Christian duty with the acquisition of land in a southern climate was very attractive.[81]

The First Crusade, led by princes from Norman Sicily, Normandy proper,

France and Burgundy, set off from Europe by sea and land in 1096. Over-land parties marched with the goodwill of the Byzantine emperor through the Balkans and then fought their way across the Seljuk Turks' lands in Asia Minor to reach Syria in 1098, where they were joined by seafaring contingents from England, Italy and Flanders. They were delayed by the length of the siege they laid to Antioch, a key place on the coastal route through Syria, but by 1099 reached the Holy Land, and on 15 July, after a whirlwind assault on the city walls, took Jerusalem. It now became the capital of a Latin kingdom under a Burgundian duke who assumed the title of King of Jerusalem; other Crusading leaders set up states along the Syrian coast and in southern Asia Minor. These Crusading kingdoms endured, with varying fortunes, until 1291, when the last of them was swept away in the Mamelukes' final counter-offensive. Western Christendom regularly revived and restored the Latin states by launching new Crusades, for which a remarkable enthusiasm persisted in France and the Holy Roman empire, but their success was one of diminishing returns as Muslims gathered forces to recover what for them also were holy places and to expel the invaders from the vital land bridge that connected Egypt and Baghdad.

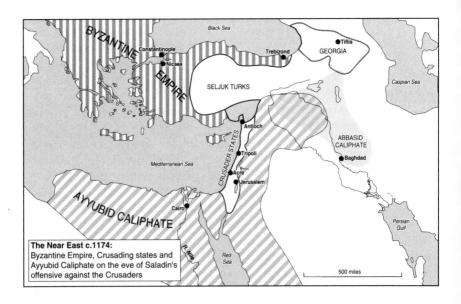

The Near East c.1174:
Byzantine Empire, Crusading states and Ayyubid Caliphate on the eve of Saladin's offensive against the Crusaders

The Islamic counter-offensive may have been essentially a response to a 'frontier problem', akin to that which troubled Islam on the border with the steppe. But the wars against the Christians achieved an intensity that the Muslims did not experience on any other front; moreover, a lamentable effect of the Fourth Crusade (1198–1204) was that it inflicted irreparable damage on Byzantium: an ill-judged intervention in a succession conflict fatally weakened the eastern empire's capacity to resist the advance of the Islamic Turks into southern Europe; the fall of Constantinople 250 years later was a delayed result of the depradations of the Fourth Crusaders.

Militarily, the Crusades provide us with the most accurate picture we possess of both the culture and the nature of European warfare in the long interregnum between the disappearance of the disciplined armies of Rome and the reappearance of state forces in the sixteenth century. Crusading warfare was a strange contest, which confronted the face-to-face warriors of the north European tradition with the evasive, harrying tactics of the steppe horsemen. It did not begin exactly like that. The Egyptian caliphate, before its usurpation by the Mamelukes, depended largely on Arab and Berber light cavalry, who fought with lance and sword rather than the composite bow and therefore competed on unequal terms with armoured Crusaders. At Ascalon in 1099, for example, Godfrey, the future king of Jerusalem, scattered such an army to the winds. But with the coming of Saladin from the Baghdad caliphate in 1174, and particularly after Baybar's establishment of Mameluke power in Egypt in 1260, it was the steppe swarm against which the Crusaders had to launch that once-for-all-charge on which their ability to win battles depended and, fighting always at an inferiority of numbers, the balance of advantage moved progressively against them.

They made, nevertheless, stalwart efforts to enhance their effectiveness against military methods that were not their own, notably by incorporating along with their mounted forces sizeable numbers of foot-soldiers who, with edged weapons, bows and eventually mechanical crossbows, presented a fierce face to light horsemen whenever they surged forward to divide and pick off in detail a body of knights. Foot-soldiers had counted for little in the wars against the Magyars and Vikings, least of all in the wars over rights that were the obsession of feudal Europe; in Europe mounted men positively discouraged the horseless from carrying arms, since they might thereby – particularly if they were the inhabitants of towns – defend and even claim rights to which the warriors did not concede their entitlement. In the Holy Land, however, foot-soldiers had value, especially to protect the baggage trains, without which Crusaders could not campaign, as well as the vulnerable flanks of the mounted body when drawn up in order of battle.

Historians have long argued that the Crusaders' Muslim opponents fixed on the stratagem of dividing horse from foot as their chief tactical principle and, though this is now disputed, it proved often the case that such a separation did lead to the Crusaders' defeat.[82] There were such separations at Ramla in 1102, at Marj'Ayyun in 1179, at Cresson in 1187 and in the disaster of Hattin in the same year, a victory for Saladin that returned to him much of the territory of the Kingdom of Jerusalem. What underlay the Crusaders' failure in all these and other defeats was not, however, tactical accident but a structural defect in their method of warmaking: dependence on the armoured charge as a means to victory against an enemy whose main intention was not to stand and receive it. The Crusaders believed that success lay in choosing 'the moment at which to deliver their charge with the certainty of striking into the main body of the enemy'.[83] In Europe it was becoming a matter of honour for a warrior not to flinch from the shock of such an attack – a continuation, in an elaborated form, of the code of the phalanx fighter. On the Crusades, the western warrior met an opponent whose tradition was quite other, and who saw no dishonour in fighting at a distance and manoeuvring to avoid the critical blow. Over time the Crusaders adapted to the unfamiliar challenge, by enlisting increasing numbers of local infantrymen and by choosing where possible, in accordance with local practice, to fight in locales where their flanks were protected by obstacles; meanwhile the Muslims moved closer to western practice also – there is evidence that, in the thirteenth century, they began to imitate the western ceremony of the joust.

The principal response of the Crusaders to the strains of warmaking in the Holy Land was, however, cultural, an ever closer assimilation of the code of warriordom by which they lived with the appeal to Christian service that drew them across the Mediterranean in the first place. Already during the eleventh century, the outline of this chivalric idea was discernible in Europe; it was no longer enough for a man to be a warrior that he should have a horse, a coat of mail and a lord to follow. The basis of fidelity was passing from the purely material enjoyment of a grant of land, by which he supported the military capability his lord expected of him, to the forging of a ceremonial and religious relationship between the two. The old oath of fealty, by which the Church had solemnised a vassal's dutiful acceptance of a benefice from a great man, was transformed into one by which a knight bound himself in personal service to his lord and swore not merely to obey but also to behave in knightly fashion, which meant to lead an honourable and even virtuous life.

It was no long step for the focus of the knightly ideal to be transferred, in the Crusading world, from the person of the lord to that of the Church itself. At the end of the twelfth century, a number of new monastic orders were founded which, though originally dedicated to such traditionally pious works as the maintenance of hospitals for pilgrims to the Holy Land and their welfare on the journey, quickly took on another function: that of fighting to defend the Holy Land itself. These knightly orders, the Hospitallers and Templars, soon became both a mainstay of the Crusading effort as well as powers in their own right, great builders of castles in Palestine and Syria and recruiters and fund-raisers for the Crusading effort in Europe.[84] Their influence was infectious, for

> their way of life turned them into exemplary warriors. They were obedient and showed discipline in battle, whilst displaying frugality and asceticism in communal life, from which women and children were excluded. They all lived under the same roof, received from their leaders clothing and nourishment and had no private possessions. They were never inactive. When they were not fighting, they were doing manual tasks . . . Their hierarchy was founded not on nobility but on merit. They had repudiated the pleasures and prestige proper to secular chivalry – love of fine arms, exaggerated care for the body and coiffure, passion for games and hunting – [in exchange for] a new order founded on poverty, communal life and devotion to Christ.[85]

In the founding of the military orders we may perceive the origins of the regimented armies that arose in Europe in the sixteenth century; there is certainly a strong case to be argued that the dissolution of the monastic orders in the Protestant lands during the Reformation carried into the state armies – through warrior-monks who secularised themselves to become lay soldiers – the system of hierarchy, of commanders and their subordinate units, that had made the orders the first autonomous and disciplined fighting-bodies Europe had known since the disappearance of the Roman legions. That, however, lay in the future. The immediate influence of the Hospitallers and Templars on the battlefield was to prompt other Christian warriors elsewhere, notably those fighting the Muslims in Spain but also the Germans waging war against the pagan Prussians and Lithuanians, to found similar orders of their own. Of these the most important was that of the Teutonic Knights who, in conquered Prussia, founded a military regime from whose secularised estates Frederick the Great, 500 years later, recruited the nucleus of his officer corps.

The decline and eventual extinction of the Crusading kingdoms at the end of the thirteenth century was too gradual to mark a watershed in European warmaking; too many Crusades had been launched for the Muslim triumphs to provoke a climactic retaliation, and in any case the European kings had their hands full with wars of their own at home. Nevertheless, the Crusades left changes in the European military world that were never effaced. They re-established the presence of Latin (Roman Catholic) states in the eastern Mediterranean, not only in Palestine and Syria but more lastingly in Greece, Crete, Cyprus and the Aegean, through which staging-places the northern Italian cities, notably Venice (where town life and commerce had never wholly died), were enabled to reopen a prosperous trade with the Middle and eventually Far East, and to revive the safe transportation of goods between ports throughout the Mediterranean itself; the money they made thereby fuelled most of the wars fought during the fifteenth century between themselves and later by France against the Habsburgs of the Holy Roman empire for dominance south of the Alps. They sent a powerful impulse to fortify the liberation of Spain from Islam (the *Reconquista*), as well as the eastward extension of the Christian frontier toward Russia and the steppe. Having undermined the strength of the Byzantines, they did nothing to check the advance of the Ottoman Turks into the Balkans; by the beginning of the fifteenth century they had reached the Danube, overwhelming in the process the Christian kingdom of Serbia and menacing that of Hungary. By way of compensation, however, the Crusaders had confronted the warring kings of Europe and their turbulent vassals with the idea of a larger purpose to warfare than that of their interminable quarrel over rights; they reinforced the authority of the Church in its efforts to contain the warrior impulse within some ethical and legal framework; and, paradoxical as it may seem, in schooling the European knightly class to the disciplines of purposive warmaking, they laid the basis for the rise of effective kingdoms. By the assertion of central power within their own borders, these eventually gave birth to a Europe where conflict ceased to be the endemic condition of everyday life and became an occasional and then external undertaking.

The development of this pattern would have been difficult for contemporaries to perceive in the troubled fourteenth and fifteenth centuries. In the great dispute over rights that led to the Hundred Years' War between France and England (1337–1457), in the wars between Habsburgs, Wittelsbachs and Luxembourgs for the crown of the Holy Roman empire, and of the emperors to do down their rebellious subjects in Bohemia and Switzerland, and in the Italian city wars, any thought that the social and political, let alone military, dominance of the man on horseback might be reaching its conclusive term would have seemed fanciful. Nevertheless, such was the case. Mounted warfare between armoured men, fought in the belief that to shrink from the blow in the line of battle was an offence not merely against legal duty but against personal honour, ultimately proved as self-defeating as had the code of phalanx warfare in classical Greece. Indeed, there is considerable evidence that, even in its heyday in the fifteenth century, knightly warfare was not what it seems to us or what its devotees believed it ought to be at the time. The ever heavier and more impenetrable armour worn by mounted warriors (plate rather than mail after the mid-fourteenth century) was better suited not to the exigencies of the battlefield – despite the appearance of more and more foot-soldiers handling the long- and crossbows in that century, the lethality of warfare did not much advance – but to the artificialities of the joust.[86] Just as the modern warfare of lightning armoured thrusts and pinpoint airstrikes achieves its theoretical perfection only on an army's training-grounds, so it may well have been that the shining suit of the fifteenth-century warrior achieved its theoretical purpose of protection rather from an opponent's lance in a tourney than from an arrow or sword-blow on the battlefield. Common sense, the quality that allowed Victor Hanson to unravel the mystery of phalanx warfare, should persuade us of the improbability of any other case.

Medieval battles, as R.C. Smail, the master of Crusader historiography, has pointed out, defy reconstruction from the evidence.[87] But in the three battles of the Hundred Years' War of which we do have detailed knowledge, Crécy (1346), Poitiers (1356), and Agincourt (1415), the English knights in all three cases fought dismounted, and supported by archers, and the bulk of the French dismounted in the second and third. The idea that armoured knights, riding knee to knee with couched lances in dense waves of successive ranks, could have charged home against each other without instantaneous catastrophe to both sides at the moment of impact defies belief.

The iron warfare of the Middle Ages, like that of the Greeks, was a bloody and 'horrible affair', made all the worse by its relentless regularity and the bloodthirsty courage of those who bound themselves to it. For all the higher motivation involved – civic independence among the Greeks, fealty and chivalry with the knights – a certain 'hard primitivism' lurked beneath the surface. The Greeks fought themselves to exhaustion by the logic of their own methods; the eclipse of the knightly way of warmaking had an external cause, the coming of gunpowder. But, in either case, the power of iron, that delusively cheap and common metal, had run its course.

Interlude 4
Logistics and Supply

Stone, bronze and iron furnished the instruments of combat, which is the central act of warfare, from its beginnings until its nature was transformed by gunpowder a mere twenty generations ago. Combat may only be joined, however, if the combatants find the means to meet on a battlefield, and to supply them on their way to such meetings has always presented difficulties second only to those of achieving success in combat itself. The horse peoples alone escaped such difficulties but, historically, they were a minority among warriors. The majority depended upon the power of legs and shoulders to carry them and their necessaries about any theatre of campaign, a restriction that limited both the range and endurance of fighting-forces, whether acting offensively or defensively, very severely. Indeed, most warmaking on land, until the most recent times, was a short-term and short-distance activity.

For that there is the simplest explanation. When a body of men join together to perform a day's task, they will need at the very least to eat once between sunrise and sunset. If the task protracts beyond a single day, and the men move from the place where they keep their food, they will have to carry their meals with them. Since all but the most primitive operations of war entail protraction and movement, warriors necessarily burden themselves with rations as well as weapons. Experience, however, borne out by modern field trials, has established that the soldier's load cannot on average be made to exceed seventy pounds' weight – of which clothes, equipment, arms and necessaries will form at least half; as a daily intake of solid food by a man doing heavy work weighs at least three pounds, it follows that a marching soldier cannot carry supplies for more than ten or eleven days, and of course the burden is only worth the effort if the food is provided in imperishable form. These figures have not varied over centuries: Vegetius, the Roman military theorist of the fourth century AD, urged that 'the young soldiers must be given frequent practice in carrying loads of up to sixty pounds, and marching along at the military pace, for on strenuous campaigns they will be faced with the necessity of carrying their rations as well as their arms';[1] the British soldiers who attacked in the Somme on 1 July 1916, carrying with them several days' rations in case of a break in the line of supply, were burdened on average with sixty-six pounds;[2] and, though the British parachutists and marines who 'yomped' across the Falklands in 1982 briefly carried, for lack of helicopter lift to supply them, loads equal to their own body weight, they were exhausted by the effort, though they were picked men in exceptional physical condition.[3]

Soldiers may 'live off the country', of course, by which is meant taking the food of the civil population, a familiar depredation that explains why, until the most recent times, the approach of even the best-disciplined army often caused the inhabitants to hide every portable consumable. Occasionally, if an army organised a market, as Wellington always took care to do in Spain, the effect might be the opposite, as peasants flocked to bring goods to sell, but Wellington was in the unusual position of having cash to spend.[4] Historically most armies have either lacked money, sought to pay by promissory notes or, if operating in enemy territory, simply taken what they wanted. It is not a policy that works for long. Even if food can be found where it has been hidden, the army must disperse to squirrel it out, thus diluting its fighting-power, and in any case soon eats out its area of operations; cavalry armies, except on extensive grasslands (where human food lacks, a complicating difficulty), will graze out an area even more quickly.

Cavalry armies, because their power derives from the speed at which they strike and then decamp, and because, too, of the noted frugality of the nomadic horsemen who most often formed them, generally escaped the constraint of overgrazing, as long as they kept to or near a grassland region. Marching armies had no such freedom of action. Moving at twenty miles a day, the very best speed to be achieved with regularity by men on foot – it was that of the legions on the Roman internal lines of communication and of Von Kluck's army on the advance from Mons to the Marne in the French campaign of 1914 – they progressed too slowly to find untouched stores close enough to their line of advance to supply their daily needs.[5] In consequence they had either to stop at intervals so as to gain time to forage at a distance, or to transport their bulk supplies with them.

The transport of bulk supplies requires access to a waterway close to the line of march – a river or coastal sea route – or else the use of wheels; pack animals, though much used in the ancient world and in difficult terrain in modern times (the Russians in their conquest of Khiva in Central Asia in 1874 employed 8800 camels to feed 5500 men), are a poor substitute.[6] Water transport has been the mainstay of many campaigns – Marlborough's advance to Bavaria in 1704, provisioned down the Rhine, is a famous example – but the axis of supply then determines that of the campaign: it may be that if a river leads in the wrong direction, the decisive battle cannot be fought. Roads for wheeled transport, if the road network is of any density, give more logistic flexibility, but until road engineering was undertaken on a major scale in Europe from the eighteenth century onward, first in France, later in Britain and Prussia, few regions furnished such a network (the lengths per thousand of population in 1860 were: 5 miles in Britain, 3 in France, 2⅓ in Prussia, only ¾ in Spain); and, until the development of macadamisation in the early nineteenth century, roads generally lacked an all-weather surface.[7]

The exception to this state of affairs prevailed only within the Roman empire and in part also in China (though Chinese waterways, particularly the Grand Canal, begun AD 608, served the main purpose of internal communication), and it was Rome's roads that made the legions who built them so effective an instrument of imperial power. Within the Roman province of Africa alone, which stretched from modern Morocco to the Nile basin, archaeologists have identified some 10,000 miles of road of greater or lesser width; and Gaul, Britain, Spain and Italy were similarly served, making it possible for Roman commanders to calculate marching-times very precisely between the military storehouses and barracks that served as revictualling stops: from Cologne to Rome sixty-seven days, from Rome to Brindisi fifteen days, from Rome to Antioch (including two days at sea) 124 days.[8] There were, however, no equivalents to the Roman roads in any of the neighbouring empires, not even in the comparatively easily engineered plains of Mesopotamia and Persia (the 'royal road' used by Alexander was not of Roman standard), and once Rome's administration collapsed in the fifth century, its magnificent roads regularly decayed also. That decay spelt an end to strategic marching everywhere for more than a thousand years. In England the Hardway, for example, by which Alfred the Great laboriously brought his army out of Somerset to fight the Danes in the middle of the ninth century, was a muddy track aligned on no route used by the Romans, though several excellent Roman roads had run near to it 400 years earlier.

Without roads, armies could not supply themselves by wheeled transport except of the roughest sort, and they had to depend on either ships or bullocks, the latter being the commonest beast of traction and burden from the fifth millennium BC (attested by archaeological finds in what today is Poland) to the early nineteenth century AD in India and

Spain.[9] In both those campaigning theatres Wellington, for example, woke and slept with the search for 'good bullocks' ever on his mind. 'Rapid movement', he wrote in August 1804, 'cannot be made without good cattle, well driven and well taken care of'; earlier, in India, he had made the same point: 'the success of military operations depends upon supplies; there is no difficulty in fighting, and in finding the means of beating your enemy either with or without loss; but to gain your objects you must feed.'[10] For a commander like Wellington with the money to buy more, bullocks had the advantage that they could be eaten as well as driven for transport, and he used them for both purposes. Few other commanders have been so well provided. Bullock trains were in general too valuable to be slaughtered for the soldiers' cooking-pot, a consideration that automatically limited an army's speed and range.

Alexander the Great, for example, was as dependent as Wellington on bullocks and oxen – the latter the more mature version of the former – for tactical mobility. But he reckoned his tactical range no more than eight days' march from the point of bulk re-supply, usually a maritime depot, since an ox ate its own load over that period. As a consequence he could campaign over long distance only if he could keep close to his fleet train or if he sent representatives ahead to purchase food and forage, either for cash or for the promise of repayment after victory, a transaction into which treacherous Persian officials were increasingly ready to enter as Alexander's offensive against Darius prospered. For his farthest march from home, that of 326 BC between the River Indus and the Makran in Baluchistan, a distance of 300 miles, he assembled a stockpile of 52,600 tons of provisions, enough to supply his army of 87,000 infantry, 18,000 cavalry and 52,000 followers for four months. Since an animal train would have consumed their loads, and the men eaten their thirty pounds of personal provisions, well before the march was complete, he counted on an accompanying fleet to re-supply him along the Indian Ocean coast, and the seasonal monsoon to refresh the rivers from which he would take water at their estuaries. The logistic calculations were well founded. The stockpile, if regularly unshipped and distributed, would have sufficed to provision his army in plenty. But that year the monsoon blew so as to confine Alexander's fleet at the Indus mouth, with the result that three-quarters of his army was lost on the march through the deserts of Baluchistan.[11]

This disaster supplies an extreme example of how heavily logistics impinge on warmaking, even that of the most care-taking and talented general; it gruesomely exemplifies Wellington's maxim that 'to gain your objects you must feed'. Few commanders in ancient or pre-modern times, except those of Roman armies operating at the extremities of the imperial road network or those keeping close to a water-borne supply train, could campaign outside their home territories with a freedom unconstrained by logistic consideration. Even the Romans ran into difficulties when they left their roadheads behind, while large armies might risk starvation within territories they controlled, as Napoleon's marshals discovered in Spain in 1809–13. A great part of the quartermastering problem derived from the perishability of food in all periods and places before canning and the provision of artificial foodstuffs was developed in the nineteenth century. Parched or milled grain was a staple for soldiers throughout history, and kept them in fighting trim when supplemented by oil, lard, cheese, fish extracts (an essential element of the legionary's diet), wine, vinegar or beer and perhaps some meat, cured, salted, dried or slaughtered at the point of consumption.[12] Even the best quartermaster's diet, however, was deficient in fresh essentials, so that in times of shortage soldiers, just as much as long-voyaging sailors, were prone to succumb to diseases of malnutrition. Resulting debility bred the epidemics that regularly struck armies massed for battle or during the prolonged operations of a siege.

Military diet was revolutionised in the middle of the nineteenth century by the appearance of canned meat (as early as 1845, though by a process that threatened lead-poisoning to those too dependent upon it, and the cause of many deaths in Franklin's Polar expedition), evaporated milk (1860), dried milk powder (1855) and margarine, invented under competitive rules set by Napoleon III to find a substitute for butter for his soldiers in the 1860s.[13] The northern armies of the American Civil War largely subsisted in the field on the products of the Chicago stockyards, though more often in salt than canned form, while their Confederate enemies had to make do with such unpalatable if traditional staples as maize meal and dried peanuts ('goober peas'), and starved for meat because supply from the great herds of Texas was denied to them by Union control of the Mississippi River; as early as 1862 a Confederate wrote to his wife, 'We have lived some days on raw, baked and roasted apples, sometimes on green corn and sometimes nothing.'[14] Northern soldiers also experimented with industrially processed dry potatoes and vegetables and a canned mixture of coffee extract, milk and sugar, all unpopular, but luxuries to the hungry rebels who captured any.

Ultimately, however, the Northern armies were better fed than the Southern because their quartermasters controlled the 30,000 miles of American railroad laid by 1860 (longer than that of the rest of the world's combined) in the ratio of 2.4:1, and continued to lay more in each month of a war in which a prime task of the Union soldiers was to pull up every stretch of Confederate track – irreplaceable from the South's narrow economic base – they crossed. Railways revolutionised warmaking on land, and the American Civil War was the first to demonstrate that trend. Indeed, it is often now represented as a purely railway war, in which the North's success in first cutting the rail connections between the populous south-east and the productive south-west at the Mississippi line, and then dividing the south-east's internal system by seizing the Chattanooga–Atlanta link in 1864, fragmented its territory into zones that lacked economic self-sufficiency, and ensured the ultimate collapse of Southern secession, through want of supply to the fighting armies, even though, ragged and hungry as they were, they could defy the Union on the battlefield to the end.[15]

That view distorts the relative contributions that combat and logistics make to victory, however. Logistic supremacy on its own rarely wins a campaign against a determined enemy, as McClellan found in the Union's Peninsula Campaign of 1862, while states economically at the end of their tether, as were both Germany and Japan in 1944–5, may continue to inflict demoralising setbacks on their opponents.[16] Nevertheless, Napoleon's blunt maxim has an overriding truth: victory goes ultimately to the big battalions, and the coming of the railway age ensured that the states which could raise big battalions were at least enabled to transport them speedily, swiftly and at all seasons to a chosen place of deployment. Those nations, the United States apart, lay in the industrialising zones of western and central Europe, where extensive networks, first laid to connect factories with ports in Britain and Belgium, were rapidly extended within France and Prussia and then, more slowly, eastward to bring the agricultural areas of Austria-Hungary and Russia into a common system; between 1825 and 1900, the length of locomotive track within Europe grew from nothing to 175,000 miles; it was carried in tunnels and on bridges, and crossed every one of the continent's natural barriers, including the Rhine, Alps and Pyrenees. The journey from Rome to Cologne, sixty-seven days' marching for a legion, by the year 1900 could be completed in less than twenty-four hours.

It was the railways' east–west axes, not their north–south, that made them militarily significant, however, for it was on the frontiers between France and Germany, Germany and Austria, and Germany and Russia that potential conflict festered. So important to national defence were the railways held by the Prussian, later Imperial German, government that by 1860 half had been taken into public ownership, and the whole twenty years later. In 1866 the Prussian Guard Corps was deployed within a week, in twelve trains a day from Berlin to the front with Austria, conclusive evidence of the superiority of rail over road movement in military operations and a stark warning that a state that did not integrate its transport and mobilisation policies must in future risk defeat at the hands of another which did. Prussia defeated Austria in 1866 largely by means of these superior numbers; it was able to hurry to the opening engagement, while its defeat of France in Alsace-Lorraine in 1870 stemmed directly from French mismanagement, admittedly on an inferior network of rail reinforcement and re-supply.[17]

The lessons of the wars of 1866 and 1870–1 were taken to heart by all European general staffs, not least the German itself, which by 1876 had established its own railway department with authority to oversee the building of new track within the Reich, so as to ensure that military needs would be served in time of war; small rural railway stations at the borders with France and Belgium were equipped with platforms a mile long, so that several troop trains might disgorge whole divisions of men and horses in a single visit. In August 1914 such feats of deployment were readily achieved. Between 1–17 August, Germany, the peacetime strength of whose army stood at 800,000, not only multiplied it six times by mobilisation of reservists, but transported in that period 1,485,000 men to the front with Belgium and France, ready and equipped to fight as soon as detrained. Its enemies matched the achievement. France's military management of its railways was as good in 1914 as it had been bad in 1870, and French transportation staffs actually showed greater flexibility in transferring needed troops to threatened sectors in the crisis of the battle of the Marne in September than the Germans did. Austrian mobilisation was as efficient as the German; even the Russians, on whose suspected organisational incapacity the German General Staff had counted to win it six trouble-free weeks on the eastern front in which to complete victory in the west, surprised itself, its allies and – very badly – the Germans by the speed with which it concentrated its First and Second Armies in Poland.

The mobilisation of 1914 justified all the efforts the European general staffs had put into the perfection of railway organisation for war in the forty preceding years of peace; enormous armies – 62 French infantry divisions (of 15,000 men each), 87 German, 49 Austrian, 114 Russian – were picked up from their peacetime garrison-places and decanted on to the field of battle, together with several million horses, within a month of the outbreak.[18] Once arrived, however, they found that the almost miraculous mobility conferred by rail movement evaporated. Face to

307

face with each other, they were no better able to move or transport their supplies than Roman legions had been; forward of railhead, soldiers had to march, and the only means of provisioning them was by horse-drawn vehicles. Indeed, their lot was worse than that of the well-organised armies of former times, since contemporary artillery created a fire-zone several miles deep within which re-supply by horse was impossible and re-provisioning of the infantry – with ammunition as well as food – could be done only by man-packing.

Of course, the loss of mobility presented itself more urgently in a tactical than a logistic form: in the heart of the fire-zone, infantry could scarcely move at all, and then at catastrophic human cost; not until the introduction of the tank in 1916 were units of men able to manoeuvre once again while in direct contact with the enemy. The logistic dimension nevertheless dogged armies throughout the First World War, not least because the effort to win superiority within the fire-zone by increasing the weight of fire delivered demanded an ever larger trans-shipment of munitions between railhead and guns, which could only be undertaken by horses. As a result, horse fodder became the single largest category of cargo unloaded, for example, at French ports for the British army on the Western Front throughout the period 1914–18.

The problem reappeared in the Second World War, when the German army, deficient in motor transport because the German engineering industry had to devote its resources to manufacturing tanks, aircraft and U-boats, and in any case because it was chronically short of fuel, actually took into service more horses than it had done between 1914 and 1918 – 2,750,000 as opposed to 1,400,000; most died in service, as did the majority of the 3.5 million horses mobilised by the Red Army between 1941 and 1945.[19] It was only the American and British armed forces that could tactically re-supply their troops in the line through motor transport alone, and then thanks to the unique productive capacity of the American oil industry and automobile plants. So ample, indeed, were American resources that they sufficed not only to supply the US army and navy with all the trucks and fuel they required but to equip the Red Army also with 395,883 trucks and 2,700,000 tons of gasoline, thus providing the means, as the Soviets themselves freely admitted later, by which it advanced from Stalingrad to Berlin.[20]

The burden thrown on rail, horse and motor transport during the great wars of the industrial era was infinitely larger than that borne by the supply trains of earlier armies, even those of the gunpowder age. Food, fodder and impedimenta – tents, tools, perhaps some bridging equipment

– were all that those of edged-weapon armies were asked to carry, while the munition needs of gunpowder armies were small. But the industry of the mass-production age, which rolled the steel and cast the engine-blocks by which transportation was revolutionised, also spewed out the shells and bullets that mass armies devoured in ever larger quantity. Rates of consumption increased exponentially. Napoleon's artillery at Waterloo, for example, numbered 246 guns which fired about a hundred rounds each during the battle; in 1870 at Sedan, one of the most noted battles of the nineteenth century, the Prussian army fired 33,134 rounds; in the week before the opening of the battle of the Somme, 1 July 1916, British artillery fired 1,000,000 rounds, a total weight of some 20,000 tons of metal and explosive.[21] The demand for quantities of that sort caused a 'shell crisis' in 1915, but the famine was staunched by a programme of emergency industrialisation in Britain and the placing of large contracts with factories working at under-capacity elsewhere. British and French industry thereafter never faltered; the French, who had planned before the war for an expenditure of 10,000 75-mm. shells per day, pushed production to 200,000 per day in 1915 and in 1917–18 supplied the arriving American expeditionary force with 10,000,000 shells for its French-built artillery, as well as 4791 of the 6287 aircraft its air corps flew in combat. Germany, though forced to find an artificial substitute for the nitrates denied it by blockade, increased production of explosive from 1000 tons a month in 1914 to 6000 in 1915; even the much despised Russian factory system pushed shell output from 450,000 per month in 1915 to 4,500,000 in 1916, a tenfold increase.[22]

The capacity and complexity of the European and American arms industries that arose in the nineteenth century had no parallels in former times. Stone Age man had mined and worked flint on a commercial basis, but the manufacture of bronze weapons and armour had always been a craft industry. The coming of iron had led to an expansion of output and even to standardisation: the Roman army maintained a network of arms factories to produce the legionary's hooped armour, helmets, swords and javelins; the workers' skills were regarded as so important to the state that in 398 a decree was issued for them to be branded as a deterrent against desertion.[23] The barbarian invasions, however, threw arms-making back into private hands, though the art of manufacturing chain-mail was thought rare enough to come under state regulation. Charlemagne ordained in 779 that any merchant caught exporting mail-shirts should forfeit all his property, an order reissued in 805; it has been estimated that the weight of chain-mail worn by his mounted men, when summoned for war, represented, at about 180 tons, the output of several years' work by the chain-smiths of his empire.

The making of plate armour, an extremely complex metallurgical and fashioning process, concentrated arms manufacture even more narrowly; the best was produced in royal workshops, of which that at Greenwich was the centre in England. However, the apogee of plate armour-making coincided with the appearance of gunpowder, which both rendered it obsolete and at the same time created a surge of demand for powder, ball, cannon and personal firearms. Metal cannonballs were at first found so expensive to purchase that masons branched out into the manufacture of stone substitutes. The production of powder was constrained by the intrinsic shortage of potassium nitrate, saltpetre, which – until an industrial process for its manufacture was developed in the nineteenth century – could only be found in places where bacterial action on urine and faeces had deposited it into the earth, usually in caves and stables where livestock was kept; its collection and use were widely taken under state control.[24] Firearms, though increasingly subjected to state manufacturing monopoly (as, for example, in Britain at the Tower of London), were made as well in quantity by private gunsmiths, located particularly in the smaller German states. The founding of cannon, however, was from the start seen by kings to be a necessary prerogative of their power, and with the coming of the artillery revolution at the end of the fifteenth century the history of state arsenals really begins.

Cannon-founding was an art first developed by bell-founders, the only craftsmen who understood how to cast molten metal in large shapes (a technique developed in the eighth century), and who worked in the only material at first considered suitable to withstand gunpowder shock, which was bronze. During the sixteenth century, however, experimentation began with cast iron; initially the products were found suitable only for use at sea, since they had to be made thicker and heavier than a bronze equivalent in order to absorb the energy of a given weight of powder. Eventually most siege-guns, as well as ships' cannons, were iron cast. Experimentation with casting meanwhile produced great improvements in bronze field-artillery. Jean Maritz, a Swiss who entered French state employment in 1734, realised that a better barrel could be produced if it were cast solid, rather than hollow, the bell-casting practice, and then bored out. Boring would make for a better fit between ball and tube, so reduce the charge of powder needed to achieve a given range, and ultimately make for a lighter and more mobile weapon. No boring-machine of the necessary power – derived hydraulically – yet existed, but one was perfected by his son, who in consequence was appointed master of the royal arsenal at Ruelle, and then of all other national gun-foundries in France.[25]

The French machine was copied and introduced into England in 1774, but French artillery production, centred in the state arsenals, nevertheless remained superior to that of all other European countries until the end of the gunpowder age, largely as a result of the programme of standardisation and rationalisation carried through by the great artillerist Jean Gribeauval in 1763–7; his guns were still in service with the French army in 1829.[26] By then, however, the state arsenal system was under threat from the commercial forces released by the industrial revolution, to which it would eventually, perhaps inevitably, succumb. Large-scale engineering in iron, heated to malleability in furnaces fuelled by the abundant supply of coal that steam-power was now lifting from mines, proved so profitable an investment for capital that successful ironmasters could, by the middle of the nineteenth century, command funds for almost any undertaking of whose profitability they could persuade a banker. Rails, locomotives, iron ships and industrial machinery were the initially favoured products; as armies (and navies) grew in size, large and small guns, for ships, for the artillery park and for the individual soldier, began to promise a seductive return. William Armstrong, a British manufacturer of hydraulic equipment, decided as a result of reading how effective artillery had proved in the Crimean War that it was 'time military engineering was brought up to the level of current engineering practice'. Soon he was manufacturing large rifled cannon for the army and even larger guns for the navy; between 1857 and 1861 he manufactured no less than 1600 rifled, breech-loading guns at his Elswick works. An English competitor, Whitworth, quickly entered the market – both enjoyed government subsidies to undertake experiments – but both found competition overseas.[27]

Alfred Krupp, a German steelmaker at Essen, began to experiment with the use of steel in gunmaking before 1850; he exhibited steel, breech-loading artillery at the Great Exhibition of 1851. Steel was an intractable material; its chemistry was not fully understood; and many of Krupp's experimental models proved too brittle and burst at proof. Eventually the technology was mastered, and in 1863 his gunmaking business went into profit when he obtained large Russian orders. By the end of the century, Krupp's steel guns, in calibres from 77 mm. to 155 mm. (420 mm. was achieved by 1914), equipped many armies, although not the British, French, Russian and Austrian, the last two having built gun factories of their own; Krupp naval guns of 11-inch calibre were superior to their British equivalents of 13.5 inches.

At the same time the manufacture of small arms had also been revolutionised by private enterprise, centred largely in the United States. American inventors and manufacturers, located chiefly in the Connecticut River valley, were the first to embrace the concept of 'interchangeable parts'. These, produced by automatic or semi-automatic water- and then steam-powered milling-machines, cut out components to a prescribed shape at high speed and with great accuracy, thereby altogether eliminating costly handwork to make parts fit. Rifles manufactured by this process – and the rifle rapidly supplanted the smooth-bore musket in the 1850s – could be assembled by semi-skilled workers from baskets of components with the supplier's certainty that the buyer would find all of equal quality. The process was soon applied to the manufacture of the metallic cartridges the new rifles accepted, with the result that the British Woolwich Arsenal, where repetitive-process machines had been installed in the 1850s, was soon capable of producing 250,000 a day.

It was indeed the perceived danger of overproduction, and consequent flooding of the home market, that prompted arms-manufacturers to persist in the search for new designs that would render the existing ones obsolete, and to search for new markets overseas. Here, again, the Americans were to be the innovators. The French had in 1870 deployed a working model of that weapon which gunsmiths had long sought to perfect, a machine-gun. In its *mitrailleuse* form it was a crude and only semi-automatic weapon. Several inventors – the Swedish Nordenfeldt, the American Gardner – raced to produce a superior, commercial model. The race was won by the American Hiram Maxim, who in 1884 set up a company to make a weapon that was a true machine, discharging 600 bullets a minute through a mechanism powered by energy captured from each successive detonation; the operator of the Maxim gun may be regarded as a uniformed industrial process-worker, since his function was limited to that of pulling the machine's starting-lever, the trigger, and moving the apparatus through a series of mechanically controlled arcs.[28]

Machine-guns, and their rather less lethal but related equivalent, the breech-loading, small-bore magazine rifle, equipped the armies of all the combatant powers that went to war in 1914. Firing as they did over a range of 1000 yards, and accurately to 500, they rapidly established a defensive dominance on the battlefield that made infantry attacks costly and often suicidal. From the first moment of the digging of trench lines in which the infantry could take refuge from this storm of steel, the generals sought to find a means of dampening its effect. Multiplication of artillery pieces was

312

the first solution tried; it resulted only in mutual attrition by the competing artilleries, devastation of the battlefield and overtaxation both of the shell-producing industries at home and of the supply services nearer the front. The invention of the tank was the second solution; but the machines produced were too few in number, too slow and too cumbersome to impose a decisive alteration to tactical conditions. Toward the end of the war both sides were looking to the newly introduced instrument of airpower to impinge directly on the civilian morale and productive capacity of the opponent, in the hope of wearing both down; however, neither the heavy aeroplane nor the airship had yet achieved the offensive capability to alter the balance. The First World War was eventually resolved not by any discovery or application of new military technique by the high commands, but by the relentless attrition of manpower by industrial output. The fact that it was Germany which went down to defeat in this *Materialschlacht* was almost fortuitous; it might as well have been any of her enemies, among whom Russia did indeed pay the penalty in 1917. The means that general staffs had convinced governments would ensure peace and, if war broke out, bring victory – ever wider recruitment of men, ever costlier purchases of arms – had cancelled each other out. Supply and logistics had damaged all the combatants in almost equal measure.

Supply and logistics were, nevertheless, to bring clear-cut victory in the Second World War, and at almost marginal cost, except in human sorrow, to the principal winner. The United States, a late entrant to the First World War and at the time largely bereft of military industry, since it had made its wealth in the years after 1865 by industrialisation for its own internal and unwarlike development, entered the Second World War at an earlier stage, in 1941, and that after two years of rearmament undertaken to supply Britain and then Russia with the means to fight Nazi Germany. Rearmament had revived American industry, badly stricken by the Great Depression, but left it still with much surplus capacity. Between 1941 and 1945 its economy underwent the largest, most rapid and sustained expansion ever known; gross national production increased by fifty per cent, while war production, which increased from two to forty per cent of output between 1939 and 1943, was largely financed out of revenue rather than borrowing. Labour productivity improved by twenty-five per cent and utilisation of plant increased from forty to ninety hours a week; as a result shipbuilding output rose ten times, rubber output doubled, steel output nearly doubled and aircraft output increased elevenfold, so that, of the 750,000 aircraft produced by the principal combatants during the war, 300,000 originated in the United States, of which 90,000 were built in 1944 alone.[29]

It was America's industry that overwhelmed its German and Japanese enemies, though only because American shipyards also supplied the transportation to move it. More than 51,000,000 tons of merchant shipping was built by United States shipyards between 1941 and 1945, representing some 10,000 Liberty and Victory freighters and T-2 tankers, produced by a revolutionary process of prefabrication which, for demonstration purposes, could take a vessel from start to launch in four days, fifteen hours; on average the United States, at the height of the Liberty-building programme, was launching three ships a day.[30] Germany's U-boats, even before they were defeated by the introduction of long-range aircraft and escort aircraft-carriers, both American-built, to the Battle of the Atlantic, could not sink such an output at the rate losses were replaced.

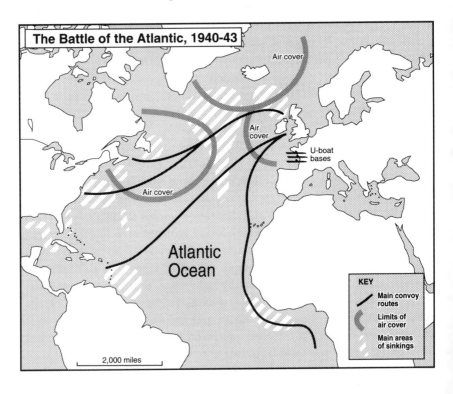

It was supply and logistics, therefore, which ensured victory in the largest and most terrible of wars ever fought. They thus determined that in any future conflict between conventional forces conducted as a struggle for national survival, industrial capacity, rather than any other factor, would be decisive. That no such conflict has yet followed the outcome of 1945 is

314

the result of a parallel effort exerted by the United States during the years of its unprecedented industrial achievement to produce an alternative to warmaking by struggle at the battlefront, the atomic bomb. That weapon was the culmination of a process of technological development begun 500 years earlier, which sought to transfer demand for the energy needed for military purposes from the muscles of man and beast to a stored source. The search had begun with the discovery of gunpowder.

—5—
Fire

FIRE IS A WEAPON of great antiquity. In the form of 'Greek fire' it was first brought into use by the Byzantines in the seventh century. They guarded the secret of its composition so carefully that even today scholars debate about the exact nature of its ingredients. All that is known for certain is that it was discharged in liquid form, by a sort of syringe, chiefly as an incendiary agent against wooden structures in siege and naval warfare. It was not 'fire' in the modern sense of a propellant or explosive. It was not, for all the fear it aroused and mystery that surrounded it, a very effective innovation. It did not revolutionise warfare, as the coming of gunpowder would do.

Gunpowder nevertheless connects with it, for it is now believed that the basis of 'Greek fire' was what the Babylonians called 'naphtha' or 'the thing that blazes', a seepage from surface deposits of petroleum.[1] They found no practical use for it. In China, however, about the eleventh century AD, it was discovered that intermixing naphtha-based substances from local surface seepages with saltpetre yielded a compound that had explosive as well as incendiary properties. The Chinese had earlier stumbled on the discovery that lighting fires, particularly of charcoal, on soils that contained high concentrations of sulphur also produced explosive effects. When purified sulphur was combined with powdered charcoal and crystalline saltpetre – this was perhaps first done for semi-magical purposes in Taoist temples about AD 950 – what we now call gunpowder resulted.[2] Whether the Chinese used it in warfare is much disputed. There is no evidence that they made cannon (as opposed to fireworks) before the end of the thirteenth century;[3] soon after that date gunpowder was certainly known also in Europe, where its secrets may have been hit upon by alchemists in the course of their eternal and fruitless search for means to turn dross into gold, and where its military utility was recognised as soon as its explosive properties were discovered. Quite how the further discovery was made that, when gunpowder and a projectile were confined within a tube, the force released by detonating the former imparted both range and direction to the latter, defies reconstruction. But it can be dated quite accurately to the beginning of the fourteenth century, since a drawing of 1326 survives that shows a vase-shaped vessel – perhaps cast by a bell-founder who was used to working in such forms – with a large arrow projecting from its neck; a gunner is applying a taper to the touchhole and the device is aimed at a castle gate.

By the fifteenth century gun technology had advanced. Cannonballs had replaced arrows and the gun had assumed tubular form, sometimes achieved by binding billets of wrought iron, barrel-fashion, with iron hoops. Nevertheless, the use of the cannon remained confined to siege warfare. Though there were apparently cannon deployed at Agincourt (1415), they could as yet do little on the battlefield but make noise or smoke; it would have been an unlucky knight or archer who got in the way of a random shot. Forty years later, however, when the French finally expelled the English from Normandy and Aquitaine, in the campaign of 1450–3, they knocked through castle walls of the English strongholds with cannon; at exactly the same time the Turks were battering down the walls of Theodosius at Constantinople with monster bombards (the Turkish taste was for guns so large that they sometimes had to be cast *in situ* before a siege began). In 1477 Louis XI of France (1461–83) further extended his area of control over his ancestral lands by using cannon against the castles of the dukes of Burgundy. By 1478, as a result, the French royal house was fully in control of its own territory for the first time since Carolingian days six centuries earlier, and ready to erect a centralised government – supported by a fiscal system in which cannon were the ultimate tax-collectors from refractory vassals – that shortly became the most powerful in Europe.[4]

GUNPOWDER AND FORTIFICATION

The cannon with which the French kings and the Ottoman Turks knocked through their enemies' defensive walls suffered, however, from defects that gravely limited their military usefulness: they were large, heavy and mounted on immobile platforms. As a result they could be brought into action only on territory their owners already controlled, as the French did the Norman countryside and the Ottomans the water and land approaches to Constantinople. For cannon to become instruments of campaign they had to be lightened enough to be transported on wheels at the same speed as the army that accompanied them, so that foot, horse and guns could move as an integrated unit within enemy territory, thus averting the dangers that the artillery might be captured while gunners struggled to keep up with the marching force or have to be abandoned in the event of a retreat.

In 1494 the French achieved the appropriate breakthrough:

> French craftsmen and bell-founders . . . by the [early] 1490s . . . had evolved a cannon that was recognisably the same creature that was going to decide battles and sieges for nearly four hundred years to come. The heavy 'built-up' bombard, firing a stone ball from a wooden platform that had laboriously to be lifted onto a cart whenever it changed position, had been replaced by a slender, homogeneous bronze-cast tube, no more than eight feet long, its proportions carefully calculated to absorb the progressively diminishing shock of discharge from breech to muzzle. It fired wrought iron balls, heavier than their stone equivalents but, because of that, of three times' greater destructive effect for a given bore.[5]

Most important of all, the guns were mobile; because the tubes were cast in one piece, 'trunnions', short flanges projecting just forward of the point of balance, could be incorporated into them, by which they could be hung in wooden two-wheeled carriages. The cannon thus became as manoeuvrable as a small cart – even more manoeuvrable when the 'trail' of the carriage was hitched to another two-wheeled 'limber', forming an articulated unit to which horses could be directly harnessed between shafts; the carriage itself could be so fashioned as to allow the muzzle of the tube, or barrel (the nomenclature of the 'built-up' gun of hooped metal staves persists to this day), to be depressed or elevated by the manipulation of wedges under the breech. To traverse the gun from right to left or vice versa, the trail of the carriage, which rested on the ground to provide stability, was shifted in the appropriate direction.

In the spring of 1494, forty of Charles VIII's new guns were shipped for him from France to the port of La Spezia, in northern Italy, whence, having brought his army across the Alps by the pass of Mont-Genèvre, he set off to march down the length of Italy to make good his claim to the kingdom of Naples. The city states and the papal lands that stood in his way gave up resistance as soon as they heard how quickly his guns had battered down the wall to the castle of Firizzano. In November he entered Florence as a conqueror. In February of the following year, having overwhelmed in eight hours the Neapolitan fortress of San Giovanni, which had once withstood a siege by traditional military means lasting seven years, he rode into Naples. The whole of Italy quaked at his passage. His guns had brought a true revolution in warmaking. The old high-walled castles against which both siege-engines and scaling-parties had so often failed were hopelessly vulnerable to the new battering-instrument. Guicciardini, an Italian contemporary, wrote that the cannon were 'planted against the walls with such speed, the space between the shots was so brief, and the balls flew so speedily, and were driven with such force, that as much execution was inflicted in a few hours as used to be done in Italy over the same number of days'.[6]

Charles VIII's Neapolitan triumph did not last. His barnstorming methods panicked the Italian states, Venice, the Holy Roman emperor, the Pope and Spain to form a league against him, and though his artillery gave him victory in the main battle of the ensuing War of the Holy League, Fornovo, he then decided to abandon Italy and return to France, where in 1498 he died. His artillery revolution, none the less, proved enduring. The new guns achieved an effect after which siege-engineers had striven for millennia without success. Hitherto the strength of a fortress had derived principally from the height of its walls. That was not exclusively the case, since water defences greatly enhanced defensibility also, as Alexander the Great found during the siege of the offshore stronghold of Tyre (332 BC), which took seven months to conclude. In general, however, the higher the wall the more difficult for the storming-party to scale the crest, while the thickness entailed by height rendered attack by siege-engines less effective. Opposed-weight engines (catapults) threw projectiles that struck only glancing blows at such walls, while torsion-machines, though working in a flat trajectory, were intrinsically underpowered. The only certain means of bringing a wall down was to attack it at its base by mining, a laborious task that ditches and moats readily defeated, and that was also open to the riposte of counter-mining.

The new cannon, because they could be brought rapidly into action close to a wall, and then handled to fire accurately in a predictable arc of impact, transferred the effect of mining to artillery. Iron cannonballs, directed at the base of a wall in a horizontal pattern of attack that did not vary in height, rapidly cut a channel in the stonework, the cumulative effect of which was to use the physics of the wall against itself: the higher the wall, the more quickly it would become unstable and the wider the breach it left when it toppled. Since in falling it automatically filled up the ditch at its foot with rubble, thus providing passage for an assault party, and probably brought down a tower as well (that would have been the artillerists' intention, thus depriving the defenders of a dominating position from which to assail the assault party with missiles), the opening of the breach amounted to the fall of the fortress also; it was already a convention

322

of siege warfare that a refusal to surrender after a breach had been made thereafter absolved the attackers from the obligation to offer quarter or abstain from looting. In the artillery age that convention became absolute.

The disasters in Naples naturally provoked a response. Existing castles were a first line of defence for many, particularly the smaller states of Renaissance Europe, their building and maintenance consuming a large part of state revenues, and fortification-engineers were put on their mettle by the ease with which Charles VIII's cannon had knocked down walls that had stood stoutly for many centuries. In the wars between France, Spain, the Holy Roman empire and the shifting alliances of city states that troubled Italy in the first half of the sixteenth century, remarkable improvisatory works to strengthen old fortifications were achieved. At Pisa in 1500, for example, the city's engineers contrived an inner earthen bank and ditch behind the city's stone wall, which stood intact after the guns of the French and their Florentine allies had battered a breach. This 'double Pisan rampart' was much copied, while there was a great deal of building of external lines of earthen and timber walls and towers, against which iron cannonballs did little damage, at least in the early stages of a siege.[7] City and fortress commanders also quickly recognised that breaches, once made, could be successfully defended by infantry equipped with firearms, effective models of which were just then coming into use, as their sharp practice at the sieges of Cremona in 1523 and Marseilles in 1524 demonstrated.

Improvisation, however, could not adapt old walls to withstand new cannon for ever. An alternative system of fortification was needed. The wonder is that it was found so quickly, so quickly indeed that the age of overwhelming artillery dominance was quite short, little more than a half-century. Measured against the pace of other adaptations to military innovation – that, for example, to armoured *Blitzkrieg* at the outset of the Second World War, which Hitler's enemies contained by radical reorganisation of their armies and the mass manufacture of anti-tank weapons by 1943 – fifty years may seem a lengthy period. But that is to overlook both the intellectual difficulties and the costs involved. An anti-artillery concept had first to be thought out; then the funds had to be found to transform the concept into architectural reality – an enormous capital undertaking, since what was at issue was nothing less than the replacement of a continent-wide system of fortification built over many centuries (some towns sheltered behind walls that, though rebuilt and restored in the Middle Ages, were Roman in origin) of which the original costs had long been amortised.

Clever minds hit upon the germ of the concept almost from the moment mobile cannon appeared. Since cannons did their worst against high walls, new walls to resist them must therefore stand low. However, a fortress so built was open to escalade, the rush-forward of a storming-party with ladders to sweep over the crest and into the fortress's interior by surprise attack. The new system of fortification had to incorporate features that resisted bombardment and, at the same time, held the enemy's infantry at a distance. The solution to this problem of surrendering height while acquiring depth was the angular bastion, which stood forward of the walls, dominated the ditch or moat, served as a fire platform for both cannon and firearms, and was strong enough not to be battered shapeless by a concentration of enemy fire. The most suitable design proved to have four faces: two forming a wedge that pointed out toward the surrounding countryside so as to present a glancing surface to enemy fire, and where attacking artillery could be mounted, and two that joined the wedge to the wall at right-angles, from the rampart of which defenders could use cannon and firearms to sweep the ditch and stretches of wall between the bastions. The bastion should be built of stone, though brick was an acceptable substitute, backed and filled with rammed earth, the whole constituting a structure of immense solidity so as to provide both a solid cannon platform and an outer face on which impacting shot would make the least possible impression.[8]

Fortress-engineers had been experimenting with bastions, and had been thickening walls and sloping their faces, for some time before Charles VIII's expedition into Italy in 1494 demonstrated that the castle had had its day. Such experiments had been scattered and piecemeal, but those who undertook them were thereby sufficiently attuned to the demand for innovation to respond with speed and energy. Giuliano da Sangallo, who with his brother Antonio founded the first and most important of a group of Italian fortification 'families', had drawn up a design for a bastioned defence of the town of Poggio Imperiale in 1487, while in 1494 itself Antonio had begun to reconstruct the fort of Civita Castellana on a bastion system for Pope Alexander VI.[9] Convinced that such systems offered the answer to artillery attack, they were soon proceeding apace with new works for any Italian government that could find the necessary money; Nettuno was outfitted with bastions between 1501 and 1503, and in 1515 Antonio undertook to construct a model fortress for Cardinal Alessandro Farnese at Caprarole. The Sangallos' commercial success attracted competitors into the field, first the San Micheli family, then the Savorgnano, Peruzzi, Genga and Antonelli.

The money to be made invited envy and drew all sorts of unlikely practitioners into the market, including both Leonardo da Vinci,[10] who was inspector of fortresses for Cesare Borgia, and Michelangelo, who in the course of an argument with Antonio da Sangallo in 1545 announced, 'I don't know much about painting and sculpture, but I have gained great experience of fortifications, and I have already proved that I know more about them than the whole tribe of the Sangallos.'[11] Michelangelo equipped his native Florence with new defences between 1527 and 1529 but, fortunately for art, thereafter found fewer commissions for his fortification skills.

The Sangallos and other fortification families were kept in almost continuous employment, not only in Italy but, as their fame spread and rulers acquired ever larger numbers of mobile cannon, in France, Spain, Portugal, the Aegean, Malta (where the Hospitaller order had settled after its expulsion from the Holy Land) and as far away as Russia, West Africa and the Caribbean. They, with the artillerists whose weapons confronted them with their challenge, were the first international technical mercenaries since the builders of chariots who had sold their skills to the warring aristocracies of the Middle East during the first millennium BC. An Italian historian has described their way of life:

> We must put ourselves in the position of these men. They were short of money, and yet they were aware of their own talents and regarded themselves as superior beings who moved among folk who were less civilised than the Italians. They were upset by the example of the few men among them who rose to the highest ranks, and they were liable to go off and serve the most distant prince who attracted them by tempting promises. And yet they did not end up any better off – their creditors were many, their purses light and the expense of long journeys made it difficult for them to return to their homelands. They had to put up with the scorn which the soldiers reserved for those among their comrades who tried to combine the theory of war with the weapons of war.[12]

If fighting soldiers, many of them also mercenaries themselves, scorned the engineers, it was for reasons of warrior pride, not because the new fortifications failed in the purposes for which they were erected, at such enormous cost and labour. The reality was quite the contrary: the bastion fortress restored the advantage of defence over offence as rapidly as cannon had reversed it at the end of the fifteenth century. By the end of the sixteenth, the frontiers of every state that aspired to preserve its sovereignty were protected at the most vulnerable points – mountain passes, river-crossings, navigable estuaries – by modern defences. The internal pattern of fortification was also altered: there were few 'star forts' in the hinterland, for kings used their monopoly of expensive artillery to push over the strongholds of their last dissident grandees and to prevent them rebuilding castles with bastions. At the frontiers, however, fortification was becoming denser than it had ever been before, and much more effective as a means both of imposing a military barrier and of defining the outlines of a government's jurisdiction. The modern frontiers of Europe are, indeed, largely the outcome of fortress-building, by which existing linguistic and the new, post-Reformation religious boundaries were teased and chivvied into neatness.

Nowhere was this more evident than in the Netherlands where 'above the rivers', the Rhine, Meuse and Scheldt, which flow together into the North Sea, the Protestant Dutch subjects of the Catholic Spanish kings (Habsburgs after 1519, who in their persons united the imperial lands of Austria, Germany and Italy as well) raised rebellion in 1566. The war, which lasted eighty years, merged with the Thirty Years' War in Germany (1618–48) and spawned such subsidiary conflicts as the campaign of the Spanish Armada against England in 1588. The Dutch were able to sustain resistance for so long for two reasons: through their access to the sea and control of the river routes upstream into central Europe they were already becoming a trading nation soon to equal Venice in wealth; and their wealth permitted them to build the fortresses that enabled them to assert their independence. The secretary to the Spanish governor, Requesens, reported in 1573 that 'the quantity of rebel towns and districts is so great that they embrace almost all of Holland and Zeeland, which are islands that can be reduced only with great difficulty or by naval forces. Indeed, if several towns decide to hold out, we shall never be able to take them.'[13] Such towns did so decide, their populations throwing up earthen bastion fortifications where stone or brick did not yet stand. Even a few such fortified places sufficed to hold the Spaniards at bay; the towns of Alkmaar and Haarlem were so strongly defended that they consumed the military effort of the whole Spanish counter-offensive in 1573.

Siege warfare was time-consuming and laborious because the means of bringing sufficient fire to bear against a bastion fortress demanded an enormous effort in excavation. The bastion fortress was a 'scientific' construction, which meant that its design was arrived at by mathematical calculation of how best to minimise the wall area that shot could strike and to maximise the area of open ground outside it that defending fire could sweep. The attack had therefore to be 'scientific' also. Siege-engineers soon worked out the principles. A trench had to be dug parallel to one side of a bastion trace, in which guns could be sheltered while they began the bombardment. Under cover of that fire, 'approach' trenches were then pushed forward until another 'parallel' could be dug closer in, to which the guns would be brought up to continue the bombardment at closer range. It was eventually found – Vauban, Louis XIV's master siege-engineer, perfected the technique in the seventeenth century – that three parallels was the necessary number to dig; from the last, sufficient weight of fire could be mounted to batter a bastion into rubble, fill the ditch with the detritus and so give the infantry massed in the last parallel the fighting chance of rushing the breach.

Infantry assault on a bastion fortress, however badly it had been knocked about, nevertheless remained always a desperate business; it was a universal defensive practice to keep handy the materials – cylindrical baskets to contain earth, called gabions, posts, rails and wooden barricades – with which an inner defence could be improvised behind a breach, while musketeers and gunners from an adjoining bastion could always direct withering fire on any assault party that crossed the ditch or even reached the sloping 'glacis' outside it. The horrors of the assault did not, however, constitute the sixteenth-century infantryman's principal objection to siege warfare. What he objected to was the labour of digging, particularly in Holland, where the water table might be struck two feet below the surface. Parma, one of the principal Spanish commanders, resorted to paying diggers extra – the practice was to become almost universal in the next few centuries – but he still 'had to do battle with the twisted pride of the Castilians, who regarded begging in the streets as more honourable than labouring for a reward'.[14]

The Spaniards nevertheless made progress during the first twenty years of the Dutch revolt, subduing the rebel towns between the Scheldt and the Meuse in what would later become northern – and Catholic – Belgium. Into the even more waterlogged country north of the Rhine and west of the Ijssel, which contained the great cities of Rotterdam, Amsterdam and Utrecht, Spain could make no progress. By 1590 the commanding general of the Dutch armies, Count Maurice of Nassau, who, with his cousins William Louis and John, was to reintroduce from classical literary models the discipline and drill of the Roman legions, had assembled sufficient force to go over to the offensive. Between 1590 and 1601 he pushed the Dutch frontier south of the Rhine, so securing such places as Breda in perpetuity for Holland and ensuring that Eindhoven would eventually fall also; meanwhile he was also reducing the Spanish garrisons in the northern Netherlands, thus clearing the way for the future kingdom of Holland to have a frontier solidly abutting against the German-speaking lands. In 1601 the Spanish caught Maurice out when he ventured beyond 'Fortress Holland' toward Ostend, a fortified Dutch outpost which they eventually took at the end of a three-year siege; however, they so exhausted themselves, financially rather than militarily, in the ensuing campaign that by 1608 they were ready to agree to a truce. It did not last the specified twelve years. By 1618 a larger war had broken out in northern Europe, the Thirty Years' War, in which gunpowder put the participants to a far more gruelling test than the static fortress battles between Dutch and Spanish had ever done.

GUNPOWDER BATTLES IN THE EXPERIMENTAL AGE

Soldiers of the fourteenth century found the mysterious power released by gunpowder far too volatile to treat it with anything but distant respect. Using it even in a primitive cannon, discharged by the application of the hot end of a long taper to the touchhole, must have demanded remarkable courage from a daring individual, all the more so if we realise that early cannon often burst from shock. To utilise gunpowder as the propellant force in a missile-throwing weapon held in the hands required, therefore, the passage of a high threshold of mistrust, anxiety and outright fear. By the mid-fifteenth century, however, some European soldiers were beginning to experiment with such a firearm and by 1550 it had come into quite general use.

The intermediary in the psychological process that allowed the soldier to move from a detached to an intimate relationship with the gunpowder weapon was the crossbow, a mechanical device which, as its clockwork was wound against a spring, stored enough energy to discharge a heavy bolt with narrow accuracy and to long range when a release mechanism, a trigger, was pulled. The crossbow, found in Chinese tombs of the fourth century BC, did not appear in Europe until the end of the thirteenth century AD, and may have been local in conception. During the fourteenth century, it came into common use on the battlefield as a potent weapon of war, most of all because of its bolt's power to penetrate armour at medium and short range.

The mechanism and shape of the crossbow readily lent itself to adaptation for gunpowder use. The crossbow's stock, which was held against the shoulder and had to be strong enough to support the sudden shock of the spring's release, provided a pattern for a similar wooden shape into which a lightened cannon barrel could be laid; the crossbow's recoil, when the trigger was pulled, would have accustomed its user to the sort of blow against the shoulder a firearm threw at the moment of detonation. The first users of firearms may well have been crossbowmen.

Commanders had never quite known, however, how best to employ crossbowmen on the battlefield, as opposed to at a siege, and they found the same difficulty with users of firearms. During the fourteenth and fifteenth centuries the English used longbowmen to great effect, but the longbow was a demanding weapon that few men had the patience to master – usually they were from remote and rustic areas; as with the composite bow, the best was brought out of it by peoples with time on their hands. The pike, or thrusting spear, was a simpler tool of war, and in the hands of hardy and fractious peasant communities from areas where the knightly class was small, such as Switzerland, could be wielded to oppose a dense barrier to cavalry attack, as long as the pikemen kept their nerve in the face of a charge. The Swiss acquired a reputation for fearlessness as pikemen and by it won during the fifteenth century both a high measure of independence from their Habsburg overlords and a name for steadfastness that brought them a living as the leading mercenaries of Europe during the next 300 years. At the 'mad battle' of St Jacob-en-Birs (1444), for example, a party of 1500 Swiss pikemen forced their way into the centre of a French army 30,000 strong and fought until all had been killed. In their battles with the Burgundians, fighting on more equal terms – Granson and Morat (1476), Nancy (1477) – they employed the same headlong phalanx-like tactics and won a series of victories that destroyed Burgundian power for good.

By the early sixteenth century, therefore, it was clear that to deploy a combination of pikemen with some missile arms – crossbow, longbow, firearm – offered a potent means of combating cavalry in an open battlefield. A better combination still was of cavalry, archers or handgunners and infantry, and it was with such a force that Charles the Rash, Duke of Burgundy, had confronted the Swiss in the battles of 1474–7; he had gone down to defeat not because his forces lacked any essential component but because his funds failed to pay an army strong enough to match that of the Swiss in numbers.[15] Nevertheless, the proportion among his different contingents – in 1471, he had 1250 armoured horsemen, 1250 pikemen, 1250 handgunners and 5000 archers – remained experimental. It may have been the wrong one, but no one as yet knew what was right. Machiavelli believed that an army should contain twenty foot-soldiers to each cavalryman, but did not specify how the infantry should be armed. A great deal of effort in the sixteenth century was devoted to establishing the correct mix.

Handgunners were clearly essential. Venice, which lived by trade and the military force necessary to protect it, decided in 1490 to replace all crossbows with gunpowder weapons and in 1508 to equip the newly formed state militia with firearms.[16] Until about 1550, however, when the prototype of the armour-penetrating musket was introduced, hand-held firearms remained relatively ineffective. They were fired by applying a burning match to an open touchhole, both prone to malfunction in wet weather, and they threw comparatively light balls only a short distance. Nevertheless they badly frightened and sometimes hurt both infantry and cavalry at close ranges, with the result that Renaissance commanders looked for some battlefield antidote. Cannon seemed best to provide it. That can be the only explanation of the unprecedented, rarely to be repeated and quite bizarre nature of the engagements at Ravenna (1512) and Marignano (1515). In each case a French and a Spanish army fought a pitched battle, freely entered into by both sides, in which the point about which they manoeuvred was formed by a large entrenchment hastily thrown up as a bastion of support for the sitting party's gunpowder weapons.

At Ravenna, the French, whose army contained a large contingent of German mercenaries, freebooters who were making the same sort of living in the Italian wars as the Greek veterans of the Peloponnesian wars had done in the Hellenistic world, advanced to check the Spaniards. The French had about fifty-four cannon, used in the mobile role, the Spanish about thirty emplaced in an entrenchment. By relentless cannonade, the French provoked the Spanish cavalry into charging, and then broke them up, but when the German mercenaries advanced they were held up at the entrenchment and a desperate hand-to-hand struggle ensued. Eventually two French cannon were brought round to the rear of the Spanish position, and their fire panicked the Spaniards into retreat.

Three years later, the roles were reversed. At Marignano it was the French who were entrenched while the enemy, a Swiss force serving the Spanish alliance, advanced to contact; they did this so rapidly – a characteristic of their headstrong style of giving battle – that they got into the entrenchment before the French artillery could make its effect felt. The Swiss were repulsed by a counter-attack but reorganised and next morning attacked again. (Marignano is an unusually early example of a battle lasting more than one day.) By then, the French artillery was well prepared and the battle at the entrenchment degenerated into a bloody stalemate that ended only when a force of Venetians, French allies, approached from the rear and menaced the Swiss into withdrawal.

Fire

Disengaging as rapidly as they had attacked, they drew clear; but their losses had been so heavy that they shortly afterward accepted the French offer of a negotiated peace, by which was laid the basis of the relationship under which Switzerland became the principal supplier of mercenaries to the French army for the next 250 years.[17]

What made Ravenna and Marignano so extraordinary was that the combatants chose to fight battles in the open field as if they were extempore sieges – the consequence, it would seem, of contemporary commanders not having thought out a better way of using artillery than from behind improvised siegeworks. They had recognised the power of artillery to disrupt the traditional offensive purpose both of cavalry and of infantry in phalanx, which was the formation in which the Swiss fought; they could not as yet improve on those tactics for their own offensive purposes.

In fact, an alternative method was available. At Cerignola (1503), the French had been repulsed from a Spanish entrenched position by the firepower of the Spanish handgunners, and at Bicocca (1522) the outcome was repeated; 3000 Swiss infantry, fighting on the French side, were killed in half an hour of senseless aggression against Spanish entrenchments strongly defended with firearms. The experience deterred the Swiss, despite their reputation for disregard of danger on the battlefield, from ever again attacking handgunners positioned behind an obstacle.

Yet it was clear that giving battle could not persist for ever along lines where one side entrenched itself and awaited attack. By so doing the entrenched army tied itself to a particular spot, which its enemy might decide to bypass in order to despoil friendly countryside or attack isolated fortresses at leisure. The invitation to battle pitched in such an extreme form would bring on an engagement only if the other side accepted the challenge; if it chose to conduct mobile operations, the defender would have to do likewise. The prosecution of mobile operations with artillery and firearms demanded, therefore, a change in the cultural attitude of Renaissance armies. Though they had admitted gunpowder technology to their traditional practices, they had not adjusted to its logic. Like the Mamelukes who bore down, sword in hand, on the firearms of the Egyptian sultan's black slaves, they were still trapped in an ethos which accorded warrior status only to horsemen and to infantry prepared to stand and fight with edged weapons. Fighting at a distance with missiles was beneath the descendants of the armoured men-at-arms who had dominated European warmaking since the age of Charlemagne. They wanted to fight from horseback, as their grandfathers had done, and they wanted such infantrymen as accompanied them to bear the manly risks of standing to receive cavalry at point of pike. If guns had to take their place on the battlefield, then let it be behind ramparts, which was where missile weapons had always belonged. What the horse soldier did not want to see was the sturdy footman reduced to the level of the cunning crossbow mercenary: what he wanted to do even less was dismount and learn the black art of gunpowder himself.

The cultural roots of the mounted aristocrats' resistance to the gun-powder revolution went deep into the past. As we have seen, the Greeks of the phalanx age were the first warriors of whom we have detailed knowledge who cast aside the evasiveness of primitive warfare and confronted their like-minded enemies face-to-face. Not for them the preliminaries of the 'conflict of champions' that, in a variety of forms, we find in the warfare of tribal peoples and that provide the high points of Homer's account of the Trojan War. The Greeks of the classical age sought to settle an issue by the quickest and most direct means possible. The Romans of the early republic accepted the logic of Greek methods also, indeed probably learnt them from the Greek colonists of southern Italy. One might suppose that it was the Romans' encounter with first the Gauls, then the Teutonic peoples from beyond the Rhine, which progressively transmitted the habit of face-to-face fighting to them as well. The Romans gave testimony that the northerners fought in such a way, for, though they despised their crude, individualistic tactics, they never denied their courage or readiness to come to hand strokes. 'Many of [the Helvetii],' Caesar observed, of an episode when his legionaries had peppered the enemy's shields with javelins, 'after a number of vain efforts at disentangling themselves preferred to drop their shields and fight with no protection for their bodies.' It was only when 'the wounds and the toil of battle [became] too much for them [that] they began to retire'.[18] However, it seems clear that the Gauls fought face-to-face before they even met the Romans, if the great swords of the Hallstatt culture offer any indication, and it appears that the Germans, whose courageous and warlike nature so impressed Tacitus, were also doing so before they met the Romans on the Rhine in the first century AD. If we recall that it was only after the arrival of the Dorians in Greece that phalanx warfare developed, and accept that the Dorians probably made their way thither from the Danube, then it may be that we can locate there both a common point of origin for this 'Western way of war', as Victor Hanson calls it, and a line of division between that battle tradition and the indirect, evasive and stand-off style of combat characteristic of the steppe and the Near and Middle East: east of the steppe and south-east of the Black Sea, warriors continued to keep their distance from their enemies; west of the steppe and south-west of the Black Sea, warriors learned to abandon caution and to close to arm's length.

The reason for this final abandonment of the psychology and conventions of primitivism in the West and for their persistence elsewhere baffles analysis. The line of division follows that prevailing between climatic, vegetation and topographical zones quite closely though the linguistic division much less exactly: Greeks, Romans, Teutons and Celts spoke Indo-European languages, but the Iranian peoples, who did so as well, did not join them in choosing to surrender the bow for the spear or the sword, preferring instead to persist in reliance on missile weapons and the tactics of rapid strike and swift disengagement. It seems dangerous to ascribe any racial explanation to the phenomenon. During the nineteenth century, both the Zulus and the Japanese acquired the disciplines of Western-style combat apparently from first principles and certainly by their own effort. All that can be said is that, if there is such a thing as the 'military horizon', there is also a 'face-to-face' combat frontier, and that Westerners belong by tradition on one side of it, and most other peoples on the other.

The force of this face-to-face tradition provoked the warrior crisis of the sixteenth century. The attitude to crossbowmen of Bayard, *chevalier sans peur et sans reproche*, is well known; he had them executed when taken prisoner, on the ground that their weapon was a cowardly one and their behaviour treacherous. Armed with a crossbow a man might, without any of the long apprenticeship to arms necessary to make a knight, and equally without the moral effort required of a pike-wielding footman, kill either of them from a distance without putting himself in danger. What was true of the crossbowman was even more true of the handgunner; the way he fought seemed equally cowardly, and noisy and dirty as well, while requiring no muscular effort whatsoever. 'What is the use, any more,' asked the biographer of the sixteenth-century warrior Louis de la Tremouille, 'of the skill-at-arms of the knights, their strength, their hardihood, their discipline and their desire for honour when such [gunpowder] weapons may be used in war?'[19]

Yet, for all the protests of the traditional warrior class, it was clear by the mid-sixteenth century that firearms as well as cannon had come to stay. The arquebus and the heavier musket, both fired by a mechanism which brought a slow match to the priming-pan by the release of a trigger, were efficient weapons, the latter capable of penetrating armour at 200–240 paces. The foot-soldier's breastplate was of decreasing value as a means of protection; even more ominously, so was the horseman's full armour. By the end of the century it was no longer worn, and cavalry itself was losing its decisive purpose on the battlefield. That purpose had always been equivocal; the effect of a cavalry charge had always depended more on the moral frailty of those receiving it than on the objective power of horse and rider. And once the horseman encountered an opponent who could muster the resolve to stand, as the Swiss pikemen had found, or a weapon that could bring a rider to the ground with certainty, as the musket could, the right of the knightly class to determine how armies should be ordered, and to retain an equivalent social pre-eminence, was called into question. In France and Germany, the aristocracies held out against the pressure 'to dismount in order to stiffen foot soldiery', but the facts of life were not on their side, and neither were the state paymasters, who increasingly wanted value for money.[20] In England, Italy and Spain the traditional military class were readier to scent the changed direction in which the breeze was blowing, to embrace the new technology of gunpowder and to persuade itself that to fight on foot might be an honourable calling after all.

In Spain the 'hidalgo' – son of somebody – most enthusiastically accepted the logic of the gunpowder tradition, perhaps because it was the Spanish who, in this experimental age, found themselves with the largest wars on their hands. In the Italian wars of the first half of the century they were situated in an environment where cannon dominated without argument. The multiplicity of ingeniously fortified places which the Italian siege-engineers had built to withstand artillery attack meant that soldiers who were not masters of the low art of gunnery could not keep the field; while in the waterlogged theatre of war in the Netherlands, cavalry automatically yielded first place to infantry, which alone had the freedom to manoeuvre in the narrow spaces between canals, estuaries and walled towns. Young Spanish noblemen readily accepted commissions as infantry officers in the Dutch wars, fighting with regulars enlisted in Spain itself and large contingents of mercenaries hired in Italy, Burgundy, Germany and the British Isles; they thus initiated a precedent that, in the eighteenth century, would make vacant places in the regiments of British, French, Russian and Prussian foot guards the most eagerly competed for by well-born young men with military ambitions.[21]

GUNPOWDER AT SEA

While armies were hesitantly and reluctantly adapting themselves to the coming of gunpowder, European mariners were adjusting to its implications in an altogether more positive spirit. The transportation of cannon on land may have confronted military quartermasters, forever strapped for means to transport heavy loads along bad roads or none, with a new, all but insoluble problem; seagoing warriors found no comparable difficulty. On the contrary: ships and cannon were made for each other. The cannon's weight was easily accommodated in what by design was a load-bearing vehicle, while the cannon's necessaries, ball and powder, could easily be housed in its cargo-carrying spaces. The only complication that the cannon imposed on the shipwright was that of absorbing its recoil within a vessel's confined dimensions. On land, a cannon's recoil was expended when it ran back on its wheels at the moment of discharge; at sea, the necessary room was not available. If mounted free, its firing would damage the ship's timbers, perhaps even knock a hole in the side or bring down a mast. It had to be harnessed to the structure and its recoil either decelerated by a braking-mechanism or else transferred to the ship's own line of least resistance.

The latter was the solution adopted by the galley-masters who first embarked cannon in the Mediterranean. The Mediterranean galley had an ancient lineage, which ascended at least to the oared ships of the Egyptians and the 'Sea Peoples' who first fought in open waters during the second millennium BC. Since the greater part of its long, narrow hull was filled by oarsmen, cannon might be mounted only at the bow or stern; since shipwrights had been familiar since the time of the Persian wars with the practice of strengthening the bow to permit ramming, it was there that they placed the cannon. When fired, the recoil was partly absorbed by the ship itself, which, if in motion at the moment of firing, was imperceptibly slowed by the shock of discharge, if at rest was driven slightly backward; it was later found desirable, as a means of absorbing primary recoil, for the largest centre-line cannon to be so mounted as to slide backward on a platform.[22]

It was with galleys so armed that the battles for control of the eastern Mediterranean were fought between the Ottoman Turks and their Christian enemies during the first half of the sixteenth century. After the Ottomans had captured Constantinople (1453), then effectively all that remained to the Byzantines of their once great possessions, they had concentrated their formidable energies on consolidating what had once been the eastern Roman empire into one of their own. Serbia came under Ottoman control in 1439, Albania in 1486 and the Peloponnese in 1499. Internal troubles then checked the Ottoman advance, but the undisputed succession as sultan of Selim I in 1512 led to the crushing of Safavid Persia in 1514 and the conquest of Egypt from the Mamelukes the following year. Thus by 1515 the borders of Ottoman territory ran from the Danube to the lower Nile and from the headwaters of the Tigris and Euphrates to the shores of the Adriatic, enclosing an area almost as large as that which the Byzantines had controlled on the eve of the great Arab offensive in the seventh century. Selim's son Suleiman, 'the Magnificent', who succeeded in 1520, set out to make the area of Ottoman control even wider. He captured Rhodes, then held by the Hospitaller order (1522), and, in an extended offensive into the Balkans, seized Belgrade (1521), destroyed the armed power of the Hungarian kingdom at the battle of Mohacs (1526) and in 1529 arrived under the walls of Vienna to challenge the Habsburg empire in the first great Ottoman siege of that city.

Meanwhile the Turks were also taking to the sea to push their advance westward against Christendom. They had already raided deep into the Adriatic to outflank the Habsburgs from the east and to serve warning on Venice that it maintained its island possessions in the Aegean only on sufferance. Christendom struck back. In 1532, Andrea Doria, admiral of the great trading city of Genoa, raided the Peloponnese, and when a second Holy League of Spain, Venice and the Papal States was formed in 1538 to contest both the Ottoman threat in the Mediterranean and that of France (which in 1536 entered into an expedient alliance with the Turks) in Italy, he became the chief of the combined fleet. The tide of battle swung wildly from end to end of the inland sea. In 1535 the great Turkish admiral Khair ed-Din took Tunis and, though driven out by Doria, then defeated him in the battle of Preveza off the western coast of Greece (1538). This victory freed the Turkish fleet to raid deeply into the western Mediterranean in the following years, as far as Nice, not then French (1543), and Spanish Minorca (1558). Despite some successful Christian counter-attacks against the Muslim pirate ports on the North African coast – notably at Djerba in 1560 – the balance of advantage lay with the Turks who, in Greece and Albania, had found an ample supply of Christian galley oarsmen willing to serve for pay. Venice and Spain, more dependent on slaves and crim-inals, had difficulty in matching their numbers. All that stood between the Ottomans and free use of the Mediterranean for offensive purposes was the island of Malta. Malta, dominating the straits that divide the eastern and western Mediterranean at the point where Sicily and North Africa adjoin, had been turned by the Hospitaller knights into a mighty fortress, but its strength was not equalled by their number. Besieged in May 1565, the fortress held out against a combined land and sea attack until September but was relieved only by the intervention of a Spanish fleet. The Ottomans' achievement of complete control of the Mediterranean had only narrowly been averted. The threat was finally ended at Lepanto, the Holy League's victory over the Turkish fleet off the Peloponnese in 1571, and then rather because of the crippling loss to the Turks of a high proportion of their corps of trained composite bowmen than because of a loss of ships, which was swiftly made good.

Mediterranean galley warfare, as the historian John Guilmartin has made so brilliantly clear, remained essentially what it had been for two millennia, an amphibious undertaking in which not only were the sea battles a variant of contemporary land battles, but the campaigns themselves were normally an extension of operations on shore. Armies and fleets accompanied each other by coastwise movement as far as possible, seeking to engage the enemy only when the inshore flank of the fleet locked with that of the army, or vice versa, preferably at a point where a fortified place could lend artillery support to both. Lepanto was an exception; in so far as a battle fought in inshore waters can be called a true naval engagement, Lepanto was that. It was won, however, not by ramming, not even by weight of artillery, but by clash of arms at short range between the shipboard soldiers of either side. The Christians had embarked arquebusiers and musketeers; the Ottomans opposed them with men using the traditional Turkish weapon, the composite bow. It was their loss – Turkish fatal casualties totalled 30,000 out of 60,000 men engaged – that made Lepanto the turning-point in Mediterranean affairs that it was. The lack of skilled naval archers, irreplaceable in a single generation, since it was a life's work to master the necessary skills, 'signified the end of a golden age of Ottoman power . . . Lepanto marked the death of a living tradition that could not be reconstituted.'[23]

Outside the Mediterranean, the contest at sea between armed ships was taking a different form, one in which the issue was decided not by bow-mounted cannon and the personal weapons of an embarked fighting-force, but instead by a great battery of artillery that filled the whole ship itself. Merchant craft had not hitherto been thought suitable for naval use, since their lack of oars, slow speed under sail and ungainly bulk unfitted them to mingle with galleys in maritime battle. In confined waters they offered easy prey, either to ramming or to bombardment from a quarter where the wind would not carry them. But in oceanic waters, the advantages were reversed. Not only were galleys unsuited by their extreme length and shallow keels to the long swells of the ocean; their need to revictual their large crews at short intervals by return to port meant that they could not keep the seas for more than a few days at a time, even if weather permitted. The load-carrying sailing-ship of northern waters, built to withstand those rougher seas, was under no such disadvantage, since its deep hull held rations and water-casks ample to supply a large crew for months at a stretch. Its defect was of a different order: since bow-mounted guns could be brought to bear only when the wind was behind, and there was no guarantee that the enemy would appear downwind, any artillery embarked would have to be fired through ports cut in the ship's sides, an arrangement that required both its own ancillary technology, in the form of a braking-mechanism to absorb recoil, and the devising of a new way of handling ships in battle.

With an adaptability akin to that shown by fortress-engineers on land, shipwrights solved the problem almost as soon as it was presented to them. The small fifteenth-century cannon had been housed in 'castles' built at bow and stem. When 'great guns' were developed at the beginning of the sixteenth century, they were placed below decks, equipped with rope tackle to prevent their careering out of control when discharged, and positioned to fire 'broadside'. The first ship so constructed is generally held to be the English *Mary Rose* of 1513; by 1545 an English ship like the *Great Harry* was mounting heavy artillery on two decks; and by 1588 great fleets of ships so equipped fought a running battle up the English Channel lasting seven days.[24]

The resulting defeat of the Spanish Armada, decisive though it was in determining the balance of advantage between Protestant and Catholic powers in the sixteenth-century wars of religion, is less representative of the significance of the armed sailing-ship, however, than the oceanic voyages of the Portuguese, Spanish, English and Dutch to the Americas, Africa, Indies and Pacific from the end of the fifteenth century onward. Sailing-ships of the northern European type, which shed dependence on the auxiliary power of oars and proceeded under sail alone, carried Columbus to America in 1492 and then the conquistadors who destroyed the civilisations of the Aztecs of Mexico, the Maya of Yucatan and the Incas of Peru. Horses rather than cannon were the important cargoes of the conquistadors in their campaigns of conquest – Cortés disembarked seventeen in Mexico in 1517, Montejo fifty in Yucatan in 1527 and Pisarro twenty-seven in Peru in 1531 – since the species, wiped out in the Western Hemisphere by the hunters of the original migrations 12,000 years earlier, was terrifyingly strange to the native warriors. Their ritualised style of combat also unfitted them to confront Europeans who

338

fought to win rather than to take sacrificial captives; but, in a contest of hundreds against thousands, it was their horses that gave the invaders the decisive advantage.

Elsewhere, cannon were the key weapons of the European maritime adventurers. In 1517 the Portuguese learned at Jiddah, in the Red Sea, whither they had sailed round the Cape of Good Hope, that it was too dangerous to close with a local (in this case Mameluke) fleet supported by cannon on shore, and their attempt to block the maritime spice route into the western Islamic lands therefore failed. Yet they had already established a naval supremacy in the Indian Ocean by their victories at Ormuz (1507) – the choke point through which Gulf oil is shipped today – and at Diu on the west coast of India (1509).[25] Soon they would reach out to establish bases in the East Indies (1511), and China (1557), and then to contest possession of the Philippines with Spain. By the end of the century, the cannon-armed forts the Iberian seafaring nations had planted along the coasts of all the world's oceans were claim stakes of empires that were to grow during the next 300 years.

The societies which the first European navigators encountered had few means with which to oppose their demands, first, for trading-rights, then for land on which to build trading-posts, finally for exclusive trading-rights enforced by military control. African coastal kingdoms, protected by a disease barrier, survived intact into the nineteenth century, but only at the cost of complicity in an ever-expanding and horribly destructive slave-gathering trade into the hinterland. The Japanese preserved their traditional society by closing their maritime borders and defying the Europeans to test their hardihood in battle against that of the *samurai*. China was protected from dissection by its enormous size and bureaucratic coherence. Much of the rest of the world proved easy prey. In the Americas, which the Spanish and Portuguese intended to colonise from the start, native societies had no effective means of resistance, not even an appropriate state of mind, with which to oppose their military power. The small sultanates of the East Indies were easily overcome, while most of the Filipinos whom the Spanish encountered were simple tribal cultivators. Only in India was there a state system organised at a level adequate to deny the Europeans intrusive footholds; yet even the Moghuls, since they were recent conquerors whose control at the periphery was not absolute, failed to exclude them altogether. Moreover, no Moghul emperor succeeded in organising a seagoing, cannon-armed fleet, the only guarantee of a coastline's security against its European equivalent.

If the navigators found little to resist them beyond the sea frontiers of the Ottoman lands, that did not mean they voyaged unopposed. On the contrary: the prizes at stake were so rich that they were rapidly driven to fighting each other, both in distant seas and in home waters, whence the expeditions to the lands of gold and spices originated. The Dutch first arrived on the Coromandel coast of India in 1601 and the English eight years later. Soon they were both fighting the Portuguese in the Indian Ocean – the Dutch fought them also off Brazil in 1624-9 – and then each other in the English Channel and North Sea in three great naval wars of 1652-74. Both nations also fell into conflict with the Spanish over trading-rights in the Caribbean which, after the introduction of sugar cane from the Canaries and slaves from Africa to raise it, was to grow into the richest colonial area in the world; and then with the French who, latecomers to voyaging, established trading-posts in India and West Africa and the beginnings of an overseas empire in North America by the mid-seventeenth century.

These gunpowder wars at sea, fought broadside with ships that by 1650 mounted fifty guns apiece in fleets seventy or more strong, emphasised the power of artillery even more strikingly than did fortress warfare on land. The best siege-engineer might take weeks to reduce a well built citadel; in the Three Days' Battle off southern England (1653), the Dutch lost twenty warships (out of seventy-five) and 3000 men killed, a result fairly representative of how intensive action at sea had become and a warning that worse was in store. By the end of the eighteenth century the largest sailing-ships would mount a hundred cannon, while losses in the Franco-Spanish fleet that fought at Trafalgar (1805), a one-day battle, exceeded 7000 dead. The warrior culture of the pikeman and the man on horseback had migrated to sea, where sailor-cannoneers stood by their guns in a hundred point-blank battles with all the steadfastness of the hoplite in the phalanx.

GUNPOWDER STABILITY

The demands made by the warfare of seaborne artillery on the courage and skill of European mariners were scarcely to vary between the appearance of the 'great ship' of the early sixteenth century and the eclipse of its direct and easily recognisable descendant, the ship-of-the-line, by the steam-powered ironclad in the mid-nineteenth century. On land, however, the developing capabilities of gunpowder weapons were to perturb soldiers throughout the sixteenth and seventeenth centuries. The mobility and firepower of cannon continued to increase, to a point where lighter pieces were actually being deployed with effect in the battlefield by the end of the seventeenth century.[26] By about the same date, the firepower and handiness of the musket also improved, allowing it to be fired without a rest; a new flintlock mechanism was less susceptible to damp than the old slow match. Yet the difficulty of arriving at the correct proportion between 'shot' and pike in the infantry, and then between infantry and cavalry, persisted.

Cavalry, challenged by shot, sought to perpetuate its battlefield role by adopting an ever more elaborate horsemastership – akin in its complexity to the *furusiyya* of the Mamelukes – which, by a routine of wheeling and caracole, was supposed to facilitate the use of firearms from horseback (the routines survive at the Spanish riding school in Vienna). The experiment was not successful. Firearms and horses do not mix, and in any case the infantry responded by elaborating its own tactics so effectively as to rob horsemen of the chance to catch musketeers at a disadvantage. That was indeed part of the reason why armies retained pikemen, in a proportion of one to two as against musketeers, well into the seventeenth century. Pikemen could deny room for manoeuvre to cavalry that threatened a battle line with sword or pistol, while protected by musketeers who held their fire to contest a charge.

Nevertheless, pikemen and musketeers could not simultaneously occupy the same space, and, while their weapons complemented each other, they could not do the same work. The battles of the Thirty Years' War (1618–48) in Germany, involving the armies of the French, Swedes and Habsburgs, were in consequence confused and messy affairs; Gustavus Adolphus, the Swedish soldier-king, was killed at Lützen (1632) precisely because he rode his horse into a static struggle between musketeers and cavalrymen. The solution to the difficulty, however, lay at hand. At the end of the seventeenth century all European armies almost simultaneously adopted a new attachment to the musket, the ring bayonet, which permitted it to serve as pike and firearm simultaneously.[27]

Yet it was not the musket-bayonet combination alone that gave eighteenth-century battles their distinctive character. Even more important was the universalisation of infantry drill. Drill had ancient origins. It is conjectured that the Macedonians drilled their phalanxes, though the simplicity of phalanx tactics makes that hard to credit. The Romans certainly subjected the legionary recruits to the school of arms, teaching them to throw their javelins at a mark and to wield shield and sword in uniform style. Nevertheless, it is most unlikely that a Roman legion's evolutions in formation, whether it was in contact with the enemy or not, resembled in any way at all those of a musket-bayonet force. The Romans did not practise the cadenced stop – a style of marching not possible for soldiers to learn until governments created large, level parade grounds in the eighteenth century – while the exertions of muscle-power fighting cannot be narrowly regularised; it seems that the legionary was encouraged to pick an individual target for his javelin.[28]

Gunpowder drill had an altogether different end in view. It undoubtedly originated in a natural concern of musketeers – which must have been felt by archers also (an unexplored subject) – not to wound each other while using their weapons. Whereas the archer risked impaling only a single neighbour, musketeers ranked in close order, especially in the early days when they scattered loose powder near to burning slow matches, threatened to set off a chain of accidental discharges unless all the men performed the many steps of loading, aiming and firing in exact unison. The musketry drill books – equivalents, in their way, of industrial safety manuals of a later age – which were widely printed from the early seventeenth century onward, divide the sequence into numerous precise actions – forty-seven in Maurice of Orange's drill book of 1607 – from the moment when the musketeer takes up his weapon to that when he pulls the trigger.

Still, the seventeenth-century musketeer was an individualist. He may not have chosen his moment to fire, but he probably chose his own target in the opposing ranks. By the eighteenth century, that freedom was disappearing. The musketeers of the royal regiments which had come into existence after the end of the Thirty Years' War – the most senior of the Austrian, Prussian and British armies, for example, were raised in 1696, 1656 and 1662, respectively – were trained to aim not at a man but at the mass of the enemy; drill sergeants, carrying an otherwise obsolete half-pike, used it to knock the muzzles of the front rank's muskets to an equal level, so that when the order to fire was given, the bullets, in theory at least, departed at a uniform height above the ground to strike a simultaneous blow across the front of the rank opposite.[29]

The soldier's loss of individualism was made manifest in numerous other ways. From the end of the seventeenth century he wore uniform clothing, as household servants did. The idea of uniform was indeed the same as that of livery. It marked its wearer out as someone in the servile employment of a master and, therefore, as a person of restricted rights and liberties. The sixteenth-century soldier gloried in the diversity of his raiment, often collected by looting; indeed, the Renaissance fashion of slashing the outer garment to display the silks and velvets worn underneath had been adopted precisely to demonstrate that a soldier could take fine things as he pleased and wear them with impunity. Their leaders indulged them. 'It was argued that soldiers should be free to choose their own clothes . . . they were thought more likely to fight bravely and cheerfully that way.'[30] Eighteenth-century soldiers were expected to fight not cheerfully but dutifully and on command; to enforce discipline, officers treated their men with a harshness that neither the free pikemen nor the mercenaries of the sixteenth and seventeenth centuries would have tolerated. They had accepted hanging or disfigurement as the arbitrary penalty for mutiny or murder, but they would not have accepted the regime of statutory flogging or casual beating by which the liveried military servants of the dynastic monarchies were kept in order.

Indeed, only an entirely different sort of individual from the anarchistic freebooters of the Italian wars and the Thirty Years' War would have acquiesced in the new regime. A high proportion of the soldiers of the seventeeth-century civil wars in France had been 'outlaws, vagabonds, thieves, murderers, deniers of God, renouncers of debts', who drifted into military service because they had turned their backs on civil life and it on them.[31] Not all, of course, belonged to those debased categories. The Spanish and, especially, the Swedes (the latter through the *Indelingsverket* system of military smallholding) succeeded in enlisting steady men from villages or farms to form their regular regiments, but 'scum' was what mercenary employers generally got. The dynastic monarchies got something else, often the younger sons of large, poor families to whom civil employment offered few opportunities, whom a notional form of conscription generally brought into the army, particularly in France; in Prussia and Russia, where the peasantry was widely enserfed from the seventeenth century onward, outright compulsion applied.[32] Though its organisers might have denied it, we can recognise this as a military slave system, close in character to that of the Ottoman janissary force, recruited by levy and kept in obedience by harsh discipline and an almost complete denial of civil rights to its members. The style of fighting it practised, that of stereotyped, almost mechanical drill-movements performed in serried ranks, exactly reflected the surrender of individuality its members had undergone.

The officers in these royal armies, too, surrendered much of the personal freedom that their real or imagined knightly ancestors had enjoyed. From the early seventeenth century onward, 'the riotousness and restlessness of younger members of noble families' had prompted Venice to set up a number of military academies to inculcate some discipline and professional learning among what would soon be recognised as, if not actually named, 'the officer class'. The reforms of Maurice, John and William of Nassau accelerated the process. Their deliberate return to the sources of classical military teaching, which resulted in a conscious effort to revive the spirit and structure of the Roman legions, led both to the emergence of a body of professional drillmasters, ready, like the fortification-engineers, to sell their knowledge on the international market, and to the establishment of military schools, designed to teach hot-headed young aristocrats parade-ground drill, fencing and advanced equitation and, in the process, to educate, even civilise them.

John of Nassau's *schola militaris* at Siegen, which existed only between 1617 and 1623, is reckoned to have been the first true military academy in Europe; 'its chief emphasis was in turning out technically competent infantry officers'. Professor John Hale has identified five other military academies founded in France and Germany between 1570 and 1629, and, while none can be counted as the ancestor of those which survive to our own day – St Cyr, Sandhurst, Breda, the Maria-Theresianer and Modena, which date from the eighteenth and early nineteenth centuries – their creation marks the coming of an idea, or at least its rebirth: that leadership in war, as the Romans had believed, required civic as well as military virtues.[33] This was a more significant development than the parallel trend to train young men from the emergent middle-class in artillery and engineer academies, the first of which was founded by Louis XIV at Metz in 1668. A mastery of mathematics was clearly essential to future gunners and sappers. The imposition of rote-learning, examination in the classical texts and the threat of the rod on young bloods were innovations of a different order. They spelled the end to the days when falconry, hunting and the joust were reckoned the only upbringing of which a warrior stood in need.[34]

Drill, discipline, mechanical tactics, scientific gunnery all worked to make eighteenth-century warmaking quite different in character from the chaotically experimental style of the sixteenth and seventeenth centuries. By 1700 the weapons with which battles were fought had assumed a form that did not alter for 150 years. The infantry was armed with a musket which, though almost harmless to combatants at ranges much above a hundred yards, could be used in mass volley-firing to create a deadly killing-zone immediately to the front of the battle line. Increasingly mobile and quick-firing field artillery offered the only certain means of shaking the solidity of drilled infantry formations; its safe deployment, however, could be threatened by the timely unleashing of cavalry, which was increasingly committed to that subordinate activity, and to charging against infantry disorganised by artillery fire or harrying fugitives driven to flight.

The opposed properties of these three elements of eighteenth-century armies, musketry, artillery, cavalry, thus brought about a strange equilibrium on pitched battlefields, leading to what Professor Russell Weigley has identified as a persistent indecisiveness in the succession of struggles fought by the dynastic monarchies in western Europe, usually over rights of succession, between the last Dutch wars at the end of the seventeenth century and the outbreak of the French Revolution. Time and again, the liveried musketeers arrayed themselves in dense formation, fired their volleys, reeled under artillery fire, repelled or more infrequently ran from cavalry, but at the end of the day parted from each other on the battlefield with their power to fight again still intact. The 'great' battles of the heyday of dynastic warfare – Blenheim (1704), Fontenoy (1745), Leuthen (1757) – were notable rather for the number of casualties suffered among the docile ranks of the participants than for any permanency of outcome achieved. It was an exhaustion of reserves of money and manpower that brought eighteenth-century wars to an end rather than decision by clash of arms.

In an effort to diminish the indecisiveness of their warmaking, European armies turned increasingly to the enlistment of traditional warrior peoples as the century drew on, hoping that their irregular methods would sharpen the offensive qualities of the liveried masses. Magyar light cavalrymen – hussars – were recruited from Hungary, sharpshooters from the forests and mountains of central Europe, and Christian refugees (loosely known as 'Albanians') from the Ottoman Balkans; the plot of Mozart's opera *Così fan tutte* turns on the allure these exotic strangers could exert on the civilised imagination. In practice, they could be found in numbers too small to shift the balance of advantage either way, and, though their recruitment set a pattern that persisted into the nineteenth century, when the opportunity to lead units of North African Zouaves, Bosnian Muslims, Tyrolese Jäger, Punjabi Sikhs and Nepalese Gurkhas would appeal to the instincts of the most dashing among young French, Austrian and British officers, their appearance on the flanks of the regulars made more for visual spectacle – the 'Turkish' costume of the Zouaves was one of the most potent sartorial influences of the nineteenth century – than for objective effect. Exotic irregulars were most useful in 'small wars' overseas; German light infantry in British service gave as good as they got against the riflemen of the American Revolutionary armies, while native Americans – 'Red Indians' – armed with European weapons humiliated regulars in the depths of the great forests.

Yet, paradoxically, armies drilled to European standards came off best in wars in which traditional warrior peoples formed the bulk of the enemy. By the end of the seventeenth century the Ottoman offensive into Europe had reached its term largely because the Habsburgs had succeeded in creating a regular army of a quality good enough to meet the Sultan's janissaries on equal terms. The janissaries – the word came from the Turkish for 'new soldiers' – were enslaved on the Mameluke pattern but, unlike them, were recruited in the Balkans through a forced levy (the *devsirme*) of Christian children who were trained as infantry.[35] 'New soldiers' the janissaries may originally have been by comparison with their Western equivalents, but by the end of the seventeenth century their discipline and steadfastness in battle were matched by that of the European regulars, whose drill, moreover, was superior to theirs. At the siege of Vienna in 1683 the janissaries made Europe tremble; twenty-five years later they had been driven out of southern Hungary and northern Serbia and their master was forced to sign a peace, that of Karlowitz (1699), which marked the beginning of the great Ottoman retreat to Constantinople that ended with the Balkan wars of 1911–12.

In the Islamic lands beyond Europe, particularly the Moghul domains in India, no local army had been brought to a janissary level of efficiency. India had been full of Turkish mercenary artillerists and siege-engineers since the beginning of the sixteenth century – the Turks, as their magnificent citadel at Belgrade still testifies, built fortifications as impressive as any in the West – and from the seventeenth century by English, Dutch, French and Swiss gunnery experts as well. In the eighteenth century the Moghuls began to want drillmasters, whom the French largely supplied, but the Moghul ethos, rooted in the steppe tradition, nullified their efforts. Babur (1483–1530), the founder of the Moghul dynasty, believed that a 'cavalry army could fight set-piece battles successfully without having an infantry "core"'. Sir Thomas Roe, English ambassador to the Moghul court between 1615 and 1619, accordingly thought its forces 'an effeminat army, fitter to be a spoyle than a terror to enemys', and told his colleagues at Constantinople, 'I see no souldiers, though multitudes entertayned in that quality.'[36] 'Quality' versus 'multitudes' proved the Moghuls' undoing: when the British in the mid-eighteenth century began to recruit and train Hindus, untouched by steppe attitudes, they rapidly produced an army whose standard of infantry drill compensated for its small numbers. At Plassey (1757), the victory on which British empire over India was to be raised, Clive's 1100 Europeans and 2100 Hindu sepoys, encircled by 50,000 Moghul infantry and cavalry, easily dispersed them with steady musketry and chased them as fugitives from the field. Drill and legionary organisation there achieved everything to which the Nassau cousins had looked forward 150 years earlier, but only because their effects came as a shock, in the true sense, to soldiers of an alternative tradition who were unprepared to withstand it.

POLITICAL REVOLUTION AND MILITARY CHANGE

Drill, and the ethos that underlay it, won spectacular victories in India, even against soldiers armed with muskets and cannon identical to those of their European opponents: Plassey and a dozen similar battles continued to lend weight to the arguments of those who held that moral factors outweigh material ones in war by three to one – Napoleon's estimate – or more. In other battles overseas, where the opponents were technically matched, notably those between the British and the American colonists and the Spanish and theirs, drill was outweighed as a determinant of outcomes by another moral factor altogether: the sense of legitimacy felt by European emigrants in fighting for what they regarded as their right to self-taxation and so to self-government. The North American colonists' war with Britain, which inspired that of the South Americans against Spain, was the first truly political war, a war detached from the traditional motivations of religious difference or usurpation of legal rights, fought to achieve recognition of abstract principles and to win not merely independence but the freedom to found a new and, it was hoped, superior society. The struggle for freedom was not short. Perhaps only a third of the colonists were actively committed; another third remained neutral and the remaining third held loyal to the old order. The army that the revolutionaries raised was at first weak and poorly armed. Based on the colonial militias, raised to defend the original colonies against attack by the native Americans and later by the French of Canada, it was hard pressed to stand against the discipline of the British regulars and achieved success largely by its ability to confront them with threat at many different points inside the vast space of the North American theatre of war. The colonists, moreover, had the confidence to take the offensive to the enemy whenever the chance offered – in 1775 they actually invaded Canada to strike at the stronghold of Quebec – while in 1779 and 1781 they transferred operations to the interior, campaigning as far away as the Ohio River and the central Carolinas. This strategy caused the British to disperse their efforts and robbed them of their chief advantage, which was the ability to deploy force against the main coastal centres of population by sea. That advantage was further eroded by the intervention of the Spanish and the French, Britain's European enemies; the despatch of a French expeditionary force and of a large fleet in 1780 was what eventually turned the tide, leading to the surrender of the main British army at Yorktown in October 1781.

Yet, despite foreign assistance, the victory was unquestionably the Americans' own and the example they gave was a major stimulus to the demands laid by the French constitutionalists against Louis XVI when, in 1789, he was finally compelled to summon his subjects, unassembled for more than a century, to agree a new system of taxation. French revenues had been exhausted, and the French fiscal system overborne, by the demands of incessant royal warmaking throughout the eighteenth century; the costs of French naval and military support to the American colonists in their war with the British had been the final straw.[37] Warmaking, except for outright predators in the steppe tradition, had always been costly, had bankrupted states before and had often enforced the succession of one dynasty by another. The threat of bankruptcy through warmaking had never yet, however, ushered in an entirely new philosophy of government. That, nevertheless, was the outcome of the summoning of the Estates General, which in rapid succession resolved that France's separate bodies of nobility, clergy and commoners should vote by head count, not rank, then that they should sit together, finally that they should remain in permanent session until the King vested his powers in a democratic constitution. Louis XVI's inept attempts to overawe by force the Estates, now calling themselves the National Assembly, led to revolt in Paris, in which units of the royal army, notably the *Gardes françaises*, joined; when the King, after a period of temporising with the Revolution, sought but failed to flee the country, he was suspended from executive office, while the Assembly warned France's neighbours, Prussia and Austria foremost among them, that it would regard their continued sheltering of anti-republican emigrés, who were organising counter-revolutionary forces, as a provocation to war. In April 1792 Louis XVI, at the instigation of the Assembly, declared war with Austria, which was quickly joined by Prussia and Russia as co-belligerents and, in 1793, by Britain. The invasion of France began in July 1792.

The wars of the French Revolution, perpetuated by Napoleon Bonaparte after he became head of government as First Consul in 1799, lasted until 1815; fought defensively at the outset by the French, who renounced wars of conquest in May 1790, they rapidly swelled into the most sustained and extensive offensive yet known in European history. Motivated at first by a desire to carry revolutionary freedoms to the subjects of neighbouring kingdoms, the French ended by committing themselves to a permanent military programme of national aggrandisement. By 1812 Napoleon had more than a million men under arms, distributed across the continent from Spain to Russia, and he directed an economy and an imperial administration whose sole object was to keep his armies in the field. The major powers of continental Europe, Russia apart, had been defeated in their own territory, the soldiers of the smaller states had been incorporated outright in the French army, and able-bodied men everywhere lived either under military discipline or in fear of the recruiting-sergeant. In the span of twenty years a European society in which only those men existing at the economic margin risked incorporation into the ranks, had become militarised from top to bottom, and the grandeurs and servitudes of the soldier's life, hitherto known only to a willing or more usually unwilling minority, had become the common experience of many in a whole generation. How had it been done?

The French did not set out to make 'every man a soldier'; the founding ideals of their Revolution were anti-militarist, rational and legalistic. To defend the sway of reason and the role of just laws – those that abolished the feudal privileges of an aristocratic class which, even if fictively, dated the winning of its place in society to its warrior past – the citizens of the Revolution had, however, sprung to arms. The American colonists had done the same thing fifteen years earlier;[38] but while the English colonists in America had turned an existing military system – that of militias maintained to defend their settlements against the Indians and the French – to their own purposes, the French had to create a new instrument of their own. The royal army was politically suspect and, moreover, had lost many of its trained officers, who were among the first to leave France in protest at the indignities the Revolution had inflicted on the King. Enthusiastic volunteers came forward to form a National Guard to defend the revolutionary institutions against the remaining royalist troops; but the legislators of 1789–91, like those of classical Greece's city states, were at first anxious to limit the right of arms-bearing to responsible, by which they meant propertied, men. The original National Guard, therefore, both lacked sufficient numbers and contained too high a proportion of home-loving bourgeois to form an effective military force. While the threat was internal, that did not much matter; *ad hoc* crowds could always be assembled in the streets to outface troops loyal to the King. After July 1792, when the threat became one of invasion, France needed a large and effective army in a hurry. By then the anti-militarism of 1789 had been forgotten; the logic of the American constitutional 'right to bear arms' had been widely accepted, possession of a firearm had come to be seen as a guarantee of a citizen's freedom, the property qualification for membership of the National Guard was hastily abolished (30 July) and an appeal for 50,000 men to join the 150,000 remaining in the regular army was issued on 12 July. Early in 1793, 300,000 men were called for, to be conscripted if they would not volunteer, and on 23 August the decree of the *levée en masse*, putting all fit males at the disposal of the Republic, was promulgated; it had already been ordered that regular and National Guard units should be amalgamated in brigades in the proportion of one to two, the regulars to provide stiffening to the volunteers until they had learned their trade.

Here was a wholly new sort of army. Discipline was enforced not by corporal punishment (though drunkards were gorged with water) but by tribunals composed of soldiers and officers. Officers, following the practice of the National Guard, were elected; pay was fixed at the comparatively generous rates allotted to revolutionary volunteers. Under the pressure of war, the election of officers was soon abolished (1794) and the disciplinary councils suppressed (1795), but by then the social transformation of the army had gone too far for these afterthoughts to be reversed. The initial impulse to volunteering among respectable men might have slowed, but the character of the officer corps had been altered out of recognition. While in 1789, more than ninety per cent of officers had been noblemen (often, admittedly, very petty noblemen whose title to heraldic arms conferred almost the only social position they enjoyed), by 1794 only three per cent remained.[39] The vacant places were taken by civilians or, more often, by former non-commissioned officers of the royal regiments to whom the Revolution did indeed offer 'a career open to talents'; of Napoleon's twenty-six marshals, Augereau, Lefebvre, Ney and Soult had been sergeants before 1789. More remarkably, Victor had been a bandsman, and three others had been private soldiers, Jourdan, Oudinot and Bernadotte (who, trumping any of Alexander's generals, ended his career as king of Sweden). These were men of large ability to whom the old army had offered no opportunities at all; as late as 1782, officers had secured the restriction of grants of commissions to candidates whose great-grandparents had been noble. Trained to arms, they drew on the self-confidence brought them by the social liberation of 1789 to become outstanding commanders.[40]

Yet the Napoleonic marshalate also contained men who had held commissions before 1789. Marmont, like Napoleon himself, was a graduate of Louis XIV's artillery school at Metz, while Grouchy had served in the *Gardes écossaises* (originally the Varangians of the Bourbon court). 'Openness to talents' sensibly meant the talents of royal officers ready to serve the Revolution, even those of emigrants who had thought better of their decision. By 1796, when Bonaparte set off to unleash his terrible swift sword against the Habsburg territories in Italy, the Republican army was an *amalgame* in the broadest sense of the word: not only of former regular soldiers and ex-National Guardsmen but also of officers from many other traditions, united in service to a new France but also greedily conscious of the rewards that a successful career under arms could bring. Promotion was one, loot another; there would be plenty of both in the next twenty years. Meanwhile the urgency was to discover means that would strip musket and bayonet warfare of its besetting indecisiveness and invest confrontation on the battlefield between revolution and the *ancien régime* with the same dynamism by which the popular will had overthrown royal government.

A solution lay to hand. Even the royal army had been perturbed by the indecisiveness of battle of the recent Seven Years' and Austrian Succession wars and many aristocratic officers, notably the Comte de Guibert, had advocated tactical reform. Guibert, like all his military contemporaries, was deeply impressed by the achievements of Frederick the Great of Prussia who, with a small army of highly disciplined regulars, frequently beat those of states much larger than his own. Frederick's ruthlessly rational approach to warmaking accorded with the spirit of the age – that 'Age of Enlightenment or Reason [which] had already brought forward the idea that all institutions of government ought to be in harmony with the spirit and desires of the people'.[41] Guibert, a typical aristocratic rationalist, believed that Prussian drill and training could transform the French army into a logical instrument of state power. As many of his contemporaries did, he rejected dependence on the old linear formations of musketeers, whose fire alone was supposed to beat down the enemy's resistance, and urged a change to manoeuvre by larger masses, whose weight would deliver a decisive effect. In this debate between 'line versus column', as it has come to be known, he and other like-minded officers effectively carried the day by 1789; but neither he nor they could follow their argument to its conclusion, since that would have required them to accept that soldiers should learn to identify with the state as well as to serve it better. He remained an absolutist at heart. Intellectually he harked back to the idea of the citizen-soldier, but his social prejudices prevented him from embracing the reality.

The Revolution dissolved that contradiction. It brought into being almost overnight a true citizen army, which found in the tactical disputes of the *ancien régime* the solution to the problems it was shortly to encounter on the battlefield with the surviving *ancien régime* armies. It has been argued that the Revolutionary armies fought as they did, in dense columns supported by heavy concentration of mobile artillery, because the amateurism of their citizen-soldiers gave their commanders no other choice. More recently it has been recognised that this view is short-sighted: change was on the way in any case and the Revolution's officers actively hurried it forward. But that does not explain why the changes worked. Under the hand of generals like Dumouriez, Jourdan and Hoche, all the difficulties that had inhibited decision and impeded the movement of armies since the building of the great chains of artillery fortresses at national frontiers in the sixteenth century dissolved as if by magic. French armies overran the borderlands of Belgium, Holland, Germany and Italy, bypassing fortresses that did not at once fall at their approach, and decisively beating the Austrians and Prussians wherever they tried to stem the flood. Part of their success was due to what later would be called 'fifth columns'; many of the Dutch, for example, were only too ready to embrace the Revolution, which also had many sympathisers in northern Italy. Partly it was due to the sheer size of the Revolutionary armies – which had grown to 983,000 in 1793, at the end of a century in which 100,000 had been an enormous force – and to their disregard for logistic convention; fortresses blocking a line of supply lost their point when the surrounding countryside filled with troops who took what they chose.

Most of all, success stemmed from the superior quality of the Revolutionary armies themselves. At least at the outset, they were composed of men who were genuinely willing soldiers, devotees of a 'rational' state (even if its nature greatly alarmed many of the surviving rationalists of the Age of Reason), and led by officers of outstanding personal qualities. It seems untrue that they were undertrained. The new officer corps put great effort into training both the surviving royal and the new volunteer units in 1793–4 – two revolutionary officials reported in June 1793 that 'the soldiers devote themselves to drill with an indefatigable zeal . . . the veteran soldiers are astonished when they see the precision with which our volunteers manoeuvre' – while the artillery, already the best in Europe, thanks to the innovations of Gribeauval, retained many of its original officers as well as gunners.[42] When led into battle, the 'amalgamated' units simply outfought their enemies, who remained trapped in the habits of doltish obedience and stereotyped tactics from which the French had escaped.

By 1800 the Revolution had been saved from its foreign enemies and secured at home by conservative reaction. The young Bonaparte had outstripped all rivals in winning French victories abroad and had also struck a decisive blow against domestic extremism in the coup of Brumaire in November 1799. Political and military power fell naturally into his hand. Between 1802 and 1803 he entered into an uneasy peace with France's enemies – Austria, Prussia, Russia, Britain – but then led the armies out again for another twelve years of lightning and even longer-range conquests: against Austria in 1805 and 1809, Prussia in 1806, finally, though disastrously, Russia in 1812. Only in Spain, where in 1809–14 his marshals had to battle against a high-quality British expeditionary force commanded by Wellington, supported by a country-wide guerrilla effort and supplied by the Royal Navy (which, since its victory at Trafalgar (1805) sailed the seas uncontested), did he meet a sustained check. His Grand Army was not the army of the Revolution; though many of its officers and some of its soldiers survived from the epic campaigns of 1793–6, it had become an instrument of state power rather than of ideology. Enough remained of its revolutionary ethos, however, for the great Napoleonic victories – Austerlitz (1805), Jena (1806), Wagram (1809) – to appear as extensions of the whirlwind tradition. On their devastating outcomes Clausewitz, a veteran of the very first Prussian encounters with the Revolutionary armies who survived to witness Napoleon's defeat in 1815, erected his theory that the harnessing of the popular will to strategic purposes brought 'real war' to approximate with 'true war', and founded his belief that warmaking was ultimately a political act.

Clausewitz's ideas were not wholly original, as he himself conceded. Machiavelli, he said, had 'a very sound judgement in military matters'. That was faint praise. *The Art of War*, which appeared in twenty-one editions in the sixteenth century alone, was a revolutionary text, because it was the first handbook that directly linked warmaking to the art of government.[43] Earlier classical writers, such as Philo, Polybius and Vegetius, had merely described how military affairs might best be regulated. Machiavelli demonstrated how a well-regulated army – by which he meant one recruited from subjects, not hired on the mercenary market – might achieve a ruler's purposes. It was of enormous value to heads of states who, at a time when the revival of the money economy had eroded the old feudal basis of recruitment, were genuinely confused about how best to raise reliable armies. Machiavelli had modest objectives, however. He merely sought to give practical advice to other men like himself, members of the political class of rich Renaissance city states. Clausewitz's intellectual ambitions verged on the megalomaniac. Like his near contemporary Marx, he claimed to have penetrated the inner and fundamental reality of the phenomenon he took as his subject. He did not deal in advice; he dealt in what he insisted were inescapable truths. War was the continuation of politics by other means, and any government which blinded itself to that truth doomed itself to harsh treatment at the hands of an unblinkered opponent.

Hence the enthusiasm with which his own Prussian government took up his ideas – transmitted to it by his pupils and followers in the War Academy and general staff – in the middle of the nineteenth century. *On War* was a book with a slow fuse. By the time the Prussian army came to fight its wars for hegemony in Germany, however, his ideas had permeated it, and the victories it won in 1866 and 1870–1 ensured that they would thereafter direct the course of the new German empire's diplomacy as well. By an irresistible process of osmosis, they then percolated throughout the whole European military establishment; by 1914, it is true to say that its outlook was as Clausewitzian as the continent's coalition of socialist and revolutionary movements was Marxist.

Since the objects of the First World War were determined in great measure by the thoughts that were Clausewitz's, in the war's aftermath he came to be regarded as the intellectual begetter of a historical catastrophe; B.H. Liddell Hart, then Britain's most influential military writer, pilloried him as 'the Mahdi of Mass'.[44] With longer hindsight, this estimate of his influence seems exaggerated. His ideas undoubtedly bore heavily on the assumptions made by generals before 1914 of the high numbers of men that would have to be deployed to gain advantage on a future battlefield and of the high proportion of loss likely to be suffered; the result was that European armies demanded even larger annual intakes of conscripts for both their field forces, which would provide an immediate line of defence, and the reserves from which casualties would be made good and new formations created. But there would have been no point in the generals wanting more soldiers, or even in states instituting the systems of compulsory recruitment necessary to find them, had the men themselves not been willing to serve. Generals had always wanted more troops since states were young, and the history of bureaucracy is littered with examples of futile and discarded schemes of enlistment. Even when a state possessed the means to identify its fit young males and their places of work or residence, as by 1914 all European states did, the best of police forces could not have sufficed to bring an entire age-group to barracks if they resisted and if society at large supported their resistance.

That they did not resist and were not supported tells us something quite different from what is said by those who believe Clausewitz was the architect of the First World War. Architects create structures, but they cannot determine moods. They reflect a culture. They cannot create one. By 1914 an entirely unprecedented cultural mood was dominating European society, one which accepted the right of the state to demand and the duty of every fit, male individual to render military service, which perceived in the performance of military service a necessary training in civic virtue and which rejected the age-old social distinction between the warrior – as a man set apart whether by rank or no rank at all – and the rest, as an outdated prejudice.

Much had worked against this mood, notably the nineteenth-century belief in benevolent progress, of which ever-increasing prosperity and the spread of liberal constitutional governments were the hallmarks. The powerful revival of religious sentiment, too, a reaction against the godlessness both of revolution and of the claims of science to explain the universe – much though the latter had fostered prosperity – resisted it as well. Optimism and the moral deprecation of violence could not prevail, however, against the other forces that hurried forward the militarisation of European life.

The United States, least militarised of Western societies at mid-century, was the first to discover the danger of that movement. Plunged into civil war in 1861, neither North nor South expected a long conflict. Each hastily assembled amateur armies which advanced to battle in the hope of quick victory. Neither contemplated full-scale mobilisation, either of manpower or industry. The South, indeed, had little industry to mobilise. Both found, as decision on the battlefield eluded them, that they were driven to enlarge their armies in pursuit of achieving a success through a superiority of numbers that generalship could not deliver. Eventually the South was to assemble nearly 1,000,000 men under arms, the North 2,000,000, out of a pre-war population of 32,000,000; a military participation ratio of ten per cent, which these figures represented, is, as we have seen, about the maximum a society can tolerate while continuing to function at normal levels of efficiency. The South might have added to its military manpower by drawing on the active males among its 4,000,000 slaves but the chattel nature of its slave system, which it had gone to war to defend, precluded such an expedient. The North,

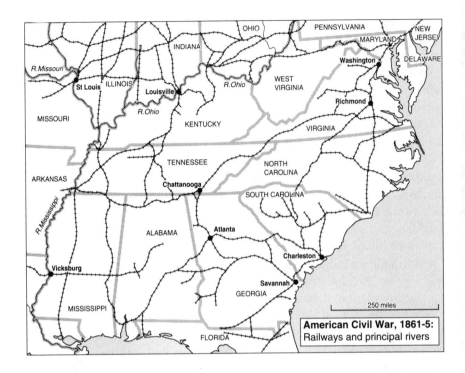

American Civil War, 1861-5:
Railways and principal rivers

drawing on its greatly superior economic resources, including a larger navy and merchant marine and a much denser railroad network, was enabled to blockade the South from the start and to transport armies to the South's points of vulnerability. By 1863 it had cut the South in half and in 1864 it bisected its most productive region from west to east. Logistic superiority, however, could not win the war as long as Southern soldiers were willing to fight and could find, as they did, the barest means to do so. The battles of 1864 therefore proved as bloody as those of 1862–3, Southerners fighting as tenaciously in defence of their heartland as they had on the offensive into the North at Gettysburg. The cost to both sides of this ever-deepening struggle was agonising. By April 1865, when the North's strangulation of the South at last achieved its result, 620,000 Americans had died as a direct result of the war, more than the total number killed in the two world wars, Korea and Vietnam.

The emotional aftermath of the war inoculated several generations of Americans against the false romanticism of uniforms and training-camps. The spectacle the war had presented of the conjuring into existence of great amateur armies nevertheless encouraged 'volunteering' by would-be citizen-soldiers elsewhere, notably in Britain, and validated also the progressive enlargement of mobilisable reserves of time-expired conscripts in Germany, France, Austria, Italy and Russia.

The swelling nationalism of such states was militarist in its thrust, while nationalism was fed by their successful imperialism overseas. Even though continental Europe was rarely at war between 1815 and 1914 – despite the international conflicts of 1848–71 and a flurry of civil wars, the period will still bear the description of the 'great peace' – European armies and navies were constantly in action in India, Africa and Central and South-East Asia, and their success in winning campaigns small in scope but spectacular in results brought strong satisfactions to the nations that sponsored them. Yet perhaps the most powerful sentiment that supplied popular consent to militarisation was the thrill of the process itself. The proclamation of egalitarianism had provided the French Revolution with one of its headiest appeals. That appeal had been rooted in the identification of equality with arms-bearing and had launched into the European consciousness the idea that to serve as a soldier made a man more not less of a citizen. The Revolution had effectively killed mercenarism and had extinguished also the claim of the old warrior class to monopolise leadership and command. The armies that emerged from the wars of the French Revolution and empire came to be seen – delusively perhaps, since the old warrior class doggedly defended its surviving claim to command appointments – as instruments of social cohesion and even of social levelling. Within them able young men of the middle class could aspire to rank and so to social standing, while all young men, by donning uniform, could display the badge of their full acceptance as equal members of the community. Mercenary and regular enlistment had each, in their different ways, been seen as forms of servility; universal conscription, by contrast, conferred respectability and even enlarged horizons. As William McNeill has written, 'Paradoxical as it may sound, escape from freedom was often a real liberation, especially among young men living under very rapidly changing conditions, who had not yet been able to assume fully adult roles.'[45]

This judgement implies that there was a measure of infantilism in Europe's enthusiastic espousal of militarising tendencies, and that may well be: 'infantilism' and 'infantry' have the same root. If so, it was the infantilism of a thinking child. Clever men and responsible governments found wordy arguments to justify themselves. Thus the report of the French Chamber of Deputies on the conscription boom of 1905, designed to increase the size of the army even further, opened with the preamble:

> It is from the lofty ideas born of the French Revolution that the military ideas of a great republican democracy . . . must be inspired: and when, after more than a century, the legislator can ask all citizens – without distinctions of wealth, instruction or education – to consent to give an equal part of their time to their country, without exceptions and privileges of any sort, the proof is there that the democratic spirit has once again bound up the chains of time.[46]

Thus spoke the parliament of the continent's foremost democracy in the City of Light nine years before the consequences of creating mass citizen armies became apparent. On 3 August 1914, the third day of the First World War, the rectors of the Bavarian universities jointly issued the following appeal:

> Students! The muses are silent. The issue is battle, the battle forced upon us for German culture, which is threatened by the barbarians from the East, and for German values, which the enemy in the West envies us. And so the *furor teutonicus* bursts into flame once again. The enthusiasm of the wars of liberation flares, and the holy war begins.[47]

In this extraordinary outburst by leading members of the German professoriat, which competed only with the officers of the Great General Staff for first place in German society, half-a-dozen, half-buried, half- or even wholly primitive elements in mankind's long experience of warmaking come to the surface. Reason and learning are cast aside ('the muses are silent'). The terror from the steppe ('barbarians from the East', meaning here Russia's Cossacks) is invoked. Germany's own barbarian past (the *furor teutonicus*, by which classical civilisation, largely reconstructed by German scholarship, had been overthrown) is suddenly found estimable again. The call to holy war – a Muslim not a Christian or even Western idea – is issued over the signatures of men who unquestionably shared in the prevailing European belief that the achievement of Islam had been to sow corruption and decay wherever the Koran was taught.

Such contradictions went unrecognised by Bavaria's – or Germany's – university students. Untrained though they were (the conscription laws exempted them from service until their studies were complete), they volunteered almost as a complete body to form the new XXII and XXIII corps, which in October 1914, after two months of drill, were thrown into action against the regulars of the British army near Ypres in Belgium. The result was a massacre of the innocents (known in Germany as the *Kindermord bei Ypern*), of which a ghastly memorial can be seen to this day. In the Langemarck cemetery, overlooked by a shrine decorated by the insignia of Germany's universities, lie the bodies of 36,000 young men interred in a common grave, all killed in three weeks of fighting; the number almost equals that of the United States' battle casualties in seven years of war in Vietnam.

FIREPOWER AND THE CULTURE OF UNIVERSAL SERVICE

One survivor of Langemarck – an odd man out among his university comrades, since a chaotic temperament had disqualified him from higher education – was Adolf Hitler. He had shown himself a good soldier and continued to serve, despite several wounds, until the end of the war. His long survival made him an odd man out also. His regiment, the 16th Bavarian Reserve, emerged from battle after a month in the line of Ypres with only 611 of its original 3600 soldiers unwounded. Within a year it contained scarcely a single original member. Such casualty lists had by then become commonplace in all the fighting-units of the combatant armies. They recorded an unprecedented shedding of blood in two respects: the total of losses, for any given period of hostility, was absolutely higher than any known before; the rate of loss, calculated as a percentage of combatant manpower, was also without parallel, because never before had such a high proportion of any population been engaged in combat. It is difficult to be categorical about casualty figures; they are, as any military historian knows, a quagmire into which the scholar sinks ever deeper the more effort he makes to wade his way out. For pre-census times, which means for all periods before the nineteenth century, accurate civilian population figures are lacking, so that even if estimates of army strengths can be relied upon, which is rarely the case, it is difficult to translate reported battle losses, again usually unreliable, into a figure that represents a verifiable proportion of a combatant nation's military manpower. Thus, for example, while it is generally accepted that the Roman republic lost 50,000 out of 75,000 soldiers committed at Cannae, we do not know how large was Rome's pool of military manpower in the third century BC and so cannot compare the scale of that disaster with, say, that of the Teutoburg forest in the first century AD.

It is a safe presumption, however, that armies in all organised states before the introduction of universal conscription formed but the smallest fraction of populations – in France in 1789, 156,000 out of 29,100,000 (though by 1793 universal conscription had raised this to 983,000); we also know that the cost of battle only exceptionally exceeded ten per cent fatalities among those engaged; and finally we know that battles were infrequent incidents in wars (the French republic fought only fifty, by both land and sea, between 1792 and 1800, or six a year, a very high number by earlier standards).[48] Thus we may conclude that news of a death in battle was a comparatively rare family tragedy at any time before the nineteenth century. Napoleon's battles, fought with field forces as large as those of the whole French army of the *ancien régime*, pushed the incidence higher. At Borodino (1812), his Pyrrhic victory outside Moscow, he lost 28,000 out of 120,000, while at Waterloo, a battle to which accurate statistical methods can be applied almost for the first time, his losses were 27,000 out of 72,000, Wellington's 15,000 out of 68,000.

Figures from the American Civil War (for which dependable figures are supplied from the pension returns of the widows of those killed) show the upward trend: some 94,000 Confederates, out of about 1,300,000 enlisted, died in the forty-eight major battles of the four-year war, and some 110,000 out of 2,900,000 Union soldiers. The higher Confederate casualty rate, about seven as opposed to three per cent, is explained by such factors as lower rates of desertion and more frequent commitment of units in a smaller army to action.[49] The deaths of some 200,000 young men in battle in four years, from a population that numbered 32,000,000

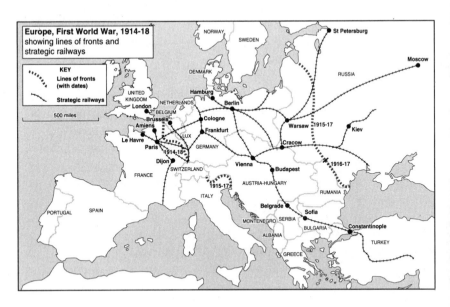

in 1860, left an emotional wound that gave war a lasting bad name in the United States; the agony was compounded by the death from disease or hardship of 400,000 more.[50]

By 1914 the age-old scourge of disease, always hitherto war's chief agent of death, had been lifted from armies; the Boer War (1899–1902) was the last in which the British army suffered more fatalities from sickness than from missiles. That, however, made the casualty lists of 1914–18 all the harder to bear. Soldiering had become a healthy life; recruits, nurtured in an environment of improved public health at home, well fed on the produce of mechanised agriculture, were kept fit and strong; indeed, in some sense, the length of the casualty lists of the First World War directly reflected the decline in infant mortality and the rise in civilian life expectancy during the previous century. Those factors combined to provide the numbers that came forward to the slaughter, which rose steeply each year. By September 1915 the French army had suffered 1,000,000 casualties, of which about a third were fatal, in the battles of the frontiers – the Marne, Aisne, Picardy and Champagne. In the battle of Verdun (1916) it lost 500,000 dead or wounded (conventionally the proportion is reckoned at one to three) and the Germans more than 400,000; on the first day of the battle of the Somme that year, 1 July, the British army lost 20,000 killed, almost as many deaths as it had suffered in the entire Boer War from wounds and disease combined.

By 1917 the French army had lost 1,000,000 dead, and, after another disastrous offensive in Champagne in April, one half its fighting divisions refused to obey further orders to attack. The episode, loosely described as mutiny, is better represented as a large-scale military strike against the operation of an unbearable probability; four out of nine Frenchmen enlisted in fighting-units suffered wounds or death by the war's close. At the end of that year, the Italian army, which its government had committed to war against Austria in May 1915, went the same way; after suffering 1,000,000 casualties in eleven profitless Alpine offensives, it collapsed in the face of an Austro-German counter-offensive and was effectively immobilised until the armistice. The Russian army, its casualties uncounted, had by then begun to 'vote for peace with its feet', in Lenin's phrase. Lenin's political victory in the Petrograd revolution of October 1917 could not have occurred but for the military catastrophes the army had undergone in East Prussia, Poland and the Ukraine, which dissolved the units on which the constitutional government counted for support.

Mechanistic explanations for this quantum leap in casualty rates are easy to supply in retrospect. Firepower, both that of the individual soldier's weapon and of the machine-guns and artillery pieces that supported him, had been multiplied several hundred times since the days of gunpowder 'indecision' in the eighteenth century. Then it had been calculated that the ratio of deaths inflicted to rounds fired (discounting artillery) had fallen to between 1 to 200 and 1 to 460.[51] However, the musketeer fired at most three times a minute, while opposed forces rarely exceeded 50,000 in strength; even so, the casualties inflicted in a few minutes' exchange of fire were usually sufficient to induce a panic flight to the rear by one party or the other, and it was indeed precisely through the infliction of such a panic that commanders sought to take possession of the field.[52] By 1914 the infantryman fired fifteen rounds a minute, a machine-gun 600, and an artillery piece, discharging shrapnel shell filled with steel ball, twenty rounds. While the infantry remained under cover, the effect of much of this fire was wasted; but when they rose to advance in attack, it might destroy a battalion of a thousand men in a few minutes. Such indeed was the experience of the 1st Newfoundland Regiment on 1 July 1916, when many others suffered almost equal loss. Moreover, flight from such a torrent of fire offered no escape, since the fugitive had a killing-zone hundreds of yards deep to cover before he could return to the protection of the trenches. Fire thus pinned him to the ground where, if he had been wounded, he might all too often lie untended until he succumbed.

All efforts by the high commands of the First World War to overcome the stalemate that firepower imposed on the fighting-fronts by the application of indirect methods elsewhere proved unavailing. The action of fleets, in particular, returned poor rewards for the enormous sums that had been expended to build them, in the sixty years which had elapsed since the supersession of the wooden by the iron ship. Wooden fleets had, as we have seen, proved extraordinarily successful instruments of European gunpowder technology in both home and distant waters. With them the European maritime states had brought their power to bear against remote peoples who, even if they had acquired access to gunpowder weapons, were culturally quite unfitted to confront their warriors on face-to-face terms.

On the European seas the successful naval nations, above all Britain, not only had managed to establish long-term dominance over trade routes and critical operational zones but had also mastered the techniques of supplying effective support to their armies on land, notably through blockade and logistic supply. It was with such objects in view that Germany had challenged Britain to the great Dreadnought building race in the first decade of the twentieth century, a competition which equipped their fleets with dozens of battleships (Britain 28 Dreadnoughts in 1914, Germany 18) capable of destroying each other at ranges of twenty miles. The German naval staff's hope was to catch the British fleet at a disadvantage in the North Sea, inflict crippling losses and so win the freedom to break out to the Atlantic trade routes and raid British commerce to destruction. Its efforts to do so, notably at the Battle of Jutland (May 1916), failed and it was thereafter narrowly confined to its own bases. It had a greater success with its own counter-blockade of Britain by its rapidly expanded U-boat fleet, which adopted a policy of sinking without warning in 1917, but that was eventually curtailed when the Admiralty reverted to the eighteenth-century practice of sailing merchant ships in convoy under warship escort.

Britain's attempt to revive its traditional amphibious strategy, by which expeditionary forces were lodged and supplied by the navy at vulnerable points on its adversary's maritime periphery, encountered a severe reverse at the only place it was attempted, Gallipoli, in Turkey (April 1915). The Turkish defenders, recent allies to Germany, displayed all the bravery that had made them so feared by Christian Europe 300 years earlier and also demonstrated that they had made themselves masters of the new firepower technology. At Gallipoli local firepower ashore defeated strategic power at sea.

Eventually strategic sea power helped to affect the great firepower struggle between the Allies and Germany on the Western Front in France, chiefly by assuring the safe passage across the Atlantic of a fresh American army, which in 1918 began to arrive in sufficient numbers to lend new heart to the demoralised French and gravely shaken British. Its arrival consonantly disheartened the Germans, whose five 'war-winning' offensives of the spring and summer had each broken on defensive lines hastily improvised to contain their advance. In October 1918 they at last began to reveal the signs of war-weariness that had overtaken the French, Russians, Italians and even the British in the previous year. All their infantry formations had, like those of their enemies, replaced their original manpower twice, sometimes three times over, and despite victory over Russia on the Eastern Front, a string of successes on other fronts, and the nearness with which they had threatened the western powers with defeat, they flinched from further and what appeared increasingly pointless sacrifice. In November the German high command, confronted by incontrovertible evidence that they had tried their soldiers too hard, treated for an armistice.

The truth was that all the combatant states had tried their soldiers too hard. The ordeal had been as much self-inflicted as imposed. The populations that had embraced the outbreak of 1914 with such enthusiasm had despatched their young men to the battlefronts in the belief that they would win not only victories but glory, and that their return with laurels would justify all the trust they had invested in the culture of universal service and commitment to warriordom. The war exploded that illusion. 'Every man a soldier', the philosophy which underlay conscription politics, rested on a fundamental misunderstanding of the potentiality of human nature.

Warrior peoples might have made every man a soldier, but they had taken care to fight only on terms that avoided direct or sustained conflict with the enemy, admitted disengagement and retreat as permissible and reasonable responses to determined resistance, made no fetish of hopeless courage, and took careful material measure of the utility of violence. The Greeks had shown a bolder front; but, while inventing the institution of face-to-face battle, they had not pushed their ethic of warmaking to the point of demanding Clausewitzian overthrow as its necessary outcome. Their European descendants had limited the objects of their warmaking also, the Romans to that of consolidating but then chiefly assuring a defensible frontier for their civilisation – quintessentially the Chinese military philosophy also – while the Romans' successors had fought, incessantly though they did, chiefly for enjoyment of rights within quite closely circumscribed territories. In a different form, battles for rights had also characterised the wars of states in the gunpowder age. Though their struggles had been exacerbated by the religious differences expressed in the Reformation, the Protestants had acted rather to challenge pre-existing rights than to throw down new ones. In none of these contests, moreover, had the combatants yielded to the delusion that the whole male population must be mobilised to prosecute the quarrel. Even had that been materially possible, which the labour-intensiveness of agriculture, to say nothing of fiscal incapacity, disallowed, no pre-1789 society considered soldiering a calling for any but the few. War was rightly seen as too brutal a business for any except those bred to it by social position or driven to enlist by lack of any social position whatsoever; mercenaries and regulars alike, poor, jobless, often criminally outcast, were judged fitted for war because peaceful life offered them nothing but equivalent hardship.

The exclusion of the industrious, the skilled, the learned and the modestly propertied from military service reflected a sensible appreciation of how war's nature bore on human nature. Its harshnesses were not to be sustained by men of comfortable, regular and productive habits. In its frenzy to equalise, the French Revolution roughly set that perception aside, by seeking to confer on the majority what hitherto had been the privilege of a minority – the title to full legal freedom represented by the aristocrat's warrior status. The Revolution was not wholly wrong to do so. Many respectable men whose fathers would have shrunk from military service proved to make excellent soldiers, in both the lower and higher ranks: Murat, most dashing of Napoleon's marshals, had studied for the priesthood, Bessières had been a medical student, Brune a newspaper editor.[53] It is true that seminarian and newspaper editor were also the respective backgrounds of Stalin and Mussolini, but they were men of savage temperament in a later age. In their time, Murat, Bessières and Brune passed for respectable *bourgeois*, and it merely chanced that their temperaments fitted them for the discipline and danger of military life. Even in Napoleon's army they stood as exceptions. A hundred years later they would not have done so. The armies of the First World War were composed from bottom to very near the top by representatives of every station and calling in society, and many of those who were spared death or wounds served for two or three or even four years with uncomplaining fortitude. But 200 or 300 per cent casualties among the infantry, the passing of the level of 1,000,000 deaths, will suffice to shatter the spirit of a nation. By November 1918 France had lost 1,700,000 young men from a population of 40,000,000, Italy 600,000 from a population of 36,000,000, the British empire 1,000,000, of whom 700,000 were from the 50,000,000 people of the British Isles.

Germany's persistence to the very end, despite the loss of more than 2,000,000 from a pre-war population of 70,000,000, is all the more remarkable. It paid the emotional price, though in a different coin from that which circulated in the victorious nations. There the cost was reckoned too high ever to be borne again. 'I am beginning to rub my eyes at the prospect of peace,' wrote Cynthia Asquith, wife of a former British prime minister in October 1918. 'I think it will require more courage than anything that has gone before . . . one will at last fully recognise that the dead are not only dead for the duration of the war.'[54] Of course, November 1918 brought an end for millions of families to four years of apprehension that a post-office boy at the door might be carrying the death telegram, but her sentiment was correct. The casualty lists had left gaps in almost every family circle and the agony of loss persisted for as long as those who felt it themselves survived. Even today the 'In Memoriam' columns of British newspapers carry remembrances of fathers or brothers who died in the trenches or no man's land nearly eighty years ago. Psychic wounds of such depth are not healed with the first dulling of memory. They fester in the collective consciousness, and the national consciousness of the British and French, in the aftermath of 1918, rebelled at the thought of a repetition of suffering.

France sought literally to wall itself off from a renewal of the trench agony by building a simulation of the trench system in concrete along its frontier with Germany, the Maginot Line, which was as costly in its first phase (3,000,000,000 francs) as that of Britain's Dreadnought building programme of 1906–13; like an enormous landlocked fleet of battleships, it was intended to prevent an offensive by any future German army – for Germany had effectively been deprived of an army under the terms of the peace – from ever setting foot again on French territory.[55] The British reacted from the prospect of another great war with the same revulsion as the French, though without their realism. In 1919, at the prompting of Winston Churchill, a former First Lord of the Admiralty and Secretary of State both for War and Air, it adopted the ruling that, 'for the purpose of framing the [defence] estimates, [it should be assumed] that at any given date there will be no major war for ten years' and this 'ten-year rule' was renewed year-on-year until 1932; even thereafter, despite the accession to power in Germany of Adolf Hitler in 1933, resolved to reverse the outcome of the First World War, Britain undertook no substantive measures of rearmament until 1937.[56] Hitler had meanwhile reintroduced universal conscription and set about recreating once more a warrior culture among a new generation of German youth.

ULTIMATE WEAPONS

For Hitler the First World War had been 'the greatest of all experiences'.[57] Like a minority of veterans in all armies, he had found the excitement and even the dangers of the trenches enlarging, indeed uplifting. His bravery had won him medals and the good opinion of his officers while his admission to a circle of comradeship, after years of life as a down-and-out in the backstreets of Vienna, had reinforced his burning belief in the superiority of the German nation above all others. And he was filled with consuming outrage at its humiliation at the peace of Versailles, the terms of which – including loss of territory, the reduction of its army to a strength of only 100,000, the deprivation of its navy of modern warships and the outright abolition of its air force – the German government had accepted only because the Allied naval blockade, at last achieving the effect it had failed to impose in the war years, gave it no option. Hitler's anger was matched by that of enough other veterans to supply him, when he took up extreme right-wing politics in 1921, with the nucleus of a paramilitary party.

Paramilitary parties were on the march in the 1920s, in almost every country that had undergone defeat or been cheated of its expectation of victory. Turkey was the exception: there Atatürk, military saviour of the Turkish heartland, after the Allies had stripped it of its Middle Eastern empire, succeeded in turning his warlike people for the first time toward a strategy of moderation. In Russia, a triumphalist Bolshevik party, victorious in civil war, was instituting a regime which, for all its egalitarian rhetoric, would far outdo the French Revolution in subordinating every aspect of public life, and much of private life as well, to command from the top, reinforced by arbitrary disciplines and a pervasive system of internal espionage. In Italy in 1923 Mussolini – voice for all those who felt that the British and French had taken an unfair share of the victor's spoils, though the Italians had made an equal blood sacrifice – actually usurped government with a party that wore military uniforms, aped military habits, exiled or imprisoned its political opponents and installed its own militia on an equal footing with the constitutional army.

Hitler deeply admired Mussolini, whom he constantly compared to Julius Caesar and whose use of legionary symbolism, including that of legionary banners and the 'Roman' salute, he adopted for his own revolutionary group. The German state, weakened though it was by defeat, proved a tougher nut, however, than the Italian. Hitler's attempt at a *coup d'état* in 1923 was easily quashed by the Bavarian police, backed by an army which was not prepared to see its national role challenged by a rabble parading in a parody of field-grey. During sixteen months in prison, Hitler reflected on his mistakes and determined never to confront the army directly again. Instead, while courting the military leadership and proceeding with the creation of a mass uniformed militia of 'storm-troopers' (which achieved a strength of 100,000 – as large as the army – in 1931), he decided to use the electoral process to bring him to power.[58] In January 1933 he scraped a plurality, was installed as Chancellor and embarked at once on measures designed to restore Germany to its former place as a great military power; on 8 February, he secretly informed his Cabinet that 'the next five years have to be devoted to rendering the German people again capable of bearing arms'.[59] The following year, on the death of President Hindenburg, the wartime commander-in-chief, he arranged for all servicemen to swear personal allegiance to himself as the new head of state (*Führer*, or 'leader'). In 1935 he renounced the clauses of the Versailles treaty which limited the size of the army to 100,000, reintroduced universal conscription, and decreed the creation of an independent air force; in 1936, the same year as he negotiated with Britain a new Anglo-German naval treaty that allowed him to build U-boats, he unilaterally reoccupied the demilitarised Rhineland with German troops. He was already building tanks – in January 1934, he had been shown some illegal prototypes at Kummersdorf by Guderian, father of the panzer arm, and had trumpeted, 'That's what I need! That's what I want to have' – and by 1935 three panzer divisions were under formation.[60] By 1937, the German army had thirty-six infantry and three panzer divisions (in 1933 there had been only seven infantry divisions) which, with reserves, yielded a war strength of 3,000,000 men, a thirtyfold increase in armed strength in four years' time. By 1938 the new Luftwaffe had 3350 combat aircraft (none in 1933), and was training parachute troops to be the airborne arm of the army, while the navy was laying down the first of a series of super-battleships and planning to build an aircraft-carrier.

Rearmament proved enormously popular, not simply because it provided a means of absorbing the youthful unemployed and of integrating into the territory of a greater Germany both the Rhineland and, in 1938, the rump of Austria and the German-speaking regions of Czechoslovakia, but also because it restored German national pride. Among the victor nations the cost of winning the First World War had left the populations determined never to bear it again; in Germany the cost of losing the war seemed to be justified only if the result could be reversed. Hitler, whose whole being was suffused with that conviction, had had the perception to detect this popular rancour, buried though it was beneath a veneer of internationalism that was the official philosophy of the post-imperial state, and had worked to excite it throughout fifteen years of political agitation. His accusations of treason against those who had signed the Versailles treaty and his relentless demands for revenge fell on ready ears.

While the French strengthened the Maginot Line and the British steadfastly refused to rearm, young Germans enthusiastically donned the field-grey uniform of the trenches, basked in the admiration of civilians as their fathers and grandfathers had done in the decades before 1914 when the conscript army had been the principal symbol of German nationhood, and thrilled to the modernity that tanks, fighter aircraft and dive-bombers represented. Mussolini's vision of what Italy might do had been inspired by the art of 'futurism'; in Hitler's Germany futurity was not merely an aspiration, as it remained in underfunded Fascist Italy, but a heady reality. By 1939 German society was not only remilitarised but suffused with the belief that it possessed the means to overcome its decadent neighbours, states which paid no more than lip service to the philosophy of 'every man a soldier', and win the victory of which it had been cheated twenty-one years earlier.

Announcing his decision to go to war against Poland, and therefore also France and Britain, on 1 September 1939, Hitler explicitly evoked the trench experience. 'I am asking', he said, 'no German man more than I myself was ready to perform during the few years of the [First World] War . . . I am from now on no more than the first soldier of the Reich. I have once more put on the coat that was most sacred and dear to me. I will not take it off again until victory is assured, or I will not survive the outcome.'[61] These were eerily prophetic words from a political leader who was to take his own life five and a half years later as enemy shells rained down on the bunker where he sheltered in the ruins of Berlin. At the outset, however, any prospect of defeat seemed chimerical. Hitler's generals had warned, as military professionals commonly do when asked to translate plans into action, that victory over Poland might not be swift. In the event Poland's forty divisions, none armoured, found themselves surrounded from the outset by sixty-two German divisions, including ten panzer, and were overwhelmed in five weeks of fighting; the Polish air force of 935 aircraft, almost all obsolete, was wiped out in the first day. Nearly 1,000,000 Poles were taken prisoner, 200,000 by the Russians who, in a secret agreement with Hitler which lifted the danger from Germany of having to fight a two-front war as in 1914, had arranged to invade and annex the east of the country once operations were under way.

The Polish campaign unveiled the new tactics for which Germany's land and air forces were equipped and trained. Called *Blitzkrieg*, 'lightning war', a journalist's term but a descriptive one, it concentrated the tanks of the panzer divisions into an offensive phalanx, supported by squadrons of dive-bombers as 'flying artillery', which, when driven against a defended line at a weak spot – any spot was, by definition, weak when struck by such a preponderant force – cracked it and then swept on to spread confusion in its wake. The technique was the same as that introduced by Epaminondas at Leuctra, used by Alexander against Xerxes at Gaugamela and employed by Napoleon at Marengo, Austerlitz and Wagram. *Blitzkrieg*, however, achieved results denied earlier commanders, whose ability to exploit success at the point of assault had been limited by the speed and endurance of the horse, whether as an instrument of force or a means to carry messages and reports. The tank not only easily outstripped infantry, but could keep up a pace of advance of thirty, even fifty miles in twenty-four hours as long as supplied with fuel or spare parts, while its radio set enabled headquarters both to receive intelligence and transmit orders at the same speed as operations invoked, a development which came to be known during the war as 'real time'.

There had been experimentation with radio during the First World War, but the early sets, needing bulky power sources, had worked well only at sea. Miniaturisation had reduced the power demand, allowing reliable sets to be installed in tanks or command vehicles, while the Germans had also achieved remarkable success in mechanising encipherment of messages. Here was the basis for an offensive revolution. Its nature was encapsulated in remarks made by the German air-force general, Erhard Milch, at a pre-war conference on *Blitzkrieg* tactics: 'The dive bombers will form a flying artillery, directed to work with ground forces through good radio communications . . . tanks and planes will be [at the commander's disposition]. The real secret is speed – speed of attack through speed of communication.'[62]

These ingredients of an offensive revolution persuaded Hitler and the more forward-looking German generals not only that the Wehrmacht could defeat the still conventionally organised armies of its enemies in the west at little loss, but that they would also spare Germany the crippling economic costs of putting German industry on a full-scale war footing. The German military establishment attributed the Allied victory in 1918 to its better ability to fight the *Materialschlacht*, 'battle of materials'; thus it preserved the illusion that the German soldier had not really been defeated at all. *Blitzkrieg*, the weapons of which were comparatively cheap, would thus allow the German people to enjoy the fruits of victory without making the financial sacrifices always previously entailed in waging all-out war.

The results of the campaign of May–June 1940 in France and the Low Countries appeared to bear this expectation out. Concentrated by stealth in the Ardennes forests north of the Maginot Line, the German panzer divisions cracked the French field defences in three days of fighting and drove forward to reach the Channel coast at Abbeville on 19 May. This advance cut the Allied armies into two, leaving the best of the French and the British Expeditionary Force isolated in the north, while to the south the French hinterland was defended only by immobile and second-rate formations. The northern pocket was eliminated by 4 June – most of the British army was evacuated by sea from Dunkirk – while the southern front was penetrated and overrun immediately after. On 17 June the French government sued for an armistice which came into effect (also with Italy, a latecomer to Germany's side) on 25 June. 'The great battle of France is over,' wrote a young German officer. 'It lasted twenty-six years.' His sentiment neatly reflected that of Hitler. On 19 July he held a victory celebration in Berlin to elevate twelve of his generals to the rank of marshal; he had already made the decision to demobilise thirty-five of the army's hundred divisions, so that industry would regain the manpower necessary to sustain output of consumer goods at peacetime levels.

It seemed in the summer of 1940, therefore, as if Germany was to enjoy the best of all worlds: victory, economic plenty and the return of the warriors to their firesides. As a precaution against the resumption of conflict, Hitler gave orders to persist in the output of the new weapons; the number of tank divisions was to be doubled, U-boat launchings increased and advanced aircraft prototypes taken to production stage. No threat of conflict, however, appeared to loom. The Soviet Union was inert, content to incorporate into its territory the eastern lands assigned to it by Hitler's pre-war agreement with Stalin, and to fulfil the deliveries of raw materials that were a condition of it. Britain, expelled from the continent where it had abandoned almost all its heavy military equipment, was bereft of means to wage offensive war; at best it would hope to defend its sea lanes or air space. By any rational calculation it ought to sue for peace. So Hitler calculated, and he waited throughout June to July to receive Churchill's overtures.

None came. Instead the war took a different course. Hitler had already turned to consideration of how safe it was to leave Russia undisturbed on his open eastern frontier. Its lack of natural frontiers and the 'tankable' expanses of its western steppe laid it open to *Blitzkrieg* on an extended scale; a successful lightning war would provide Germany with the material and industrial resources to make it Europe's unassailably dominant power in perpetuity. No such *Blitzkrieg* would be launched if Britain would agree to an armistice, since that would avert the danger that the United States might eventually intervene in Europe, as it had done in 1917, to reverse the balance of power. However, Britain proved recalcitrant, even under the weight of a full-scale air offensive launched against it in August. While Hitler watched to see how long British air defences could sustain resistance, therefore, he decided to halt the demobilisation of divisions that had taken part in the Battle of France and to begin a precautionary deployment of his panzer formations to the east.

Hitler must be seen in retrospect as the most dangerous war leader ever to have afflicted civilisation, since he combined in his outlook three savagely complementary beliefs, often found separately but never before combined in a single mind. He was obsessed with the technology of warmaking, preening himself on his mastery of its details and holding unfailingly to the view that superior weapons could supply the key to victory; in this he stood in outright opposition to the traditions of the German army, which reposed its trust in the fighting-power of the German soldier and the professional skills of the general staff to bring victory.[63] He nevertheless also believed in the primacy of the warrior class, which in his political messages to the German people he invested with a ruthless racial content. Finally, he was a convinced Clausewitzian: he really did see war as a continuation of politics, did not distinguish, indeed, between war and politics as separate activities. Like Marx, though he contemptuously rejected his collectivism, since it was invented to liberate all races indifferently from economic slavery, he conceived of life as struggle, and warfare therefore as the natural means by which racial politics was to achieve its ends. 'Not one of you', he threw at a Munich audience in 1934, 'has read Clausewitz, or if you have read him, you haven't learnt how to relate him to the present'; in his last days of life in Berlin in April 1945, when he sat down in the bunker to compose his political testament to the German people, the only name he cited was that of 'the great Clausewitz' in justification of what he had tried to achieve.[64]

Revolutionary weapons, the warrior ethos and the Clausewitzian philosophy of integrating military with political ends were to ensure that, under Hitler's hand, warmaking in Europe between 1939 and 1945 achieved a level of totality of which no previous leader – not Alexander, not Muhammad, not Genghis, not Napoleon – had ever dreamed. At the outset he acquiesced in the declaration issued by the British and French governments that they would not direct aerial attack against civilian targets. Once the prohibition was breached – by, as it happened, a German attack mistakenly delivered against the German city of Freiburg on 10 May 1940, which expediency required should be blamed upon the French – inhibitions were cast aside.[65] An Italian military theorist, Douhet, had already advanced the proposition that wars might be won by airpower alone (the Italians, coincidentally or not, had been the first to use aircraft for military purposes, against the Turks in Libya in the war of 1911–12) and, though the bombing of each other's cities by aircraft and airships in the First World War had caused few casualties and trifling damage, Hitler was persuaded that his new Luftwaffe, with its thousand bombers, could break both the Royal Air Force and British civilian morale with a concentrated blow.[66] On what is still called in London 'the first day of the bombing', 7 September 1940, the Luftwaffe burnt out the London docks and wide swathes of the city on each side of the Thames; on 31

December, it destroyed much of the City of London; and on 10 May 1941, the first anniversary of the panzer attack in the west, it devastated Whitehall and Westminster, including the chamber of the House of Commons. Despite causing the deaths of 13,596 Londoners in 1940 alone, the Luftwaffe eventually found its own losses – of 600 bombers in August and September – the deciding factor, and abandoned the effort to give Douhet's doctrine of 'victory through air power' force.[67] During 1941–3 it confined itself to launching sporadic raids only at night against British targets.

Hitler, frustrated in his efforts to bring Britain to concede defeat by the effect of bombing attack, therefore reverted to using his other revolutionary weapons system, the panzer force, to achieve the total victory in Europe that he craved. By the spring of 1941 his precautionary deployment of divisions to the east was complete and his resolve to attack the Soviet Union, which had refused to acquiesce in his diplomatic reordering of southern Europe, was absolute. After a subsidiary campaign to conquer Yugoslavia and Greece, which resisted his demands to accept subordination, he launched his tank forces against Russia on 22 June.

Blitzkrieg worked as spectacularly in the first six months of the Russian war as it had done in the west in the spring of 1940. By December, German tanks had overrun the Ukraine, the Soviet Union's agricultural heartland and source of much of its industrial and extractive wealth, and stood at the gates of both Leningrad and Moscow. Hitler's Clausewitzian philosophy had, or so it appeared, been fulfilled in its objectives by applying to its operations the revolutionary military technology of which Hitler (though not Clausewitz, who discounted the superiority of weapons as a significant factor in warmaking) was such an ardent protagonist. Hitler's fervent championship of the warrior ethos also played its part; indeed, too large a one. Though German soldiers had observed prevailing legal codes of combat in the west, in the east they too often behaved as if the alleged barbarism of their opponents – a barbarism woven into existence by the propagandists of the Reich from folk memories of the steppe menace and evocations of Red Revolution bloody in tooth and claw – justified barbaric behaviour against the soldiers of the Red Army, even after they had been made prisoner, which, following the encirclements at Minsk, Smolensk and Kiev, they were in hundreds of thousands. More than 3,000,000 of the 5,000,000 Soviet soldiers taken prisoner by the Wehrmacht died of mistreatment and privation in captivity, the majority in the first two years of the campaign.[68]

Blitzkrieg worked on land, at least up until the German embroilment in the Battle of Stalingrad, deep within the steppe, in the autumn of 1942. But elsewhere Hitler's reliance on revolutionary weapons and strategic extremism encountered a series of unforeseen checks. At sea, his expectation of consummating the U-boat blockade of Britain, which had been denied the German navy in 1917–18 for want of numbers of submarines, was foiled in 1943 by the Allies' success in extending long-range air cover across the whole zone in which transatlantic convoys operated, in supplying them with local air cover provided by escort carriers of their own, and in outdoing the German cryptographic organisation by decoding the cyphers by which U-boats were instructed to intercept convoys and then diverting the latter to elude them.[69]

In continental air space, meanwhile, his enemies were moving to achieve a decisive advantage. Germany's economic policy of committing industrial capacity only to weapons of direct battlefield efficiency – tanks, dive-bombers, automatic infantry weapons – had meant that the Luftwaffe did not have the resources of a true strategic force. Even before the war began, Hitler's infatuation with the idea of *Blitzkrieg* had forced it to abandon earlier plans to build large, long-range bombers.[70] The policy of the British and the American air forces was precisely contrary. Indeed, it had been with some difficulty that the British government had compelled the Royal Air Force to divert resources from bomber to fighter production before the war, so convinced were its leaders of the rightness of Douhet's doctrine of 'victory through air power'. The early British bombers were strategic in conception rather than capacity, but the American air force, which began to arrive in Britain in 1942 to share with the Royal Air Force the prosecution of a strategic bombing campaign against Germany, did so with an aircraft, the B-17, that met all the necessary desiderata: it was fast, had a long range, dropped a heavy bomb load with great accuracy and was designed to defend itself against fighter attack.

Hitler's abrogation of the tacit agreement to spare civilian targets prompted Britain to begin bombing German cities during 1940. The bombers achieved little effect that year or the next, but in February 1942 a new chief of Bomber Command, Air Marshal Arthur Harris, set aside the policy of directing attacks only at identifiable military targets and inaugurated that of 'area bombing'. It is ironical in context to recall that the Wright brothers, inventors of the practicable aeroplane in 1903, had foreseen its use as a means of bringing the family of mankind into closer community; a British Air Staff directive of 14 February laid down that operations 'should now be focused on the morale of the enemy civilian population and in particular of industrial workers'.[71] Soon a thousand

374

British bombs at a time were deluging chosen German cities with high-explosive – in the Hamburg night raids of 24–30 July 1943, eighty per cent of the city's buildings were damaged or destroyed, 30,000 of the inhabitants killed and the streets left choked with 40,000,000 tons of rubble – while in coordinated daytime raids the United States Army Air Force sustained the assault. Once it had acquired a force of long-range fighters to escort its formations to their targets, its bombers flew over Germany almost with impunity.

The Allied strategic air attack on German cities was a revolutionary development in warmaking, and a few brave individuals rightly denounced it as a moral regression, and yet it was outmatched in strategic scope by the deployment of amphibious air power in the Pacific. Japan, another of the nominal victors of the First World War (it had declared against Germany in order to seize its enclave in China) that felt cheated of a fair share of the spoils, had spent a major proportion of its military budget since 1921 in building up the largest and best-equipped naval air force in the world. Its fleet of six large carriers had been of no use when, in 1937, an army-dominated Japanese government embarked on an all-out assault on China, but it proved the essential strategic prop when, during 1941, the decision was taken in Tokyo to outface the United States' insistence that it terminate its offensive into the Chinese heartland and desist from deployments southward that threatened British and Dutch possessions in Malaya and the East Indies (conquered by sailing-ship in the gunpowder age). Yamamoto, Japan's leading naval strategist and one of the few Japanese to know the United States at first hand, warned of the relative frailty of the fleet he commanded: 'we can run wild for six months to a year,' he forecast, but after that, 'the oil wells of Texas and the factories of Detroit'[72] would supply the means to mount an inevitable and decisive counter-offensive. His protests were overruled, and in the first six months of 1942 the Japanese navy, acting as both spearhead of and escort to the Japanese army, conquered almost the whole of the western Pacific and South-East Asia, and carried the perimeter of what was intended to be an impenetrable zone of strategic control to the northern approaches of Australia.

Whence the Japanese derived the warrior ethos which made them one of the most formidable military peoples the world has ever known remains as mysterious today as it was on 7 December 1941, when the departing pilots of the First Air Fleet left the United States Pacific Fleet's battleships a row of burning hulks at Pearl Harbor. They were a warrior people already and during the thirteenth century, the only one, besides the

Turkish Mamelukes of Egypt, to have confronted and seen off (assisted, admittedly by a timely typhoon) the conquering impulse of the Mongols. They were warriors none the less, of a recognisably 'primitive' sort, practising a highly ritualised style of combat and valuing skill-at-arms largely as a medium for defining social status and subordinating the unsworded to the rule of the samurai. It was to perpetuate that social order that they had banished gunpowder from their islands in the seventeenth century, and thereafter resisted the intrusions of foreign traders until, on the arrival of an American steam warship fleet in 1854, they recognised that the means to deny the outside world no longer availed.

Unlike the Chinese Manchu, who responded to Western technical challenge by counting on the resilience of traditional culture to negate its destabilising effects, the Japanese, from 1866 onward, took a conscious decision to learn the secrets of the West's material superiority and bend them to the service of their own nationalism. In a bitter civil war, the samurai backwoodsmen who resisted the programme of reform were crushed by armies which for the first time admitted commoners to their ranks. The victorious regime, dominated by feudal families, but by those which had embraced the necessity for change, proceeded to introduce into Japan the institutions that their envoys in the West had identified as those that made Western states strong: in the economy, repetitive-process industries; in the public domain, an army and a navy recruited by universal enlistment and equipped with the most advanced weapons, including armoured warships which, by 1911, were being built in Japanese yards.

Other non-European states that attempted this emulation of the West's military power, notably Muhammad Ali's Egypt and nineteenth-century Ottoman Turkey, had failed. The purchase of Western weapons did not, it proved, entail with it the transfer of the West's military culture. But Japan succeeded in acquiring the one with the other. In 1904–5 it defeated Russia in a war for control of Manchuria in which all Western observers testified to the exemplary fighting-power of the common Japanese conscript.[73] This was demonstrated again in the campaigns of 1941–5 in South-East Asia and the Pacific, notably in the opening stages, when trained units of the 'martial peoples' of India – scions of successive waves of militant conquerors, and commanded by British officers – were consistently outmatched in combat by the descendants of Japanese cultivators who, a hundred years earlier, had been forbidden the right to bear arms altogether.

The personal qualities of the Japanese fighting man were eventually overcome by exactly the means of which Yamamoto had warned: the 'surge' capacity of American industry to exceed Japan's output of warships and aircraft delivered to the front. But to say that is in no way to denigrate the courage or skills of the American servicemen who opposed the Japanese in the Pacific theatre. The performance of the United States Marine Corps in the battles to conquer the island of Iwo Jima or Okinawa (1945), in particular, gave the lie to Hitler's deluded and racialist dismissal of the Americans as a people emasculated by material plenty. Nevertheless, the consistency with which the Japanese demonstrated their determination to fight literally to the death – after the assault in Tarawa (1943) only eight out of the Japanese garrison of 5000 were found alive – persuaded the American high command by 1945 that an assault on the Japanese home islands would be too costly – a million casualties or sometimes deaths was the figure invoked – to be risked unless no other means prevailed.[74] By the middle of 1945 such a means was available.

The United States had already deployed a plethora of advanced technical means against Japan in the effort to beat down courage with firepower. Its carrier fleet, outnumbered but vigorously handled in the battles of Coral Sea and Midway, had restored a naval equilibrium in the Pacific in 1942. Thereafter its size had grown so fast – between 1941 and 1944 the United States launched twenty-one fleet carriers, Japan only five – that the US Pacific Fleet could move virtually at will, supported by a fleet train that allowed its ships to remain at sea for weeks at a time. By the end of 1944 the American submarine force had sunk half Japan's merchant fleet and two-thirds of its tankers, while in the summer of 1945 the US strategic air force was engaged in an incendiary campaign against Japan's wooden-built cities that left sixty per cent of the ground area of the sixty largest completely burnt out. It was still doubted, however, if not by American air force generals, whether bombing alone would bring the Japanese to concede defeat.

Strategic bombing had not defeated Germany. In the last months of the European war, the Anglo-American combined bomber offensive put out of action all of Germany's synthetic oil plants, its only surviving source of such supply, and brought movement on its railways to a standstill. By then, however, the Anglo-American armies that had landed in France in June 1944, and the Red Army which had simultaneously broken through the Wehrmacht's last line of defence in White Russia, were fighting deep within German territory. The battles they fought were those of attrition: the increase in the numbers of tanks in all armies had robbed that armoured weapon of the revolutionary properties it had apparently brought to warmaking in the brief era of *Blitzkrieg* in 1941–2. The bomber offensive also, moreover, had passed through a long period of attrition in

1943–4, when air crew losses of five, sometimes ten per cent per mission had threatened to break morale and concede advantage in the skies over Germany to its fighter and anti-aircraft defences. The manned bomber was a fragile weapon of offence, as Hitler had learned to his cost in the campaign of 1940 against Britain. That was the principal reason for his enthusiastic espousal of a programme of unmanned aircraft development, generously funded by the army since 1937. In October 1942 a test firing of a rocket with a range of 160 miles, designed to carry a ton of high-explosive, had taken place, and in July 1943 Hitler declared it 'the decisive weapon of the war' and decreed that 'whatever labour or materials [the designers] need must be supplied instantly'.

The rocket, designated by the Allies the V-2, was not brought into service until September 1944, and only 2600 were ever fired, against first London (in which they killed 2500 people) and then Antwerp, the Anglo-American armies' main logistic base during the assault against Germany's western frontier.[75] But the potentiality of the weapon was plain for all to see; word of its development had greatly alarmed the British when first received, by a mysterious disclosure by a German well-wisher to the Allied cause, in November 1939. This 'Oslo Report' supplied British technical intelligence research with much of its thrust during the first two years of the war. Simultaneously, however, British scientific intelligence had become even more alarmed by the possibility that Germany might be experimenting with the applicability of atomic energy to military purposes.

Thus far the threat was purely theoretical; no one had yet succeeded in causing a chain-reaction by fission, the process through which atoms yield their explosive power, and the machinery to produce it did not exist. In the United States, however, Albert Einstein sent an intermediary to President Roosevelt on 11 October 1939, to warn of the atomic danger, and the President at once set up a committee, from which would develop the Manhattan Project, to take stock of it.[76] Meanwhile the British themselves began to gather the manpower and materials necessary to carry atomic research forward, while seeking to deny them by every means to the Germans. Immediately after Pearl Harbor, the personnel of the British organisation, which bore the cover name of Tube Alloys, was transhipped bodily to the United States to join that of the equally misleadingly named Manhattan Project, and together the teams proceeded, with an urgency fuelled by the fear that Germany might be outstripping them, to uncover the processes by which the theory of fission could be translated into the reality of an ultimate weapon. The outcome of their efforts was not demonstrated until after Germany's defeat; frantic investigations by teams of Allied experts disclosed that even then the Germans were still far away from the discovery of how to initiate a chain-reaction.

When Winston Churchill was informed of the successful explosion of the first atomic bomb at Alamagordo in the New Mexico desert on 16 July 1945, he uttered prophetic words: 'What was gunpowder? Trivial. What was electricity? Meaningless. This Atomic Bomb is the Second Coming in Wrath!'[77] He was speaking to Henry Stimson, the American Secretary of War, who was already centrally involved in the American government's debate over whether so terrible a weapon should be used, even to bring the surrender of the Japanese, whose treacherous attack on Pearl Harbor, ferocity in combat, and inhumanity to prisoners and subject peoples had robbed the American people of all sympathy for them. It did not take long to reach a decision: the anticipated million casualties or deaths among the American servicemen then gathering to assault the Japanese home islands turned the trick. As Stimson himself later explained, speaking for most who endorsed President Truman's order, 'I felt that to extract a genuine surrender from the Emperor and his military advisers they must be administered a tremendous shock which would carry convincing proof of our power to destroy the Empire.'[78] The shock, administered first at Hiroshima on 6 August 1945 and then at Nagasaki three days later, killed 103,000 people. Called on to cease resistance or 'expect a rain of ruin from the air', the Japanese emperor broadcast to his people on 15 August the news that the war was at an end.

LAW AND WAR'S END

The end of the Second World War and the advent of atomic weapons did not bring an end to warmaking, either immediately or in the decades that followed. Japan's destruction of the European empires in the East, and its humiliation of the European governors and settlers under the eyes of their former subjects, ensured that after 1945 colonial rule there could be re-established only by force, if at all. The British judged the effort to be impossible in Burma, to which it conceded independence in 1948, and it recognised that a Communist-inspired rising that broke out the same year in Malaya could be suppressed only if the population was promised self-government as the condition for supporting the counter-insurgency campaign. The Dutch rapidly abandoned their attempt to restore colonial rule in the East Indies where, as in Burma, a Japanese-fostered independence movement captured the populist loyalties. France alone took a different view. Confronted in Indochina by a Communist-led nationalist party, which had acquired arms from the Japanese, it despatched an expeditionary force to re-impose the pre-war imperial regime, but from the moment of its appearance in 1946 it found itself embroiled in guerrilla operations which the enemy showed it knew how to conduct with the greatest skill and persistence. The Viet Minh, as the nationalist movement became known, had learned its guerrilla techniques from Mao Tse-tung's Communist army in China; there, in a country impoverished and destabilised by eight years of occupation by and war against the Japanese, the Communists rapidly seized power from the established government of Chiang Kai-shek in the civil war of 1948–50. Mao's army won its victory by conventional tactics; during its years in the wilderness, however, it had refined its own philosophy of warmaking, in which the traditional Chinese strategy of evasion and delay was reinforced by Marxist conviction in the inevitability of revolutionary triumph. Translated to Indochina, where terrain greatly favoured operations based on surprise, piecemeal offensives and rapid disengagement, 'protracted war', as Mao had entitled his method, successfully wore down the resistance of the French expeditionary force. In 1955, the French government gave up the struggle and conceded power to the Viet Minh.

The Viet Minh example inspired subject peoples throughout what remained of the European colonies to rise in arms, notably in French North Africa but also in British Arabia and Portuguese Africa. During the 1960s the European imperial powers conceded defeat on every front, often in colonies that still remained at peace. The 'wind of change' blowing against European dominance was strong enough to shred to tatters the self-confidence of the European maritime powers whose venturers had sailed forth with such certainty in their moral and material superiority at the outset of the gunpowder age.

The Western-style militarisation of the new independent states of Asia and Africa in the four decades after 1945 was as remarkable a phenomenon as it had been with the non-warrior populations of Europe in the nineteenth century. That it had many of the same doleful effects – overspending on arms, subordination of civilian to military values, superordination of self-chosen military élites and even resort to war – could be expected. It was equally to be expected that most of the hundred or so armies brought into being after decolonisation were of little objective military worth; Western 'technology transfers', a euphemism for selfish arms sales by rich Western nations to poor ones that could rarely afford the outlay, did not entail the transfusion of culture which made advanced weapons so deadly in

Western hands. Only the Vietnamese, against whom the United States was drawn into an unavailing ideological war between 1965 and 1972, made the same transition that the Japanese so spectacularly achieved after the Meiji restoration of 1866. Elsewhere militarisation served only to bring the trappings of militarism without the redeeming military virtue of discipline.

The many small wars of the post-colonial era, affronting though they were to those of liberal conscience among the ex-imperial peoples, did not greatly alarm any of the victor nations of 1945 with the fear that the peace won then was threatened. Their fears on that score came from another source: the nuclear weapons by which the Second World War had been brought to so abrupt a halt. The United States' initial monopoly of the nuclear secret briefly held such fears at bay. When in 1949, however, it became known that the Soviet Union had exploded its own atomic bomb, and when during the 1950s both it and the United States proceeded to the development of the far more destructive hydrogen bomb, the industrial world was forced to take stock of the nature of the nightmare it had created for itself. In the space of 500 years, it had progressed from practising a form of international hostility in which the harm threatened was limited to what could be delivered by power of human and animal muscle, via an interlude in which chemical energy supplanted and enhanced this but did not psychically transcend it, to an unintended state of affairs, suddenly arrived at, in which the practice of hostility, for the objects that prevailing military theory laid down as proper and correct, would destroy the earth. Stimson's judgement on the atomic bomb, at first hearing news of it – 'more than a weapon of terrible destruction . . . a psychological weapon' – was even truer than he guessed.[79] Nuclear weapons preyed upon the mind of man, and the fears they aroused exposed the hollowness of the Clausewitzian analysis once and for all. How could war be an extension of politics, when the ultimate object of rational politics is to further the well-being of political entities? The nuclear dilemma drove thinking people, statesmen, bureaucrats, and members of the professional military class perhaps most of all, to cudgel their brains for discovery of some means of escape from the terrible predicament they had created for themselves.

Some very clever men, many of them academics recruited to the policy-making institutions of Western governments, painfully worked their way toward an accommodation with the predicament by constructing a step-by-step argument to show that Clausewitzian logic held good as never before: nuclear weapons, it ran, could be made to work for political ends not by their use but by the threat of their use alone.

This 'deterrence' theory had deep roots. Military men for centuries past had justified the raising and training of armies by reference to the tag, Roman in origin, 'If you wish for peace, prepare for war.' By the early 1960s, this thought had been reformulated into the doctrine known in the United States, where it originated, as 'mutually assured destruction', the capacity to 'deter a deliberate [nuclear] attack . . . by maintaining at all times a clear and unmistakable ability to inflict an unacceptable degree of damage upon any aggressor – even after absorbing a surprise first strike'.[80] When the numbers of nuclear warheads and of the aircraft and missiles (developments of the German V-2) assigned to deliver them remained low, 'mutually assured destruction' could, if only barely, be justified as a tolerable system of containing nuclear power within manageable limits, especially since the mutual suspicions of the two principal nuclear powers imposed an intransigent resistance to productive measures of disarmament. By the 1980s, when the number of intercontinental nuclear missile-launchers had risen to some 2000 on each side, and the number of warheads to tens of thousands, some alternative and better means of managing the preservation of peace was a clear necessity.

Man has long sought to restrain war by laws, laws defining both when war is or is not permissible (*ius ad bellum*, as international jurists term it) and what is permissible in war (*ius in bellum*) if and when it has begun. In the ancient world a 'just war' was so recognised merely if insult or injury had been given to the state or its officials. The first Christian theologian of the state, St Augustine of Hippo (354–430), challenged to judge whether to take part in war was permissible at all to a man who wished to avoid sin, affirmed that it was, provided that the cause was just and that it was waged with 'right intention' – to achieve good or avert evil – and under constituted authority. These three principles formed the basis for ecclesiastical adjudication between warring parties until the coming of the Reformation; they were subsequently elaborated by such Catholic jurists as Francisco de Vittoria (1480–1546), who argued that an infidel, if fighting under constituted authority, must be accorded respect for his belief that his cause was just, but most importantly by the great Dutch Protestant lawyer Hugo Grotius (1583–1645), whose concern was as much to define 'unjust' as 'just' war and to propose measures by which those who waged unjust wars might be punished for wrongdoing.

During the eighteenth and nineteenth centuries his distinctions were overlooked, for national policy was largely permeated by the amoral Machiavellian view that sovereignty supplied a state with all the justification it needed in its choice of action; in the absence since the

Reformation of any supranational authority to gainsay that philosophy, it prevailed unchallenged throughout the gunpowder age. As a leading international lawyer, W.E. Hall, put the matter in 1880:

> International law has . . . no alternative but to accept war, independently of the justice of its origin, as a relation which the parties to it may set up if they choose, and to bury itself only in regulating the effect of the relation. Hence both parties to every war are regarded as being in an identical legal position, and consequently as possessed of equal rights.[81]

The development of weapons of mass destruction by the end of the nineteenth century made this indifferentist doctrine appear dangerous even to the strongest states, and in the Hague Conventions of 1899 and 1907, the leading powers agreed on modest measures to limit their unfettered freedom to make war if and when they chose. (How they might fight had already begun to be regulated by the Geneva Conventions, the first of which was signed by twelve major powers in 1864.) Since the circumstances in which the First World War broke out made a mockery of the Hague movement, its spirit was entrenched after 1918 in the Covenant of the League of Nations, set up at American inspiration, which imposed the necessity of arbitration on states in dispute, to be reinforced by international sanction on the party that rejected an unwelcome decision. In 1928 the direction in which legal restraint and warmaking was tending took definitive form in the Pact of Paris, properly known as the General Treaty for the Renunciation of War, which, independent of the League Covenant, explicitly committed the signatories to resolve all disputes in future 'by pacific means'.[82] Thereafter, all warmaking was technically illegal, and it was the flagrant disregard of this new principle of international law that made the United States government in 1945 determined to translate the moralistic affirmation of the anti-German and anti-Japanese alliance, the self-styled United Nations, into a permanent organisation of that name. Largely at American insistence, the United Nations Organisation's Charter reaffirmed both the Pact of Paris and the League Covenant, and it added to the League's machinery of arbitration and sanctions a set of provisions that allowed the United Nations to act with military force against a transgressor.

The frustration of the spirit of the United Nations Charter during the forty years of Russo-American nuclear confrontation is a story too well known to rehearse here. Even before that confrontation was resolved by the sudden collapse of the Marxist regime in the Soviet Union in 1990, however, the two superpowers had agreed substantive measures of nuclear disarmament, for they were both alarmed by the relentless heightening of danger of surprise attack into which the perfection of missile technology was driving them. The relaxation of tension thus produced was the most hopeful development in the arena of international relations since the foundation of the United Nations Organisation in 1945.

It was, however, neither nuclear disarmament nor the new mood of harmony induced by Russia's rejection of Marxism that has offered the best hope that a world steeped in warmaking is at last turning into peaceful paths, but, paradoxically, the Soviet Union's decision, in the last months of its existence, to endorse the United Nations' decision to take military action against Iraq's unprovoked invasion of Kuwait in the autumn of 1990. Iraq, by any measure, had violated every provision of 'just war' morality and all the legalities laid down successively by international treaty in the League Covenant, the Pact of Paris, and the United Nations Charter itself. The whirlwind victory of the forces sent to punish Iraq and deprive it of its illegal sequestration of territory, achieved without the infliction of civilian casualties and authorised throughout by United Nations resolution, was the first genuine triumph of just war morality since Grotius had defined its guiding principles at the height of the Thirty Years' War in the seventeenth century.

Those who repose their trust in the hope that the United Nations will succeed in perpetuating its peacemaking function – no better instrument offers itself – have nevertheless a long road to travel before that hope is fulfilled. Man has a potentiality for violence; that cannot be denied, even if we concede that it is a minority, rather than a majority, in any society that is likely to carry potentiality into effect. Man has learned, over the course of the 4000 years in which organised armies have existed, to identify in that minority those who will make soldiers, to train and equip them, to supply the funds they need for their support, and to endorse and applaud their behaviour at those times when the majority feel at threat. We must go further: a world without armies – disciplined, obedient and law-abiding armies – would be uninhabitable. Armies of that quality are an instrument but also a mark of civilisation, and without their existence mankind would have to reconcile itself either to life at a primitive level, below 'the military horizon', or to a lawless chaos of masses warring, Hobbesian fashion, 'all against all'.

There are places in the world, riven by communal rancour, saturated by the cheap weapons which are the industrial world's most shameful product, where the war of all against all already confronts us, and we can see this on our television screens, a spectacle that gives an awful warning. It teaches us to what afflictions war may subject us when we refuse to deny the Clausewitzian idea that war is a continuation of politics, and refuse to recognise that politics leading to war are a poisonous intoxication.

To turn away from the message Clausewitz preached, we do not need to believe, like Margaret Mead, that war is an 'invention'. Nor do we need to ponder the means of altering our genetic inheritance, an intrinsically self-defeating process. We need not seek to break free of our material circumstances. Mankind already masters the material world to a degree which the most optimistic of our ancestors only two centuries ago would have thought beyond apprehension. All that we need to accept is that, over the course of 4000 years of experiment and repetition, warmaking has become a habit. In the primitive world, this habit was circumscribed by ritual and ceremony. In the post-primitive world, human ingenuity ripped ritual and ceremony, and the restraints they imposed on warmaking, away from warmaking practice, empowering men of violence to press its limits of tolerability to, and eventually beyond, the extreme. 'War', said Clausewitz the philosopher, 'is an act of violence pushed to its utmost bounds.' Clausewitz the practical warrior did not guess at the horrors toward which his philosophical logic led, but we have glimpsed them. The habits of the primitive – devotees themselves of restraint, diplomacy and negotiation – deserve relearning. Unless we unlearn the habits we have taught ourselves, we shall not survive.

Conclusion

'WHAT IS WAR?' was the question with which I began this book. Now that I have finished it, and if the reader has followed me to the end, I hope I have called into doubt the belief that there is a simple answer to that question or that war has any one nature. I hope, too, that I have cast doubt on the idea that man is doomed to make war or that the affairs of the world must ultimately be settled by violence. The written history of the world is largely a history of warfare, because the states within which we live came into existence largely through conquest, civil strife or struggles for independence. The great statesmen of written history, moreover, have generally been men of violence for, if not warriors themselves, though many were, they understood the use of violence and did not shrink to use it for their ends.

In this century the frequency and intensity of warmaking have also distorted the outlook of ordinary men and women. In western Europe, the United States, Russia and China, the demands of warfare have touched a majority of families over two, three or four generations. The call to arms has taken sons, husbands, fathers and brothers in their millions away to the battlefield and millions have not returned. War has scarred the gentler emotions of whole peoples and left them inured to the expectation that the lives of their children and grandchildren might go untouched by the ordeals they themselves have suffered. Yet, in their everyday lives, people know little of violence or even of cruelty or harsh feeling. It is the spirit of cooperativeness, not confrontation, that makes the world go round. Most people pass most of their days in a spirit of fellowship and seek by almost every means to avoid discord and to diffuse disagreement. Neighbourliness is thought the best of common virtues, and kindness the most welcome trait of character.

Neighbourliness flourishes, we must recognise, inside firm bounds of restraint. The civilised societies in which we best like to live are governed by law, which means that they are policed, and policing is a form of coercion. In our acceptance of policing we silently concede that man has a darker side to his nature which must be constrained by fear of superior force. Punishment is the sanction against those who will not be constrained and superior force is its instrument. Yet, despite a potentiality for violence, we also have an ability to limit its effects even when no superior force stands ready to spare us from the worst of which we are capable. It is for that reason that the phenomenon of 'primitive' war, with a study of which this book began, is so instructive. Because the wars of this century have taken such an extreme and ruthless form, it has become all too easy for modern man to slip into the supposition that the trend to extremity in warfare is an inevitable one. Modern war has given moderation or self-restraint a bad name; humanitarian intermissions or mediations are cynically seen as a means by which the intolerable is palliated or disguised. Yet warmaking man, as the 'primitives' show, does have a capacity to limit the nature and effects of his actions. Primitives have recourse to all sorts of devices which spare both themselves and their enemies from the worst of what might be inflicted. Exemption is one, the exemption of specified members of society – women, children, the unfit, the old – from combat and its consequences. Convention is another, particularly the conventions of choice of time, place and season of conflict, and of pretext for it. Most important of such devices is that of ritual, which defines the nature of combat itself and requires that, once defined rituals have been performed, the contestants shall recognise the fact of their satisfaction and have recourse to conciliation, arbitration and peacemaking.

It is important, as has been said, not to idealise primitive warfare. It may take a very violent turn, in which exemptions, conventions and rituals are discarded and violence rises to a high level. It may, even when constraints are observed, have material effects undesired by those who suffer them. The most important is the progressive displacement of the weaker party from familiar territory to worse land. Such displacement may eventually damage or even destroy the culture which the cultural constraints on warmaking normally protect. Cultures are not infinitely self-sustaining. They have fragilities which are vulnerable to hostile influences, and among those influences warmaking is one of the more potent.

Culture is, nevertheless, a prime determinant of the nature of warfare, as the history of its development in Asia clearly demonstrates. Oriental warmaking, if we may so identify and denominate it as something different and apart from European warfare, is characterised by traits peculiar to itself. Foremost among these are evasion, delay and indirectness. Given the extraordinary dynamism and ruthlessness of the campaigns of Attila, Genghis and Tamerlane, such a characterisation may seem wholly inappropriate. Those excursions, however, must be seen in context. Over the 3000-year span in which the riding-horse was a principal instrument of warmaking, they appear as quite widely spaced interruptions rather than as a constant and regular feature in the military history of Eurasia. The threat posed by the horse warrior was, of course, a constant in those millennia; but it was normally containable, not least because of his preferred style of fighting. That was, indeed, one in which evasion, delay and indirectness were paramount. The horse warrior chose to fight at a distance, to use missiles rather than edged weapons, to withdraw when confronted with determination and to count upon wearing down an enemy to defeat rather than by overthrowing him in a single test of arms.

For that reason, mounted warmaking could usually be successfully checked by a defender who had recourse to fixed defences built at the perimeter of terrain where the horseman had his home. Off that terrain he found the management of his large horse herds difficult in any case; if free movement were further impeded by obstacles – the Great Wall of China, the Russian *cherta* – his ability to campaign might be altogether nullified. Nevertheless, some horse warriors did eventually succeed in penetrating the settled lands and establishing themselves as rulers in permanency. Notable among them were the Moghuls of India and the Ottoman Turks, together with the bodies of Mamelukes who, at various times, wielded power within the Arab lands. Yet, as we have seen, even these successful horse conquerors did not succeed in transforming the conquering impulse into a creative and constructive style of government. They remained wedded to the culture of the camp, the horse and the bow, living still as nomad chiefs even when luxuriously accommodated in the capitals of the empires they had overthrown. When eventually confronted by new powers which had adapted to real technological change in warfare, their cultural rigidity denied them the opportunity to respond effectively to the challenge and they were eventually extinguished.

Yet, paradoxically, there was a dimension to Oriental warmaking, which came only later to the West, that invested it with formidable but self-limiting purpose. That dimension was ideological and intellectual. Long before any Western society had arrived at a philosophy of war, the Chinese had devised one. The Confucian ideal of rationality, continuity and maintenance of institutions led them to seek means of subordinating the warrior impulse to the constraints of law and custom. The ideal could not be and was not always maintained. Internal disorder and irruptions from the steppe, the latter often the cause of the former, prevented that. Nevertheless, the most persistent feature of Chinese military life was moderation, designed to preserve cultural forms rather than serve imperatives of foreign conquest or internal revolution. Among the greatest of Chinese achievements was the sinicisation of successful steppe intruders and the subordination of their destructive traits to the civilisation's central values.

Restraint in warmaking was also a feature of the other dominant civilisation of Asia, that of Islam. The perception is contrary. Islam is widely seen as a religion of conquest and one of its most widely known tenets is that of the obligation to wage holy war against the unbeliever. The history of Islamic conquest and the exact nature of the doctrine of holy warmaking are both misunderstood outside the Muslim community. The era of conquest was comparatively short-lived and came to an end not simply because Islam's opponents learnt how to mobilise opposition to it but also because Islam itself became divided over the morality of warmaking. Riven by internal disputes which set Muslim against Muslim, in defiance of the doctrine that they should not fight each other, its supreme authority chose the solution of devolving the warmaking role on to a specialist and subordinate class of warriors recruited for the purpose, thus freeing the majority from military obligation and allowing the pious to emphasise in their personal lives the 'greater' rather than the 'lesser' aspect of the injunction to wage holy war, 'the war against self'. As the specialists chosen by Islam to wage war in its name were chiefly recruited from steppe horsemen who refused to adapt their military culture to changed circumstances even when their monopoly of arms brought them to power, Islamic warmaking eventually became almost as circumscribed as within Chinese civilisation. Within the culture the effects were widely beneficial. Once that culture encountered the full force of another, which recognised none of the constraints the Oriental tradition had imposed upon itself, it succumbed to a ruthlessness it was not prepared or able to mobilise even in self-defence.

That culture was Western. It comprised three elements, one derived from within itself, one borrowed from Orientalism and a third brought to it by its own potentiality for adaptation and experiment. The three elements are respectively moral, intellectual and technological. The moral element is owed to the Greeks of the classical age. It was they who, in the fifth century BC, cut loose from the constraints of the primitive style, with its respect above all for ritual in war, and adopted the practice of the face-to-face battle to the death. This departure, confined initially to warfare among the Greeks themselves, was deeply shocking to those outside the Greek world who were first exposed to it. The story of Alexander the Great's encounter with Persia, an empire whose style of warmaking contained elements both of primitive ritual and of the horse warrior's evasiveness, is both real history, as narrated by Arrian, and a paradigm of cultural difference. The emperor Darius is a genuinely tragic figure, for the civilisation that he represented was quite unprepared to contend with enemies who could not be bought or talked off after they had won an advantage, who sought always to bring the issue to the test of battle and who fought in battle as if its immediate outcome took precedence over all other considerations, including that of personal survival. The death of Darius at the hands of his entourage, who hoped that by leaving his body to be found by Alexander they might save their own skins, perfectly epitomises the cultural clash between expediency and honour in these two different ethics of warmaking.

The ethic of the battle to the death on foot – we must say on foot for it is associated with infantry rather than cavalry fighting – then made its way from the Greek to the Roman world via the presence in southern Italy of Greek colonists. How it was transmitted, as it certainly must have been, to the Teutonic peoples with whom Rome fought its conclusive and eventually unsuccessful battles for survival has not been, and perhaps never will be reconstructed. The Teutonic invaders were, nevertheless, face-to-face warriors without doubt; but for that they would surely not have defeated Roman armies even of the debilitated state to which they descended in the last century of the western empire. A peculiar achievement of the Teutonic successor kingdoms was to assimilate the face-to-face style with combat on horseback, so that the Western knight, unlike the steppe nomad, pressed home his charge against the main body of the enemy, rather than skirmishing against it at a distance. Against the Arab and Mameluke opponents they eventually encountered in the Crusading campaigns for the Holy Land the face-to-face style often foundered; charging home could not be made to work against an enemy who saw no dishonour in avoiding contact. There was, nevertheless, a cultural exchange of great importance that resulted from the conflict of Muslim and Christian in the Middle East. The conflict resolved the inherent Christian dilemma over the morality of warmaking by transmitting to the West the ethic of holy war, which was thereafter to invest Western military culture with an ideological and intellectual dimension it had thitherto lacked.

The combination of the face-to-face style – in which the ethic of personal honour was embedded – with that ideological dimension then only awaited the addition of the technological element to produce the final Western manner of warmaking. By the eighteenth century, when the gunpowder revolution had been accepted and gunpowder weapons perfected, it had arrived. Why Western culture should have been open to the changes that technology offered, while Asian was not (and primitivism, of its nature, not at all), is a question that belongs elsewhere; we should, however, recognise that a major factor closing Asian culture to such adaptation was its adherence to a concept of military restraint that required its élites to persist in the use and monopoly of traditional weapons, however obsolete by comparison with those coming into fashion elsewhere, and that this persistence was a perfectly rational form of arms control. The Western world, by forsaking arms control, embarked on a different course, which resulted in the form of warfare that Clausewitz said was war itself: a continuation of politics, which he saw as intellectual and ideological, by means of combat, which he took to be face-to-face, with the instruments of the Western technological revolution, which he took for granted.

The Western way of warfare was to carry all before it in the years after Clausewitz died. During the nineteenth century all Asian peoples, with the exception of the Chinese, Japanese, Thais and the subjects of the Ottoman Turks, came under Western rule; the primitives of the Americas, Africa and the Pacific stood no chance at all. A few peoples of remote and inaccessible regions – Tibet, Nepal, Ethiopia – alone proved too difficult to bring under the sway of empire, though all experienced Western invasions. During the first half of the twentieth century even China succumbed, at the hands of the Westernised Japanese, while most of the Ottoman lands were overrun by Western armies also. Only the Turks of Turkey, that tough, intelligent and resourceful warrior race, who had taught their enemies so many harsh military lessons even through the unsatisfactory medium of the horse and the bow, remained unsubdued to emerge in mid-century as an independent nation.

The triumph of the Western way of warfare was, however, delusive. Directed against other military cultures it had proved irresistible. Turned in on itself it brought disaster and threatened catastrophe. The First World War, fought almost exclusively between European states, terminated European dominance of the world and, through the suffering it inflicted on the participant populations, corrupted what was best in their civilisation – its liberalism and hopefulness – and conferred on militarists and totalitarians the role of proclaiming the future. The future they wanted brought about the Second World War which completed the ruin initiated by the First. It also brought about the development of nuclear weapons, the logical culmination of the technological trend in the Western way of warfare, and the ultimate denial of the proposition that war was, or might be, a continuation of politics by other means.

Politics must continue; war cannot. That is not to say that the role of the warrior is over. The world community needs, more than it has ever done, skilful and disciplined warriors who are ready to put themselves at the service of its authority. Such warriors must properly be seen as the protectors of civilisation, not its enemies. The style in which they fight for civilisation – against ethnic bigots, regional warlords, ideological intransigents, common pillagers and organised international criminals – cannot derive from the Western model of warmaking alone. Future peacekeepers and peacemakers have much to learn from alternative military cultures, not only that of the Orient but of the primitive world also. There is a wisdom in the principles of intellectual restraint and even of symbolic ritual that needs to be rediscovered. There is an even greater wisdom in the denial that politics and war belong within the same continuum. Unless we insist on denying it, our future, like that of the last Easter Islanders, may belong to the men with bloodied hands.

References

1 WAR IN HUMAN HISTORY

1   Carl von Clausewitz, *On War* (tr. J.J. Graham), London, 1908, I, p. 23
2   Luke 7: 6–8, Authorised Version
3   Address to the Michigan Military Academy, 19 June 1879, in J. Wintle, *The Dictionary of War Quotations*, London, 1989, p. 91
4   R. Parkinson, *Clausewitz*, London, 1970, pp. 175–6
5   R. McNeal, *Tsar and Cossack*, Basingstoke, 1989, p. 5
6   A. Seaton, *The Horsemen of the Steppes*, London, 1985, p. 51
7   Parkinson, op. cit., p. 194
8   Seaton, op. cit., p. 121
9   Ibid., p. 154
10 Parkinson, op. cit., p. 169
11 G. Sansom, *The Western World and Japan*, London, 1950, pp. 265–6
12 W. St Clair, *That Greece Might Still Be Free*, London, 1972, pp. 114–15
13 Marshal de Saxe, *Mes rêveries*, Amsterdam, 1757, I, pp. 86–7
14 P. Contamine, *War in the Middle Ages* (tr. M. Jones), Oxford, 1984, p. 169
15 M. Howard, *War in European History*, Oxford, 1976, p. 15
16 L. Tolstoy, *Anna Karenin*, London, 1987, pp. 190–5
17 M. Howard, *Clausewitz*, Oxford, 1983, p. 35
18 P. Paret, *Understanding War*, Princeton, 1992, p. 104
19 P. Paret, *Clausewitz and the State*, Princeton, 1985, pp. 322–4
20 M. Howard, op. cit., p. 59
21 Carl von Clausewitz, *On War* (tr. M. Howard and P. Paret), Princeton, 1976, p. 18
22 Ibid., p. 593
23 M. Sahlins, *Tribesmen*, New Jersey, 1968, p. 64
24 S. Engleit, *Islands at the Centre of the World*, New York, 1990, p. 139
25 M. Wilson and L. Thompson (eds.), *Oxford History of South Africa*, Vol I, Oxford, 1969
26 K. Otterbein, 'The Evolution of Zulu Warfare', in B. Oget (ed.) *War and Society in Africa*, 1972
27 Wilson and Thompson, op. cit., pp. 338–9
28 G. Jefferson, *The Destruction of the Zulu Kingdom*, London, 1979, pp. 9–10, 12

29   E.J. Krige, *The Social System of the Zulus*, Pietermaritzburg, 1950, Chapter 3 passim

30   Wilson and Thompson, op. cit., p. 345

31   Ibid., p. 346

32   D. Ayalon, 'Preliminary Remarks on the *Mamluk* Institutions in Islam', in V. Parry and M. Yapp (eds.), *War, Technology and Society in the Middle East*, London, 1975, p. 44

33   Ayalon, ibid., pp. 44–7

34   D. Pipes, *Slave Soldiers and Islam*, New Haven, 1981, p. 19

35   P. Holt, A. Lambton and B. Lewis (eds.), *The Cambridge History of Islam*, Cambridge, 1970, Vol. IA, p. 214

36   H. Rabie, 'The Training of the Mamluk Faris', in Parry and Yapp, op. cit., pp. 153–63

37   D. Ayalon, *Gunpowder and Firearms in the Mamluk Kingdom*, London, 1956, p. 86

38   Ibid., pp. 94–5

39   Ibid., p. 70

40   A. Marsot, *Egypt in the Reign of Muhammad Ali*, Cambridge, 1982, pp. 60–72

41   N. Perrin, *Giving Up the Gun*, Boston, 1988, p. 19

42   R. Storry, *A History of Modern Japan*, London, 1960, pp. 53–4

43   J. Hale, *Renaissance War Studies*, London, 1988, pp. 397–8

44   Sansom, op. cit., p. 192

45   Storry, op. cit., p. 42

46   Perrin, op. cit., pp. 11–12

47   I. Berlin, *The Crooked Timber of Humanity*, New York, 1991, p. 51

48   Ibid., pp. 52–3

49   Clausewitz (tr. Graham), op. cit., p. 25

50   J. Shy 'Jomini', in P. Paret, *Makers of Modern Strategy*, Princeton, 1986, p. 181

51   A. Kenny, *The Logic of Deterrence*, London, 1985, p. 15

52   J. Spence, *The Search for Modern China*, London, 1990, p. 395

53   Ibid., p. 371

54   B. Jelavich, *History of the Balkans (Twentieth Century)*, Cambridge, 1983, p. 270

55   F. Deakin, *The Embattled Mountain*, London, 1971, p. 55

56   N. Beloff, *Tito's Flawed Legacy*, London, 1985, p. 75

57   K. McCormick and H. Perry, *Images of War*, London, 1991, pp. 145, 326, 334

58   Deakin, op. cit., p. 72

59 M. Djilas, *Wartime*, New York, 1977, p. 283
60 Spence, op. cit., p. 405
61 A. Horne, *A Savage War of Peace*, London, 1977, pp. 64, 537–8
62 R. Weigley, *The Age of Battles*, Bloomington, 1991, p. 543
63 J. Mueller, 'Changing Attitudes to War. The Impact of the First World War', *British Journal of Political Science*, 21, pp. 25–6, 27

LIMITATIONS ON WARMAKING

1   *Mariner's Mirror*, Vol. 77, no. 3, p. 217
2   A. Ferrill, *The Origins of War*, London, 1985, pp. 86–7
3   See J. Guilmartin, *Gunpowder and Galleys*, Cambridge, 1974, especially Chapter 1, for argument that the galley's usefulness was not immediately extinguished by the appearance of cannon
4   J. Keegan, *The Price of Admiralty*, London, 1988, p. 137
5   O. Farnes, *War in the Arctic*, London, 1991, pp. 39 ff.
6   See 'Adrianople' in index of R. and T. Dupuy, *The Encyclopedia of Military History*, London, 1986
7   J-P. Pallud, *Blitzkrieg in the West*, London, 1991, p. 347
8   J. Keegan, *The Second World War*, London, 1989, p. 462
9   *Punch*, 1853, quoted in T. Royle, *A Dictionary of Military Quotations*, London, 1990, p. 123
10 *The Times Atlas* (Comprehensive Edition), London, 1977, plate 5
11 I. Berlin, *Karl Marx*, Oxford, 1978, p. 179
12 A. Van der Heyden and H. Scullard, *The Atlas of the Classical World*, London, 1959, p. 127, and C. Duffy, *Siege Warfare*, London, 1979, pp. 204–7, 232–7
13 N. Nicolson, *Alex*, London, 1973, p. 10
14 See A. Fraser, *Boadicea's Chariot*, London, 1988

2 STONE

1   J. Groebel and R. Hinde (eds.), *Aggression and War*, Cambridge, 1989, pp. xiii–xvi
2   A. J. Herbert, 'The Physiology of Aggression', in ibid., p.67
3   Ibid., pp. 68–9
4   R. Dawkins, *The Selfish Gene*, Oxford, 1989
5   A. Manning, in Groebel and Hinde, op. cit., pp. 52–5
6   Groebel and Hinde, op. cit., p. 5
7   A. Manning, in Groebel and Hinde, op. cit., p. 51

8   R. Clark, *Freud*, London, 1980, p. 486 ff.
9   K. Lorenz, *On Aggression*, London, 1966
10 R. Ardrey, *The Territorial Imperative*, London, 1967
11 L. Tiger, *Men in Groups*, London, 1969
12 M. Harris, *The Rise of Anthropological Theory*, London, 1968, pp. 17–18
13 D. Freeman, *Margaret Mead and Samoa*, Cambridge, Mass., 1983, pp. 13–17
14 Ibid., Chapter 3
15 Harris, op. cit., p. 406
16 A. Kuper, *Anthropologists and Anthropology*, London, 1973, p. 18
17 Ibid., pp. 207–11
18 A. Mockler, *Haile Selassie's War*, Oxford, 1984, p. 219
19 A. Stahlberg, *Bounden Duty*, London, 1990, p. 72
20 H. Turney-High, *Primitive War: Its Practice and Concepts* (2nd edition), Columbia, SC, 1971, p. 5
21 Ibid.
22 Ibid., p. 55
23 Ibid., p. 142
24 Ibid., p. 14
25 Ibid., p. 253
26 Ibid., p. v
27 R. Ferguson (ed.), *Warfare, Culture and Environment*, Orlando, 1984, p. 8
28 M. Mead, 'Warfare is Only an Invention', in L. Bramson and G. Goethals, *War: Studies from Psychology, Sociology, Anthropology*, New York, 1964, pp. 269–74
29 R. Duson-Hudson, in *Human Intra-specific Conflict: An Evolutionary Perspective*, Guggenheim Institute, New York, 1986
30 Ferguson, op. cit., pp. 6, 26
31 M. Fried, M. Harris and R. Murphy (eds.), *War: The Anthropology of Armed Conflict and Aggression*, New York, 1967, p. 132
32 Ibid., p. 133
33 Ibid., p. 128
34 *US News and World Report*, 11 April 1988, p. 59
35 W. Divale, *War in Primitive Society*, Santa Barbara, 1973, p. xxi
36 A. Vayda, *War in Ecological Perspective*, New York, 1976, pp. 9–42
37 Ibid., pp. 15–16
38 Ibid., pp. 16–17
39 J. Haas (ed.), *The Anthropology of War*, Cambridge, 1990, p. 172

40 P. Blau and W. Scott, *Formal and Informal Organisations*, San Francisco, 1962, pp. 30–2

41 M. Fried, *Transactions of New York Academy of Sciences*, Series 2, 28, 1966, pp. 529–45

42 J. Middleton and D. Tait, *Tribes Without Rulers*, London, 1958, pp. 1–31

43 R. Cohen, 'Warfare and State Formation', in Ferguson, op. cit., pp. 333–4

44 P. Kirch, *The Evolution of the Polynesian Chiefdoms*, Cambridge, 1984, pp. 147–8

45 Ibid., p. 81

46 Ibid., pp. 166–7

47 Vayda, op. cit., p. 115

48 Kirch, op. cit., pp. 209–11

49 Vayda, op. cit., p. 80

50 Turney-High, op. cit., p. 193: 'The Caytes of the Brazilian coast ate every wrecked vessel's crew. At one meal they ate the first Bishop of Bahia, two Canons, the Procurator of the Royal Portuguese Treasury, two pregnant women and several children.'

51 Ibid., pp. 189–90

52 I. Clendinnen, *Aztecs*, Cambridge, 1991, pp. 87–8

53 R. Hassing, 'Aztec and Spanish Conquest in Mesoamerica', in B. Ferguson and N. Whitehead, *War in the Tribal Zone*, Santa Fe, 1991, p. 85

54 Ibid., p. 86

55 Clendinnen, op. cit., p. 78

56 Ibid., p. 81

57 Ibid., p. 116

58 Ibid., p. 93

59 Ibid., pp. 94–5

60 Ibid., pp. 95–6

61 Ibid., pp. 25–7

62 I. Clendinnen, *Ambivalent Conquests, Maya and Spaniard in Yucatan, 1515–70*, Cambridge, 1987, pp. 144, 148–9

63 J. Roberts, *The Pelican History of the World*, London, 1987, p. 21

64 Ibid., p. 31

65 H. Breuil and R. Lautier, *The Men of the Old Stone Age*, London, 1965, p. 71

66 Ibid., p. 69

67 Ibid., p. 20

68 Ibid., p. 69
69 A. Ferrill, op. cit., p. 18
70 W. Reid, *Arms Through the Ages*, New York, 1976, pp. 9–11
71 Breuil and Lautier, op. cit., p. 72
72 C. Robarchak, in *Papers Presented to the Guggenheim Foundation Conference on the Anthropology of War*, Santa Fe, 1986; also Robarchak, in Haas, op. cit., pp. 56–76
73 H. Obermaier, *La vida de nuestros antepasados cuaternanos en Europa*, Madrid, 1926
74 F. Wendorf, in F. Wendorf (ed.), *The Prehistory of Nubia*, II, Dallas, 1968, p. 959
75 Ferrill, op. cit., p. 22
76 M. Hoffman, *Egypt Before the Pharaohs*, London, 1988, pp. 87–9
77 Roberts, op. cit., p. 51
78 J. Mellaert, 'Early Urban Communities in the Near East, 9000–3400 BC', in P. Moorey (ed.), *The Origins of Civilisation*, Oxford, 1979, pp. 22–5
79 H. de la Croix, *Military Considerations in City Planning*, New York, 1972, p. 14
80 Y. Yadin, *The Art of Warfare in Biblical Lands*, London, 1963, p. 34
81 Mellaert, op. cit., p. 22
82 B. Kemp, *Ancient Egypt. Anatomy of a Civilisation*, London, 1983, p. 269
83 S. Piggott, 'Early Towns in Europe', in Moorey, op. cit., pp. 3, 44
84 H. Thomas, *An Unfinished History of the World*, London, pp. 19, 21
85 J. Bottero et al. (eds.), *The Near East: The Early Civilisations*, London, 1967, p. 44
86 Ibid., p. 6
87 Roberts, op. cit., p. 131
88 Hoffman, op. cit., pp. 331–2
89 Kemp, op. cit., pp. 168–72
90 Ibid., pp. 223–30
91 Ibid., p. 227
92 Yadin, op. cit., pp. 192–3
93 Kemp, op. cit., pp. 43, 225
94 Hoffman, op. cit., p. 116
95 W. Hayes, 'Egypt from the Death of Ammanemes II to Seqenenre II', in *Cambridge Ancient History* (3rd edition), Vol. II, Part 1, p. 73
96 Kemp, op. cit., p. 229

97 The first of the intermediate periods (2160–1991 BC) between the Old and Middle Kingdoms is held to have been an era of warmaking between local strongmen: a text of the period (quoted Bottero, op. cit., p. 337) reads, however, as follows: 'I armed my bands of recruits and went into combat . . . There was no one else with me but my own troops, while [the mercenaries from Nubia and elsewhere] were united against me. I returned in triumph, my whole city with me, with no losses'; scarcely evidence that Egyptian domestic warfare was hard-fought.

98 Bottero, op. cit., pp. 70–1

99 W. McNeill, *The Pursuit of Power*, Oxford, 1983, p. 5

100 J. Laessoe, *People of Ancient Assyria*, London, 1963, p. 16

101 Yadin, op. cit., p. 130

102 G. Roux, *Ancient Iraq*, New York, 1986, p. 129

103 P.J. Forbes, *Metallurgy in Antiquity*, Leiden, 1950, p. 321

104 Ibid., p. 255 and fig. 49

105 W. McNeill, *A World History*, New York, 1961, p. 34

106 R. Gabriel and K. Metz, *From Sumer to Rome*, New York, 1991, p. 9

FORTIFICATION

1 D. Petite, *Le balcon de la Côte d'azure*, Marignan, 1983, passim

2 A. Fox, *Prehistoric Maori Fortifications*, Auckland, 1974, pp. 28–9

3 F. Winter, *Greek Fortifications*, Toronto, 1971

4 N. Pounds, *The Mediaeval Castle in England and Wales*, Cambridge, 1990, p. 69

5 S. Johnson, *Roman Fortifications on the Saxon Shore*, London, 1977, p. 5

6 Kemp, op. cit., pp. 174–6

7 S. Piggott, 'Early Towns in Europe', in Moorey, op. cit., pp. 48–9

8 A. Hogg, *Hill Forts of Britain*, London, 1975, p. 17

9 Piggott, op. cit., p. 50

10 W. Watson, in Moorey, op. cit., p. 55

11 S. Johnson, *Late Roman Fortifications*, London, 1983, p. 20

12 E. Luttwak, The *Grand Strategy of the Roman Empire*, Baltimore, 1976, pp. 96, 102–4

13 B. Isaac, *The Limits of Empire*, Oxford, 1990; A. Horne, *A Savage War of Peace*, London, 1987, pp. 263–7

14 Q. Hughes, *Military Architecture*, London, 1974, pp. 187–90

15 C. Duffy, *Siege Warfare*, London, 1979, pp. 204–7

16 J. Fryer, *The Great Wall of China*, London, 1975, p. 104; A. Waldron, *The Great Wall of China*, Cambridge, 1992, pp. 5–6

17 O. Lattimore, 'Origins of the Great Wall', in *Studies in Frontier History*, London, 1962, pp. 97–118

18 J. Needham, *Science and Civilisation in China*, I, Cambridge, 1954, p. 144

19 S. Johnson, *Late Roman Fortifications*, Maps 25, 44, 46

20 P. Contamine, *War in the Middle Ages*, Oxford, 1984, p. 108

21 Ibid., p. 46

22 Pounds, op. cit., p. 19

23 Winter, op. cit., pp. 218–19

24 Yadin, op. cit., pp. 158–9, 393, 409

25 S. Runciman, *A History of the Crusades*, I, Cambridge, 1951, pp. 231–4

26 Pounds, op. cit., p. 115

27 Ibid., p. 213

3 FLESH

1 A. Azzarolli, *An Early History of Horsemanship*, London, 1985, pp. 5–6

2 S. Piggott, *The Earliest Wheeled Transport*, London, 1983, p. 87

3 Ibid., p. 39

4 Azzarolli, op. cit., p. 9

5 R. Sallares, *The Ecology of the Ancient Greek World*, London, 1991, pp. 396–7

6 Piggott, op. cit., pp. 64–84

7 W. McNeill, *The Rise of the West*, Chicago, 1963, p. 103

8 A. Friendly, *The Dreadful Day*, London, 1981, p. 27

9 Yadin, op. cit., pp. 150, 187

10 J. Guilmartin, op. cit., p. 152; P. Klopsteg, *Turkish Archery and the Composite Bow*, Evanstown, 1947

11 Yadin, op. cit., p. 455

12 Y. Garlan, *War in the Ancient World*, London, 1975, p. 90

13 O. Lattimore, op. cit., pp. 41–4

14 Piggott, op. cit., pp. 103–4

15 H. Creel, *The Origins of Statecraft in China*, Chicago, 1970, pp. 285–6

16 Guilmartin, op. cit., p. 157

17 Lattimore, op. cit., p. 53

18 *Cambridge Ancient History*, Vol. II, Part 1, Cambridge, 1973,

pp. 375–6
19 Laessoe, op. cit., pp. 87, 91
20 *Cambridge Ancient History*, Vol. II, Part 1, pp. 54–64
21 J. Gernet, *A History of Chinese Civilisation*, Cambridge, 1982, pp. 40–5
22 H. Saggs, *The Might That Was Assyria*, London, 1984, p. 197
23 Ibid., pp. 199, 255
24 Ibid., p. 100
25 Ibid., p. 101
26 Ibid., p. 258
27 Creel, op. cit., pp. 258, 265
28 Ibid., p. 259
29 Ibid., pp. 266, 264
30 Robert Thurton, 'The Prince Consort in Armour', in M. Girouard, *The Return of Camelot*, New Haven, 1981; Hubert Lanzinger, 'Hitler in Armour', in P. Adam, *The Arts of the Third Reich*, London, 1992
31 Yadin, op. cit., pp. 100–3; *Cambridge Ancient History*, Vol. II, Part 1, pp. 444–51
32 Yadin, op. cit., pp. 103–14
33 Ibid., pp. 218–21
34 McNeill, *The Rise of the West*, p. 15
35 Saggs, op. cit., p. 169
36 J. Saunders, *The History of the Mongol Conquests*, London, 1991, pp. 9–10
37 Ibid., p. 14; Gernet, op. cit., pp. 4–5
38 W. McNeill, *The Human Condition*, Princeton, 1980, p. 47
39 D. Maenchen-Helfen, *The World of the Huns*, Berkeley, 1973, p. 187
40 Ibid., p. 267
41 Ibid., p. 184
42 Ibid., p. 180
43 J. Jakobsen and R. Adams, 'Salt and Silt in Ancient Mesopotamian Agriculture', *Science*, CXXVIII, 1958, p. 257
44 L. Kwantem, *Imperial Nomads: A History of Central Asia, 500–1500*, Leicester, 1979, p. 12
45 A. Jones, *The Later Roman Empire, 284–602*, Oxford, 1962, p. 157
46 J. Bury, *A History of the Later Roman Empire*, 1927, I, p. 300, n. 3
47 R. Lindner, 'Nomadism, Horses and Huns', *Past and Present*, 92 (1981), pp. 1–19
48 J. Lucas, *Fighting Troops of the Austro-Hungarian Army*, New York, 1987, p. 149

49 Marquess of Anglesey, *A History of British Cavalry*, IV, London, 1986, p. 297
50 Maenchen-Helfen, op. cit., pp. 152–3
51 P. Ratchnevsky, *Genghis Khan*, Oxford, 1991, p. 155
52 Kwantem, op. cit., p. 21; the Ephthalites appear to have spoken Tocharian, an extinct Indo-European language
53 Saunders, op. cit., p. 27
54 Ibid.
55 J. Keegan, *The Mask of Command*, London, 1988, p. 18
56 Ferrill, op. cit., p. 70
57 A. Hourani, *A History of the Arab Peoples*, London, 1991, p. 19
58 Koran 9: 125
59 P.M. Holt and others, *Cambridge History of Islam*, Vol. IA, Cambridge, 1977, pp. 87–92
60 *Cambridge History of Islam*, op. cit., p. 42
61 Sallares, op. cit., p. 27
62 D. Hill, 'The Role of the Camel and the Horse in the Early Arab Conquests', in Parry and Yapp, op. cit., p. 36
63 Ibid., pp. 57–8
64 *Cambridge History of Islam*, op. cit., p. 60
65 Ibid.
66 Pipes, op. cit., pp. 109–13
67 Ibid., p. 148
68 Saunders, op. cit., p. 37
69 Kwantem, op. cit., p. 61
70 *Cambridge History of Islam*, op. cit., p. 150
71 Ratchnevsky, op. cit., p. 109
72 Kwantem, op. cit., pp. 12–13
73 Chen Ya-tien, *Chinese Military Theory*, Stevenage, 1992, pp. 21–30
74 Gernet, op. cit., p. 309
75 Ibid., p. 310
76 Ratchnevsky, op. cit., pp. 194–5
77 Kwantem, op. cit., p. 188
78 Ratchnevsky, op. cit., pp. 4–5
79 B. Manz, *The Rise and Rule of Tamerlane*, Cambridge, 1989, p. 4
80 Saunders, op. cit., pp. 196–9
81 Kwantem, op. cit., p. 192
82 Ibid., p. 108
83 Saunders, op. cit., p. 66
84 Ratchnevsky, op. cit., pp. 96–101

85 *Cambridge History of Islam*, op. cit., p. 158
86 Kwantem, op. cit., p. 159; S. Shaw, *History of the Ottoman Empire and Modern Turkey*, Vol. II, Cambridge, 1976, p. 184
87 D. Morgan, 'The Mongols in Syria', in P. Edburg (ed.), *Crusade and Settlement*, Cardiff, 1985, pp. 231–5
88 P. Thorau, 'The Battle of Ain Jalut: A Re-examination', in ibid., pp. 236–41
89 Ibid., p. 238
90 Manz, op. cit., pp. 14–16
91 B. Spuler, *The Mongols in History*, London, 1971, p. 80
92 Shaw, op. cit., I, p. 245
93 Ratchnevsky, op. cit., pp. 153–4
94 See Keegan, *Mask of Command*, esp. Chapter 2
95 C. Duffy, *Russia's Military Way to the West*, London, 1981, p. 2
96 J. Fairbank, 'Varieties of Chinese Military Experience', in F. Kierman and J. Fairbank, *Chinese Ways in Warfare*, Cambridge, Mass., 1974
97 Ibid., p. 7
98 Ibid., p. 15
99 Ibid., p. 14
100 Gernet, op. cit., p. 493

ARMIES

1 Parkinson, op. cit., p. 176
2 J. Elting, *Swords Around a Throne*, London, 1989, Chapters 18–19
3 H. Roeder (ed.), *The Ordeal of Captain Roeder*, London, 1960
4 N. Jones, *Hitler's Heralds*, London, 1987, passim
5 S. Andreski, *Military Organisation and Society*, London, 1968
6 W. McNeill, *Plagues and People*, New York, 1976
7 Andreski, op. cit., p. 33
8 Ibid., pp. 91–107, 75–90
9 Ibid., p. 26
10 Seaton, op. cit., p. 57
11 Andreski, op. cit., p. 27
12 Ibid., p. 37
13 M. Lewis, *The Navy of Britain*, London, 1948, pp. 128–44
14 G. Jones, *A History of the Vikings*, Oxford, 1984, p. 211
15 Manz, op. cit., p. 17
16 Ratchnetsky, op. cit., p. 66

17   Hourani, op. cit., pp. 139–40
18   S. Blondal, *The Varangians of Byzantium*, Cambridge, 1978, p. 230–5
19   P. Mansel, *Pillars of Monarchy*, London, 1984, p. 1
20   Garlan, op cit., p. 95
21   M. Mallet, *Mercenaries and their Masters*, London, 1974, pp. 60–1
22   L. Keppie, *The Making of the Roman Army*, London, 1984, p. 17
23   P. Paret (ed.), *Makers of Modern Strategy*, p. 19
24   W. Doyle, *The Oxford History of the French Revolution*, 1989, pp. 204–5

4 IRON

1   R.J. Forbes, *Metallurgy in Antiquity*, London, 1950, p. 380
2   Ibid., pp. 418–19
3   R. Oakeshott, *The Archaeology of Weapons*, London, 1960, pp. 40–2
4   N. Sandars, *The Sea Peoples*, London, 1985, pp. 56–8
5   P. Greenhalgh, *Early Greek Warfare*, Cambridge, 1993, pp. 10–11
6   Ibid., pp. 1–2
7   N. Hammond, *A History of Greece to 322 BC*, Oxford, 1959, p. 73
8   Ibid., p. 81
9   Ibid., p. 99
10   Ibid., p. 100
11   Ibid., p. 101
12   V. Hanson, *The Western Way of War*, New York, 1989
13   V. Hanson, *Warfare and Agriculture in Classical Greece*, Pisa, 1983, p. 59
14   Ibid., pp. 50–4
15   Ibid., p. 42
16   Ibid., pp. 67–74
17   Hanson, *Western Way*, p. 6
18   Ibid., pp. 4, 34
19   M. Finley and H. Plaket, *The Olympic Games*, New York, 1976, p. 19
20   D. Sansome, *Greek Athletics and the Genesis of Sport*, Berkeley, 1988, pp. 19, 50–3, 63
21   M. Poliakoff, *Combat Sports in the Ancient World*, New Haven, 1987, pp. 93, 96
22   Finley and Plaket, op. cit., p. 21
23   Poliakoff, op. cit., pp. 93–4
24   A. Snodgrass, 'The Hoplite Reform and History', *Journal of Hellenic Studies*, 85 (1965), pp. 110–22

25   M. Jameson, 'Sacrifice before Battle', in V. Hanson (ed.), *Hoplites*, London, 1991, p. 220
26   E. Wheeler, 'The General as Hoplite', in ibid., pp. 150–4
27   J. Lazenby, 'The Killing Zone', in ibid., p. 88
28   Hanson, *Western Way*, p. 185
29   Ibid., pp. 64–5
30   Ibid., pp. 180–1
31   Ibid., p. 36
32   Ibid., p. 4
33   Roberts, op. cit., p. 178
34   E. Wood, *Peasant, Citizen and Slave*, London, 1981, pp. 42–4
35   Hanson, *Western Way*, pp. 10, 16
36   Sandars, op. cit., pp. 125–31
37   Garlan, op. cit., pp. 130–1
38   Hammond, op. cit., pp. 289–90
39   Ibid., pp. 661–2
40   Keegan, *Mask of Command*, pp. 78–9
41   Ibid., p. 80
42   Ibid., p. 82
43   Hammond, op. cit., p. 615
44   L. Keppie, op. cit.
45   Hammond, op. cit., p. 236
46   Keppie, op. cit., p. 18
47   W. Harris, *War and Imperialism in Republican Rome*, Oxford, 1979, pp. 54–67
48   Ibid., p. 56
49   Ibid., p. 51
50   Ibid., p. 48
51   Keppie, op. cit., p. 18
52   Harris, op. cit., pp. 44–6
53   Ibid., pp. 11–12
54   Keppie, op. cit., p. 53
55   J. Keegan, *The Face of Battle*, London, 1976, p. 65
56   G. Watson, *The Roman Soldier*, London, 1985, pp. 72–4
57   Van der Heyden and Scullard, op. cit., p. 125
58   Keppie, op. cit., pp. 61–2
59   J. Balsdon, *Rome*, London, 1970, p. 91
60   A. Ferrill, *The Fall of the Roman Empire*, London, 1986, p. 25
61   Luttwak, op. cit., pp. 191–4
62   D. Breeze and B. Dobson, *Hadrian's Wall*, London, 1976, pp. 247–8

63 Balsdon, op. cit., pp. 90–1
64 Ferrill, *Fall of the Roman Empire*, pp. 48–9
65 Ibid., p. 140
66 Ibid., p. 160
67 J. Fuller, *The Decisive Battles of the Western World*, London, 1954, pp. 307–29
68 A. Jones, *The Decline of the Ancient World*, London, 1966, pp. 297–9
69 Ibid., p. 102
70 J. Beeler, *War in Feudal Europe, 730–1200*, Ithaca, 1991, pp. 2–5
71 Ibid., p. 17
72 M. Van Crefeld, *Technology and War*, London, 1991, p. 18
73 Ibid., p. 20
74 Beeler, op. cit., pp. 228–32
75 Johnson, *Late Roman Fortifications*, pp. 8–16
76 G. Jones, *Vikings*, pp. 182–92
77 Ibid., p. 76
78 H. Cowdray, 'The Genesis of the Crusades', in T. Murphy (ed.), *The Holy War*, Columbus, 1976, pp. 17–18
79 Beeler, op. cit., p. 12
80 Runciman, op. cit., pp. 106–8
81 Ibid., pp. 91–2
82 R. Smail, *Crusading Warfare*, Cambridge, 1956, pp. 115–20
83 Ibid., p. 202
84 G. Sainty, *The Order of St John*, New York, 1991, pp. 105
85 P. Contamine, *War in the Middle Ages*, p. 75
86 Ewart, op. cit., pp. 283–4
87 Smail, op. cit., pp. 165–8

LOGISTICS AND SUPPLY

1 Watson, op. cit., pp. 63–5
2 P. Liddle, *The 1916 Battle of the Somme*, London, 1992, p. 39
3 J. Thompson, *No Picnic*, London, 1992, p. 89
4 Keegan, *Mask of Command*, p. 134
5 Luttwak, op. cit., map 2.2
6 C. Callwell, *Small Wars: Their Principles and Practice*, London, 1899, p. 40
7 T. Derry and T. Williams, *A Short History of Technology*, Oxford, 1960, p. 433
8 R. Chevallier, *Roman Roads*, London, 1976, p. 152

9   Piggott, op. cit., p. 345
10 Keegan, *Mask of Command*, p. 114
11 D. Engels, *Alexander the Great and the Logistics of the Macedonian Army*, Berkeley, 1978, p. 112
12 M. Grant, *The Army of the Caesars*, London, 1974, p. xxiii
13 Derry and Williams, op. cit., pp. 691–5
14 B. Wiley, *The Life of Johnny Reb*, Baton Rouge, 1918, p. 92
15 J. McPherson, *Battle Cry of Freedom*, New York, 1988, pp. 11–12
16 Ibid., pp. 424–7
17 D. Showalter, *Railroads and Rifles*, Hamden, 1975, p. 67
18 J. Edmonds, *A Short History of World War I*, Oxford, 1951, pp. 9–10
19 J. Piekalkiewicz, *Pferd und Reiter im II Weltkrieg*, Munich, 1976, p. 4
20 J. Beaumont, *Comrades in Arms*, London, 1980, p. 208
21 J. Thompson, *The Lifeblood of War*, London, 1991, p. 38
22 McNeill, *Pursuit of Power*, pp. 322, 324, 329
23 Watson, op. cit., p. 51
24 Derry and Williams, op. cit., p. 269
25 McNeill, *Pursuit of Power*, pp. 166–7
26 Ibid., p. 170
27 Ibid., p. 238
28 Ibid., p. 290
29 A. Milward, *War, Economy and Society, 1939–45*, London, 1977, pp. 64–9, 76
30 D. Van der Vat, *The Atlantic Campaign*, London, 1988, pp. 229, 270, 351

5 FIRE

1   Derry and Wells, op. cit., pp. 268–9, 514
2   J. Needham, *Science and Civilisation in China*, I, Cambridge, 1954, p. 134
3   McNeill, *Pursuit of Power*, p. 39
4   Ibid., pp. 82–3
5   Duffy, *Siege Warfare*, pp. 8–9
6   Ibid., p. 9
7   Ibid., p. 15
8   Ibid., p. 25
9   Ibid., pp. 29–31
10 Mallet, op. cit., p. 253
11 Duffy, *Siege Warfare*, p. 40

12 Ibid., pp. 41–2
13 Ibid., p. 61
14 Ibid., p. 64
15 G. Parker, *The Military Revolution*, Cambridge, 1988, p. 17
16 Ibid., p. 17
17 Mallet, op. cit., pp. 254–5
18 Grant, op. cit., pp. 15–16
19 Hale, *Renaissance War Studies*, p. 396
20 J. Hale, *War and Society in Renaissance Europe*, Leicester, 1985, p. 96
21 G. Parker, *The Army of Flanders and the Spanish Road*, Cambridge, 1972, pp. 27–9
22 Guilmartin, op. cit., p. 207
23 Ibid., pp. 251–2
24 Lewis, op. cit., pp. 76–80
25 Guilmartin, op. cit., pp. 8–11
26 Weigley, op. cit., pp. 15–16
27 Ibid., pp. 76–7
28 Watson, op. cit., pp. 57–9
29 C. Duffy, *The Military Experience in the Age of Reason*, London, 1989
30 G. and A. Parker, *European Soldiers 1550–1650*, Cambridge, 1977, pp. 14–15
31 Hale, *War and Society*, p. 87
32 A. Corvisier, *Armies and Society in Europe*, Bloomington, 1979, pp. 54–60
33 Hale, *Renaissance War Studies*, pp. 285, 237–42
34 Weigley, op. cit., p. 44
35 Shaw, op. cit., Vol. I, pp. 113–14
36 B. Lenman, 'The Transition to European Military Ascendancy in India', in J. Lynn, *Tools of War*, Chicago, 1990, p. 106
37 Doyle, op. cit., pp. 67–71
38 J. Galvin, *The Minute Men*, McLean, 1989, pp. 27–33
39 J. Lynn, 'En avant: The Origins of the Revolutionary Attack', in Lynn, op. cit., pp. 168–9
40 Elting, op. cit., pp. 123–56
41 Weigley, op. cit., p. 265
42 Lynn, in Lynn, op. cit., p. 167
43 F. Gilbert, 'Machiavelli', in P. Paret, *Makers of Modern Strategy*, p. 31

44 B. Liddell Hart, *The Ghost of Napoleon*, London, 1933, pp. 118–29
45 McNeill, *Pursuit of Power*, op. cit., p. 254
46 R. Challener, *The French Theory of the Nation in Arms*, New York, 1955, p. 58
47 M. Eksteins, *Rites of Spring*, New York, 1989, p. 93
48 C. Jones, *The Longman Companion to the French Revolution*, London, 1989, pp. 156, 287
49 T. Livermore, *Numbers and Losses in the American Civil War*, Bloomington, 1957, pp. 7–8
50 McPherson, op. cit., p. 9
51 Duffy, *Experience of War*, p. 209
52 A. Corvisier, 'Le moral des combattants, panique et enthousiasme', in *Revue historique des armées*, 3, 1977, pp. 7–32
53 Elting, op. cit., pp. 30–1, 143
54 T. Wilson, *The Myriad Faces of War*, Cambridge, 1986, p. 757
55 A. Horne, *To Lose a Battle*, London, 1969, p. 26
56 R. Larson, *The British Army and the Theory of Armoured Warfare 1918–40*, Newark, 1984, p. 34
57 Keegan, *Mask of Command*, p. 238
58 A. Bullock, *Hitler and Stalin*, London, 1991, p. 259
59 Ibid., p. 358
60 C. Barnett (ed.), *Hitler's Generals*, London, 1989, pp. 444–5
61 Keegan, *Mask of Command*, p. 235
62 G. Welchman, *The Hut Six Story*, London, 1982, pp. 19–20
63 Keegan, *Mask of Command*, p. 302
64 Ibid., p. 286
65 T. Taylor, *The Breaking Wave*, London, 1967, pp. 114–15
66 Ibid., p. 97
67 K. Wakefield (ed.), *The Blitz Then and Now*, London, 1988, p. 8
68 O. Bartov, *The Eastern Front 1941–5*, Basingstoke, 1985, pp. 107–19
69 D. Kahn, *Seizing the Enigma*, London, 1991, pp. 245–58
70 W. Murray, *Luftwaffe*, London, 1985, pp. 8–12
71 J. Terraine, *The Right of the Line*, London, 1985, p. 474
72 R. Spector, *Eagle Against the Sun*, London, 1984, pp. 79–82
73 R. Connaughton, *The War of the Rising Sun and the Tumbling Bear*, London, 1988, pp. 166–7
74 Spector, op. cit., pp. 259–67
75 N. Longmate, *Hitler's Rockets*, London, 1985, p. 59
76 M. Gilbert, *Second World War*, London, 1989, pp. 20–1
77 L. Freedman, *The Evolution of Nuclear Strategy*, London, 1989, p. 16

78   Ibid., p. 19
79   Ibid.
80   Ibid., p. 246
81   G. Draper, 'Grotius' Place in the Development of Legal Ideas about War', in H. Bull et al. (eds.), *Hugo Grotius and International Relations*, Oxford, 1990, pp. 201–2
82   G. Best, *Humanity in Warfare*, London, 1980, pp. 150–1

Select Bibliography

Adam, P. *The Arts of the Third Reich*, London, 1992

Andreski, S. *Military Organisation and Society*, London, 1908

Anglesey, Marquess of, *A History of British Cavalry*, IV, London, 1986

Ardrey, R. *The Territorial Imperative*, London, 1967

Ayalon, D. *Gunpowder and Firearms in the Mamluk Kingdom*, London, 1956

Azzarolli, A. *An Early History of Horsemanship*, London, 1985

Balsdon, J. *Rome*, London, 1970

Bar-Kochva, B. *The Seleucid Army*, Cambridge, 1976

Barnett C. (ed.) *Hitler's Generals*, London, 1989

Bartov, O. *The Eastern Front 1941–5*, Basingstoke, 1985

Beaumont, J. *Comrades in Arms*, London, 1980

Beeler, J. *War in Feudal Europe, 730–1200*, Ithaca, 1991

Beloff, N. *Tito's Flawed Legacy*, London, 1985

Berlin, I. *Karl Marx*, Oxford, 1978

Berlin, I. *The Crooked Timber of Humanity*, N.Y., 1991

Best, G. *Humanity in Warfare*, London, 1980

Blau, P. and Scott, W. *Formal and Informal Organisations*, San Francisco, 1962

Blondal, S. *The Varangians of Byzantium*, Cambridge, 1979

Bottero J. et al (eds.) *The Near East: the Early Civilisations*, London, 1967

Bramson, L. and Goethals, G. *War: Studies from Psychology, Sociology, Anthropology*, New York, 1964

Breeze D. and Dobson, B. *Hadrian's Wall*, London, 1976

Breuil H. and R. Lautier, *The Men of the Old Stone Age*, London, 1965

Bull, H. et al (eds.) *Hugo Grotius and International Relations*, Oxford, 1990

Bullock, A. *Hitler and Stalin*, London, 1991

Bury, J. *A History of the Later Roman Empire*, London, 1923

Callwell, C. *Small Wars. Their Principles and Practice*, London, 1899

Challener, R. *The French Theory of the Nation in Arms*, New York, 1955

Chevallier, R. *Roman Roads*, London, 1976

Clark, R. *Freud*, London, 1980

Clausewitz, Carl von, *On War* (tr. M. Howard and P. Paret), Princeton, 1976

Clausewitz, Carl von, *On War* (tr. J. J. Graham), London, 1908

Clendinnen, I. *Ambivalent Conquests, Maya and Spaniard in Yucatan, 1515–70*, Cambridge 1987

Clendinnen, I. *Aztecs*, Cambridge, 1991

Connaughton, R. *The War of the Rising Sun and the Tumbling Bear*, London, 1988

Contamine, P. *War in the Middle Ages* (tr. M. Jones), Oxford, 1984

Corvisier, A. 'Le moral des combattants, panique et enthousiasme' in *Revue historique des armées*, 3, 1977

Corvisier, A. *Armies and Society in Europe*, Bloomington, 1979

Creel, H. *The Origins of Statecraft in China*, Chicago, 1970

Dawkin, J. *The Selfish Gene*, Oxford, 1989

de la Croix, H. *Military Considerations in City Planning*, New York, 1972

Deakin, F. *The Embattled Mountain*, London, 1971

Derry, T. and Williams, T. *A Short History of Technology*, Oxford, 1960

Divale, W. *War in primitive Society*, Santa Barbara, 1973

Djilas, M. *Wartime*, New York, 1977

Doyle, W. *The Oxford History of the French Revolution*, 1989

Duffy, C. *Russia's Military Way to the West*, London, 1981

Duffy, C. *Siege Warfare*, London, 1979

Duffy, C. *The Military Experience in the Age of Reason*, London, 1987

Dupuy, R. and T. *The Encyclopaedia of Military History*, London, 1986

Edburg, P. *Crusade and Settlement*, Cardiff, 1985

Edmonds, J. *A Short History of World War I*, Oxford, 1951

Eksteins, M. *Rites of Spring*, New York, 1989

Elting, J. *Swords Around a Throne*, London, 1989

Engels, D. *Alexander the Great and the Logistics of the Macedonian Army*, Berkeley, 1978

Engleit, S. *Islands at The Centre of the World*, N.Y., 1990

Farnes, O. *War in the Arctic*, London, 1991

Ferguson, B. and Whitehead, N. *War in the Tribal Zone*, Sante Fe, 1991

Ferguson, R. (ed.) *Warfare, Culture and Environment*, Orlando, 1984

Ferrill, A. *The Fall of the Roman Empire*, London, 1986

Ferrill, A. *The Origins of War*, London, 1985

Finley, M. and Plaket, H. *The Olympic Games*, New York, 1976

Forbes, P.J. *Metallurgy in Antiquity*, Leiden, 1950

Fox, A. *Prehistoric Maori Fortifications*, Auckland, 1974

Fraser, A. *Boadicea's Chariot*, London, 1988

Freedman, F. *The Evolution of Nuclear Strategy*, London, 1989

Freeman, D. *Margaret Mead and Samoa*, Cambridge, Mass., 1983

Fried, M. *Transactions of New York Academy of Sciences* Series 2, 28,

1966

Fried, M., Harris, M. and Murphy, R. (eds.) *War: The Anthropology of Armed Conflict and Aggression*, New York, 1967

Friendly, A. *The Dreadful Day*, London, 1981

Fryer, J. *The Great Wall of China*, London, 1975

Fuller, J. *The Decisive Battles of the Western World*, London, 1954–6

Gabriel R. and Metz, K. *From Sumer to Rome*, New York, 1991

Galvin, J. *The Minute Men*, McLean, 1989

Garlan, Y. *War in the Ancient World*, London, 1975

Gernet, J. *A History of Chinese Civilisation*, Cambridge, 1982

Gilbert, M. *Second World War*, London, 1989

Girouard, M. *The Return of Camelot*, New Haven, 1981

Grant, M. *The Army of the Caesars*, London, 1974

Greenhalgh, K. *Early Greek Warfare*, Cambridge, 1973

Groebel, J. and Hinde, R. (eds.) *Aggression and War*, Cambridge, 1989

Guilmartin, J. *Gunpowder and Galleys*, Cambridge, 1974

Haas, J. (ed.) *The Anthropology of War*, Cambridge, 1990

Hale, J. *Renaissance War Studies*, London, 1988

Hale, J. *War and Society in Renaissance Europe*, Leicester, 1985

Hammond, J. *A History of Greece to 322 B.C.*, Oxford, 1959

Hanson V. (ed.) *Hoplites*, London, 1991

Hanson, V. *The Western Way of War*, New York, 1989

Hanson, V. *Warfare and Agriculture in Classical Greece*, Pisa, 1983

Harris, M. *The Rise of Anthropological Theory*, London, 1968

Harris, W. *War and Imperialism in Republican Rome*, Oxford, 1979

Hayes, W. 'Egypt from the Death of Ammanemes II to Seqemenre II' in *Cambridge Ancient History*, 3rd ed., Vol. II, Part 1

Hoffman, M. *Egypt Before the Pharaohs*, London, 1988

Hogg, A. *Hill Forts of Britain*, London, 1975

Holt P., Lambton A., and Lewis B., (eds.), *The Cambridge History of Islam*, Vol IA, Cambridge 1970

Horne, A. *A Savage War of Peace*, London, 1977

Horne, A. *To Lose a Battle*, London, 1969

Hourani, A. *A History of the Arab Peoples*, London, 1991

Howard, M. *Clausewitz*, Oxford, 1983

Howard, M. *War in European History*, Oxford, 1976

Hughes, Q. *Military Architecture*, London, 1974

Isaac, B. *The Limits of Empire*, Oxford, 1990

Jakobsen, J. and Adams, R. 'Salt and Silt in Ancient Mesopotamian Agriculture', *Science*, CXXVIII, 1958

Jefferson, G. *The Destruction of the Zulu Kingdom*, London, 1979

Jelavich, B. *History of the Balkans (Twentieth Century)*, Cambridge, 1983

Johnson, S. *Late Roman Fortifications*, London, 1983

Johnson, S. *Roman Fortifications on the Saxon Shore*, London, 1977

Jones, A. *The Decline of the Ancient World*, London, 1966

Jones, A. *The Later Roman Empire*, Oxford, 1962

Jones, C. *The Longman Companion to the French Revolution*, London, 1989

Jones, G. *A History of the Vikings*, Oxford, 1984

Jones, N. *Hitler's Heralds*, London, 1987

Kahn, D. *Seizing the Enigma*, London, 1991

Keegan, J. *The Mask of Command*, London, 1987

Keegan, J. *The Face of Battle*, London, 1976

Keegan, J. *The Price of Admiralty*, London, 1988

Kemp, B. *Ancient Egypt*. Anatomy of a Civilisation, London, 1983

Kenny, A. *The Logic of Deterrence*, London, 1985

Keppie, L. *The Making of the Roman Army*, London, 1984

Kierman, F. and Fairbank, J. *Chinese Ways in Warfare*, Cambridge, Mass., 1974

Kirch, P. *The Evolution of the Polynesian Chiefdoms*, Cambridge, 1984

Klopsteg, P. *Turkish Archery and the Composite Bow*, Evanstown, 1947

Krige, E. J. *The Social System of the Zulus*, Pietermaritzburg, 1950

Kuper, A. *Anthropologists and Anthropology*, London, 1973

Kwantem, L. *Imperial Nomads: A History of Central Asia, 500–1500*, Leicester, 1979

Laessoe, J. *People of Ancient Assyria*, London, 1963

Larson, R. *The British Army and the Theory of Armoured Warfare 1918–40*, Newark, 1984

Lattimore, O. *Studies in Frontier History*, London, 1962

Lewis, M. *The Navy of Britain*, London, 1948

Liddell Hart, B. *The Ghost of Napoleon*, London, 1933

Liddle, P. *The 1916 Battle of the Somme*, London, 1992

Lindner, R. 'Nomadism, Horses and Huns', *Past and Present*, (1981)

Livermore, T. *Numbers and Losses in the American Civil War*, Bloomington, 1957

Longmate, N. *Hitler's Rockets*, London, 1985

Lorenz, K. *On Aggression*, London, 1966

Lucas, J. *Fighting Troops of the Austro-Hungarian Army*, New York, 1987

Luttwak, E. *The Grand Strategy of the Roman Empire*, Baltimore, 1976

Lynn, J. *Tools of War*, Chicago, 1990
Maenchen-Helfen, M. *The World of the Huns*, Berkeley, 1973
Mallet, M. *Mercenaries and Their Masters*, London, 1974
Mansel, P. *Pillars of Monarchy*, London, 1984
Manz, B. *The Rise and Rule of Tamerlane*, Cambridge, 1989
Marsot, A. *Egypt in the Reign of Muhammad Ali*, Cambridge, 1982
McCormick, K. and Perry, H. *Images of War*, London, 1991
McNeal, R. *Tsar and Cossack*, Basingstoke, 1989
McNeill, *The Pursuit of Power*, Oxford, 1983
McNeill, W. *A World History*, New York, 1961
McNeill, W. *Plagues and People*, New York, 1976
McNeill, W. *The Human Condition*, Princeton, 1980
McNeill, W. *The Rise of the West*, Chicago, 1963
McPherson, J. *Battle Cry of Freedom*, N.Y., 1988
Middleton, J. and Tait, D. *Tribes Without Rulers*, London, 1958
Milward, A. *War, Economy and Society, 1939–45*, London, 1977
Mockler, A. *Haile Selassie's War*, Oxford, 1979
Moorey, P. (ed.) *The Origins of Civilisation*, Oxford, 1979
Mueller, J. 'Changing Attitudes to War. The Impact of the First World War', *British Journal of Political Science*, 21
Murphy, T. (ed.) *The Holy War*, Columbus, 1976
Murray, W. *Luftwaffe*, London, 1985
Needham, J. *Science and Civilisation in China*, I, Cambridge, 1954
Nicolson, N. *Alex*, London, 1973
Oakeshott, E. *The Archaeology of Weapons*, London, 1960
Obermaier, H. *La vida de nuestros antepasados cuaternanos en Europa*, Madrid, 1926
Oget, B. (ed.) *War and Society in Africa*, 1972
Pallud, J-P. *Blitzkrieg in the West*, London, 1991
Paret, P. (ed.) *Makers of Modern Strategy*, Princeton, 1986
Paret, P. *Clausewitz and the State*, Princeton, 1985
Paret, P. *Understanding War*, Princeton, 1992
Parker, G. *The Army of Flanders and the Spanish Road*, Cambridge, 1972
Parker G. *The Military Revolution*, Cambridge, 1988
Parker, G. and A. *European Soldiers 1550–1650*, Cambridge, 1977
Parkinson, R. *Clausewitz*, London, 1970
Parry, V. and Yapp, M. (eds.) *War, Technology and Society in the Middle East*, London, 1975
Perrin, N. *Giving Up the Gun*, Boston, 1988
Petite, D. *Le balcon de la Côte d'Azure*, Marignan, 1983

Piekalkiewicz, J. *Pferd und Reiter im II Weltkrieg*, Munich, 1976

Piggott, S. *The Earliest Wheeled Transport*, London, 1983

Pipes, D. *Slave Soldiers and Islam*, New Haven, 1981

Poliakoff, M. *Combat Sports in the Ancient World*, New Haven, 1987

Pounds, N. *The Mediaeval Castle in England and Wales*, Cambridge, 1990

Ratchnevsky, P. *Genghis Khan*, Oxford, 1991

Reid, W. *Arms Through the Ages*, New York, 1976

Robarchak, C., in *Papers Presented to the Guggenheim Foundation Conference, On the Anthropology of War*, Santa Fe, 1986

Roberts, J. *The Pelican History of the World*, London, 1987

Roeder, H. (ed.) *The Ordeal of Captain Roeder*, London, 1960

Roux, G. *Ancient Iraq*, New York, 1986

Royle, T. *A Dictionary of Military Quotations*, London, 1990

Runciman, S. *A History of the Crusades*, I, Cambridge, 1951

Saggs, H. *The Might That Was Assyria*, London, 1984

Sahlins, M. *Tribesmen*, N.J., 1968

Sainty, G. *The Order of St. John*, New York, 1991

Sallares, R. *The Ecology of the Ancient Greek World*, London, 1991

Sanders, N. *The Sea Peoples*, London, 1985

Sansom, G. *The Western World and Japan*, London, 1950

Sansome, D. *Greek Athletics and the Genesis of Sport*, Berkeley, 1988

Saunders, J. *The History of the Mongol Conquest*, London, 1971

de Saxe, Marshal. *Mes rêveries*, Amsterdam, 1757

Seaton, A. *The Horsemen of the Steppes*, London, 1985

Showalter, D. *Railroads and Rifles*, Hamden, 1975

Smail, R. *Crusading Warfare*, Cambridge, 1956

Spector, R. *Eagle Against the Sun*, London, 1984

Spence, J. *The Search for Modern China*, London, 1990

Spuler, B. *The Mongols in History*, London, 1971

St. Clair, W. *That Greece Might Still Be Free*, London, 1972

Stahlberg, A. *Bounden Duty*, London, 1990

Storrey, R. *A History of Modern Japan*, London, 1960

Taylor, T. *The Breaking Wave*, London, 1967

Terraine, J. *The Right of the Line*, London, 1985

Thomas, H. *An Unfinished History of the World*, London, 1979

Thompson, J. *No Picnic*, London, 1992

Thompson, J. *The Lifeblood of War*, London, 1991

Tolstoy, L. (tr. R. Edmonds) *Anna Karenin*, London, 1987

Turney-High, H. *Primitive War. Its Practice and Concepts* (2nd Edn), Columbia, S.C. 1971

Van Crefeld, M. *Technology and War*, London, 1991

Van der Heyden A. and Scullard H. (eds.), *Atlas of the Classical World*, London, 1959

Van der Vat, D. *The Atlantic Campaign*, London, 1988

Vayda, A. *War in Ecological Perspective*, New York, 1976

Wakefield, K. (ed.) *The Blitz Then and Now*, London, 1988

Waldron, A. *The Great Wall of China*, Cambridge, 1992

Watson, G. *The Roman Soldier*, London, 1985

Weigley, R. *The Age of Battles*, Bloomington, 1991

Welchman, G. *The Hut Six Story*, London, 1982

Wendorf, F. (ed.) *The Prehistory of Nubia*, II, Dallas, 1968

Wiley, B. *The Life of Johnny Reb*, Baton Rouge, 1918

Wilson, T. *The Myriad Faces of War*, Cambridge, 1986

Winter, F. *Greek Fortifications*, Toronto, 1971

Wintle, J. *The Dictionary of War Quotations*, London, 1989

Wood, E. *Peasant, Citizen and Slave*, London, 1988

Ya-tien, Chen *Chinese Military Theory*, Stevenage, 1992

Yadin, Y. *The Art of Warfare in Biblical Lands*, London, 1963

Index

Abbasid dynasty, 197–9, 200, 209
Abbeville, 370
Abu Shama, 35, 211
Achilles, 247
Acre, 210
Adler, Alfred, 3
Adrianople, battles and sieges of, 70–1, 73, 185, 280
Aegospotami, battle of (405 BC), 257
Aëtius, 186, 280, 281
Afghanistan, 34, 128, 198
    conquered by Arabs, 195
Agincourt, battle of (1415), 297, 320
Agrigentum, Sicily, siege of (262 BC), 146
Ain Jalut, battle of (1260), 35, 210–11
Ajnadain, battle of (634), 196
Akhenaten, Pharaoh, 125
Akkadians, 133
al-Ansari (historian), 38
al-Mansur, 291
al-Mu'tasim, Caliph, 34, 198
al-Muzt'asim, Caliph, 200, 209
al-Nasir, Caliph, 199
Alamagordo, New Mexico, atomic bomb
    exploded (1945), 379
Alans of Iran, 184, 186
Alaric, 185
Albania, Ottoman occupation of, 335
Aleppo, massacre by Mongols, 210
Alesia hill-fort, 146
    siege of, 273
Alexander the Great, 10, 74–5, 192, 206, 277, 284, 303, 322, 369
    battles with Persians, 145–6, 174, 178, 194, 258–63, 304, 389–90
    campaign in Asia, 260–3
    employment of Greek mercenaries, 231
Alexander VI, Pope, 324
Alfred the Great, 303
Algerian war (1954–62), 55, 108, 147
Algiers, conquered by Mamelukes, 39
Alkmaar, 326
Alp Arslan, 199
America
    American Anthropological Association, 80, 93
    Civil War, 6, 305–6, 356; casualties, 360–1

discovery of (1492), 388
nuclear confrontation with Russia, 383
Vietnam War, 56, 92, 359, 381
War of Independence, 67, 345–6, 347–8
    see also First and Second World Wars
Ammianus Marcellinus, 162
Amosis, 168
Amphictyonic Council, 258
Amr, 196
An Lu-shan, 203
Anatolia, 168, 239
    iron production, 238
Andreski, Stanislav, 223–5, 227
    Military Participation Ratio (MPR), 223, 224
Antarctic Treaty (1959), 69
anthropologists, war and the, 84–94
Antioch, surrender to the Crusaders (1098), 151, 292
Antonine Wall, 146
Antoninus Pius, Emperor, 276
Antwerp, rocket attack on (1944), 378
Arab Guard of Frederick II, 230
Arabs, 191–200
    Afghanistan conquered, 195
    Byzantium defeated, 195, 196
    Chinese defeated at Talas River (751), 191, 282
    Persian Empire destroyed, 192, 195, 196
    slave armies, 198, 199
    Syria and Egypt conquered, 195, 282
    Turks, encounter with, 191
Ardrey, Robert, 85, 86, 119
Arene Candide skeleton, 117
Argos, 243, 252
Ariovistus, 272
Aristotle, 3, 46
Armada, defeat of (1588), 67, 68, 326, 338
Armenia and Armenians, 276, 278
armies, 221–34
Arminius, 276
arms manufacture, 309–15
Armstrong, William, 311
Arrian (biographer of Alexander the Great), 260, 263, 389
artillery revolution, 321–2
Aryans, 155, 168

Ascalon, battle of (1099), 293
Ashur-nasir-pal, 171
Ashuruballit, King, 169
Askut, 143
Asquith, Cynthia (Lady), 365
Assassins, 209
Assinboin tribe, 91
Assur, 169, 172
Assyria and Assyrians, 169, 170, 171, 172–3,
  176, 216, 229, 239, 244, 266
  and the chariot, 169–77
  fall of empire, 177–6
  Roman conquest of, 276
  system of military bureaucracy, 169–72,
    192, 267
  warhorse, 177
Atatürk, 367
Athens and Athenians, 241, 243, 249, 250,
  252–7, 258, 262, 264
Atlanta, Georgia, burning of, 6
Atlantic, battle of (1940–3), 68, 314
Attica, 241
Attila, 183, 184, 186–8, 189, 205, 281
Augereau, Marshal, 350
Augsburg, 287
  battle of (910), 287
Augustus, Emperor (Octavian), 274–5, 278,
  279, 282, 283
Ausculum, battle of (299 BC), 263
Austerlitz, battle of (1805), 353, 369
Australopithecus, 115–16, 117
Austria
  defeat by Prussia (1866), 307
  German occupation (1938), 368
  Napoleon's conquest (1805), 353
Avars, 47, 190, 194
Aztecs and warfare, 106–14
  destroyed by conquistadors, 338
  flower battles, 111, 131, 214

Babur (founder of Moghul dynasty), 201,
  346
Babylon and Babylonians, 171, 178, 262
Baghdad, 197, 198, 292
  captured by Mongols (1258), 200, 209
Balaclava, battle of (1854), 9
Baldwin, Emperor, 70fn
Bantu, 120
Bavaria, advance by Marlborough (1704),
  303
Bavarian Trabanters, 230
Baybars, 210, 211, 293
Bayard, Pierre du Terrail, 38, 333
beginnings of warfare, 115–26
Belgrade, seized by Ottomans (1521), 336
  citadel, 346
Belisarius, 281
Benedict, Ruth, *Patterns of Culture*, 87
Beneventum, battle of (295 BC), 263
Berenger, King of Italy, 286
Berlin, 369, 371

'Red Revolution' (1919), 222
Berlin, Sir Isaiah, 47
Bernadotte, Marshal (later King of Sweden),
  350
Berthier, Marshal, 222
Bessières, Marshal, 365
Bicocca, battle of (1522), 331
Bigeard, Colonel, 113
Biskupin, Poland, 144
Bismarck, sinking of, 67
Blake, Admiral Robert, 65
Blenheim, battle of (1704), 345
Blitzkrieg warfare, 71, 323, 369–70, 371,
  373, 374
Boas, Franz, 87
bodyguards, 230
Boeotian League, 256
Boer Trekkers, 224–5
Boer War (1899–1902), 188, 361
Bohemond, 210
Bokhara, 195
  Mongol occupation, 205
Boniface, St, 289
Borgia, Cesare, 325
Borodino, battle of (1812), 8, 9–10, 16, 360
Bougainville, Louis Antoine de, 27
bow, composite, introduction of, 162–3, 176
  longbow, 329
Breda, 327
Bredow, von, 38
Brenta, River, battle of (899), 287
Breuil, H., 117
Britain
  Boer War, 188, 361
  Crimean War, 9, 311
  Dutch wars, 340
  Danish invasion, 303
  Falklands War, 302
  French maritime conflict, 340
  Gulf War, 57, 384
  Hundred Years' War with France, 296,
    297, 320
  Norman conquest, 142, 288, 290
  Roman occupation, 265, 273, 276, 279,
    287; withdrawal, 279
  Viking invasion, 288
  see also First and Second World Wars
    and Napoleonic Wars
Brune, Marshal, 365
Bulgars, 70fn, 190
Burgundy, 320
  power destroyed by Swiss pikemen, 329
Burmese independence (1948), 379
Bush, George, 58
Byron, George Gordon (6th Baron), 10
Byzantium, 190, 191, 192, 194, 216, 286, 319,
  335
  damaged by Fourth Crusade, 293, 296
  defeated by Arabs, 195, 196
  defended by Rome, 281–2
  Persian wars, 194, 195

Saracens driven out of southern Italy, 286
Varangian guard, 230

Caesar, Julius, 71, 146, 279, 332, 367
  assassination, 274
  battle against the Nervii, 269
  conquest of Gaul, 266, 272–3, 274
  triumph in civil war, 274
Cairo, 197
  surrender to Ottomans, 37
Cambodian civil war, 56
Camperdown, battle of (1797), 67, 68
Cannae, battle of (216 BC), 271–2, 359
cannon, introduction of
  becomes mobile on wheels, 321, 324, 325
  founding of, 310–11
  increase in mobility and fire power, 340–1
  on board ship, 335, 338, 340
  siege warfare transformed, 321–3
Capprarole, 324
Cartagena, 265, 272
Carthage, 254
  Punic wars with Rome, 265, 267, 270–2, 283
Catal Hüyük excavations, 124
cavalry revolution, 188–9
cave paintings, 118, 119, 120
Celts, 146, 239, 273
Cerignola, battle of (1503), 331
Chaeronea, battle of (338 BC), 258
Chagnon, Napoleon, 94, 96–7
Chaldaeans, 171, 172
Châlons, battle of (451), 186–7, 281
chariots and charioteers, 135, 139, 155–68
  Assyrian, 169–77
  first recorded chariot battle, 175
  Greek, 240–1
Charlemagne, Emperor (King of the Franks), 309–10
  campaigns of, 284, 289
  effort to create pan-European state, 149
  empire of, 284–5
  includes Lombard Kingdom and Rome within his empire, 284
  overcomes Avars, 190
Charles VII of France, creation of
  compagnies d'ordonnance, 13
Charles VII of France
  deployment of mobile artillery, 14
  Neapolitan triumph (1494–5), 321–2, 323, 324
Charles the Bald (King of West Franks), 285
Charles the Rash (Duke of Burgundy), 329
Château-Gaillard, 151
Cherokee, 247
Chetniks, 51, 52, 54
Chiang Kai-shek, 51, 53
Chin, 206

China
  Ch'in dynasty, 148, 201
  Ch'ing dynasty, 215
  Chou dynasty, 165, 168, 173
  Communist seizure of power (1948–50), 203, 380
  conflict with India (1962), 68
  defeated by Arabs at Talas River (751), 191, 195, 203
  fortifications in, 145, 148–9
  Grand Canal, 303
  Great Wall, 147–8, 149, 201, 202, 203, 204, 206, 215, 278, 388
  gunpowder discovery, 319
  Han dynasty, 182, 190, 203–4
  Japanese offensive (1937), 375, 391
  Manchu dynasty, 162, 215–16, 228, 278, 376
  Ming dynasty, 212, 215
  Mongol occupation, 200, 201–4
  Northern Wei dynasty, 190–1
  Opium Wars, 216
  protected by size, 339
  Shang dynasty, 167, 168
  Sui dynasty, 202
  Sung dynasty, 203, 204
  T'ang dynasty, 191, 202, 203, 278
  way of warfare, 214–15, 221;
    restraint in, 202, 388
  Yuan dynasty, 200, 215
Christians and warmaking, 193, 198, 284, 290, 291–6
  pacification and conversion in Western Europe, 289–90
  victory over Ottomans at Lepanto (1571), 337
  see also Crusades and Crusaders
Churchill, Winston (later Sir), 366, 371, 379
Cimmerians, 178
civilisation and war, 126–35
Civita Castellana, fort of, 324
Clair, William St, 11
Clausewitz, Carl von, 3, 28, 39, 40, 50, 58, 98, 106, 109, 277, 355, 372, 373
  affronted by savagery of Cossacks, 7, 8–9, 10, 11, 217, 221
  army service: Prussian Army, 14, 15;
    tsarist army, 16; military dilemma, 16–17
  belief in war as a continuation of politics, 46–7, 222, 233, 353, 385, 391
  deterrent logic, 48, 49
  Essential Points on the Formation of a Defence Force (1813), 221
  intellectual ambitions, 354
  on the burning of Moscow, 6–7
  On War, 3, 18–22, 354
  philosophy of war, 3, 5, 6, 11–12, 18–24, 26–7, 46, 221
Claudius, Emperor, 275

Index

Clendinnen, Inga, 108, 109, 113
Clermont, Council of (1095), 290–1
Clive, Robert (Baron Clive of Plassey), 347
Clovis, King of the Franks, 198
Cnidus, battle of (384 BC), 257
Columbus, Christopher, 338
Commandos, 4
conscription, 228, 233–4, 343, 366, 376
Constantine, Emperor, 70, 192, 280
Constantinople (Istanbul), 70–1, 186, 195, 209, 320
    capture by Turks (1453), 189, 212, 281, 293
    Ottoman retreat to, 346
    sacked by Crusaders (1204), 71
    siege by Avars, 190
    Topkapi Palace, 163, 181–2
Constantius, 280
Cook, Captain James, 24
Copenhagen, battle of (1801), 65, 67, 68
Coral Sea, battle of (1942), 377
Corinth, 252, 256
Corsica, 271, 281, 286
Cossacks, 7–10, 11, 147, 224, 225
    battle of Balaclava, 9
    burning of Moscow (1812), 7, 8
    savagery of, 7, 8, 9, 10, 217, 221
    slaughter of the retreating French (1812), 8, 9
Covenant of the League of Nations, 383
Creasy, *Fifteen Decisive Battles of the World*, 67
Crécy, battle of (1346), 297
Creel, Professor, 174
Cremona, siege of (1523), 323
Cresson, battle of (1187), 294
Crete and Cretans, 240, 242, 282
    destruction of Minoan civilisation, 169
Crimean War (1854), 9, 311
Croesus of Lydia, 253
crossbow, 328–9, 330, 333
Crusades and Crusaders, 151, 198, 199–200, 208–9, 210, 211, 214, 291, 294, 390
    decline and extinction of kingdoms, 292, 296
    fall of Antioch (1098), 151, 292
    First Crusade, 291–2
    Fourth Crusade, 293
    Hospitallers and Templars, 295
    Jerusalem: capture (1099), 151, 199–200, 208, 292; loss to Saladin (12th century), 208; recapture (13th century), 209
    sack of Constantinople (1204), 71
Cultural Determination, 87–8, 91, 92
culture, war as, 24–46
culture without war, 46–60
Cyprus, 282
Cyrus the Great, 243
Czechoslovakia, German occupation (1938), 368

Dacia, 276, 279
Dalton, Francis, 86
Damascus, capture by Mongols, 210
Dandolo, Doge, 70fn
Danish invasion of England, 303
Darius, Emperor, 174, 178, 192, 253, 254, 257
Darius III, 259, 260–2, 304, 389–90
Darwin, Charles, 82
Dawkins, Richard, *The Selfish Gene*, 83
Deakin, Sir William, 52, 54
Delhi, Slave Kingdom of, 198
Delian League, 256
Delion, battle of (424 BC), 250
Demeunier, 86
Demosthenes, 258
Dien Bien Phu, surrender of, 113
diet, military, 305
Diocletian, Emperor, 280
Diu, battle of (1509), 339
Divale, W., *War in Primitive Society*, 98–9
Djerba, battle of (1560), 336
Djilas, Milovan, 52, 54–5
    Wartime, 54
Doria, Admiral Andrea, 336
Dorians, 169, 241, 242, 332
Dorstadt, Viking devastation, 288
double patriotism, 16
Douhet, 372, 373, 374
Dreadnought, HMS (1906), 66
Duffy, Christopher, 214
Dumouriez, General, 352
Dunkirk evacuation (1940), 370
Dutch East Indies, gaining of independence, 379

Eanatum II, King of Lagash, 133
Easter Island, 392
    decadent phase, 26
    Polynesian civilisation, 24–5
    war as culture, 24–8
Egypt and Egyptians, 150, 166, 169, 239, 376
    Arab conquest (642), 195, 282
    Ayyubid dynasty, 209, 210
    defeat of Mongols at Ain Jalut, 35, 210–11
    establishment of Mameluke power, 210, 211, 293
    Hyskos invasion, 155, 167, 168
    Middle Kingdom, 130, 131, 169
    Napoleon's invasion and Battle of the Pyramids (1798), 39
    New Kingdom, 130, 131, 168, 169, 176, 247
    Nubian forts, 142–4, 147
    Old Kingdom, 169
    Ottoman Turks victory over Mamelukes (1515–16), 36, 37–40, 336
    Roman occupation, 272, 279
    Site 117, Jebel Sahaba, 120–1, 122, 129
    stabilisation, 132

Twelfth Dynasty, 130, 142, 144
violent prehistory, 120−1, 122, 129−31
see also Mamelukes of Egypt
Einstein, Albert, 84, 378
El-Amarna, 125
Elamites, 133, 172−3
Elis, 246
Epaminondas (Theban general), 258, 261, 369
Ephthalites, 190, 191
equus caballus, 156−7
Erickssson, Leif, 104
Esarhaddon, 171
Etruscans, 263
Europe after Rome, 281−98
Evans-Pritchard, Edward, 89

Fabius Maximus, 271
face to face traditional combat, 331−2, 333, 364, 390
Fairbank, John King, 214
Falklands War, 302
Farajallah, 38
Farnese, Cardinal Alessandro, 324
Ferrill, Arthur, 119, 121
Finisterre, battle of (1747), 66
Finley, Professor M. I., 174
fire, 319−85
    firepower and the culture of universal service, 359−66
    gunpowder and fortification, 320−8
    gunpowder battles in the experimental age, 328−34
    gunpowder at sea, 334−40
    gunpowder stability, 340−7
    law and war's end, 379−85
    political revolution and military change, 347−59
    ultimate weapons, 366−79
firearms, introduction of, 328−31, 333−4
Firizzano, castle of, 321
First Punic War (262 BC), 146
First World War, 21, 22, 40, 89, 234, 313, 354−5, 358−9, 361−4, 365−6, 372, 391
    casualties, 50, 358−9, 361−2, 365
    Gallipoli (1915), 363
    German advance from Mons to the Marne (1914), 302
    Jutland, battle of (1916), 67, 68, 363
    mobilisation of armies, 307−8
    sea battles, 66, 67, 68, 363
    Somme battle (1916), 302, 309, 361
    Verdun, battle of (1916), 361
    Ypres (1914), 358−9
Florence
    equipped with new defences, 325
    falls to French (1494), 321
Fontenoy, battle of (1745), 345
Fornovo, battle of, 322
fortification, 139−52

and gunpowder, 320−8
Fox, Robin, 85, 86
France
    Arab invasion, 195
    army mutiny (1917), 234
    battle with Spanish at Ravenna (1512), 330
    battle with Swiss at Marignano (1515), 330−1
    conflict with Dutch and English, 340
    conscription under First French Republic, 233, 234
    defeat of Burgundy, 320
    fall of (1940), 370
    Hundred Years' War, 296, 297, 320
    Neapolitan triumph (1494−5), 321−2, 324
    Norsemen secure foothold, 288
    overseas empire in North America, 340
    Prussian defeat in Alsace-Lorraine (1870), 307
    Revolution, 15, 17, 18, 46, 50, 57, 235, 348, 349, 352, 353, 357, 365, 367
    Thirty Years' War, 341
    war in Indochina, 302
    wars of the French Revolution, 348−53
    wars against the Habsburgs, 296
    see also Napoleon, Napoleonic Wars, and First and Second World Wars
Franco, General, Moorish Guard of, 230
Franklin, Benjamin, 305
Franks, 309−10
    Avars defeated, 190
    Carolingian dynasty, 284−5, 287, 290
    conversion to Christianity, 198
    defeated by Magyars at Augsburg (910), 287
    empire of, 284−5
    feudalism, 285
    Lombard kingdom and Rome included in empire, 284
    victory over Muslims at Poitiers (732), 284
Frazer, Sir James, *The Golden Bough*, 87
Frederick the Great, 27, 233, 296, 351
Frederick I (Barbarossa), Emperor, 149
Freiburg, 372
Freud, Sigmund, 3, 88
    psychological basis advanced for theory of aggression, 84−5
    Totem and Taboo, 85

Gaiseric, 281
Gallipoli (1915), 363
Gardner, 312
Gaugamela, battle of (331 BC), 146, 174, 260, 261−2, 369
Gaul, 263, 264, 281, 332
    barbarian invasion of, 149, 183, 186
    conquered by Caesar, 266, 272−3, 274
    inroads by Rome, 271, 332

Gelimer, 281
General Treaty for the Renunciation of War (Pact of Paris 1928), 383
Geneva Conventions, 383
Genghis Khan, 35, 75, 189, 200–1, 204, 205, 206, 207, 211, 212, 213, 214, 228–9
Genoa, 336
Gerasimov, Sergei, 53
Géricault, Jean, 53
Germany
  Blitzkreig tactics, 71, 323, 369–70, 373, 374
  collapse of army (1918), 234
  Hitler's rise to power, 367–8
  invasion of Poland (1939), 369
  Magyar invasion, 287
  militia system, 232
  occupation of Austria and Czechoslovakia (1938), 368
  revolt against Rome, 276, 332
  Roman defeat at Teutoburg Forest (AD 9), 270, 276, 359
  Thirty Years' War, 326, 341
Gettysburg, battle of, 356
Gibbon, Edward, 279
Gilgamesh, King, 133
Glorious First of June, battle of the (1794), 66
Gneisenau, General, 15
Gobi Desert, 179, 191, 206
Godfrey, King of Jerusalem, 293
Golikov, General, 72
Goths, 184–5, 188, 192
  victory over Rome at Adrianople, 185, 195, 280
Gotland mass grave, 121
Gracchus brothers, 274
Granicus river, battle of (334 BC), 146, 260, 261
Gratian, Emperor, 185
Great Harry, 338
Greenland, 288
Greeks, 144, 233, 265, 266, 272, 297, 364
  alliance of states with Persia, 257–8
  amphibious strategy, 255–7
  charioteers, 240–1
  city-states, 145, 242, 244, 245, 252, 256
  competitive sports, 246–7
  enforced unification by Macedonia, 256
  fortifications, 145
  hatred of Persia, 192
  mercenaries, 231, 255, 259, 261
  overthrown by Rome, 263
  Peloponnesian Wars, 256
  Persian Wars, 243–4, 253–6, 258–63
  phalanx warfare, 244–54, 266, 297, 332; culmination of, 257–63
  ritual sacrifice, 248
  siege warfare, 150
  technique of pitched battle, 192, 216, 232

War of Independence from Turkey (1821), 10–11, 40, 53, 196
Greenwich, 310
Gregory VII, Pope, 290, 291
Gribeauval, Jean, 311, 352
Grotius, Hugo, 382, 384
Grouchy, Marshal, 351
Guderian, Heinz, 368
Guibert, Comte de, 351
Guicciardini, 322
Guilmartin, John, 65, 166, 337
Gulf War, 57, 384
gunpowder revolution, 36–7, 42–5, 298, 310, 319–20, 390
  at sea, 334–40
  battles in the experimental age, 328–34
  cavalry resistance to, 331–2
  Chinese discovery, 319
  fortification and, 320–8
  stability, 340–7
  Thirty Years' War, 328
Gurganj, siege of, 205
Gurkhas, 231
Gustavus Adolphus, King of Sweden, 341
Gutians, 135, 168

Haarlem, 326
Habsburgs, 296
  conflict with Ottomans, 336, 346
  Military Frontier, 147, 222
  Napoleonic wars, 351
  overlords of Swiss, 329
  Thirty Years' War, 341
Hadrian, Emperor, 276
Hadrian's Wall, 142, 146, 270, 279
Hague Conventions, 383
Hale, Professor John, 344
Hall, W.E., 383
Hallstatt culture, 239, 332
Hamburg night raids (1943), 375
Hammurabi, 155, 167, 168
Hannibal
  defeat of Romans at Cannae, 271–2
  march across the Alps, 271
Hanson, Victor Davis, 73–4, 245, 246, 249, 251, 253, 297, 332
Harold, King, 290
Harran, battle of, 178
Harris, Air Marshal Arthur, 374
Harris, William, 265–6
Hasdrubal, 271, 272
Hassing, R., 109
Hastings, battle of (1066), 290
Hattin, battle of (1187), 294
Hayek, F.A., 6
Hector, 247
Helvetii, 272, 332
Henri IV, 290
Henry the Fowler, 287
Herbert, A.J., 81
Herodotus, 247, 249, 253

A HISTORY OF WARFARE

Hezekiah, siege of, 172
Hidetada, 44
Hideyoshi, Toyotoi, 42, 43
Hindenburg, President, 367
Hirohito, Emperor, 16, 379
Hiroshima bomb (1945), 379
Hitler, Adolf, 222, 377
    conduct of Second World War, 323, 369,
        370, 371−4, 378
    infatuation with *Blitzkrieg*, 374
    rise to power, 367−8
    service in First World War, 359, 366
Hittites, 168, 238
Ho Chi Minh, 53, 55, 202
Hoche, General, 352
Holy League (1538), 336
    defeat of Ottomans at Lepanto (1571),
        337
Homer, 169, 174
    Iliad, 240−1, 246, 249, 332
homo erectus, 116
homo sapiens sapiens, 115, 117, 118
Hopi of Arizona, 247
horse peoples of the steppe, 179−82
    Arabs and Mamelukes, 191−200
    decline of, 207−17
    horizon (453−1258), 188−207
    Huns, 182−8
    Mongols, 200−7
Howard, Sir Michael, 13, 16
Huaxtecs, 111
Hülegü, 200, 208, 209, 210
human nature, war and, 81−4
Hundred Years' War, 296, 297, 320
Hungary, destruction of kingdom by
    Ottomans (1526), 336
Huns, 47, 161, 162, 180, 182−8, 189, 205
    collapse and disappearance, 187−8, 190
    invasion of Roman empire, 182, 183,
        184−7, 281
Huron tribe, 107, 108, 247
Hurrians, 135, 167, 168, 169
Huxley, Aldous, 227
Hysiae, battle of, 243
Hyskos people
    chariot battle with Egypt, 175
    expulsion from Egypt, 169
    invasion of Egypt, 155, 167, 168
    origins, 167

Ibn Khaldun, 227
Ibn Zabul, 37
Ice Age, 121, 156
Iceland, 288
Ieyasu, Tokugawa, 42, 43, 44
Incas of Peru, destroyed by Conquistadors,
    338
indecisiveness of war, 57
India
    arrival of Dutch and English, 340
    Aryan invaders, 168

conflict with China (1962), 68
defeat of Moghuls by Clive at Plassey
    (1757), 346−7
Moghul empire (1526), 201, 339, 346,
    388
North-West Frontier, 143
slave kingdom of Delhi, 198
Wellington's campaign, 304
India-China conflict (1962), 68
Indochina war (1946), 380
    surrender of Dien Bien Phu, 113
Indus valley, 128−9
intoxication of war, 226−7
Iran, 126, 160, 168, 170
    Alans of, 184, 186
    Medes of, 178
    Parthians of, 194−5
    Scythians of, 177−8, 180
    war with Iraq, 56, 195
Iraq, 134
    conquered by Mamelukes, 39
    Gulf War, 57, 384
    invasion of Kuwait (1990), 384
    war with Iran, 56, 195
    see also Sumer and the Sumerians
Iron Age forts, 144
Iron Age revolution and warfare in the
    Middle Ages, 237−98
Iroquois tribe, 91
irregulars, 5−11, 13
irrigation societies, 127−30, 132
Isaac, Benjamin, 147
Isocrates, 192
Israel, 169
    Jewish revolt against Romans (AD 66),
    276
    warrior kings, 192, 193
Issus, battle of (333), 260−1
Istemi Khan, 191
Italy
    Charles VIII's expedition (1494−5),
    321−2, 323, 324
    defeat of Vandals, 281
    enters Second World War, 370
    Magyar invasion, 286−7
    Mussolini and the fascists, 367, 368
    Norman occupation, 288
    strengthening of fortifications, 324−5
    war of 1911−12 with Turks in Libya, 372
Ivan the Terrible, 7

Japan
    acquires discipline of Western-style
    combat, 333
    battle of Nagashino (1575), 43
    battle of Uedahara (1548), 43
    closure of maritime borders, 339
    cult of the sword, 45−6
    defeat of Russia (1904−5), 66, 67, 376
    emulation of the West's military power,
    376

424

gunpowder development, 42−5
Hiroshima and Nagasaki bombs (1945), 379
Mongol offensive (1274−81), 68; defeat of, 42, 376
Pearl Harbor attack (1941), 67, 375, 379
Second World War, 375, 376−7, 379
Shimbara Rebellion (1637), 44
shoguns, 41
successful offensive in China (1937), 375, 391
Tokugawa shogunate, 43−6
Jebel Sahaba, Upper Egypt (Site 117), 120−1, 122, 129
Jena, battle of (1806), 8, 353
Jericho, 150
  discovery of town, 124−5, 142
  fortifications, 139, 141, 142, 143
Jerusalem, 172, 291
  falls to Crusaders (1099), 151, 199−200, 208, 292
  loss to Saladin, 208
  recaptured by Crusaders, 209
Jiddah, 339
John, King, 151
John of Nassau, 327, 344
Johnson, Dr Samuel, 159, 223
Jourdan, Marshal, 350, 352
Juan-Juan, 190−1
Julian the Apostate, Emperor, 185, 195, 280
Jung, Carl G., 3
Justin II, 191
Justinian, Emperor, 281
Jutland, battle of (1916), 67, 68

Kaiser II, 222, 230
Kamatari, Jujiwara, 41
Kant, Immanuel, 5
Kardelj, 52−3
Karlowitz, peace of (1699), 346
Kassites, 135, 167, 168
Khair ed-Din, Admiral, 336
Khalid, 196
Khiva, conquest of (1874), 302
Khmer Rouge savageries, 56
Khwarazamians, 206
Khyber Rifles, 143, 144
Kiersey, Capitulations of, 285
Kiev, 72, 373
Kitbuga, 210
Kluck, von, 302
Knossos, 240
Krupp, Alfred, 311
Kubla Khan, 200, 208, 212
Kurtbay (Mameluke chieftain), 37−8
Kuwait, invasion of (1990), 384

La Spezia, 321
Labaume, Eugène, 10
Lamarck, Jean Baptiste, 82
Langemarck cemetery, 358−9

Larrey (Napoleon's senior surgeon), 9−10
Latifau, 86
Lattimore, Owen, 147, 148, 164−5
Lautier, R., 117
law and war's end, 379−85
lawful bearer of arms, 4−5
Lebanon, 134
  war, 56
Lech river, battle of (955), 287
Lefebvre, Marshal, 350
Lenin, Vladimir Ilyich, 17, 361
Leningrad (St Petersburg), 71, 373
  battle of (1942), 374
Leo, Emperor, 281
Leo I, Pope, 187
Leo III, Pope, 284, 289
Leonardo da Vinci, 325
Leonidas, King of Sparta, 254
Lepanto, battle of (1571), 65, 67, 68, 337
Leuctra, battle of (371 BC), 258, 261, 369
Leuthen, battle of (1757), 345
Lévi-Strauss, Claude, 88−9, 91
Leyte Gulf, battle of (1944), 68
Libya, war of 1911−12 (Italy-Turks), 372
Licinius, 70fn
Liddell Hart, Captain Basil, 48, 354
Liguria, 266
Ligustinus, Spurius, 268−9
Lindisfarne monastery, 288
Lisbon earthquake (1755), 6
List, King, 134
Litorius, 183
Livy (Roman historian), 268−9
logistics and supply, 301−15
London blitz (1940), 372−3
  rocket attacks (1944), 378
Lorenz, Konrad, 85, 86, 119
Louis XI, 320
Louis XIV, 147, 327, 344, 351
Louis XVI, 348, 349
Louis the Child, 287
Luttwak, Edward, 278, *The Grand Strategy of the Roman Empire*, 146
Lützen, battle of (1632), 341

Macedonia, 74−5, 216, 232, 256
  campaign in Asia, 260−3
  enforces Greek unification, 256, 258
  overthrown by Rome, 263, 265
  Persian wars, 145−6, 174, 178, 194, 259−63, 304, 389−90
  use of phalanx, 260−1, 262, 341
Machiavelli, 232−3, 329, 353−4
McClellan, George W., 306
McNamara, Robert 49
McNeill, William, 75, 160, 177, 180, 181, 357
  Plagues and Peoples, 223
Madras, 304
Mäenchen-Helfen, 187
Maginot Line, 366, 368, 370
Magyars, 13, 47, 190

conversion of, 289
 threat to the West, 286−7, 288, 293
Maiden Castle (massacre by Romans), 265
Malaya, Communist uprising (1948), 379
Malik Shah, 199
Malinowski, Bronislaw, 88
Malta, besieged by Ottomans (1565), 336−7
Malthus, Thomas Robert, population
 theory, 223
Mamelukes of Egypt, 23, 32−40, 189, 225,
 227, 228, 388
 defeat by Ottoman Turks (1515−16),
  36, 37−40, 336
 establishment of power in Egypt, 210,
  211, 293
 massacre in Cairo by Muhammad Ali
  (1811), 39
 military slavery, 23, 32−8
 part in defeat of Mongols at Ain
  Jalut, 35, 210−11, 376
 routed by Napoleon in Battle of the
  Pyramids (1798), 39
 sweep away Crusader kingdoms, 292
Mantinea, battle of (362 BC), 258
Manzikert, battle of (1071), 199, 291
Mao Tse-tung, 50, 51, 53, 73, 196, 202
 Long March (1934−5), 54−5
 seizes power from Chiang Kai-shek, 380
Maoris and warfare, 103−6, 140
Marathon, battle of (490 BC), 253, 255
Marco Polo, 187
Marcus Aurelius, Emperor, 276
Mardonios, 253
Marengo, battle of, 369
Marignano, battle of (1515), 330−1
Maring and warfare, 98−103, 119, 121, 140,
 161
Maritz, Jean, 310
Marius, Consul, 274
Marj'Ayyun, battle of (1179), 294
Marj Dabiq, battle of (1515), 37, 38
Marjorian (puppet emperor), 281
Marlborough, Duke of, 303
Marmont, Marshal, 351
Mars-la-Tour, battle of (1870), 38
Marseilles, siege of (1524), 323
Martel, Charles, 284
Marx, Karl, 17−19, 21, 22, 50, 55, 73, 74,
 224, 354, 372
 Kapital, 18
Mary Rose, 338
Maurice of Nassau, Count, 327−8, 342, 344
Mauritania, 279
Maxim, Hiram, 312
Maya of Central America, 114
 destroyed by Conquistadors, 338
Mead, Margaret, 90, 92, 385
 Coming of Age in Samoa, 87−8
Mecca, 193
Medes of Iran, 178
Medina battle (625), 193

Megiddo, battle of, 175−6
Mehmet the Conqueror, 281
Memphis, 155
mercenaries, 228, 231, 233, 255, 334, 343,
 357
 Swiss, 329
Mesopotamia and Mesopotamians, 127, 128,
 134, 135, 150, 160, 166, 167, 168,
 169, 170, 178, 183, 209, 238, 261,
 262, 276
 Amorite dynasty, 155, 168
Messenia, 243
Metaurus river, battle of, 272
Metz artillery school, 344, 351
Mexico, 108, 109, 110, 113, 338
 see also Aztecs of
Michael VII, Emperor, 199
Michelangelo, 325
Midway, battle of (1942), 67, 68, 377
Mihailovic, Draga, 51
Milch, General Erhard, 370
military academies, viii-ix, x, 344
military slavery, 23−4, 32−8, 198, 199, 212,
 228, 343
militia principle, 221−2, 228, 232−3, 234
Milvian Bridge battle, 192
Minoans, 145, 240
 destruction of civilisation in Crete, 169
Minorca, Ottoman raids (1558), 336
Minsk, 373
Mitrović, Golub, 54
Mohacs, battle of (1526), 336
Moltke, General Helmuth von, 20, 23, 39, 40
Mongols, 47, 75, 161, 164, 181, 186, 189,
 200−7, 212, 214, 215, 216, 229,
 265, 266
 defeated by Egyptians at Ain Jalut, 35,
  210−11, 376
 disintegration, 208, 212
 extend dominions into China, 200,
  201−4
 founding of Moghul empire in India
  (1526), 201
 occupation of Baghdad (1258), 200, 209
 offensive against Japan (1274−81), 68;
  defeated by Samurai, 42, 376
 Persian conquest, 209
 victorious campaigns, 200
Montgomery, Field Marshal Bernard (later
 1st Viscount), 68
Morosini, Francesco, 230
Moscow, 71
 burning by Cossacks (1812), 6−7, 8, 217
 German advance in Second World War,
  72, 373
 Napoleon's retreat, 8−9, 221, 222
Mu'awiya, Caliph, 195
Mueller, John, 58−9
Muhammad, Prophet, 194, 195, 197
 preacher and practiser of war, 193
Muhammad Ali, 376

defeats Ottomans at battle of Nezib (1839), 39–40
massacre of Mamelukes in Cairo (1811), 39
Mujesinovic, Ismet, 53
Murat, Marshal, 365
musketeers, 320, 333, 341, 342, 344, 345
Mussolini, Benito, 365, 367, 368
Mycale, battle of (481 BC), 255
Mycenaeans, 167, 168–9, 240, 241

Nagasaki bomb (1945), 379
Nagashino, battle of (1575), 43
Naples, 288
    fortress of San Giovanni, 321
    occupied by France (1495), 321–2, 323
Napoleon Bonaparte, 6, 15, 27, 151, 221, 222, 305, 306, 309, 347, 348, 349, 351, 352, 360, 369
    Army of Italy, 233
    campaign in Russia (1812), 6–7, 8, 9–10, 217, 353, 360; retreat, 8–9, 221, 222
    defeat of (1815), 17, 22, 353
    defeat of Prussians (1806), 15, 16, 353
    Grand Army, 8, 22, 353
    invasion of Egypt (1798), 39
    see also Napoleonic Wars
Napoleon III, 305
Napoleonic Wars, 6–7, 8–10, 15, 39, 65, 66, 67, 68, 221–2, 234, 302, 304, 305, 309, 340, 348–53
    casualties, 360
Naram-Sin, King, 134, 135
Narmer, Pharaoh, 131
Narses (Byzantine general), 82, 281
naval warfare, 63–8, 287–8
    armed sailing ship, 337–8
    gunpowder and, 334–40
    Mediterranean galleys, 335–7
Navarino, battle of (1827), 67, 68
Nazarenko, Tatyana, 53
Neanderthal man, 117, 118
Nedeljković, Raja, 54
Nelson, Admiral Lord, 65, 66
Nero, Emperor, 276
Nerva, Emperor, 276
Nervii, 269
Netherlands
    conflict with Spain and Portugal, and France, 340
    wars with England, 340
Nettuno, 324
New Carthage (Spanish Cartagena), 265
New Hebrideans, 91
Ney, Marshal, 350
Nezib, battle of (1839), 40
Nice, Ottoman raids on (1543), 336
Nicholas I, Tsar, 7, 72
Nile, battle of the (1798), 65, 66, 67, 68
Nimrud excavations, 169

Nineveh, 170, 171
    excavations at, 169
Nizam al-Mulk, 199
Nobunaga, Oda, 42, 43
nomadism, 148, 164–6, 181–2, 183, 189, 207, 226, 285, 286
Nordenfeldt, 312
Norman castellation of England, 142
    invasion of England, 288
North Africa, occupied by Arabs, 195, 282
Nubia, Egyptian forts in, 142–4, 147
nuclear weapons, 56, 378–9, 381–2, 391
    bombing in Hiroshima and Nagasaki (1945), 378
    deterrence theory, 48–9, 382
    disarmament, 383–4
    Manhattan Project, 378
    Russo-American confrontation, 383
Numidians, 279

Obermaier, Hugo, 120
Odoacer, 281
Offa's Dyke, 147
Old Smyrna, 144
Olduvai gorge excavations, Tanzania, 115
Olympia, 246
    games, 246, 247, 252
Opium Wars, 216
Oppenheim, Professor, 174
Orestes, 281
Orléans, siege by Huns, 186
Ormuz, batle of (1507), 339
Osaka fortress, siege of (1614), 42
Ostend, 328
Otto I, Emperor, 287
Oudinot, Marshal, 350
Oxus river, 47–8

pacifism, 4
Palestine, 295
Papago chiefs of North America, 91
peace-making efforts, 58–60
Paris commune of 1871, defeat of, 19
Parma (Spanish commander), 327
Parthians of Iran, 194–5
pastoralists, 160–1, 163, 165, 166
Patroclus, 247
Pearl Harbor attack (1941), 67, 375, 379
Peloponnese, occupied by Ottomans, 335
Peloponnesian League, 254, 256
Peloponnesian Wars, 256–7, 260
Pericles, 256
Pérouse, La, 24
Perry, Commodore, 43
Persia and Persians, 134, 178, 191, 192, 286
    alliances with Greek states, 257–8
    Byzantium war, 194
    crushed by Ottomans, 336
    defeat by Macedonia and Alexander, 259–63
    empire destroyed by Arabs, 192, 195, 196

Greek wars, 243–4, 253–6
war with Ephthalites, 190, 191
wars with Alexander the Great, 145–6,
174, 178, 194, 259–63, 304,
389–90
wars with Rome, 185, 195, 280
Pevensey, 142
Philhellenism and Philhellenes, 10–11, 196
Philip of Macedonia, 258, 259
Philip V of Macedonia, 271
Philippines possession contested between
Spain and Portugal, 339
Philo, 353
Phoenicians, 144, 170, 255, 270
Phrygians, 169
Picq, Ardant du, 271
Piggott, Stuart, 144, 158, 159
pikemen, 329, 334, 341, 343
Pipes, Daniel, 34
Pisa, fortifications of, 149, 323
Plassey, battle of (1757), 346–7
Plataea, 253
battle of (481 BC), 255
Plato, 247
Poggio Imperiale, 324
Poitiers battles: (732) 284; (1356) 297
Poland
German invasion (1939), 369
walled settlements (6th century), 144
political revolution and military change,
347–59
Polybius (Roman historian), 151, 265, 353
Pompey, Emperor, 274
population theory of warmaking, 223–4
Portuguese
conflict with Dutch and English, 340
dispute control of Red Sea, 36, 37
failure to block spice route, 339
Far East bases, 339
naval supremacy in Indian Ocean, 65,
339
Preveza, battle of (1538), 336
primitive people and their warfare, 94–115
Aztecs, 106–14
Maoris, 103–6
Maring, 98–103
Yanomamö, 94–8
Prussian army, 14–17, 20–1, 295–6, 309,
351, 354
conscription, 233, 234
defeat by Napoleon (1806), 15, 16, 353
defeat of Austria (1866), 307
defeat of France in Alsace-Lorraine
(1870), 307
Guard Corps, 307
modernising Turkish army, 39–40
ruthlessness, 27
victory in wars against Austria and
France (1871), 20
Punic Wars, 267, 270–2
Second, 265, 271

Pylos, palace of, 240
Pyrrhus, 263, 270

Qadesh, battle of (1294), 176, 177
Qadisiyah, battle of (637), 195, 196
Quebec, 347
Quiberon Bay, battle of (1759), 65, 67, 68
Qutuz, Sultan, 210, 211

Radagaisus, 186
Rameses II, Pharaoh, 131, 176
Rameses III, Pharaoh, 64
Ramla, battle of (1102), 294
Rapaport, David, 93
Ravenna, 282
battle of (1512), 330, 331
Raydaniya, battle of (1516), 37, 38
Reculver, 142
regiment, emergence of, 12–15, 20, 27
regular enlistment, 228, 229, 267, 270, 357
Requesens, 326
rewarding soldiers, ways of, 228–9, 230–4,
264, 275
Rhodes, capture by Ottomans (1522), 336
Ricimer, 281
roads and railways, 303–7
Roberts, J.M., 115, 116, 122–3
Rochester, siege of (1215), 151
rocket attacks by Germans (1944–5), 378
Roe, Sir Thomas, 346
Roeder, Captain Franz, 222
Roggeveen (Dutch voyager), 26
Romans, 182, 183, 216, 232, 302, 305, 309,
341–2, 344, 364
Antonine emperors, success of, 276, 278
centurionate cadre, 268–9
civil war (50–44 BC), 274
confrontation with Goths, 184–6, 280
conquests, 146–7, 263–74, 276, 332
defence of Byzantium, 281–2
dilectus selection process, 267–8
disaster at Teutoburg forest (AD 9),
270, 276, 359
encounters with Teutonic peoples, 267,
272, 285, 332, 390; infiltration into
Roman army, 280–1, 282–3
ferocity in war, 265–6
fortification against barbarian assaults,
149, 182–8
Gaul, conquest of, 264, 266, 272–3,
274, 332
German revolt, 276, 332
Hun invasion, 182, 183, 184–7, 281
influx of barbarians into army, 185, 192,
280–1, 282–3
Julio Claudians, 276, 278
mother house of modern armies,
263–81
occupation of Britain, 265, 273, 276
papacy, 289–91
payment of stipend to legionaries, 264

Persian wars, 185, 195, 280
Punic wars against Carthage, 165, 267, 270–2
return of Rome to imperial rule, 282
revolt in the empire, 276
road-building, 303
Rome included in kingdom of Charlemagne, 284
sack of Rome by Vandals of Gaiseric, 281
Saracen attack, 286
Rommel, Field Marshal Erwin, 68
Romulus (puppet emperor), 281
Roosevelt, President Franklin D., 378
Rostopchin (governor of Moscow), 6
Rousseau, Pierre, 46
Rusa, King of Urartu, 173
Russia and Russians, 266
collapse of army (1917), 234
conquest of Khiva (1874), 302
Crimean War, 9, 311
fortifications (*Cherta*), 147, 388
invasion of Poland (1939), 369
Japanese war (1904–5), 66, 67, 376
Marxist regime, 367; collapse of, 383, 384
Napoleon's conquest (1812), 6–7, 8, 217, 353; retreat, 8–9, 221, 222
nuclear confrontation with America, 383
Revolution (1917), 19, 22, 361, 367
Second World War, 71–2, 373–4, 377

Sa'adat Muhammad, Sultan, 38
Saddam Hussein, 195
Saguntum, siege of (219 BC), 271
St Augustine of Hippo, 382
St Jacob-en-Birs, battle of (1444), 329
Saladin (Salah el-Din), 199, 200, 208, 209, 210, 214, 293, 294
Salamis, battle of (480 BC), 65, 67, 68, 254
Samarkand, 47, 195
Mongol occupation, 205
Samnites, 263
San (Bushmen) of Kalahari, 120
Sandhurst, Royal Military Academy, viii–ix, x, 344
Sangallo, Antonio da, 324, 325
Sangallo, Giuliano da, 324
Sansom, G.B., 45
Saracens, 13
threat to the West, 286, 288
Saragossa, 144
Sardinia, 271, 281, 286
Sargon of Agade, Emperor, 133, 134, 142, 168, 169
Sargon II, 171, 173, 176, 177
Sarmatians, 181
Saxe, Marshal de, 11
Scandinavia
conversion of, 289

sea raiders, 149, 287–8
Scharnhorst, General, 15
Scipio Africanus, 265, 272
Scipio, Cornelius, 272
Scottish Archers of the French kings, 230
scourge of war, 59
Scythians of Iran, 177–8, 180
Second World War, 89, 369–79, 391
Allied bombing offensive, 374–5, 377–8
Allied landings in France (1944), 377
Arctic skirmishes, 69
Battle of the Atlantic, 68
battle of France (1940), 370–1
bombing of Hiroshima and Nagasaki, 378
casualties, 50, 373
Dunkirk evacuation (1940), 370
German *Blitzkrieg* into France (1940), 71
human cost, 57
Japan's conquest of Malaya, 68
kamikaze pilots, 38
Leyte Gulf, battle of (1944), 68
logistics and supply, 308, 313–14
London blitz (1940), 372–3, 378
Midway, battle of, 67, 68, 377
North African campaign, 68
partisan warfare and civil war in Yugoslavia, 51–5
Pearl Harbor attack (1941), 375
Polish campaign (1939), 369
rocket attack by Germans (1944–5), 378
Russian front, 71–2, 373–4, 377
sea battles, 66–7, 377
Sedan, battle of (1870), 309
Seleucus, 194
Selim I, Sultan, 37, 336
Selous, Frederick, 120
Semai tribe, 120
Semna, Nubia, 143, 144
Sennacherib, King of Assyria, 170, 171, 172–3, 176
Senusret III, Pharaoh, 143
Seqenenre the Brave, Pharaoh, 131
Serbia, 70, 296
Servius Tullius, 263
Sève, Colonel, 40
Seville
statement condemning belief in man's violent nature (1986), 80–1
Viking raid (844), 288
Shaka (Zulu chief), 29, 30–1, 32, 131
Shelley, Percy Bysshe, *Hellas*, 11
Sherman, General William Tecumseh, 6
Shimbara Rebellion (1637), 44
Sicily
acquired by Rome, 270–1
base of Vandals, 281
expedition by Athens, 257

Saracen occupation, 286
siege of Agrigentum by Romans (262 BC),
    146
  siege warfare, 150−1, 172, 205, 326−7
  transformed by use of canon, 321−3
Siegen, *schola militaris*, 344
Silk Road, 182, 195, 206
Singapore, fall of, 113
Skidi Pawnee tribe, 107
Smail, R.C., 297
Smith, Adam, *Wealth of Nations*, 18
Smith, Professor Gertrude, 174
Smolensk, 373
Socrates, 250
Somme, battle of (1916), 302, 309, 361
Soult, Marshal, 350
Spain
  Arab occupation, 195; liberation from,
      214, 296
  battles with France, 330−1
  Civil War (1936−9), 230
  Conquistadors in South America,
      338−9
  defeat of Armada (1588), 67, 68, 326,
      338
  Netherlands rebellion, 326−8
  Peninsular War, 302, 304, 305, 353
  walled cities, 149
Spartans, 233, 242−3, 249, 252−6, 257, 260,
    262
Special Air Service (SAS) Regiment, 230
Spitzbergen, 69
Srednij Stog culture, 156
Stahlberg, Alexander, 89
Stalin, Joseph, 172, 365, 371
Stanwix, 279
Stilicho, 185, 186
Stimson, Henry, 379, 381
Stone Age Man, 156−7, 160; and warfare,
    79−135
  New Stone Age, 118, 119, 120, 121, 122,
      123−4, 125
  Old Stone Age, 117, 118
strongholds, 139−52
Structural Functionalism, 88, 91, 97
Suleiman the Magnificent, 336
Sumer and the Sumerians, 115, 123, 126−8,
    132−5, 142, 157, 161, 162, 216,
    229, 234
  see also Iraq
Sun Tzu, 202
  Art of War, 202, 353
Sung, Duke of, 173
Sweden, Thirty Years' War, 341
Switzerland and the Swiss
  battle with French at Marignano (1515),
      330−1
  débâcle against Spanish at Bicocca
      (1522), 331
  Habsburg overlords, 329
  mercenaries, 329, 331

pikemen, 13, 329, 334
Syracuse, 257
Syria, 126, 134, 169
  conquered by Arabs (636), 195, 282
  falls to Rome, 272
  siege of Antioch by Crusaders (1098),
      151, 292

Taginae, battle of (455), 281−2
Takashima (Japanese military reformer), 10
Talas river, battle of (751), 191, 195, 203
Tamerlane, 47, 75, 211−12, 227, 266
Tanais river, battle of, 184
Tarawa, assault on (1943), 377
Tartars, 204, 222
Teutoburg forest, battle of (AD 9), 270, 276,
    359
Teutonic barbarians
  encounters with Rome, 267, 272, 285,
      332, 390
  infiltrate Roman army, 280−1, 282−3
  Teutonic Knights order, 295−6
Thebes, 143, 233, 252, 255, 256, 258, 259
Themistius, 192
Themistocles, 254
Theodosius, Emperor, 185, 192, 280, 320
Thermopylae, battle of (480 BC), 254
Third Sacred War (355−46 BC), 258
Thirty Years' War (1618−48), 326, 328, 341,
    384
Three Days' Battle (1653), 340
Thucydides, 248, 250
Tiger, Lionel, 85, 86
Timurids, 265, 266
Tito, Marshal Josip Broz, 50, 51, 53, 54
Tolstoy, Leo Nikolaievich, 8
  Anna Karenina, 14
Toulouse, battle of (439), 183
Trafalgar, battle of (1805), 65, 67, 340, 353
Trajan, Emperor, 276
Trasimene, Lake, battle of (217 BC), 271
Tremouille, Louis de la, 333
Tricameron, battle of (453), 281
Trieste, 117
Troy, 240
  Trojan War, 241, 246−7, 251, 332
Truman, Harry S., 379
Tsushima, battle of (1905), 67, 68
Tungu, 179
Tunis, 39
  falls to Ottomans (1535), 336
Turkey, 126, 128, 134, 169
Turks of the steppes, 47, 161, 180, 181, 190,
    191, 204, 205, 206−7, 211, 216,
    266, 286
  barbarian empire, 119; overthrown by
      Arabs, 191, 192
Turks, Ottoman
  arrival in Mesopotamia, 183
  attempt by Prussia to modernise army,
      39−40

Balkan wars of 1911–12, 346
battles at Adrianople with Serbs and
    Bulgars, 70fn
capture of Constantinople (1453), 189,
    212, 281, 320, 335
capture of Rhodes (1522), 336
challenges Habsburg empire, 336, 346
compromise between steppe heritage
    and urban West, 212
conquest of Balkans, 214, 296, 336
conquest of Egypt from Mamelukes
    (1515–16), 36, 37–40, 336
control of Albania and Peloponnese,
    335
control of Bulgars, 190
crushing of Safavid Persia, 336
defeated at Lepanto by Holy League
    (1571), 337
defeated by Muhammad Ali at Nezib
    (1839), 39–40
destruction of Hungarian kingdom
    (1526), 336
empire a major military factor in
    Europe, 23, 212
Gallipoli (1915), 363
Janissaries (military slaves), 24, 212, 346
loss of empire in First World War, 40
naval warfare, 335–7
peace of Karlowitz (1699), 346
retreat to Constantinople, 346
siege of Malta fails (1565), 336–7
siege of Vienna (1529), 336
siege of Vienna (1683), 48, 212, 346
Serbia overwhelmed, 296, 335
succession procedure, 209
Topkapi Palace of the sultans, Istanbul,
    181–2
war in Libya with Italy (1911–12), 372
Turks, Seljuk, 198
conversion to Islam, 198
enter Baghdad, 198
exploits, 199
Turkish Republic and moderation under
    Atatürk, 367, 391
Turner, Frederick Jackson, 147
Turney-High, Harry, 93, 94, 102, 115, 189
Primitive Warfare extracts, 89–92, 107
Tuthmosis III, Pharaoh, 175, 176
Tyre, siege of (322 BC), 322

Uedahara, battle of (1548), 43
ultimate weapons, 366–79
United Nations Organisation, 383, 384
    Charter, 383
Ur death-pit excavations, 133
Urartu, 171, 173
Urban II, Pope, 290–1
Uruk, 133, 157

Valens, Emperor, 70fn, 185, 280
Vandals, 186, 281, 286

Varro, 271
Vauban, Marshal, 327
Vayda, Andrew, 99, 101
War in Ecological Perspective extracts,
    100, 105
Vegetius, 301–2, 353
Veneti of Brittany, 273
Venice, 226, 230, 296, 322, 326, 330, 336, 343
Vercingetorix, 146, 273
Verdun, battle of (1916), 361
Versailles, treaty of, 366, 367, 368
Vespasian, Emperor, 276
Vico, Giambattista, 47
Victor, Marshal, 350
Victoria, Queen, 201
Vienna, Ottoman sieges: (1529) 336; (1683)
    48, 212, 346
    Spanish riding school, 341
Viet Minh, 1131, 380
Vietnam War (1965–72), 56, 92, 359, 381
Vikings, 13, 64–5, 150, 226, 288, 293
    atrocities, 227
Virginia Capes, battle of (1781), 67, 68
Visby, battle of (1361), 121
Vittoria, Francisco de, 382
Voltaire, 46

Wagram, battle of (1809), 353, 369
War of the Holy League, 323
warhorse, 177–8, 285–6
warmaking, limitations on, 63–76
Waterloo, battle of (1815), 8, 309; casualties,
    360
Weber, Max, 103
Weigley, Professor Russell, 57, 345
Wellington, Duke of, 46, 304
    Peninsular War, 302, 353
    Waterloo casualties, 360
Wendorf, F., *The Prehistory of Nubia*
    extract, 120–1
Western Hsia (Tanguts), 206
Whittaker, C.R., 147
Whitworth, 311
why do men fight?, 79–80
William the Conqueror, 290
William Louis of Nassau, 327, 344
Wilson, Professor, 174
Woolwich Arsenal, 312

Xerxes, Emperor, 192, 254, 255, 257, 369

Yakutsk, 179
Yamamoto, Admiral, 375, 376
Yanomamö and warfare, 94–8, 119, 121,
    161
Yeomen of the Guard, 230
Yoritomo (first shogun), 41
Yorktown, surrender of British (1781), 348
Ypres, battle of (1914), 358–9

Yugoslavia
civil war in 1990s, 55
partisan warfare and civil war during
Second World War, 51–5

Zama, battle of (202 BC), 272
Zulu warriordom, 23, 24, 28–32, 333
imperialism, 31